A SOCIAL HISTORY

OF

ANCIENT IRELAND

FIG. 167B.—Cormac's Chapel on the Rock of Cashel.
From Miss Stokes's Early Christian Architecture in Ireland

FIG. 167A

Shrine of St. Patrick's Bell, made by order of Donall O'Loghlin, king of Ireland (died 112)
now in the National Museum, Dublin   See vol. I., p 374, *supra*

(From Miss Stokes's Early Christian Art in Ireland.)

A SOCIAL HISTORY

OF

ANCIENT IRELAND

TREATING OF

The Government, Military System, and Law;
Religion, Learning, and Art; Trades, Industries, and Commerce,
Manners, Customs, and Domestic Life,
of the Ancient Irish People

BY

P. W. JOYCE,

LL.D., TRIN. COLL., DUB. ; M.R.I.A.

VOL. II

ARNO PRESS

A New York Times Company
New York • 1980

First Published 1913
Reissued 1968
by Benjamin Blom, Inc. Bronx, New York 10452
and 56 Doughty Street London, W.C. 1
Reprint Edition 1980 by Arno Press Inc.
LC79-8880
ISBN 0-405-08677-6
Manufactured in the United States of America

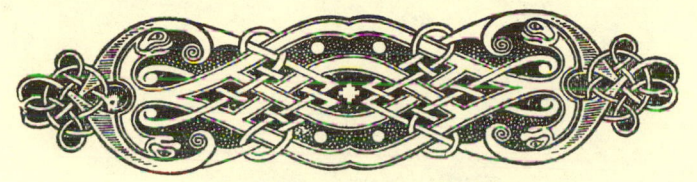

Ornament composed from the Book of Kells.

CONTENTS OF VOL. II

PART III

SOCIAL AND DOMESTIC LIFE

CHAPTER XIX

CHAPTER XX

CHAPTER XXI

CHAPTER XXX

CHAPTER XXXI

Sculpture on a Capital: Priest's House, Glendalough: Beranger, 1779.
(From Petrie's Round Towers.)

LIST OF ILLUSTRATIONS IN VOL. II.

PART III

SOCIAL AND DOMESTIC LIFE

Sculpture on Window, Cathedral Church, Glendalough: Berringer, 1779.
(From Petrie's Round Towers).

CHAPTER XIX

THE FAMILY

SECTION I. *Marriage.*

ANCIENT Ireland it was a very general custom, as it was in Wales, and in Greece in the time of Homer, that when a couple got married the man was bound to bring the marriage portion or dowry, not the woman. Instances of this custom are mentioned everywhere in our literature : and so well was it recognised, that the ancient Irish writers—as was their wont in such cases—assign a legendary origin for it. The legend is found in the Book of Leinster, into which it was copied from the still more ancient Book of Dromsnechta. When the sons of Milesius arrived in Ireland, they found there some Hebrew women who had been driven thither from the Tyrrhene or Mediterranean sea by a tempest. The newcomers proposed marriage to them : but the women answered that they preferred to return to their own country ; and that they would not abandon it to marry the Milesians unless they got *Tinnscra* or dowry as a sort of compensation : to which the Milesians agreed. And the old account goes on to say :—" It is from this circum-
" stance that in Erin it is the men that purchase wives
" always : while it is the husbands that are purchased in
" all the rest of the world."*

* O'Curry, MS. Mat., 15, bottom : LL, 190, *c*, 27

There were several terms in common use to designate dowry : and according to an ancient manuscript in Trinity College, Dublin, quoted by O'Donovan,* the several names were used for different sorts of dowries. The *Tinnscra* was a gift of gold, silver, copper, or brass : the *Coibche* [cōv-kĕ] consisted of clothes and warriors : the *Slabra* of cattle and horse-bridles : and the *Tochra* of sheep and swine. But there is good reason to believe that these distinctions were not rigidly adhered to, and that the several terms were in some measure used indiscriminately. Thus O'Clery, in his Glossary, explains *Tinnscra* by *Coibche* : and many other such instances might be cited. Moreover, the dowry might consist of other things besides those named above, such as land, or houses, or the concession of some valuable favour or privilege. " Give me," said Oengus mac Natfree, king of Munster in the fifth century, " your foster-child [Eithne Uathach] as a wife, and I will give you land as *Tinnscra*."† There were other terms, too, for ' dowry,' such as *fola* and *foluch*. Occasionally time was given for payment of the dowry : if it was paid in hand, it was called by the general name *Ellam*,‡ from *lam*, ' the hand.'

In Ireland, as among all the Aryan nations,§ the original conception was that the man purchased his affianced wife from the father or other guardian, and the dowry he brought in was the bride-price. It was usually paid over by the bridegroom to the father of the bride. Accordingly, Cormac's Glossary interprets *coibche* as meaning *cendach*, i.e. ' buying.' The bride-price often consisted of a yearly payment from the husband after marriage : and we find it laid down in the Brehon Law that the woman's father was entitled to the whole of the

---

* In Hy F, 207, note *r* : see also Silva Gad., 525, 18.

† LU, 54, *b*, 2: and Sullivan, Introd., 174, note 295. For houses as dowry, see O'Curry, MS. Mat., 133.   ‡ Corm. Gloss., 67, " Ellam."

§ De Jubainville, Cours de Litt. Celt., VI. 303.

first year's *coibche*, to two thirds of the second year's, to one-half of the third : and so on, diminishing to the twenty-first, when the claim ceased.* In each case, what was left of the *coibche* belonged to the wife.†

We meet many instances where the dowry consisted of a privilege. When Fergus mac Roy, king of Ulaid (Ulster) in the first century of the Christian era, proposed marriage to the beautiful widow Ness, she refused to marry him except on this condition as *Tinnscra* :—That her son Concobar, then a mere boy, should be permitted to reign as king, instead of Fergus, for one year : to which Fergus, with the consent of his nobles, agreed. But at the end of the year—just as the wily widow expected—when Fergus claimed his throne, the nobles refused to supersede Concobar, who—by the help of his mother—had so completely won them over that he remained king for the rest of his life.‡

Within late historical times we find a still more interesting example of this sort of bride-price. Early in the fourteenth century, it happened on one occasion that Cormac O'Clery, a learned young *ollave* or doctor of laws, visited the house of Matthew O'Sgingin, professor of history to the O'Donnells of Tirconnell. For many generations the O'Sgingins had been hereditary historians to the O'Donnells : but this Matthew was destined to be the last *ollave* of the name, for his only surviving child was a daughter, a beautiful young girl. The two young people soon fell in love with each other : and the father consented to their union, but demanded from O'Clery as *Tinnscra*, that the first son born of the marriage should be sent to study history, so as to succeed to the position held by the

* Br. Laws, II. 347 ; III. 315.

† In remote times the idea of sale and purchase of the woman in marriage must have been prominent and familiar : see an instance of Concobar mac Nessa *buying* a woman after the death of her first husband : Br. Laws, IV., p. 9, note. 2.

‡ LL, 106, *a*, 30: MS. Mat., 274, 636 : Stokes, Lives of SS., XXXV., top.

O'Sgingins. The young man willingly agreed: and he faithfully kept to his promise. His first son, who became a historian, was the ancestor of the O'Clerys of Kilbarron in Donegal, who succeeded the O'Sgingins as hereditary ollaves of history to the O'Donnells.* They were a race of scholars who have left us many precious works in Irish, illustrating the history and antiquities of Ireland, including the Annals of the Four Masters, the greatest and most important of all.†

The fact that the husband paid the bride-price did not prevent the bride bringing goods or valuables of her own, if she had them. Any number of cases might be cited where the young woman brought jewels, or gold, or herds, or land: and after the marriage, these continued to be her own special property. Sometimes the friends of the young couple made a collection for them, which was called *Tinól* (i.e. 'collection': pron. tinnole), of which two-thirds belonged by law to the man, and one-third to the woman.‡ This custom was common among high and low, and we meet with instances everywhere in the tales. Our present custom of making a young married couple presents is not unlike the old Irish *tinnole*.

It was usual that girls should be married in order of age, beginning with the eldest. We are told in the story of the *Boroma* that Tuathal the Legitimate, king of Ireland (A.D. 130–160), had two daughters, of whom Eochaid [Ochy], king of Leinster, married the elder, though he preferred the younger, who was more beautiful. "For at that time"—says the story—"it was not the custom in Erin for the younger sister to be married before the elder."§ The lady Emer, when Cuculainn sought her in marriage, says :—
" I may not marry before Fial my sister, who is older than

* FM, Vol. I., Introd. Remarks, xx. For Kilbarron, see vol. I., p. 524, *supra*.

† For examples of other sorts of dowries, see Oss. Soc., IV. 299 (head of a destructive wild boar), and Bec Fola, p. 175 (a brooch).

‡ Br. Laws, II. 347, 350, 351.   § Rev. Celt., XIII. 37 : Silva Gad., 402

I am." It was expected, too, that a girl should marry a man of a family equal to her own in social standing.*

Marriages, as stated elsewhere (Chap. xxix., p. 439, *infra*), formed a prominent feature of the fair of Tailltenn, held during the last days of July and first days of August. But it would appear from a passage in Cormac's Glossary (p. 82, " Gam ") that throughout Ireland in general the favourite and fashionable month for getting married was November. According to some authorities quoted by Sullivan in his Introduction to O'Curry's Lectures (p. 240), a tribute had to be paid—at least in some cases—to the king, on the marriage of every maiden of his people. This tribute was usually a *fáinne maighdena* [fawnya myděnă], or ' maiden's ring ' ; for it was often a gold ring : but it might be an ounce of gold, or less, or it might be the bride's wedding-dress.

The general custom was to have only one wife† : but there were exceptions, for in very early times we some-times find a king or chief with two. In the story of the Cattle Spoil of Fraech in the Book of the Dun Cow, referring to far distant pagan ages, it is related how Fraech, a powerful chief of Erris, goes to the house of Ailill and Maive, king and queen of Connaught, as a suitor for the hand of their daughter Finnabair, though it was well known that he had at the time a wife and three sons. Cobthach Coel Brég, king of Ireland before the Christian era, had more than one queen.‡ Coming to Christian times, Dermot, king of Ireland, A.D. 544–565, had two queens.§ In the time of St. Finnchua (seventh century) old Nuada the sage, king of Leinster, had two wives (*da bainchéle*), who, as might be expected, kept the poor old king in hot water by their jealousies and bickerings.||

* Br. Laws, II. 347.

† On Monogamy, the basis of Greek, Roman, and Celtic society, see De Jubainville, Cours de Litt. Celt., VI. chap. iv.

‡ Orgain Dind Ríg, in Zeitschr. Celt. Phil., III. 9.

§ See page 255, farther on. || Stokes, Lives of SS., p. 237.

That chastity and modesty were prized we know from many passages, such as that in the Life of St. Finnchua, in which he leaves blessings to the Leinster men, among them " chastity in their queens and in their wives, and modesty in their maidens."* A wedding was called *banais* contracted (from *ban-theis*, meaning " woman's feast ") : a married couple was *lánamain* : marriage, *lánamnas* : a widow was *tedb* and *bantrebthach*.

2. *Position of Women and Children.*

In ancient Ireland free women (as distinguished from slaves) held a good position : and it may be said that as to social rights and property they were in most respects quite on a level with men. Husband and wife continued to own the respective shares they brought in at marriage, such as land, flocks, household goods, &c., the man retaining his part and the woman hers, each quite independently of the other. Of this custom we find illustrations everywhere ; and there are many records of married women taking legal proceedings on their own account against outsiders, quite independently of the husband, in defence of their special property.†

But notwithstanding this separate ownership, as both portions were worked more or less in conjunction, and naturally increased from year to year, it was generally impossible—even if so desired—to keep them distinct, so that a part at least of the entire possessions might be looked upon as joint property : and for this state of things the law provided. It is from the Brehon Law we get the clearest exposition of the rights of women regarding property. The respective privileges of the couple after marriage depended very much on the amount of property

---

* Stokes, Lives of SS., p. 239.

† For the law on the point, and instances, see Br. Laws, ii. 361, 363, 379 : O'Curry, Man. & Cust., ii. 89 : Stokes, Lives of SS., 165, 235 : Féilire, 75 : Reeves, Adamn., 305 : and vol. i., p. 216, *supra* (the *glaisin* crop).

they brought in.   If their properties were equal at marriage " the wife "—says the Senchus Mór—" is called the wife of equal rank," and she was recognised as in all respects, in regard to property, on an equality with her husband.*   In this case all transactions affecting the joint property, such as buying and selling, had to be made with the consent of both parties : and any contract made by either, for his or her own special benefit, without the consent of the other, was null and void in a court of law.   But if it could be shown that the transaction tended equally to the advantage of both, the law confirmed it.   If profit accrued from any transaction (such as selling) it was apportioned to husband and wife in the ratio of their respective shares.

That the husband and wife were on terms of equality as to property is made still more clear from the provisions laid down to meet the case of separation : and from the evident care with which these are set forth, we may conclude that the separation of married couples was, in those days, by no means an uncommon occurrence.   Sometimes they separated by mutual consent and sometimes as the outcome of legal proceedings.   Seven different kinds of injury are enumerated in the law, which if inflicted on a wife by her husband, gave her the right to separate from him : most of which would at this day lead to a decree of " separation from bed and board."   If she proved her case home, she was entitled to her dowry (or that part of it that remained with her after marriage) in addition to personal damages as *Eneclann* or honour-fine.†

If the couple separated by mutual consent, the woman took away with her all she had brought on the marriage day ; while the man retained what he had contributed. Supposing the joint property had gone on increasing

---

* Br. Laws, II. 357 : and Preface, lvi.
† Br. Laws, v. 293 : see also II. 357, 359, 361, 381, 383 : and Sullivan, Introd., 176.

during married life : then at separation the couple divided the whole in proportion to the original contributions.*

But all this might be modified by special circumstances, which are detailed in the law with much exactness. One of these was whether the woman was a " great worker " or a "small worker." She was a " great worker " if she had, of her own, all the utensils necessary for her feminine occupations : such as a mill, a sieve, a loom, a spinning wheel, a distaff, spindles, &c. : she was a " small worker " if these were supplied by the husband.† In the division of property a great worker took a larger share than a small worker. For instance, in case of flax at the time of pulling and drying : a great worker got one-sixth of it ; a small worker one-ninth.‡

If the woman was a " great worker " during married life, and helped by her industry to increase the property, she was entitled, at separation, to one-ninth of the increase, even though she had no property (beyond the utensils) at the time of marriage.§ And in like manner the man, under similar circumstances, if he had been a "great worker," could claim just one-ninth of the increase. Here, in the words of the law tract (II. 391), " the man goes in the place of the woman, and the woman in the place of the man."

As to household articles manufactured by the woman's hand, she was entitled to a part, as in case of other goods —even though having no property at the time of marriage : but the exact amount depended on the state of advancement of the work. Take woollen goods as an example, which were generally managed exclusively by women. If the wool was in the fleece at the time of separation, she took one-eighth. If it had been separated into locks or flakes ready for combing, she took one-sixth ; if after being combed ready for spinning, one-third : after spinning, or

---

* Br. Laws, II. 397 : O'Curry, Man. & Cust., II. 118.
† Br. Laws, II. 411.   ‡ Br. Laws, II. 419.
§ Br. Laws, II. 391, 393, 395.

when in cloth, one-half.* So also flax : one ninth-growing " on foot " ; one-sixth after drying ; one-third after scutching ; one-half after that. Similar arrangements were laid down for dye-stuffs in the several stages of preparation ; and for various other materials and products. From all this, moreover, as well as from many separate passages, it may be inferred that great importance was attached to hand-work of all kinds.

Women, as has been said, might take actions at law on their own account, and if successful might distrain the goods of the defendant. But the distress should be confined to such things as were understood to specially pertain to women, in their daily life, of which a list is given in the Senchus Mór. These included sheep, lap-dogs, and cats ; all utensils used in the manufacture of cloth, such as spindles, wool-bags, needles, weavers' reeds, &c., and also such articles as looking-glasses, sieves, and kneading-troughs.†

When the wife owned land, it was subject to the same law of succession as that of the husband ; viz., if she had sons it descended to them, whether there were daughters or not : if she had no sons it went to the daughters. Here however, there were proper safeguards to prevent the land passing from the tribe, in case the woman married a man of another tribe.‡ When land passed by any right to a woman, she entered into formal possession, by a process which was attended with very curious ceremonies.§ When a woman came into possession of land, she was bound to send men for war-service like male land-owners : but she was set free of this obligation on giving up to the *finè* or tribe half the land ; a privilege which was not accorded to men.||

* Br. Laws, II. 369, 373 : O'Curry, Man. & Cust., II. 118.

† General list in Senchus Mór, Br. Laws, I. 151 ; and see 149. See also IV. 9, note ₂; and 13, 19.

‡ See Br. Laws, IV. 17 and 19, 39 and 41, 45, 47, top : and Introduction, cxvi, cxvii.   § Ceremonies : for which see Br. Laws, IV. 9, 11, 13.

|| Br. Laws, IV. 19, 8 to end of par. ; 21, note ₂; 41, mid par. ; 45 ; 47, 11; 49 ; and Introd., cxvii., bottom

Husband and wife stood on equal terms in a brehon's court, so that if the husband gave evidence against his wife, she was entitled to give evidence against him. For, as the Senchus Mór expresses it, " though the Law cedes " headship to the man [husband] for his manhood and " nobility, he has not the greater power of proof upon the " woman on account of it, for it is only contract that is " between them."* But her father could give evidence against his daughter, whether married or single, and she was not permitted to rebut it by her evidence.†

The testimonies hitherto brought forward are mostly legal and historical. But the general popular conception of the position of married women may be also gathered from the old romantic tales and legends, including those of the Dinnsenchus, in which women hold as high a place as men. We read of great female physicians, such as Airmeda the daughter of the leech-god Dianket ; and of distinguished female brehons or lawyers, such as Brigh Briugaid, whose decisions were followed as precedents for centuries after her death.

But with all that has been said so far in commendation of the position of women, there were some features, which, regarded from a moral point of view, were very objectionable. These were not indeed peculiar to Ireland, but were common enough among European nations at the time ; but they were not the less repulsive for that. It is manifest from Irish literature in general, and especially from the Brehon Laws, that the practice of separation of man and wife, either by mutual consent or by process of law, was unpleasantly common. Concubinage was very general, especially among the higher classes, and does not appear to have been regarded by the general public as in any degree reprehensible : indeed the Brehon Law provides for it as a recognised custom. Female slaves too were treated with great grossness, at least till the time of

* Br. Laws, II. 351.

† Ibid., 347.

Adamnan (at the end of the seventh century), by whose exertions some much-needed improvements were effected in their position, as well as in that of women in general.*

It is worthy of remark that the good old lawyers who compiled the Brehon Law tracts, while doing full justice to the position of women, are sometimes given to a rather pompous assertion of the superiority of their own sex. We have seen the lofty expression in last page : and the commentator, explaining why the Senchus Mór, though treating as much of women as of men, is still called the " Senchus of the *Men* of Erin," says " it is proper indeed " that it should be so called, so as to give superiority to " the noble sex, *i.e.* to the male : for the man is the " head of the woman, and the man is more noble than the " woman."†

The son was under the father's control till formally emancipated : but what was the age or in what the ceremony of emancipation consisted I have not found.‡

We have seen (vol. I., p. 165, *supra*) that, even as late as the twelfth century, it was common among the English to sell their children and other relatives, especially to the people of Ireland. In Ireland illegitimate children were sometimes sold, but not legitimate children. It is laid down in the Brehon Law that the children begotten illegitimately of a woman who has been abducted belong to the woman's family, who may sell them if they choose.§ That fathers also sometimes sold their illegitimate children is shown by a story in the Life of St. Brigit, who—according to this legend—was the illegitimate daughter of a pagan chief named Dubthach. When she was a girl living in her father's house, she was so charitable that everything in the house she could lay hands on she gave away

---

* Trip. Life, Introd., xxii.   † Br. Laws, I. 35.
Br. Laws, IV. 231, 12; V. 357, 11; 439, 5. See De Jubainville, Cours de Litt. Celt., VI. 312 : and " Saer, Leicthe " in Atkinson's Br. Law Glos As to the duty of the son to support the parents, see p. 495, *infra*.
§ Br. Laws, III. 403, 541.

to the poor and the needy : till her father became at last so incensed that he resolved to rid himself of her by selling her for a slave. He actually brought her away in his chariot with this object but was diverted from his purpose by the advice of a friend : and so Brigit was saved from bondage.* In the annals and other ancient writings we sometimes come across references to times of famine and distress so severe that people were driven to sell their legitimate children to procure food. But these entries, so far from showing that the practice was customary in Ireland, prove, as acknowledged exceptions, the very reverse.

Adoption, whether of individuals, of familes, or of whole septs, has been already dealt with (vol. I., p. 166, *supra*).

A child was called in Irish *lenab*, now *leanbh*, pron. lannav : an infant was *noidiu*. A son was *mac*, corresponding with the Welsh *map* : a daughter, *ingen* [ing-een] : a grandson was *ua, hua*, or *haue*. A father was *athair* : a mother, *máthair* : a brother, *dearbhráthair*, now pron. drahaar : a sister, *deirbhshiúr*, pron. drihoor.

3. *Fosterage.*

One of the leading features of Irish social life was fosterage (Irish, *altram* or *altrum*), which prevailed from the remotest period. It was practised by persons of all classes, but more especially by those in the higher ranks. The most usual type of fosterage was this :—A man sent his child to be reared and educated in the home and with the family of another member of the tribe, who then became foster-father, and his children the foster-brothers and foster-sisters of the child. While young persons were generally fostered in this manner, in families, some were put in care of distinguished ecclesiastics : and many of the Irish saints

* Stokes, Lives of SS., 187

were fostered in this way, whose early training in a great measure determined their future life. St. Columkille was fostered and educated during childhood by a holy priest named Cruithnecan.* For a number of individual examples of the fosterage of well-known historical personages, the reader may refer to O'Curry's Manners and Customs of the Ancient Irish, I. 374, 375.

The foster-father was denoted by the word *aite* or *oide* [2-syll.] : the foster-mother by *muime* [mummě] : the foster-child by *dalta*. *Dalta* is still in use as a term of endearment to denote a favourite or a petted child, but is now always applied to a boy. A foster-brother was *comalte* [3-syll.]. Fosterage was subject to stringent regulations, which were carefully set forth in the law. A special portion of the Senchus Mór—occupying twenty-four pages, Irish type, of the second volume—is devoted to it ; in which the rights, duties, and obligations of the parties are detailed with minute particularity : and it is referred to in other parts of the law. I give here a few of the most important of these regulations.

A child might be sent to fosterage at one year of age. Boys might be kept till seventeen and girls till fourteen, which were considered the marriageable ages : then they returned to their parents' house. There were **two** kinds of fosterage—**for affection and for payment.** In the first there was no fee : in the second the fee varied according to rank. The fosterage fee (*iarrad*) sometimes consisted of land, but more generally of cattle. For the son of an *og-aire* or lowest order of chief, the fee was three cows ; and from that upwards to the son of a king, for whom the fee was from eighteen to thirty cows. For girls, as giving more trouble, requiring more care, and as being less able to help the foster-parents in after-life, it was something higher than for boys. The child, during fosterage, was treated in all respects like the children of the house : he worked at

* Reeves, Adamnan, 191.

some appropriate employment or discharged some suitable function for the benefit of the foster-father : and he had to be educated in a way that suited his station of life : as has been already described (vol. I., p. 441). There were minute regulations regarding clothes, food, and means of amusement, all of which varied according to rank. How far the foster-father was liable for injuries suffered by the foster-child at the hands of others, or for his misdeeds, is set forth with great care.

Precautions were taken, in the shape of penalties, to prevent the fosterage being terminated before the time by either party without sufficient cause. At the termination of the period of fosterage the foster-father gave the foster-son a parting gift, the amount of which was regulated according to rank and other circumstances. If in after-life the foster-father fell into poverty, and had no children of his own to support him, he had a claim on his foster-son for maintenance, provided he had duly discharged all the duties of fosterage, including that of the parting gift. The foster-mother had a similar claim. It was usual for a chief to send his child to be fostered to one of his own sub-chiefs : but the parents often chose a chief of their own rank. Sometimes a chief had a large number of children at fosterage : in the Book of the Dun Cow we are told that at one time Ochy Beg, king of Cliach, the district round Knockainy in Limerick, had forty boys in his charge, sons of the nobles of Munster.* In cases where children were left without parents or guardians, and required protection, the law required that they should be placed in fosterage under suitable persons at the tribe's expense.†

The children of kings, chiefs, or other distinguished persons were eagerly sought after for fosterage ; and in order to satisfy such claims, it sometimes happened that such children had two or more foster-fathers, with whom

* O'Curry, Man. & Cust., I. 357.   † Br. Laws. II., Pref. lvii.

they lived in succession or in turn. Thus the great
Dedanann chief, Lugh the Ildana, had nine fosterers ;* and
coming to historic times, Lewy Mac Con, king of Ireland
(A.D. 250–253), was fostered by Olioll Olum, king of
Munster, and by Olioll's brother, Lewy Laga.† To be
fostered by several was considered a mark of distinction.
Laegaire's daughters, when inquiring from St. Patrick about
God (who they thought might be some great chief), asked,
among many other questions, did many foster His Son—
implying that this would be a sure indication of rank and
dignity.‡

Although it was more usual to send boys to be fostered
than girls, still we often find in the old tales pleasant
pictures of girls in their homes with their foster-sisters.
In the story of the courtship of Emer, the young hero
Cuculainn, going to the house of her father, Forgall Monach,
at Lusk, north of Dublin, to woo the young lady, found
her on the lawn of the fort with her foster-sisters, who
were learning embroidery and hand-dexterity with her.§

Fosterage was the closest of all ties between families.
The relationship was regarded as something sacred. The
foster-children were often more attached to the foster-
parents and foster-brothers than to the members of their
own family : and cases have occurred where a man has
voluntarily laid down his life to save the life of his
foster-father or foster-brother. This attachment is noticed
by many English writers from Giraldus down‖ : and
illustrations are found everywhere in Irish writings both
ancient and modern. At the great Battle of Moyrath,
fought in 637 by the monarch Domnall against his
rebellious foster-son, Congal Claen, the king, both before
and during the battle, shows himself most anxious for the
personal safety of Congal, now his mortal enemy.¶ For a

---

* Rev. Celt., XII. 89.   ‡ Todd, St. Patk., 453 : see also Trip. Life, clxix.
† Silva Gad., 349.   § Kilk. Archæol. Journ., 1870–1, p. 404.
‖ Girald., Top. Hib., III. xxiii.   ¶ Moyrath, 135, 155, 161, 305.

modern illustration, see Carleton's story of " The Foster-Brother."*   The custom of fosterage existed in Ireland—though in a modified form—even so late as the seventeenth or eighteenth century.

There was also a **literary fosterage,** when a boy was sent to be reared up by an ollave or professor, and instructed for a degree.   The foster-father was " to instruct him with-" out reserve, to prepare him for his degree, to chastise " him without severity, and to feed and clothe him while " learning his legitimate profession."   The amount of fee was regulated by law.   All gains earned by the pupil while learning were to be paid to the tutor, and also the first fee he earned after leaving him.   If the teacher fell into poverty in after-life, his foster-pupil was bound to support him.   The relationship of literary fosterage was regarded as still more close and sacred than that of ordinary fosterage.   On this see also vol. i., p. 423.

Gossipred.—When a man stood sponsor for a child at baptism, he became the child's godfather, and gossip to the parents.   Gossipred was—and is still—regarded as a sort of religious relationship between families, and created mutual obligations of regard and friendship.†

After the Anglo-Norman invasion the people of the English colony, from the great lords down, often sent their children to be fostered by the Irish: and as might be expected, these young persons grew up speaking the Irish language, and thoroughly Irish in every way.   Mainly for this reason the two customs of fosterage and gossipred were bitterly denounced by early English writers,‡ most of whom were anxious to keep the two races apart: and we know that the Government passed several stringent laws forbidding them under the penalty of high treason: but these laws were generally disregarded.   Gossipred in

---

* Irish Penny Journal, 338.

† For full accounts of Fosterage, see Br. Laws, ii. 147, 349 ; v. 97 : and for both customs, Ware, Antiqq., chap. xi.   ‡ Instance, Spenser, 112.

a modified form exists to this day all over the empire ; and the custom of fostering was formerly common among the Welsh, the Anglo-Saxons, and the Scandinavians.

4. *Family-Names.*

Hereditary family-names became general in Ireland about the time of Brian Boru, viz. at the end of the tenth and the beginning of the eleventh century : and some authorities assert that they were adopted in obedience to an ordinance of that monarch. The manner of forming the names was very simple. Each person had one proper name of his own. In addition to this, all the members of a family, and of their descendants in the male line, took as a common surname the name of their father, with *Mac* (son) prefixed, or of their grandfather or some more remote ancestor, with *Ua* or *O* (grandson or descendant) prefixed. Thus the O'Neills are so called from their ancestor *Niall* Glunduff, king of Ireland (A.D. 916), and ' John O'Neill ' means John the descendant of *Niall* : the Mac Carthys of Desmond have their surname from a chief named *Carrthach*, who lived about the year 1043. The same custom was adopted in Scotland : but while in Ireland *O* was much more general than *Mac*, in Scotland the *O* was very rarely chosen, and nearly all the Scotch Gaelic family-names begin with *Mac*.

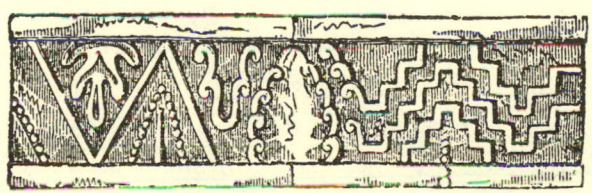

Sculpture on a Column, Church of the Monastery, Glendalough.
(From Petrie's Round Towers, 260.)

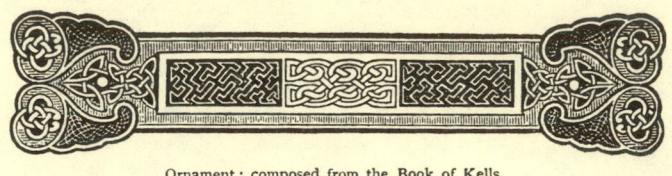

Ornament: composed from the Book of Kells.

CHAPTER XX

THE HOUSE

SECTION I. *Construction, Shape, and Size.*

BEFORE the introduction of Christianity, buildings in Ireland, whether domestic, military, or sepulchral, were generally round or oval. The quadrangular shape, which was used in the churches in the time of St. Patrick, came very slowly into use, and round structures finally disappeared only in the fourteenth or fifteenth century. But the round shape was not universal, even in the most ancient period. The great Banqueting Hall of Tara was rectangular, as we see by its ruins at the present day. The *Craebh-ruadh* [Creeveroe], a similar hall at Emain, was of a like shape ; and the *bruden* or feasting-hall at Dun-da-benn (the fort overhanging the waterfall in the Bann near Coleraine) was square : both of these made in imitation of the hall of Tara.* And in case of many of the ordinary good-sized dwelling-houses, the expressions used regarding them show that the walls were straight and parallel, and that consequently the shape was rectangular. Some of the old lisses or forts still to be seen are of this shape : and even where the surrounding rampart was round the wooden houses it enclosed were often rectangular.†

* Táin bo Fraich, 160, 161 : Mesca Ulad, 13.
† See for example Sick Bed, Atlantis, II. 105, first line : also O'Curry, Man. & Cust., II. 31.

The common Irish word for a house is *tech*, Lat. *lectum*; whence come the compounds *tegduis* or *teaghdais*, one of the names for a homestead; and *teaghlach*, ' a family or household.' A dwelling in general is denoted by *árus* or *áross*; a homestead by *baile*, now generally anglicised *bally*, but used in a more extended sense to denote a townland. The word *brug* or *brugh* [broo] was also applied to a large dwelling: in Peter O'Connell's Dictionary, taken from old authorities, we find :—" *Brug*, the same as *baile*, a mansion, manor, or farmhouse." But this word *brug* had other applications, which will be found fully set forth in Hennessy's Introduction to the Mesca Ulad, p. 7.

It has sometimes been stated that there were no towns or cities in ancient Ireland: but this statement is misleading. There were many centres of population, though they were never surrounded by walls; and the dwellings were detached and scattered a good deal—not closely packed as in modern towns. In our old writings, both native and Anglo-Irish, we have many records of towns and cities. As a comparatively late example—in the twelfth century—may be mentioned Downpatrick, which Giraldus Cambrensis, in his account of John de Courcy's invasion of Ulster, calls the " City of Down " : but it was quite open and undefended. Then we know that some of the large monasteries had two or three thousand students, which implies a total population much larger. Some of the provisions of the Brehon Law show that numbers of lis-dwellings must have been clustered together: one statement, for instance, that a mill or a fishing-weir was sometimes the common property of the *finè* or tribe.

The dwelling-houses, as well indeed as the early churches, were nearly always of wood, as that material was much the most easily procured. The ordinary kinds of timber were used according to circumstances, but the most common were deal, oak, and yew. The custom of building in wood was so general in Ireland that it was considered

FIG. 168.

Clochan or beehive-shaped house in Inishmurray : of unhewn stones : no mortar. Nearly circular : 13 feet across, and 14 feet high. The doorway (which is at the far side, and does not appear in the figure) is strikingly Cyclopean, formed of a few great stones : the opening shown in the figure was for ventilation, light, and smoke. A good type of the pagan and very early Christian clochan. (From Kilk. Archæol. Journ. for 1885-6, p. 204 : in which, on p. 206, is a sketch of the doorway. Drawn by Wakeman.)

a characteristic of the Irish—*more Scottorum*, " after the manner of the Scots "—as Bede expresses it. Yet we know that the Britons, Saxons, and Franks, also very generally built in wood. When Henry II. was in Ireland, 1171–2, " he had a royal palace constructed for himself of " planed wood, built with wonderful taste, in which he and " the kings and princes of Ireland kept the festival of " Christmas."* Of course this house was the work of Dublin builders and tradesmen. Some of the houses in Waterford in 1168 were of wood : and it was by pulling one of them down that Raymond le Gros effected an entrance into the city. Wooden houses, highly ornamented, continued in use in Dublin, Drogheda, and other towns, down to the last century.†

But although wood-building was general in Ireland before the twelfth century, it was not universal : for some stone churches were erected from the time of the introduction of Christianity : beehive-shaped houses, as well as cahers and cashels (pp. 57, 58, below), were built of stone, without mortar, from pre-historic times : and the remains of these primitive structures—churches, houses, and cahers —are still to be seen in many parts of Ireland.‡ In all these mortarless buildings, the stones, though in their natural state—not hammered or chiselled into shape—are fitted to each other with great skill and accuracy : or, as Petrie expresses it, " with wonderful art."§

The dwelling-houses were almost always constructed of wickerwork : *tech-figthi* or *tech-fithi*, a ' wickerwork house ' : from *figim*, ' I weave.' The wall (*fraig*) was formed of long stout poles (*slat*, ' a pole ') placed in a circle, if the house was to be round, standing pretty near each other, with their ends fixed deep in the ground, the

* Hoveden, quoted in Cambr. Ev., II. 173.

† Dublin Penny Journal, I. 89 and 268.

‡ For a whole town of pre-historic circular stone houses in Kerry, see Macalister's article in Trans. Roy, Ir. Acad., vol. XXXI., p. 209.

§ See Stokes's Life of Petrie, p. 135.

spaces between closed in with rods and twigs neatly and firmly interwoven ; generally of hazel. The poles were peeled and polished smooth. The whole surface of the wickerwork was plastered on the outside, and made brilliantly white with lime, or occasionally striped in various colours ; leaving the white poles exposed to view. The residence of O'Murphy at Dunflin in Sligo in the thirteenth century is called in HyF (265) " a white wattled edifice of noble polish."* When the house was to be rectangular the poles were set in two parallel rows, filled in with wickerwork.

Building in wicker-work was common to the Celtic people of Ireland, Scotland, and Britain.† It is very often referred to in Irish writings of all kinds. An instance has been already cited in vol. I., p. 10. Adamnan (p. 106) relates that Columba on one occasion sent his monks to bring bundles of rods (*virgarum fasciculos*) to construct one of the houses of a hospice. The same incident is told in the Irish Life of St. Columba ; and here the rods or wattles are called by the Irish term *caelaig* (sing. *caelach*, ' anything slender,' ' a slender wattle,' from *cael*, ' slender,' pron. *kail*). The *cliath* [clee-a] or hurdle and the wattles or laths for building houses are often mentioned in the Brehon Laws.‡ In some large houses the standing poles were very thick and high : in describing the construction of Bricriu's house at Dun-Rury, the writer of the " Feast of Bricriu " (p. 5) states, probably with some exaggeration, that it took seven strong men to put each pole in its place. But more usually they were of moderate dimensions.

From the curious details given in the Brehon Law tract called Crith Gabhlach,§ it appears that, after the

* On all this, see O'Curry, Man. & Cust., II. 32 : HyF, 265, 279 : Three Irish Homilies, 77 bot. : and vol. I., p. 10, *supra*

† Bede, Eccl. Hist., III. x. : Rhys, The Welsh People, 199, 200 : Ware, Antiqq., xxv.

‡ As in vol. IV. 253, 305, 313.   Br. Laws, IV. 305.

poles had been fixed in the ground, the spaces were filled up with wickerwork in the following manner, to form the *fraig* or side wall. Beginning at the bottom, a strip of a certain width was woven all round ; another strip was woven above that : and so on till the eave was reached ; after which a sloping-drip board was fixed all round at the junction of each adjacent pair of strips, and one at the eave over all.

FIG. 16.

Maynooth Castle at present: photograph. Erected originally in 1176 by Maurice Fitzgerald : but greatly altered and enlarged subsequently. One of the Anglo-Norman castles referred to in page 65 farther on. (From Journal of the Kildare Archæological Society, I., p. 223.)

This last description, and that of Bricriu's house-poles above, go to show that the side wall was often very high : and this is borne out for other buildings by many passages, both direct and incidental. Keating (page 333), drawing from old authorities, says that the Banqueting-Hall of Tara was 300 feet long by 75 feet wide and 45 feet high : and Kineth O'Hartigan, in the tenth century, makes a similar statement as to length and height.* Now Keating understates both the length and breadth, as appears by actual measurement of the present

* Petrie's Tara, 190.

existing ruin,* so we may take it that the height was not under 45 feet. Again, three great heroes contend in another banqueting-hall, the feat consisting in throwing a heavy *roth* or wheel-quoit upwards towards the roof. Laegaire the victorious throws it half-way up the wall: Conall Cernach throws it to the ridge pole: but Cuculainn sent it right through the roof.† Lastly, in the Battle of Rossnaree (p. 5), Concobar, speaking of the devastation committed by the Connaughtmen in Ulster, says :—" Our " fine dwellings were burned so that they were left no " higher than single rooms or outhouses." This passage seems to point to two-storied houses, with which other passages concur. But in some cases the wall, or part of it, was so low that the eave was within reach of the hand, like the eaves of some " Swiss cottages " of the present day: for the Crith Gabhlach‡ lays down a penalty for taking away any portion of the straw from the thatch of a *bo-aire's* house. When there was more than one apartment in a house, each had a separate wall and roof: except, of course, where one apartment was over another.

In the Highlands of Scotland wattled or wicker houses were used, even among high-class people, down to the end of the eighteenth century§; and it is probable that they continued in use in Ireland to as late a period.

In the superior classes of houses, and in churches, a better plan of building was adopted, by forming the wall with sawed planks instead of wickerwork. The little hut erected at Iona for St. Columba's special use was constructed of wood planks (*in tuguriolo tabulis suffulto*).|| The oratory built at Rahan in the present King's County in the year 747 was of boards; and we are told that it was unusually large, so that it took a thousand boards to build

---

* For actual dimensions, see p. 85, below.
† Kilk. Arch. Journ., 1870, p. 438.
‡ Brehon Laws, IV. 313.
§ Stuart, in Book of Deer, Pref. cli. note 1.
|| Adamnan, p. 54; and see 177.

it.* But the dwelling-houses of monasteries, as well as the smaller oratories, were generally of wickerwork: of which one instance has already been cited at p. 24 from Adamnan. In the houses of the higher classes the door-posts and other special parts of the dwelling and furniture were often made of yew, carved, and ornamented with gold, silver, bronze, and gems. We know this from the old records; and still more convincing evidence is afforded by the Brehon Law (IV. 313, 315), which prescribes fines for scratching or otherwise disfiguring the posts or lintels of doors, the heads or posts of beds, or the ornamental parts of other furniture.

Small square timber houses, consisting generally of just one apartment, have often been found deep in bogs, and sometimes in clay. They consist of beams and planks of oak and other timber, joined together with much rude skill by tenon-and-mortise without nails. They seem to have served some temporary purpose, as they are too small for permanent residence; perhaps they were intended to shelter workmen for the time who were cutting turf, or for those who attended to cattle when they were grazed in the booleys. Or possibly some may have been the little buildings connected with ancient mills (see chap. xxv.). From the position in which some of these houses have been found, it seems plain that they are very archaic: belonging probably to a time beyond the reach of history.†

The roof of the circular house was of a conical shape, brought to a point, with an opening in the centre for the smoke. It was of wickerwork or hurdles supported by rafters sloping upwards from the tops of the wall-poles all round, to the centre at the very top. From its shape and material this sort of roof was often called *cua-chlethe,*

---

* O'Curry, Man. & Cust., II. 37.

† Instances: Kilk. Arch. Journ., 1879–82, pp 307, 561 : see also Wood-Martin, Pagan Ireland, p 223 *et seq*

FIG. 170.

Wooden hut found, with many antique tools, in a bog in Donegal. Nearly square—16 feet each way; 9 feet high: divided into two stories. Evidently used, not as a residence, but as a shelter and sleeping-place. Open-air fireplace a little distance off, with remains of fires. The house was covered with bog to a depth of 25 feet, which must have taken an immense time to grow. (From Col. Wood-Martin's Pagan Ireland, p. 222. Drawn by Wakeman.)

' cup-shaped wicker roof.'*　The roof of the quadrangular houses was much like that of the common run of houses of the present day.　If the house was large, the conical roof of those of circular form was supported by a tall, strong *tuireadh* or pole standing on the centre of the floor† ; in case the house was quandrangular, there was a row of such supporting poles, or two rows if the structure was very large.　The circular building with conical roof was in shape exactly like the buildings called ' tholos ' among the Greeks.

Straw was used for roof-covering from the earliest times, and its use has continued to the present day.　In 1596 the straw thatch of O'Madden's Castle was ignited by a firebrand thrown by the besiegers, so that the roof was burned (Hy Many, 150).　The word *tuga* was used to denote a roof-covering, whether made of straw or of any other material.　In the Tripartite Life of St. Patrick (p. 157) we are told that a certain person built a house in Ess Macc n-Eirc ;　but that a *rush* of the thatch (*simni tuga : simni*, ' a rush ') had not been put upon it before it was demolished by another person.　Reeds were often employed ;　and for this purpose they were sometimes cultivated in special plots of ground.‡　We have seen that St. Finan roofed his church at Lindisfarne with reeds (*harundine texit*).　Whatever the material, the covering was in all cases put on with some degree of art and neatness, such as we see in the work of the skilled straw-thatchers of the present day.

A better class of roof than any of the preceding was what is called in Irish *slinn*, commonly rendered by *shingle*.　The house of Ailill and Maive at Cruachan had a roof of *slinn* (*tuga slinned*).§　*Slinn*, in Old Irish,

---

* Sullivan, Introd. 299, note 531 : and LU, 19, *a*, 17.
† O'Curry, Man. & Cust., II. 32.　　　　　　　　‡ Adamnan, 163.
§ Táin bo Fr., 141 : Ir. Texte, I. 281, ₁₁: and see " Slind " in Wirterbuch, same vol. : also Fled Bricrenn, § 55.

glosses *imbrex*, 'a brick or tile,' and it has the same meaning in the modern language : but *tuga slinned* generally means a roofing of thin boards. For instance, in an Irish poem written by Mac Conmidhe early in the thirteenth century, the church of Armagh is said to be roofed with *slinns* of oak (*slinntech darach*)* ; and in another much older authority shingles made of yew are mentioned.† The covering was constructed by making the small flat pieces overlap as in modern slated or tiled roofs. Sometimes, anticipating modern usage, they employed materials superior to any of the preceding. The Annals of Ulster record that in the year 1008, the oratory of Armagh was roofed with lead.

The thatch of ladies' greenans (see p. 42, *infra*) was sometimes formed of birds' wings. In a poem composed by the hero Cael O'Nemnann about the lady Crede [Cray], daughter of the king of Kerry, it is stated that her beautiful greenan was thatched with the wings of birds, so arranged as to form bright stripes of brown, reddish purple, and other colours‡ : and King Cormac Mac Art, when he visited Tairngire or Fairyland, saw people thatching a house with the wings of white birds.§

Over the top of the principal room on the inside extended a ridge-pole or roof-tree called *féici* [faika], from which lamps were suspended to light the apartment : whence Cormac's Glossary (p. 81) derives the word from *feighe* [fay], ' illumination.' This last word again is derived from *féig*, which Zeuss (998, 38, 39) explains ' bright, or illuminated,' and which is connected with the modern Gaelic verb, *féuch*, ' see.' This word *féici* was also applied to the ridge-pole of a tent, and sometimes to the lintel of a door.‖ The *féici* was used in houses of a rectangular shape, and possibly in round houses also. It was supported

---

* O'Curry, Man. & Cust., II. 58. † *Ibid.*, p. 34.
‡ O'Curry, MS. Mat., 309 : Man. & Cust , II. 12, 13 : Silva Gad., 120.
§ Ir. Texte, III. 213. ‖ Moyrath, 200, 13.

by the posts already mentioned, which also supported the roof. In Cormac's Glossary (34, under ' *clii* ') a house-post is mentioned as tapering from floor to ridge.

There were windows in the *fraig* or wall, and often a skylight in the roof. A window was called by two names *seinester* and *fuinneóg*, the first derived from Lat. *fenestra*, and the second—which is the word now in use—from A.-Sax. *windeage*.* A skylight was called by the native name *forless* (' top-light '), from *less* or *les*, ' light.' On one occasion persons kept a lady in concealment in a wicker-work house, door and windows all closed up except one *seinister* and a *forleas*, ' a window and a skylight.'† The house of Ailill and Maive at Croghan had a shutter of brass to each of its windows, and a fastening of brass to its *forles*.‡

Glass was known among various ancient nations from the most remote period: the Celts of Britain were well acquainted with it: and from constant references to it in our oldest writings, it is obvious that it was well known to the ancient Irish.§ Beads and other small ornamental objects of glass, variously coloured, are constantly found in Irish pre-Christian graves and crannoges: and in one of the Loughcrew graves were found a number of them, one about an inch long, and—says Mr. Fergusson—obviously shaped by being softened by fire.‖ The statement that this bead was softened by fire is quite true indeed, inasmuch as all the objects of this kind wherever found in Ireland were formed while the material was heated to softness. More-over the manufacture of these little articles was an art requiring long training and much delicate manipulative skill, for most of them are made of different coloured glass

---

* Stokes, in Lives of SS., Pref. c.   † Stokes, Da Derga, 19, 20.
‡ Crowe, Tain bo Fr., 141 top.
§ See, for examples, Miss Stokes, in Trans. Roy. Ir. Acad., xxx. 283: Fled Bricrenn, 208: Todd, St. Patrick, 222: and Kilk. Arch. Journ., 1879–82, p. 532.   ‖ Fergusson, Rude Stone Mon., 218.

or porcelain—blue, white, yellow, pale red, &c.—blended and moulded and beautifully striated in the manner shown imperfectly here in the black-and-white figures. They were used for ornamentation, very often forming the heads of pins, but sometimes made into rings, or strung together for beads.*

One of the testimonies to the use of glass at a remote period in Ireland is the fact that it has two native Irish names—not derived—viz. *gloine* or *glaine* [2-syll.], which signifies clearness and purity, from *glan*, 'pure,' 'clear,' 'bright' : and *bus*, which is explained by O'Davoren as 'crystal or glass.' We often read of *copans* or cups of *bus*, *corns*

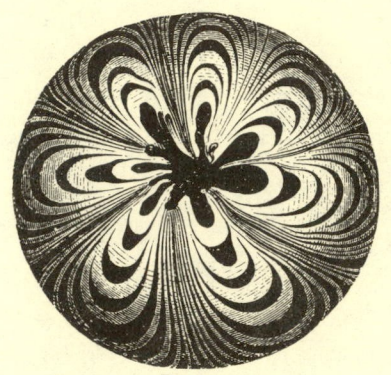

FIG. 171.

FIG. 172.   FIG. 173.   FIG. 174.   FIG. 175.

Glass and porcelain ornaments, full size, now in National Museum. In figures 172, 173, and 175, the coloured ornaments form part of the substance, and were worked into shape while the whole mass was softened by heat. Figure 172, made of clear glass, with a yellow spiral ornament. Figure 173, of opaque light-green glass, grooved from top to bottom. Figure 174, body of deep blue, on which is twisted, and fastened while soft, an ornament of white enamel. Figure 175, pin-head of fine light-red porcelain decorated with wavy stripes, some white, some yellow : found with part of bronze pin attached, as shown in figure.

There are in the Museum many ornaments of coloured glass, with variously coloured patterns of enamel on the surface, of which the most beautiful is shown, full size, in figure 171. It is a circular disk, half-inch thick, the body of dark blue glass, with a wavy pattern of white enamel, like an open flower, on the surface. (All, both figures and descriptions, from Wilde's Catalogue, pp. 162-165.)

or horns of *bus*, &c. These words were also applied to natural crystal as well as to glass. Glass was turned to various uses. Glass drinking-vessels were known to the Irish at least as early as the sixth century. Adamnan (p. 147) relates that a druid named Broichan, foster-father

* See Wilde's Catalogue, 162 to 169.

of the Pictish King Brude, in the time of St. Columba, had a glass drinking-cup (*vitream biberam*) of great value which, as he was about to drink from it, fell and was broken into fragments : and vessels of glass are mentioned in the *Lebar Brecc**. In the Tripartite Life of St. Patrick (p. 95) there is a legend of a stone altar found in a cave in Connaught with four glass chalices (*ceitri cailig glainidi*) at the four corners.

Glass and vessels of glass are frequently mentioned in the most ancient of the tales. In several passages of the Voyage of Maildune we read of *lestars* or drinking-vessels of glass : and in one part of the voyage he sails over a transparent sea " like green glass." In a sermon in LU, on the Day of Judgment, the six kinds of mercy by which heaven is to be attained are called " the six glass doors " through which comes the light of eternal life into the " church."† Add to all this that the remains of a regular glass factory have been found by the Rev. Mr. Ffrench in the townland of Moylisha, almost beside the ancient church of Aghowle in Wicklow, where great quantities of lumps of glass, chiefly of the three colours, blue, green, and white, have been—and can still be—dug up. The fuel used in the manufacture was charcoal, bits of which are found among the fragments (Kilk. Arch. Journ., 1885–6, p. 420).

Glass was used in England for church windows in the seventh century ; and it had been long previously in use for this purpose on the Continent : so we may conclude that the knowledge of the use of glass for windows found its way into Ireland from Gaul, Italy, and England, through missionaries and merchants.‡ At all events glass windows are mentioned in many of the ancient Irish tales, which shows that this use of glass was familiarly known to the original writers. In the Feast of Bricriu in LU, which was

---

* Atkinson, Pass. & Homil., p. 48, 265.
† Rev. Celt., IV. 249 : LU, 32, *a*, 29.
‡ See Petrie, Round Towers, 201.

copied in 1100 from earlier books, we are told that Bricriu made an apartment for his own special use, with windows of glass (*senistre glainide*) on every side ; and he placed one over his own couch in his *grecnan*, so that he could have a full view of the banquet-hall and company through it.*   In the same tale the house of Ailill and Maive, king and queen of Connaught in the first century, is described as having twelve windows closed up with glass.†   There is of course bardic exaggeration in all this : still we are forced to believe that glass of some kind was used in Ireland for windows, certainly before 1100, and probably as early as the beginning of the historical period.

There was one large door leading to the principal apartment of the dwelling-house, with smaller doors, opening externally, for the other rooms.   Generally the several rooms did not communicate with each other internally. In the outer *lis* or rampart surrounding the homestead (for which see p. 54, below), there was a single large door.   The doors of some great houses were very large and heavy.   In the Boroma, Branduff and his companions " went forth " outside and shut the great royal doorleaf of the palace " behind them " (*ro iadsadar in ríg-comlai móir in rígthigi dara néise*), " for the strength of nine men was in each of them‡ " :   which implies that the *comla* or door was very massive.   But such doors were exceptions, and those of ordinary houses were not larger than was necessary.   The common Irish word for door was, and is, *dorus* : a single leaf of a door was *comla*.

Sometimes there was a *cairthe* or stone column or pillar —or more than one—standing at the side of the outer or *lis* doorway.   In the Mesca Ulad a person, seeing certain white objects in the distance, mistakes them for shields : but his companion says :—" They are not shields at all but

* Ir. Texte, I. 254 ; and Fled Bricrenn (Henderson), p. 5
† Ir. Texte, I. 281 : Henderson, 69.
‡ Rev Celt., xiii. 61 Silva Gad., 410.

" the [white] stone columns (*colomna cloch*) that are in the
" doors of these royal raths "* : and in the " Destruction of
Dind Rîg " we are told that at the door of the dun outside
there was a *cairthe* or standing-stone. The knocker was
a small log of wood called *bas-chrann*, i.e. ' hand-wood,'
which lay in a niche by the door. It is everywhere
mentioned in the old tales that visitors knocked with the
bas-chrann. In rich people's houses there was a special
doorkeeper (Irish *dóirseoir, dóirside* or *dóirsire*), to answer
knocks and admit visitors. At the bottom of the door
was a *tairsech* or threshold. Cormac, in his Glossary
(p. 161), derives this word from *tairis*, ' over it,' because
" people pass inwards over it." It is a derivative from the
Irish *tars* or *tarsa*, ' across,' connected with Latin *trans*.

The jamb was anciently called *aursa* or *irsa*, but in the
modern language it is *ursa* : the lintel was *for-dorus* (i.e.
' on the door '), now usually *fardorus*. A certain student
was making prostrations near the door of his hut, when he
struck his head against the *fordorus* and fell dead.† On
the outside of the large door of the *lis* was a porch called
aurdúine (lit. ' front part of the *dún* '). Cormac's Glossary
explains *aurdúine* as a structure " at the doors of the *dúns*,
which is made by the artisans "—implying ornamentation.
The *lis* door was always closed at night. A more usual
name for a door-porch was *immdorus* (*imm* or *im*, ' about ' :
' about a door '). In the Vision of Mac Conglinne (90, 91)
persons are spoken of as carrying offal " from the *immdorus*
of the great house to the *immdorus* of the *dun* or rampart
on the outside." In O'Clery's Glossary *immdorus* is stated
to be the same as *fordorus*, from which it would seem that
the two words were sometimes used one for the other.

The door was secured on the inside either by a bolt
or by a lock. We have the best evidence to show that
locks were used in Ireland in very early times. When

---

* Mesca Ulad, 21
† *Fordorus* : so in LL : see Stokes, Lives of SS., Pref. xi. note 5.

St. Columba went to visit the Pictish King Brude, " the
door of the fortress "—as the Irish Life of the Saint relates
—" was shut against him, and at once, through Colum-
cille's prayer, the iron locks (*glais iarnaidhi*) opened."
We are told by Adamnan that a certain disciple on an
important occasion peeped at St. Columba in his hut at
Iona through the keyhole, and was soundly rated by the
saint next day for his curiosity. Another similar occurrence
ended less harmlessly. While Columba was surreptitiously
copying St. Finnen's Book of Psalms at Drumfinn (vol. I.,
p. 501, *supra*), Finnen sent a messenger to spy out what he
was doing, who looked through the keyhole and saw him
at the work. But the saint's pet crane, happening to be
with him, walked over to the door and neatly picked out
the man's eye through the keyhole.*

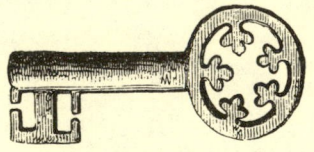

FIG. 176.   FIG. 177.

Bronze Keys. Figure 176, a very perfect and highly decorated key, 2⅞ inches long,
with a pipe in the shaft: found in Tory Island. Figure 177, 1⅝ inch long. (From
Wilde's Catalogue.)

In the romantic literature notices of locks and keys
are equally common. In the story of Mongan in the Book
of the Dun Cow, mention is made of a beautiful chamber
locked and opened by a key.† And in the story of the
Demon Chariot of Cuculainn in the same old book, we are
told that the king's palace in the Isle of Skye had iron
locks.‡ Locks were used for other purposes, as, for
instance, to fasten fetters. In the seventh-century Life
of St. Patrick by Muirchu, it is related that Maccuil put
on his feet an iron fetter which he locked, and threw the
key into the sea.§ The common word for a lock is *glas*.

* Adamnan, 226, and note *c*.
† Voyage of Bran, I. 55: LU, 134, *a*, last line, and *b*, first line.
‡ Kilk. Arch. Journ., 1870–1, p. 385.   § Trip. Life, 288, 28.

A key is denoted by *echuir* or *cochuir* (gen. *eochrach*), which in Cormac's Glossary (p. 68) is derived from two words signifying ' crooked-straight ' : *i.e.* partly crooked and partly straight. A keyhole is *poll-eochrach* (*poll*, ' a hole '). Sometimes a door had a chain (*slabrad*) attached, which was probably used to fasten it. When Labraid and his men were about to set fire to the palace of Dinnree, they drew out the chain that was attached to the *comla* or double door, and put it on or round the pillar-stone outside, apparently to prevent the escape of those inside, who in a little time were all burned to death.* Mention is made of the *aradh* or ladder, which must have been in constant use.

The houses were generally small, according to our idea of size. But then we must remember that, like the people of other ancient nations, the Irish had very little furniture. In the main room there was probably nothing—besides the couches—but a sufficient number of small movable seats and a large table of some sort, or perhaps a number of small tables. On this point it has been remarked that the Grianan of Ailech on Greenan-Ely near Derry, a circular building of uncemented stones, which was the palace of the Ulster kings, " gives a very poor idea of the extent of an ancient Irish regal abode† " : inasmuch as it was, as its ruins show, only seventy-seven feet in diameter. But this was merely the central keep or citadel. The dwelling of the king himself may have been within this enclosure, which afforded space enough for a respect-ably large house. The whole hill is surrounded by several earthen ramparts, one outside another, now nearly levelled, with broad spaces between (for which see page 91 below). In the intervening spaces timber houses were built, in which the chiefs and numerous dependents of the king lived : and probably the king himself had one or more

---

* Stokes, Destruction of Dinnree, Zeitschr. Celt. Phil., III. 13.

† Hennessy, Book of Fenagh, 63, note 3.

outside the circular fortress. Many of the English and Anglo-Irish square castles, of which the ruins are seen to this day all through the country, were small and inconvenient to live in—often much smaller than the Greenan-Ely fortress : but most of them were merely citadels, which were originally surrounded by buildings of a lighter construction and more convenient size, in which the family and dependents customarily lived.

FIG. 178

Trim Castle, originally built by Hugh de Lacy the Elder, end of twelfth century ; but afterwards rebuilt. One of the Anglo-Norman strongholds referred to at p. 65 farther on. (From Cromwell's Tours. Drawn by Petrie.)

Still the general run of houses were small in early times, in Ireland as elsewhere. Moreover the standard of living was in all countries low and rude compared with what we are now accustomed to ; a fact that ought to be borne in mind by the reader of the account given here of the domestic arrangements in ancient Irish houses. In England, even so late as the time of Holinshed—sixteenth century—hardly any houses had chimneys. A big fire of logs was kindled against the wall of the principal room, the smoke from which escaped through an orifice in the roof right overhead. Here the meat was cooked, and here the family dined. In very few houses were there beds or bedrooms, and the general way of sleeping was on a pallet of straw covered with a sheet, under coverlets of various coarse materials, with a log of wood for a pillow : while the manner of eating, which is noticed farther on (page 111), was correspondingly rude. All this is described for England by Roberts.*

It is not easy to understand the statements given in the Brehon Laws as to the size of houses. For instance, the text of the Crith Gablach (IV. 311) says that a brewy or public hospitaller had " a house of 27 teet," and a backhouse or kitchen of 17 feet. But this is obviously a partial and imperfect statement—like so many others in the Brehon Laws ; for elsewhere we are told that he should be provided with all the necessary appliances to accommodate numerous guests, including, in case of one high class of brewy, 100 beds. It is probable that the " house of 27 feet "was his own special residence, rectangular in shape, 27 feet wide : the length undetermined. In this case the little apartments for the family beds (see p. 46, *infra*) might be along one or both side walls : but if it was a circular house 27 feet in diameter, some at least of the family beds must have been in separate houses outside. As for the beds for the brewy's guests, there must have been a number of separate houses for these.

St. Patrick, in laying out the ecclesiastical buildings in Armagh, imitated the ancient fashion of the country, as he wisely did in most other things : for we are told in the Tripartite Life (p. 237) :—" In this wise then Patrick " measured the *ferta*, namely, seven score feet in the *lis* " [*i.e.* the circular rampart enclosing the whole establish- " ment], and twenty-seven feet in the great house, and " seventeen feet in the kitchen, and seven feet in the " oratory : and in that wise it was that he used to found " the *congbala* [ecclesiastical homesteads] always."

* See Roberts, Soc. Hist., p. 318.

We know that many of the great houses were very large. The present remains of the *Tech Midchuarta* or Banqueting-Hall of Tara measure 759 feet long and 46 feet wide : and Petrie states that it must have been originally about 90 feet wide.* In the " Wooing of Emer " (p. 69) we are told that the measurement of the hall of Emain was " fifteen feet and nine score " : which refers to a square shape.

FIG. 179.

King John's Castle in Limerick.   Erected in the beginning of the thirteenth century by one of the Anglo-Norman chiefs.   Stanyhurst states that it was built by the order of King John.   One of the Anglo-Norman castles referred to at p. 65 farther on.   (From Mrs. Hall's Ireland.)

We may form some idea of the better class of dwellings from an enumeration, in the Crith Gabhlach, of the various buildings in the homestead of a well-to-do farmer of the class *bo-aire*, who rented land from a chief and whose property was chiefly in cattle. His dwelling consisted of (at least) seven different houses, each as already observed with a separate wall, door, and roof :—1. Dwelling-house (*tech*), at least 27 feet in diameter : 2. Kitchen or cooking-

* Petrie's Tara, p. 185.

house (*ircha*, or *cuchtair*, or *cuile*), at the back of the dwelling-house : 3. A kiln (*aith*) for drying corn : 4. A barn (*saball*) in which corn was stored : 5. A sheep-house (*lías* cáirach*) : 6. A calf-house (*lías láeg*) : 7. A pigsty (*muc-fóil* or *muccál*, from *muc*, ' a pig,' and *foil* or *fail*, ' a house '—*fail*, ' demus,' Z., 5, 43).† These were all in one

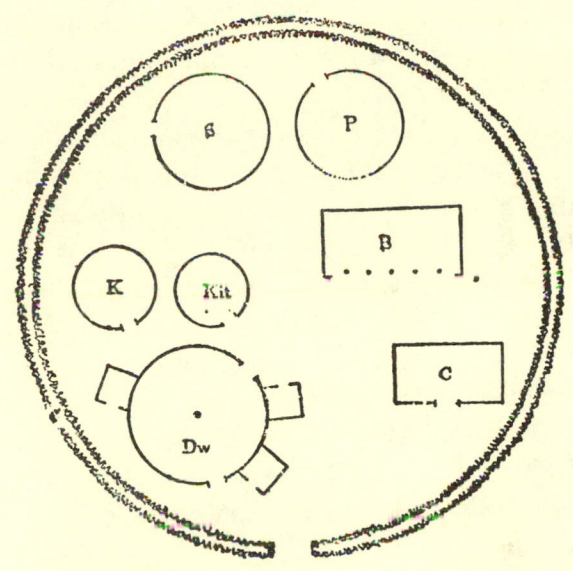

FIG. 180.

Conjectural plan of homestead of a well-to-do farmer of the *bo-aire* class, constructed from the descriptions given in the Brehon Laws. "Dw," family dwelling-house, of wickerwork, 27 feet in diameter, with three outside sleeping-rooms (which might be either round or rectangular): "Kit," kitchen: "K," kiln (chiefly for corn-drying): "B," Barn: "C," calf-house: "P," pig-house: "S," sheep-house. The whole group surrounded by a circular rath or defensive entrenchment. with one entrance. The cows and horses were kept outside this enclosure.

group close together ; and each generally, though not always, consisted of the usual round-shaped wicker-house with conical roof, except the barn, which was oblong : the whole group surrounded by the *lis* or *rath*, described farther on (p. 54). In all houses of the more comfortable class the

* This word *lias* (leece) was in very general use to denote a hut for the smaller animals—calves, sheep, lambs, &c　It must be distinguished from *les*, *lios*, or *lis*, ' a rath or fort."　　　† Brehon Laws, IV. 309, 311.

kitchen was separate from the dwelling-house and placed at the back : and there was a separate pantry for provisions, called in Irish *seallad,* a word which glosses *cellarium* in some Old Irish documents.*

From a fanciful derivation of *sabhall,* given in Senchus Mór (Br. Laws, I. 141), we may infer that a barn was oblong and had one side quite open, with the roof supported at that side on posts. From the same derivation, and from other passages,† it would appear that while in some cases the barn belonged to the owner of the homestead individually, in others it was common to the several families of the same *finè,* each householder using his own compartment for storing his corn : but in this case it must have been very large and detached—not situated within the enclosure of any private homestead. This arrangement could be adopted when the *lisses* and houses were near each other, forming a village or hamlet.

The women had a separate apartment or a separate house in the sunniest and pleasantest part of the homestead. This was called a *grianan* [greenan], which signifies a *solarium, solar,* or summer-house : a diminutive derivative from *grian,* ' the sun.' The women's greenan is constantly mentioned in Irish writings : and sometimes the master of the house had a greenan for himself, to which he could retire when he pleased. In Cruachan the greenan was placed over the *fordorus* or lintel, as much as to say it was placed in front over the common sitting-room : and probably it occupied some such position in most houses.

In great houses there was one apartment called the house of conversation (*tech immácallamae*), answering to the modern " drawing-room," where the family often sat, especially to receive visitors. Prince Fraech, when he visited Maive at the palace of Cruachan on important

* Stokes, Ir. Glosses in Tract on Declension, No 741.
† And see also Brehon Laws, IV. 305, mid.

business, was always brought into the "house of conversation" to discuss matters when an interview was needed.*

Sometimes there was a small side-room beside the principal apartment, from which a door opened directly into it : having no separate outside door. This was called *erdam* or *erdomh* or *aurdom*, as it is given in Cormac's Glossary (p. 3 : 'on or by a house' : *dam* or *dom*, 'house'). This plan was often adopted in Christian churches where a small apartment was placed at the side of the church.†

FIG. 181.

Bunratty Castle in the south of Clare, on the Bunratty river, where it joins the Shannon : built about the end of the thirteenth century by Thomas de Clare, an Anglo-Norman lord. One of the Anglo-Norman castles referred to in sect. 3 below. (From Kilk. Archæol. Journ., 1890-91, p. 292.)

The privy was called *fialtech*, i.e. 'veil-house' (*fial*, 'a veil' : *tech*, 'house') : the urinary was *fualtech*, from *fual*, 'urine.' In the Rule for the Culdee Monks, both houses are said to be the abode of demons ; and whoever goes to them is enjoined to bless them and also to bless himself— *i.e.* to make the sign of the cross.‡ The *fialtech* and

* Táin bo Fr., 143, 145.
† See the Erdamh or Erdam discussed at length in Petrie's Round Towers (Index). ‡ Reeves, Culdees, 91.

the *fualtech* are often referred to incidentally, but most often in connexion with monasteries.

Maigens or Sanctuaries.—The plot of land around the house of a person of rank was a sort of asylum. This was called a *maigen* or precinct : and within it no man should break the peace without the consent of the owner. The higher the rank the larger the maigen. The maigen of a *bo-aire*, the lowest rank entitled to the privilege, was the smallest : it extended the cast of a spear all round his house. That of an *aire-desa* extended two casts. The extent doubled for each rank upwards to the king of the *tuath*, whose maigen extended sixty-four casts round his residence. The maigen of a provincial king or of the king of Ireland included the whole plain on which the palace stood. There was also a maigen—varying according to rank—round the dwelling of an ecclesiastic, and also round a church : the sanctuary of a church was often called Termon land (i. 358, *supra*). The Archbishop of Armagh had the same extent of maigen as the king of Ireland. It will be mentioned farther on (page 173) that every *bruden* or first-class hostel was also an asylum.

A fugitive, no matter what his crime, and also whatever property he had with him, whether belonging to himself or to the pursuer, once he entered on a maigen, were safe for the time, provided the regulations were complied with. The following conditions and formalities were necessary to ensure his safety :—1. The owner, or some member of his family legally entitled to act for him in such cases, should give permission to the fugitive to enter on the precinct, and should persist in claiming asylum for him. 2. The owner or his deputy should inform the pursuer that the place was a precinct. 3. The owner or deputy should guarantee that no loss should accrue to the pursuer or aggrieved party by the temporary shelter afforded to the fugitive—that the original claim should hold good—that the fugitive should not be enabled to finally escape from justice. If any one of these failed he might be arrested on the maigen. A person who committed any act of violence within a maigen—provided he knew it was one, and that the necessary formalities were observed—had to pay damages to the owner, the amount depending on honour-price, on the extent of the violence, and on other circumstances.

This law of sanctuary in and around a house existed also in early times in England, and in a form almost identical with that laid down in the Brehon Law.*

This is a proper place to observe that there was an all-important distinction between the asylum-right of a private residence and that of a church or a hostel. The right accorded to the maigen of a dwelling was for the protection of the owner against scenes of violence on his premises by outsiders—not primarily in the interest of the fugitive ; and as it depended on the will—or caprice—of the owner, it was uncertain. It was indeed not an asylum at all in the proper sense of the word. But the sanctuary of a church or the asylum of a bruden was absolute and inviolable, depending on no conditions and on no man's will or caprice.

2. *Interior Arrangements and Sleeping Accommodation.*

It will be shown farther on (p. 52) that in large houses there were separate sleeping-rooms. But among the ordinary run of comfortable, well-to-do people, including many of the upper classes, the family commonly lived, ate, and slept in the one principal apartment,† as was the case in the houses of the Anglo-Saxons, the English, the Germans, and the Scandinavians of the same period. In the better class of houses in Ireland there were, ranged along the wall, little compartments or cubicles, each con-

* Brehon Laws, III., Introd. by Richey, ciii. For the whole law of Precincts see Brehon Laws, IV. 277. See also III. 119 to 145.

† For examples, see Mac Conglinne, 58 ; and Tromdamh, 51, 55, 61.

taining a bed, or sometimes more, for one or more persons, with its head to the wall. The wooden partitions enclosing the beds were not carried up to the roof ; they were prob- ably about eight or nine feet high, so that the several com- partments were open at top. A little compartment of this kind, whether open or closed overhead, was called an *imda*. The primary meaning of *imda* is a ' bed,' as is clearly indicated in Cormac's Glossary (p. 6), where it is stated that the *adhart* or ' pillow ' is so called because it is higher than

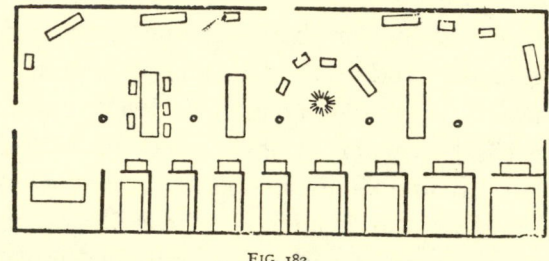

FIG. 182.

Conjectural plan of a good-class house, where the family lived, ate, and slept in the one large apartment: constructed from the descriptions in Tales and Brehon Laws. (House here made quadrangular, but might be round or oval. Eight *imdas*, cubicles, or sleeping-places, each with one bed : some beds for one person, some for two, some for three. Four low, small tables and a number of seats are shown, all movable. Seats at ends of cubicles outside are fixed. Five supporting posts (shown by little circles) : fire near middle. The openings or windows in walls are not marked ; neither are the doors in doorways of house and cubicles.

the rest of the *imda* or bed. But by a natural extension of meaning the word is often used to denote the whole compartment or cubicle with its bedstead. Sometimes the word *imda* was applied to a large room : for example, in Kineth O'Hartigan's poem it is stated that in Tara there were fifty *imdas*, each with fifty men in it.* But the usual meaning was either a bed or the little room containing a bed. In the Bruden Da Derga, Ingcel goes to reconnoitre the hostel that his party are about to attack. He sees many *imdas* of different sizes with men in them varying in number from one up to nine. From the whole context it

* Petrie's Tara, p. 190

is plain that these *imdas* were not couches but little compartments open in front, so that all those in them could be seen sitting or reclining on couches : and accordingly the persons are described all through, not as *on* the *imda*, but as *in it*. Let us add that Dr. Stokes, in his edition of this story, always translates *imda* by ' room.'

At the foot of each *imda* outside, and projecting into the main room, there was a low fixed seat, often stuffed with some soft material, for use during the day. Besides these there were on the floor of the main apartment a number of detached movable day couches or seats—all low—with one or more low tables of some sort.

The preceding description of the disposition of the beds applies to the better class of houses. The lower classes of people probably slept, like those of Wales and Scotland of those times, on beds or pallets ranged along the wall with little or no attempt to screen one from another. Giraldus describes the Welsh as sleeping in this manner with their heads to the circular wall and their feet towards the fire.

The fire was in or near the middle, and the people sat or reclined by day all round it ; while the smoke escaped through an opening in the roof : a custom which, as Scott records, existed in Scotland down to 200 years ago.* In England also, down to the time of Elizabeth, before coal was brought into domestic use, and when wood was the general fuel, there were hardly any chimneys, and the fire was lighted—as in Ireland and Scotland—in the centre of the single big room or hall, or up against one of the walls, the smoke escaping through a hole in the roof.†

That these arrangements for living and sleeping were in general use in Ireland is abundantly plain from many passages in the old writings. We find the expression, so many " *imdas* from fire to side wall in the house all

* Rob Roy, chap. xxviii.

† Roberts, Social Hist. pp. 325, 348 : see also Mr. P. H. Newman in " Social England," I. 225.

round "* constantly used in the tales. That there were
seats distinct from those at the ends of the cubicles appears
from a passage in the Crith Gabhlach describing the house
and furniture of an *aire-tuisi* chief, in which we read that
there were " *eight imdas* with their proper furniture [namely,
" bedsteads with beds and end-seats], besides *six* couches
" [*brothrach*, ' a couch ' : pl. *brothracha*], with their proper
" furniture both pillows and sitting-skins " (*i.e.* skins stuffed
with feathers).† All this shows that the ancient Irish of the
higher classes had two distinct kinds of couches : a couch
or bed for sleeping on, and another sort for sitting or reclining on at meals, or on other occasions during the day ;
just as the Romans had their two kinds of *lecti* or couches
for the same two purposes.

The bedstead within the *imda*, in the best class of
houses, consisted of four pillars connected by rails, with
a canopy overhead, and curtains running by rings on
copper rods.‡ Such a bed was designated *lige cumtachta*,
i.e. a ' protected,' enclosed, or testered bed : and this
designation occurs so often that such beds must have
been pretty common. Near the foot of the bed and
within the *imda* there was a rack with pins or hooks
for hanging clothes or other articles on.§ *Lige* or *ligi*
[lee] was a usual term for a bed, cognate with Lat. *lectus* :
but the commonest name was *lepad*, which, in the form
leaba or *leabadh* [labba], is the term in use at the present
day. This word was also used to denote a couch for day
use, which had generally a little table beside if for food
and drink. St. Patrick, when at Tara, was summoned to
King Laegaire's *lepad* in the banquet-room to have some
food.‖ Both *lige* and *lepad* were applied to a grave. The
word *sceng* [skeng] also means ' a bed,' though not often
used : and hence the enclosure round a bed or couch was

* Táin bo Fr., 139.   ‡ Silva Gad., 120.
† Brehon Laws, IV. 326, ₆; 327, ₁₁.   § Brehon Laws, IV. 75, bot.
                    ‖ Trip. Life, 55

often called *imscing* (*im*, ' about '). In Cormac's Glossary (p. 98) we have " imscing, a little house [or apartment] in which a bed [*imdae*] fits " : and again (p. 150), " sceng, *i.e. iumdha*, a bed, whence imscing, a small *both* or tent which surrounds a bed." *Sceng* and *imscing*, like *lepad*, were applied also to day-couches. King Domnall, at the banquet of *Dun-nan-gedh*, sat or reclined at the head of the table in his golden *imscing* (Moyr. 29) : *i.e.* an *imscing* ornamented with gold.

A bedframe or bedstead is often called *tolg*. We are told in an ancient book of Irish annals, and also in the story of the Boroma, that Feredach, king of Ossory, in the sixth century, falling very sick, had to lie abed : and he caused to be brought to him all his treasures, which he kept beside him in his *tolg* :—" For it was [then] the " custom of kings to have couches (*tolgs*) of yew around " them, in which they had a collection of their bars and " ingots of silver, and their [valuable] cups and vessels, and " their chessmen and chessboards, and their *camans* or " hurleys."* The fierce old warrior *Cellach*, unable to walk or move about on account of his great age, had a brass *tolg* as his bed, in which he always remained : and his only treasure and consolation was his sword, which he kept unknown to all, hidden under the bedclothes.† The practice of keeping a sword in bed must have been common : Dallan mac Moire, chief poet to Cerball king of Leinster (A.D. 885–909), in his poem addressed to Cerball's sword, asks : " from the day that Cerball departed, with whom shalt thou have bed-fellowship ? " (*lepthanas*).‡

As distinct from the *imda* and bedstead, the bed-tick or mattress was called *dergud* [dergu], a distinction clearly pointed out in this passage from the voyage of Maildune :— " There were seventeen canopied *imdas* in the house, with

* Three Fragments of Annals, 9 : Silva Gad., 416.
† Moyrath, 43.
‡ Kuno Meyer in Rev. Celt., xx., p. 12 : LL, 47, *b*, 13 from bottom.

good *derguds* (*dagdergudhaib*) set in them."* The word *colcaid* (a loan-word from Lat. *culcita*) was also often applied to a bed or bed-tick : O'Donovan always renders it ' a flock-bed ' : but whatever sort of bed it was, it must have been regarded as a luxury, for we are told in Cormac's Glossary (p. 44) that it was used by nobles. This word was also often applied to a quilt or other bed-covering ; having undergone a change of meaning like the English word *quilt*, which also comes from *culcita*. The blanket (*setigi*) and other bed-covering were brought out by day to be aired and sunned.† White linen sheets were used, and in grand houses they were often embroidered with figures.‡

Beds of the best class were stuffed with feathers. St. Columba is made to prophesy of a certain king that he would not be killed in battle, but that he would die on his own feather-bed (*plumatiunculam*).§ Some of the beds in the guest-house of the Cork monastery were made of feathers. Straw was sometimes used : Mac Conglinne (p. 14) growls by way of contempt that the attendant who waited on him in Cork monastery had no better way of lighting the fire in the guest-house than by pulling a wisp of straw from the bed. The Book of Aicill,‖ defining the penalty for stealing straw, lays down a double fine if the straw was intended to be put as beds under people ; which indicates that it was subjected to some sort of preparation. Rushes were sometimes used for beds—as in Wales¶—especially in cases of emergency or for temporary use. When Cuculainn and Ferdiad had finished their day's fighting, their attendants prepared beds of fresh rushes for them.** When the Fena of Erin were out on their hunting excursions, they put up hunting-booths each evening, after which—to use the words of Keating :—

* Rev. Celt., x. 65.   † Mac Conglinne, 10, 22.
‡ Leahy, Courtship of Ferb. 29 : LL, 256, *b*, top line: Three Fragm., 11, 17.
§ Adamnan, 44.   ¶ Giraldus, Descr. of Wales, i. x.
‖ Brehon Laws, iii. 151, 15, 14.   ** O'Curry, Man. & Cust., ii. 439.

" Each man constructed his bed of the brushwood of the
" forest, moss, and fresh rushes.　The brushwood was laid
" next the ground ; over that was laid the moss ; and the
" fresh rushes were spread over all : which three materials
" are designated in old books *tri cuilcedha na Féine*, ' the
" three bed-materials of the Fena.' "　The people often
used beds of hides stuffed with some soft material : or
perhaps they simply spread the skin on the top of straw
or rushes.　The Senchus Mór mentions " a poor sick man
lying on the hides."*

FIG. 183.

Castle of Athlone : erected by John de Grey, Lord Justiciary, or Governor, or
Ireland, 1210-1213.　One of the Anglo-Norman castles referred to at p. 65, *infra.*
(From Mrs. Hall's Ireland.)

A pillow was used for the head.　The most common
word for a pillow was *adart* [ey-art], which is used to
this day by speakers of Irish.　A fanciful derivation of
the word given in Cormac's Glossary (p. 6) indicates
clearly the nature of the article :—" *Adart*, i.e. *ath-ard*,
" additional height, because it is higher than the rest
" of the bed,"　Sometimes *frithadart* was used ; and a

* Brehon Laws, I. 195.

passage in Fiach's Hymn, in which this word occurs, also indicates the distinction between the bed and the pillow :—" He [St. Patrick] slept on a bare flagstone, a pillar-stone was his pillow " (*frithadart*).* Another name for a pillow was *cerchaill* or *cenncherchaill* (where *cenn* is ' head '). Cormac's Glossary (p. 38) defines *cerchaill* as " head-protection." From the same passage we learn that a pillow was filled with feathers, and that the case was [sometimes] made from the skin of a wild deer (" It is of " his hide [the hide of a wild deer] that the case for the " feathers is made.").

Often two, and sometimes three, persons slept in the same bed. St. Patrick placed the youth Aed, the king of Leinster's son, in charge of Cascorach the minstrel, saying :—" Let the king of Leinster's son be in one bed (*in* " *aeinlebaid*) and in one condition with thee till we reach " Leinster."† When St. Caillin visited the O'Cahalans of Connaught, they received him so well that he blessed them and prophesied that there should be always among them some chief who would be [so much esteemed as to be] selected as a king's bed-fellow.‡ It was a mark of distinction to set apart a bed for one. Maildune and his men came to a certain house in which were a number of bed-couches, one intended for Maildune alone, and each of the others for three of his people§ : and in another place was a house with a number of large beds, each for three of the household, and one smaller bed for the master of the house.‖ One of the complaints of the unreasonable demands of the poets who were on a visit to Guaire king of Connaught was that they insisted on a separate bed for each.¶

In great homesteads there were sleeping-houses or apartments distinct and separate both from the sitting-

* Trip. Life, 408–9.   § Joyce, Old Celtic Romances, 141.
† Silva Gad., 205.   ‖ *Ibid.*, 125.
‡ Book of Fenagh, 179, 185.   ¶ Tromdamh 41, 15; 109, verse.

or banquet-room and from one another, each probably circular and having a conical roof of its own : often called *tech-leptha*, i.e. ' bed-house.'　When the three Red Branch champions came to the palace of Cruachan, Ailill and Maive gave them the choice of a house (*tech*) for each, or one house for the three : and they selected three houses, in each of which was a bed.*　" We have distinct " statements in our ancient records "—says O'Curry—" that " different members of the same family had distinct houses " (and not apartments) within the same *rath, dun, lis*, or " *cathair* : that the lord or master had a sleeping-house, " his wife a sleeping-house, his sons and daughters, if he " had such, separate sleeping-houses, and so on, besides " places of reception for strangers and visitors."†　But this applies to the great houses belonging to people of rank.　Even in high-class houses, however, it was usual to put two or three in the same room, with a bed for each.‡

People of the upper classes sat upon seats covered with skins.　St. Patrick's chariot-seat was covered with the skin either of a cow or of a seal : both are mentioned in the Tripartite Life (p. 75) as in use.　Skins for sitting on (*Gaimniu suidi*) are noticed in the Crith Gabhlach§ as in the house of an *aire-tuisi* chief.　In Kuno Meyer's Liadain and Curithir (p. 23) is mentioned a couch covered with white fleeces of [sheep-] skins ; and Cormac's Glossary (p. 81) quotes this verse from a poem, ancient in his time : " It is delightful for me to be [sitting] on a yearling calf's skin in Garbhán's house."

It was a common practice in the better class of houses to strew the floor with rushes : and when distinguished visitors were expected, the old rushes were removed and fresh ones supplied.　The women-servants always managed this business.　When Murkertagh of the Leather Cloaks

---

* Fled Bricr., 69.　　　　　　　　† Man. & Cust., ii. 70.
‡ See Silva Gad., 52 mid. and 102, 9; and Hyde, Lit. Hist., 295.
§ Brehon Laws, iv. 326, 8.

was approaching Ailech his home, with many royal captives, after his circuit round Ireland, A.D. 941, he sent on a page the day before with directions that women should be sent to cut rushes for the floor.* The use of rushes for this purpose was so well understood that there was a special knife for cutting them ; and such a knife is enumerated among the household articles in the house of a *brugh-fer* or brewy.† Sometimes the floor was covered with soft green-leaved birch-branches with rushes strewn over them.‡ We know that this custom of covering the floor with rushes also prevailed in England, where it was continued down to the time of Elizabeth. In some of the inferior apartments of Irish houses, straw was used : for example, it was expected that the kitchen of a *bo-aire* chief should be kept strewn with fresh straw,§ which one would think a dangerous practice.

3. *Outer Premises and Defence.*

The homesteads had to be fenced in to protect them from robbers and wild animals. This was usually done by digging a deep circular trench, the clay from which was thrown up on the inside. This was shaped and faced ; and thus was formed, all round, a high mound or dyke with a trench outside, and having one opening for a door or gate. Whenever water was at hand the trench was flooded as an additional security : and there was a bridge opposite the opening, which was raised, or closed in some way, at night. The houses of the Gauls were fenced round in a similar manner. Houses built and fortified in the way here described continued in use in Ireland till the thirteenth or fourteenth century (see Westropp's " Anc. Forts of Ireland," p. 624).

* Circuit, 53 and note : see also Mesca, 13 top : and O'Curry, Man. & Cust., II. 13, 21.   † Brehon Laws, IV. 311.
‡ Leahy, Courtship of Ferb. 8 ; LL, 253, *b*, 23.
§ Brehon Laws, IV. 315 top.

These old circular forts are found in every part of Ireland, but more in the south and west than elsewhere ; many of them still very perfect—but of course the timber houses are all gone.   Almost all are believed in popular superstition to be the haunts of fairies.   They are now known by various names—*lis, rath, brugh, múr, dún, moat, caiseal* [cashel], and *cathair* [caher] : the cashels, múrs, and cahers being usually built of stone without mortar.   These are generally the very names found in the oldest manuscripts.   The forts vary in size from 40 or 50 feet in diameter, through all intermediate stages up to 1500 feet : the size of the homestead depending on the rank or means

FIG. 184.

The great " Moat of Kilfinnane," Co. Limerick, believed to be *Treda-na-Ree*, the triple-fossed fort of the kings, one of the seats of the kings of Munster.   Total diameter 320 feet. (From a drawing by the author, 1854.)

of the owner.   Very often the flat middle space is raised to a higher level than the surrounding land, and sometimes there is a great mound in the centre, with a flat top, on which the strong wooden house of the chief stood.*

Forts of this exact type are still to be seen in England, Wales, and Scotland, as well as in various parts of the Continent ; and the figure of an existing one near Geiselberg in Germany, given by Borlase (p. 1128), might be mistaken for a drawing of some of those in Ireland. Round the very large forts there are often three or more

* On this point see the instructive letter of the Welsh antiquary, Mr. Geo. T. Clarke, in Stokes's Life of Petrie, p. 216 ; showing that the same custom existed in England and Normandy : and see also Mr. Westropp's Essay (Ancient Forts of Ireland), p. 585, in which are given, from the Bayeux Tapestry, representations of houses on the tops of forts.

great circumvallations, sometimes as many as seven.* The "moat or fort of Kilfinnane," figured above, has three.

A *dún*, sometimes also called *dind*, *dinn*, and *dingna*, was the residence of a *Ri* [ree] or king : according to law it should have at least two surrounding walls with water between.† Round the great forts of kings or chiefs were grouped the timber dwellings of the *fudirs* and other dependents who were not of the immediate household, forming a sort of village.   Any great fortified residence of this kind was often called *port* : in Cuimmin's Poem on the Saints of Ireland, Armagh is called *Port Macha*.‡

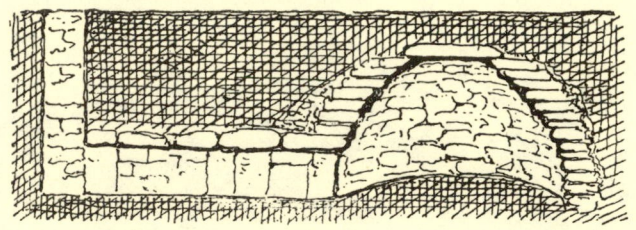

FIG. 185.

Section of an underground beehive-shaped hut.   (From Wood-Martin's Pagan Ireland, p. 205.)

In most of the forts, both large and small, whether with flat areas or with raised mounds, there are underground chambers, commonly beehive-shaped, which were probably used as storehouses, and in case of sudden attack as places of refuge for women and children.   In the ancient litera-ture there are many references to them as places of refuge.§ The Irish did not then know the use of mortar, or how to build an arch, any more than the ancient Greeks ; and these chambers are of dry-stone work, built with much

* See Kilk. Arch. Journ., 1870–71, p. 387, verse xi.

† O'Curry, quoting Brehon Laws, Man. & Cust., II. 3, 4.

‡ Stokes, in Zeitschr. Celt. Phil., I. 72.

§ Miss Stokes, Early Chr. Art, 3 : Kinahan, On *Luscas* [or caves] in Raths, in Kilk. Arch. Journ., 1883–4, p. 11 : and Westropp, Ancient Forts, p. 666.

rude skill, the dome being formed by the projection of one stone beyond another, till the top was closed in by a single flag.

Where stone was abundant the surrounding rampart was often built of dry masonry, the stones being fitted with great exactness. In some of these structures the stones are very large, and then the style of building is termed cyclopean. Many great stone fortresses of the kind described here, usually called caher, Irish *cathair*, still remain near the coasts of Sligo, Galway, Clare, and Kerry, and a few in Antrim and Donegal : two characteristic examples are Greenan-Ely, the ancient palace of

FIG. 186.

Staigue Fort in Kerry. Of stones without mortar. External diameter 114 feet ; internal, 88 feet : wall 13 feet thick at bottom, 5 feet at top. (From Wood-Martin's Pagan Ireland, p. 180, and that from Wilde's Catalogue, p. 120, where a further description of this fort will be found.)

the kings of the northern Hy Neill, in Donegal,* and Staigue Fort near Sneem in Kerry. The most magnificent fortress of this kind in all Ireland is Dun Aengus on a perpendicular cliff right over the Atlantic Ocean on the south coast of Great Aran Island (see next page).

At the most accessible side of some of these stone cahers, or all round if necessary, were placed a number of large standing stones firmly fixed in the ground, in no order—quite irregular—and a few feet apart. This was a very effectual precaution against a sudden rush of a body of assailants. Beside some of the existing cahers these stones, or large numbers of them, still remain in their places (shown in figs. 187 and 188).

* For which see sect. 5 of this chapter below.

The *caiseal* or cashel was a strong stone wall round a king's house, or round a monastery ; of uncemented stones in pagan times, but often built with mortar when in connexion with monasteries. The caher was distinguished from the cashel by being generally more massive in structure, with much thicker walls. The cahers are almost confined to the south and west of Ireland.* Buildings like our cahers are also found on the Continent, as mentioned by Borlase (pp. 1126–1129).

That the wooden dwelling-houses were erected within the enclosing *lios*, *les*, or *rath*, is abundantly evident from

FIG. 187.

Dun-Aengus on the great Island of Aran, on the edge of a cliff overhanging the sea : circular Firbolg caher : without mortar : the standing-stones were intended to prevent a rush of a body of enemies. (Drawn for Dr. Wilde : published in Arch. Cambr., 1858 : and subsequently in Wilde's Lough Corrib.)

the records. Queen Medb (or Maive) Lethderg (not Queen Maive of Croghan) is recorded to have built the rath near Tara, now called from her, Rath-Maive : " and she built a choice house within that rath."† There were often several dwelling-houses within one large rath : inside the great rath at Emain there were at least three large houses, with others smaller‡ : the Rath-na-Righ at Tara had several houses within it : and in the romantic story of Cormac in Fairyland, we are told that he saw " a very large kingly *dún* which had four houses within it."

* On these fortified residences, see the valuable article in Stokes's Life of Petrie, p. 216, *et seq.*

    † O'Curry, MS. Mat., 480.   ‡ O'Curry, Man. & Cust:, II., II.

There is good reason to believe that originally the word *rath* was applied to the surrounding embankment or rampart, and *lios* or *les* to the space enclosed. Thus a person who was making his way towards the palace, leaped over the three *raths*, until he was on the floor of the *les*, and from that until he was on the floor of the royal house (*for lár ríg-thige*)* : a passage which moreover affords additional testimony that the houses were built within the enclosure. Again, in the tale of the sons of Usna, it is told that the child shrieked " so that it was heard all over the *lis*."† But these distinctions have long since ceased to be observed : and the words *rath* and *lis* are now applied to the whole structure.

The rampart enclosing a homestead was usually planted on top with bushes or trees, or with a close thick hedge, for shelter and security : or there was a strong palisade on it :—*Co n-accai in liss m-bileach m-barrach* : " so that I saw a *liss* topped with trees."‡ *Tuittid cnói cuill cairmessa dobilib rath* : " the fair-fruit hazel-nuts fall from the trees of the raths."§ Lisses and raths such as we see through the country are generally round or oval : but they are occasionally quadrangular or square.|| Vitrified forts, *i.e.* having the clay, gravel, or stone of the rampart converted into a coarse glassy substance through the agency of enormous fires, are found in various parts of Ireland as well as in Scotland : and similar forts are still to be seen in several parts of the Continent.¶

Sometimes outside the outer earthen or stone rampart there was a timber palisade of strong stakes, enclosing a

* Voyage of Bran, I. 47, 17, and 51, 10: see also Kilk. Arch. Journ., 1868–9, p. 223 : and 1870–1, p. 447.

† O'Curry, 3 Sorrowful Stories, Atlantis, III. 399.

‡ Mac Conglinne, 68.   § LL, 118, *a*, 16.

|| Kilk. Arch. Journ., 1849–51, pp. 23, 24 ; 1867, p. 4 : and Mr. West-ropp's Essay on the Ancient Forts of Ireland, p. 583.

¶ See Wood-Martin, Pagan Ireland, 183 : Kilk. Arch. Journ., 1879–82, p. 756 : Borlase, 1126 : Stokes's Petrie, 223, 357 : Proc. Roy. Ir. Acad., v., p. 69 ; and Adamnan, 151, note *b*.

large area : this palisade was called *sonnach* (and sometimes *tonnach*), from *sonn*, a *cuaille* or ' stake.'   Aed Guaire, king of Connaught in the sixth century, built, in preparation for a marriage-feast for his wife, a new [wooden] house (*tech*) within a *dún* or double circular rampart ; and round the *dún* again, that is, outside all, he made " a *sonnach* of red oak."   Just as it was finished Aed Baclamh, the king of Ireland's spear-bearer, made a circuit round the kingdom to test obedience and discipline among the provincial and minor kings : and he demanded that all doors should be

Fig. 188.

Ballykinvarga Stone Fort (mortarless) near Kilfenora in Clare.   Shape, oval ; 155 feet by 135 feet. Showing *chevaux de frise* of standing-stones, to prevent a rush.   (See Mr. Westropp's description of this fort in Journ. Roy. Soc. Antiqq., Irel., for 1897, p. 121 ; and p. 57, *supra*.)

broken open wide enough to permit him to enter freely with his long spear held crosswise.   Things went well with him till he came to Aed's new house.   Aed went so far as to break an opening in the outer palisade : but when the ill-grained visitor demanded that a corresponding opening should be made in the elaborately carved door of the house, he found to his cost that he had met his match ; for Aed, flying into a rage, struck off his head with one blow of his sword.*

* O'Grady, Silva Gadelica, 70.

Immediately outside the outer door of the rath was an ornamental lawn or green called *aurla*, a name often varied to *urla* and *erla*, which was regarded as forming part of the homestead : " then queen Maive went out through the " door of the *liss* into the *aurla* [*isin n-aurlainn*], and three " times fifty maidens along with her."* So also prince Cummascach, when he visited Branduff, king of Leinster at Baltinglass, pitched his tent on the *erla* of the king's *baile*

FIG 189

Carlow Castle in 1845 : believed to have been erected by Hugh de Lacy, who was appointed Governor of Ireland in 1179   One of the Anglo-Norman castles referred to at p. 65, *infra.* (From Mrs. Hall's Ireland.)

or homestead.† Beside the *dun* or *lis*, but beyond and distinct from the *aurla*—and outside the *sonnach* if there was one—was a large level sward or green called a *faithche* [*faha*]—commonly Latinised *platea* or *plateola*‡—which was chiefly used for athletic exercises and games of various kinds : it was sometimes called *blai.*§ Some idea of its

* Ir. Texte, 1. 280 : Fled Bricr., 69.   † Silva Gad., 408.
‡ Adamnan, 98 (*e*) ; 360 ; 450.
§ See Windisch, Würterbuch, Ir. Texte, 1., " Bla," land

size may be formed from the statement in the law that the *faithche* of a brewy extends as far as the voice of a bell (*i.e.* of the small bell of those times) or the crowing of a cock can be heard.*   Finn mac Cumail when a boy, coming one day to a *dún*, found a number of youths hurling (*oc imáin*) on the *faithche*.†   The law lays down certain regulations regarding the striking of the ball on the *faithche* in hurling.‡   When not formally measured and enclosed, the four fields nearest the house were understood to constitute the *faithche*.§   A visitor was free to go upon the *faithche* and could not be sued for trespass, " for every *faithche* is free " [to all comers],‖   The *faithche* was not to remain profitless : animals, commonly sheep, were kept grazing on it.¶   The haggard for grain-stacks, which was always near the homestead, was called *ithla* (gen. *ithlann*), from *ith*, ' corn.'   The *ithla*, like the barn, sometimes belonged to an individual, and sometimes to the *finè* or clan, of which each householder had his share**: but in this case the *ithla* was very large, standing apart, and unconnected with any one homestead.   A garden or enclosure at the back, fenced in for general purposes, was often called *airlis*.††   The *lubgort*, or ' kitchen-garden,' will be spoken of at p. 148, *infra*.

At a little distance from the dwelling it was usual to enclose an area with a strong rampart, into which the cattle were driven for safety by night.   This was what was called a *badhun* (bawn], *i.e.* ' cow-keep,' from *ba*, pl. of *bo*, ' a cow,' and *dún*‡‡ : and sometimes *bo-dhaingen* [bo-ang-in], which has the same meaning (*daingen*, ' a stronghold ').   This custom continued down to a late

* Brehon Laws, IV. 195.   As to these measurements, see pp. 374 and 375, *infra*.

† Oss. Soc., IV. 295.

‡ Brehon Laws, III. 253.

§ Corm. Gloss., 78.

‖ Brehon Laws, III. 253.

¶ Br. Laws, IV. 311 bottom.

** *Ibid.*, I. 125, 141 : III. 285.

†† *Ibid.*, IV. 313 bottom.

‡‡ See Moylena, 183 (whole page): and Joyce, Irish Names of Places, I. 308.

time : and was adopted by the English and Scotch settlers. One class of the planters who were settled in Ulster in the time of James I. were required to build a castle and a bawn. The ruins of many of these settlement-bawns still remain.*

The outer defence, whether of clay, or stone, or timber, that surrounded the homestead was generally whitened with lime. When Nuada the druid built a dun on *Almu*, now the Hill of Allen in Kildare, " he rubbed the *sund* or *sunn* " or outer rampart with *alamu* (*ro colmed alamu dia sund*) " until it was all white."† The text does not tell us what this colouring stuff *alamu* or *almu* was. Stokes (Acallamh 283) makes it alum ; and we know that alum is a native product, with which people have been familiar from early times.‡ It is indeed probable that alum was in the writer's mind ; for the impossibility of procuring so much of it as would whiten a whole immense rampart would be no difficulty to an etymologist who invented the episode to account for the name. The dún was made white at any rate ; and it is pretty certain that lime was the real material ; which seems borne out by an old verse relating to Almu, quoted in the story in the Book of the Dun Cow :—

> " All white is the dun of battle renown
>   As if it had received the lime of Ireland."

That the outer rampart of duns or homesteads was often whitened with lime is shown by many other passages. Maildune comes to a little island with a large dun on it surrounded by a white wall (*múr gel*), as white " as if it " had been built of burnt lime or carved out of one unbroken

---

* See the article on Bawns, Ulster Journ. Archæol., v. 125 ; and a particular *bawn* described by Dr. J. P. Mahaffy, in the Athenæum of 10th August, 1901.

† See LU, 41, *b*, 26 and 29 : Hennessy in Rev. Celt., II. 89 ; Silva Gad., 132, 9.   ‡ See Kinahan, Geol., 358 ; and p. 357, below.

" rock of chalk."*   " The colour of the dun of the lady
Crede "—says another story—" is like the colour of lime."†
The great ramparts of Tara must have shone brilliantly
over the surrounding plain : for it is called " White-sided
Tara," in the " Circuit of Muirchertach mac Neill " : but
this was a memory only, for when the poem was written,
Tara had been deserted for centuries.

FIG. 190.

Dundrum Castle, near Newcastle, County Down. Built at the end of the twelfth
century by John de Courcy, on the very site of the old Irish fortress called Dun
Rury, which covered the summit of the rock. The great earthworks belonging to
the original *dún* still remain at the base of the rock at one side, but are not seen in
this figure. (From Kilk. Archæol. Journ. for 1883-4, p. 158.)

The treatment of forts here is necessarily very brief.
Those who wish to study the subject farther may consult
Mr. Westropp's essay in Trans. Roy. Ir. Acad. on " The
Ancient Forts of Ireland," in which the whole subject is
examined for the first time scientifically and in considerable
detail, and the similarity of the ancient Irish forts to those
of Greece, Thessaly, Italy, France, Austria, Germany, and
other parts of the Continent, is pointed out.

In modern times, when the native knowledge of Irish
history and antiquities had greatly degenerated, and the
light of our own day had not yet dawned, many writers
attributed the ancient Irish raths and duns to the Danes,

* Joyce, Old Celtic Romances, 131.   † O'Curry, Man. & Cust., II. 13.

so that it became the fashion to call them "Danish raths or forts": but this idea has been long since exploded, as the reader will have seen who has glanced through the preceding pages. The peasantry have the same notion: but their error arose from confounding the *Dedannans* or *Dananns* with the *Danes*, through similarity of sound.*

The Anglo-Normans built stone castles in Ireland according to their fashion: and not unfrequently they selected the very site, or the very vicinity, of the old Irish fortresses: for an Anglo-Norman had at least as keen an eye for a good military position as an old Irish warrior. Accordingly the circumvallations of the ancient native forts still remain round the ruins of many of the Anglo-Norman castles; as at Rahinnane in Kerry, Knockgraffon near Cahir in Tipperary, and Dundrum in County Down.† Several of those Anglo-Norman or Anglo-Irish castles are figured throughout this chapter. It is to be observed that the Irish began to abandon their earthen forts and build stone castles—many of them round like the older earthen forts and cahirs—shortly before the arrival of the Anglo-Normans in 1169: but this was probably in imitation of their warlike neighbours.‡

Crannoges.—For greater security, dwellings were often constructed on artificial islands made with stakes, trees, and bushes, covered with earth and stones in shallow lakes, or on small flat natural islands if they answered. These were called by the name *crannóg* [crannoge], a word derived from *crann*, ' a tree,' as they were constructed almost entirely of wood. Communication with the shore was carried on by means of a small boat, commonly dug out of one tree-trunk. At night, and at other times when precaution was necessary, it was kept in a boat-house on the island. But in ordinary times, for the convenience

* On this see Stokes's Petrie, 218: and Wilde, Boyne, 70.
† See Kilk. Arch. Journ., 1854-5, pp. 394-7.
‡ Stokes's Petrie 212 *et seq.*

of the residents and visitors coming and going, it was usually left floating in the lake-channel, with a cable from boat to island and another from boat to mainland, so that whether arriving or departing the person could pull it towards him.*   Usually one family only, with their attendants, lived on a crannoge island ; but some-times several families, each having a separate wooden house.   Where a lake was well suited for it—pretty large and shallow—several crannoge islands were formed, each with one or more families, so as to form a kind of little crannoge village.

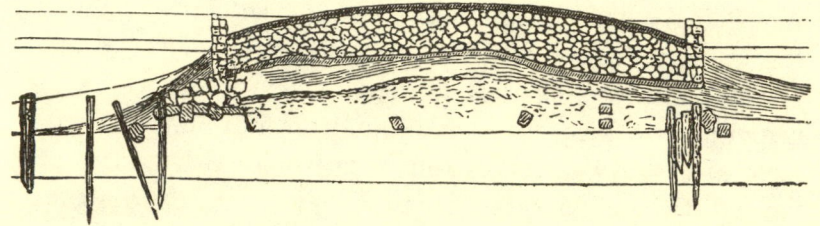

FIG. 191.

Section of Crannoge in Ardakillen Lough, near Strokestown, Co. Roscommon. Gives a good idea of the mode of constructing these little islands. The three horizontal lines at top show the level of the water according to season. (From Wilde's Catalogue, p. 226.)

Crannoge dwellings were in use from the most remote prehistoric times, as is clearly shown by the remains found in them, implements of various kinds, which belonged to primitive ages.   They are very often noticed, both by native Irish and by English writers, and they continued in use down to the time of Elizabeth.   They are referred to in the Tripartite Life by the name *insola in gronna*, 'an island in a bog.'   Cambrensis describes them as he saw them in the twelfth century, though he does not use the name *crannoge* :—" These lakes [of Ireland] encompass " some slightly elevated spots, most delightfully situated, " which, for the sake of security, and because they are " inaccessible except by boats, the lords of the soil appro- " priate as their places of refuge and seats of residence."†

* Bec Fola, 179.   † Top. Hib., I. vii.

Great numbers of crannoges have of late years been explored, and the articles found in them show that they were occupied by many generations of residents. In most of them rude "dug-out" boats have been found, many specimens of which are preserved in the National Museum, Dublin, and elsewhere. In some cases the original crannoge dwelling was, in later ages, replaced by a stone-and-mortar castle, of which the finest existing example is the Hag's Castle in Lough Mask in Mayo. This is circular like

FIG. 192.

A Crannoge Village in Lough Eyes, near Lisbellaw, County Fermanagh. The little artificial islands are there still, but the wooden dwelling-houses are all gone: and this is an attempted resto- ration, by Mr. Wakeman, of the appearance of the whole group when a house stood on each. (From Colonel Wood-Martin's Traces of the Elder Faiths, I. 223.)

the original structure, occupying almost the whole of the little island: and it is perhaps the earliest stone-and-mortar castle erected in Ireland before the Anglo-Norman invasion.* Lake-dwellings similar to the Irish crannoges were in use in early times all over Europe, and explorers have examined many of them, especially in Switzerland.†

* See Wilde, Lough Corrib, 260: and Kilk. Arch. Journ., 1872–3, p. 11.

† Numerous descriptions of individual crannoges and of their exploration will be found in the Proc. Roy. Ir. Acad., and in the Kilk. Arch. Journ. and its continuation, the Journ. of the Roy. Soc. Antiqq., Irel. Easily found out by glancing through the Indexes.

The word 'crannóge' was also used by the ancient Irish
to designate a small wooden vessel of some sort.   In the
"Colloquy of the Ancients," Feredach, king of Ossory, is
spoken of as using gold and silver for decorating such
things as drinking-horns, *crannoges*, swords, chessboards,
and chessmen.*   In later times the 'crannóge' was familiar
among the Anglo-Irish—a sort of basket of a certain
size used as a measure for corn.†   In the Senchus Mór
'crannóg' is used simply to denote a rod.‡

4. *Domestic Vessels.*

The material in most general use for vessels was wood ;
but there were vessels of gold, silver, bronze, and brass, all
of which however were expensive.   Occasionally we read
of iron being used : among the treasures possessed by Ailill
and Maive, as we find stated in the Táin, were *iarn-lestair*,
'iron vessels.'§   There were also vessels of

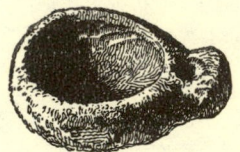
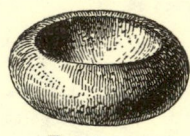

FIG. 193.   FIG. 194.

Figure 193, Stone Drinking-cup, 4⅜ inches wide across
the bowl. Found, buried deep, in the bed of the Shannon.
Figure 194, Stone Cup. (Wilde's Catal., p. 114.)

stone : but these were not much in use.   A stone bottle,
of the kind hitherto known only in Egypt, has been found
in the big rath near Lucan‖ : and two stone drinking-cups
are figured here.   Drinking-goblets of glass have been
already noticed ; and leather vessels for holding liquids
will be described in chap. xxvi., sect. 5.

* Silva Gad., 416.   † Ware, Antiqq. 223.
‡ Brehon Laws, I. 152, 29 ; 153, 9 from bot.
§ O'Curry, Man. & Cust., II. 89 : LL, 54, *a*, 33.
‖ Stokes's Petrie, 420 : see Wilde, Catal., 114.   Petrie and his biographer,
Dr. William Stokes, seem to have regarded this as an Irish imitation of an
Egyptian bottle.   Many years later Miss Margaret Stokes calls it an
" Egyptian alabaster bottle," and looks upon it as brought hither by some
of those Egyptian monks mentioned in vol. I., p. 413, *supra*. See Miss
Stokes, Inscr., II. 137.

For making wooden vessels beech was oftenest employed : but the best were made of yew. In one of
O'Curry's Lectures,* he gives, from an old MS., a curious
list of vessels, all made from the trunk of one immense
yew-tree. A large proportion of the timber vessels used
were made of staves bound by hoops, like those in use
at present, indicating skill and accuracy in planing
and jointing. This is proved by many passages. St.
Finnchua's mother during her pregnancy—according to

FIG¹ 195.

Carrickfergus Castle in 1840. On a rock over the sea. Built originally by John
de Courcy in the end of the twelfth century, on the site of an older Irish fortress, but
greatly enlarged and altered after his time. One of these Anglo-Norman castles
referred to at p. 65, *supra*. (From Wright's Ireland Illustrated.)

the legend†—once longed for a drink of ale, and asked
the brewers for a little : but the churlish fellows refused.
She went away : but scarcely had she turned her back
when the hoops (*circalla* : sing. *circall*, a ' circle ' or ' hoop ' :
Lat. *circulus*) slipped off the vats, and the ale all ran
about. In the list of yew-tree vessels noticed above,
several are mentioned as having grown so old that *the
hoops at last fell off*. There was also a native term for
a hoop—*fonnsa* : the Brehon Law (v. 483) enumerates
the material for *fonnsa* or hoops—*i.e.* plantations of the

* Man. & Cust., II. 61.　　　　† Stokes, Lives of SS., 85, 232.

proper timber, such as sallow-trees—as forming part of the " Commons " property of a territory.

A large open hooped tub or vat was called by several names. One was *dabach* or *dabhach* [dauvagh], of which the derivation in Cormac's Glossary (p. 52) shows that the vessel was a two-handled tub like that of the present day :—" *Dabach*, derived from *de-oach*, two *o*'s or ' ears,' " meaning two handles upon it : for at first there used to " be no handles on vessels." It may be remarked that the side-handle of a vessel was often called an *o* or ' ear,' of which the word *oach* is a modification. In O'Clery's Glossary it is stated that a *coimde* was the same as a *dabach*. Another name for this sort of vessel was *lotar* or *lothar* [lōher] : " a trough wherein are kept *braichles* or grains left after brewing," says Cormac's Glossary (p. 105). A moderately-sized tub with two handles, called a *drolmach*, was used by women for bringing water. This word is still in use and pronounced *drowlagh*.

There was a special drinking-vessel, originally made of yew (*ibar*), and thence called *ibrach*, or in modern spelling *iubhrach* [yooragh]. This was until lately in use in Mayo, and called by its old name : it was deep, and grew narrow from bottom to top.

The people used a sort of pitcher or hand-vessel called a *cilorn* [keelorn], having a *stuag* or circular handle in its side, from which it was also called *stuagach*, i.e. ' circle-handled ' : sometimes called *milan-duirn* and *metair-duirn*, i.e. ' hand-vessel ' ; for *milan* and *metair* (or *medar*) both mean ' a small vessel ' : and *dorn*, gen. *duirn* is a ' hand ' or ' fist.' In Zeuss (p. 41, 26) *cilornn* glosses *urceus*, ' a pitcher.' In the Cóir Anmann we read that a certain Lugaid went with a *cilorn* in his hand to bring water for drinking at dinner.* *Milan* glosses *urna* in the Tract on Lat. Decl. (No. 138) ; and it must have been intermediate in size between the *cilorn* and the *medar* : for in the list of

* Ir. Texte, III. 319.

yew vessels mentioned above (p. 69) it is stated that when the original *cílorn* became worn out from age, the owner made a *milan* out of what was left : and when this *milan* again became decayed and worn, there was only as much sound wood left as made a *medar*.　In the Voyage of Maildune it is related how a certain man gathered up a great many valuable articles, and among them a number of brazen *cílorns*.*　This ancient term is still preserved in the south of Ireland, where it passes quite current as an English word, in the form of *keeler*, though the people apply it now to a vessel of a different shape and with a different use.　A broad, shallow tub about 18 inches across and 6 or 8 inches deep, and having two handles formed by

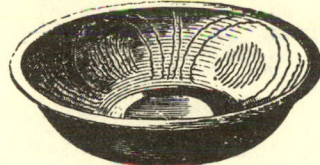 

FIG. 196.　　　　　　　FIG. 197.

Two bronze Drinking-vessels in National Museum. Figure 196 is 7¾ inches wide : hammered out and shaped with great skill from one single thin piece of metal : found in a crannoge in County Roscommon. Figure 197, oval, 5¾ inches in the long diameter. Handle decorated, and terminating at top in an animal's head. Found near Keshcarrigan, County Leitrim. (Both from Wilde's Catalogue, pp. 533, 534.)

the projection upwards of two of the staves, is universally called a ' keeler.'　Milk is ' set ' in a keeler for a night to throw the cream to the top for churning.

A *corn* [curn] or horn was a drinking-vessel, usually made from a bullock's horn, hollowed out and often highly ornamented with metal-work and gems.　A *corn* mounted with silver was sometimes called a *fethal* (Corm. 80). This word *corn* seems to be borrowed from Latin *cornua* : but there was a native name also, viz. *buabaill* [boovill], from *bo* or *bu*, ' a cow ' : and another, *adarc* [ey-ark], which is now the common Irish word for ' horn ' : but *buabaill* may be a borrowed word.　Conn the Hundred Fighter, on a

* Rev. Celt., x. 83.

certain occasion during the *féis* of Tara, stood up from where he sat on his throne, and with a polished *buabaill* in his hand, spoke to the assembled nobles.* That a *corn* is the same thing as a *buabaill* is proved by this :—that while in one version of the *Boroma* it is stated that certain messengers, arriving at the palace of Ailech, found king Aed mac Ainmirech drinking mead from a *corn*, in another version the self-same drinking-horn is called a *corn-buabaill*.† Drinking-*corns* were made at home from cows' or bullocks' horns ; but very large ones were imported and much valued. Among the " foreign " valuables mentioned in the Brehon Law, the glossator enumerates *cuirn-buabaill* (*cuirn*, pl. of *corn*): these no doubt were genuine buffalo-horns, as is perhaps indicated by the Irish word *buabaill*.‡

FIG, 198.

The " Kavanagh Horn," drawn from an exact model in National Museum, Dublin : 22 inches along the convex or under side. On a brass plate round the top is this inscription : — "TIGERNANUS O'LAUAN ME FECIT DEO GRACIAS. I. H. S.": which gives the name of the artist, Tiernan O'Lavan. This is not a very old specimen. (From Wilde's Catalogue. p. 266.)

These *corns* were sometimes given as a part of the stipend due from one king to another, as we find by many entries in the Book of Rights, where they are often called *curved corns* from their shape. Sometimes they were coloured : part of the stipend or *taurcrec* due to the king of Offaly from the king of Ireland was four *corns* " of various colours " (Bk. of R., 253). According to the bardic history, ornamented drinking-horns covered with gold and silver were first introduced into Ireland by king Tigernmas, many centuries before the Christian era, a

* Silva Gad., 143 : Ir. Texte, 131, 10.   † Rev. Celt., XIII. 63.
‡ Brehon Laws, V. 220, 23 ; 221, 29.

record which, though, legendary, indicates the general costliness of the workmanship. Some of these *corns* are preserved in our museums, of which one is figured on page 72.

The *escra* was a drinking-goblet: Cormac's Glossary (p. 69, twice) says it was a copper vessel for distributing

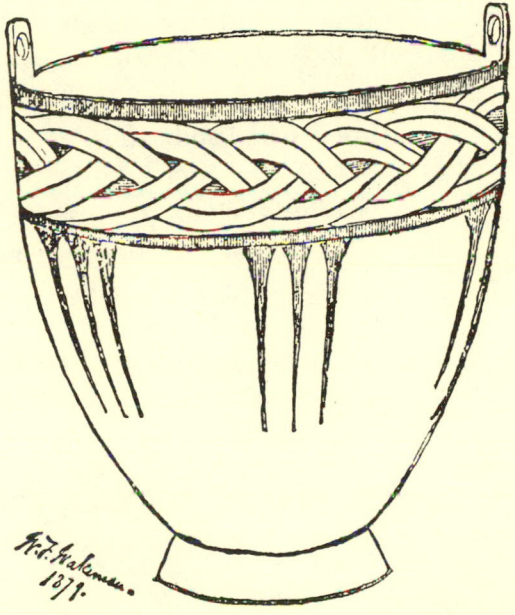

Fig. 199.

Ancient Irish vessel, 15 inches high, and 15 inches in width at the mouth : made out of a single piece of oak, except the bottom, which is of alder. The carving on the side is the *Opus Hibernicum* or interlaced work. It had a lid when found, similarly carved ; but this has been lost. The whole outer surface was originally painted in a kind of dark enamel, portions of which still remain. This very ancient vessel was found five feet deep in a bog in County Fermanagh. (From Kilk. Archæol. Journ. for 1879-82, p. 98.)

water ; but it was sometimes made of silver. The sons of O'Corra, in the course of their voyage, landed on an island, where a lady came towards them having in one hand a copper *cílorn* full of food like cheese, and in the other a silver *escra*. And she gave them the food to eat : and she brought them water in the *escra* from a well on the strand : " and there was no delicious flavour that was "ever tasted by man that they did not find in this food "and drink."* In the Life of St. Darerca it is stated that the *escra* was a silver drinking-cup from which great people were wont to drink.†

The word *lestar* was applied to vessels of various kinds, among others to drinking-vessels : it was often used as a generic term for vessels of all kinds, including ships. In the Life of St. Brigit it is related that on one occasion the king of Teffia was drinking out of a *lestar* covered with

FIG. 200.
Grotesque figure of a man drinking : from the Book of Kells (seventh century). (From Wilde's Catalogue, p. 299.)

gems, when a careless man took it from his hand and let it drop so that it was broken into bits.‡ The beautiful *lestar* represented in fig. 199 was found some years ago, as stated in the descriptive note, but what special name was applied to it we cannot tell. There was a drinking-cup of some kind called *indtile* which Cormac (p. 58) defines "a little *lestar* or vessel in which drink fits," *i.e.* for holding drink : which agrees with O'Reilly's "*inntille*, a drinking-cup."

The simple word *cua*, and its derivatives *cuad* and *cuach*, all mean 'a cup.' In the gloss on the Senchus Mór we are told that a *folderb* (see below) is a *cua* in the shape of a bell (*cua cluic*)§ : and the Crith Gabhlach speaks of a *cuad* 12 inches high for drinking milk out of.‖ *Cuach*, which is the common word for 'cup,' is retained in Scotland to this day and used as an English word, in the forms of *quaigh* and *cogue*, for a drinking-cup. It was prophesied for Finn mac Cumail by his wife that on

---

*Rev. Celt., XIV. 47 : Joyce, Old Celtic Romances, 415. This food like cheese, containing every delicious flavour, is a stock incident in ancient Welsh, as well as in Irish, tales.

† Three Fragments, 9, *i.*

‡ Stokes, Three Irish Homilies, 73.

§ Brehon Law, I. 134, 5.

‖ *Ibid.*, IV. 306, 9.

whatsoever day he should drink from a horn (*adarc*), he would die. Accordingly he took good care always to drink from a *cuach*. But one day in his old age, being overcome with thirst, and not having his *cuach*, he drank from an *adarc* : and on that same day he was killed on the Boyne.* *Ian*, gen. *ena*, means 'a vessel' : it is often applied to a small drinking-mug. The Crith Gabhlach mentions a vessel, *ian-óil* [drinking-*ian*], three hands high, used for drinking milk.† Cormac's Glossary (p. 34) describes a sort of drinking-goblet called a *cingit*, in such a way that we may infer it was slender in the middle and opened out at the top and bottom, so that the two halves were alike, or nearly so, in shape and size, and were probably intended to be reversible.

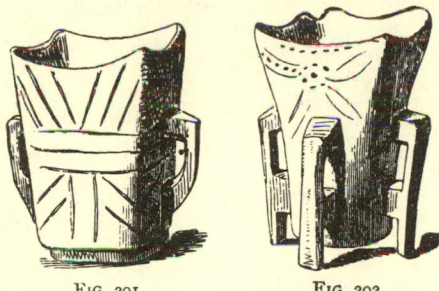

FIG. 201.   FIG. 202.

Wooden Methers.   From Wilde's Catalogue, p. 214.

The usual drinking-vessel among the common people, especially at meals and drinking-bouts, was a *medar* or *mether* (so called from the drink called *mead*), made of wood, with two or four handles : it circulated from hand to hand, each passing it to his neighbour after taking a drink. Many of these *methers* are preserved in museums, of which two are figured here.‡ People drank from the corners. A sort of hamper or vessel called a *rúsc* [roosk], made of bark-strips on a wicker-work frame, was much used in farmhouses.§

A churn was known by several names—among others *cuinneóg*, which is the present name. In the Senchus

---

* Silva Gad., 98.   † Brehon Laws, IV. 302, 23.

‡ See Dub. Pen. Journ., I. 300 : Kilk. Arch. Journ., 1860–61, p. 54 : and Wilde, Catal., 214.

§ Stokes, Lives of SS., line 1277, and p. 320 bot. Also Three Irish Homilies, 62, 11 : and "Rusc" in Windisch's Wörterbuch.

Mór it is called *comm*; and in the gloss, this again is interpreted by three names:—*cuairt* ('round-vessel'), *belcumang* ('narrow-mouth'), and *muide*,* showing that it was something like the hand-churn still in use. *Derb* is another name for a churn, according to O'Clery's Glossary, which explains this word as meaning either a churn (*cuinneóg*) or a cup (*ballán*). A saying quoted in the same glossary, "my ear to the ear of the *derb*," shows that the ancient churn had two ears or handles, which the modern hand-churn has not. The compound *foilderb* was also used; but from the words of the gloss in the Senchus Mór, it would seem to denote here an ordinary drinking-cup:—

Fig. 203.

Pail or bucket, made out of one piece of red deal: 1 foot long, 6½ inches deep, and 10½ inches broad. Cover made of yew, pressed into shape when softened (see "cantair," 'a press,' in Index). Now in National Museum. (From Wilde's Catalogue, p. 213.)

"*Folderb* which has a ring or handle (*fóil* or *fáil*) out of its side, and it is a bell-shaped *cua*."† Another compound of *derb* is given in Cormac's Glossary (p. 58) to denote a churn—*derb-loma*, i.e. the *derb* of *lóim* or milk. From all the preceding we may infer that *derb* and its compounds were used to denote both a drinking-cup and a churn.

The form of churn used among the ancient Irish was that in which the cream or milk is agitated by a dash worked with the hand. The churn-dash was—and is still—called *loinid*, and sometimes *loimdha*, from *loim*, 'milk.'‡

For bringing home milk from the milking-place, Adamnan (pp. 126, 445) mentions a wooden vessel of such a make that it could be strapped on the back. The lid was kept in its place by a wooden cross-bar (*gercenn*) which ran through two holes at opposite sides near the rim. Adamnan tells a story of a young member of the Iona community bringing home on his back a vessel full of milk

---

* Brehon Laws, I. 124, 4; and 134, 2, 3.   † *Ibid.*, 124, 5.
‡ O'Curry, Man. & Cust., I. 133.

into which a demon had entered : and when St. Columba, blessing the milk according to his custom, made the sign of the cross, it became agitated, and the bar which fastened the lid was driven through the two holes and shot away to a distance. Adamnan, writing in Latin, uses the original Irish word for this bar in the form *gergenna*. The word is elsewhere explained as a slender bar which passes through two openings and fastens the lid. In " Mac Conglinne's Vision " (p. 87, 19) it is used for an ordinary door-bolt— which seems its primary meaning. It appears that this term is not found in any other Latin document besides Adamnan's : and it is probably an original Gaulish or Celtic word.*

Fig. 204.

Natural Boulder-Stone : height 3 feet, with three artificial *ballans*. (From Col. Wood-Martin's Pagan Ireland, p. 411. Drawn by Wakeman.)

It will be seen from what precedes that there was in old times in Ireland quite as great a variety of vessels of all kinds, with distinct names, as there is among the people of the present day ; and there are, besides, other names not yet noticed. The cup that St. Patrick was drinking out of at Tara, when the druid attempted to poison him, is called *ardig* in the Tripartite Life (p. 54, 7) : *ardig* or *airdig* being a common old word for a drinking-goblet. A *ballán* seems to have been a simple, cheap, wooden drinking-cup in very general use : in one place,

* See Kuno Meyer in Rev. Celt., XIII. 506.

Cormac's Glossary (p. 25) defines it as "a poor man's vessel": and elsewhere (p. 27) as a vessel used by lepers. Keating applies it to a drinking-cup, and it was sometimes also applied to a milk-pail.* In Connaught it is used to designate round holes in rocks usually filled with water: which use modern antiquarians have borrowed, and they now apply "ballaun" to those small cup-like hollows, generally artificial, often found in rocks, and almost always containing water.†

FIG. 205.

Earthenware glazed Pitcher, 13 inches high. Found in a crannoge in County Down. (From Wilde's Catalogue, p. 158.)

Esconn, escand, or *escann* is described in Cormac's Glossary as a vessel for distributing water, derived from *esc,* 'water,' and "*cann,* the name of a vessel." This last phrase is interesting as showing the existence in ancient Gaelic of a term for a drinking-vessel identical with the English word *can.* There was a pail or vessel of some kind called *sitheal,* which was sometimes made of silver.

The word *cernín* [kerneen] is given in Cormac's Glossary (p. 37) as meaning *miass,* i.e. a dish on which food is placed at table; in which sense it is also found in an ancient satire given in the Book of the Dun Cow, said to have been the first satire ever composed in Ireland. *Cernín* is a diminutive of the simple word *cern*—modern form *cearn*—which is used to denote a dish of any kind, for measuring commodities, such as grain: Peter O'Connell explains it "a certain dry measure": and Keating has the expression *cearn-arbhair,* a 'cern of corn.' *Bleid* or *bleide* was the name of a goblet or vessel of some kind, mentioned both in the Brehon Laws and in the Tales. The word

* Corm. Gloss., 54 ("Del").   † *Ibid.,* 25.

miass or *mias*, given above from Cormac's Glossary, is very commonly used for a platter or dinner dish.* *Coire*, ' a caldron '; *cusal*; *criol*; and some other terms, as well as the vessels they denote, will be dealt with elsewhere in this book. Most of those named in this section will be found mentioned in vol. v. of the Brehon Laws, p. 407, and the following pages.

Earthen vessels of various shapes and sizes were in constant use. They were made either on a potter's wheel, or on a mould, or on both. This appears from a curious commentary on the Latin text of a passage in the Psalms (II. 9), written in the Irish language by an Irishman, in the eighth or ninth century, contained in a manuscript now in Milan. This old writer, evidently taking his illustration from his native country, explains " a potter's wheel " as " a " round wheel on which the potters [Irish *na cérda*, ' the " *cairds* or artisans '] make the vessels, or a round piece of " wood about which they [the vessels] are while being " made."† The " round piece of wood " was the block or mould on which they were first formed roughly, to be afterwards perfected on the wheel.

5. *Royal Residences.*

Almost all the ancient residences of the over-kings of Ireland, as well as those of the provincial and minor kings, are known at the present day; and in most of them the circular ramparts and mounds are still to be seen, more or less dilapidated after the long lapse of time. As there were many kings of the several grades, and as each was obliged to have three suitable houses (vol. I., p. 58), the royal residences were numerous; of which the most important will be noticed here.‡ In addition to these,

* See the story of Bóthar-na Mias in Joyce, Ir. Names of Places, II. 191.
† Stokes and Strachan, Thesaurus, I., p. 23.
‡ The present appearance of several of the royal residences will be found described in Mr. T. O. Russell's " Beauties and Antiquities of Ireland."

several of the great strongholds described in vol. i., pp. 84 to 90, were royal residences.

Tara.—The remains of Tara* stand on the summit and down the sides of a gently-sloping, round, grassy hill, rising 500 feet over the sea, or about 200 over the surrounding plain, situated six miles south-east of Navan, in Meath, and two miles from the Midland Railway Station of Kilmessan. It was in ancient times universally regarded as the capital of all Ireland, or, as Muirchu, in his seventh-century Life of St. Patrick calls it, *caput Scotorum*, the ' capital of the Scots ' ; so that in building palaces elsewhere it was usual to construct their principal houses and halls in imitation of those of Tara. It was the residence of the supreme kings of Ireland from prehistoric times down to the sixth century, when—as already mentioned—it was deserted in the time of King Dermot the son of Fergus Cervall on account of St. Ruadan's curse. Although it has been abandoned to decay and ruin for thirteen centuries, it still presents striking vestiges of its ancient importance.

Preserved in the Book of Leinster and other ancient manuscripts there are two detailed Irish descriptions of Tara, one written in the tenth century by Kineth O'Hartigan, and the other in the eleventh by Cuan O'Lochain (for whom see vol. i., p. 462, *supra*). Both these distinguished men examined the remains personally, and described them as they saw them, after four or five centuries of ruin, giving the names, positions, and bearings of the several features with great exactness. These two interesting documents are published with translations and learned annotations in Petrie's essay on Tara. More than sixty years ago Dr. Petrie and Dr. O'Donovan made a most careful detailed

---

* Old Irish name *Temair* (modern *Teamhair*), gen. *Temrach*, dat. *Temraig*, which is represented by the present name " Tara." For more about this name, and for other places of the same name, see Joyce, Ir. Names of Places, i., p. 294.

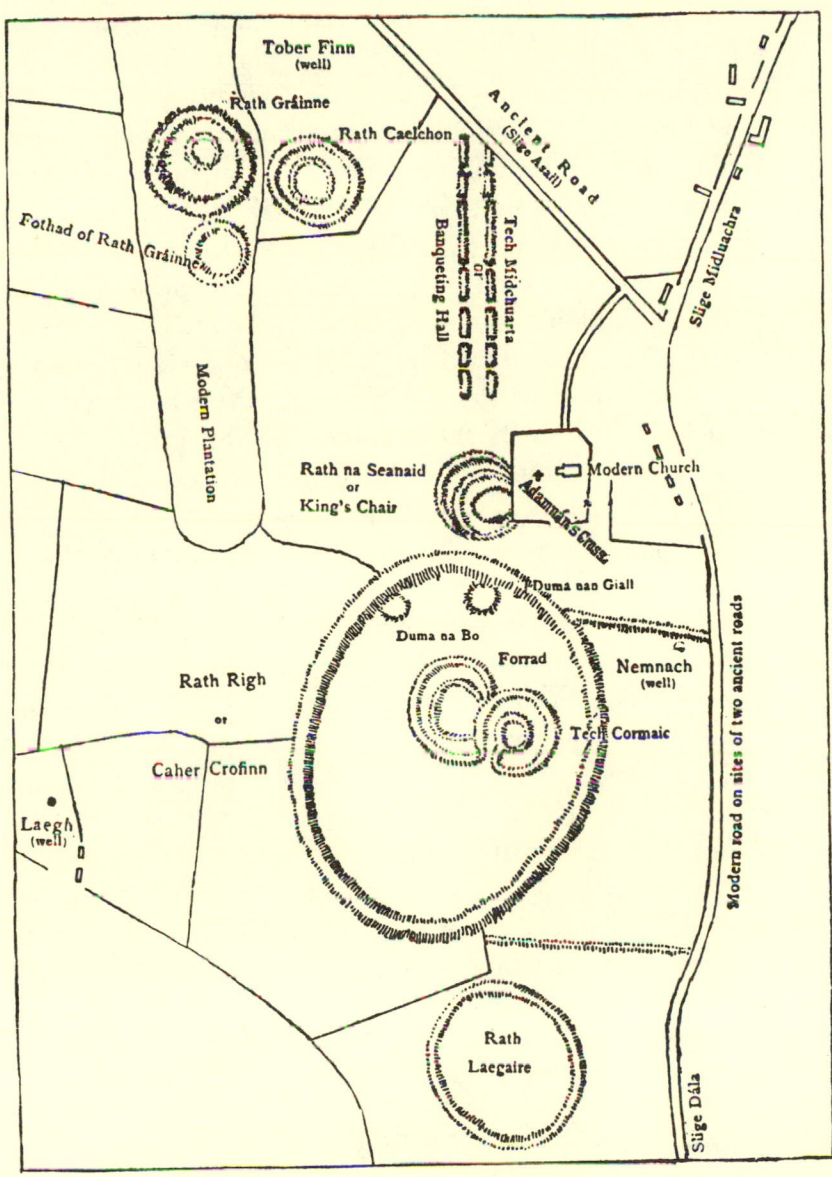

FIG. 200.

Plan of Tara, as it exists at the present day.   (From the two plans given by Petrie in his Essay on **Tara**.

examination of the hill and its monuments; and with
the aid of those two old topographical treatises they
were able, without much difficulty, to identify most of the
chief forts and other remains, and to restore their ancient
names. The following are the most important features
still existing, and they are all perfectly easy to recognise
by any one who walks over the hill with the plan given here
in his hand. A much more detailed description of them,
with their full history and all extracts relating to them
from Irish manuscripts, is given in Petrie's essay on Tara,
from which most of the account given here has been con-
densed. It is to be borne in mind that the forts now to be
seen were the ramparts or defences surrounding and protecting the houses. The houses themselves, as has been
already explained (p. 55), were of wood, and have of
course all disappeared.

The principal fortification is *Rath Righ* [Rath-Ree] or
Rath-na-Righ, the 'fort of the kings,' also called *Caher
Crofinn*, an oval occupying the summit and southern slope
of the hill, measuring 853 feet in its long diameter. The
circumvallation can still be traced all round; and judging
from the existing remains, it consisted originally of two
walls or parapets with a ditch between. Moreover it is
pretty certain that one at least of these two ramparts was
of stone, as the " caher " (Irish *cathair*) in the name
" Caher Crofinn " would indicate; and as a matter of fact
the stones still remain for about a fifth of the whole circuit.
This seems to have been the original fort erected by the
first occupiers of the hill and the most ancient of all the
monuments of Tara.

Within the enclosure of Rath Righ are two large
mounds, the *Forrad* or *Forradh* [Forra] and *Tech Cormaic*,
beside each other, and having portions of their ramparts in
common. The Forradh has two outer rings or ramparts
and two ditches: its extreme outer diameter is nearly 300
feet. The name " Forradh " signifies ' a place of public

meeting,' and also a judgment-seat, cognate with Lat. *forum*; so that it seems obvious that this is the structure referred to by the writer of the ancient Norse work called " Kongs Skuggsjo " or ' mirror for kings,' already referred to (vol. I., pp. 226, 300). This old writer, speaking' of Tara says :—" And in what was considered the highest " point of the city the king had a fair and well-built castle, " and in that castle he had a hall fair and spacious, and in " that hall he was wont to sit in judgment."

On the top of the Forradh there now stands a remarkable pillar-stone six feet high (with six feet more in the earth), which Petrie believed was the *Lia Fáil*, the inauguration-stone of the Irish over-kings, the stone that *roared*

FIG. 207.

The Mound called the Forradh, at Tara. (From Mrs. Hall's Ireland. Drawn by Wakeman.)

when a king of the true Milesian race stood on it (see vol. I., p. 45) ; but recent inquiries have thrown grave doubts on the accuracy of this opinion.

Tech Cormaic (' Cormac's house ') was so called from the illustrious King Cormac mac Art, who reigned A.D. 254 to 277. It is a circular rath consisting of a well-marked outer ring or circumvallation, with a ditch between it and the inner space : the extreme external diameter being 244 feet. We may probably assign its erection to King Cormac, which fixes its age.

Duma nan Giall or the ' mound of the hostages, situated just inside the ring of Rath Righ, is a circular earthen mound, 13 feet high, 66 feet in diameter at the base, with a flat top, 25 feet in diameter. The timber house in which the hostages lived, as already mentioned (vol. I., p. 54), stood on this.

A little to the west of the Mound of the Hostages stands another mound called *Duma na Bo* (the ' mound of the cow '), about 40 feet in diameter and 6 feet high. It was also called *Glas Temrach* (the ' Glas of Tara ') which would seem to indicate that the celebrated legendary cow called Glas Gavlin, which belonged to the Dedanann smith Goibniu,* was believed to have been buried under this mound.

About 100 paces from Rath Righ on the north-east is the well called *Nemnach* (' bright ' or ' sparkling ') so cele-brated in the legend of Cormac's mill—the first mill erected in Ireland, for which see chap. xxv. (page 330), below. A little stream called *Nith* (' shining ') formerly ran from it, which at some distance from the source turned the mill. The well is now nearly dried up ; but it could be easily renewed.

Rath na Seanaid (the ' rath of the synods '), now popu-larly called " the King's Chair," has been partly encroached upon by the wall of the modern church : the two ramparts that surrounded it are still well-marked features. Within the large enclosure are two mounds, 106 and 33 feet in diameter respectively.   Three Christian synods are recorded as having been held here, from which it had its name :— one by St. Patrick on the occasion when he preached to King Laegaire and his nobles at Easter, A.D. 433 ; one by St. Ruadan or Rodanus when he pronounced the curse that caused Tara to be abandoned (for which see page 437, below) ; and the last by Adamnan, probably in the year 697, in which he procured acceptance for the law exempting women from taking part in battles (see vol. I., p. 96, *supra*).

* For Goibniu, see vol. I. 261, *supra* : and for the wonderful cow, Glas Gavlin, see Joyce, Ir. Names of Places, I. 163 : and FM, I., p. 18, note *s*.

Near the Rath of the Synods, and within the enclosure of the modern church, stood *Adamnan's Cross*, of which the shaft still remains, with a human figure rudely sculptured in relief on its side. A little to the south-east of this cross was situated the house which—as already related, vol. i. p. 307—was burned round young Benen and the druid Lucet Mail, when Benen escaped and the druid was reduced to ashes.

On the northern slope of the hill are the remains of the Banqueting-Hall, the only structure in Tara not round or oval. It consists of two parallel mounds, the remnants of the side walls of the old Hall, which, as it now stands, is 759 feet long by 46 feet wide ; but it was originally both longer and broader. It is described in the old documents as having twelve (or fourteen) doors : and this description is fully corroborated by the present appearance of the ruin, in which six door-openings are clearly marked in each side wall. Probably there was also a door at each end : but all traces of these are gone.

The whole site of the Hall was occupied by a great timber building, 45 feet high or more, ornamented, carved, and painted in colours. Within this the Féis or Convention of Tara held its meetings, which will be found described in chap. xxix. (p. 436), farther on. Here also were held the banquets from which the Hall was named *Tech Midchuarta*, the ' mead-circling house ' ; and there was an elaborate subdivision of the inner space, with the compartments railed or partitioned off, to accommodate the guests according to rank and dignity. For, as will be seen in chap. xxi. (p. 105), they were very particular in seating the great company in the exact order of dignity and priority. From this Hall moreover, the banqueting-halls of other great houses commonly received the name of *Tech Midchuarta*.

Rath Caelchon was so called from a Munster chief named *Caelchu* (gen. Caelchon), who was contemporary with Cormac mac Art, third century. He died in Tara, and was interred in a *leacht* or carn, beside which was raised the rath in commemoration of him. The rath is 220 feet in diameter ; and the very carn of stones heaped over the grave still remains on the north-east margin of the rath.

Rath Gráinne is a high well-marked rath, 258 feet in diameter. It received its name from the lady Gráinnĕ [Graunya : 2-syll.], daughter of King Cormac mac Art, and betrothed wife of Finn mac Cumail. She eloped with Dermot O'Dyna, and the whole episode is told in detail in the historic romance called ' 'The Pursuit of Dermot and Gráinne.''* This mound, and also the smaller mound beside it on the south called the *Fothad of Rath Gráinne*, are now much hidden by trees.

A little north-west of the north end of the Banqueting-Hall, and occupying the space north of Rath Grainne and Rath Caelchon, was the *sheskin* or marsh of Tara, which was drained and dried up only a few years before Petrie's time : but the well which supplied it, Tober Finn (Finn's well), still remains.

Rath Laegaire [Rath Laery], situated south of Rath Righ, was so called from Laegaire, king of Ireland in St. Patrick's time, by whom, no doubt, it was erected. It is about 300 feet in diameter, and was surrounded by two great rings or ramparts, of which one is still very well marked, and the other can be partially traced. Laegaire was buried in the south-east rampart of this rath, fully armed and standing up in the grave, with his face, towards the south as if fighting against his enemies, the Leinster men. The whole account of his interment will be found at page 551, farther on.

West of Rath Righ was the well called Laegh [Lay], a name signifying ' calf ' : it is now dried up, though the ground still remains moist. In this well, according to

* This fine story will be found in Joyce's Old Celtic Romances.

the seventh-century Annotations of Tirechan, St. Patrick
baptised his first convert at Tara, Erc the son of Dego
who afterwards became bishop of Slane, and who is commemorated in the little hermitage still to be seen beside
the Boyne (vol. i., p. 320). This well is called *Laeg* by
Cuan O'Lochain ; and Tirechan calls it *Loig-les*, which he
translates *vitulus civitatum*, the ' calf of the lisses or cities.'
Probably there was some legend accounting for this very
old name of *Laeg* or ' calf,' but it is not now known.

The five main *sliges* [slees], or roads, leading from
Tara in five different directions through Ireland, will be
found described at pp. 393 and 395, below. Of these,
portions of three are still traceable on the hill. The
modern road traverses and covers for some distance the
sites of two of them, *Slige Dala* and *Slige Midluachra*, as
seen on the plan : *Slige Asail* still remains, and is sometimes
turned to use.

In one of the ancient poetical accounts quoted by
Petrie (Tara, 147, top), it is stated that the houses of the
general body of people who lived near Tara were scattered
on the slope and over the plain east of the hill.

In connexion with Tara, two other great circular forts
ought to be mentioned. A mile south of Rath Righ lies
Rath Maive, which is very large—673 feet in diameter ; it
forms a striking object as seen from the hill, and is well
worth examining. It was erected, according to one
account, by Queen Maive, wife of Art the solitary, the
father of King Cormac mac Art, which would fix the period
of its erection as the beginning of the third century. This
lady, observe, was different from Queen Maive of Croghan.

The other fort is *Rathmiles*, 300 feet in diameter, lying
one mile north of the Banqueting-Hall : but nothing is
known of its history.

After the abandonment of Tara the kings of Ireland
took up their abode where they pleased, each commonly
in one of his other residences, within his own province or

immediate territory.   One of these seats was **Dun-na-Sciath** (the ' Fort of the Shields ' : pron. Doon-na-Skee), of which the circular fort still remains on the western shore of Lough Ennell in County Westmeath (MS. Mat., 24).   Another was at Rath near the western shore of *Loch Leibhinn* (now Lough Lene in Westmeath), two miles from the present town of Castlepollard.   This residence was occupied for a time by the Danish tyrant Turgesius, so that the fort, which is one of the finest in the country, is now known as **Dun-Torgeis** or Turgesius's fort ; while the Old Irish name has been lost (Petrie, Tara, 128).   In the time of St. Fechin, Dermot, one of the joint kings of Ireland (A.D. 656–664), had a residence in an island in Lough Lene, which, accord-ing to a local tradition, was also occupied for a time by Turgesius.*   The tradition is probably correct, for the island is now known by the name of **Turgesius's Island.**

Cenannus.—In the second century Conn the Hundred Fighter, while yet *roydamna*, before he became king of Ireland, resided in his stronghold at *Cenannus*, now Kells, County Meath : and four centuries after his time Dermot (son of Fergus), king of Ireland (544–565), had a palace here, probably the very stronghold occupied by Conn.

Fremainn.—The kings of Tara had two royal residences at two different places called Fremainn (LU, 129, *b*, 25). One of these is still well known, and retains its old name : now locally designated Frewen Hill, rising over the western side of Lough Owel in Westmeath, on the top of which the old fort still stands (see MS. Mat., 285).

Raeriu.—There were two very ancient palaces at two places called by the same name Raeriu, both of which still retain the name slightly altered.   One was at the place now called Reary-more near the village of Clonaslee in the north of Queen's County.   The other at Mullagh-Reelan, **five** miles south-east of Athy in Kildare, where the old

---

* See FM, I., p. 501, note *r* : Three Fragments, 169, note *c* : and Rev. Celt., XII., 343.

mound still remains near Kilkea Castle.   In this anglicised name, the termination " Reelan " represents *Raerenn*, the genitive of the old name, by the usual change of *r* to *l*.*

Maistiu (gen. form *Maistenn*).—A better-known royal homestead stood five miles nearly east from Ath-I (now called Athy), where on the summit of a low hill the large circular fort remains, and is now well known by the name of the " Rath of Mullamast," in which the last syllable represents the old name.   (This is mentioned farther on, at pages 366, 442, 552.)

It has been already stated (vol. I., p. 38) that Tuathal the Legitimate, king of Ireland in the second century, built four palaces at **Tara, Tailltenn, Ushnagh,** and **Tlachtga.**   The fort of Tlachtga still remains on the summit of the Hill of Ward near the village of Athboy in Meath.   There were royal residences also at Dunseverick in Antrim, the ancient **Dun-Sobairce ;** at the Old Head of Kinsale in Cork, called in Irish **Dun-mic-Patraic ;** at **Derry ;** at **Rathbeagh** on the Nore, where the rath is still to be seen ; at **Dun-Aenguis** on Great Aran Island (for which see p. 57, *supra*) ; and on the site of the present Baily Lighthouse at Howth, where several of the defensive fosses of the old palace-fort of **Dun-Criffan** can still be traced.

Emain.—Next to Tara in celebrity was the palace of Emain or Emain-Macha, or, as its name is Latinised, Emania.   It was for 600 years the residence of the kings of Ulster, and attained its greatest glory in the first century of the Christian era, during the reign of Concobar (or Conor) Mac Nessa, king of Ulster.   It was the centre round which clustered the romantic tales of the Red Branch Knights.†   The most ancient-written Irish traditions assign the foundation of this palace to Macha of the

* As to these two mansions, see FM, I., p. 38, note *r* ; and Book of Rights, pp. 210, 211.

† For the Red Branch Knights, and the literature connected with them, see vol. I., pp. 83 and 536, *supra.*

Golden Hair, wife of *Cimbaeth* (Kimbay], king of Ireland three or four centuries before the Christian era. From that period it continued to be the residence of the Ulster kings till A.D. 335, when it was burned and destroyed by three brothers, cousins of Muredach, king of Ireland—Colla Uais, Colla Menn, and Colla Dachrich, commonly known as the Three Collas—after which it was abandoned to ruin. The imposing remains of this palace, consisting of a great mound surrounded by an immense circular rampart and fosse half obliterated, the whole structure covering about eleven English acres, lie two miles west of Armagh. Nay, the ruin retains to this day the old name " Emain " slightly disguised ; for it is familiarly called " The Navan Fort or Ring," in which " Navan " correctly represents the sound of *'n-Emain*, i.e. the original name with the Irish article *'n* prefixed.

When the Red Branch Knights came to the palace each summer to be exercised in feats of arms, they were lodged in a great house near Emain, called the *Craobh-Ruadh,* commonly Englished the ' Red Branch,' from which the whole body took their name. But according to an old glossary, *ruadh* here means not ' red,' which is its usual sense, but ' royal ' : so that *Craobh-Ruadh* should be translated ' royal branch ' : but the designation " Red Branch Knights " is now too well established to be displaced. The name of this house is also preserved : for " Creeveroe," which very well represents the sound of *Craobh-Ruadh,* is still the name of a townland near the Navan fort. So far as we can judge from old tales, the *Craobh-Ruadh* seems to have been altogether built of wood, with no earthen rampart round it, which explains why the present townland of Creeveroe contains no large fort like that of Emain.* (See also Allen, vol. I., p. 88, *supra*).

---

* According to LL, as quoted by O'Curry, Man. & Cust., I. 332, there were, in the time of Concobar, three chief houses in Emain :—The *craeb ruaid*, or ' royal branch,' where the kings and chiefs feasted : the *craeb*

Ailech or the Grianan of Ailech.—Another Ulster palace, quite as important as Emain, was Ailech, the ruins of which are situated in County Donegal, on the summit of a hill 800 feet high, five miles north-west from Derry, commanding a magnificent view of Lough Foyle and Lough Swilly with the surrounding country. It is a circular stone cashel of dry masonry, 77 feet in internal diameter, the wall about 13 feet thick at the base, and on the outside sloping gradually inwards. This central citadel was surrounded at wide intervals by five concentric ramparts, three of which may still be traced, the whole area originally including many acres. According to the old tradition it was founded by the Dedannans, and continued to be a royal residence to the time of its destruction, sometimes of the king of Ulster, and sometimes of the king of Ireland. After the fourth century it was the recognised residence of the northern Hy Neill kings, down to the year 1101, when it was destroyed by the Munster King Murkertagh, in retaliation for the destruction of Kincora by the Ulstermen thirteen years before. After this it was abandoned ; and the kings of Ailech transferred their residence to **Inis-Eanaigh**—now called Inchenny—in the County Tyrone, near Strabane, where they probably resided till the arrival of the Anglo-Normans. For nearly eight centuries Ailech continued in a state of ruin, the wall being reduced to a height of about 6 feet : but during the years 1874–8, it was rebuilt—in the face of great difficulties—by Dr. Bernard of Derry, a man of culture, with antiquarian tastes, who, as far as he could, restored it to its original shape. The wall

derg, or ' crimson branch,' where were kept their spoils and trophies and the skulls of their enemies : and the teite brecc, or ' speckled house,' wherein were deposited the heroes' arms, so as to have them safely out of reach in case the owners should quarrel over their cups. There was also, according to Keating (p. 271), a hospital for the sick and wounded, called Brón-Bherg, or the " Warrior's Sorrow." See the Paper on the Plan of Navan Fort, by M. D'Arbois de Jubainville in Rev. Celt., xvi., p. 1 : Joyce, Irish Names of Places, i., p. 90 : and Mr. T. O. Russell, p. 58.

is now about 17 feet high. It still retains—has all along retained—its ancient name, in the form of Greenan-Ely, where *Ely* correctly represents the sound of *Ailigh*, the genitive of *Ailech.**

The Dalaradian princes had their residence in the sixth and seventh centuries, in a place of great repute called **Rathmore-Moylinny.** The fort still remains in the townland of Rathmore two miles from the town of Antrim. Adjoining Rathmore townland is another called **Rathbeg,** which takes its name from the rath of another palace of much celebrity, where Dermot, the son of Fergus Cervall king of Ireland, lived for some time after he had left Tara, and where he was slain in the year 565, by Aed Dubh, king of Dalaradia.†

Cruachan.—The chief palace of the kings of Connaught was *Cruachan* (or as it is now called, Croghan) from times beyond the reach of history down to the death of King Raghallach, who, as already related (vol. I., p. 409), was assassinated A.D. 648. It figures in various parts of this book, and is chiefly celebrated as being the residence of Ailill and Maive, king and queen of the province, in the first century of the Christian era. Here they held their court, which is described in the Tales of the Red Branch Knights in a strain of exaggerated magnificence : and from this the warlike queen set forth with her army to ravage Ulster and bring away the great brown bull which was the main object of the expedition, as described in the epic story of the " Táin bo Chuailnge " [Quelna].

The remains, which are situated three miles north-west from the village of Tulsk in Roscommon, are not imposing : for the main features have been effaced by cultivation. The principal rath, on which stood the timber palace and

* See Ordnance Survey of Londonderry, p. 217. In this work, Dr. Petrie, with the assistance of O'Donovan and O'Curry, has given an elaborate historical, literary, and topographical description of Ailech.

† See Reeves, Eccl. Antiqq., pp. 69 and 278–281 : Adamnan, p. 68, note : FM, A.D. 558 : and Voyage of Bran, I. 58.

the subordinate houses, is merely a flat, green, circular moat about an English acre in extent, elevated considerably above the surrounding land, with hardly a trace of the enclosing circumvallation. There are many other forts all around, so that, in the words of O'Donovan, who has described the place in some detail in the Four Masters under A.D. 1223—the whole site may be said to be " the " ruins of a town of raths, having the large rath called " Rathcroghan placed in the centre ' : but they are scattered much more widely and at greater distances than those at Tara. Besides the homestead forts there are also, in the surrounding plain, numerous other antiquarian remains, indicating a once busy centre of royalty and active life—cromlechs, caves, pillar-stones, and mounds, including the cemetery of Relig-na-ree (about half a mile south of the main rath), which will be described at p. 556, below.

Durlus Guaire or **Dungory.**—The royal house known by this name was the abode of Guaire [Goorie], the hospitable king of Connaught in the seventh century. It was built on a little island beside the seashore, half a mile north-east from the present village of Kinvarra on Galway Bay. On the site of the old *dun* a stone castle was subsequently erected, the ruin of which is now called " Dungory Castle," a name that commemorates the fortress of the hospitable monarch.*

Ailenn or Ailend, now Knockaulin. The most important residences of the kings of Leinster were Ailenn, Dinnrigh, Naas, Liamhain, and Belach-Chonglais or Baltinglass, in all of which the raths still remain. Ailenn is a round hill, now commonly called Knockaulin (*Aulin* representing ' Ailenn ') near Kilcullen in Kildare, rising 600 feet over sea-level, and 200 or 300 feet over the Curragh of Kildare which lies adjacent, and over all the plain around. The whole summit of the hill is enclosed by a huge oval embankment, 514 by 440 yards, enclosing an area of 37 statute acres,

* See Tromdamh, p. 120, note 2.

one of the largest forts, if not the very largest, in Ireland. Within this great enclosure stood the spacious ornamental wooden houses in which, as we learn from our records, the Leinster kings often resided : for each king had at least three palaces (vol. i., p. 58, *supra*) which he occupied in turn, changing from one to another as it suited his pleasure or convenience. On the present 6-inch Ordnance map the fort is called the " Hill of Allen," instead of the proper modern popular name Knockaulin, which tends to confound it with the equally celebrated hill, now properly and universally called the Hill of Allen near Newbridge in Kildare, Finn mac Cumail's residence already described (vol. i., p. 88) : a mistake evidently committed without O'Donovan's knowledge, when he and others were employed sixty or seventy years ago to settle the local names of Ireland.*

Dinnrigh.—One of the most noted, and probably the oldest, of the Leinster palaces was *Dinnrigh* [Dinnree : the ' *dinn* or fortress of kings '], also called by two other names,

---

* I am informed on the best authority, that this mistake will be rectified in future editions of the 6-inch map.

The fact that there are no remains of a fort on the Hill of Allen—*i.e.* the hill properly so-called, near Newbridge—a place of such celebrity as having been the residence of the renowned hero Finn mac Comail—seems so unaccountable as to lead some to conjecture that the ancient Irish writers confounded the names of the two hills—names which are somewhat like each other ; and that the fort of Ailenn above described may have been really Finn's residence. But this is pure conjecture without a shadow of evidence to support it. The absence of remains on the Hill of Allen has been already satisfactorily accounted for (vol. i., p. 90). As to the two names : they have never been confounded by any old writer, and could not possibly be, except by an amount of stupidity never exhibited by the writers of the Book of Leinster or the Book of the Dun Cow. The oldest form of the name of Finn's residence was *Almu*, gen. *Alman*, dat. *Almain* ; which dative—in accordance with a well-known linguistic law—is often used as a nominative, on which a second genitive *Almaine* has been formed. The oldest form of the name of Knockaulin is *Ailend* or *Ailenn*. The names of both vary somewhat in form ; but there is one obvious and never-failing distinction :—that however *Almu* is varied, it always has the *m* : however *Ailenn* is varied, it never has an *m* The evidence that Finn lived at *Almu*, or what is now properly called the Hill of Allen, is quite as clear as that by which we know that Brian Boru lived at Kincora.

Tuaim-Tenba and *Duma-Slainge*, ' Slainge's burial-mound,' because the Firbolg king Slainge died and was buried there (FM, A.M. 3267). Besides being very often mentioned in the records, it was the scene of a tragedy which is related in detail in the historical story called " The Destruction of Dinnree," contained in the Book of Leinster, which has been edited and translated by Dr. Whitley Stokes.*　　Some two centuries and a half before the Christian era, Cobthach the Slender of Brég murdered the king

FIG. 208.

Dinnree, the most ancient residence of the kings of Leinster.　Now Ballyknockan Fort, on the west bank of the Barrow, half a mile below Leighlin-bridge, Carlow. (From Mrs. Hall's Ireland.)

of Ireland—his own brother—and also the king's son Ailill, and usurped the throne. But Ailill's son Labra Loingsech, or Lavra the Mariner, who fled to the Continent, returned after some years with a party of Gauls, and landed at Wexford, where he was joined by large contingents of the men of Leinster and Munster, who hated the usurper. Marching quickly and silently by night to Dinnree, where the king then happened to be holding court, he surrounded the palace, and setting fire to the houses while

* In Zeitschr. Celt Phil., vol. III.

the company were engaged in feasting, he burned all—palace, king, and courtiers—to ashes.*

Dinnree continued to be used as a royal residence far into Christian times. From a passage in the Life of St. Finnchua,† we know that it was occupied early in the seventh century by " Old Nuada the Sage," king of Leinster : but when it was abandoned is not known. The old documents define very clearly the position of this palace : and the fine old fort still exists in good preservation. It is situated on a high bank over the River Barrow on the west side, half a mile south of Leighlinbridge, and is now commonly known by the name of " Ballyknockan Moat." The moat or mound—figured in the illustration, p. 95—is 237 feet in diameter at the base ; the circular plateau on the top is 135 feet in diameter, and 69 feet over the River Barrow (FM, vol. i., p. 15, note *l*).

FIG. 209.

North Moat, Naas : remains of ancient palace.   House on top modern.
(From a drawing by the author, 1857.)

Naas.—In old times Naas was a place of great celebrity, where the Leinster tribes held some of their periodical *aenachs* or fair-meetings, from which it got the name of *Nás-Laigen* [Naas-Lyen], *i.e.* the ' assembly-place of Leinster,' corresponding exactly with the name of Nenagh in Tipperary. There were here two royal houses, the forts of which still remain. One is an ordinary circular, flat

* See O'Curry, MS. Mat., 252 to 257 : Keating, 253 : and Joyce, Irish Names, I. 93.   † Stokes, Lives of SS., pp. 237, 238.

rath, now called the south moat, situated near the southern end of the town. The other, called the north moat, is a high, flat-topped mound on which the citadel once stood, but which is now occupied by an ugly modern house. Naas continued to be a residence of the Leinster kings till the death of King Cerball (already referred to, p. 49), who was slain by the Danes in 908.*

Belach Chonglais.—Another of the Leinster palaces was at Baltinglass in the county Wicklow, whose old name was *Belach-Chonglais* (Cuglas's road) : but a still older name was *Belach Dubthaire* [Duffera].† Here resided in the sixth century Branduff, the powerful king who defeated and slew Aed mac Ainmirech, king of Ireland, in the Battle of Dunbolg, A.D. 598 (vol. I., p. 141, *supra*). On the hill rising over the town are two great raths or forts, the remains of the old residences. One, now called Rathcoran, is on the very summit, 1256 feet over sea-level. It is an oval, about a quarter of a mile in its longer diameter, having two ramparts, and containing about twenty-five statute acres. The other and smaller fort, now called Rathnagree, is on the northern slope of the hill : it has also two ramparts and covers about seven acres.

Liamhain.—The name of *Liamhain* or *Dun-Liamhna* [Dun-lavna] is still preserved in that of Dunlavin, a small village in the county Wicklow. The mound of this residence is still to be seen a mile south of the village : but it has lost its old name and is now called " Tornant Moat." (Tornant, ' nettle-mound ' : ominous of ruin.)

Side-Nechtain.—The Hill of Carbery in Kildare has a dim legendary history as a royal residence. It was anciently called *Side-Nechtain* [Shee-Nechtan], *i.e.* ' Nechtan's Shee or fairy-hill ' : showing that it was the site of one of those elf-mounds described in vol. I., p. 254, *supra*. This Nechtan, according to the old documents, was king of Leinster, and

---

* FM, vol. II., p. 573, note *o* : see Tromdamh, p. 166, for a further account of Naas.   † Rev. Celt., XIII. 57 : Silva Gad., 411

also a poet.   But the place contained a residence of a less shadowy kind ; for on the north-west slope there are still two remarkable and very perfect military raths or forts. Near the base of the hill is Trinity Well, the source of the Boyne, the enchanted well that in old times burst up and overwhelmed Boand, Nechtan's queen, as described in vol. I., p. 284, *supra*.   But in subsequent times the Christian missionaries—as in case of many another well (vol. I., p. 366)—removed its heathenish character and

Fig. 210.
Carbury Castle, County Kildare.   (From a photograph.)

associations, and dedicated it to the Holy Trinity.   The Anglo-Norman De Berminghams, who took possession of the district, having an eye to something more substantial than Dedannan fairy palaces, took advantage of the selection of their immediate Milesian predecessors and built a splendid castle not far from the old Irish fortresses, near the summit, the ruins of which are now conspicuous for leagues round the hill.*

Cashel was one of the most renowned seats of the North Munster kings, though not the oldest as a royal

* See Wilde's Boyne, pp. 24 to 32.

residence. Its chief feature is the well-known lofty isolated rock overlooking the surrounding plain—the magnificent Golden Vale, as it is called, from its fertility. The most ancient name of the rock was *Sidh-Dhruim* [Sheedrum or Sheerim], ' fairy-ridge ' ; but it was also called *Lec-na-gcéd* [Lack-na-gade], the ' rock of the hundreds,' and *Druim-Fiodhbhuidhe* [Drum-Feevee], ' woody-ridge ' ; and in Christian times *Lec-Phatraic*, ' St. Patrick's Rock.' An ancient legend still preserved in old Irish MSS., and

FIG. 211.

Rock of Cashel (top of Round Tower appears to the right). (From Brewer's Beauties of Ireland. Drawn by Petrie.)

given by Keating, relates that two swineherds, while feeding their flocks in the woods round the hill, in the beginning of the fifth century, saw an angel as bright as the sun standing on the rock, blessing the place with voice more melodious than any music, and prophesying the coming of St. Patrick. Corc mac Luighdheach, king of Munster, coming to hear of this, immediately took possession of the whole place, and on the summit of the rock built a stronghold, which was known as Lis-na-Laochraidhe [Laikree], the ' fort of the heroes,' and which then became the chief residence of the Munster kings, and continued so till the beginning of the twelfth century. In 1101 King Murkertagh O'Brien dedicated the whole place to the church, and handed it over to the ecclesiastical authorities, since which time it figures chiefly in ecclesiastical history. Then began to be erected those splendid buildings which remain to this day ; so that the " Rock of Cashel " is now well known as containing the most imposing group of ecclesiastical ruins in the united kingdom.*

Grianan Lachtna.—One of the ancestral residences of the Dalcassian kings of Thomond or North Munster was Grianan-Lachtna or Greenan-Lachna, the fine old fort of which is still to be seen occupying a noble site on the south slope of Craig-Liath or Craglea in Clare, over the western shore of Lough Derg, two miles north of Killaloe.

Kincora.—But when Brian Boru ascended the throne, he came to live at Kincora, where the remains of the palace have all disappeared, inasmuch as the site is now occupied by the town of Killaloe. The O'Briens, as kings of Thomond, continued to reside at Kincora for two centuries after the Battle of Clontarf : but about 1214 they removed their residence to **Clonroad** near Ennis. One of the outlying forts—a very fine one—still remains, however, beside the Shannon, a mile north of Killaloe, and is now known by the name of Beal Boru.

Dungrud.—In East Munster there were, from remote times, two royal residences. One was *Dun-gcrot*, now called Dungrud or Dungrott, in the Glen of Aherlow, at the foot of the Galtys, on the site of which the English of Galbally erected a strong castle.

Caher.—The other East Munster palace was on a little rocky island in the river Suir at the town of Caher, in Tipperary. It was oringially called *Dun-iasgach*, the ' fish-abounding dun,' from the *dun* that constituted the original

* On all this, see O'Curry, MS. Mat., 485 and 623 : Comyn's Keating, I. 123 : and for a description of the buildings on it, Petrie's article in the Irish Penny Journal, p. 17.

fortress-palace. This was succeeded by a circular stone caher, which gave the place its present name. The castle was built by the Anglo-Normans on the site of the caher.*

Another of these Munster palaces was **Dun-gcláire** [Doonglara], the fort of which is still in good preservation, standing at the northern base of the mountain of Slievereagh near Kilfinnane, two miles nearly north-west from Ballylanders, on the left of the road as you go from

FIG 212.

Caher Castle in 1845 : on site of the old palace. (From Mrs. Hall's Ireland.)

this village to Knocklong. It covers about four statute acres, and is now called Doonglara, or more often Lis-Doonglara.

Brugh-righ.—Bruree in the county Limerick, situated beside the river Maigue, was from remote times one of the seats of the kings of South Munster, as its Irish name *Brugh-righ* indicates, signifying the 'House of Kings.' It was also called *Dun Eochair Mhaighe*, the 'fort on the

* See Petrie's article on Caher Castle in Irish Penny Journal, p. 27. For all these Munster palaces, see Comyn's Keating, pp. 121 to 129.

brink (*eochair*) of the River Maigue.'* The illustrious King Ailill Olom, ancestor of many of the chief Munster families, lived there in the second century† : and it continued to be occupied by the Munster kings till long after the Anglo-Norman Invasion. The Anglo-Norman chiefs also adopted it as a place of residence, as they did many others of the old Irish kingly seats : and the ruins of two of their fine castles remain. There are still to be seen, along the river, several of the old circular forts, the most interesting of which is the one now universally known in the neighbourhood by the name of Lissoleem, inasmuch as it preserves the very name of King Ailill Olom, whose timber house was situated within its enclosure. It is situated on the western bank of the river, a mile below the village, in the townland of Lower Lotteragh, in the angle formed by the Maigue and a little stream joining it from the west. It is a circular fort with three ramparts, having the reputation—like most other raths—of being haunted by fairies : and as it is very lonely and much overgrown with bushes, it is as fit a home for fairies as could well be imagined.

This king's name, Ailill Olom, signifies ' Ailill Bare-Ear,' so called because—as already mentioned (vol. i., p. 263)— one of his ears was cut off in a struggle with the fairy lady Aine of Knockainy. *Olom* is accented on the second syllable, and is compounded of *o*, ' an ear,' and *lom*, ' bare,' : in the name " Ailill Olom " it is in the nominative case : " Ailill Bare-Ear " (not " of the Bare-Ear ") : like the English names William Longsword, John Lackland, Richard Strongbow. But when placed after " Lis," it takes —as it should take—the genitive form, " Oluim " : and " *Lis-Oluim*," which is exactly represented in sound by " Lissoleem," signifies ' Olum's *lis* or residence.' Many examples of the preservation of very old personal and other names in our existing topographical nomenclature

* Comyn's Keating, p. 123 † Silva Gad., p. 348.

are given in my " Irish Names of Places " ; and this case of Lissoleem—which has not been noticed before—is fully as interesting as any of them.

Temair-Luachra.—In the time of the Red Branch Knights and of the Munster Degads (vol. I., p. 86), and from immemorial ages previously, the chief royal residence of South Munster was Teamair or Tara-Luachra, the fort of which in all probability still exists, though it has not been identified. Mr. W. M. Hennessy, in his Introduction to the Mesca Ulad, has brought together the several notices bearing on its position : and the Rev. Dr. Hogan has a remark on the subject in Rossnaree (p. 23, note 7). It was well known in the time of Elizabeth ; and anyone acquainted with the country, who would take the trouble to walk over the exact locality indicated, and make inquiry among the old people, would be able, as I believe, to light on and identify the very fort.

Knockgraffon.—Another noted Munster palace was *Cnoc-Rafonn*, now called Knockgraffon, three miles north of Caher in Tipperary, where the great mound, 60 or 70 feet high, still remains, with the ruins of an English castle beside it. Here resided, in the third century, Fiacha Muillethan [Feeha-Mullehan], king of Munster, who, when the great King Cormac mac Art invaded Munster in an attempt to levy tribute, defeated him at Knocklong and routed his army : an event which forms the subject of the historical tale called *Forbais Droma Damhghaire*, or the " Siege of Knocklong." The fort is now as noted for fairies as it was in old times for royalty (see Crofton Croker's story " The Legend of Knockgrafton.")*

* A full list of the royal seats of Munster, annotated by O'Donovan, is given in the Book of Rights, pp. 89 to 95.

Ornament: composed from the Book of Kells

CHAPTER XXI

FOOD, FUEL, AND LIGHT

SECTION I. *Meals in General.*

DINNER, the principal meal of the day, was called in Irish *prainn* or *praind*, probably a loan-word from the Latin *prandium*, which is explained by the Irish *proind* in Zeuss (67, 2). Hence the refectory of a monastery was called *praintech*, literally ' dinner-house.' Dinner was taken late in the evening both among the laity and in monasteries. "At the end of the day his [Patrick's] "charioteer said to him: ' Thou hast left a cross to-day "in thy path without visiting it.' Thereupon Patrick left "the guest-house and his dinner (*a tech-nóiged ocus a* "*praind*), and went back to the cross."* In the notes to the Feilire of Aengus (p. 62), it is stated that Ciaran's dinner (*praind*), *every night*, consisted of a little bit of barley-bread, two roots of a vegetable, and a drink of water.

It was usual to have a light meal between breakfast and dinner corresponding with the modern luncheon. It was called *etsruth* or *etrud* which Cormac (p. 68) explains

---

* Trip. Life, 125 : see also Silva Gad., 113, 24.

104

as "*eter-shod* ['middle-meal'], the middle-meal of the day." The time is given more definitely in an entry (quoted by Stokes under this explanation) in an ancient MS. :—" *Etrud*, i.e. *etar-suth* ('middle-fruit'), *i.e.* between " morning and evening ; or *rith-etir*, or 'middle-running,' " *i.e.* [running] at midday." It was a custom among the laity, as well as in the monastic communities, to have better food on Sundays and church festivals than on other days, as appears from many passages in the Laws, and in ecclesiastical and general literature.

Among the higher classes great care was taken to seat family and guests at table in the order of rank ; any departure from the established usage was sure to be resented by the person who was put lower than he should be ; and sometimes resulted in serious quarrels or wars. The placing of Prince Congal by Domnall king of Ireland below his proper place at the banquet of Dun-nan-gedh was one main cause of the great Battle of Moyrath (fought A.D. 637).* It was especially necessary to observe the proper formalities at banquets and on all state occasions, where the arrangements were under the direction of the *rechtaire* or 'house-steward' (for whom see vol. I., p. 64). At the banquet given by King Concobar mac Nessa at Dun-da-Benn, as narrated in the Mesca Ulad (p. 13) of which the original is in the Book of Leinster, the banqueting-hall was " arranged by Concobar according to " deeds and parts and families ; according to grades and " arts and customs, with a view to the fair holding of the " banquet." (Any great banquet or feast was called *fléd*, and sometimes *imdell*.)

The account given by Keating (pp. 302–3), which he took from ancient documents now lost, of the seating of the guests at the state banquets of Tara, is very interesting. The persons entertained were of three main classes :—

* Moyrath, 29, 31. For the battle, see Joyce, Short History of Ireland, p 153.

Lords of territories; the commanders of the bands of warriors who were kept permanently and maintained at free quarters by the king at Tara; and the ollaves or learned men of the several professions. The territorial lords were regarded as of higher rank than the military commanders; and each chief of both classes was attended by his " shield-bearer " or squire. It was the duty of the ollave shanachie to have the names of all written in two separate rolls, in exact order of precedence: and in this order they sat at table.

The banquet-hall was a long narrow building, with tables arranged along both side-walls. Immediately over the tables were a number of hooks in the wall at regular intervals to hang the shields on. One side of the hall was more dignified than the other, and the tables here were for the lords of territories: those at the other side were for the military captains. The upper end was reserved for the professional ollaves: the dependents—always a large company—sat at the lower end.

Just before the beginning of the feast all persons left the hall except three :—A *Shanachie* or historian : a *Bollscari* or marshal to regulate the order : and a trumpeter (*fear-stuic*) whose duty it was to sound his trumpet just three times. At the first blast the shield-bearers or squires of the lords of territories came round the door and gave their masters' shields to the marshal, who, under the direction of the Shanachie, hung them on the hooks according to ranks, from the highest to the lowest : and at the second blast the shields of the military commanders were disposed of in like manner. At the third blast the guests all walked in leisurely, each taking his seat under his own shield (which was marked with his special cognisance : see vol. i. p. 125). In this manner all unseemly disputes or jostling for places were avoided. No man sat opposite another, as only one side of each row of tables was occupied, namely, the side next the wall.

Keating does not, in this passage, give the arrangement when the king was present : but this is described in other authorities ; as well as elsewhere in Keating (415). The king was always attended at banquets by his subordinate kings, and by other lords and chiefs : and great formality was observed in seating all. In the " Wooing of Emer " (p. 69), it is stated that when the company sat drinking in the banquet-hall of Emain, " no man of them would touch the other." Those especially on the immediate right and left of the king had to sit at a respectful distance. At the feasts of Tara, Tailltenn, and Ushnagh, it was the privilege of the king of Oriell to sit next the king of Ireland, but he sat at such a distance that his sword just reached the high king's hand : and to him also belonged the honour of presenting every third drinking-horn brought to the king.* According to Kineth O'Hartigan, while King Cormac mac Art sat at dinner, fifty military guards, or " heroes," remained standing beside him.† The arrangements for seating subordinate kings, at banquets given by the Hy Neill Monarchs, may be seen in the Battle of Moyrath, pp. 29, 31 ; and a much more detailed account of those for king and guests at Brian Boru's banquets at Kincora is given, from old authorities, in O'Curry's Lectures.‡ At Tara it often happened that the women did not sit at banquets with the men : they had a banquet-hall for themselves. But in the feasts at other places men and women always, or nearly aways, banqueted in the same hall : the women, however, generally sitting apart : and they often wore a mask—sometimes called *fethal*—which hid or partly hid the face.§

This rigid adherence to order of priority at table continued in Ireland and Scotland down to a recent period :

* Book of Rights, 137. † Petrie, Tara, 191, 192.
‡ Man. & Cust., I. 121. See also Petrie's Tara, p. 199 *et seq.*, for the detailed arrangements in Tara.
§ See Law Tract quoted by O'Curry, Man. & Cust., II. 114.

and it continues still in a modified and less strict form everywhere. Readers of Scott will call to mind the scene in " The Lord of the Isles," when the seneschal—corresponding with the Irish *rechtaire*—seated the unknown strangers next the prince :—

> " Then lords and ladies spake aside,
>   And angry looks the error chide
>   That gave to guests, unnamed, unknown,
>   A place so near their prince's throne."

An odd instance of the Irish " pride of place " in the eighteenth century is related by Hardiman* concerning Arthur O'Neill, the celebrated Irish harper. He was universally respected, partly on account of his musical abilities, but more because he belonged to the illustrious family of O'Neill : and he always sat at table among the highest people. Once at a public dinner in Belfast, which was attended by all the local nobility and gentry, the noble lord who presided apologised to him for being accidentally placed so far down from the head of the table. " O my lord," replied he, " apology is unnecessary : wherever an O'Neill sits, that is the head of the table."

The host stood up before the meal and formally welcomed his guests.† At all state banquets particular joints were reserved for certain chiefs, officials, and professional men, according to rank. These are set forth in several authorities, though with some differences : they may be seen in detail in Petrie's Tara (pp. 199 *et seq.*), taken from the Book of Leinster. The following shorter statement is given in the treatise on Irish Ordeals translated by Stokes, which is almost identical with that given by the commentator on the Senchus Mór — " A thigh " [*laarg*] for a king and a poet : a chine [*croichet*] for a

---

* Ir. Minstr., II. 412.

† See Moyrath, 25 : Ir. Texte, I. 99. paragraph, 6, with a translation in Hib. Minora, 59.

"literary sage [*sai litri* : vol. I., p. 434] : a leg [*colptha*]
"for a young lord [*ógtigern*] : heads [*cuind*] for charioteers :
"a haunch [*les*] for queens."* A similar custom existed
among the ancient Gauls and also among the Greeks.†
A remnant of this old custom lingered on in the Western
Islands of Scotland to the time of Martin (p. 109), 200
years ago. When the chief of an island killed an animal,
he gave head, feet, entrails, and such like, to his dependents, the head being due to the smith, the udder of a cow
to the piper, &c. At a still later time—1773—Dr. Johnson,
in his account of his visit to the Hebrides, records the
prevalence of the custom there in the following words :—
"When a beef was killed for the house, particular parts
"were claimed as fees by the several officers or workmen.
". . . The head belonged to the smith, and the udder of a
"cow to the piper : the weaver had likewise his particular
"part : and so many pieces followed these prescriptive
"claims that the laird's was at last but little." Even so
late as 1839, when Petrie wrote his Essay on Tara, the
custom was partially kept up in some parts of Ireland,
where the farmers, when they killed a beef or a pig, always
sent the head to the smith, whose kitchen was often
garnished with from fifty to a hundred heads, obtained in
this manner.‡ Sometimes the marrow-bones were assigned
to a particular member of the household, to whom everyone
passed his bone after picking it : and woe betide anyone
else who broke a bone for marrow.§

In the time of the Red Branch Knights, it was the
custom to assign the choicest joint or animal of the whole
banquet to the hero who was acknowledged by general
consent to have performed the bravest and greatest exploit.
This piece was called *curath-mir*, i.e. ' the hero's morsel or

---

* Ir. Texte, III. 206 : Br. Laws, I. 49 : see also " Milgitan " in Corm.
Gloss., 107 : and for a further detailed account see Ulster Journ. Archæol.,
III. 119.

† Iliad, XXII., and VII. 320 : Odyss., IV. 66.

‡ Petrie's Tara, p. 212.   § For instance, see Moyrath, 71.

share' (*mir*). There were often keen contests among the Red Branch heroes, and sometimes fights with bloodshed, for this coveted joint or piece : and some of the best stories of the Táin hinge on contests of this kind.* This usage, which, according to Diodorus Siculus, prevailed among the continental Celts in general, and which also existed among the Greeks,† seems to have continued in Ireland to comparatively late times : for the Senchus Mór mentions among the offences for which penalty was due "Carrying away the hero's morsel from the person to whom it belongs." The word used here is *dantmir*, which the gloss explains by *curath-mir*. O'Donovan, the translator of the Senchus Mór, considers the marrowbones mentioned above—assigned to one particular individual— as a sort of *curath-mir*.‡

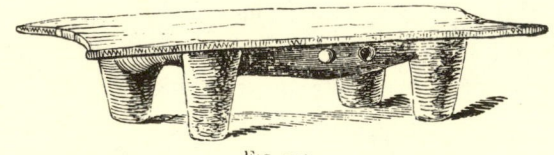

FIG. 213.

Small Table : 28 inches long, 16 inches broad, and 5 inches high : made of willow : found in a bog in Tyrone, five feet under the surface. (From Wilde's Catalogue, p. 211.)

Tables were, as we have seen, used at the great feasts. But at ordinary meals, high tables, such as we have now, do not seem to have been in general use. There were small low tables, such as that in the illustration, each used no doubt for two or more persons, who sat or reclined on low couches or seats of some kind at meals. Often there was a little table laid beside each person, on which his food was placed—the meat on a platter.§ In late times— the sixteenth century—Derrick, in his " Image of Ireland,"

* See Fled Bricrend, p. 15. Nearly the whole of this tale is occupied with the contests of the three Red Branch heroes, Cuculainn, Loegaire the Victorious, and Conall Cernach for the *curath-mir*.

† De Jubainville, Cours de Litt. Celt., VI., pp. 3, 4.

‡ Br. Laws, I. 177, 181, bottom, and note 1.

§ Joyce's Old Celtic Romances, 125.

represents the Irish at their meals in this fashion : but Derrick's words and pictures must be received with caution, for they are all more or less caricatures. According to Giraldus,* his countrymen, the Welsh, had no tables at all at their meals : and very probably this was the case in the general run of the houses of the Irish peasantry.

Forks are a late invention : of old the fingers were used at eating. In Ireland, as in England and other countries in those times, each person held his knife in the right hand, and used the fingers of the left instead of a fork : just as we see described in the " Vision of Mac Conglinne " (p. 64). Sometimes—as at banquets, and among very high-class people—the carvers cut off great pieces from the joint, which they brought round and put on the platters. The attendants who supplied food and drink in this manner at great dinners were called *dáilemain*, ' carvers, distributors, or spencers ' (from *dáil*, ' to cut or divide ') ; and *deogbhaire*, or *deochbhaire*, ' cupbearers ' (from *deoch* ' a drink '). But more commonly each person went to the joint, and using his left-hand fingers to catch hold, cut off a piece for himself and brought it to his own platter. Even so late as the sixteenth century this was the custom in England, according to Roberts (p. 342), who says that dinner was served without knives or forks, but each had his own clasp-knife, and going to the dish, cut off a piece for himself : and he gives this illustrative verse from " The Mirror of Good Manners," by Alexander Barclay (sixteenth century) :—

> " If the dish be pleasant, either flesche or fische,
> Ten hands at once swarm in the dishe."

Even towards the end of the seventeenth century " they " scarce ever make use of forks or ewers, for they wash " their hands by dipping them into a basin of water " (Social Engl., IV. 490). That this was the manner of dining

* Description of Wales, x.

in very early times in Ireland appears from a passage in the "Second Battle of Moytura," where it is said of the inhospitable King Bres :—" Their knives [*i.e.* the knives of " his subjects the Dedannans] were not greased [*nibtar* " *beoluide a sceanai*] by him, and their breaths did not smell " of ale at the banquets."*   The Greeks and Romans had no knives or forks at meals : they used the fingers only, and were supplied with water to wash their hands after eating : yet the meat must have been cut in some way either by the guests or by the attendants.   The Irish people picked the bones as many do now, partly with the knife and partly with the teeth.†   In the story told in vol. I., p. 414, *supra*, the bishop, being suddenly called on deck, came up from his dinner holding in his hand a big bone, which no doubt he was picking in the good old fashion.

As early as the eighth or ninth century the higher classes used napkins at table, for which they had a native word, *lámbrat*, i.e. ' hand-napkin ' (*lám*, ' hand ' : ' *brat*, a cloth '). In a manuscript quoted by Zeuss (653, ₄₅) the Latin words *mappa* and *mantile* are explained by the eighth-century Irish Glossator, *lambrat bis tar glune*, ' a napkin that is usually placed over the knees ' : and in another part of the same manuscript the Latin *gausape* is explained by the single Irish word *lambrat* (Z., 854, ₂₂). In the Latin version of the Voyage of St. Brendan there is a more direct reference to the use of napkins.   The voyagers went into a mansion on an island, in which they found a large hall with couches and seats and water to wash their feet, and plenty of food.   " St. Brendan ordered " the serving-brother to bring forward the meal which God " had sent them : and without delay the table was laid with " napkins (*linteamina*) and with white loaves and fish for " each brother."‡   But perhaps *linteamina* here means

---

* Rev. Celt XII. 69.   † See for example Moyrath .p. 71.
‡ Brendaniana, 121 : Card. Moran, 93, ₁₃.

' tablecloths.' I suppose the chief use they made of the napkins was to wipe the left-hand fingers ; which was badly needed.   They sometimes used dried hides as tablecloths. Cathal the king-glutton (eighth century : for whom see Index) was once eating apples as part of his dinner, and " he began supplying his mouth from both " hands with the apples that were on hides round about " him." Mac Conglinne (pp. 46, 50) was there and began importuning him for some of the apples, so that the king threw him one after one ; till at last he " flung him hide, apples, and all."

It was the custom, both in monastic communities and in secular life, to take off the shoes or sandals when sitting down to dinner ; which was generally done by an attendant. The Romans we know had the same custom : " the covering of the feet was removed before reclining at meals."* It is related in the " Vision of Mac Conglinne " (p. 46) that the gluttonous king of Munster mentioned above, who had a *lón-craos*, i.e. a ' demon of gluttony ' in his stomach, sitting down one day to dinner, was in such a hurry that he fell to before the attendant had loosed the thong of one shoe (*bróc*). And Adamnan tells us in his " Life of St. Columba" (pp. 121, 122) that St. Canice, in his monastery of Aghaboe (sixth century), while in the act of breaking the bread in the refectory, having a revelation that St. Columba and his companions were in great danger on sea, hastily left the table and went to the church to pray " with one shoe on his foot, the other being left behind in his great haste." Another similar incident is related in Oengus's Feilire (p. 9, 15). We may infer from the existence of this custom that the Irish, like the Romans, reclined during meals on couches on which the feet also rested.

The Irish, like the people of all other countries, had their meals commonly served hot, immediately after

* Smith's Dict. Greek & Rom. Antiqq., " Calceus."

cooking. But at great banquets the food must have been generally taken cold ; for in such cases, with the appliances then available, it would have been impossible to serve hot. Accordingly, we constantly read that before a banquet the whole of the food was cooked and laid out on tables in the first instance. Just before the guests came into the hall to the Feast of Dun-nan-gedh, Prince Congal is brought in to view the viands, all laid out and ready, and eats part of a goose-egg. When Lomman, king of Hy Fidgente, prepared a feast for St. Patrick, a youth named Nessan, as soon as he heard of it, came with his mother, bringing a cooked ram as a contribution.*

2. *Drink.*

In old times people were quite as fond of intoxicating drinks at·dinners and banquets as they are now : and we are constantly told in the tales that when the cups went round, the company became *mesca medarchaini*, ' exhilarated and right merry.' They sometimes drank more than was good for them too ; and on one occasion of this kind the Ulstermen marched southwards in a drunken raid on Munster, which is the subject of the old tale in the Book of Leinster called *Mesca Ulad*, the " Intoxication of the Ultonians," edited by Mr. Hennessy in the MS. series of the Proc. Roy. Ir. Acad. Yet drunkenness was looked upon as reprehensible. In Cormac's Glossary (p. 116) is a derivation for the word *mesci*, ' drunkenness,' implying that radically it meant " more of reproach than sense or sobriety " : and in the Tripartite Life (p. 137) it is related that when St. Patrick was in Connaught, a certain king, while in a state of intoxication, came to visit him : at which the saint was sorely displeased, and prophesied that that king's descendants would be ale-tipplers and would go to the bad in the end. At their feasts they often

* Trip. Life, 205.

accompanied their carousing with music and singing. Maildune and his men visiting a certain island, saw the people feasting and drinking and " heard their ale-music " (*corm-cheól*).*

In very early times ladies often sat with the men at the banquets, and joined in the festivities. It appears, too, that the Irish ladies of those times could take a moderate part in a drinking-bout with their male friends, like those of Wales and Scandinavia, as we read of them in the tales of those countries ; like the Egyptian ladies of four or five thousand years ago ; and like English ladies of much later times (Soc. Engl., II. 422 ; and IV. 161). At Bricriu's Feast, where the ladies were present, after the revelling had gone on for some time, Fedelma, wife of Loegaire the Victorious, went forth from the banquet-hall with her fifty hand-maidens, " after heaviness of drinking " (*iar trommi óil*), as much as to say, they went out to shake off the effects by a walk in the fresh air.† In the ancient tale called the " Vision of Cahirmore," king of Ireland A.D. 174–177, we read that on one occasion, while the king was celebrating the *Féis* of Tara, the whole company, after dinner, got so drunk that they fell asleep, and a thief slipped in and stole the queen's diadem‡ : which seems to imply that the queen herself was present taking a comfortable nap like the rest.

Besides plain water and milk, the chief drinks were ale. mead or metheglin, and wine. Giraldus Cambrensis (Top. Hib., I. v.) remarks that Ireland never had vineyards : but that there was plenty of wine supplied by foreign commerce ; and he mentions Poitou especially as supplying vast quantities in exchange for hides. This account is corroborated by the native records, from which we learn that wine (Irish *fín*, pron. feen : a loan-word from Latin) was imported in very early ages ; and it is frequently

* Rev. Celt., x. 81.
† Fled Bricr., 17, 154 : see also Bec Fola, 179 and note 23.
‡ Kilk. Archæol. Journ., 1872–3, p. 29.

mentioned as an accompaniment at banquets. Muirchu, writing in the seventh century, tells us that when St. Patrick came to Tara on Easter Sunday A.D. 433, the kings, princes, and druids were feasting and drinking wine in the palace with King Laegaire.* In the year A.D. 533 the palace of Cletty was set on fire by a revengeful woman while Murkertagh mac Erca, king of Ireland, was feasting in it with his nobles ; and the king, to avoid the fire, plunged into a butt of wine, in which he was drowned.† Domnall, king of Ireland (A.D. 627 to 641), in preparation for the banquet of Dun-nan-gedh, provided three kinds of drink—wine, mead, and ale. Wine is also often mentioned in Cormac's Glossary and in other Irish authorities as a well-known drink.

Of all the intoxicating drinks ale was the most general, not only in Ireland, but among all the peoples of northern Europe : and the more intoxicating it was the more esteemed. One of the attractions of Midir's wonderful fairyland was " ale which is strongly intoxicating."‡ Irish ale was well known from the earliest period, even on the Continent, as we see from the statement of Dioscorides in the first century :—" The Britons and the Hiberi or Irish, " instead of wine, use a liquor called *courmi* or *curmi*, made " of barley."§ This author caught up correctly the ancient Irish name for ale, which was *cuirm* or *coirm* (gen. *corma*) : and hence *coirmthech*, ' ale-house,' *i.e.* a house in which ale was made. The present word for ale is *linn* or *leann* : and although this, too, was one of the words for ale in old times, it was often used to denote drink in general. Ale was a native product, and was reddish in colour as now. Its manufacture was understood everywhere ; and the whole process is given in detail in the Senchus Mór, and in the commentaries and glosses on it.|| The grain chiefly

---

* Hogan, Docum., 37.   ‡ O'Curry, Man. & Cust., II. 191.
† Petrie, Tara, 120.   § Ware, Antiqq., 183.
  || Br. Laws, II., pp. 241 to 245, from which the following details of the processes are chiefly taken.

used was barley; and what grew on rich land was most valued for the purpose: but it was also often made from rye, as well as from wheat and oats.

The corn, of whatever kind, was first converted into malt: Irish *brac* or *braich*: gen. *bracha*. For this purpose it was steeped in water for a certain time, after which the water was let off slowly, and the wet grain was spread out on a level floor to dry. During this time persons turned it over and over and raked it into ridges to bring all parts in turn to the surface. It was next dried in a kiln (*aith*, pron. ah) till the grain became hard. This dried grain was malt. If not intended to be kept in grains, it was ground with a quern or in a mill, and was then either put into sacks as it came from the mill, or made into cakes and dried. Malt cakes were often so hard that before using they had to be broken in pieces with a mallet and ground again

FIG. 214.

Bronze Strainer, found in the crannoge of Moylarg, County Antrim. Cup-shaped, 4½ inches wide and 1½ inch deep. Observe, the holes are not at random; they form curve-patterns. (From the Journ. Roy. Soc. Antiqq. for 1894, p. 319.)

in a mill to reduce them back to meal.* Whether as unground kiln-dried grains, or as meal in bags, or as dried cakes, this *brac* or malt kept for any length of time; and it was often given in payment of rent or tribute, as repeatedly mentioned in the Book of Rights.

* Fled Bricrend, 67 ; O'Curry, Man. & Cust., I. 309.

When the ale was to be prepared, the ground malt was made into a mash with water, which was fermented, boiled,* strained, &c., till the process was finished. Conall Derg O'Corra had in his house strainers (men) with their cries always at work *ag sgagadh leanna,* ' a-straining ale,' in hospitable preparation for guests.† Malt, and of course the ale, might be spoiled by mismanagement at any stage of the process ; and the Senchus Mór mentions three successive tests : one after kiln-drying and before being ground, by putting a grain under the tooth to try whether it was sound and free from bitterness : another after grinding, before it was made into a cake, to ascertain if it was free from mawkishness ; and a third when it was in mash, before it was put to ferment.

Ale was often made in private houses for family use : for everywhere among the people there were amateur experts who understood the process. But there were houses also set apart for this purpose, where a professional brewer carried on the business. Some ale-making houses were what were called " lawful " (*dligtech,* ' lawful,' ' legalised,' or ' licensed '), that is, the law took cognisance of them and received their certificates : others were unlawful—unlegalised or unlicensed, which meant, not contrary to law, but merely that the law took no cognisance of them—did not accept their certificates. This made an important difference in cases of dispute ; for whenever a tenant paid part of his rent or tribute in ale which had been made in a lawful ale-house, if he proved that the three tests had been applied with satisfactory results while the malt was in the house, he was free from responsibility, even though the ale turned out bad.‡ But if ale which had been made in an unlawful house proved to be bad after being sent in payment to the chief, it was forfeited, and the tenant had to

---

* Boiled : see Br. Laws, IV. 311, 12.   † Rev. Celt., XIV., 27.
‡ On this see Br. Laws, V. 167, in addition to the passages in Br. Laws, vol. II. referred to in note ||, p. 116, above.

make good the loss, even though the three tests had been applied : for the certificate from the unlawful house counted for nothing. Probably the proprietor of a licensed ale-making house took advantage of his privilege to make higher charges, like legally recognised experts of all kinds at the present day.

Among the members of St. Patrick's household was a brewer—a priest named Mescan. A professional brewer was called *cerbsire* or *cirbsire* [kirvshirrĕ], a loanword from Latin *cervicia* or *cerviciarius* (which is itself a borrowed Gaulish word). But there was also a native term for a brewer, *scoaire* [3-syll.], which is given in Cormac's Glossary (p. 31) to explain *cerbsire*. It is probable that a " lawful " alehouse had always one of these men, and not a mere amateur, in charge of it.

When people felt indisposed or out of sorts, it was usual to give them a draught of ale to refresh or revive them, as we now give a cup of tea or a glass of wine. At Easter time, and after the restraint of Lent was over, the people sometimes indulged in a good drink of ale : and a supply was commonly kept in the churches, so that members of the congregation might take a drink when it was lawful to do so. At a certain Easter time, as we are told in the Life of St. Brigit, she brewed ale to supply the churches all round her : and this she did as a kindly and charitable act. St. Domangart or Donard, a disciple of St. Patrick, always kept a pitcher of ale and a *larac* or leg of beef with its accompaniments every Easter at his church of Maghera near Slieve Donard : " and he gives them to Mass-folk " [*i.e.* those that have been at Mass] on Easter Tuesday " always."*

Yeast or leaven—called in Irish *descad* and *serba*— made from malt, was used in brewing, and also in baking. The house of the hospitable *brewy* Conall Derg O'Corra

was never without a " sack of malt for preparing yeast "
(*miach bracha re frithealamh ndeasgadh*).*

There was a kind of ale called in Cormac's Glossary
and elsewhere *brocoit, bracaut*, or *braccat*, which, although
made and named from *brac* or malt, was somewhat different
from the ordinary *cuirm* or ale. Cormac (p. 19) says that
brocoit is a Welsh word. It has descended to our day,
and is found in English dictionaries as *bragget*, used to
designate a sort of ale sweetened with honey and seasoned
with spices. The Glossary states that " braccat is a goodly
ale [or goodly drink : *sain-linn*], made from malt " [and
honey] : and we know that honey was also used in making
the Welsh *bragget*. This kind of ale is often mentioned in
later Irish writings under the name of *brogoit*.

Mead or metheglin (Irish *mid*, pron. mee) was made
chiefly from honey : it was a drink in much request, and
was considered a delicacy, which is indicated in the designation applied to it in the " Vision of Mac Conglinne " (p. 98)—
the " Dainty drink of Nobles " (*sercoll sochenélach*). It was
intoxicating, though not so much so as ale : the O'Caith-
niadhs are spoken of in " Hy Fiachrach " as " the host who
are most excited by mead." Where mead abounded the
people of the district were the more thought of for it ; so
that we often meet with such laudatory expressions as
" the mead-abounding murrisk," " the O'Gillens who have
encouraged mead-drinking," " the mead-drinking men of
Meath." A visitor on arrival was often treated to mead :
when the king of Leinster came to visit St. Brigit at her
nunnery, she gave him a cup of mead to drink. Mead is
mentioned, in our most ancient authorities. The rule of
St. Ailbe, a contemporary of St. Patrick, directs that when
the monks sit down to dinner, they " shall get on clean
" dishes herbs or roots washed in water, likewise apples,
" and mead from the hive to the depth of a thumb."† In

---

* Rev. Celt., XIV. 27.   † Lynch, Cambr. Ev., II. 137

the story of the Children of Lir, Finola, speaking of their former happy life, says that they often drank " hazel-mead " (*miodh cuill*)* ; from which we may infer that hazel-nuts were sometimes used as an ingredient in making mead, probably to give it a flavour. Mead continued to be made in the south of Ireland till about the year 1824.†

Sullivan, in his Introduction to O'Curry's Lectures (p. 378), states that the Irish made a kind of cider called *nenadmim*, from the wild- or crab-apple ; and that the people kept wild-apple trees planted in hedgerows to supply the fruit. He also says that they made another drink bearing the same name from " wood-berries," which are probably the berries still well known as *fraechóga* or *fraecháin*, anglice " froghans," the *Vaccinum myrtillus*, better known in Munster as " whorts " or " hurts." No doubt he had good authority for these statements, but I have found none.

In old times it would appear that people consumed their drink in large quantities : but then it was only mildly intoxicating. The law-tracts assign the quantity of ale allowed at dinner to laymen and to clerics respectively. There are some contradictions and obscurities in these statements‡ : but it seems probable that the following are the allowances meant :—Six pints to a layman, and three to a cleric. It is added that the latter were so restricted in order that the clerics " may not be drunk and that their canonical hours may not be set astray on them " : in which there is an implication that a man was liable to get drunk on six pints but not on three.

The word *beoir* is used in Irish for ' beer '—obviously the same as the English word. There is a late tradition that a kind of beer was made from heath, or from the

---

* Three Sorrowful Stories, 141 ; and old Celt. Rom., 24. See also " a cup with hazel-nut mead " in K. Meyer's King and Hermit, p. 17.
† For mead see also Ware, Antiqq., 183 : and Sullivan, Introd., 377.
‡ Br. Laws, iii., 337 and note.

red heather-berries called *mónadan* ("bog-berries": not "hurts" or whortleberries), which was designated in English "bog-berry wine," and in Irish *beoir Lochlannach*, *i.e.* "Lochlann or Norse wine": but I have not met with any reference to it in old Irish literature.*

Whiskey is a comparatively modern innovation. The first notice of it in the Irish annals appears to be at A.D. 1405, where there is the ominous record that Richard Mac Rannall, chief of Muinter Eolais, died from an over-dose of *uisge beatha* [ishkĕ-baha] or whiskey.

3. *Cooking.*

In great houses there were professional cooks, who, while engaged in their work, wore a linen apron round them from the hips down, and a flat linen cap on the head.† Among ordinary families the women did the cooking: and in monasteries a few of the monks, specially skilled, were always assigned for this part of the work of the community. Among St. Patrick's household his cook was Athcen, who is still remembered as the patron saint of Bodoney in Tyrone.‡ The Irish for 'a cook' is *coic*, which is a loan word from Latin *coquus*: and the Irish *cucenn*, 'a kitchen,' is from the Latin *coquina*: both Irish words are found in Cormac's Glossary (p. 31).

Meat and fish were cooked by roasting, boiling, or broiling. The word *inneónadh* [innōna] was commonly applied to the process of broiling or roasting, as distinguished from *fulachta*, 'seething, stewing, or boiling.' A spit (*bir*) for roasting—made of iron—was an article in general use, and was regarded as an important household implement. But the spits commonly used in roasting, as well as the skewers for trussing up the joint, were pointed hazel-rods, peeled and made smooth and white.§ Meat,

---

* See Sullivan, Introd., p. 378.   ‡ Trip. Life, 265 : FM, A.D. 448.
† Mac Conglinne, 62.   § For spits, see Petrie, Tara, 213, 214.

and even fish, while roasting, were often basted with honey or with a mixture of honey and salt* ; and it is to be presumed that the joint or animal was kept turning round simply by hand. Meat and fish were often broiled on a gridiron, or something in the nature of a gridiron. In a very ancient story in Cormac's Glossary (p. 130), we read that on a certain occasion Finn mac Cumail found one of his men, Coirpre, in an empty house, cooking fish upon an *indeoin* [innone]. There is some doubt about the exact meaning of *indeoin* in this passage. Stokes translates it ' stone,' while O'Donovan renders it ' spit ' : but in another place he makes it ' gridiron.' An *indeoin* was no doubt a gridiron or griddle of some kind : probably of stone in primitive times, but subsequently of metal. This word *indeoin* has, however, several meanings : as may be seen by reference to the Index at the end.

When bodies of men marched through the country, either during war or on hunting excursions, they cooked their meat in a large way. Keating and other writers give the following description of how the Fena of Erin cooked, a plan which is often referred to in the ancient tales, and which was no doubt generally followed, not only by the Fena but by all large parties camping out. The attendants roasted one part on hazel spits before immense fires of wood, and baked the rest on hot stones in a pit dug in the earth. The stones were heated in the fires. At the bottom of the pit the men placed a layer of these hot stones : then a layer of meat-joints wrapped in sedge or in hay or straw ropes to keep them from being burned : next another layer of hot stones : down on that more meat : and so on till the whole was disposed of, when it was covered up ; and in this manner it was effectively cooked. The remains of many of these cooking-pits are still to be seen in various parts of the country, and are easily recognised by the charred wood and blackened stones ; and sometimes

* Mac Conglinne, 62.

the very pits are to be seen.*   To this day they are called
fulachta-na-bhfiann [fullaghta-na-veen], the *fulachta* or
' cooking-places of the Fena ' : for in popular legend they
are still attributed to the Fena of Erin.   These cooking-
places are referred to in Cormac's Glossary (p. 69, " Esnad")
where they are called *fulacht-fiansae* ; and it is stated that
while the cooking was in progress the hunters chanted a
kind of music called *esnad* (see vol. I., p. 592, *supra*).   A
pit in which meat was cooked in this manner was called
brothlach.

In the house of every chief and of every brewy there
was at least one bronze caldron for boiling meat.   Its
usual name was *coire* or *caire* [2-syll.] : but it was sometimes called *aighean*, or more correctly *adhan* [ey-an],
which is now its usual name in Scotland.   It was highly
valued, as a most important article in the household ; and
it was looked upon as the special property of the chief or
head of the house—much in the same way as his sword
and shield.   Everywhere we meet with passages reminding
us of the great value set on these caldrons.   One of them
was regarded as a fit present for a king.   St. Patrick when
a boy in slavery in Ireland was sold to some mariners at
the mouth of the Boyne for two caldrons of bronze.†   The
caldron of a chief or of a brewy was supposed to be kept
in continual use, so that food might be always ready for
guests whenever they happened to arrive.   A common
appellation for one of these was *coire ainsec*, or *caire ainsic*,
or *caire ainsecan*, the ' un-dry caldron.'   It is laid down in
the Senchus Mór‡ that a brewy of the highest class should
have a *caire ainsec*, which is defined as " a caldron which
" should be always kept on the fire for every party that
" should arrive " : and the old book goes on to give several
derivations for *ainsec*, of which one—from *an*, a negative,
and *sic*, ' dry '—' not dry,' ' always wet '—is probably

* Kilk. Archæol. Journ., 1885–6, p. 390.   † Trip. Life, 417.
‡ Br. Laws, I. 41, 47, 49.

correct ; reminding one of the modern Irish invitation to
" a dry bed and a wet bottle."

Some caldrons were believed to possess magical properties, one of which was that, whatever quantity of food
was put into the vessel to boil, it cooked just as much
as was sufficient for the company and no more : and when
the attendant (*luchtaire*) thrust in the fleshfork to serve
any particular individual, he always—by the same magic
virtue—brought forth the very joint specially allotted to
him (p. 108, *supra*).   This virtue is alluded to in Cormac's

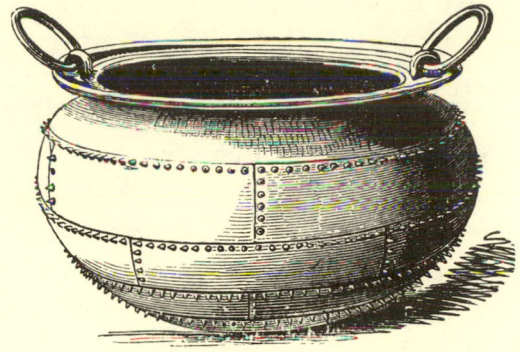

Fig. 215.

Ancient Bronze Caldron : 12 inches deep : now in National Museum :
formed of separate pieces, beautifully riveted, the head of each rivet
forming a conical stud or button, like the rivets of the gold gorgets and
of some of the bronze trumpets. (From Wilde's Catalogue.)

Glossary (p. 45, " *Caire ainsic* ") in a derivation of the
name :—it was called *caire ainsic* " because it returns
(*aisces*) his right to everyone."   The Welsh, too, had their
magical caldrons, to which they attributed magical virtues
something like those in Ireland.*

If we are to believe the tales and other old writings,
some caldrons were large enough to hold two or three
sheep or hogs together, cut up into joints ; the Brehon
Law (IV. 327) tells us that in an *aire-tuisi* chief's house
there must be a caldron in which a cow and a hog will fit ;
and in other parts of Irish literature these very large

* Ulst. Arch. Journ., v. 85 : Mabinogion, p. 31.

caldrons are continually referred to. Many bronze caldrons have been found from time to time, and are now
preserved in the National Museum, Dublin—several of
beautiful workmanship—but none are large enough to hold
all the chief joints of a cow and a hog.

All those caldrons that have been preserved have a
pair of ears or rings at the sides by which they were hung
over the fire on hooks ; and this use is alluded to in the
expression *sadail ar cairi da drol*, " cozy our caldron on
the hook," in the story of the cave of *Ben Etair* or Howth.*
Caldrons appear to have been always made of brass or
bronze—most often the latter. Those hitherto found are
all of that material ; and the Brehon Law says that in
every brewy's house there should be a *cairi humai*, 'a
bronze (or brazen) caldron.' Caldrons were manufactured
at home : but that some at least, and those among the
most valuable, were imported, is shown by Muirchu's
record, written in the seventh century, that Daire gave
Patrick an *aeneum mirabilem transmarinum*, ' a wonderful
brazen caldron from over sea.'†

Accompanying every caldron was an *áel* or fleshfork,
for lifting out pieces of meat. On one occasion, soon
before the Battle of Dunbolg, A.D. 598 St. Maidoc of
Ferns, as we are told in the " Boroma," brought to Branduff,
king of Leinster, a present of a three-pronged fleshfork
(*áel-trébend*), a caldron, a shield, and a sword‡ : an odd
combination, quite characteristic of the times. But in
early ages kitchen utensils were everywhere regarded as
important. The inventory of the jewels of the English
King Edward III. gives a list of this king's frying-pans,
gridirons, spits, &c.§ A fleshfork was also called *gabal*
[goul], which was, and is now, the ordinary word for a fork
of any kind. There is a curious provision in the Brehon

---

* Rev. Celt., XI. 133.   † Trip. Life, 291.
‡ Rev. Celt., XIII. 57 : Silva Gad., 408, 409 : Wilde, Catalogue, 529 :
Man. & Cust., I. 338.   § Roberts' Soc. Hist., p. 318.

Law that if any accident occurred to a bystander by the lifting of the joint out of the boiling caldron, the attendant was liable for damages unless he gave the warning : " Take care : here goes the *ael* into the caldron ! "*

4. *Flesh-meat and its accompaniments.*

The flesh of wild and domestic animals, boiled or roast or broiled, much as at the present day, formed one of the staple food-materials in old times in Ireland as in other countries.

Pork (*muicc-fheóil*, i.e. ' pig-flesh,' pron. *muckole*) was a favourite among all classes, as it was among the Greeks and Romans. When the fairy-king Midir tried to entice Befinn to Fairyland, one of the allurements he held out was that—among other choice viands—it had plenty of fresh pork (vol. I., p. 295). This preference is noticed in later ages by Stanyhurst.—" No meat they fansie so much " as porke and the fatter the better. One of John O'Nel's " household demanded of his fellow whether beefe were " better than porke : ' that ' (quoth the other) ' is as intricat " a question as to ask whether thou art better than O'Nele." And the partiality for this meat continues to the present day among the peasantry, but they generally eat it in the form of bacon. Pork was made into bacon as at present by being salted and hung up on the wall over the fire. Old bacon was considered good for chest-disease.†

Beef, or as it was called in Irish *mairt-fheóil* (i.e. ' ox-flesh ' : pron. *morthole*), was much in use. The animal seems to have been generally killed with a spear.‡ The flesh of fattened calves, either boiled or roast, was considered a dainty food. Mutton—in Irish *caer-fheóil* or *muilt-fheóil* (' sheep-flesh,' ' wether-flesh ' : pron. *kairole* and *multhole*)—was perhaps in more request than beef. Boiled mutton (*muilt-bruithi*, ' boiled wether ')is mentioned in the " Vision of Mac Conglinne " (98) as a savoury viand.

* Br. Laws, III. 267.   † Mac Conglinne, 98.   ‡ Br. Laws, IV. 311, 18.

Venison was in great favour : everywhere in the tales we read of hunters chasing deer and feasting on the flesh. It was sometimes called *fiadh-fheoil*, ' deer-flesh ' [pron. fee-ole] : and there were other names. It was food fit for kings : one of the seven prerogatives of the king of Ireland was to receive a tribute of the *milradh* [milra] or venison of Naas.* On a certain occasion an envoy promised Finn mac Cumail among other choice viands the *feoil daimh* (' flesh of deer ') of Knockclare. Salted venison, which is sometimes called *serccol-tarsain* (' dainty-condiment ') is mentioned in the Brehon Law (IV. 309, ₁₇) as one of the refections due to an *óg-aire* or ' junior chief.' Goats were quite as common in old times as now, and their flesh was as much used, as well as their milk.

Some of the animals mentioned in the records as supplying food are no longer used for this purpose. That badgers were eaten we have certain proof. Cormac Gaileng, preparing a grand feast for his father Teige, held it as a point of honour to have the flesh of all eatable animals, and put himself to much trouble to procure badgers from a neighbouring warren.† Deirdre, when recalling the life she had led in Scotland, says that the sons of Usna brought her for food fish and venison and the flesh of badgers : and badger-flesh from Beare in Cork was one of the dainties promised on a certain occasion to Finn mac Cumail by Molling the Swift.‡ Badgers were eaten in Ireland until lately. In a comic description of a wedding in an Irish poem by a Connaught poet named Mac Sweeny, of about a hundred years ago, " the badger of the glen " is enumerated as among the animals to be procured for the feast.§ A small animal named a *togmall* is mentioned in some of the oldest of the Irish tales (see chap. xxx., page 519, *infra*). O'Curry makes it a squirrel : but it

---

* Book of Rights, 3, 9.
† Joyce, Irish Names of Places, II. 244 : see also vol. I. 287, *supra*.
‡ Rev. Celt., XIII. 47.   § Hardiman, Iar C., 286, note ; 290, ₁₀.

appears that the squirrel is not a native Irish animal, and that it was introduced only in late times. About the *togmal* we only know that it was sometimes tamed as a pet, and as such was often carried on the shoulder—as was then the custom—so that it must have been small: and that its flesh was used as food; for " speckled *togmalls* from Berramain " (in Kerry) are included in the Colloquy as part of the food-supplies of the Fena of Erin.*

Seals were valued chiefly for their skins, but partly also for their flesh as food. Adamnan mentions the seal and calls it by two Latin names, *phoca*, and *marinus vitulus* (' sea-calf ') : the Irish name was, and is, *rón* [roan]. There was a little rocky island near Mull where seals congregated and bred, and which—according to Adamnan (p. 78)—was regarded as a preserve belonging to Iona : but he does not state what use the monks made of the animals : probably for the skins. We have direct evidence however that seals were anciently used as food in Ireland. In the Book of Lismore it is related that the seven bishops of Tulla in the east of Leinster (near Killiney) came on a visit to St. Brigit, on which she sent one of her people to sea to fish. This man succeeded in spearing a seal, which, with some difficulty, he brought home for the use of the visitors.†
The flesh of seals is now seldom used as food, for which —at least in parts of the west—there is a very good reason. There is a legend that at some former time several members of a certain family were metamorphosed into seals, so that a latter-day member who sat down to a dinner of seal could never be quite sure that he was not feasting on his own great-great-great-grandfather.‡ Martin, in his description of the Hebrides in 1703 (p. 64), says that seals were eaten by the meaner people, who salted the flesh with " burnt sea-ware." The higher classes however ate only the hams.

* Silva Gad., 119 (Irish text, 110, 19).
† Stokes, Lives of SS., 196 : see also Hardiman in Iar C., 95.
‡ Iar C., 27, *t* ; 95, *z*.

Corned meat was everywhere in use A dead pig salted was usually called *tinne* [tin'ně] : but this word was also often applied to a salted joint of any animal. A number of whole pig-*tinnes* commonly formed part of the tribute paid to a superior king or chief.* The word *saill* or *saille* [sal, sal-le] from *sal*, ' salt,' was applied to any sort of salted meat : and it is still in use in this sense.

Besides the main joints boiled or roast, we find mention of various preparations of the flesh of animals, mixed up with many ingredients. A pottage or hash formed of meat chopped up small, mixed with vegetables, was called *craibechan* [craiv'ahan]. We find it stated in an Irish document that Esau sold his birthright to Jacob for a *craibechan*† : and elsewhere the term is defined " fine or small meat."   In the " Vision of Mac Conglinne " (p. 34) is mentioned as a dainty food " sprouty *craibechan* with purple-berries " : " sprouty," *i.e.* mixed with vegetable sprouts. The " purple-berries " were probably the quicken-berries or rowan-berries added to give a flavour. There are several other terms used to designate meat-preparations of this kind : such as *brothchán* (a dim. of *broth*), *follach*, and *scaiblin*. No doubt each of these pointed to some special mode of preparation : but the distinction—if it ever existed—is now lost.

Simple broth or meat-juice without any mixture of minced-meat was called by several names :—*beochail, bruth, broth,* and *enbruithe*. This last, which is still a living word for broth, is given in Cormac's Glossary ; and is there said to be derived from *en*, ' water,' and *bruith*, ' flesh,' *i.e.* ' water of flesh,' a natural interpretation. The Irish *broth* or *bruth*, which is also a living word, is the same as the English *broth*.   In later times broth was a favourite with the Irish, and also among the Scottish Highlanders, as is noticed in " The Fair Maid of Perth " :—" The hooped " cogues [Gaelic *cuach* : see p. 74, *supra*] or cups, out of

* Br. Laws, II. 201, bottom.   † Trip. Life, Introd., XVIII. 12.

" which the guests quaffed their liquor, as also the broth or
" juice of the meat, which was held a delicacy."

Sausages or puddings were a favourite dish, made
much the same as at the present day, by filling the intestines
of a pig, cow, or sheep with minced-meat and blood.
They were known by the terms *indrechtan* and *maróc*, the
latter of which (spelled *maróg*) is still in use among the
Highland Scotch.* In O'Clery's Glossary *innreachtan* is
given as equivalent to *putóg*, ' a pudding.' In the " Vision
of Mac Conglinne " (p. 88) we find mention, as a delicacy,
of *indrechtana finda bo-bán-méthi*, ' white-coloured puddings
of white fat cows.' Puddings and sausages got a boil after
making, so as to half cook them, and were then put aside
till wanted : when about to be brought to table they were
fried and served hot as at the present day. Accordingly
in the same piece (p. 66) we find mentioned *maroca arna
cétberbad*, ' puddings first-boiled,' *i.e.* having got a boil
after making. The belly of a pig, called *tarr*, when
properly cleaned and boiled, was much in use, but was
regarded as rather an inferior meat food.†

In the " Vision of Mac Conglinne " is mentioned, as good
food, the *dressan* of an old wether : and Kuno Meyer, the
editor, on the authority of an ancient Glossary, translates
dressan, ' the spleen.' The word is a diminutive of *dress*
or *driss*, which is familiarly applied to things of a branchy
nature, such as a bramble or the smaller intestines : and as
applied to an article of food is still in use in Cork in the
form of *drisheen*, which has the Irish diminutive *in* instead
of the *án* of Mac Conglinne. The name *drisheen* is now
used in Cork as an English word, to denote a sort of
pudding made of the narrow intestine of a sheep, filled
with blood that has been cleared of the red colouring
matter, and mixed with meal and some other ingredients.
So far as I know, this viand and its name are peculiar to
Cork, where *drisheen* is considered suitable for persons

* Mac Conglinne, 32, 66, 86.　　† Rev. Celt., v. 252.

of weak or delicate digestion. The fact that the word *drisheen* (old form *drisín*) is now used in this sense makes it probable that the other diminutive *dressan* was used in a wider sense than that of ' spleen,' as given in the above-mentioned Glossary. Perhaps the *drisheen* of Cork is the same as the *dressan* of Mac Conglinne.

Sometimes the gullet (*lonlongin*) of an ox was filled with minced-meat and cooked like a sausage : and this appears to have been regarded as a delicacy, for it is designated in " Mac Conglinne's Vision " (98, 15) " the choice " easily discussed thing for which the hosts contend—the " gullet of salted beef " (*lónlongin bóshaille*). The contents only were eaten, not the enveloping gullet, which was not fit for food. Tripe, whether of pig or sheep, was designated by the word *caelán** (kailaun], which means something slender, ' a slender gut ' (from *cael*, ' slender '). In Cormac's Glossary (p. 44), it is stated that the *coelan* or small gut is " the slenderest thing in the body " : and farther on in the Glossary the word *innbi* is found as another name for a *caelán*. Spenser says that in his time the northern Irish used to draw the blood of living beasts " to make meat [*i.e.* puddings] thereof " : but I find no mention of this custom in old Irish literature.

Lard was known by three names, *geir, úsca,* and *blonog,* which last is the word now in use. It was much used as an *annlann* or condiment, and entered into cooking in various forms. It is very often mentioned in " Mac Conglinne's Vision," showing how much it was in request. The Culdee monks were allowed lard on festival-days.† We also find mention of *olar,* ' rich gravy ' ; and of *inmar,* ' dripping,' both used as a condiment or relish.‡

Most of the birds used for food at the present day were eaten in old times : and frequent allusions to birds as food are found in ancient Irish writings. Among the food of

---

* Mac Conglinne, 38, 88, 98.   † Reeves, Culdees, 85.
‡ Mac Conglinne, 32.

the Fena are enumerated " birds out of the trackless oak woods " : " wood-cocks (*cailig fheda*) out of [the wood of] Fidrinne " : and " speckled nests from the mountain peaks."* This last entry shows that they made some use of birds' nests in cooking : but how is not known : for we have in Ireland no edible nests. Stokes (Acall. 279) throws out the suggestion that the nests may have been used to make fires as a charm : just as in India milk-porridge boiled on a fire of birds' nests was used as a charm against certain evil spirits. Giraldus Cambrensis says that the Irish loathed the flesh of the heron ; but that Henry II. induced those kings and chiefs he entertained in Dublin at Christmas, 1171, to taste it. They do not seem to have much relished it : for ever since that time the Irish people have let the herons alone.

Eggs were extensively used : they seem to have been often boiled hard and eaten cold. One of the relaxations allowed to Culdee monks on festivals was " a dry [*i.e.* a hard] egg."† Goose-eggs, if we are to judge from their frequent mention, were a favourite. In a legendary account of Bishop Erc of Slane given in the " Feast of *Dun-nan-gedh*," we are told that he kept a flock of geese to lay eggs for him, and that his dinner every evening was " an egg and a half and three sprigs of the cresses of the Boyne."‡ At the great banquet itself, some of these eggs were on the table, cold, and Congal, going in to view the feast, ate a part of one. And when the company sat down, a goose-egg [cold] on a silver dish was placed before each chief.§ From all this we may infer that the eggs were boiled hard.

All the fish used for food at the present day were eaten in Ireland in old times, so that there is no need to go into details. Only it may be remarked that salmon was then the favourite ; and we meet with constant reference to it as

---

* Silva Gad., 119.　　‡ Moyrath, 19.
† Reeves, Culdees, 85.　　§ *Ibid.*, 25, 29.

superior to all other fish. The salmon of the " salmon-full Boyne," of *Linnmhuine* or Lough Neagh, and of the Barrow, were much prized. The subject of fishing, will be treated of in chapter xxix., p. 472, below.

Any viand eaten with the principal part of the meal as an accompaniment or condiment, or *kitchen* as it is called in Ireland and Scotland—anything taken as a relish with more solid food—was designated by one of the words *annlann, tarsunn, ionmar*, all equivalent to the Latin *obsonium*. The Brehon Laws, when setting forth the refections legally due to various classes of persons, specify the *tarsunns* with much particularity :—butter, salt, bacon, lard, salt meat of any kind (when used in small quantities and not the principal part of the meal), honey, kale, onions, and other vegetables, &c. Thus in one place (IV. 119) we find mentioned " three cakes with their *annlann* of butter or bacon," as the fine for a hen's trespass in a garden. According to the Rule of the Culdees, while they could not increase the quantity of bread on festival-days, they were allowed the use of various *annlanns* such as kale, apples, &c.*

Salt—Irish *sal, salann*—was used for domestic purposes much the same as at the present day—for corning various kinds of provisions, especially butter, pork, and beef, and at meals with all viands requiring it. It was not so easily made or procured then as now, so that the supply was limited, and people kept it carefully, avoiding waste. In rich people's houses it was kept in small sacks. In the Life of St. Senan it is related that on a certain occasion the saint sent, as a present to St. Brigit of Cluain Infide, a basket containing certain articles, among which were two masses of salt (*dá cloich t-salainn*, ' two stones of salt '), one for herself and the other for St. Diarmait of Inis Cleraun in Lough Ree.† The Senchus Mór mentions salt as one of the important articles in the house of a brewy, on which

* Reeves, Culdees, 84.   † Stokes, Lives of SS., line 2408.

the glossator remarks that it is " an article of necessity at all times, a thing which everyone desires "* : and in confirmation of this we find, in the story of the " Voyage of the O'Corras," that the house of the rich brewy Conall Derg O'Corra was never without certain plentiful supplies, among them a sack of salt (*miach salainn*) " to make each food taste well."† It was kept in lumps or in coarse grains ; and at dinner each person was served with as much as he needed. In the sixteenth century in England —as we are told by Roberts—each guest at dinner was given a little lump of salt, which he ground into powder with the bottom of his glass or drinking-goblet : and something of the same plan may have been followed in Ireland. English salt was largely imported, and was considered the best. Mac Conglinne (p. 60), when calling for a number of viands specially delicious, has among them " English salt (*salann saxanach*) on a beautiful polished dish of white silver." In this last point the Irish accounts are corroborated by an English authority of a later time, Higden's " Polychronicon," which mentions the export of salt from England to Ireland :—" Also Flanders " loveth the wolle of this lond [England], Ireland the oor " [ore] and the salt."‡ But there were at home professional salt-makers, as we find by a passage in the story of the *Tromdamh* (119), where it is related how a ship's crew from Ireland meets on the coast of the Isle of Man (then occupied by the Irish) a person who was every alternate year a maker of salt. At a much later time, A.D. 1300, salt was exported from Ireland, as we know from the fact that it was one of the commodities sent to Scotland to supply the army of Edward I. (for which see p. 433, *infra*). The salt must have been manufactured either from sea-water, or from rock-salt taken from the earth, or more

---

* Br. Laws, I. 127, 143.
† Stokes, Rev. Celt., XIV, 27 ; Joyce, Old Celtic Romances, 401.
‡ Quoted by Kuno Meyer in Mac Conglinne, 142.

likely from both. For, according to Kinahan,* there are plenty of salt deposits in Ulster : and we have seen above how St. Senan sent to his friend a present of " two *stones* (or rocks) of salt." But of salt mines, or of the mode of preparing the salt, the ancient literature—so far as I know —contains no details. The word *salannán* (a dim. of *salann*) is still used in the Irish language to signify a salt-pit.

5. *Milk and its products.*

There are several ancient Irish words for milk, three of which are *ass*, *loim*, and *melg* or *melc* : this last evidently cognate with Latin *mulgeo* and with English *milk* ; and from it is derived the old verb *omalgg* ("mulxi;" Zeuss, 61, 15). The most general word in modern use is *bainne* [bon-yă], which is also an ancient word. Another old word for milk, according to Cormac's Glossary (149), is *séig*, whence comes *ségamlae*, ' milkiness,' " as in the saying of the Bretha Nemed :—' a cow is estimated by her *ségamlae*.' "

The milk chiefly used in Ireland was that of cows ; but goats' and sheep's milk was also in much request. Deer's milk was sometimes made use of, and the milking of the doe is often mentioned in the records, but always in a manner implying that it was exceptional. In the Tripartite Life (73) we read that St. Patrick left at *Ath-da-laarg* (the ancient abbey of Boyle in Roscommon) three brothers with their sister Cathnea : " She it is that used to milk the hinds " (*eillti* : sing. *eillit*, ' a hind '). Nia Ségamain, who was king of Ireland, A.M. 4887, was so called because " during his time cows and does were milked alike : and it is for him that does were cows." This it seems was effected through the incantations of his mother, who was an enchantress.†

Milk was used in a variety of ways, as at the present day. For drinking, the choice condition was as new milk

* Geology of Ireland, 358, 359.
† Cóir Anmann in Ir. Texte, III. 295 : FM, A.M. 4887 : Keating, 260. For other instances of milking does, see Trip. Life, 233 and Dr. Healy, 211.

(*lemnacht* or *lemlacht*): and cream was sometimes added as a luxury. But skimmed milk, *i.e.* milk slightly sour, and commonly thick, from which the cream had been skimmed off, was considered a good drink. This was called *draumce* and also *bláthach* [draumkĕ, blawhagh], which last word is the name used at the present day. Thick milk was improved by mixing new milk with it,* as I have often seen done in our own day.

The people made butter (Irish *im* or *imm*) in the usual way, in a small churn: the churn has been already described (p. 75, *supra*). The process of churning was called *maistred*. In the description of an imaginary house, all made of choice viands, in "Mac Conglinne's Vision" (p. 92), is mentioned "a pure-white bed-tick of butter," from which it may be inferred that a whitish colour was a mark of good fresh butter.

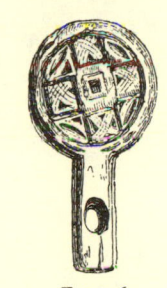

Fig. 216.

Ancient Butter-print of willow: 5½ inches in diameter: in National Museum. (From Wilde's Catalogue, p. 214.)

Butter of any kind was considered a superior sort of condiment. Salt butter was called *gruiten* and sometimes *grusden*. In Cormac's Glossary (86) *gruiten* is derived from *groit*, 'bitter,' and *sen*, 'old.' Its inferiority to fresh butter is brought out clearly in the Brehon Law provision (II. 149) that, in fosterage, the sons of farmers are to have *gruiten* with their stirabout, the sons of chiefs fresh butter, and the sons of kings honey. A lump of butter shaped according to fancy was called a *mescan*, a word given in Cormac's Glossary (116), where it is stated that a *mescan* was so called because it was produced by the *mescad* or agitation of the milk. This word is still in very general use even among the English-speaking people, who pronounce it *miscaun* or *miscan*. A carn on a mountain top is sometimes called a *miscaun* from its shape, as, for

* Br. Laws, IV. 303, 4 from bottom: and 306, 10.

example, Miscaun Maive on the top of Knocknarea hill near Sligo. Another name for a roll or *miscaun* of butter was *brechtan*: a *brechtan úr-imme*, a 'roll of fresh butter,' was portion of the viands procured for the May-day feast according to an old Irish poem*: and in O'Clery's Glossary *brechtan* is explained 'wheat,' and also *im úr*, 'fresh butter.' But *brechtan* was also applied to a viand like what we call a custard, made of flour, milk, and perhaps eggs, sweetened with honey : a *brechtan cruthnechta* (of wheat) is mentioned in " Mac Conglinne's Vision " (123, 24).

FIG. 217.

A firkin of Bog-butter 26 inches high : made from a single piece of sallow. Top and bottom and part of side of firkin, with butter inside, still remain. In the National Museum. (From Wilde's Catalogue, p. 212.)

In later times it was customary to sink butter deep down in bogs, closed up in casks or wrapped up in cloths, to give it a flavour, or, as some think, as a mode of preserving it.† Among the food of the Irish, Dineley (A.D. 1675) mentions butter " mixed with store of . . . a kind of garlick, " and buried for some time in a bog to " make a provision of an high taste for " Lent." Sir William Petty also mentions butter made rancid by keeping in bogs ; and other authorities to the same effect might be quoted. Whether this custom existed in ancient times I am unable to say ; but at any rate, its prevalence, even at this late period, is a sufficient explanation of the fact that butter is now very often found in vessels of various shapes and sizes, deeply embedded in bogs ; sometimes in firkins not very different from those now in use.‡ Several specimens of this " bog butter," as it is commonly called, are to be seen in the National Museum. In all cases the

* Sick Bed, Atlantis, I. 271.

† Rev. James O'Laverty, in Kilk. Arch. Journ., 1892, p. 356, thinks so, and advances good reasons for his opinion. See Sullivan, Introd., 367; and the authorities referred to by Wood-Martin, Pagan Ireland, 601.

‡ Wilde, Catalogue, p. 212.

butter is found to be changed, by the action of the bog water, into a greyish cheese-like substance, partially hardened, not much like butter, and quite free from putrefaction.

Curds—called in Irish *gruth* [gruh]—formed one important article of diet. Milk was converted into curds and whey by calves' rennet, Irish *binit*, so called, according to the fanciful derivation in Cormac's Glossary (p. 20), because "it strikes (*benait*) in milk till it [the milk] is thick and coagulated."* A light collation of curds, butter, and milk, flavoured with *crem* or wild garlic, was known by the names *samit* or *sam-ith* and *crimmes*. It was well recognised as a summer dainty, for the wild garlic grows only in summer. The second name *crimmes* means 'wild-garlic harvest,' from *crim*, another form of *crem*, and *mes*, 'harvest or produce.''

Curd was converted into cheese of various sorts, which was greatly valued as an article of food. Cheese was denoted by several different words, of which the most common were *cáisse* or *cáise* [cawsha], and *maethail* [maihil]: but this last word was often applied to dried curd. Cheese was made from curd as now, by pressing in a mould, from which it was turned out in firm shapes. Curds were much used in an intermediate stage, not quite turned into cheese, but sufficiently pressed to squeeze out all the whey, so as to form a mass moderately firm and capable of keeping for a long time. In this state curd was a well-recognised food : in the " Circuit of Muirchertach of the Leather Cloaks " (p. 55) we are told that on a certain occasion he contributed to a banquet, among many other supplies, three score vats of curds (*gruidh*). This soft material, half curd, half cheese, was often called *milsen*, which O'Clery in his Glossary explains by *gruth-caisse*, or 'curd-cheese.' It was also called *maethail*, and *mulchan*, words understood to mean soft unpressed cheese.† This sort of food was

---

* For Curds, see Sullivan, Introd., 368 ; and Reeves, Culdees, 85, middle.
† Corm. Gloss., p. 117 : Mac Conglinne, 80, 189.

often given as rent or tribute : thus we are told in the Tripartite Life (p. 15) that the steward of a certain king came to St. Patrick's foster-mother for tribute of curd (*gruth*) and butter.

Cheese pressed tightly in a mould, and turned out very hard, was called *tanag*. Its hardness is illustrated in one version of the death of Queen Maive of Connaught in her old age :—That her nephew Furbaide, who had a grudge against her, catching sight of her one day in some distance, put into his sling a piece of *tanag* that he happened to be eating, as he had no stone, and flung it with so true an aim that he struck her on the forehead and killed her on the spot.* Masses of cheese have been found in bogs, of which some specimens may be seen in the National Museum.

Whey—Irish *médg* [maig]—was made use of ; but it was considered a poor drink, so much so that it was in constant use among monks as a fasting beverage. Mac Conglinne, grumbling at the beggarly reception he got in Cork monastery, complains that they gave him nothing but the whey-water (*médg-usci*) of the church to drink. New milk from a cow that had just calved, now called *beestings*, was in Old Irish called *nús*, a word still in use, which in Cormac's Glossary (126) is derived—probably erroneously—from Latin *novus*, ' new.' This milk was not fit for drinking ; but it was turned into curds and whey by merely heating, and in this form it was used as food. But more often the curd was made into thin pancakes. It was evidently valued—as it is at the present day—for one of the blessings brought on the country by Cormac Mac Art's benign reign, was that the cows after calving had their udders full of *nús* or beestings.†

Milk and all food-preparations from it, such as curd, cheese, butter—as distinguished from flesh-meat—were called *bán-bid* [bawn-bee], ' white-meat.' They were con-

* LL, 125, *a*, 19.   † Silva Gad., 97, 7 (Ir. Text, 90, 2).

sidered inferior in nutritive qualities to flesh-meat : and they were often permitted—and are permitted still—by the Roman Catholic ecclesiastical authorities, on fast days, when flesh-meat is forbidden. Mac Conglinne mentions the constant consumption of white-meats as one of the causes of his low condition of health.

6. *Corn and its preparations.*

It will be seen in chapter xxiii., sect. 2 (pp. 271, 272, below), that all the various kinds of grain cultivated at the present day were in use in ancient Ireland. Corn was ground and sifted into coarse and fine, *i.e.* into meal and flour, which were commonly kept in chests.* The staple food of the great mass of the people was porridge, or as it is now called in Ireland, stirabout, made of meal (Irish *min*), generally oatmeal. It was eaten with honey, butter, or milk, as an *annlann* or condiment. So well was it understood, even in foreign countries, that stirabout was almost the universal food in Ireland—a sort of characteristic of the country and its people—that St. Jerome takes occasion to refer to the custom in a letter directed against an Irish adversary, generally believed to be the celebrated heresiarch Celestius, the disciple of Pelagius. Jerome could use tongue and pen in hearty abuse like any ordinary poor sinner : and he speaks revilingly of Celestius, who was a corpulent man, as " a great fool of a fellow swelled out with Irish stirabout."†

The common word for stirabout was, and still is, *littiu*, modern *leite*, gen. *leitenn* [letthĕ, letthen] ; but in the Brehon Laws and elsewhere it is often called *gruss*. Gruel was called *menadach* : it is mentioned as part of the fasting-fare of the Culdees.‡ The Senchus Mór annotator, laying down the regulations for the food of children in fosterage,§

---

* Todd, Book of Fermoy, 17.
† Todd, St. Patrick, 190, 191 : Lanigan, I. 17 ; FM, vol. I., Pref. li.
‡ Reeves, Culdees, 86.   § Br. Laws, II. 149 and note ; 151 and note.

mentions three kinds of *leite* or stirabout :—of oatmeal, wheatmeal, and barleymeal : that made from oatmeal being the most general. Wheatmeal stirabout was considered the best : that of barleymeal was inferior to the others. For the rich classes, stirabout was often made on new milk : if sheep's milk, so much the better, as this was looked upon as a delicacy.* *Finn-leite*, ' white-stirabout,' *i.e.* made on new milk, is designated by an epicure,† in an exaggerated strain—" the treasure that is smoothest and sweetest of all food " : it was eaten with honey, fresh butter, or new milk. For the poorer classes stirabout was made on water or buttermilk, and eaten with sour milk or salt butter : but butter of any kind was more or less of a luxury. All young persons in fosterage were to be fed, up to a certain age, on stirabout, the quality and condiment (as distinguished above) being regulated according to the rank of the parents.‡

All the various kinds of meal and flour were baked into cakes or loaves of different shapes. The usual word for a cake was *bairgen*, now pronounced *borreen* : hence *borreen-brack*, ' speckled cake ' (speckled with currants and raisins), eaten on November eve, now often written *barn-brack*, sometimes corrupted to *barm-brack*. Flour was usually mixed with water to make dough : but bread made of flour and milk was also much in use. Honey was often kneaded up with cakes as a delicacy : and occasionally the roe of a salmon was similarly used.§ The word *tort* was applied to a cake, or to a loaf of bread of any shape ; whence the diminutive *tortine* [torteena], ' a little cake '‖ : connected with Lat. *torta* : Span. *tortilla*.

By a curious custom, often referred to in the Brehon Laws, what was called a " cake of man-baking " (*bairgen*

---

* Mac Conglinne, 32, 34.
† *Ibid.*, 98, 29.
‡ Br. Laws, II. 151, top ; 177.
§ Fled Bric., 9 bottom : Sullivan.

Introduction, 365, note : and Tromdamh, 73.
‖ Corm. Gloss., 156.

fer-fuine) was twice the size of a " cake of woman-baking."
" Three cakes of man-baking," says the Brehon Law, " are
the equivalent of six cakes of woman-baking " ; and this
proportion is given in many parts of the law.* Accordingly the Crith Gabhlach, when setting forth the legal
allowances of an *og-aire* chief, includes among them
either one cake of man-baking or two of woman-baking.†
Perhaps the meaning of these terms is that the larger cake
was considered as a meal for a man, and the smaller for a
woman. There is something like a confirmation of this
conjecture in the " Small Primer," where it is stated that
under certain circumstances each man of a company is
allowed two cakes of men's baking per night as his refection : *i.e.* presumably supper (or dinner) and breakfast.‡
If this is so, the allowance was liberal : for the Senchus
Mór states in one place that a cake of woman-baking was
two " fists " or ten inches in width, and one fist or five
inches thick.§ Wheaten bread was considered the best,
as at present : barley-bread was poor. St. Finntan, the
son of Gaibréne, never ate anything but " woody bread of
barley," and a drink of muddy water.‖

We have seen that yeast, or barm, or leaven, was used
in brewing. That it was used also in baking appears
from the fact that in this application there was a native
word (*descaid*) for it, as well as from an eighth-century
commentary on I Corinth. v. 7, 8, written in the Irish
language by some Irish writer, in which the use of *descaid*
or leaven in souring dough is spoken of in such a manner
as to show that the writer was quite familiar with the
process.¶

The several utensils used in making and baking bread
are set forth in the Senchus Mór ; and baking and the

---

* Br. Laws, II. 177, 24 ; IV. 119, 9.

† *Ibid.*, IV. 307, 15 : see also V. 31
and 47.

‡ *Ibid.*, V. 47, III.

§ *Ibid.*, II. 255, 8.

‖ Féilire, 52.

¶ Zeuss, 777, 28 to 32 : Stokes and
Strachan, Thesaurus, I 552. Here
the word for sour is *serb* ; modern
Irish, *searbh* [sharrav].

implements employed therein are always spoken of as specially pertaining to women.* The woman had a *criathar* [criher] or sieve for separating the fine part of the flour from the coarse, which was done on each particular occasion just before baking.† Having made the flour into dough (Irish *toes*, now written *taos*), she worked it into cakes on a *losat* [losset] or kneading-trough—sometimes also called *lethech*‡—a shallow wooden trough, such as we see used for making cakes at the present day. The cake was baked on a griddle of some kind, which was called *lec* or *lec-fuine*.§ *Lec* signifies a flat flagstone : *lec-fuine*, 'flag of baking' : which shows that whatever may have been the griddle or baker in later times, it was originally a *lec* or flagstone, heated to the proper degree. In some Irish Glosses, *lapisfulta* is explained by *lec-an-aráin*, 'the flag or griddle of the bread.'|| And O'Davoren, as quoted by Stokes, has "*cert-fuine*, i.e. the stone (*lec*) on which cooking is done."¶ In the "Courtship of Emer" in LU (123, *b*, 9 from bot.), it is called *lec* or flagstone, without any qualifying epithet : Cormac's Glossary (103) calls it *lecc*, which is the same word. We know that in Ireland, down to the time of Elizabeth, cakes were sometimes baked on a hot stone.** A common metal griddle was usually called *gretel* or *greidel* ; and sometimes *lann*, which however means any thin plate of metal.

7. *Honey.*

Before entering on the consideration of honey as food, it will be proper to make a few observations on the management of bees by the ancient Irish. From the earliest times Ireland was noted for its abundance of honey. A foreign writer, Solinus, who lived in the third

* Br. Laws, I. 123, 149.
† Miss Hull, Cuch. Saga, 97.
‡ Corm. Gloss., 102.
§ Br. Laws, III 275 ; IV. 11, 9 from bottom

|| Stokes in Corm. Glossary, 103 ("Lecc").
¶ Corm. Gloss., XII. 5.
** Tribes of Ireland, 51 and note 2.

century, says that there were no bees in Ireland : but in this he was undoubtedly misinformed, as he was in many other particulars regarding this country.* Giraldus expresses the curious opinion that honey would be still more abundant in Ireland if the bee-swarms were not checked by the bitter and poisonous yews with which the woods abounded.

The management of bees was universally understood, and every comfortable householder kept hives in his garden. Wild bees, too, swarmed everywhere—much more plentifully than at present, on account of the extent of woodland. Before cane-sugar came into general use —sixteenth century—the bee industry was considered very important, so that a special section of the Brehon Laws is devoted to it. The Irish name for a bee was *bech* or *beach* : a swarm was called *saithe* [saeha]. The hive was known by various names, such as *cliabh* [cleeve], which means ' basket ' ; *bechdin*, ' little bee-house ' ; and *cesach-bech*, ' bee-basket ' : but the name now universally in use is *corcóg*. A honeycomb was called *criathar* [criher], literally a ' sieve.' Hives stocked with bees were sometimes given as part of a tribute to a king.†

The Brehon Law tract on " Bee-judgments," of which the printed Irish text occupies twenty pages (of vol. iv.), enters into much detail concerning the rights of the various parties concerned, to swarms, hives, nests, and honey : of which a few examples are given here. If a man found a swarm in the *faithche* or green surrounding and belonging to a house : one-fourth of the produce to the end of a year was due to the finder, the remaining three-fourths to the owner of the house. If he found them *in a tree* growing in a *faithche* or green : one-half produce for a year to the finder : the rest to the owner. If they were found in land which was not a green : one-third to the finder and two-

---

* See Keating, Pref., xxiv : and Gir. Cambr., Top. Hib., i. v.
† Book of Rights, 245, 3rd verse.

thirds to the owner of the land. If found in waste land not belonging to an individual, but the common property of the tribe, bees and honey belonged to the finder, except one-ninth to the chief of the tribe. As the bees owned by an individual gathered their honey from the surrounding district, the owners of the four adjacent farms were entitled to a certain small proportion of the honey : and after the third year each was entitled to a swarm. If bees belonging to one man swarmed in the land of another, the produce was divided in certain proportions between the two. It is mentioned in " Bee-judgments " that a sheet was sometimes spread out that a swarm might alight and rest on it : as is often done now. At the time of gathering the honey the bees were smothered. The Senchus Mór prescribes a penalty for stealing bee-hives with their bees.

The Book of Aicill has a long enumeration of injuries done by bee-stings to men and animals, with the corresponding fines, and also the fines for killing bees. Great care is exhibited on the one hand to protect bees from wanton or unnecessary destruction, and on the other to provide compensation for men and animals injured by their stings* : but some of the provisions are so minute and trifling that we may doubt if they were ever seriously intended to be carried into practice. The whole article however shows that the subject of bees and bee-culture much occupied the attention of the public.

One of the circumstances indicating the great plenty of honey in historic times in Ireland is the large size of the vessels sometimes used in measuring it, as instanced in chap. xxvii. (p. 376, below). It was used with most kinds of food, sometimes mixed and sometimes separately as a condiment. In the Book of Aicill the penalty for a certain class of offences is laid down as " a full meal of honey "† : taken of course with other food.

* Br. Laws, iii. 433–441.
† *Ibid.*, iii. 433, ₁₂ from bottom.

In the tale of the Feast of Bricriu (p. 9) we are told
that in a certain house, among other choice viands, were
one hundred wheaten cakes kneaded up with honey. A
mixture of milk and honey was sometimes drunk: the
Culdee monks were allowed to drink thick milk mixed
with honey on the eves of Christmas and Easter* : a drink
which would be hardly relished nowadays by either monk
or layman. A mixture of lard and honey was sometimes
used as a condiment.† When the gluttonous Munster King
Cathal—eighth century—was cured of the *craes lon* or
wolf in his stomach, he was ordered to get one more good
meal before toning down to his natural appetite. So they
boiled, according to directions, a mixture of new milk,
fresh butter, and honey, in a great caldron, of which he
drank a prodigious quantity ; and " that was the last great
" bellyful that Cathal took under the influence of the
" glutton-demon."‡ After this he fell asleep, and woke
up well. In another part of the same story (p. 78) is
mentioned *brechtan-ƒo-mil*, some sort of custard mixed
with honey, with probably flour and eggs.

Honey was sometimes brought to table pure, and
sometimes in the comb.§ Often at meals each person had
placed before him on the table a little dish, sometimes of
silver, filled with honey ; and each morsel whether of meat,
fish, or bread was dipped into it before being conveyed to
the mouth.‖ Stirabout was very generally eaten in the
same way with honey as a delicacy. Honey was used to
baste meat while roasting, as well as salmon while broiling.
In the " Táin bo Fraich " (p. 153) we read that Ailill and
Maive, king and queen of Connaught, had a salmon broiled
for the young chief, Fraech, which was basted with honey
that had been " well made by their daughter, the Princess
Findabair " : from which again we learn that the highest

---

* Reeves, Culdees, 84, top
† Mac Conglinne, 90, , from
bottom.

‡ Mac Conglinne, 106.
§ *Ibid.*, 60.
‖ *Ibid.*, 64, 8.

persons sometimes employed themselves in preparing honey. It has been already stated that honey was the chief ingredient in mead ; and it is probable that it was used in greater quantity in this way than in any other.

8. *Vegetables and Fruit.*

Table vegetables of various kinds were cultivated in an enclosure called *lúbgort* [loo-ort], *i.e.* ' herb-garden ' or kitchen-garden : from *lúb*, ' an herb,' and *gort*, a fenced-in cultivated plot. The manner in which the kitchen-garden is mentioned in literature of all kinds—lay, ecclesiastical, and legal—shows that it was a common appanage to a homestead. We find it often noticed in the Book of Armagh (eighth century) : and in the eighth-century glosses of Zeuss (37, 28) *lubgartóir*—which is still the common word for a gardener, and pronounced *looartore*—explains the Latin word *olitor*, a ' kitchen-gardener.' The word *lub*, now spelled *luibh* [luv or liv], glosses *frutex* in Zeuss, and is cognate with the English *leaf*. Another and more usual Irish word for herb is *lus* : but this term was often used specifically to designate the leek.

Cabbage of some kind was an important food-herb among the early Irish, so that it is often mentioned in old authorities. Its Irish name was *braisech* [brasshagh], borrowed probably from the Latin *brassica* : but this word *braisech* was sometimes applied to a pottage made of herbs of any kind.* Among the articles of food noticed in the " Vision of Mac Conglinne " is " boiled, leafy, brown-white kale or cabbage." In the Culdee rule the monks were permitted on festival days to add kale as a condiment to their customary scanty allowance of bread.

Among the vegetables cultivated in kitchen-gardens and used at table were leeks and onions. " Mac Conglinne's Vision " mentions the leek by one of its Irish names *lus*,

---

* As in Stokes, Lives of SS., 362, *a*, 10.

and the onion by the name *cainnenn*. *Lus* is now the general word for a leek, and was often used in this special sense in old writings : in the Rule of the Culdees " three or four sprigs of *luss* " are mentioned as part of the refection of the monks : but *lus* primarily means an herb in general. A leek had a more specific name, *folt-chep* (*folt*, ' hair ' : " hair-onion " : *chep* or *cep*, corresponding with Lat. *cepa*, ' an onion '). A pregnant woman, as we are told in the Tripartite Life (201), once longed for leeks, so that she was like to die ; whereupon St. Patrick miraculously changed a rush into a *folt-chep*, which she ate and was cured : and Patrick declared that " all women who shall eat of this herb (the leek) shall be cured of their [longing-] illness." That the word *cainnenn* or *cainne* signifies an onion there can be no doubt, for an old Irish authority remarks that a *cainnenn* will draw tears from the eyes.* Under this name onions are mentioned as part of the refection due to a chief from his tenant.† But *cainne* was also occasionally applied to a leek : as in the expression in the Crith Gabhlach, " a handful of *cainne* with their heads."‡ Garlic appears to have been a pretty common condiment, and the same word *cainnenn* was often applied to it. O'Donovan sometimes translates *cainnen* and *coinne* by garlic in the Brehon Law :§ from the Law also we see that garlic was cultivated in gardens. But in individual passages it is often doubtful whether *cainnen* or *cainne* means onion or garlic.

Wild garlic, called in Irish *crem* or *creamh* [crav or craff] was often used as a pot-herb, gathered no doubt from the fields, for I find no evidence that it was cultivated. The facts that it is often mentioned in Irish literature, and that it has given names to many places,‖ show that it

---

* Mac Conglinne, 163, last line.   † Br. Laws, IV 339.
‡ Br. Laws, IV. 303, 6 from bottom
§ *Ibid.*, II. 255, 11: IV. 117, 16; 119, 27.
‖ For which see Joyce, Irish Names of Places, II. 347.

was a well-recognised plant and pretty generally used. The Chronicon Scotorum records the winter of A.D. 1006 as being so mild that *creamh* (which is a summer plant) grew in the fields. Sprigs of *creamh* are mentioned as portion of the food of the Fena of Erin,* no doubt as an *annlann* ; and in the Brehon Law (II. 327, note 2), a certain food allowance is mentioned as given to a chief in the time of the " *creamh* harvest " (see also *crim-mes*, p. 139, *supra*).

Tap-rooted plants were designated by the general term *mecon* [mackan], with qualifying terms to denote the different kinds : but *mecon* used by itself means a parsnip or a carrot. Both these vegetables were cultivated in kitchen-gardens, and are often mentioned in old writings. St. Ciaran of Saigir had for his dinner every evening a small bit of barley-cake and two *mecons* of *murathach*, with a drink of water.†

Good watercress (*birir*) was prized and eaten raw as a salad or *annlann*, as at present. It is often spoken of in connexion with brooklime, which is called *fochlocon* in Cormac's Glossary (p. 72), but more commonly *fothlacht* [fullaght], and which was also eaten. Constant references to both are found in the ancient tales. In the Story of the Colloquy a certain well is praised for producing large *birir* and *fothlacht*‡ : and St. Caillin, when the people of Magh-Ae in Connaught had received him well, left them, among other blessings, the palm of pure water and brook-lime.§ Among the prerogatives of the king of Ireland mentioned in the Book of Rights were the cresses of the river Brosna in Westmeath. The three drink-bearers of Conaire, king of Ireland in the first century, are repre-sented in the story of Bruden Da Derga, as having before

---

* Silva Gad., 119 (*creamh* here translated " gentian " by O'Grady).

† Féilire, 62, *b*, ₃. Stokes does not translate *murathach* : Sullivan makes it equivalent to *gort*, ' an enclosed garden ' ; Introd., 366 : but ?

‡ Silva Gad., 103, 104.   § Book of Fenagh, 179, and note 10.

each of them, ready for the use of the guests, a cup of water in which was a bunch of *birir*.* From all this it is plain that both watercress and brooklime were in constant use as salads. In Cormac's Glossary (p. 19) the first syllable of *birir*, ' watercress,' is derived from *bir*, ' a well or stream,' which is certainly correct.

Poor people sometimes ate a pottage made of the tender tops of nettles, as I have seen them do in my own day in time of scarcity : but they mixed a little oatmeal with it when they could get it. Once when St. Columba was walking near the monastery of Iona, he saw a poor old woman cutting nettles ; and he asked what she wanted them for. She replied :—" I have but " one cow that I am expecting to calve soon : and until " that happens I live on nettle-pottage, which I have eaten " for a long time back." He was much impressed with this, and said :—" This poor woman eats nettles, and " endures hunger, waiting for an uncertain event—the " calving of her cow : why should I not live on that same " pottage too, since the thing I look for is very certain— " namely, heaven ? " Whereupon he ordered his cook to give him for supper thenceforward nettle-pottage without milk or butter. But as time went on, the brethren, who had heard with dismay of the change for the worse in his diet—which was poor enough before—were rather surprised to observe that he still continued in excellent condition. Their talk among themselves coming to his ear, he began to suspect some kindly pious fraud on the part of the cook. So he sent for him and asked him :— " What do you put into my pottage every day ? " The cook, looking as innocent as a lamb, replied : " I know " nothing that goes into the pottage unless it could come " out of the iron of the pot or out of the potstick." The saint, who was not so easily hoodwinked, examined the potstick, and found that the cook had ingeniously made

* O'Curry, Man. & Cust., II. 150.

it hollow like a pipe, and thus contrived to pour in some milk or meat juice unknown to Columba, to keep his master from starving. The saint at once put a stop to the thing : but with characteristic kindness of heart left a blessing on the cook for his affectionate solicitude.*

We find it stated by several Anglo-Irish writers that in former times the Irish occasionally ate the shamrock. Spenser, for instance, mentions that in time of famine the poor people who were reduced to the last stage of starvation were glad to eat water-cresses and shamrocks ; Fynes Morrison has a passage of much the same import ; while Thomas Dinely, who made a tour through Ireland in 1675, tells us that the people ate shamroges to cause a sweet breath. In the time of Elizabeth, Aengus O'Daly, the notorious satirist (for whom see vol. I., p. 455), reviling one of the Irish clans, represents them as at certain seasons making an onslaught on the shamrocks.† All this has led some persons to believe that the true shamrock is the *Oxalis acetocella*, or wood-sorrel. I see no reason, however, why these passages should not refer to the white trefoil, which is quite as fit to be used as a food-herb as wood-sorrel ; for I think we may assume that neither cress nor shamrocks were eaten in any quantity except under pressure of extreme hunger, but only as an *annlann* with other food, as watercress is eaten now.

Moreover *seamar* and *seamróg* are given in Irish dictionaries as meaning *Trifolium repens*, which is the name of the true shamrock, while wood-sorrel is designated by *samhadh-coille* and *seamsóg*. And as corroborating the dictionary explanations, we find the compound *scoith-sneamrach* (translated by O'Donovan " abounding with flowers and shamrocks " : *scoth*, ' a flower ') a favourite term among Irish writers to designate a green, open plain. The old records, for instance, tell us that *Fiacha*

---

* Stokes, Lives of SS., 302 : Féilire, 100.
† Tribes of Ireland, 51. note 8 ; 53, note 2.

Finnscothach (*Fiacha* of the white flowers), king of Ireland before the Christian era, was so called because " every plain in Ireland was *scoith-sheamrach* in his time " : and the same term is used by the Irish poet, Ferfeasa O'Cointe, about the year 1617 (Misc. Celt. Soc., 1849, p. 355), and by the writer of the Life of St. *Scuithin* (O'Cl. Cal., p. 5).   In these passages *seamar* cannot mean ' wood-sorrel,' which is not produced in sufficient abundance, and moreover does not grow in open plains, but in shady places under trees and hedges.*

The sea-plant called in Irish *duilesc*, and in English *dillesk, dulse, dulsk,* or *dilse* (*Rhodymenia palmata*), growing on sea-rocks, was formerly much used as an article of food, that is, as an accompaniment.   It was eaten with butter, a practice that Martin (p. 68) found in the Western Isles of Scotland in 1703.   According to the Brehon Law, seaside arable land was enhanced in value by having rocks on its sea-border producing this plant, and there was a penalty for consuming the *duilesc* belonging to another without leave.†   Among the various choice articles used by the Fena as food was *duilesc* from the coves of Cape Clear.‡ In the Crith Gabhlach *duilesc* is included with other food as part of the refection due to an *og-aire* or junior chief :§ and it is mentioned in the " Vision of Mac Conglinne " (p. 88) as a desirable viand.   On one occasion St. Senan, while at Scattery, sent one of his disciples to cut some for him on the island-rocks.‖   Dillesk is still used ; and you may see it in Dublin hawked about in baskets by women : it is dry and, people eat it in small quantities raw, like salad.

The marine-plant called *Porphyra vulgaris*, a species of *laver*, found growing on rocks round the coast, was

---

* See this whole question well discussed by Mr. Nathaniel Colgan in Journ. Soc. Antiqq., Irel., 1896, pp. 211 and 349.

† Br. Laws, I. 171, middle.   § Br. Laws, IV. 309.

‡ Silva Gad., 119.   ‖ Stokes, Lives of SS., line 2331.

esteemed a table luxury : it is now often sold in fish-shops and eaten with pepper, vinegar, &c. It is called in Gaelic *sleabhacán* [slavacan, sloakan], which in the anglicised forms *sloakan, sloke,* and *sluke,* is applied to it all over the Three Kingdoms.*

Though there is not much direct mention in old Irish literature of the management of fruit-trees, various detached passages show that they were much valued and carefully cultivated. It would appear from a remark in the Irish language on St. Paul's Epistle to the Romans, xi. 24, written in the eighth century by some Irish commentator, that the art of grafting was probably understood in Ireland : at least this old writer shows himself familiar with the process : but whether he saw it practised at home is not made clear. The remark in question is :—" For they " [the Romans] have a custom to cut a tree and to insert " another tree therein."† One of the Brehon Law tracts (IV. 149) has a curious provision showing much thoughtfulness and knowledge in the management of trees—though the case instanced in not a fruit-tree. If a person stripped off part of the bark of a growing oak-tree belonging to another—a thing sometimes done for tanning—he had not only to pay a fine, but also to secure the tree against injury from weather by covering the wound *and two fingers beyond all round* with a plaster made of fine clay, cow-dung, and new milk. The apple (*ubhall*, pron. ooal) appears to have been as much cultivated and used in old times as at the present. Apples, when gathered, were hoarded up to preserve them as long as possible : they were generally eaten uncooked. During the great festivals, the Culdees, though not permitted to increase the quantity of bread at meals, could use various condiments as an indulgence, and among them apples.‡ According to

* S e Sullivan, Introd., 367.

† Stokes and Strachan, Thesaurus, I. 529. See also Stokes, in Trip. Life, Preface, cl.   ‡ Reeves, Culdees, 85.

O'Donovan, the word *abhall* (fem.) was used in the best and most ancient Irish MSS. to denote the apple-tree, and *ubhall* (masc.) its fruit* : but this distinction has long ceased to be observed.

The hazel-nut was much used for food. This is plainly indicated by the high value set on both tree and fruit, of which we meet with innumerable instances in tales, poems, and other old records, in such expressions as " Cruachan of the fair hazels " : " Fidh-cruaiche of the white banquets, in which are shower-shaken hazels of white bark " : " Doire-na-nath, on which fair-nutted hazels are constantly found." The Brehon Law classes the hazel among the " noble " trees, partly on account of its nuts (for which see p. 287, *infra*) : a plain indication of the value set on them. Abundance of hazel-nuts was a mark of a prosperous and plenteous season. The year 1031 is mentioned by the Four Masters as of such abundance that, among other great bargains, you could buy in Armagh one-third of a *sesedhach* " of the nuts of the fair hazel-hedge " for one *pinginn* or penny. It is expressly stated in the Colloquy of the Ancients that part of the choice food of the Fena of Erin was " nuts from the hazels of Cantire " (*cno do chollaib cintire*).† Among the blessings a good king brought on the land was plenty of hazel-nuts :—" O'Berga [the chief] for whom the hazels stoop " [with the weight of their fruit] : " Each hazel is rich from [the worthiness of] the hero " (HyF, 253, 221).

In many similar entries nuts are mentioned without the hazel being specified : but there can be no doubt that hazel-nuts are meant. An old Irish poem enumerating the viands for the Mayday festival has among them *cno mes*, ' nut-mast.'‡ A young man comes up to St. Patrick

* HyF, 285, *d*. The distinction seems to indicate that the fruit was imported long before the tree was naturalised in Ireland.

† Silva Gad., 119.

‡ Hib. Minora, 49 : see also Br. Laws, v. 407, bottom.

and his companions with a present of fruit :—" An armful of yellow-headed nuts, and of beautiful golden-yellow apples* : and on a certain occasion the cook of St. Mochta of Louth brought him a dish of nuts.† Nuts are often referred to as a dainty : a lady sends to her lover kernels (*ettne*), and apples, and many sweets.‡ In the Book of Leinster it is recorded that in the year 1056 there was a remarkable nut-harvest (*cno-mess* : " Trip. Life," 525). It has been stated elsewhere (at p. 121, *supra*) that hazel-nuts were sometimes used as an ingredient in making mead : but this was an exceptional and minor use. It appears that nuts were hoarded up for use like corn, another illustration of the value set on them.

From all these references and quotations it may be inferred that hazel-nuts were regarded as an important article of human food. No doubt they were generally eaten raw, as they are at present. Tacitus tells us that some of the Celtic nations of Gaul ground acorns and other wild nuts into meal of which they made a sort of coarse bread : but I find no evidence that the Irish ground nuts for food. The Irish name for the hazel-tree is *coll*, gen. *coill*, *caill*, or *cuill*. A nut of any kind is *cno* or *cnu*, cognate with Latin *nux* and English *nut*, both of which have lost the initial hard *c*, which the Irish has preserved. A hazel-nut is called *cno-coill*.

The sloe-tree or blackthorn was called *droigen* (Corm. 60), modern *droigheann* [dree-an], which generally takes a diminutive form *droigheannan* [dreenan] : hence *dreenan-donn* or *drinan-donn* (*donn*, ' brown ') is a common name for the blackthorn, even among English-speaking people. The sloe is called *áirne* [awrna] : a less usual word, *grannmhuine* [granwinna], is given in O'Clery's Glossary as meaning *sloes*. That sloes were used as food, or as an *annlann* or

---

* Silva Gad., 112.   † Stokes, Three Irish Homilies, 99.
‡ Mac Conglinne, 4, 13; see also Three Sorrowful Stories, Atlantis, III. 385, verse.

condiment, and that the sloe bush was cultivated, is evident from the manner in which both are mentioned in Irish literature. Annagh Island in Lough Conn is called by way of praise " a district of sloes and apples."* The year 1031 was so plentiful that, as the Four Masters tell us, a large measure of black-red sloes could be bought for a penny. When King Domnall was endeavouring to placate his angry foster-son Congal, he offered him, among many other privileges [the produce of] an apple-tree and of a sloe-tree out of every homestead in a certain district :† and among the many dainties promised to Finn mac Cumail on a certain occasion, as related in the story of the Boroma, were sloes from one of the glens of *Ebliu*, now Slieve Felim, east of Limerick city. St. Brigit once came to a certain church round which grew abundance of apples and fragrant sloes ; and one of the nuns gave her a basketful of the fruit.‡

Strawberries (sing. *sub*, pl. *suba* : pron. *soo, sooa*) are often mentioned as dainties. In the passage above referred to from the Boroma, Finn was also promised strawberries from *Sliab Bairrche*, now Slieve Margy near Carlow. We are told in the Book of Rights (p. 9) that one of the prerogatives of the king of Erin was to have the heath-fruit (*fraechmeas*) of *Brigh-Leithe* (now Slieve Golry in Longford) brought to him. The *fraechmeas* was no doubt the whortleberry (called *whorts* or *hurts* in Munster), as is indicated by the fact that the whortleberry is now called *fraechóg* and *fraechán*, two diminutives of the same word *fraech*, heath. Most Dublin people have seen women with baskets of " froghans," as they call them, for sale, picked on the neighbouring mountains. The passage referred to shows that they were eaten in old times even by kings.

Beechmast and oakmast were greatly valued for feeding pigs, which were kept in droves among the woods. The

* HyF, 283.   † Moyrath, 131.
‡ Stokes, Lives of SS., 326.

general name for mast was *mes* or *mess*. On one occasion the *badb* [bauv] or war-witch, predicting evils for Ireland, included among them " woods without masts."* (*feda cin mess*). The Four Masters signalise the year A.D. 835, for " great produce both of beechmast and acorns, which so choked up the brooks that they ceased running." And in the Brehon Laws (IV. 257 bot.) mast is coupled with grass and corn as a part of the valuable produce of the land. In the Bodleian copy of the Dinnsenchus we are told that " in the west of the plain of Macha there was a fruitful " oak wood, of which the odour was so fragrant, that when " the swine in the country all round smelled the wind that " blew over it, it was a heartbreak to them, and they " rushed quite mad to get to the wood." The same story is told in the Book of Leinster.†

9. *Fuel and Light.*

Fuel.—as the country abounded in forests, thickets, and brakes, the most common fuel for domestic use was wood. Firewood or " firebote " was called *condud*, or as it is now spelled, *connadh* [conna]. Two other names given in Cormac's Glossary (p. 73) are *fochonnad* and *geltine*. Firewood, made up in faggots, is mentioned in the Book of Rights as a portion of the tribute of the unfree tribes of Leinster to the king of that province. A bundle of firewood was called a *brossna*, a word found in the oldest authorities and used to this day all over Ireland, even by the English-speaking people, as meaning a bundle of withered branches, or of heath, for fuel. We read in the Tripartite Life (p. 10) that when St. Patrick was a boy, his foster-mother told him to bring her a *brossna* of withered branches to make a fire.

Peat or turf was much used as fuel. The Senchus Mór speaks of the cutting of turf from a bank (*port*) and carting

---

* Rev. Celt., XII. III.

† Folklore, III. 514 : LL, 169, *a* (" *Sruthair Matha* ").

it home when dry ; and mentions a penalty for stealing it.*   It is recorded in the Annals that Ragallach, king of Connaught in the middle of the seventh century, having exasperated some men who were cutting turf (*oc buain mónadh*) in a bog, they fell on him and killed him with their sharp *ruams* or turf-spades.†   The whole bog was the " commons " property of the *finè* or group of related families : but a single turf-bank might belong for the time to an individual.‡   The word *ruam*, used above, was a general word for any spade.   At the present day the sharp spade used in cutting turf is designated by the special name of *sleaghan* [pron. *slaan*, the *aa* long like the *a* in *star*].   This word is a diminutive of *sleg*, modern *sleagh*, a ' spear ' (see vol. I., p. 108, *supra*) : *sleaghan*, a little spear '—though a *slaan* is not very like one.

Metal-workers used wood charcoal ; for neither plain wood nor peat afforded sufficient heat to melt or weld. We have seen (vol. I., p. 565) that charcoal made from birch afforded the highest degree of heat then available ; and was used for fusing the metals known at that time. Allusions to the use of charcoal—which in Irish is designated *gual* or *cual*—are met with in all sorts of Irish literature.   In the Book of Rights (253) it is stated that the king of Hy Gabla was entitled to certain stipends, and, among other things, to " a ring of gold from the white [-hot] coal " (*fáil óir o'n gheal ghual*) : and in the Crith Gabhlach we find mention of " a sack of coal (*gual*) for the irons."§   In a poem in the Book of Leinster the fuel kept in a blacksmith's forge is designated *cual craing*, a form of *cual craind*, ' coal of *crand* or wood,'‖ which plainly points out its material.   From the Crith Gabhlach passage, as well as from the special manner in which the

* Br. Laws, I. 133 ; also IV. 221, 223.
† Silva Gad., 431 : Keating, 476. See also p. 92, *supra*.
‡ Br. Laws, I. 133, 165 : a law still observed.
§ *Ibid.*, IV. 311, bottom.
‖ O'Curry. Man. & Cust., I. 147 : LL, 35, *a*, ₄.

cual craing is mentioned in this last entry, it appears that it was usual for smiths to keep it in sacks. The pit on which charcoal was made was called *clas-guail* or *gual-chlais*. The remains of some of the old charcoal-pits are still recognisable. I know one in which the soil is mixed up and quite black with quantities of charcoal-fragments and dust. In the story of " Fingal Ronain " a man says :— " If I were to be thrust into a *cual-chlais tened* (a ' fiery charcoal-pit.'), I would not do it " [a certain evil deed].*

That coal from mines was used at some very early time is rendered certain by the fact that old coal-mines have recently been found exhibiting all the marks of extreme antiquity (chap. xxiv. page 289, *infra*). But as the word *gual* or *cual*, which is constantly used in the old accounts of the Irish metal-workers, will stand for either mine-coal or wood-charcoal, the literature alone—or that portion of it available—would not enable us to infer with certainty that mine-coal was used by the old Irish smiths and braziers, or used at all for fuel.

A live coal from a turf fire was called *smeróit* or *smeróid*† : a mixture of *smeróids* and hot ashes was, and is still, called *gríosach* [greesagh]. A mass or fire of burning coals, especially of charcoal or coal, was called *richis* or *righis*,‡ a word which has long dropped out of use. O'Clery explains *righis* as *lasair* (flame), and O'Davoren has *richis* as meaning *tine* (fire). Straw, when plentiful and not otherwise wanted, was sometimes used as fuel in the absence of better. That this was so we know by a provision of the Book of Aicill, which mentions a penalty for stealing it.§ If it was intended for cattle-feeding, there is a certain fine : but if for burning, the fine was less. Probably the straw for burning was wheaten straw, and was subjected to some sort of preparation, such as trussing it up into wisps. Sometimes when fuel was

* Rev. Celt., xiii. 376, 377.   ‡ Rev. Celt., xi, 435, top.
† Corm. Gloss., 149.   § Br. Laws, iii. 151.

scarce, the poor people burned dried cowdung, gathered in the pasture fields in summer, as they do to this day : they call it *bóithreán* [boraun], a word formed by suffixes from *bo*, ' a cow.'*

Flint and steel with tinder were used for striking and kindling fire. In the ancient Latin version of the voyage of St. Brendan, so celebrated all over Europe in the middle ages, the old hermit Paul says that on a certain occasion he struck fire with flint and steel (*silice ferro percusso*) and cooked his fish.† And in the Mediæval Irish Tract on Latin Declension, edited by Stokes (No. 720), *igni ferrium* (' steel-fire ') is glossed by the Irish *teine-creasa*, literally ' fire of the girdle,' so designated because the whole kindling-gear, or *tenlach-teined*, as it is called,‡ *i.e.* the flint, steel, and tinder, was carried in the girdle-pocket, so as to be ready to hand. The spark produced by flint and steel was called *tenlam*, which in Cormac's Glossary (158) is derived from *tene*, ' fire,' and *lám*, ' the hand ' : that is to say, it means ' hand-fire ' : and O'Clery again explains this word *tenlam* by *teine-creasa*, ' girdle-fire.' Tinder was, and is, commonly called *sponc* [spunk], which is obviously the same as the Latin *spongia*, English sponge. Spunk or tinder was sometimes made from the dried leaves of the coltsfoot, so that this plant is now always called *sponc* :§ but in recent times it was more usually made of coarse brown paper steeped in a solution of nitre and dried. " Spunk " is now used as an English word both in Ireland and Scotland : " a spunk of fire on the hearth."

Light.—In the better class of houses dipped candles were commonly used. The usual Irish word for a candle is *caindel* or *cainnel*, which seems borrowed from the Latin *candela* : but there is also an old native word for it—*innlis*,

* See O'Curry, Man. & Cust., II. 65.
† Brendaniana, 171 : Card. Moran, Act. Brend., 127.
‡ Silva Gad., 302, top : Ir. Text, 267, s.
§ See Kilk. Archæol. Journ., 1868–9, p. 449.

which O'Clery's Glossary explains by *cainneal*. There are numerous references to candles in ancient Irish authorities. The Senchus Mór mentions candles of " eight fists " (about forty inches) in length, made by [repeated] dipping of peeled rushes in melted tallow or meat grease*: from which we learn that the wicks of candles were, sometimes at least, made of peeled rushes : but other kinds of wicks were used. In the Tripartite Life (p. 53) St. Patrick is made to say, when about to present himself at Tara, that he would not make of himself a candle under a vat (*caindcl fo dabaich*). In the Irish Life of St. Senan in the Book of Lismore (which however seems a comparatively late piece, though copied from older books), we are told that the saint—when young—once asked for a candle to light him while grinding corn at the mill : and the cook answered " I have no dipped candles [*coinnle tumtha*] just now but one : take this and you will get more if they are dipped."† In the ancient tract called the " Law of Adamnan," it is stated that before the time of that saint one function of a *cumal* or female slave was to dip a candle (*cainnel*), four hand-breadths in length, in butter or lard, and to hold it in her hand to light the company at supper till they separated for bed.‡

As bees were so abundant, beeswax (Irish *céir*, pron. care), as might be expected, was turned to account. Beeswax candles must have been in use at some early period in the houses of the rich. In the Book of Rights (15 and xlvi) it is stated that one of the prerogatives of the king of Leinster was " to drink by the light of wax candles [*coindle ciarrtha*] at Dinnree " ; which was one of the most ancient of the royal residences of Leinster (p. 94, *supra*). Add to this that beeswax " found in square masses, and " also in the form of candles, has been discovered under

---

* Br. Laws, ii. 251, 253.   † Stokes, Lives of SS., line 1995.
‡ Trip. Life, Introduction, xxii. See also for candles, Ware, Antiqq., 183, bottom.

" circumstances which leave no doubt as to the great
" antiquity of such articles."*   Several specimens of this
ancient wax are in the National Museum, Dublin.

Although, in very early times, candles were sometimes
held in the hands of slaves, they were more commonly
placed on candlesticks.   The ancient Irish word for a
candlestick is *caindelbra*, modern Irish *coinnleoir* [conlore],
both of which are modified forms of the Latin *candelabra*.
The Senchus Mór and the Crith Gabhlach mention a
caindelbra as a usual article in a house ; O'Donovan here
translates the word ' branch-light ' : and the old Irish commentator explains it as " the straight wand upon which the
" beautiful light is placed, like a candle, in the house of
" each person."†   The ancient Latin Hymn of Secundinus
makes mention of a light placed on a *candelabrum*‡ : and
in the description of the Banqueting-House of Tara in
the Book of Leinster it is stated that there were seven
coindelbruig in it.§

It was usual to keep a *ríchaindell* [reehannel], or ' king-
candle ' (*rí*, ' a king '), or royal candle, of enormous size,
with a great bushy wick, burning at night in presence of a
king ; in the palace it was placed high over his head ;
during war it blazed outside his tent-door ; and on night-
marches it was borne before him.   This custom is mentioned very often in the records.   We are told in the
Annals that Cerbhall [Kerval], king of Ossory, coming
out of his chamber in the middle of the night to attack
the Danes, A.D. 860, had " a large king-candle carried
before him, the light of which shone far on every side."‖
In Táin-bo-Fraich (O'Curry, II., 219), Froech visits his aunt
with a spear shining like the candle of a king-house (*caindel*

---

* Wilde, Catalogue, 255.   See also Kilk. Archæol. Journ., 1892, p. 184.
† Br. Laws, I. 126, 5; 143, bottom ; also IV. 310, 11.
‡ Trip. Life, 387, 14.
§ Petrie's Tara, p. 188.   On Candlesticks, see also Reeves, Eccl.
Antiqq., 210 ; and Joyce, Irish Names of Places, II. 204.
‖ Three Fragments, 145.

ríg-thigi) in the hand of each of his fifty attendants : and in *Bruden Da Derga* in LU, three heroes are described as sitting in presence of King Conare with the candle of a royal house burning over the head of each of them.* A hero's spear is sometimes compared (as above) to a royal palace candle for the brightness of its polished bronze head† ; and in this sense a spear is sometimes called,

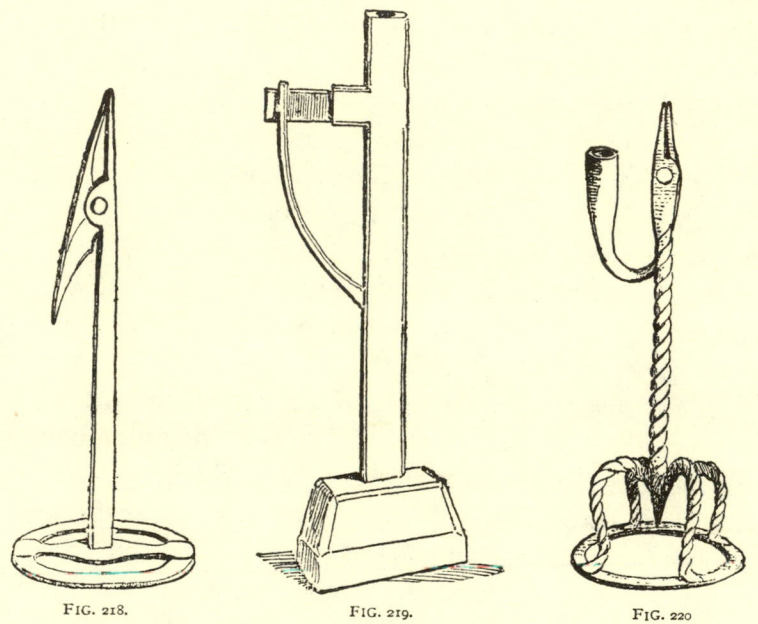

FIG. 218.   FIG. 219.   FIG. 220.

Rush and Candle-holders : found in different parts of Ireland. These are 10 or 12 inches high, and when in use were placed on a table. Those intended to stand on the floor were about 36 inches high. (From Proc. Roy. Ir. Academy for 1889-91, p. 629.)

figuratively, a *caindell rigthaige*; as in LL, 97, *a*, $_{14}$ from bot.: See also Rev. Celt. xxiv., 128, note. In regard to size, the Four Masters are fairly definite in the passage already quoted, vol. I., p. 62, *supra*, where the " king-candle " kept burning at night before Shane O'Neill's tent (A.D. 1557) is described as " a huge torch thicker than a man's body " : a passage which shows moreover that this custom continued till the sixteenth century. (See also Ware Antiqq., 183 bot.)

* O'Curry, Man. & Cust., II 140.
† O'Curry, Man. & Cust., II. 219, $_{19}$; and 220, note, 1st col., line 9.

The poorer classes commonly used a rush-light, *i.e.* a single rush peeled (leaving one little film of rind the whole length to keep it together) and soaked in grease, but not formed into a candle by repeated dippings.   It gave a poor light and burned down very quickly ; and it was known by two names, *adann* and *itharna* [ey-an : ïharna].   It is well characterised in a verse ascribed to St. Colman, founder of Cloyne (died A.D. 604), quoted in Cormac's Glossary (p. 10), in which a warrior, praising his sword, is made to say :—
" As blackbirds are to swans, as peasant women are to
" queens, as an *adann* is to a candle [so is any other] sword
" to my sword."   The word *adann* means ' to kindle ' ; and hence *adannadh* was applied to a candle-lighter in a church. The other word *itharna* is also given in Cormac's Glossary (p. 92) as equivalent to *adann* : and it is derived, says the Glossary, " according to ancient writers " (*i.e.* ancient when the Glossary was written —ninth or tenth century),

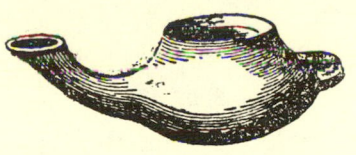

FIG. 221.

Ancient Irish bronze Lamp.   Found in a *crannoge* (i.e. an island-dwelling in a lake) in County Roscommon.   The vessel held the oil, and the wick projected from the pipe. From Wood-Martin's Lake Dwellings in Ireland, p. 235.

from *ith*, ' fat,' *i.e.* " the fat of the cattle they used to melt in the rushes " (*simnib*).   There were simple holders for rushlights : and several specimens have been found, which however do not appear to be old : nevertheless they are probably the representatives of the holders of more ancient times.   They are of iron or of wood, or of both combined, and are often so formed as that each will hold either a rush or a dipped candle, or both at one time.*   (See last page.)

Oil lamps of various kinds were used ; and they are often mentioned in the oldest records† under two names— *lespaire* [les-pe-rĕ] and *luacharnn* or *lochrann* (from Lat. *iucerna*).   *Luacharnn* occurs several times in the eighth-

* See Kilk. Archæol. Journ., 1890–1, p. 473 ; and Proc. Roy. Ir. Acad., 1889–91, p. 626.   † Corm. Gloss., 103 : Stokes, Lives of SS., line 342.

century Glosses of Zeuss, as the equivalent of *lampas* and *lucerna*, which shows the remote time in which lamps and lanterns were used in Ireland. Some were made of bronze (fig. 221) : some of clay. A rude unglazed earthenware lamp, shallow, and with a snout to support a wick, was found some time ago among prehistoric remains near Portstewart.* It has been already stated (p. 30) that it was usual to light the principal apartment in a house from above by a row of lamps or candles suspended from the ridgepole.

In modern times, long, dried slits of bogdeal have been used by the peasantry instead of candles. Probably the same practice prevailed in early times, but I have found no notice of it.

10. *Free Public Hostels.*

This seems a proper place to give some information regarding the provision made for lodging and entertaining travellers and officials. Hospitality and generosity were virtues highly esteemed in ancient Ireland ; in the old Christian writings indeed they are everywhere praised and inculcated as religious duties (I. 330, *supra*) ; and in the secular literature they are equally prominent. The higher the rank of the person the more was expected from him, and a king should be lavish without limit. In the story of the Battle of Moyrath (p. 105), Erin is lauded for many virtues during the reign of King Domnall, among them hospitality :—" Her habitations were hospitable, spacious, " and open for company and entertainment, to remove the " hunger and gloom of guests." The duty of dealing out plenty to guests was so universally recognised that even the Brehon Law (IV. 337) is careful to specify the cases where a king may be excused for deficiency of food if there should occur an unexpected arrival of a number of guests :—such as failure or refusal, at the wrong moment, of a tributary chief to send in the expected food-supply.

* Kilk. Archæol. Journ., 1883-4, p. 318.

Guaire, king of Connaught in the seventh century, is celebrated and lauded everywhere in tales and poems for his generosity and hospitality. He was so constantly stretching out his hand to give away that—as the legends have it—his right hand grew longer than his left : and to this day he is known as " Guaire the Hospitable." We often find generous persons praised in terms like those applied to Owen O'Madden, a Connaught chief, of whom it is said in an old Irish document (HyM, 141) that " he does " not refuse anyone gold or horses, food or kine. and he is " the wealthiest of the race of Gaedhal for bestowing them." Even St. Patrick himself is represented as blessing the district of Moy Rein in this fashion :—" I leave prosperity " to the place so that it shall provide for all [requiring " help] even though every cleric should be poor "—as much as to say that in case the clergy and the monasteries had not the means to discharge the duty of hospitality expected of them, the lay people of the district should be so prosperous that they could and would provide for all without any clerical help.*

If by any accident a person found himself unable to discharge the due rites of hospitality, it was supposed that his face became suffused with a *ruice* [ruckĕ] or blush—a blush of honourable shame—called also *enech-ruice* or *ainech-ruice*, ' face-blush,' as it is explained in Cormac's Glossary (p. 66). The brewy or head of a hostel took care to have " the snout of a rooting-hog '†—meaning he had plenty of pork—" to break or prevent his face-blush " : when there was plenty there was no reason to blush. If anyone through the default of another ran short of provisions when visitors came, so that he had reason to feel ashamed of his scanty table, the defaulter had to pay him as compensation what was called a " blush-fine."‡

---

* Book of Fenagh, 273.   † Br. Law, IV. 311 *et seq.*
‡ Br. Laws, I. 123, ₁₁; 129, note I. ; IV. 345, middle ; ₃₄₇, ₁₃: and Corm. Gloss., 103 (" Leos ").

As illustrating what was expected of the higher ranks, the Brehon Law (IV. 237) lays down that " the chieftain " grades are bound to entertain [a guest] without asking " any questions "—*i.e.* questions as to his name, or business, or where he was bound for, and the like. It is added that the *Féinè* or farmers were not so bound—*i.e.* they might make reasonable inquiry about a guest before entertaining. Once a guest had partaken of food in a house, his host was bound to abstain from offering him any violence or disrespect under any circumstances.* Bede's testimony as to the hospitality of the Irish has been already quoted (vol. I., p. 414).

This universal admiration for hospitality found its outward expression in the establishment, all over the country, of public hostels for the free lodging and entertainment of all who chose to claim them. At the head of each was an officer called a *brugh-fer*, or *brugaid*, or *briuga* [broo-fer, brewy, broo-a], a public hospitaller or hosteller, who was held in high honour. He was bound to keep an open house for the reception of certain functionaries—king, bishop, poet, judge, &c.—who were privileged to claim for themselves and their attendants free entertainment when on their circuits : and also for the reception of strangers. He had a tract of land and other large allowances to defray the expenses of his house : the names *brugh-fer* and *brugaid* indeed literally signify ' landholder,' from *brugh*, land, a farm of land. *Brugaid* was often used in the sense of a farmer merely, but we have here to do only with its special application to a keeper of a public hostel.

The brewys were of two main classes. The lowest was the *brugaid cedach* or ' hundred hospitaller,'† who should have at least one hundred of each kind of cattle, one hundred labourers, and corresponding provision for feeding

---

* As illustrative, see how Branduff treated Glasdam, p. 483, below.
† See Stokes, Rev. Celt., xv. 431 : HyF, 239, *h* : and Kilk. Archæol Journ., 1872–3, p. 47, verse xlii.

and lodging guests. The *brugaid cedach* is constantly met with in all kinds of Irish writings. " But "—says the gloss on the Senchus Mór—" there is a *brugaid* who is better than this man " : this was the *brugaid-lethech*, who should have two hundred of each kind of cattle. His house should be supplied with all necessary furniture and appliances, including one hundred beds for guests ; for he was not allowed to borrow.* In order to be at all times ready to receive visitors, a brewy of either class was bound to have three kinds of meat cooked and ready to be served up to all who came ; three kinds of raw meat ready for cooking ; besides animals ready for killing. In one of the law tracts a brewy is quaintly described as " a man of three snouts " :—viz. the snout of a live hog rooting in the fields to break the blushes of his face ; the snout of a dead hog on the hooks cooking ; and the pointed snout of a plough : meaning that he had plenty of live animals and of meat cooked and uncooked, with a plough and all other tillage appliances.† He was also " a man of three sacks " :—for he had always in his house a sack of malt for brewing ale ; a sack of salt for curing cattle-joints ; and a sack of charcoal for the irons ; this last referring to the continual use of iron-shod agricultural implements calling for frequent repair and renewal. We are told also (IV., pp. 310, 311) that his kitchen-fire should be kept perpetually alight, and that his caldron should never be taken off the fire, and should always be kept full of joints boiling for guests. The whole description is a picture of lavish abundance, reminding one strongly of Chaucer's description of the Franklin :—

> " An householder, and that a grete was he
>   Seint Julian‡ he was in his Contree,
>   His brede, his ale, was alway after on ;
>   A better envyned§ man was wher non.

---

* Br. Laws, I. 47, bottom.   † *Ibid.*, IV. 311.   ‡ St. Julian, the patron saint of travellers and of hospitality.   § Supplied with wine.

> Withouten bake mete never was his hous,
> Of fish and flesh, and that so plenteous,
> It snewed [snowed] in his hous of mete and drinke,
> Of alle deintees that men coud of thinke,
> After the sundry sesons of the yere,
> So changed he his mete and his soupere.
> Full many a fat partrich hadde he in mewe,
> And many a breme, and many a luce [a fish] in stewe.
> Wo was his coke but-if [*i.e.* unless] his sauce were
> Poinant and sharpe, and ready all his gere.
> His table dormant in his halle alway
> Stode redy covered all the longe day."

There should be a number of open roads leading to the house of a brewy, so that it might be readily accessible ; and on each road a man should be stationed to make sure that no traveller should pass by without calling to be entertained ;* besides which a light was to be kept burning on the *faithche* [faha] or lawn at night to guide travellers from a distance. The noble brewy, Da Derga, mentioned below, kept his doors open day and night, except at the windy side of the house.†

As visitors and their followers were constantly coming and going, the house-furniture and other property of a brewy were jealously protected by law from wanton or malicious damage, the various possible injuries being set forth in great detail, with the compensation for them. He was moreover a magistrate, and was empowered to deliver judgment on certain cases that were brought before him to his house : " He is a *bo-aire* for giving judgment." We have already seen (vol. I., p. 44) that a court was held in his house for the election of the chief of the tribe. Keating says that there were ninety *brugaids* in Connaught, ninety in Ulster, ninety-three in Leinster, and a hundred and thirty in Munster, all with open houses ; and though it is not necessary to accept these numbers as strictly accurate,

---

* Br. Laws, v. 17, 17; and 79, 22.
† Da Derga, 36. See also, about the *brugaid*, Br. Laws, v. 77, 79.

they indicate at least that the houses of hospitality were very numerous. The house of a brewy answered all the purposes of the modern hotel or inn, but with the important distinction, that guests were lodged and entertained with bed and board, free of charge. With great probability the rule prevailed here, as in case of private hospitality, that an ordinary guest was supposed to be kept—if he wished to stay—for three nights and three days : after which the obligation to entertain ceased : but I have not found this specifically mentioned.

There were a few brewys of a higher class than the preceding, who had large tracts of land and held a very exalted position. They often entertained kings, chiefs, and warriors, of the highest classes, with whom also they were on terms of familiar intercourse. The hostel of one of these was called a *brudin* or *bruden* [now pronounced breen or bryan], a word which Mr. Crowe* connects with the Greek *prytaneum*, meaning the same thing as the Irish *bruden*—a house of public or state-endowed hospitality. In the time of the Red Branch Knights there were six of these " chief courts of hospitality in Erin," each situated at the meeting of four roads,† all of which figure in the Romantic Tales. The most remarkable of them was the " Bruden Da Derga," kept by the great hosteller Da Derga. The ancient story of the " *Togail* or Destruction of Bruden Da Derga," gives a detailed and very vivid account of the sack of this hostel and the slaughter of its people, including Conari I., king of Ireland—who happened to be staying in it at the time with all his retinue—by a band of Irish and British marauders, in the first century of the Christian era : in which however the assailants suffered still greater loss than those they attacked. This fine story has been lately edited and translated by Dr. Stokes in the Revue Celtique, vol. xxii. The narrative fixes the position

---

* In Kilk. Archæol. Journ., 1868–69, p. 326.
† According to the poem referred to in note *, p. 173, *infra*

of the Bruden Da Derga with great precision, as situated on the river Dodder, where it was crossed by the " Slige Cualann " (for which see chap. xxviii., p. 395, *infra*), the great road leading from Tara across the Liffey at Dublin, and on across the Dodder through the district of Cualann towards Bray.

In 1879, during the preparation of a piece of ground for building near Donnybrook, a remarkable discovery was made, which, as in many other like cases, goes to confirm the truthfulness of the old saga. A large, low, earthern mound situated beside the Dodder on the south side, at a spot now called Mount Erroll, a little east of the Roman Catholic Church of Donnybrook, was levelled, in which vast quantities of human bones were found, not interred as in an ordinary cemetery, but flung in heaps and otherwise exhibiting unmistakable evidences of a general massacre. The whole mound and its contents were carefully examined by Dr. Frazer of Dublin, whose account of the exploration is given in the Proc. Roy. Ir. Academy, 1879–1886, p. 29. Sir Samuel Ferguson, in an instructive note to his poem of Conary, has rightly identified the place where this mound was situated, with the site of Da Derga's hostel.

We have seen that each bruden was placed at the meeting of four roads : *i.e.* where two main roads crossed. The two roads here were the *Slige Cualann* and another leading from the old district of the once powerful tribe of Hy Donohue which lay along on both sides of the Dodder from Glennasmole down. This road passed by Bohernabreena and Rathfarnham till it crossed Slige Cualann at the Bruden, and on towards the mouth of the Liffey, then and afterwards a great resort of trading vessels. O'Curry (Man. & Cust., II. 136) states that Bohernabreena took its name from the old Bruden or *breen*, in which he is undoubtedly correct : for " Bohernabreena " is the proper anglicised phonetic form of *Bóthar-na-Bruidne*, i.e. the road of the Bruden, meaning the road leading to it. But he is certainly mistaken in asserting, as he does, that the present Bohernabreena was itself the site of Da Derga's Bruden ; as anyone may see who glances through the story. The destruction of this Bruden is recorded in the Annals of Tigernach.

Another of these six hostels was Bruden-Da-Choca (or Choga), kept by the hospitaller Da Choca. This was the scene of another tragedy, in which Cormac Conlingeas, son of Concobar mac Nessa, perished, as related in the historical tale called " The Destruction of Da Choca's Bruden," which has also been translated by Dr. Stokes in the Revue Celtique, vol. xxi. The old fort, the only remaining relic of this *bruden*, is still well known. It is situated in Westmeath, a few miles from Athlone ; and to this day it retains the name " Bruden," in the phonetic form of Bryan. Forgall Monach, or Forgall the Wily, Cuculainn's father-in-law, kept another of these brudens at *Lusca*, now Lusk, north of Dublin, which figures much in the tales of the Red Branch. The remaining three were the bruden of Mac Datho in Leinster ; Bruden Blai Briuga (or Brugaid) in Ulster ; and Bruden mic Dareo (or Bruden da Ger) in Brefney.*

Every *bruden* was a place of refuge for a homicide, where he might claim protection from the immediate vengeance of his victim's friends till he could obtain a fair trial before a brehon ; as appears from a statement in the " Destruction of the Bruden Da Choca " :—" Every Bruden is an asylum of the red hand," *i.e.* for the manslayer.† In this function the Irish *bruden* answered to the " asylum " of the Greeks : and Dr. Stokes has called attention to the curious correspondence of the *six* refuge *brudens* of Ireland

* An account of the whole six may be seen in a short poem published and translated by Stokes, in Rev. Celt., XXI. 397 : of which a very corrupt version was published in Proc. Roy. Ir. Acad., 1870–76, p. 253. They are also enumerated in the Battle of Moyrath, pp. 51–53.

† Rev. Celt., XXI. 315. In the Br. Laws, v. 319, a manslayer is called a man of red weapons."

with the *six* Jewish cities of refuge for manslayers against the avengers of blood.*

The word *bruden* is still preserved in the names of several townlands in different parts of Ireland, from which it is probable that the term was applied to other houses of hospitality as well as to the six mentioned above. Or perhaps the multiplication of the name may have arisen from this circumstance : that *bruden* was—as we know—sometimes applied to any great banqueting-hall, as, for instance, to that of Tara and of Dun-da-benn, now the fort called Mountsandal, over the Bann, near Coleraine ; and also to the royal house of refuge for aged warriors at Emain (vol. I., p. 97, *supra*).† " *Bruighean* "—says Peter O'Connell's Dictionary—' a sumptuous house, a court or palace.'‡

There was another sort of public victualler called *biatach* or *biadhtach* [beetagh], who was also bound to entertain travellers, and the chief's soldiers whenever they came that way. In order to enable the *betagh* to dispense hospitality, he held a tract of arable land free of rent, called a *baile-biadhtaigh* or ballybetagh, equal to about 1000 of our present English acres, with a much larger extent of waste land. The distinction between a brewy and a betagh is not very clear. They are distinguished in a passage in the Book of the Dun Cow,§ which, among other classes of people, mentions the *briugaid* and the *biatach* : but there was probably little substantial difference between them. The Four Masters record the death of several individual *biataghs* : thus at A.D. 1225 (p. 219) : " Auliff O'Boland, Erénach of Drumcliff, a wise and learned

---

* Numbers xxxv. ; Deuteronomy iv. : Joshua xx.

† See Petrie's Tara, 199, bottom : Mesca Ulad, 13, 8: and Rossnaree, 20, last line.

‡ Zeitschr., Celt., Phil. I. 427. At the present day *Bruden*, in its modern form *bruighean* [bree-an], means a ' fairy-palace " ; for which, and for the local names derived from it, see Joyce's Irish Names of Places, vol. I. 289, 290.   § LU, p. 123, *b*, 4 and 5 from bottom.

man, and a general *biatach*, died." In later times the English of the Pale used the word *betaghe* to denote a servile class of farmers, like the English villeins : those on the king's manors are indeed sometimes called ' the king's villeins or betaghes.' But from the descriptions of these persons given by Anglo-Irish authorities, it appears that they were a class of dependent tenants who held small farms, probably on betagh lands, from which in course of time they came to be erroneously called *betaghs*. It is clear they were not the *biataghs* of Irish records.*

The Irish missionaries carried this fine custom to the Continent in early ages, as they did many others : for we are told, on the best authority, that before the ninth century they established ' hospitalia,' chiefly for the use of pilgrims on their way to Rome, some in Germany, but most in France, as lying in the direct route to the Eternal City.†

In the legendary history we read of female brewys. Just before Cormac mac Art's accession there was a *ban-brugaid* or ' she-brewy ' at Tara ; the lady already mentioned (I., 216), whose sheep ate up the queen's crop of *glaisin* : and in Cormac's Glossary (p. 130) is given the legend that through the country there were several female brewys who entertained Finn and the Fena on their hunting excursions.

---

* About the Anglo-Irish betaghes, see Ware, Antiqq., chapter xx. : Reg. of All Hallowes, xv. : and Statute of Kilkenny, pp. 4, 5.

† See Lynch, Cambr. Ev., II. 244–5.

Ornament composed from the Book of Kells

Sculpture on a Capital: Priest's House, Glendalough: Beranger, 1779.
(From Petrie's Round Towers.)

CHAPTER XXII

DRESS AND PERSONAL ADORNMENT

———

SECTION I. *The Person and the Toilet.*

arks of Aristocracy.—An oval face, broad above and narrow below, golden hair, fair skin, white, delicate, and well-formed hands with slender tapering fingers: these were considered by the ancient Irish as marking the type of beauty and aristocracy.* Among the higher classes the finger-nails† were kept carefully cut and rounded: and beautiful nails are often mentioned with commendation. It was considered shameful for a man of position to have unkempt nails: among several opprobious terms applied by Conan Mael to the warrior Cairell is *créchtingnech*, 'ragged-nailed.' Crimson-coloured finger-nails were greatly admired. In the Táin a young lady is described as having, among other marks of beauty, "regular, circular, crimson nails"; and ladies sometimes dyed them this colour. Deirdre, uttering a lament for the sons of Usna, says :—

* All the above characteristics are mentioned so often in Irish writings that it is unnecessary to give references.
† *Inga* or *ionga*, 'a finger-nail.' As to the nails, see Silva Gad., 381, with Irish text, 339, ₅: Tromdamh, 71, bottom: Hyde, Lit. Hist., 258, bottom: Sons of Usna, 413, note 44: and Sullivan, Introd., 72, 73.

" I sleep no more, and I shall not crimson my nails : no
" joy shall ever again come upon my mind."*

Ladies sometimes dyed the eyebrows black with the
juice of some sort of berry, as appears from the following
expression in Cael's poem in praise of the lady Crede
[cray] :—" A bowl she has whence berry-juice flows, with
which she colours her eyebrows black."† We have already
seen (vol. I., p. 343) that the Irish missionary monks sometimes painted or dyed their eyelids black. An entry in
Cormac's Glossary plainly indicates that the blush of the
cheeks was sometimes heightened by a colouring matter
obtained from a plant named *ruam*. The Glossary thus
explains the word :—" *Ruam*, i.e. *ro-eim*, an herb that
gives colour to the face until it is red."‡ The *ruam* was
the alder : but the sprigs and berries of the elder-tree were
applied to the same purpose, as appears by the " kenning "
or figurative name—the " reddening of faces "—given to
this tree in a passage in the Book of Ballymote.§ It is to
be hoped that bedecking the face with an artificial blush
was practised only by ladies : but the authorities do not
enlighten us on the point : or perhaps it would be more
correct to say they leave a sort of presumption that the
practice was common to men and women. In connexion
with all this, it is proper to remark that among Greek and
Roman ladies the practice was very general of painting
the cheeks, eyebrows, and other parts of the face.

The Hair.—Both men and women wore the hair long,
and commonly flowing down on the back and shoulders—a
custom noticed by Cambrensis, and pronounced by him,
in his narrow-minded way, barbarous, because among the
Anglo-Normans of his time it was the fashion to trim the

---

* Sons of Usna, Atlantis, III. 413 : Ir. Texte, I. 79, II. This is like the
practice of the Egyptian ladies dyeing their finger-tips with henna.

† O'Curry, MS. Mat., 309, 595, 6: Silva Gad., 120 (Irish text, 111).
Berry-juice is here called *sugh-subh*, from *sugh*, ' juice,' and *subh* ' a berry.'

‡ Corm. Gloss., 144 : Three Ir. Gloss. 39 (for the Irish).

Kuno Meyer, in Rev. Celt., XIII 220, note.

hair short.   The hair was combed daily after a bath, as is shown by the passage from the Battle of Rossnaree, quoted at p. 185, *infra*.   The heroes of the Fena of Erin, before sitting down to their dinner after a hard day's hunting, always took a bath and carefully combed their long hair. The Irish derived this fashion of the hair from old times ; for we know that part of Gaul was called " Gallia Comata," from the long hair worn by the people.*

Among the higher classes in very early times great care was bestowed on the hair : its regulation constituted quite an art ; and it was dressed up in several ways.   Very often the long hair of men, as well as of women, was elaborately curled.   Conall Cernach's hair, as described in Da Derga (p. 199), flowed down his back, and was done up in " hooks and plaits and swordlets."   The accuracy of this and other similar descriptions is fully borne out by the most unquestionable authority of all, namely, the figures in the early illuminated manuscripts and on the shrines and high crosses of later ages.   In nearly all the figures of the Book of Kells, for example (7th or 8th century) the hair is combed and dressed with the utmost care, so beautifully adjusted indeed that it could have been done only by skilled professional hairdressers, and must have occupied much time.   Whether in case of men or women, it hangs down both behind and at the sides, and is commonly divided the whole way, as well as all over the head, into slender fillets or locks, which sometimes hang down to the eyes in front.   In some cases the fillets are combed down straight, though kept carefully separate ; but in others each is beautifully curled or twisted spirally the whole way down, which must have been done with a curling-iron of some kind.   These descriptions apply to the hair of priests and nuns as well as to that of lay people. In the seventh century this elaborate arrangement of the hair must have been universal among the higher classes :

* Ware, Antiqq., 176

for the artist who drew the figures in the Book of Kells has represented the hair dressed and curled in the manner described, not only on the figures of men and women, whether lay or ecclesiastical, but even on those of angels. The three nuns represented on the *Breac Moedoc* [Brack Mogue : thirteenth century] have the hair hanging down on each side to the waist : not divided into fillets, but each a single mass twisted spirally. Two other figures from the same shrine, given here—both ecclesiastical—show very well how men had the hair and beard dressed, which is seen still better in the figure of the Evangelist at page 197, below. I do not find mentioned anywhere that the Irish dyed their hair, as was the custom among the Greeks and Romans.

FIG. 222.

Figures of two ecclesiastics worked in bronze on the *Breac Moedoc*, the 'Shrine of St. Maidoc or Mogue,' dating from about the thirteenth century. See vol. I., p. 570, note *. (From Miss Stokes's Early Christian Art, p. 107.)

For women, very long hair has been in Ireland always considered a mark of beauty. For example, in the Táin, a lovely lady is described as having her yellow hair parted in four wreaths, three of them braided round her head, and the fourth hanging down to her ankles.* This admiration has come down to the present ; for you constantly find mentioned in the Irish popular songs of our own day, a maiden " with golden hair that swept the dew off the grass "—or some such expression. The long fair hair hanging down at the back was called *cúilfhionn* [coolin] ; from *cúl*, the back of the head, and *finn* or *fionn*, white : whence the well-known anglicised word *coolin* or *coolun*,

* O'Curry, Man & Cust., II. 110

which is often applied to a fair-haired person, but which is now better known as the name of a beautiful Irish air, and of Moore's exquisite song to it.

In the fifteenth, sixteenth, and seventeenth centuries, it was usual, among the general run of people, for unmarried girls to wear the hair carefully combed out and hanging down loosely on the back : while married women more commonly bound it up round the head, with bright-coloured ribbons and long pins, in tasteful knots and wreaths : generally with a covering of some kind—a cap or folded kerchief.*

The practice of braiding the hair must have been very general among men as among women. One test of the activity of a candidate for admission to the ranks of the Fena of Erin (vol. I., p. 87, *supra*) was that he should be able to run and escape from pursuers through a wood without letting the braids of his hair be disordered by the branches.† It was considered an accomplishment for a young man to be able to plait hair well.‡

FIG. 223.

Portions of the plaited hair of a woman whose body, clothed in antique woollen costume, was found buried in hard gravel, under a bog, 4¼ feet deep, in the County Down, in the year 1780. (From Proc. Roy. Irish Academy, IX. 102.) For more about this find, see note under illustrations, p. 352, *infra*.

Very often—especially in active life—the hair was bound up and confined with rings or circlets, called by various names, such as *fáinne*, *flesc*, *buinne* (or *bunde*), of gold, silver, or white bronze ; or with ribbons or fillets of different materials, or with thin flexible gold plates (called *lann* or *niamlann* : see pp. 249, 250, below). This mode of disposing of the hair—both of men and women—is constantly referred to in the tales.§ That these binders were often of gold we know, partly from the literature

---

* On this see Lynch, Cambr. Ev., II. 169.

† O'Grady, Silva Gad., 100 : Keating, 350.   ‡ Three Fragm., 35.

§ For example, Voyage of Bran, I. 60, 11; 72, 21: O'Curry, Man. & Cust., 159, 9; 169, top ; 188, bottom : Joyce, Old Celtic Romances, 248. Such references might be indefinitely multiplied.

and partly from the testimony of the National and other museums, in which may be seen many long plates and ribbons of gold, most of them probably used to confine the hair.   One beautiful golden ribbon of this kind in the National Museum, 5 feet long, will be mentioned in section 3 of this chapter.   The forehead-band or fillet usually worn by a charioteer, sometimes of bronze or *findruine*, sometimes of a woven fabric, was called *gipne**—a word also applied to a doctor's cupping-horn (I. 621,

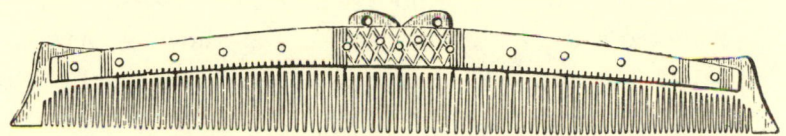

FIG. 224.

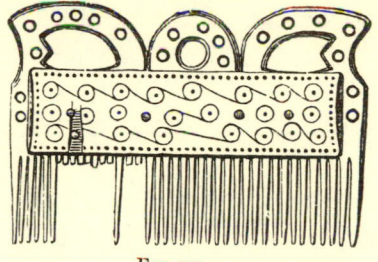

FIG. 225.

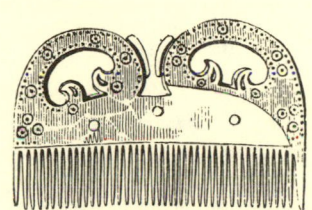

FIG. 226.

Ancient Irish Combs, of bone, now in National Museum. Fig. 224 is 10 inches long: fig. 225 2½ inches: fig. 226, 2¼ inches. (They are not drawn here to uniform scale.) Fig. 224 is of one single piece, with thin metal plates riveted on the sides. The other two have each two plates riveted together, with the teeth inserted between, and firmly riveted; so that if a tooth got broken, it could be withdrawn and a new one inserted. (From Wilde's Catalogue, p. 271.)

supra).   At the end of this chapter will be found a notice of the custom of suspending light, hollow gold balls from the ends of the hair-wreaths.   In later times the long locks worn on the back and sides of the head by men were called *glibbes* by Anglo-Irish writers.†

Combs.—From what precedes it will be understood that combs were in general use with men as well as with women : and many specimens—some made of bone, some of horn—some plain, some ornamented—have been found

* Wooing of Emer, p. 72, 19: LU, p. 122, *b*, 26, 27.
† Ware, Antiqq., 176, bottom.

in lisses, crannoges, and such like places. In the Crannoge of Cloonfinlough near Strokestown in Roscommon have been found combs in an incomplete state of manufacture, indicating a combmaker's workshop.* The comb—Irish *cir* or *cíor* [keer]—is, as we might expect, often mentioned in ancient Irish writings. In the story of Maildune, two great birds are said to have " picked and sleeked the plumage [of another bird] as if it were done with a comb."†

As long hair was so much admired, so baldness was considered a serious blemish‡ : and as showing the notice it attracted, we find it classified in Cormac's Glossary (p. 143, " Rangc ") into six different kinds, which the author names and describes. *Mail, mael*, or *maol* is the Irish word for bald ; and baldness is designated by *maile* [meela].

The Beard.—The men were as particular about the beard as about the hair. The common Irish names for the beard were *ulcha* and *feasóg* [faissoge], of which the last is still in use. It was also called *grend* or *greann* (Corm. 90) : in O'Clery's Glossary *greann* is explained by " *ulcha* or *feasóg*." In very early times the men—especially the soldiers and higher classes of people—wore the full beard. The soldiers of King Domnall, marching to the Battle of Moyrath, had " tufted beards covering and " surrounding their cheeks and mouths, their faces and " their heroic chins : great is the length of their beards, " which reach to their navels."

The fashion of wearing the beard varied. Sometimes it was considered becoming to have it long and forked, and gradually narrowing to two points below. King Concobar mac Nessa—like many of his attendant heroes—is described as having " a double-forked beard upon his chin " : and other kings and mighty heroes are constantly

---

* Proc. Roy. Ir. Acad., v. 211. † Rev. Celt., x. 77.
† O'Curry, Man. & Cust., ii. 144, bottom : Da Derga, p 286.

described as wearing their beards in this fashion. On several panels of the high crosses at Monasterboice and elsewhere, as well as on the shrines, and in the Book of Kells, are figures of men with full beards : in some the beard is forked ; in others it falls down in a single mass : while in a few it is cut rectangularly not unlike Assyrian beards (see the figures on St. Manchan's shrine, p. 204, below). Nearly all have a mustache, in most cases curled up and pointed at the ends as we often see now. In some there is a mustache without a beard : and a few others have the whole face bare. In many the beard is carefully divided into slender twisted fillets, as described above, for the hair. All this must have taken great trouble and a long time to arrange : but among the higher classes there was provision for it ; for kings and chiefs had their barbers (p. 184, *infra*). Indeed men must have given more time to this part of the toilet than women ; for they had both hair and beard to attend to.

It was disgraceful to have the hair and beard trimmed short. When Cuculainn had his hair and beard cut off by Curoi mac Dáire, who had vanquished him in single combat, and inflicted this humiliation on him, he remained in a hiding-place till both grew sufficiently long to be presentable. None others but nobles, chiefs, and warriors were permitted to wear the full beard : and those who wore it were bound by laws of honour to be brave and generous, never to retreat in battle, never to resort to mean ways of fighting, never to engage in manual or servile labour, and to be always ready to relieve distress. Working people were prohibited from wearing beards, so that they were expected to shave at least once a month.*

The beard that grew on the upper lip, when the lower part of the face was shaved, was called *crombéol* (' stoop-mouth '), what we now designate a mustache. This term

* All this is laid down in a short ancient Irish piece called *Geisi Ulchai*, or Prohibitions of Beard, edited by O'Looney, in Bec. Fola, 191.

is often met with in Anglo-Irish writings in the form *crommeal*. This was the fashion sometimes adopted by soldiers marching to battle, who probably regarded the long beard on the chin as an encumbrance. Among the silly measures passed by the Anglo-Irish Parliament in 1465, was one prohibiting the *crommeal*—commanding all the Irish within the Pale to shave the upper lip like the English.*

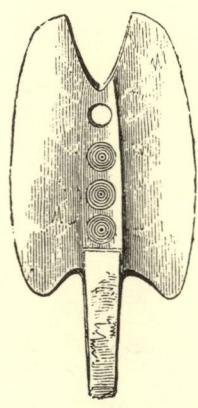

Fig. 227.

Bronze cutting-instrument, believed to be a Razor. It is all of one piece, 3½ inches long, 1¼ inch wide, with the two edges very thin, hard, and sharp. In National Museum, where there are others like it. (From Wilde's Catalogue, p. 549.)

That the ancient Irish used a razor (in Irish *alt* or *altan*) is proved by the fact that it is mentioned in our very oldest documents, and in such a way as shows it to have been a very familiar article. In a poem in the Book of Leinster, *alt*, 'a razor,' is mentioned twice :—"as sharp as a razor was his spear."† In Cormac's Glossary (p. 10) *altan* is derived from *ail*, 'edge,' and *teinn*, 'sharp-cutting.' In a still older authority, the Milan eighth-century glosses on the Psalms, the Latin *rasorium acutum* is explained by the Irish commentator :—*Amal inscrissid, edon, amal innaltain náith* : or in English, "as a scraper, that is, as a sharp razor."‡

This shows moreover that the razor was then used in shaving as it is now, by a sort of scraping movement against the beard. In the Book of Leinster it is stated that the " man of shaving" (*i.e.* barber) to the sons of Miled was Maen of the Mighty Deeds, and that he received as fee for his office the district of Berramain, lying along the shore near Tralee in Kerry, which was so called—says the legend—from *berrad*, 'shaving,' and *main*,

* See Lynch, Cambr. Ev., II. 219 : and Ware, Antiqq., 176, bottom.
† MS. Mat., 481.
‡ Stokes and Strachan, Thesaurus, I., p. 245. See also Zeuss, 657, 16.

' riches or reward ' :—*Berrad-main*, ' pay for shaving.'*
A razor was also called *berr-scian* : " shaving-knife."

The Bath.—Bathing was very usual, at least among the
upper classes, and baths and the use of baths are constantly
mentioned in the old tales and other writings. The bath
was a large tub or vat usually called *dabach*, but sometimes
ammor, *omur*, or *lothomur* : bathing—taking a bath—was
designated *fothrucud*.† People bathed daily, generally in
the evening ; and it was usual to prepare a bath for a
guest. In the " Battle of Rossnaree " (pp. 33, 35), we read
that when King Concobar's army were encamped for the
night, after a day's march, " fires were kindled, food and
" drink were prepared, they went into baths where they
" were carefully cleansed, their hair was smooth-combed,
" after which they had supper." In one of the houses that
Maildune came to he found a bath ready : and a certain
person who entertained St. Brendan and his companions
in their voyage, had a bath prepared for them on their
arrival.‡ In the story of Goll and Garb we read that
when Concobar and his retinue were entertained at the
house of Conall the brewy, a bath was prepared for them
after supper.§ In the commentaries on the Senchus Mór
it is incidentally mentioned that Fergus mac Leide, king
of Ulster, took a bath every day. There was a bath for
the use of visitors in the guest-house of every monastery :
when St. Cairnech of Tuilen came on a visit to the
monastery of Duleek, a bath was prepared for him in a
dabach : and we are told in the Crith Gabhlach that every
brugh-fer or brewy had in his house a bathing-vessel (*long-
foilcthe*).‖ Kings and chiefs were in the habit of bathing

---

* Silva Gad., 525, middle, and 478, 33: LL, 167, *b*, 6; and " Contents,"
43, *b*, middle. Other references to razors and shaving, Br. Laws, I. 125, 2;
and 133, 23: Ir. Texte, I. 277, 3: Moyrath, 20, 3, and 21, 4.

† Mac Conglinne, II, 22: Corm. Gloss., 73. ‡ Brendan., 144.
§ Rev. Celt., XIV. 417.

‖ Br. Laws, IV. 311, 14. See Foilcim in Glossary of Atkinson, Pass. &
Hom.

and anointing themselves with oil and precious sweet-scented herbs : as we find in the case of Cellach, king of Connaught, who, before a battle, bathed and anointed himself in this manner.* So Ulysses bathes and anoints himself with olive oil after being shipwrecked on the coast of Phæacea (Odyss. VI.). A king of Leinster died at Naas while in a bath, as sometimes happens people at the present day.

Every bath was furnished with a number of round stones. Among the articles of furniture in the guest-house of the Cork monastery was " a bath-tub with its stones."† They must have been moderately small : for in the Gloss on the Senchus Mór we read that Fergus mac Leide being once angered by the bond-woman Dorn, he killed her with a bath-stone (cloch-fothraicthe)‡ : no doubt by flinging it at her. The bath stones are constantly referred to in all sorts of Irish documents : but what the use of them was is a puzzle. It has been suggested that the water was heated by throwing the heated stones into it : and this view receives countenance from an incident related in Jocelin's " Life of St. Patrick " (Cap. C.), that the saint cursed the stones of Ushnagh, after which " they cannot be heated by " fire, nor when plunged into water [after coming out of the " fire] do they hiss like other stones " : which seems to show that Jocelin believed the stones were used to heat the water. In the far older Tripartite Life, where the same circumstance is told, nothing is said about heating the stones, but merely that after the curse, nothing good is made of them, " not even bathing-stones."

But it seems incredible that they heated bath-water in this uncouth fashion ; for we know they often heated it in the ordinary way. In the Battle of Moyrath (275, 20;

---

* Three Fragments, 107, top : and Silva Gad., 443, bottom. Other references to baths and bathing, Silva Gad., 77, bottom : Miss Hull, Cuch. Saga, 130, 12 (LL, 59, 7) : Mesca Ulad, 47 : Ir. Texte, I. 295, 6

† Mac Conglinne, 10, 26.   ‡ Br. Laws, I. 69, 19.

277, 3) we are told that in the house of a certain chief, the women were preparing a bath " for washing and bathing " ; and that they heated the water with firewood.   In the tale of the Sons of Usna (Atlantis, III., p. 409), Deirdre is represented as preparing a bath for Naisi " over the fire " : and such examples might be multiplied.*

Cormac's Glossary distinguishes between *fothrucud*, bathing the whole body, and *indlot* (or *indlut*), washing the feet or hands ; and this distinction is generally recognised in the old writings.   As the people had a full bath some time down late in the day, they did not bathe in the morning, but merely washed their hands ; for which purpose they generally went out immediately after rising and dressing, to some well or stream near the house.   This practice is constantly referred to.   " At early morning," says Mac Conglinne (70 : also 58), " I rose and went to the well to wash my hands."   In the Sick Bed of Cuculainn, Eochaid Iuil goes out early in the morning to wash (*do ilnut*) his hands at the spring ; and a better-known example is where, as we are told in the Lives of St. Patrick, the two daughters of King Laegaire came out in the early morning to the well of Clebach near Cruachan " to wash their hands as was their custom."†

In both washing and bathing they used soap (*sléic*, pron. slake).   In the Crith Gabhlach we are told that foulness is washed away from a person's honour as the face is washed with soap (*sléic*) and water and a linen cloth.‡

---

* In O'Grady's Silva Gadelica, p. 283 (transl.), the quarrel between King Fergus and his queen is related " anent precedence in the use of the bath-*stone*."   But in the corresponding part of the Irish text, as given in the first volume (p. 250, ₂₄)—*tre imremim fothraicthe*—it will be observed that the word for " stone " (*cloiche*) does not appear—perhaps a printer's error.   The original manuscript is inaccessible to me : and, as matters stand, this passage teaches us nothing on the point.

† Trip. Life, 101, top line : see also Táin bo Fraich, 165.

‡ Br. Laws, IV. 319.

Small Toilet Articles.—Mirrors of polished metal must have been common from very early times, for they are often mentioned ; generally by one or the other of the two names, *scathán* [skahan] and *scadarc*, this last spelled variously *scaiderc*, *scadarcc*, and the oldest form *scaterc* [all now pron. sky-ark]. The great antiquity of the article is shown by its mention in Zeuss's Glosses (854, 18), where *scaterc* glosses *lucar*, i.e. *speculum*, and where it is derived from *scáth-derc*, 'shadow-seeing,' or a 'shadow see-er.' From *scáth* [skaw], 'a shadow,' is also derived the other name *scathán*, which is merely a diminutive form. In the

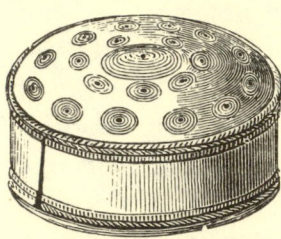

FIG. 228.

A gold box : 2¾ inches across : 1 inch deep. Found in a grave in County Cork. Probably one of the articles of a lady's toilet. (From Wilde's Catalogue, Gold, 84.) .

Senchus Mór, among many household articles, is mentioned a *scadarc*, which is explained by the other word *scathán*; and a man is spoken of as looking into it to see his image (*scáth*).* In the same authority (I., 235, 3 from bottom) the white cloth and " the *nitairic*, i.e. the *scathán* or mirror," are mentioned as among the articles of the toilet : which gives another name for the mirror—*nitairic*. In both these entries certain regulations are laid down against removing the mirror when one is using it, " looking at his image." In the romantic story of the Death of Fergus mac Leide, king of Ulster, we are told that this king was struck with a deformity in his face which he was not aware of, and care was taken that a mirror (*scathán*) should not be left in his way. But one day when he and his queen had a quarrel, she, in her anger, brought him a mirror, in which he saw his face with his mouth all awry.†

Small articles of the toilet, and especially combs, were kept by women in a little bag which they carried about

* Br. Laws, I. 124, 13 ; 125, 17 ; 138, 30 ; 139, 34.
† Silva Gad., 283.

with them, called a *ciorbholg* [keerwolg], *i.e.* ' comb-bag '
(*cíor*, ' a comb ' : *bolg*, ' a bag '). The Book of Aicill lays
down that a woman is exempt from liability in certain cases
of quarrel, if she shows her comb-bag and her distaff (*cuigél*)
in presence of her guardian (Br. Laws, III. 291, top).

2. *Dress.*

Materials.—Woollen and linen clothes formed the dress
of the great mass of the people. Both were produced at
home ; and elsewhere in this book the mode of manufacturing them will be described. Silk and satin, which were
of course imported, were much worn among the higher
classes, and we find both constantly noticed in our literature.
The flags and banners used with armies were usually made
of silk or satin, as we find mentioned in the Book of Rights
and in many of the historic tales. The ordinary word for
silk was *sída* [sheeda] ; but it was also sometimes called
siriac, a word coming from the same origin as the English
silk, and Lat. *sericum* : from which again comes the adjec-
tive *sirecda*, ' silken.' But *siriac* was also occasionally
applied to satin. The common word for satin is *srôll*
[srole], both in the old and in the modern language.

The furs of animals, such as seals, otters, badgers,
foxes, &c., were much used for capes and jackets, and
for the edgings of various garments, so that skins of all
the various kinds were valuable. They formed, too, an
important item of everyday traffic, and they were also
exported.* St. Molaise of Devenish wore a hood of
badgers' skins, which, after his death, was cherished as a
relic, and called the *brocainech* [bruckănăgh], from *broc*, ' a
badger.'† In 1861 a cape was found in a bog at Derry-
keighan in Antrim, six feet beneath the surface, made altogether of otter skins. " The workmanship of the sewing "
—says Mr. Robert Mac Adam, who gives an account of it‡

---

* Wilde, Catalogue, 279.   † Silva Gad., 21, bottom.
‡ In Ulst. Journ. Archæol., IX. 294.

—" is wonderfully beautiful and regular : and the several " parts are joined so as not to disturb the fur, so that from " the outside it looks as if formed of one piece."

In Scotland the tartan is much used—a sort of cloth, generally of wool, sometimes of silk—plaided or cross-barred in various colours. In some English dictionaries the word is conjectured to be derived from the French *teretaine*, which is not a good guess : but both the material and the name originated in Ireland. The original Gaelic name is *tuartan*, as we find it used several times, both in the Senchus Mór, and in the glosses on it, where *tuartan* is defined to be a sort of material " containing cloth of every colour."*

Colours.—Before entering on the particular forms of dress it will be well to say a few words on colours. The ancient Irish loved bright colours. In this respect they resembled many other nations of antiquity—as well indeed as of the present day ; and they illustrated Ruskin's saying (speaking of poppies) :—" Whenever men are noble they " love bright colour, . . . and bright colour is given to " them in sky, sea, flowers, and living creatures." The Irish love of colour expressed itself in all parts of their raiment : and in chapter xxvi. (p. 356), below, it will be shown that they well understood the art of dyeing.

Everywhere in our ancient literature we find dress-colours mentioned. Cahirmore, king of Ireland, saw in his sleep a vision, namely, the daughter of a brewy, with a beauteous form, and every colour in her dress.† Ailill and Maive, king and queen of Connaught in the first century, when showing off their treasures—as related in the " Táin " in the Book of Leinster‡—brought forward their stores of apparel, " purple, blue, black, green, yellow, speckled, grey, brownish-grey, pied, and striped." In the Ulster army, as

---

* Br. Laws, I. 188, ₁₈; 189, ₂₄, ₂₅; 239, ₄.
† Kilk. Archæol. Journ., 1872–3, p. 31.
‡ LL, 54, *a*, ₃₆: Man. & Cust., 90.

described in the Táin, was one company with various-coloured mantles :—" some with red cloaks ; others with " light blue cloaks ; others with deep blue cloaks ; others " with green, or blay, or white, or yellow cloaks, bright and " fluttering about them : and there is a young red-freckled " lad, with a crimson cloak in their midst."*

The king of Tara, as recorded in the Book of Rights, was bound to give, as stipend every year to the provincial king of Emain, who was his subordinate, " twelve suits of clothes of every colour " : and in the same book we often find notices of such articles as a purple cloak, a cloak with purple border, " ten red cloaks and ten blue cloaks."

King Domnall, in the seventh century, on one occasion sent a many-coloured tunic (*inar-ildathach*) to his foster-son Prince Congal† : like Joseph's coat of many colours. The fashion of dyeing a single cloak variously was so usual that we sometimes find it specially mentioned, as a thing worthy of notice, that a man's cloak had only one colour.‡ Colours are also depicted in the few drawings that have come down to us, as for instance in the Book of Kells ; but Dr. Keller is of opinion that no inference can be drawn from these figures as to the hues of the several garments in real life ; for he thinks that the colours are often flung in any way, according to the fancy or caprice of the artist.§ In several of the figures in this same book the upper mantle has a uniform pattern consisting of little spot-clusters about three inches asunder, irregularly placed : each cluster formed of three little white circular spots close together like a shamrock—but not a shamrock. This pattern is seen in the figure of the Evangelist at p. 197, *infra*, and it so often occurs that in this case at least we may conclude it represents a fabric often worn in real life.

* MS. Mat., 38, bot. For another good example, see Rev. Celt., XIV. 413.
† Moyrath, 39.   ‡ Voyage of Bran, p. 72, 19, 20.
§ Ulst. Journ. of Archæol., VIII. 229.

We are told in our legendary history that exact regulations for the wearing of colours by the different ranks of people were made by King Tigernmas [Teernmas] and by his successor, Eochaid Edguthach ('Ochy the cloth-designer'), many centuries before the Christian era :—a slave was to be dressed in clothes of one colour ; a peasant or farmer in two ; and so on up to a king and queen and an ollave of any sort ; all of whom were privileged to wear six (FM, A.M. 3656, 3664). Whatever degree of credence may be accorded to this legend, it is certain that in historic times there was some such arrangement : for the commentator on the Senchus Mór lays down with some detail the colours to be worn by children in fosterage, the clothes of those of kings and high-class chiefs having more varied, brilliant, and costly colours than those of the lower grades.* All people, young and old, wore brightly-coloured clothes, so far as they could afford, or were allowed them : and we may infer from this Brehon Law example that the distribution of colours among various classes of people in ordinary life was subjected to some sort of supervision and regulation.

At the present day green is universally regarded as the national colour : but this is a very modern innovation. It is well known that at the Battle of the Boyne in 1690, the Irish wore little strips of white paper in their caps, while the Williamites wore sprigs of green. In ancient times some colours were preferred to others. Purple, for instance, was a favourite with kings, for no other reason apparently than its great scarcity and expensiveness (for which see p. 363, below). On this account it is now sometimes designated the imperial or royal colour : but its preference had certainly nothing to do with nationality : and as a matter of fact the ancient Irish had no national colour.

* Br. Laws, II. 147, 149

Classification of Upper Garments.—The upper garments worn by men were of a variety of forms and had many names : besides which, fashions of course changed as time went on, though, as I think, very slowly.   Moreover, the several names were often loosely applied, like the English words " coat," " mantle," " frock," &c. ; so that it is often impossible to fix exact limitations.   But the articles themselves were somewhat less vague than their names ; and so far as they can be reduced to order, the upper garments of men may be said to have been mainly of four classes :—

1. A large cloak, generally without sleeves, varying in length, but commonly covering the whole person from the shoulders down.

2. A short tight-fitting coat or jacket with sleeves, but with no collar.

3. A cape for the shoulders, commonly, but not always, carrying a hood to cover the head.

4. A sort of petticoat, the same as the present Highland kilt.   There was nothing to correspond with our waistcoat.

Sometimes only one of those was used, viz. either the outer mantle or the short frock—with of course in all cases the under and nether clothing ; but often two were worn together ; sometimes three ; and occasionally the whole four.

1. **Loose Upper Garment.**—The long cloak assumed many shapes : sometimes it was a formless mantle down to the knees ; but more often it was a loose though shaped cloak reaching to the ankles.   This last was so generally worn by men in out-door life that it was considered characteristic of the Irish.   It had frequently a fringed or shaggy border, round the neck and down the whole way on both edges, in front ; and its material was according to the rank or means of the wearer.   Among the higher classes it was of fine cloth edged with silk or satin or other costly material.   Sometimes the whole cloak was of silk or satin ; and it was commonly dyed in some bright colour, or more

often—as we have said—striped or spotted with several colours. In the numerous figures in the Book of Kells (7th or 8th century) the over-garment is very common : sometimes it is represented full length, but often only as far as the knees or the middle of the thigh.

The large outer garment of whatever material was known by several names, according to shape, of which the most common was *brat* or *bratt*, gen. and pl. *bruit*, dat. *brut* : which appears to have been a general term for any outer garment, and which is still in common use, though somewhat altered in meaning. The word *fallainn* [folling : from Eng. *falding*] was applied to a loose cloak or mantle, reaching about to the knees : but it has nearly dropped out of use. This was the name given to Giraldus Cambrensis by his informant in 1185 : and he gave it the Latin form *phalingium* :—" Under which [*i.e.* under the " hooded cape : see p. 200, *infra*] they wear woollen " *phalingiums* instead of *palliums* or cloaks "* (that is, instead of the long cloaks that Giraldus was accustomed to).

There were other names for a mantle, which evidently point to some difference in material or make. The *lummon* was a cloak or 'wrap' of coarse material. In Peter O'Connell's Dictionary the word is explained " a coarse cover, a large great coat, sackcloth " : and it was sometimes applied to a sack. According to the Dinnsenchus legend, Limerick derived its name from the circumstances that a high tide once flowed over a number of men standing on the brink, and carried off their loose *luimne* or lummons ; whence the place was called *Luimnech*, i.e. a spot full of *lummons*. Mac Conglinne, the *ecclesiastical* student, on his way to the Cork monastery, travels in his cloak, which he calls more than once his " white lumman "†; and in the story of Mongan in LU, a *lay* student is described

---

* Top. Hib., III. x. ; see also Book of Rights, 38, note *f* : and Lynch, Cambr. Ev., II. 201.   † Mac Conglinne, pp. 9, 27; and 25, 15.

as wrapped in his lummon while learning his lesson.*   In Cormac's Glossary (p. 104) the word *lend*, which was in common use for some sort of coat or mantle, is derived in this manner :—" *Lend*, the name for a white *brat* or mantle, from *lee-find*, ' white wool.' "   This entry, and Mac Conglinne's " white lummon," point to the practice, which we know from other sources (vc'. I., p. 343, *supra*) was common enough, of making these coarse garments from undyed wool—the natural colour just as it came from the sheep's back.   If the sheep from which the wool was taken were black, then of course the lummon was black ; and black sheep must have been—at one time at least—very general, for Giraldus says that nearly all the woollen clothes the Irish wore in his time were black, " that being the colour of the sheep in this country " (Top. Hib. III. x.).

The *fuan* or *fuaman* was a loose *brat* or mantle : O'Clery's Glossary explains it as meaning a kind of *brat*. In the " Demon Chariot " Cuculainn is described as wearing a *fuan* of bluish-crimson around him with borders of pure white silver,   The word *matal* was applied to some sort of loose cloak, apparently—as O'Donovan believes†—another name for the *fallainn*.   The term seems borrowed from Norse *mottul*, both words being masculine, and both probably connected with Lat. *mantelum*, the *n* of this dropping out, as usual, in the transfer.   In the Lebar Brecc the garment worn by our Lord is called a *matal*.   The outer garment was called by another name, *tlacht* : " *tlacht*, that is, a *brat* or cloak," says O'Clery's Glossary.   Momera, the Spanish princess, made a *tlacht* or cloak of bright-coloured wool for her intended husband Eoghan Mór, king of Munster.‡   Still another name for the *brat* was *fola*, which is given in O'Clery's and Cormac's Glossaries (Corm. 73).

It was a very common fashion to have, on the loose cloak, five folds or plaits, called in Irish *cóic diabail* :

* Voyage of Bran, I. 54.   † In Book of Rights, p. 38, note *f*.
‡ Moylena, 163.

from *cóic*, five : *diabal*, a plate or fold : *diabul*, duplex (Z., 980, 31). In the story of Laegaire Liban, a warrior is seen emerging from the mist wearing a purple five-fold *brat** : Mac Conglinne's cloak is in one place called *lummon-coic diabalta*, a five-fold *lummon* : while Cuculainn, in the " Courtship of Emer," is described as wearing a beautiful five-fold *fuan* around him. The folds apparently ran across, not lengthwise.

Women wore similar cloaks called by the same names. The woman that was to wait on Mac Conglinne (p. 96, 14) was to have a purple five-fold *bratt* about her : and in the Táin bo Fraich in the Book of Leinster, the fifty women from the *shee* are described as wearing purple tunics (*inar*), green head-dresses, and brooches of silver.† Women often wore a variously-coloured tunic down to the very feet, with many folds and much material—twenty or thirty yards—which was different from the *bratt* and from the hooded cloak mentioned below. Under this was a long gown or kirtle. Linen, whether used by men or women, was commonly dyed saffron. The long cloak worn by women had often a hood attached at top which commonly hung down on the back over the cloak, but which could be turned up so as to cover the head at any moment when wanted. A woman represented on one of the crosses at Clonmacnoise appears with a hooded-cloak of this kind, the hood hanging down behind : and the country-women wear this sort of cloak to the present day all through Ireland.

The loose cloak, of whatever shape or by whatever name called, was almost always fastened at the throat by a brooch. Cloaks in their various forms and with their several names were an important commodity of inter-change, and very often constituted part of the tribute given by or to kings.

* Stokes, Lives of SS., xxxiv
† Tain bo Fr., 149.

It is difficult or impossible to embrace all varieties of clothing in any formal classification : and as a matter of fact there was another article of full-covering dress worn in very early times by both men and women, hardly included in any of the preceding descriptions. In the Book of Kells (7th or 8th century) a large number of the figures, both of men and women, have the usual

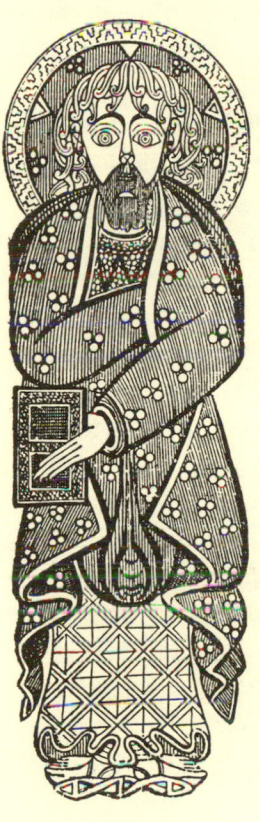

FIG. 229.   FIG. 230.

Figure 229, representation of an Angel. (From the Book of Kells : Dr. Abbott's Reproductions, Plate XIV.)
Figure 230, representation of one of the Evangelists. (From same, Plate XVIII.)

outside mantle generally reaching to about the knees, and under it a long narrow garment like a petticoat (but not a kilt), from the shoulders down to the insteps, widening towards the bottom, yet so narrow that it would obviously interfere with the free movement of the feet in quick walking. I do not find this mentioned in the written records anywhere—at least so as to be recognisable ; but it is depicted so often in the Book of Kells that it must have been in general use. It is quite conspicuous on the Blessed Virgin and on the Infant Jesus, on angels and evangelists, on our Lord in the representation of His arrest, and on the two soldiers who are in the act of arresting Him.*   It is well shown here in figs. 229 and 230, both from the Book of Kells.

Distinct apparently from the preceding over-mantles was the loose-flowing tunic—worn over all—usually of linen dyed saffron, commonly called *léine* [2-syll.], which was in very general use and worn by men and women in outdoor life. This is noticed by Spenser (p. 102) as prevalent in his time. It had many folds and plaits and much material—sometimes as much as thirty yards ; so that in later times the Anglo-Irish Parliaments made laws forbidding the use of more than a certain quantity of stuff. It has been already remarked that the Irish generally wore this garment in battle. It seems to have been the *lend-brat* which the royal army are described as wearing in the Battle of Moyrath (p. 181, note *c*), intermediate between the loose *brat* and the close-fitting *lend* : made not too loose to impede the action of the limbs in fighting, with probably a waistbelt. Part of the Boroma tribute consisted of " three times-fifty hundred *lend-brats*." The saffron-tunic was used in the Hebrides down to the time of Martin : there it took twenty-four ells of material. It was he says, called *leni-croich*, because it was dyed with the *croch* or saffron-plant ; and when worn it was tied round the waist with a belt.

The outer covering of the general run of the peasantry was just one loose sleeved coat or mantle, generally of frieze, which covered them down to the ankles ; and which they wore winter and summer. This is the garment that

* Hodges & Figgis's Reproductions, Plates XXVII., XXVIII., XXXI., XLI., XLII., L.

drew from Spenser (View, 87) the well-known denunciation that stands to this day an astonishing example of blind irrational prejudice and intolerance. Here are a few extracts; which are applied, be it remembered, to an ordinary everyday garment, worn with no more malignant intentions than are our present overcoats :—

> "It is a fit house for an outlaw, a meet bed for a rebel, and an apt cloke for a theife. First the outlaw being for his many crimes and villanyes banished from the townes and houses of honest men, maketh his mantle his house, and under it covereth himselfe from the wrath of heaven, from the offence of the earth, and from the sight of men. . . . Likewise for a rebell it is as serviceable. For in his warre, when he still flyeth from his foe, and lurketh in thicke woods and straite passages, it is his bed, yea and almost his household stuff. . . . Lastly for a theife it is so handsome [convenient] as it may seem it was first invented for him, for under it he may clearly convey any fit pillage that cometh handsomely in his way. Besides this, he, or any men els that is disposed to mischief or villany, may under his mantle goe privily armed without suspicion of any, carry his head-piece, his skean [dagger], or pistol if he please, to be always in readiness."

And so he continues, throwing in a passage about the uses to which women turned it, that could not well be reproduced her.

2. **Tight-fitting Upper Garments.**—The tight-fitting sleeved upper garment was something like the present frock-coat ; but it had no collar, and was much shorter, usually reaching to about the middle of the thigh, and often only a little below the hips ; with a girdle at the waist. It was generally called by one or another of three names :—*lenn* or *lend, inar,* and *léine, léne,* or *léinid* : but *léine* was also applied to a shirt, as well as to the saffron-dyed loose tunic. Persons are very often described as wearing this short coat with a *brat* or mantle over it : as for example in the Bruden Da Derga.* Cuculainn's charioteer wore a tight

---

* O'Curry, Man. & Cust., 147, note 218 : LU, 95, *a*, ₃ and ₄

inar of leather, over which was a *for-brat* (' over-brat ') or loose mantle.* Sometimes the tight coat was fastened at the throat with a brooch like the loose over-cloak. But *lend*, like many other terms for garments, was often used vaguely. The short coat is very well represented in the figures given below, which, however, belong to a comparatively late time, but serve to show how this garment held on in fashion.

A sleeve, no matter to what article of dress it belonged was denoted by two names :— *lamos* and *munchille*, both

Fig. 231.

Figures carved on a bone book-cover, Now in National Museum. Probably of the thirteenth or fourteenth century. "Five figures"—says Wilde—"engaged in some sort of game. . . . The external figures are represented in the act of throwing rings or quoits." The tight-fitting *inar* or jerkin well represented here: with striped sleeves and plaited skirts: confined by a waist-belt: all probably parti-coloured. (From Wilde's Catalogue, p. 320.)

given in Cormac's Glossary (pp. 100, 116). He derives *lamos* from *lam-fhoss*, the *foss* or case of the *lam* or arm. The other word he derives from *man*, the hand, and *cail*, a case : *mun-chille*, equivalent to *man-cail*, ' hand- or arm-keeper.' *Muinchille* is the present Irish word for a sleeve.

3. **Cape and Hood.**—The short cape, with or without a hood, was called *cuchull* or *cocholl*, corresponding in shape and name with the Gallo-Roman *cucullus*, English *cowl* :

* Kilk. Archæol. Journ., 1870–71, p. 423, 5, 8, 36, 40 : LU, 79, *a*, top line and those that follow.

but this English word *cowl* is now often applied to a hood simply. The *cochull* just covered the shoulders : and it is quite usual to find in the tales persons described as wearing " a short *cochull* reaching as far as the elbows."* Sometimes in old writings the diminutive *cochline* [3-syll.], " little *cochull*," is used. Cuculainn wears a *cochline ettach immi con urslocud for a dib n-ulendib*,† " a winged cochline about him with openings at the two elbows." Here the word *ettach*

FIG. 232.

Meeting of Mac Murrogh Kavanagh and the Earl of Gloucester in 1399. (From an illuminated contemporary English manuscript. Reproduced in Gilbert's Facsim. National Manuscripts, from which this illustration was copied.) The English appear on the left-hand side.

' winged,' refers to the loose extremities of the sleeves flying open at the elbows, where they terminated. Both cape and hood were dyed in colours: Giraldus says that in his time they were made with variously-coloured pieces of cloth sewed together. The hood was called *cenniud* [ken-yŭ], from *cenn*, the head ; or more usually *culpait*. It covered the whole head except the face. The followers of Art mac Murrogh Kavanagh‡ (fourteenth

* Man. & Cust., 138, 16 : Da Derga, 181 : Rev. Celt., XII. 87.
† LU, 122, *b*, 28, 29 : Demon Chariot, 376, last line ; 379, top line.
‡ For whom see Joyce's Short History of Ireland, p. 323.

century) are shown wearing these odd-looking hoods : and
it is worthy of remark that the English standing beside
them wear head-dresses and capes not very different.
This hood was generally attached to the cowl or cape so
as to form part of it ; as appears clear from the following
examples. In the Bruden Da Derga, Ingcel, describing
certain persons that he saw among many others in Da
Derga's hostel, says that each wore a little *cochall* or cape,
and a white hood (*cenniud*) on each cape, and a red tuft
(*cuirce*, pron. cur-kĕ) on each *cenniud*, and an iron brooch
in each *cochull** [fastening it at the throat in front].
The three Pictish kings who were in the same hostel
are described by Ingcel as having each a short black *cowl*
with a long hood on it† ; and again he says, about three
others, that they wore three short black capes reaching
to the elbows, and hoods on the capes. This fashion
continued long, for we find it mentioned in the story of
O'Donnell's kern as in use in the fifteenth century.‡ In
this same century, too, the hood was sometimes worn in
the Scottish Highlands.§ Still later, Thomas Dineley
(in 1675) observed that the men, in parts of Ireland,
covered their heads with their cloaks.|| *Cochall* is now
applied, as anciently, to any short cape covering the
shoulders.

The word *cochall*, like many other terms designating
articles of dress, in ancient as well as in modern times,
was often used loosely. It was applied to a monk's cowl :
and the chasuble worn by a priest was sometimes called a
" *cassal* or *cochall*."¶ We know that the long leathern
cloaks, reaching down to the feet, worn by the soldiers of
Murkertagh mac Neill during his celebrated circuit through
Ireland in the winter of A.D. 941, were called by this name,

* Man. & Cust., II. 150, top paragraph.   † Stokes, Da Derga, 181.
‡ Silva Gad., 315, top line : Irish Text, 279, ₁₀.
§ Rob Roy, Introduction. || Kilk. Archæol. Journ., 1856–7, p. 186.
¶ Trip. Life, 384, ₄: 399, ₂₃; LB, " Contents," p. 6, bottom.

whence he is known in history as *Muirchertach na g-cochall g-croicenn*, i.e. ' of the leathern *cochalls* or cloaks.'* The fact that these long cloaks were called *cochalls* renders it pretty certain that they were furnished with hoods to protect the head ; a thing we might expect under the circumstances.

4. **The Kilt.**—The Gaelic form of this name is *celt* [kelt], of which " kilt " is a phonetic rendering. In Cormac's Glossary (p. 47) *celt* is vaguely explained by the Latin *vesta*, and also by the Irish *edach*, ' raiment ': and in another old authority quoted by O'Donovan in his translation, it is said to be " anything used as a protection." This seems nearest to its primary meaning : for *celt* means ' concealing.' The word occurs so seldom, and is used so vaguely, that we might find it difficult to identify the particular article it designates, if the Scotch had not retained both the article itself and its name : for the Highland kilt is the ancient Irish *celt*. In Ireland the garment itself was very common, though it was seldom called a *celt*. On one of the panels of Muiredach's cross at Monasterboice are represented three soldiers dressed in kilts reaching to the knees† : and all the figures on the shrine of St. Manchan—a work of about the eleventh century—are similarly attired—the kilts here being very decided and characteristic, as well as highly ornamented.‡ The kilt—commonly falling to the knees—is very frequently met with on the figures of manuscripts, shrines, and crosses, so that it must have been very much worn both by ecclesiastics and laymen. The kilt and the *bratt* outside it are seen in some of the figures of the illustration in vol. I., p. 59, where also, as in all other representations, the plaits run up and down, like what we see at the present day. The present Highland article of dress is called *kilt*

* Joyce, Short History of Ireland, pp. 197, 198.
† Kilk. Archæol. Journ., 1872, p. 109, 1a.
‡ See on this shrine Stokes's Petrie, 285.

everywhere except among the Highlanders themselves, whc usually designate it by another Gaelic term, *filleadh*, or more generally *filleadh-beg* ('little garment'), anglicised *philibeg*.

FIG. 233.

The figures on one face of the shrine of St. Manchan (for which see vol I., p. 564, *supra*): dating from about the eleventh century. They all represent laymen, and they diminish in size to the right to suit the shape of the panel. (From Kilk. Archæol. Journ. for 1874-5, p. 145.)

In the story of the Táin we read that one of the games in which the boys of Emain contended was tearing off each other's outer garments—truly a rough play. The little boy Cuculainn entered the field against a number of them, and while they were not able even to disturb his

brooch, he tore off the *de-chelt* from a number of them.*
This *de-chelt* or ' double celt ' was a loose jacket and *celt*
combined, as it is defined in Cormac's Glossary (p. 47) :—
" *Dechelt,* that is to say, a *brat* and a *leine* " [joined] :
whereas the *celt* proper extended only from the waist
down.

In several passages of the Bruden Da Derga persons
are described as wearing *berbróca,* a term which both
O'Curry and Stokes translate aprons : though Stokes in
one place—and only one (Da Derga, p. 57)—makes it
' drawers '—apparently on the authority of Zimmer.   The
word is always used in LU in the plural number—*berr-
bróca* : but whether the singular is the same, or *berbróc,* is
at present uncertain.   The name of the article seems to
indicate that it was an apron—or possibly some special
sort of kilt—reaching down to the *bróca* or shoes.   For
berr means to shave : *berr-bróca,* ' shave-brogues,' because
it just brushed them with its lower hem : exactly as the
word *tond,* ' a wave,' is said in Cormac's Glossary (p. 161)
to be derived from *tondeo,* ' I shave,' " because it *shaves*
[*berrad*] the grass from off the sea-marsh," where, it will be
observed, the same Irish word (*berr*) is used.†

Of the four upper garments hitherto mentioned,
Giraldus (A.D. 1185) notices two :—the *cochall* and the
fallainn, with the trousers (to be presently dealt with
here).   He says :—" It is their custom to wear small
" tightly-fitting hoods (*caputium* is the word he uses)
" hanging the length of a cubit below the shoulders [*i.e.*
" the cape to which the hood was attached hung so far]
" and generally made of variously coloured-strips sewn
" together."‡   Three of them are mentioned in an ancient

* Miss Hull, Cuch. Saga, 139 : LL. 63, *a*, 6 from bottom : Kuno
Meyer, Ventry, 83, 1.

† On *berr-broca* see O'Curry, Man. & Cust., II. 147 (twice), 148, 149,
183 : and Stokes, Da Derga, 57, 289, 309.   Several of the original
passages where the word is used will be found in pp. 94, 95, of LU.

‡ Top. Hib., III. x. : Book of Rights, 38, note *f*.

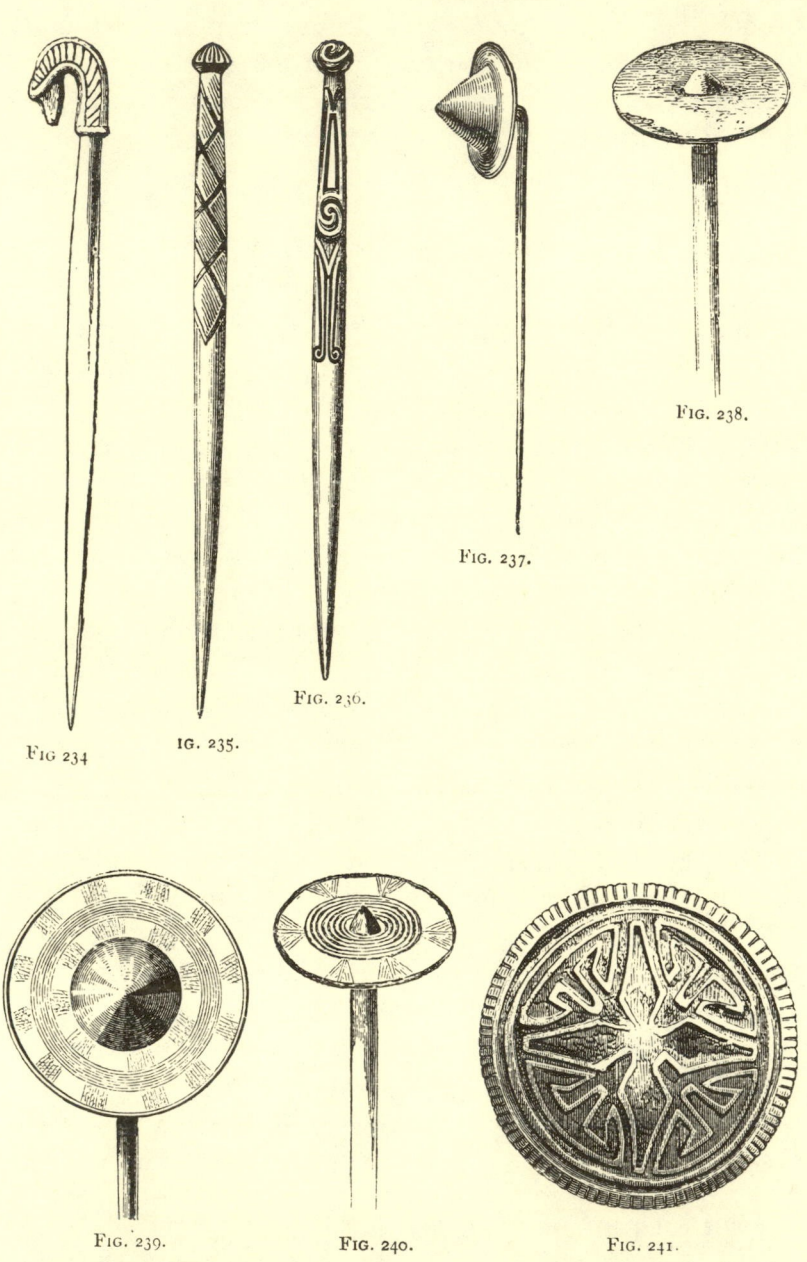

FIG. 238.

FIG. 237.

FIG. 236.

FIG 234

IG. 235.

FIG. 239.

FIG. 240.

FIG. 241.

Bronze pins and button: all very ancient. Figures 234, 235, and 236, drawn natural size. Those with circular disk-heads are generally very long: figure 240 is 13½ inches, with a disk 2¾ inches in diameter Figure 241, drawn natural size, a highly-decorated bronze button, enamelled in red and green, with a a small metal fastening-loop behind. (All from Wilde's Catalogue. pp. 555, 557, 558, 572.)

Irish poem copied at Armagh in 1139 by Mael-Brigte hua Mael-Uanaig, noticed by Stokes,* which states that on each of the Magi who came to visit the Infant Jesus were three [upper] garments (*tri-etaige im cach fer dib* : " three garments round each man of them "). The three were no doubt the cape with hood, the loose cloak, and the short tight-fitting coat (with of course the nether garment to correspond) : the Irish writer attributing to outsiders the fashion of his native country.

Fasteners for Upper Garments.—The over-garments were fastened by brooches, pins, buttons, girdles, strings, and loops. Brooches will be treated of next section. Simple pins were generally ornamented, head, or shank, or both, as seen in the annexed figures, of which the originals are all in the National Museum, with many others.

Nether Garments.—The ancient Irish wore a trousers which differed in some respects from that worn at the present day. It generally reached from the hips to the ankles, and was so tight-fitting as to show perfectly the shape of the limbs. When terminating at the angles it was held down by a slender strap passing under the foot, as seen in one of the figures in the Book of Kells.† Like other Irish garments it was generally striped or speckled in various colours. The usual Irish name was *triubhas* [truce], which is often correctly anglicised *trews*, and from which the modern word " trousers " is derived. The people of other ancient nations wore parti-coloured trousers as well as the Irish ; the Gauls and Britons for example ; among whom it was called *braccae*. The Romans saw this article of dress in general use for the first time among the Gauls : so that they gave the name *Gallia Braccata* to a part of Transalpine Gaul. It would seem, that the Irish and British trousers were also called *braccae*,‡ from which

* In Rev. Celt., VIII. 346.   † Abbott's Reproductions, Plate I.
‡ Ware, Antiqq., 176 : Lynch, Cambr. Ev., II. 213 : De Jubainville, Cours, Litt. Celt., VI. 371, 372

comes the modern word *breeches* : and which, as some think, is itself derived from the Celtic *brecc*, speckled.

In the time of Giraldus Cambrensis, the Irish trousers, hose, and shoes were all one garment :—" The Irish "—he writes—" wear breeches ending in shoes, or shoes ending in breeches "* : a fashion also described by Lynch in his " Cambrensis Eversus " (II. 209) :—" The breeches used by " the Irish was a long garment, not cut off at the knees, " but combining in itself the sandals, the " stocking, and the drawers, and drawn " by one pull over the feet and thighs. " It was not flowing (to use the words of " Tacitus), but tight, and revealing the " shapes of the limbs : not " unlike what Sidonius " describes :—

' A closely-fitting dress their limbs compresses,
No trailing robe their legs conceals.' "

Fig. 242.

Showing the tight trews or trousers, with a *fallainn* or short cloak, dyed olive-green. (From an illuminated copy of Giraldus of A.D. 1200. From Wilde's Catalogue, p. 311.)

This fashion continued in use to the time of Lynch, who tells us (II. 211) that the people generally abandoned it before 1641, partly in consequence of the exhortation of the clergy—which implies that that part of the Irish dress bordered on indelicacy—and partly of their own accord. But I do not find any statement that this combined garment was used in very early ages. It may be worth mentioning that there was an old canon of the Irish church, which is still extant, forbidding the clergy to wear those close-fitting trousers. The figures on the shrine of St. Manchan (p. 204, *supra*) have no trousers : but they wear long kilts reaching below the knees, with legs and feet bare.

* Top. Hib. III. x.

The trousers, as has been said, usually went below the ankles. But in some figures on the high crosses it terminates immediately below the knee, like the Irish knee-breeches of our own day : and two of the figures of the S.-E. cross of Monasterboice wear breeches terminating just above the knees, where they are closely bound, and fitting skin-tight on the thighs.

Leggings of cloth, or of thin soft leather, were worn, probably as an accompaniment to the kilt. They were called *ochra* or *ochrath*. In " Mac Conglinne's Vision " (88) a person is mentioned as having " *ochra* encircling his shins." It will be observed that this word *ochra* is almost identical with the Latin term *ocrea* applied by the Romans to *their* leggings. The Irish leggings were laced on by strings tipped with *findruine* or white bronze, the bright metallic extremities falling down after lacing, so as to form pendent ornaments. Bove Derg's cavalcade had all of them strings [with tips] of *findruine* hanging from their *ochraths*.* The *ochra* reached about to the ankle : for in a passage in one of the ancient Gaelic Triads it is mentioned that there was a *bas* or handbreadth between the shoe and the lower edge of the *ochrath*.†

I think it likely that the trousers and kilt were not worn together : at least in all the kilted figures that have come down to us the legs are bare. As bearing on this point it is worthy of remark that there are many passages in our ancient literature showing that it was pretty usual with those engaged in war to leave the legs naked : a fashion perpetuated by the Scotch to this day. In the ancient account of the battle of Mucrime (fought A.D. 250) the jester Dodera says to Maccon, the leader of one side :—
" Eoghan [one of the leaders of the opposing army] will
" seek thee through the battle, and if he catch sight of thy
" legs [*colptha*, legs or calves] he will strike thee down."‡

* O'Curry, Man. & Cust., II. 157.　　　　　† *Ibid.*, 107.
‡ Silva Gad., 350 : Rev. Celt., XIII. 441.

And a little farther on we are told that " through the host
" Eoghan saw Maccon's two calves which were as white as
" the snow of one night "—the whiteness being noticed as
a matter deserving praise.

That it was customary to leave the legs naked is also
shown by such personal names—or nicknames—as Niall
Glúnduff (black-knee) which was the name of a brave king

FIG. 243.

Group showing arms and costumes of the sixteenth century. Irish soldiers and
peasants, from a drawing by Albert Durer in 1521, preserved at Vienna. Over the
two soldiers is an inscription in German: " Here go the war-men of Ireland beyond
England." Over the three peasants: " Here go the poor men of Ireland beyond
England." Between the two is the date A.D. 1521. (From Kilk. Archæol. Journ.,
1877, p. 296, where the original drawing is reproduced.)

of Ireland (A.D. 916–919) : Amergin Glúngel, of the white
knee (*gel*, white) ; Brocshalach Crion-Ghlúinech,* of the
withered knee ; Irial Glúnmár (big-knee)† : Glún-iarainn
(iron-knee). Eber Glúnfhind was so called—says the
Book of Lecan—" because he had white marks on his
knee " (*find*, white).‡   Scott gives a corresponding explanation of the cognomen of one of the Mac Gregors of
Scotland of two centuries ago, " Gregor Ghlune Dhu, Black

* Silva Gad., 527, top line : Rev. Celt., XVI. 273.
† Rev. Celt., XVI. 411.
                                        ‡ Ir. Texte, III. 409.

" Knee, from a black spot on one of his knees, which his
" Highland garb rendered visible," like Nial Glúnduff.*
It was considered a blemish to have dark-coloured knees,
as we see from a passage where it is said of a splendid-
looking young man, that his dark-coloured knee was his
only blemish. On the other hand, to have white legs
and knees was considered a
point of beauty, as in case of
Lugaid Maccon mentioned
last page.

As illustrative of all that
precedes, two series of costumes of the years 1521 and
1600 respectively are presented here : pp. 210, 211.

FIG. 244.

FIG. 245.　　　　　　　FIG. 246.

Irish Costumes, A.D. 1600. (From map of Ireland published by Speed in 1611.) Figure 244,
gentleman and lady of the high classes. Figure 245, persons of the middle rank. Figure 246,
peasants (Speed, after the fashion of Englishmen of the time, calls them " wilde Irish.")

Underclothing.—Both men and women wore a garment
of fine texture next the skin. This is constantly mentioned
in the tales, and, whether for men or women, is denoted by
the word *léine* or *léne* [2-syll.], which is now the common
Irish word for a shirt. It was usually made of wool or
flax. It is said of St. Columkille that—by way of morti-
fication—he never wore linen or wool next his skin.† But
sometimes it was made of silk, occasionally of satin, highly

* Rob Roy, Introduction.　　　　† Three Irish Homilies, 123.

ornamented. One party of Queen Maive's forces wore " pure-white shirts [*lénti glegela*] next their skin "* : and such expressions are very common. Sometimes a silken shirt was shot with threads of gold. In the Battle of Moylena, (p. 129) the hero Fraech Mileasach who was surprised sleeping in his tent, started up and had to fight for life in his " shirt of many devices ornamented with threads of gold." Very often the shirt is called *caimse*, a word which in Cormac's Glossary (p. 33) is derived from the Latin *camisia*. All these notices about shirts refer to the higher classes : whether the lower order of people wore shirts is a matter on which I have found no information.

Girdles and Garters.—A girdle or belt (Ir. *criss*) was commonly worn round the waist, inside the outer loose mantle, and it was often made in such a way as to serve as a pocket for carrying small articles. We read in the Tripartite Life that on one occasion St. Patrick met six young clerical students having their books in their *crisses* or girdles. Sometimes a *bossan* or purse (also called *sparán*) was hung from the girdle, in which small articles were kept, such as rings.† The girdles of chiefs and other high-class people were often elaborately ornamented and very valuable. In the Brehon Law the value of a *bo-aire* chief's girdle is set down as three *séds* or cows, which might represent £40 or £50 of our present money : and those of higher chiefs and kings were still more costly.‡

Garters were worn, sometimes for use, and sometimes for mere ornament, or to serve both purposes. There are two words for a garter, *ferenn* and *id* ; and the use of the article is made quite clear by the explanation given in Cormac's Glossary (p. 72) :—" *Ferenn*, a garter (*id*) which is round a man's calf." Cormac goes on to say that the

---

* Miss Hull : Cuch. Saga, 119 : LL., 55, *a*, bottom, and *b*, top.
† Kuno Meyer, in Rev. Celt., XII. 460 : LL, 250, *a*, 23, 24.
‡ Br. Laws v. 417.

ferenn was made of different materials according to the rank of the wearer, and he instances the garter of a king as made of gold. This agrees with an expression in an ancient panegyric written on the hero Couri mac Dáire, king of South Munster in the first century, in which it is stated that he gave his bard, among other valuable presents, garters of gold.* But this word *ferenn* was also used, according to Cormac, to denote a girdle :—" *Ferenn* " —he says—" is also a name for a girdle (*criss*) that is round the man " : and he gives as an instance " the snow reached the men's girdles " (*ferna*), referring to the snow the druids brought down by magic in their contest with St. Patrick at Tara. The Tripartite Life relates this incident fully, which bears out the correctness of Cormac's reference : the expression used in the Tripartite being *cotoracht* [*in snuchta*] *fernu fer,* " so that [the snow] reached the *ferna* or girdles of the men."†

Gloves.—That gloves were commonly worn is proved by many ancient passages and indirect references. The common word for a glove was *lámann* or *láminn*, from *lám* [lauv], ' the hand or arm ') ; which is the word still in use. Cormac (p. 100) clearly defines *laminn*, when he derives the word from *láim-inn*, i.e. ' arm-end,' because— as he says—" the end of the arm is clothed by it." And in the mediæval tract on Latin declension, edited by Stokes (p. 4, No. 34), the meaning is made equally clear, where *lámann* glosses the Greek word " chirotheka." Sometimes the word used was *lamagan*, which is a diminutive form. Another word for a glove was *braccaile*, which Cormac's Glossary (p. 19) also explains :—[From] " *bracc*, a hand, and *cail*, a case [a case for the hand], i.e. a *lamann* or glove " : exactly corresponding with the Greek word given above, *chirotheka*, ' hand-case.'

We often find notices of people wearing gloves. In one passage of the old tale called the Acallamh it is

* O'Curry, Man. & Cust., II. 152   † Trip. Life, 56, line 2.

incidentally mentioned that two persons closing a contract by joining hands had first to remove their gloves, showing how usual it was to wear them in common life (see vol. I., p. 182, *supra*). In the " Vision of Mac Conglinne " (p. 90), an imaginary personage is spoken of as having " two glove on his hands " (*cona di lámainn bá lamaib*). St. Patrick, when traversing the country in his chariot, wore gloves when necessary.*

They appear to have been common among all classes— poor as well as rich. One of the good works of charity laid down in the Senchus Mór is " sheltering the miserable," which the gloss explains, " to give them staves and gloves and shoes (*lorga, lamanna, cuaraind*) for God's sake."† The evangelist depicted in the Book of Kells (fig. 230, p. 197, *supra*) wears gloves, with the fingers divided as in our present glove, and having the tops lengthened out beyond the natural fingers.

Sometimes gloves were highly ornamented. In the Voyage of Maildune we are told that a certain lady in one of the islands visited by the voyagers, wore gloves on her hands " with gold embroidery " (*lámanna co n-órphill imma lámaib*).‡ Besides the two names already given for gloves, there were two others, which appear to be very old words :— *Bracand*, which is given in Cormac's Glossary (p. 27), and derived from *brac*, a hand : and *mana ma* in O'Clery's Glossary (from *man*, a hand : Corm. 108) : both which the glossaries explain as meaning gloves.

As to material : probably gloves were made, as at present, both of cloth and of animal skins and furs. We have an example of this last, where gloves were on one occasion made from part of a fur mantle worn by St. Molaise of Devenish.§ The importance and general use of gloves as an article of dress are to some extent indicated by their frequent mention and by the number of names for them.

---

* Trip. Life, 295, ₉. ‡ Rev. Celt., x. 65.
† Br. Laws, III. 19. § Silva Gad., 33.

Head Gear.—The men wore a hat of a conical shape, without a leaf, called a *barréd* [barraid], a native word, of which the first syllable, *barr*, signifies top, and according to some, the second, *éd*, is from the Irish *éda*, dress ; in which case *barréd* would mean ' head-dress ' or " head cover.' But the word exists in several other languages, as French, *barrette* ; Spanish, *birreta* ; Italian, *berretta* ; and German, *pirete* ; all meaning a head-covering of some kind : which makes one doubt that the second syllable of the old Irish name is from *éda*. The word *at* also occurs in Old Irish documents for a head-covering, and of course is the same as the English *hat*, both derived from Norse *hattr* : but *at* has several other meanings in Irish which will be referred to farther on (p. 240).* The helmet and its designations have been treated of under " Warfare."

Among the peasantry, the men, in their daily life, commonly went bare-headed, wearing the hair long behind so as to hang down on the back, and clipped short in front. Sometimes men, even in military service, when not engaged in actual warfare, went bare-headed in this manner. In the panels of one of the crosses at Clonmacnoise are figures of several soldiers : and while some have conical caps, others are bare-headed. Camden describes Shane O'Neill's galloglasses, as they appeared at the English court in the sixteenth century, as having their heads bare, their long hair curling down on the shoulders and clipped short in front just above the eyes.†

Married women usually had the head covered either with a hood (*caille*, pron. cal-lĕ) or with a long web of linen wreathed round the head in several folds. This last is probably what was designated in ancient writings by the word *callad* [cal-la] : a term different from *caille*, though no doubt derived from the same root. In the Feast of Dun-nan-gedh it is related that a certain queen cried

* See also Ware, Antiqq., 177.
† See Joyce, Short History of Ireland, p. 409.

aloud in a fit of grief, and wrung her hands, " and cast her royal *callad* into the fire in presence of all." This word is now obsolete in Ireland, though it is retained in Scotch Gaelic to signify a cap or wig. But the other word *caille* is still used in Ireland for a hood or veil, from which again comes *caillech* (the veiled or hooded one), a nun : a different word from *caillech*, an old woman. It should be remarked that the veil was in constant use among the higher classes, and when not actually worn was usually carried, among other small articles, in a lady's ornamental hand-bag.

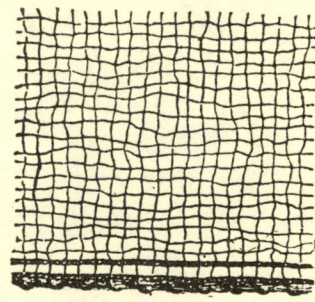

FIG. 247.

Portion of "a light gauzy woollen veil, of the most delicate texture" (Wilde). Found on the body of the woman mentioned at p. 180, *supra*. From Proc. Roy. Ir. Acad., IX. 103.)

There was another word for a woman's head-covering—*meli*—which had grown old in the ninth century, and which in Cormac's Glossary (page 120) is explained by *cop-cailli*, a woman's hood. The head-dress of a woman was also sometimes called *cenn-barr* ('head-top') as in the Táin bo Fraich (p. 148, 20) : and in a Gloss on a portion of the Brehon Laws (IV. 28, 22) it is called *cenbar no caille*—'head-dress or head-veil.'

Foot-Wear.—The most general term for a shoe was *bróc, brócc,* or *bróg* (plural *bróga*), which was applied to a shoe of any kind : it is still the word in common use, and it is correctly perpetuated in sound by the well-known Hiberno-English word *brogue*. The *bróg* was very often made of untanned hide, or only half-tanned, free from hair, and retaining softness and pliability like the raw hide. This sort of shoe was also often called *cuarán* or *cuaróg*, from which a brogue-maker was called *cuaránaidhe* [cooraunee]. A fox once stole St. Ciaran's brogues and proceeded to make a meal of them ; but was caught just when he had eaten the ears and thongs : these must have

been of untanned hide.*   Shoes of untanned hide are worn
to this day in the Aran Islands.   Mac Conglinne (p. 8),
before beginning his journey to Cork, made for himself two
pointed *cuarans* of " brown leather " of seven doubles—
meaning seven folds or layers of hide in the sole—for his

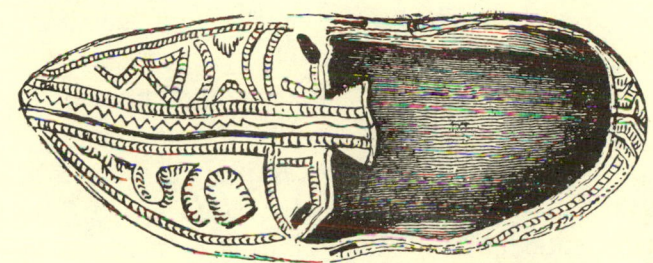

FIG. 248.

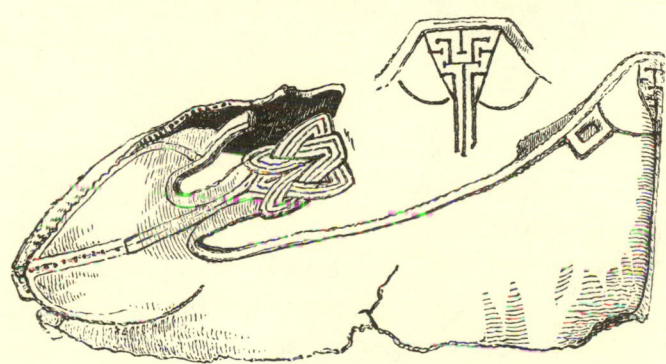

FIG. 249.

Ancient Irish shoes, of tanned leather, in National Museum, Dublin. **Figure 248** is a complete
shoe, formed of a single piece.   **Figure 249** represents the upper only: it had **a** separate sole,
which is gone: the ornament at top is a separate figure, and is merely an enlargement of the
decoration at the top of the heel.   The *opus Hibernicum* on the strap in the middle of this shoe
betokens Christian origin but great antiquity.   (From Wilde's Catalogue, p. 284.)

long walk.   When he arrived at the guest-house of the
Cork monastery he took off his *cuarans*, and having washed
his feet in the bath-tub, he next washed the shoes in it—
the usual plan of cleaning the mud off shoes of this kind.
The *cuaran* had generally a single sole ; but sometimes
two or more thicknesses were used, as we see in the case

* O'Grady, Silva Gad., 3, bottom.

of Mac Conglinne. This shoe had no lift under the heel. The whole shoe was stitched together with thongs cut from the same hide.*

There are two other words for a shoe common in ancient writings, *as* or *ass* and *maelan* : but these appear to have been applied to a more shapely shoe than the *cuaran* ; made of fully tanned leather, and furnished with a serviceable sole and heels. Many passages could be quoted showing that shoes were made of tanned leather : but the subject of tanning will be taken up again in chapter xxvi., p. 367. One example will suffice here :— We find it related that on one occasion St. Molaise gave some students, among other articles of clothing, " thick bark-soaked *brogues* as if of tanner's leather."† Most of the shoes preserved in the National Museum are of tanned leather : but some are of untanned hide.‡

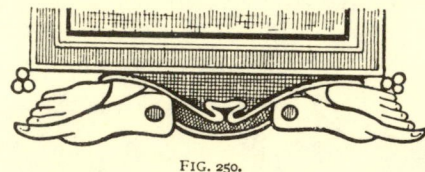

FIG. 250.

Small portion of a panel, showing the sandals under the feet, with the rosettes.   (From Book of Kells: Dr. Abbott's Reproductions, Plate XXXIV.)

Maelan is a diminutive of *mael*, blunt, and means a shoe or sandal with a wide rounded top—not pointed. A shoe of this shape is sometimes called *ass* or *as* (pl. *assa*, *assai*) and occasionally we find *mael-assa*, i.e. blunt-topped *assa* or shoes. Another compound of this word applied to a shoe is *folasai*, which is given in Cormac's Glossary (p. 76) : and O'Clery gives *folasa* as equivalent to " shoes." A shoe was also sometimes called *iallachran* (*iall-acrann*, ' thong-shoe ') which in O'Clery's Glossary is given as equivalent to *broga*, i.e. shoes. Still another name for a shoe, according to O'Clery's Glossary, was *foirtchi*, connected with *fortcha*, clothing of any kind.

Most of the figures depicted in the Book of Kells and on the shrines and high crosses have shoes or sandals,

* See Ware, Antiqq., 178.   † Silva Gad., 33.
‡ Wilde, Catalogue, 280.

though some have the feet bare. One wears well-shaped narrow-toed shoes seamed down along the instep, something like the shoes here represented (figs. 248, 249), but much finer and more shapely. Some have sandals consisting merely of a sole bound on by straps running over the foot : and in all such cases the naked toes are seen. On many of the sandals there are what appear to be little circular rosettes just under or on the ankles, one on each side of the foot—perhaps mere ornaments. They are seen in the figure of the angel, p. 197, *supra* ; and more plainly in fig. 250 on the opposite page, both from the Book of Kells.

From a passage in the story of Da Derga's Hostel (p. 189) we may infer that the shoes or sandals were often fastened to the feet by two or three or more straps across the instep. In this passage the sandals (*bróic*) of a gigantic warrior are compared to two *currachs* or hide-boats, each with five thwarts or cross-benches, referring evidently to the five fastening straps : a record which, as we see, is corroborated by the figures in the manuscripts and on the crosses. The shoes of the higher classes were often highly and beautifully ornamented ; as we know, partly from the records, and partly from the specimens preserved in museums : as illustrated in figures 248, 249, and 251.

In the tales we often find it mentioned that persons wore *assa* or *maelassa* or sandals of silver or of *findruine* (white bronze). On one of the islands visited by Maildune and his people they see a lady richly dressed approaching them, with two sandals (*da maelan*) of silver on her feet.* Dermot, king of Ireland (A.D. 656–664), saw a lady in a chariot with two pointless shoes (*da maelassa*) of white bronze on her feet† : and any number of such references might be given. Such sandals must have been worn only on special or formal occasions : as they would be so inconvenient as to be practically useless in real everyday

* Rev. Celt., IX. 491 ; and XXIV. 129, 10.   † O'Curry, Man. & Cust., II. 160

life. This seems also to be indicated by the fact that in at least one shoe—namely that of which measurements are given below—the sole was fastened on by leaden solder, and would at once give way under any rough usage, such as walking. As confirming this idea of temporary and exceptional use, we have in the Museum a curious pair of (ordinary leather) shoes—shown in the illustration—connected permanently, so that they could only be used by a person sitting down or standing in one spot.

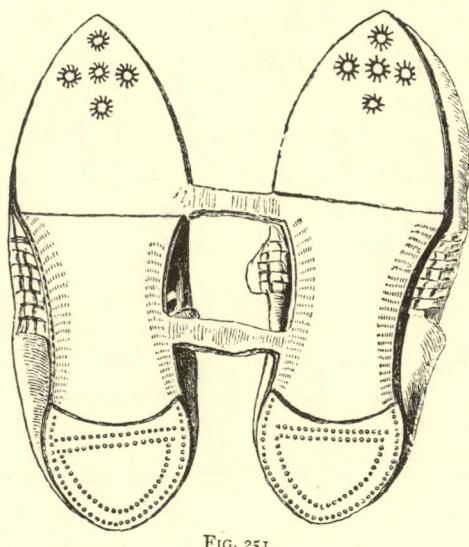

Fig. 251.

A pair of shoes permanently connected by straps: the two soles and the straps are cut out of one piece. Most ingeniously and beautifully made. (From Wilde's Catalogue, p. 287.)

In whatever way and for whatever purpose the metallic shoes were used, they must have been pretty common, for many have been found in the earth, and some are now preserved in museums. There were tradesmen, too, who made and dealt in them; as is proved by the fact that about the year 1850 more than two dozen ancient bronze shoes were found embedded in the earth in a single hoard near the Giant's Causeway. One of these was presented some years ago to the Museum of the Royal Irish Academy (now the National Museum), the dimensions of which were :—$13\frac{1}{4}$ inches long ; breadth, $4\frac{1}{2}$ inches ; height at heel, $2\frac{1}{2}$ inches ; height of instep, $3\frac{3}{4}$ inches ; weight, $9\frac{3}{4}$ ounces. This was larger than an ordinary shoe or slipper, no doubt to allow for a thick woollen stocking ; or a wisp.*

* Proc. Roy. Ir. Acad., v. 27, 28. For another bronze shoe, see Ulst. Journ. Archæol., IV. 23.

The custom of using bronze shoes descended far into Christian times. In the National Museum, Dublin, may be seen a shoe of this kind, of thin hammered bronze, engraved all over with an ornamental pattern (not the *opus Hibernicum*), and with the name " St. Brigit, patroness of Kildare " (in Latin), dated 1410.

The finding of bronze shoes, and in such numbers, is a striking illustration of how the truthfulness of many old Irish records, that might otherwise be considered fabulous, is confirmed by actually existing remains.

Sometimes people placed soft wisps of hay or fine straw in the shoes under the feet. This we know from the Senchus Mór, which provides that if a man is delayed in the performance of certain legal functions by such necessary things as " changing the wisp of his shoe " (*dlui n-assa* : see for *dlui*, vol. I., p. 224), *i.e.* removing the old wisp and putting in a fresh one, he is exempt from blame and responsibility. The gloss on this makes the matter clear :—" That is, while the cleric is changing the wisp of " his *as* or his *cúran*, i.e. a wisp of straw which is between " his foot and his shoe (*bróg*) when his shoe (*cúran*) is " hurting him."* A passage from an old Irish tale is quoted by O'Curry,† in which Dill, the famous blind druid of Ossory, is made to say, " I am putting incantations on the wisp which is in my shoes ; " preparing some spell (see vol. I., p. 224).

Laws relating to Dress.—Whenever dress came under the eye of the Law there was much particularity. This happened sometimes when it became necessary to set forth the privileges of persons of different classes, as in the case of children in fosterage. On this point the following regulations are laid down in the Senchus Mór. Whenever a boy had clothes of washing materials he should have two suits, so that one might be worn while the other was in the wash.

---

* Br. Laws, I. 268, 7 ; 269, 8 ; 301, 25.
† Man. & Cust , I. 207, 22 (and correction, p. xviii, bottom).

The sons of kings, when in fosterage, were to have satin mantles, dyed scarlet, purple, or blue : the scabbards of their little swords should be ornamented with silver, and there should be brass rings on their *camáns* or hurling sticks : while the sons of lower grade chiefs had tin scabbards. The children of the *ard-ri* or of a provincial king should have their mantle fastened with a brooch ornamented with gold, bearing a crystal : and those of inferior kings with ornaments of silver. The sons of chiefs were to be dressed in red, green, and brown clothes, and those of inferior ranks in grey, yellow, black, and white. The Law goes on to lay down many other arrangements for the dress of foster-children of various social grades, the quality depending on the grade : and all were to dress in their best on Sundays and festival days.* We must suppose that the regulations made compulsory here for children in fosterage were merely what were commonly carried out by their fathers and mothers in their own homes.

3. *Personal Ornaments.*

Legendary Origin.—In the ancient Irish tales and other records, referring to both pagan and Christian times, gold and silver ornaments, especially gold, are everywhere mentioned as worn by the upper classes : and these accounts are fully corroborated by the great numbers of objects of both metals found from time to time in various parts of Ireland, and now preserved in the Dublin Museum, and elsewhere. Gold naturally figures more prominently in the old literature than silver : and so well was the general custom of wearing gold ornaments recognised, that the legendary annalists, after their manner in such cases, thought it necessary to assign a distinct origin for it. We are told that King Tigernmas (who first smelted gold in Ireland : vol. I., p. 69) was the first to introduce orna-

* Br. Laws, II. 147, 149.

ments of gold and silver : that another king, Muinemon, first caused necklets of gold to be worn round the necks of kings and chiefs ; and that a third, Fáil-derg-doid (whose name signifies " of the red-ring-arms or fingers "), was the first to cause rings of gold to be worn on the hands of chiefs in Ireland. Perhaps these records are a dim traditional memory of the institution by these monarchs of certain orders of nobility or knighthood distinguished by peculiar gold ornaments : for we know that in Ireland there were knightly orders marked by some such badges (see vol. I., p. 99).   Most of the ornaments described in this chapter are mentioned as in use in Christian as well as in pagan times ; and records of them are found in ecclesiastical writings as well as in the lay literature.   The manufacture of gold and silver ornaments was of native growth. M. Salomon Reinach, a Continental scholar, who has carefully examined this question, says of the gold ornaments in the Dublin National Museum :— " Of objects of gold attesting imitation of Greek or Roman models there is no trace."*

In the National Museum there is a great collection of ancient artistic ornamental objects, some of pure gold, some of silver, and some of mixed metals and precious stones. All, or nearly all—of whatever kind or material— are ornamented in various patterns, some simply, some elaborately.   Those decorated with the peculiar patterns known as *opus Hibernicum* or Irish interlaced work (described in vol. I., p. 545) were made in Christian times by Christian artists, and are nearly all of mixed metals and precious stones.   Those that have no interlaced work, but only spirals, circles, zigzags, lozenges, parallel lines, &c., are mostly of pagan and pre-Christian origin, many of them dating from a period long antecedent to the Christian era.   Nearly all the gold objects, except closed rings and bracelets—and most even of these—belong to

* Rev. Celt , XXI. 75.

this class—made in pagan times by pagan artists. All the articles of gold are placed in one compartment of the Museum, and they form by far the largest collection of the kind in the British Islands: eleven or twelve times more than that in the British Museum.*

Rings and Bracelets.—Among the high classes the custom of wearing rings and bracelets of gold, silver, and

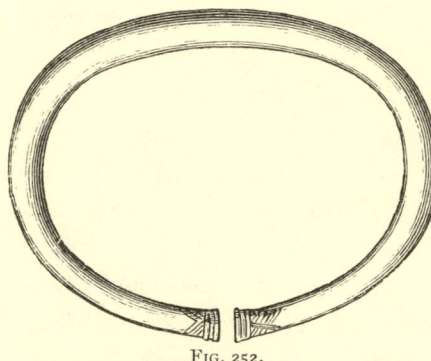

FIG. 252.

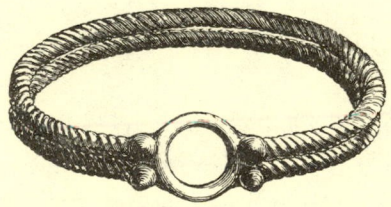

FIG. 253.

Figure 252, Irish Bracelet or Armlet, of solid gold. It is double the size of the picture, of beautiful shape and workmanship, and weighs 3¾ oz. Many of the Irish bracelets were of gold, like this: but many also were bronze, one of which is shown in figure 253. Both in National Museum. From Wilde's Catalogue, pp. 52 (Gold) and 570.

findruine (white bronze) on the fore-arm, wrist, and fingers — including the thumb — was universal, and is mentioned everywhere in ancient Irish literature. The words for a ring, whether for finger or arm, are *fáil* (pl. *fáilge*): *fáinne* [faun-yĕ]: *nasc*, which was applied to a ring, bracelet, collar, or tie of any kind — obviously cognate with Latin *nexus*, a tie: and sometimes *flesc* and *tinde*.† The word *id* was applied to a ring, collar, circlet, or chain; thus Moran's judgment-collar was called *id Moráin*. The *ordnasc* and *ordús* were rings for the *ord* or thumb: the *dornasc* was for the wrist (from *dorn*, the shut hand): the *fiam* was worn round the neck. Still another name for a bracelet or circlet or ring was

* At the end of this chapter will be found a short list of the gold objects in the National Museum, Dublin. See vol. I., p. 556, for a comparison of the gold collections of the Dublin and British Museums.

† *Tinde*, Corm. 58, under "Doss": *flesc*, Keat., 162.

buinne or *bunne* [2-syll.].   These several names were no doubt applied to rings of different makes or sizes : we know for instance that *fail* and *fáinne* are distinguished in the *Táin bo Quelna** : but these distinctions have been in many cases lost.

A passage in the Bruden Da Derga describes nine harpers, each with a crystal ring (*fail*) on his hand, and a thumb-ring (*ord-nasc*) on his thumb.   The lady Bec Fola, going through a wood, sees a young warrior whose two arms were covered with bracelets (*failge*) of gold and silver up to his elbows.†   According to the Book of Rights (p. 7) when the provincial kings attended the supreme monarch at the meeting of Ushnagh, each was bound to wear on his hand a *bunne niad d'ór dearg*, a ' hero's ring of red gold,' which, on the breaking up of the assembly, he left on his seat as a sort of tribute and mark of respect to the high king.   So jealous were the monarchs of this privilege that on one occasion a provincial king was expelled from the assembly for neglecting to bring his ring.   It was the custom with some warriors to wear a ring of a certain kind for every king they had killed in battle.   Lugaid Laga (or Lewy Law), a famous Munster champion, wore seven *bunne* in commemoration of seven kings he had slain at different times : whence King Cormac (whose father Art was one of the seven) says of him :—" In case of Laga his hand does not conceal that he has slain kings."‡

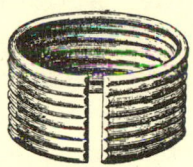

FIG. 254.

Ancient Irish Finger-ring, of pure gold. Now in the National Museum. (From Wilde's Catal., Gold, p. 81.)

Both men and women belonging to the highest and richest classes—as for example King Nuada's wife, a Leinster lady—had the arm covered with rings of gold, partly for personal adornment and partly to have them

* O'Curry, Man. & Cust , 90 : LL, 54, *a*, 35.
† O'Curry, Man. & Cust., II. 161.
‡ *Ibid.*, II. 156, 177.

ready to bestow on poets, musicians, story-tellers, and ollaves of other arts, who acquitted themselves satisfactorily.* Cailte, once travelling through Connaught with the little musician Cas Corach, meets a chief's wife with her attendants. She asks him who the little man was : " The best musician in Erin or Alban," said he. " He must be very skilful," replied she, " if his music is as good as his countenance." So the little harper took his timpan and played a tune, which so charmed her that she gave him the two gold *fáils* she had on her wrists.† This custom is like that of ladies of the present day, who often wear many thin bracelets together on the wrist—though not to give them to poets or musicians. Circlets of gold, silver, or *findruine* were also worn round the legs above the ankle : but these have been already noticed. Fully answering to all these entries and descriptions we find in the National Museum in Dublin, and in other museums, gold and silver rings and bracelets of all makes and sizes : some pagan, some Christian.

Precious Stones and Necklaces.—Ireland produced gems of many kinds—more or less valuable—which were either worn as personal ornaments by themselves—cut into shape and engraved with patterns—or used by artists in ornamental work. Precious stones are often mentioned in ancient Irish writings, the term commonly used being *lec-lógmar* or *lia-lógmar* : *lec* or *lia*, ' a stone ' : *lógmar*, ' very costly, precious ' (from *lóg* or *luach*, ' price '). In Kerry were found—and are still found—" Kerry diamonds," amethysts, topazes, emeralds, and sapphires : and several other precious stones, such as garnet, were found native in other parts of the country.‡ In crannoges and prehistoric sites in various parts of the country, have been found beads, rings, and other small ornaments, of such

* Man. & Cust., 169 : Bec Fola, 196, 197.
† Man. & Cust., II. 169, 170.
‡ Ware, Antiqq., 172 : Petrie, Tara, 195.

stones as red jasper, rose-coloured quartz, jet, amber, diorite, &c.*

A pearl was usually designated by the word *séd* [shade], old form *sét*: but this word, as we shall see in chapter xxvii., sect. 4, was also applied to a cow regarded as an article of value or exchange; and it was often used to designate a gem or jewel of any kind. *Séd* or *séad* is still in use in this last sense. Several Irish rivers were formerly celebrated for their pearls; and in many the pearl mussel is found to this day. Solomon Richards, an Englishman, who wrote a description of Wexford about the year 1656, speaking of the Slaney, says: "It ought to precede all "the rivers in Ireland for its pearle fishing, which though

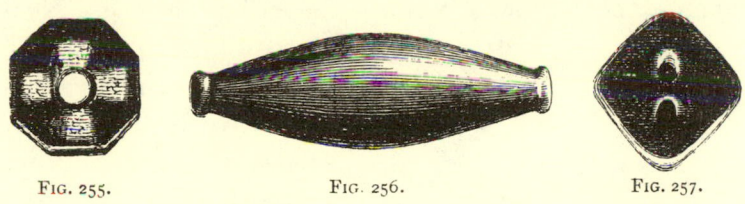

FIG. 255.   FIG. 256.   FIG. 257.

Beads or studs of jet. In National Museum. Used as buttons or fasteners, or strung together for Necklaces. (From Wilde's Catalogue, p. 241.)

"not abundant are yet excellent, for muscles are daily "taken out of itt about fowre, five, and six inches long, in "which are often found pearles, for lustre, magnitude, and "rotundity, not inferior to oriental or any other in the "world."† O'Flaherty (Iar C., 53) states that in the Fuogh river or Owenriff, flowing by Oughterard in Galway, "muscles are found that breed pearles"; and to this day they are often found in the same river. In Harris's Ware (Antiqq., 172) it is stated that pearls are found in the fresh-water mussels of the Bann, as well as in those of several streams of Tyrone, Donegal, and elsewhere; and Harris goes on to show that a present of an Irish pearl was made to Anselm, archbishop of Canterbury, by Gillebert, bishop

* See an article by Mr. Knowles in Kilk. Arch. Journ., 1879–82, p. 522.
† Kilk. Arch. Journ., 1862–3, p. 61.

of Limerick, about 1094. The same authority (Antiqq., p. 178) quotes a record of Nennius that the kings of the Irish wore pearls in their ears : but he gives no reference, and I have not been able to find the original passage in Nennius. Petrie says that he has not found the use of pearls in any Irish ornament older than the fourteenth century* : and I do not remember seeing them mentioned —or at least any stones that could be identified with pearls—as used in personal ornament, in any of the old Irish writings ; though there are several rivers and places in Ireland that derive their names from *séds* or precious stones.†

Of the various ornaments worn on the person, the common necklace was perhaps the earliest in use. Neck-

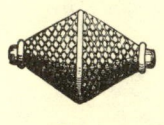
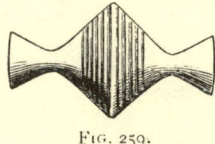

laces formed of small shells are common among primitive people all over the world, and they have been found with skele-tons under cromlechs in several parts of Ireland,

FIG. 258.   FIG. 259.

Gold Beads: portions of Necklaces: natural size.
In National Museum. (From Wilde's Catalogue, Gold, p. 37.)

of which specimens may be seen in the National Museum in Dublin, belonging to prehistoric ages. In historic times necklaces formed of expensive gems or of beads of gold were in use in Ireland. The word for necklace in Cormac's Glossary is *cuibrech-braiget* (or *cuimriug-braiget*), i.e. 'neck-binder' (*cuibrech*, a yoke or binder : *brage*, modern *braghad*, the neck, gen. *braiget*) : but this has long gone out of use, the present term being *ursgar-bhraghaid* [ursgar-vraw-id]. Cormac notices the necklace under the word *basc*, which he states was an old term denoting 'red' ; and he goes on to say that it was also a name for a neck-lace, but that the necklaces called *basc* were properly those

---

* Stokes's Life of Petrie, p. 305.

† For more information on Irish pearls and on places taking their names from them, see Joyce, Irish Names of Places, II. 375.

made of " draconic beads " (*dona mellach dracondai*).*
This alludes to the draconite or dragon-stone, a red jewel-
stone, which, according to the legend perpetuated by Pliny
and Solinus, was taken from the brain of a living dragon.
These dragon-stones are mentioned in even an older Irish
authority than Cormac's Glossary—the *Fled Bricrenn* : and
in a manner that shows it was considered very beautiful
and valuable.   When Cuculainn visited Ailill and Maive
in their Connaught palace, a golden goblet of wine was
given to him, and two dragon-stones the size of his two
eyes† : and elsewhere in the same old tale a splendid-
looking young hero is described with *ocht n-gemma deirg
dracondai for lár a da imlisen* : [the brightness of] " eight
" gems of red dragon-stone in the middle of his two eye-
" pupils."

Whether real dragon-stones found their way to Ireland in those early ages is a question that cannot now be
determined with certainty.   Indeed the words of Cormac's
Glossary, quoted above, would seem to imply that the
necklaces in use in his time with the name of *basc* were
made of gems which were not real dragon-stones, but
only stones like them.   Still we see, from the Glossary
and from the other passages quoted above, that this stone
was known in Ireland : and as there was communication
with the Continent from very early ages, it is quite possible
that real dragon-stones may have been occasionally used
among the higher classes of the Irish.

I do not know if carbuncle is mentioned as having
been worn on necklaces in Ireland : but according to the
records it was much used in artistic metal work : and it
is very often noticed in Irish writings.   The Irish name
was *carmogal*, with some slight varieties of form :—
carmhogal, carbunculus, Zeuss, 42, 8.   The house built

* Corm. Gloss., 20 ; Ir. Text in Three Ir. Glossaries, p. 7.
† Ir. Texte, I. 284, 285 : Henderson, 79 : see also Voyage of Bran,
I. 8, verse 12.

by Bricriu for Concobar mac Nessa was ornamented with gems of *carmogal* (*co n-gemaib carrmocail*).* In Tara, as we find mentioned in the old account (Petrie, 192), there were a hundred and fifty drinking-vessels ornamented with gold, silver, and *carmogal*; and part of the stipend paid by the king of Ireland to the king of the Gailenga consisted of twenty splendid bridles adorned with red bronze and *carmogal*.† According to Petrie (Tara, 195) the word *carmogal* was " applied loosely by the ancient, " Irish to any shining stone of a red colour, such as garnet, " a production of the country " : but as in the case of dragon-stone, real carbuncle may have found its way hither ; though no doubt in the greater number of cases the stones called *carmogal* were only imitations.

There was a sort of necklace called an *episle* or *epistil*. In the " Vision of Mac Conglinne " (39, 10) certain persons are mentioned as sitting round a fire, each having seven *episles* round his neck : and the celebrated judgment-collar of the just judge Morann, which is called a *sín* in Cormac's Glossary (p. 152), and *id* eleswhere, is called " a *sín* or an *epistil* that was round the neck for declaring truth," in a later copy of the same Glossary. It is also called *eibistil* in an ancient treatise on Irish ordeals in the Book of Ballymote, where moreover there is the legend that Morann got it from the Apostle Paul.‡ It seems obvious that this term made its way into Irish literature under Christian influences : and that it originally meant a few verses from one of the Epistles enclosed in a little case or box, and hung round the neck as part of a necklace : as Roman Catholics now wear a scapular.

Torques or Muntorcs.—Besides the necklaces properly so called, there were various kinds of gold and silver ornaments for wearing round the neck, of which perhaps

---

* Fled Bricr., 2, 17; Ir. Texte, I. 254, 15, 16.

† Bk. of Rights, 267, verse 5. For other examples, see Man. & Cust., II. 190, top ; and Táin bo Fraich, 137. ‡ Ir. Texte, III. 208.

the best known was the torque (Ir. *torc*).   The torque was
often formed of a single square or triangular bar of gold
from which the metal had been hollowed out along the
flat sides, so as to leave four, or three, ribbons along the
corners, after which it was twisted into a spiral shape,
something like a screw with four, or three, threads.   There
is one in the Museum only half made, having three leaves
or ribbons the whole length, untwisted.   But they were
formed in other ways, as may be seen by an inspection of
those in the Museum.   Torques are repeatedly mentioned
in our literature, sometimes by the simple name *torc*, but
generally by the word *muntorc*,
i.e. ' neck-torque,' from *muin*,
the neck.   When the great
King Cormac mac Art (A.D.
254) was arrayed in his kingly
robes at the *Féis* of Tara, he
wore his *muntorc* of gold about
his neck* : and we read that
when King Eochaid Airgthech
(A.D. 298) was buried, his jewels
were placed on his stone coffin,
among which was his silver

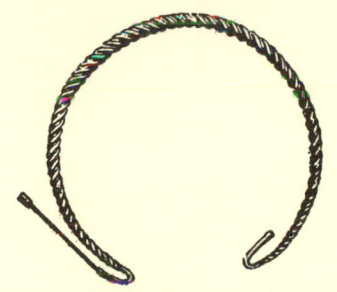

FIG. 260.

Gold torque : in National Museum :
15⅝ inches in diameter : found in 1810 in
a mound at Tara.   From Petrie's Tara.
p. 181.)

muntorc.†   In the Irish version of the Aeneid it is stated
that one of the presents Aeneas gave Dido was a *muntorc
óir* : Williams, the editor, translates it ' golden necklace ' :
but it was not a necklace properly so called.‡ There
are in the National Museum in Dublin many *muntorcs*
or various shapes and sizes.   Some are barely the size
of the neck, while others are so large that when worn
they extended over the breast almost to the shoulders :
and there are all intermediate sizes.   A number of gold
torques are figured in a group at p. 13, vol. I. of this
book, of which the two large outer ones were found at

* O'Curry, Man. & Cust., II. 180.   † Voyage of Bran, I. 48, 52.
‡ Zeitschr. Celt. Phil., II. 434, 15.

Tara in the year 1810. (The largest is shown separately here in figure 260.) The one represented in figure 261 is of unusual make, being formed by twisting a single plate of gold, and having two apples or balls of gold at the ends. The custom of wearing torques, as well as rings and bracelets, was in ancient times very general, not

FIG. 261.

Gold Torque, half the size of the original, which is now in the National Museum: found near Clonmacnoise. (From Wilde's Catalogue, Gold, p. 74.)

only among the Irish, but among the northern nations, both of Europe and Asia, especially the Gauls, as all who have read Roman history will remember. The statue of the Dying Gladiator has a torque round the neck, almost the same as some of those in our museums.*

* A fact first noticed by Robert Ball, LL.D., in a paper read before the Roy. Ir. Acad. in 1854, and published in the Proc., VI. 153. For torques, see Petrie's Tara, 181–4: the article in Kilk. Arch. Journ., 1883–4, p. 182: and Wilde's Catalogue, Gold.

Crescents, Gorgets, or Necklets.—The word *muince* [moon-kĕ] denotes a neck-circlet, from *muin*, the neck. It was used in different applications, as for instance to denote the ferrule of a spear, and also the collar round a greyhound's neck : but it is as a personal ornament that the *muince* concerns us here. The word seems to have been applied to almost any kind of neck ornament. Thus Maildune, entering a certain house, saw " a row of " *muntorcs* of gold and silver, like [in size] to the hoops of " a vat " : but a few lines farther on, in the paragraph where the same incident is re-told, one of these *muntorcs* is called a *muince*.* Nevertheless the necklets that we find constantly mentioned in the ancient tales by the names *muince* are to be generally understood as golden gorgets or collars for the neck, worn by both men and women, now often conveniently called " crescents." Thus a lady is described as wearing " a *muince* of burnished gold round her neck "† : and when Conn the Hundred Fighter was preparing to engage in the Battle of Moylena, he put on the various articles of his kingly apparel : and among the rest, his *muince* round his neck.‡

These golden crescents are of **three** main types. The FIRST is quite flat, thin, and brightly burnished. Most of those of this kind are ornamented in delicate line patterns, which are thus described by Wilde (Catalogue, Gold, 10) :—" The ornamentation, which is very minute " and elaborate, was in this, as in almost all similar " specimens, evidently effected by a series of fine chisel- " edged punches, the indentations made by which can in " some instances, be observed on the plain reverse side. " The lines which surround the edges would however " appear to have been produced by the graver." But it is probable that all the lines were produced by punches, as Mr. Johnson—an experienced goldsmith—has stated

---

* LU, 23, *a*, 34 and *b*, 4 : also Rev. Celt., IX. 477, 478.
† Man. & Cust., II. 160 and note.   ‡ *Ibid.*, 179.

was the case with the line-ornamentation of another class of gold objects (vol. I., p. 566, *supra*). Crescents of this kind are often called by the name *lunula* or *lunette*. Figures 262 and 263 represent two of those beautiful objects, of which there are now more than thirty in the National Museum.

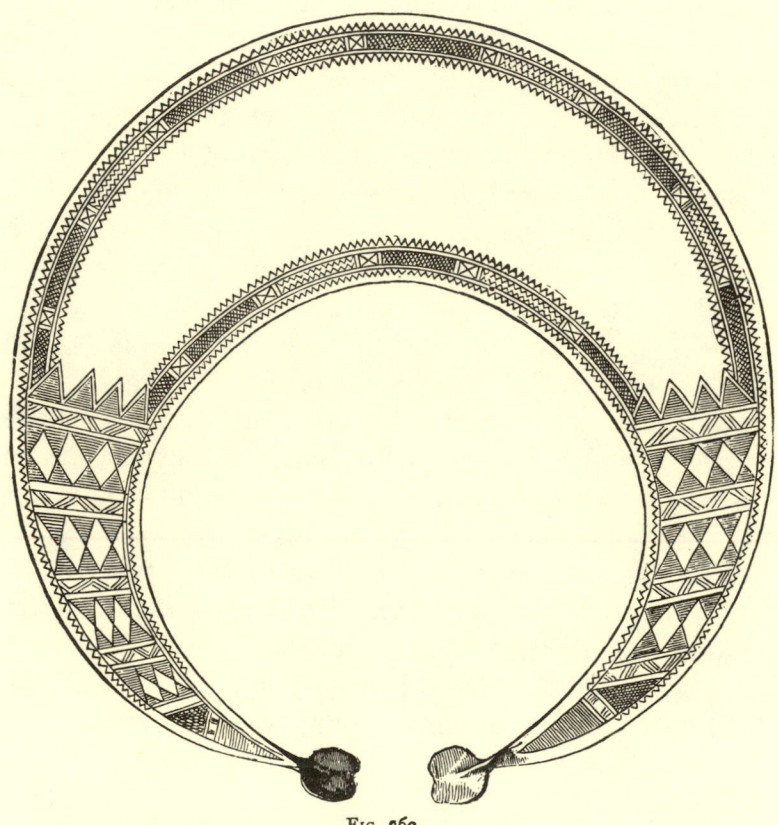

FIG. 262.

Gold Crescent, *Muince*, or Necklet of the first type, one continuous bright plate: sometimes called lunula or lunette. Diameter 9 inches: opening for the neck, 5⅞ inches: weight, 3¼ oz. Found near Killarney. Now in National Museum, Dublin. (From Wilde's Catalogue, Gold, p. 11.)

Any thin strip or plate of metal, whether of gold, silver, or *findruine* (white bronze), was called *land* or *lann*, *i.e.* 'blade': and if it was smooth and polished, it was usually designated *niam-lann* [neev-lann], 'lustrous-blade.' This term was often applied to those bright flat crescents or *muinces* now under consideration. Each of the seven horsemen who formed the retinue of the fairy chief Bove-Derg wore " a *niam-lann* of radiant gold round his neck."[*] It will be seen farther on that a long strip of gold or other metal for the forehead was also called *lann*.

The SECOND type, and by far the most elaborate, is dish-shaped in general make, convex on one side, concave

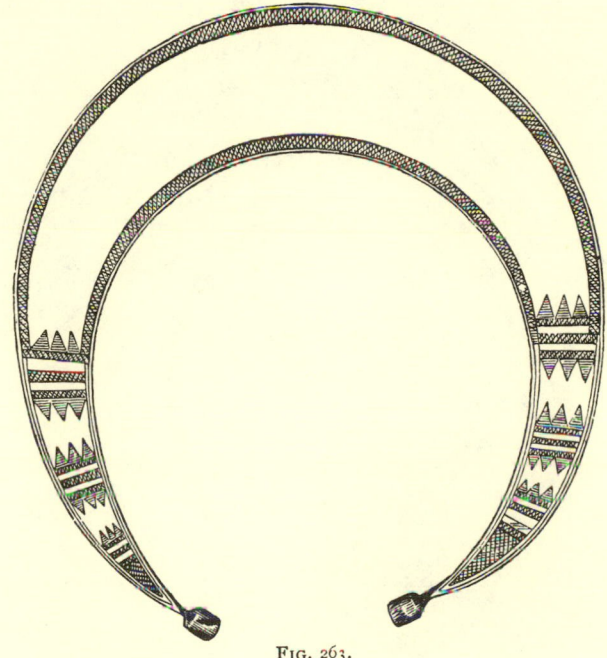

FIG. 263.

Another specimen of gold Crescent of first type : 7 inches in diameter : the opening, 5⅜ inches : weight, 18 dwts. In National Museum. (From Wilde's Catalogue, Gold, p. 14.)

on the other : covered all over with ornamental designs. The illustrations (on next two pages) give a good idea of the general shape, but represent the ornamentation only imperfectly. There are five specimens of these gorgets in the Museum, all of very thin gold. Both the general convex shape and the designs were produced either by stamping, or more probably by hammering with a mallet

[*] Man. & Cust., II. 157, note, col. 2, line 1.

and punches on a shaped solid mould. The designs are all raised from the surface (with corresponding hollows on the back); and in this respect they differ from those of the other two kinds of crescent in which the lines are indented. The patterns and workmanship on these are astonishingly fine, showing extraordinary skill of manipulation: they are indeed so complicated and perfect that

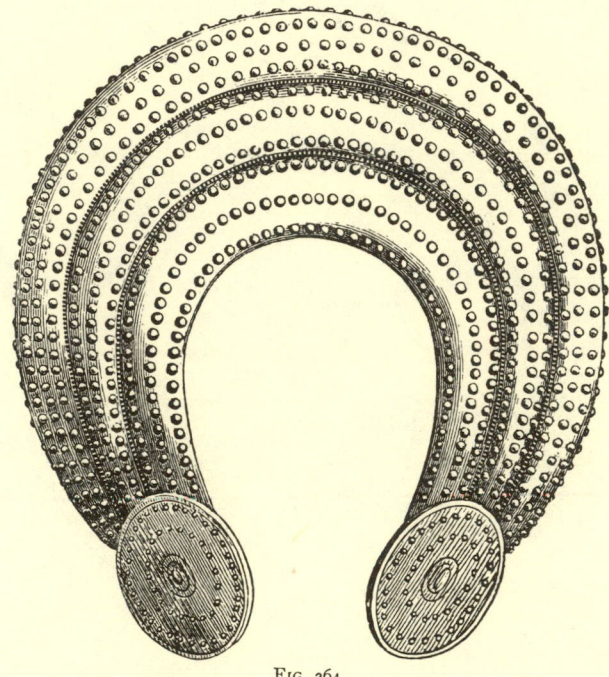

FIG. 264

Gold Muince, Crescent, or Gorget of the second type: the largest and most beautiful of this kind in the collection. "The arched or lunated portion"—says Wilde—"consists of three elevated rolls, with rows of conical studs on each—four on the upper, and three on each of the two others. A very minute rope-shaped fillet occupies the sunk space between each two elevations." Diameter 11 inches: weight, 16½ oz. Found in County Clare. Now in National Museum. (From Wilde's Catalogue, Gold, p. 22.)

it is difficult to understand how they could have been produced by mere handwork with moulds, hammers, and punches. Yet they could have been done in no other way.

The circular bosses at the ends of these gorgets deserve special notice. Two of them are shown half-size at page 238. They were made separately from the general body of the crescent, to which they are securely fastened : and the ornamentation on them is of extraordinary delicacy and beauty. Each of the circular ornaments forming the rows between centre and edge consists, in one specimen, of three delicate raised concentric circles, in another of six, and in a third of seven, each series of circles round a central conical stud or button, with point projecting outwards : and in the centre of the whole boss is a large

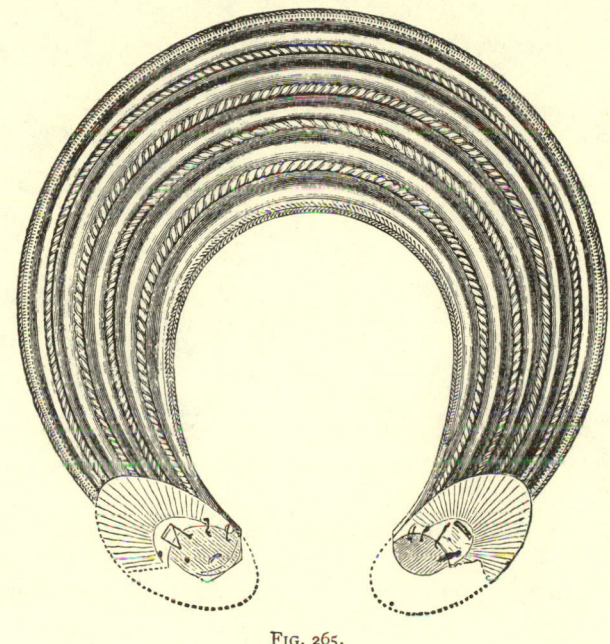

Fig. 265.

Another specimen of gold Crescent of the second type : now in National Museum. Nearly 11 inches in diameter : weight, 7½ oz. (From Wilde's Catalogue, Gold, p. 25.)

projecting stud of the same shape : all of pure gold. Each boss consists of two saucer-shaped discs, fastened (not soldered) together all round the edge, with the convex sides outwards, so as to enclose a hollow space. Wilde thus describes the disc shown in fig. 266 (*i.e.* the front disc of the two that form the complete boss):—"It is com-"posed of a very thin plate, most elaborately tooled, and "hammered into a high central umbo, surrounded by nine

'cones, each encircled with a series of minutely-raised
"lines of the most delicate tracery. A transversely
"decorated bur surrounds the edge, and another of a like
'description encircles the central elevation."*

Of the five gorgets of this class in the Museum, Wilde
truly observes :—" It may with safety be asserted that
"both in design and execution, they are undoubtedly the
"most gorgeous and magnificent specimens of antique
"gold work which have as yet been discovered in any
"part of the world."† In weight they vary from four to

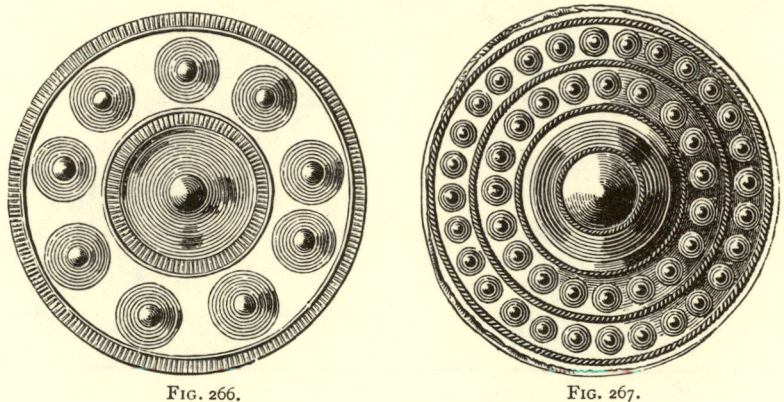

Fig. 266.   Fig. 267.

Two of the gold Bosses (front view) at the ends of the Crescents of second type : described on
pp. 236-7-8. Drawn half size. (From Wilde's Catalogue, Gold, p. 26.)

sixteen ounces: and taking material and workmanship
into account they must have been of immense value in
their time.

The necklets of the THIRD kind, of which the Museum
contains five specimens, are of a semi-tubular make, the
plate being bended round so as to form, in some specimens,
about a half tube, in others less than half. The gold is
much thicker than in those of the other two types. The
one represented in fig. 268, which is the largest and most
perfect of the five, is ornamented at the ends with a
punched herring-bone pattern. In an adjacent case of

* Wilde, Catal., Gold, p. 26.   † *Ibid.*, p. 19.

the Museum are five models of the type of these five real ones, of which the originals—all pure gold—were found in Clare in the great hoard mentioned below.

All the *muinces* of the three types were intended, and were very suitable, for the neck. The inside circular-opening is in every case of the right size, and on account of the flexibility of the plates they can be put on and

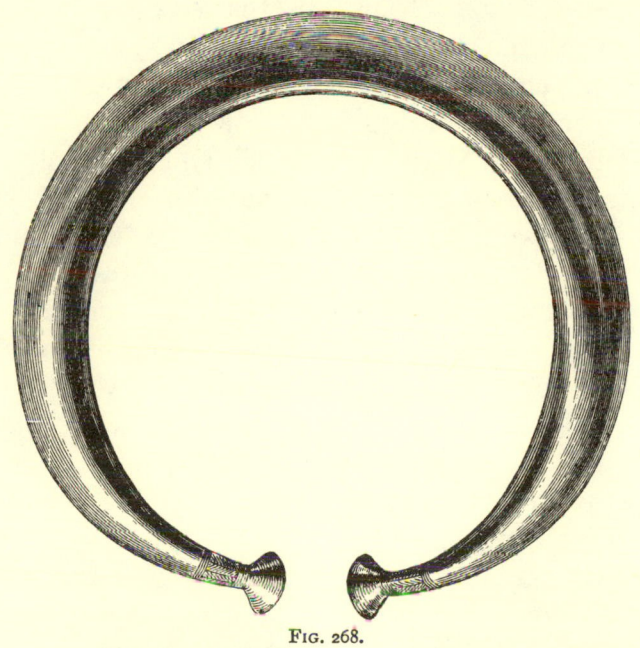

Fig. 268.

Gold Crescent or Necklet of the third type: in National Museum: described above: 7½ inches across on the outside: opening, 5½ inches: weight, a little over 7 oz. (From Wilde's Catalogue, Gold, p. 34.)

taken off with perfect ease, even though the opening at the ends is only a couple of inches, or less. What Wilde says of those of this third kind (fig. 268)—which he set down as gorgets—applies to all :—" As, owing to its shape " and material, it is very flexible, it can be easily passed " round the neck by bringing one end forward and pressing " the other backwards."* This he found by actual trial— as any one else may do.

* Wilde, Catal., Gold, p. 34.

As to the splendid crescents of the second type (figs. 264, 265), the elaborateness as well as the exquisite beauty of the bosses at once settles the question as to how they were worn. When on the neck the ends were in front, so as to exhibit the bosses to full advantage : and of course all the other necklets were worn in the same manner. Indeed the more simple necklets—those of the first and third types—show, of themselves, that this was the manner of wearing them : for where there is ornament at all, the ends are much more highly decorated than the rest, as may be seen in the illustrations.

The opinion of Sir William Wilde and others, that the crescents of the first and second types (figs. 262 to 265) were diadems and worn on the head, will be examined farther on (p. 251).

The Do-at and the Muince-Do-at.—In connexion with this part of our subject, we now come to an Irish descriptive epithet, *do-at*, used as part of two compound terms, and—so far as I am aware—of only two :—*muince-do-at* and *bunne-do-it*, which are often met with in the old tales to designate, respectively, two—and only two—classes of objects.

At each extremity of all the *muinces* or crescents of the three types is a disc or boss or button—seen in the illustrations—generally circular, or nearly so : very elaborate in one of the types, simple in the other two. Their primary use was as fasteners, to catch the ornamental string by which the necklet was secured. These terminal appendages were known in ancient Irish records by the name of *at*. In Zeuss, 67, $_{21}$, *att* glosses ' tuber ' : and to this day it has the same meaning, namely, a ' swelling ' of any kind : but the special sense here is a terminal knob, button, or disc. In accordance with this we find these gorgets—of whatever kind—designated *muince-do-at*, ' the necklet of the two *ats* or terminal discs ' (*do*, two : *do-at* has the same form in the nom. and gen.)

Ferceirtne the poet, lamenting the death of his master *Curoi-mac-Daire*, king of South Munster, states that he received as presents from him, among other precious articles, many a *muince-do-at*.*

The Bunne and the Bunne-do-at have now to be considered. The word *bunne* [2-syll.], with various forms,

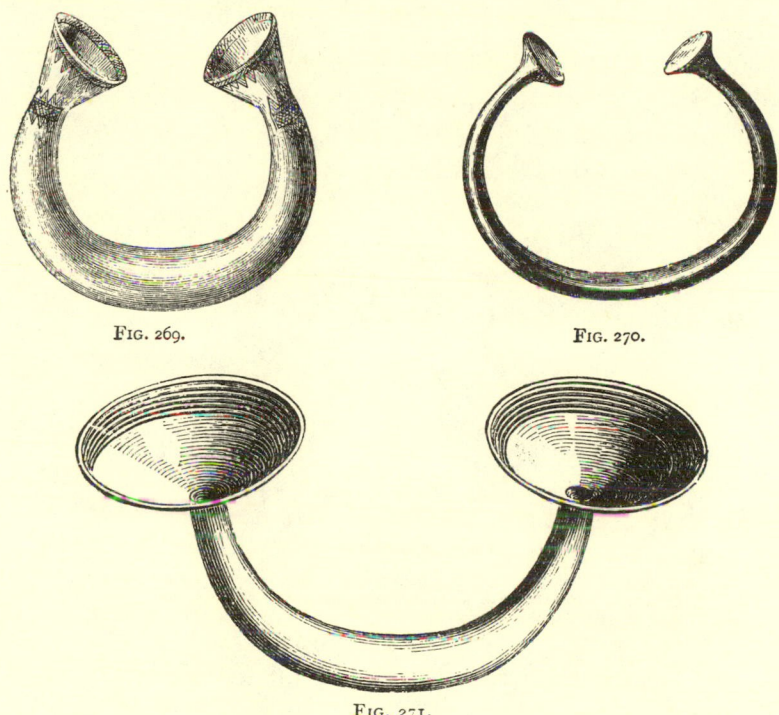

FIG. 269.   FIG. 270.

FIG. 271.

Three examples of the gold *Bunne-do-at* or fibula, all drawn half size: all in National Museum. Figure 269, hollow; weight, 2¼ oz. Figure 270, solid: over 3½ oz. Figure 271, hollow: 5¼ oz. (From Wilde's Catalogue, Gold, pp. 53, 55, 57.)

buinne, buinde, bunde, bouinde, has several significations. It denotes :—1, a wave or stream : 2, a branch : 3, a tube or anything like a tube or cylinder ; for instance the pipe of a spout, a musical pipe, the snout or horn of an anvil (*ur-buinde*), the round, thick edging on the top of a wicker basket, or any such twisted or corded rim ; and in the Rennes Dinnsenchus it is used to denote a man's shin-

* Man. & Cust., II. 179.

bone*: 4, a ring or circlet, either completely closed up or having a narrow opening or gap at one side. We are concerned here only with the last two applications (3 and 4). That *bunne* was applied to a hand- or finger-ring is placed beyond doubt by this fact :—that while in one part of the Book of Lecan we are told that Lugaid Laga had seven *bunnes* of gold on his hand or fingers, in another part of the same book, when the statement is repeated, they are designated seven rings (*fáilge*) of gold.† Under this name gold and silver rings of various forms are often mentioned. Among the treasures promised by

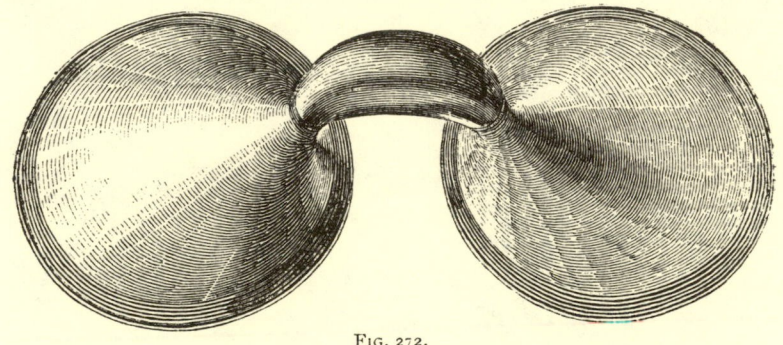

FIG. 272.

Gold *Bunne-do-at*: in the National Museum: the largest of the whole collection: drawn one-third size. The buttons, or discs, or *do-ats*, are unusually large—each 5 inches in diameter. The whole ornament is 11 inches in length: weight, nearly 17 oz. (From Wilde's Catalogue, Gold, p. 58.)

Queen Maive to Ferdiad to fight Cuculainn is "a great reward in rings" (*buinne*)‡: and in the Book of Rights (p. 6, 16) we read of a *bunne* of red gold for a king's hand. In the same Book of Rights (p. 75) we find mentioned mantles, each with a *bunne d'ór*, which O'Donovan explains "a ring-clasp of gold": and in the Voyage of Maildune a splendidly-dressed lady wears a *bunne* of gold round her hair. This brings us to the consideration of a class of gold articles in the National Museum: open rings with *ats* or buttons at the two ends, now commonly called

*Rev. Celt., XVI. 44.
† O'Curry, Man. & Cust., II. 177, bot. : see also p. 225, *supra.*
‡ *Ibid.*, 414, 415, bot.

fibulæ, of which three typical illustrations are given on p. 241.   Other examples are on pp. 242–3–4.

These have been somewhat of a puzzle : all the more so inasmuch as they are far more numerous and more varied, both as to shape and size, than any other class of articles among our gold antiquities.   There are such numbers of them that they must necessarily have been mentioned in the records, as well as the other gold articles : but no one has hitherto identified their Irish name.   There are altogether about 150 of them, varying in size from the great specimens pictured in figs. 272 and 275 down through all gradations to the two diminutive ones shown in their real size in figs. 273 and 274.   As in case of other articles of native manu- facture, some have been found half made—left for some reason unfinished, like the torque men- tioned at p. 231, *supra*.*   But however they vary in pattern all have the disc or button on

FIG. 273.   FIG. 274.

Two specimens of the very small gold *Bunne-do-at* : full size : originals in the National Museum.   (From Wilde's Cata- logue, Gold, p. 63.)

each of the two ends, already noticed in connexion with the crescents.   Seeing then that the terms *muince-do-at* and *bunne-do-at* were anciently applied to two classes of gold objects, and that there are two, and only two, classes now in the Museum to which the epithet *do-at* would apply, one the *muinces* or necklets, the other the objects now under consideration, it obviously follows that the " *fibulæ* " are the very ornaments called *bunne-do-at* in the ancient writings. A plain ring, whether closed or open, was a *bunne* or *buinne* simply :   an open ring with the two terminal buttons was a *bunne-do-at*.†

* See for example Journal of Cork Archaeological Society, 1902, p. 230.

† It is right to state that, so far as I am aware, this explanation of *muince-do-at* and *bunne-do-at*, and their identification, with the actually existing objects, have not been given before, and that I am entirely responsible for them.   On all this see also Appendix, *infra*.

That the *bunne-do-at* was used as a personal ornament is obvious from the way in which it is mentioned in the tales : the size and value of course depending on the rank and means of tne wearer. In the list of precious articles belonging to the usurping King Eochaid Airgthech (A.D. 298), and buried with him, are included his two *fáils*, wrist-rings or bracelets, his *muintorc*, and his two *bunne-do-ats** : and each individual in the retinue of Bodhbh Derg wore a *bunne-do-at* worth thirty *ungas* or ounces of gold.† From the two last entries we may conclude that these articles were sometimes worn singly and sometimes

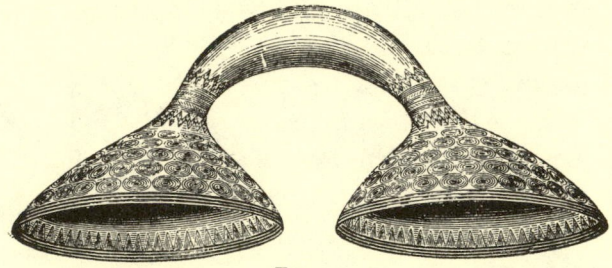

Fig. 275.

Solid gold *Bunne-do-at*, drawn one-third size. Now in the Museum of Trinity College, Dublin : 33 oz. So far as is known, the heaviest of its kind in existence. (From Wilde's Catalogue, Gold, p. 60.)

in pairs. The old writer, when describing this retinue, probably exaggerates its magnificence : but yet—in regard to the "*bunne-do-at* worth thirty *ungas* of gold," equal $22\frac{1}{2}$ oz. Troy (see chap. xxvii., sect. 3)—it should be remarked that there is not necessarily any exaggeration, inasmuch as the Trinity College *bunne-do-at* figured here is much heavier, weighing 33 Troy ounces. The *bunne-do-at* was used partly as an ornament and partly as a mark of affluence like many valuable articles of the

* Voyage of Bran, I. 48, 14 ; 52, 7.

† Man. & Cust., II. 157, where *bouinde-do-at* is translated 'twisted ring.' There is no English word to translate this Irish term : " two-disc-ring," though exact, is cumbrous. It would probably be better to transfer it to English as it stands—*bunne-do-at*; as Petrie does, with his habitual caution. He queries whether the *bunne-do-at* is not a bracelet : Round Towers, 109.

present day. It was probably worn on the breast at one side, suspended from a button like that shown at p. 206, *supra*, fig. 241, or if there was a pair, one was placed on each side. The question as to its use as money will be discussed in chap. xxvii., sect. 4.

Circular Gold Plates.—Among the gold ornaments in the National Museum are a number of very thin circular plates, with raised ornamental patterns punched from the back, varying in diameter from 1½ inch up to 4 inches. Fig. 276 represents one of these, 3¼ inches in diameter, found near Ballina in Mayo. All of them have the two holes at the centre for fastening on the dress. According to Wilde they are often found in pairs: and they were worn on the breast, like the *bunne-do-ats*, as mere ornaments, and as a mark of opulence. Petrie, in an article in the Dublin Penny Journal (I. 244), says:—" The figures of " the kings sculptured in *relievo* " on the great stone cross at " Clonmacnoise, are represented with round plates of this " description, placed upon the breast."*

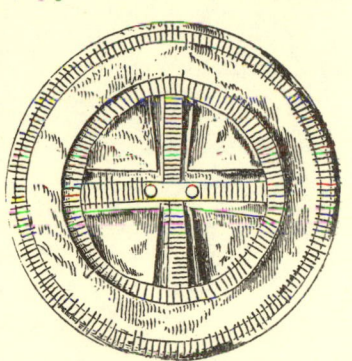

Fig. 276.

Circular gold Plate. One of those in the National Museum. (From Wilde's Catalogue, Gold, p. 83.)

Brooches.—The brooch was worn by both men and women, and was the commonest of all articles of jewellery. It was used to fasten the mantle at the throat and was fixed crosswise. In the descriptions of the warriors in the Táin in the Book of Leinster, nearly all wore brooches of gold, silver, *findruine*, or iron. The value of the brooch— like that of the *bunne-do-at*—depended on the rank and means of the wearer. The poorer people wore a plain

---

* For Bishop Gibson's story of the finding of one of these plates near Ballyshannon, through the description given by an Irish bard in a song: see Wilde, Catalogue, Gold, 82: and Dub. Pen. Journ., I. 244.

one of iron or bronze, with little or no ornamentation : but kings, queens, and other persons of high rank wore brooches made of the precious metals set with gems and, in Christian times elaborately ornamented with the peculiar Irish interlaced work. These must have been immensely expensive. That the descriptions given of brooches in old Irish writings are not exaggerated we have ample proofs in some of those now preserved in our Museums, of which the Tara Brooch, figured in vol. I., p. 562, is the most perfect.

What is called the Dalriada brooch was found in 1855 by a man digging in a field near Coleraine : it is now preserved in the National Museum. It is chiefly interesting as being of pure gold, in which probably it is unique. The circle is $2\frac{1}{8}$ inches in diameter, and the pin is 5 inches long : total weight $2\frac{1}{8}$ oz. The ornamentation is of the usual Christian Irish character, but not at all so elaborate as that of the Tara brooch. In Dr. Petrie's opinion it is not older than the end of the eleventh or the beginning of the twelfth century.* It is figured and described in the Ulster Journ. of Archæol., IV., p. I.

The general run of brooches had the body circular, from two to four inches in diameter, with a pin from six to nine inches long. But some were much smaller, while others again were larger and longer, and reached in fact from shoulder to shoulder. These great brooches are often noticed in the records. In the Story of Etain in the Book of the Dun Cow, a certain mounted warrior is seen with a brooch (eó) of gold in his cloak reaching to his shoulders at both sides. In the Bruden Da Derga, Keltar of the Battles (whose residence is figured in vol. I., p. 85) had his cloak fastened with a *cuaille* or stake-brooch, which reached from one shoulder to the other. These descriptions are corroborated by the Brehon Law, which mentions a fine for injuries caused by the points of

* Proc Roy. Ir. Acad., VI 302.

brooches extending beyond the shoulders* : and still more decisively by the existence of very large brooches in the Museum, as mentioned in vol. I., p. 22.

These large brooches were generally heavy. Queen Maive's brooch of gold (*i.e.* ornamented with gold) which fastened her mantle, weighed according to O'Curry's calculations about 4 ℔. troy (or more correctly about 3 ℔.).† This of course cannot be insisted on as historical fact : but it shows that the writers were familiar with large and heavy brooches.

The various names applied to a brooch will be exemplified in the following notices. One of the most common, and probably the earliest, was *delc* or *delg*, which primarily signifies a thorn. In the story of the *Táin*, Laegaire the Victorious is described as having a *delg* of gold fastening his cloak at the breast. When Queen Macha of the Golden Hair gave orders for the building of Emain she took the golden *eó* [yo] or brooch from her neck, and with the long pin marked the outline of the palace-rath.‡   This term *eó* was in very general use. Another word was *cassan*, a diminutive of *cas*, a twist, which evidently refers to some peculiarity of make, probably in the pin : King Concobar's son Causcraid had his cloak fastened with a silver *cassan*.   In another part of the Táin, three warriors are described as having *tanaslaidhe* [tonnaslee] of gold in their cloaks : and the nine comrades of Cormac Connlingas had their mantles fastened with nine *tanaslaide*.§ The brooch with this name must have been long and slender : for *tana* means slender and thin.   There was a very large circular brooch which was called a *roth* [ruh], *i.e.* a wheel, either from its great size, or because it was made with radii or spokes like a chariot-wheel. In the story of the Bruden Da Derga

---

* O'Curry, Man. & Cust., II. 163.   † *Ibid.*, 102.
‡ Corm. Gloss., 63 (under " Emain "   Keat. 247.
§ Stokes, Da Derga, 175.

we meet with notices of such brooches. Conari Mór, king of
Ireland in the first century, is described in a prose passage
as wearing a mantle [of silk] which " is even as the mist
" of Mayday.   Diverse are the hue and semblance each
" moment shown upon it : lovelier is each hue than the
" other."   This cloak was fastened with a *roth* or wheel-
brooch of gold, so large that it covered his whole breast,
from chin to waist.   In the accompanying poetry the same
brooch is called a *delg.**

Another word for a brooch much in use is *bretnas.*
Queen Maive once saw a lady wearing a speckled cloak
in which was a round heavy-headed *bretnas*† : on one of
the islands discovered by Maildune, he saw a lady richly
dressed wearing in her mantle a silver *bretnas* with chains
of gold‡ : and in the Palace of the Little Cat he saw a row
of *bretnases* of gold and silver with their pins fixed in the
wall and their heads outward.   The word *duille,* which
literally means a leaf, was applied—commonly with the
termination *nd* or *nn*—to a large brooch of a special make.
Queen Maive's great golden brooch was named *duillend-
delc,* ' leaf-brooch ' : and in a passage already quoted
Cuculainn wears a great *dulenn* at his breast.   The last
term I will mention is *milech* : in the story of the Bruden
Da Derga one of the champions is described as wearing a
silver *milech* in his cloak§ ; and Mac Conglinne (p. 9, 27)
arraying himself roughly for his journey, fastens his cloak
in front with an iron *milech.*

Illustrations of brooches of the usual Irish type have
been already given (vol. I., pp. 21, 562).   Two others of
a different make are represented here, figs. 277, 278.

That elaborate and costly brooches continued to be
made at least as late as the end of the twelfth century is
proved by the following stanza (quoted by O'Curry) of an
Irish poem written about 1190 by an Ulster poet, Gillabride

* Stokes, Da Derga, 202, 203, 204.   For the Roth croi, vol. I., p. 59.
† Man & Cust., II. 110.   ‡ *Ibid.,* II. 159.   § *Ibid.,* 137, 138.

mac Conmee :—" The gold brooch (*dealg-óir*), though it "gets the praise when the artist makes it lustrous by his "art, it is to the artist the praise is really due, who has " beautified the brooch."*

The brooches mentioned in this article are all Celtic, some pre-Christian, others made in Christian times ; and they were as common among the Celts of Scotland as among those of Ireland. Numerous beautiful specimens

FIG. 277.

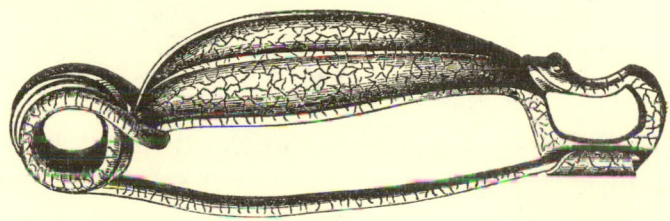

FIG. 278.

Specially-shaped Brooches. Figure 277, bronze brooch, natural size, pin turning on a hinge: one of the most beautiful bronze articles in the Museum, both as to design and workmanship. Ornamentation on the ends produced by punching or hammering from behind. Fonnd in a crannoge in Roscommon. Figure 278, bronze spring brooch, serpent pattern, natural size, also in National Museum. Both of great antiquity. (From Wilde's Catalogue.)

have been found in Scotland, many of which are figured and described in Dr. Joseph Anderson's work " Scotland in Early Christian Times " (Second Series).

The Lann, Blade, or Plate.—It was customary to wear a band or ribbon of some kind round the forehead to confine the hair. It was generally of some woven fabric ; and it will be mentioned farther on that a charioteer wore

* Man. & Cust., II. 168.

a bright yellow *gipne* or fillet in this manner as a distinctive mark. Among the higher and richer classes the band was often a very thin flexible plate, strip, or ribbon of burnished gold, silver, or *findruine*. This was what was called a *lann* or *land*, i.e. ' blade,' or more commonly *niam-lann*, ' bright-blade ' : and we have seen (p. 234) that the same terms were applied to the bright golden crescents for the neck. The *lann* is very often referred to in the old literature. In the story of Da Derga (p. 289) three men are mentioned as wearing *teóra lanna óir for airthiur a cind*, " three plates of gold on the front of their heads " : in the next page (290) nine others wear similar ornaments : and in the Acallamh (Ir. Texte, iv. 185) a woman is mentioned having a *lann d'ór buidhe re hétan*, a " blade of yellow gold on her forehead." In one of the eighth-century Irish Glosses on St. Paul's Epistles to the Corinthians (I., chap. ix., ver. 24), the Irish commentator thus explains the Latin word *brabium* (the prize in a race) :—" *i.e.* the *lann* which is sought therein is the remuneration of the soldier's service."* Several long thin gold plates are to be seen in the National Museum, no doubt of the kind and use referred to in the records. There is one beautiful thin ribbon less than a quarter of an inch wide and five feet long, with an *at* or button at each end for fastening, which was probably wound round and round the head, passing in front over the forehead, to confine the hair.

The *minn* or diadem (treated of below) and the *lann* or plate were always distinguished : for example, in the Brehon Law (v. 382, 18 ; 383, 22, 23), a lady's ornamental *tiag* or hand-bag is mentioned as containing, among other articles, a *mind óir* and *land óir*, i.e. a " golden diadem," and a " golden *lamina* or thin plate " (either for neck or forehead).

---

* Stokes and Strachan, Thesaur., I. 565.

The Minn, Diadem, or Crown.—Kings and queens wore a diadem or crown, commonly called *minn* or *mind* : often designated *minn óir* or *mind n-óir*, ' diadem of gold ' : but often also called *barr* or *cenn-barr* [kan-bar]. This last, meaning ' head-cover,' was also, as we have seen, the usual name of a helmet. That *minn* means ' diadem ' there can be no question, for it is used to explain " diadema " in the eighth-century Glosses of Zeuss. On account of the designation *minn óir*, ' golden diadem,' it is usually described as made wholly of gold : but this, as we shall see, has arisen from a misconception. The *minn*, however, was not confined to kings and queens, but was worn by men and women belonging to all the higher classes, probably indicating rank according to shape and make, like the coronets of modern nobility. It was not worn in common, but was used on special occasions : a lady usually carried her *minn-óir* in her ornamental work-bag, along with other such valuable or ornamental articles, ready to be used at any moment.*

As there has been much misconception regarding the Irish *minn*, it will be well to look into the question somewhat closely here.   Wilde, in his Catalogue (Gold, pp. 12 *et seq.*), assumes that the crescents of the first two types already described (figs. 262 to 265, pp. 234 to 237) are the objects designated by the Irish term *minn* or *mind* : and states his opinion—an opinion not originated by him however—that they were worn as diadems ; in which he is followed by Dr. Frazer of Dublin, and by others : but those of the third kind (fig. 268, p. 239) he sets down as gorgets. He does not however put forward the diadem idea quite positively, as is indicated by several expressions of doubt, such as :—" While the precise use and mode of wearing " the lunulæ or moon-shaped plates (fig. 262, p. 234) are " questions open to discussion, no doubt can exist as to " the object of the articles termed ' gorgets ' " (fig. 268,

* See O'Curry, Man. & Cust., II. 113.

p. 239).* But none of these Irish crescents are formed for head-wear, for they do not make any approach to the shape of the head, as any one who tries to fit them on will find out for himself. And to make matters worse, in order to force one of them into position, it would be necessary to have " the flat terminal plates applied behind the ears "† [and turned inwards] ; which, besides the unnatural wrench necessary to bend them back on each occasion, and the obvious violent incongruity of the whole adjustment, would have the effect—as M. Reinach observes in the passage quoted below—of completely hiding the most beautifully ornamented portions of the crescents (as in fig. 264). Moreover, it is incomprehensible why a use should be assigned to one type of crescent different from that for the others, as they. have similar flat outlines—differing only in non-essential details : all three are equally suitable for the neck, and all three equally unsuitable for the head.‡

But it is needless to follow this matter farther : one of these crescents—of whatever type—is no more fitted to be worn on the head than a stocking is to be used as a glove. Hear what a common-sense and learned foreigner —M. Salomon Reinach—who has no preconceived notions, says on this point :—" The Irish crescents should be con-
" sidered as collars or gorgets. Frazer, following [Wilde
" and] others, has had the idea that they were diadems,
" and assimilated them to decorations of that kind which
" ornament the heads of the Roman empresses on coins.
" But the form of the extremities suffices of itself to con-

* Wilde, Catal., Gold, p. 30.

† These are Wilde's words. *Ibid.*, p. 12.

‡ Sir William Wilde is sometimes mistaken in his opinions regarding Irish antiquities, as he is in the present case : for Irish antiquarians of those days had not the advantages and facilities now available to us. But he has done great service to Irish archæology by the publication of his Catalogue of Irish Antiquities, and of his two Essays on Irish Medical Science, in connexion with the Census Reports : service which I think has hardly received due acknowledgment. How much I owe him is well evidenced in this book.

" demn this explanation."*   O'Curry too, who has at great
length examined this question,† pronounces decisively that
the *minn* is not a crescent.   His words are (Man. & Cust.,
II. 193) :—" That the *mind-óir* was not an ordinary *land,*
" that is, a frontlet or a crescent of gold, must be at once
" acknowledged, when we find both mentioned together as
" different articles belonging to one and the same person,
" and when, besides this fact, it will be shown that, whilst
" the *land* was worn either at the neck or on the forehead,
" the *mind* invariably covered or surrounded the whole of
" the head."

Let us now inquire what the Irish *minn* really was.
There are two circumstances that have helped to lead
antiquarians astray on this question.   One is the representation of Roman empresses on coins—as mentioned by
M. Reinach above—in which they wear a crescent on the
front of the head : from which some have jumped to the
conclusion that the same fashion must have prevailed in
Ireland : and to illustrate this supposed Irish custom there
is actually in Gough's Camden (III. 476) a picture of a
lady wearing a crescent-ornament or diadem evidently
drawn from a Roman coin, and having nothing to do with
Ireland.   The other misleading circumstance is the term
minn-óir, ' diadem of gold,' which is constantly used, and
which many persons took to mean that the *minn* was
made wholly of gold—no mixture of any other material :
and as the crescents are all pure gold, this was considered
to indicate that a crescent was a *minn.*   But the term
minn-óir merely means that it was ornamented with gold ;
a mode of expression found everywhere in all sorts of
Irish literature.   We read of steeds having bridles and
reins of gold : Cuculainn's chariot had " a frame of tin " : a
chariot had " iron wheels " (meaning of course shod with

* Translated from M. Saloman Reinach's " Les Croissants d'or
Irlandais," Rev. Celt., XXI. 75.

† In Lects. XXVIII. and XXIX. of his Man. & Cust.

iron rims) : *camans* or hurling-sticks are described as " of silver " : chariot-shafts are " of white bronze " : all which mean that the several articles were mounted or ornamented with, or partly made of, the metals—the unmixed metals being impossible.   Such expressions are so numerous that references are needless.

The *minn* was an article wholly different from a crescent of any kind.   It was not a plate of gold, but a regular crown or cap of elaborate workmanship, made of a combination of various materials, and so formed as to cover the whole head : all which will be obvious from the following quotations and references.   The *barr* or *minn* of Brunn the son of Smetra, mentioned in the " Adventures of Nera,"* and designated as the " *mionn n-óir* which the king wears on his head," was a wonder of workmanship, one of " the three chief articles of manufacture in Erin." This same *mionn n-óir* is described in another story relating to the same adventure, as " a cathbarr of the pure " purple of eastern countries, with a ball of gold above it as " large as a man's head, and a hundred strings around it of " mixed carbuncle, and a hundred combed tufts of red " burnished gold, and stitched with a hundred threads of " *findruine.*"† Here it will be observed that the *mionn n-óir* is described as a diadem made of mixed materials, not of gold only.   It is not meant of course that this gorgeous description should be accepted as literally true : but it shows that the writer had something in view very different from a crescent of gold.

In the Táin it is related that on one occasion Cuculainn, seeing a number of maidens coming towards him headed by one beautiful lady with a *mind-n óir* on her head, whom he took to be Queen Maive, flung a stone from his sling, which struck the golden *minn*, and *broke it into three pieces.*‡ How could this be if it was a plate of tough gold ?

* Rev. Celt., x. 218, line 71.
† O'Curry, Man. & Cust., II. 200, 201, 202.   ‡ *Ibid.*, 196, top.

The manner in which Queen Maive's diadem is spoken of, too, indicates an article delicately made and easily soiled. During the march of the Connaught army north to prosecute the war of the Táin, King Ailill and the queen each wore a golden diadem—*mind-óir*. Queen Maive, as the story tells us, had nine splendid chariots for herself and her attendant chiefs, her own in the centre, with two abreast in front, two behind, and two on each side, right and left ; and—in the words of the old tale—" the reason " for this order was, lest the clods from the hoofs of the " horses, or the foam-flakes from their mouths, or the dust " raised by that mighty host should, strike and tarnish the " golden diadem [*mind-óir*] on the head of the queen."* All this elaborate precaution could hardly be needed for a simple plate of gold.

But a still better idea of the size, general shape, and use of the *minn-óir* is given in the very pretty legend of Queen Mairenn† : which shows that it was made to encircle and cover the whole head. Dermot, king of Ireland (A.D. 544–565), had two wives, Mugain, who was barren, and Mairenn Mael, who had children. Mairenn was quite bald, and always wore a diadem—*minn-óir*—to hide the blemish (see p. 182, *supra*) : and the barren Mugain was filled with jealousy and hate for the fruitful Mairenn. Once upon a time at the assembly of Tailltenn, when all were seated in state according to rank, the men on one side with the king, and the women apart on the other side with the two queens, Mugain, burning with jealousy, called to her a bitter-minded female satirist or jester (*bancáinte*, vol. I., p. 454, *supra*), and promised her whatever reward she asked, to pull the diadem off Queen Mairenn's head where she sat before all the assembly. The satirist went to Queen Mairenn and asked for a present (a usual request from a poet) ; but the queen said she had nothing to give. " You shall have this for me

* LL, 59, last four lines.
† O'Curry, Man. & Cust., II. 193 : Silva Gad., 89.

then," said the satirist, seizing the diadem and lifting it off her head. The poor queen in her agony and shame at being thus publicly exposed, cried out :—" God and St. Ciaran help me in this need ! " whereupon, quick as lightning, says the legend, and before anyone had time to notice the blemish, a beautiful crop of bright golden hair sprang from her head in ringlets and fell in glorious masses down over her shoulders, so that the whole assembly were struck with wonder and delight. For a long time after that incident Queen Mugain was in disgrace.

In numerous other old authorities the *minn* or *mind* is mentioned in terms implying that it covered the whole head. In the tenth-century version of the story of King Labra the mariner, who, like Midas, had horse's or ass's ears, we are told that he constantly wore a " *mind n-órdha* upon his head " to hide the deformity,* which certainly could not be done if the *minn* was a crescent placed on the top front of the head. Moreover, a little farther on in the tale, the same *mind n-órdha* is called a *cathbarr* or helmet : *cathbarr imom cenn*, " a helmet round my head," as the king expresses it.

All that has been said is borne out by the form of expression often used when the *minn* is mentioned. In the Acallamh it is related that St. Patrick and his companions see a band coming towards them with two warriors at their head. One wears a *cathbarr* or helmet, the other a *mind-óir* : and in both cases the same words are used, *im a chenn*, " round his head," " encircling his head "† : *im* or *imm*, circum, circa, Z., 654, 20. This shows that the *minn* was not a mere *lunula* or ornament on the front of the head, but a covering for the whole head.

Fully confirming the preceding literary testimonies, comes the most unquestionable evidence of all, the actual

---

* Prof. Kuno Meyer in " Otia Merseiana," vol. III., 1903, p. 46, where he edits the story (about King Eochaid) with translation.

† Stokes, Acallamh, Ir. Texte, IV., pp. 162, 235.

representation of a native crown worn by an Irish king, seated, carved on one of the panels of the south side of the Durrow high cross, which was erected about A.D. 1010.* It is reproduced on the cross in Miss Stokes's book, " The High Crosses of Castledermot and Durrow," from which the illustration here has been copied. The original crown of which this is a representation was about five inches high, quite flat on top, with a slender band all round, above and below, the two bands connected by slender little fillets or bars, about two inches asunder. It covers the whole head like a hat, and there are two bosses over the ears, three or four inches in diameter.†

FIG. 279.

Crowned Irish King, seated, with shield, sword, and spear; a dog on each side. (From the High Cross of Durrow.)

The Irish crown varied in shape however ; but in no case did it resemble a crescent or lunula. It is pretty certain that some had rays or fillets standing up detached all round. Crowns of this kind, belonging to the O'Conors, kings of Connaught, as represented in the thirteenth-century fresco-painting in Knockmoy Abbey, are shown in vol. I., p. 59. They are probably native Irish, though it is just possible that these particular forms might have been adopted under Anglo-Norman influence. That some such crown however existed in Ireland at an earlier period is shown by the literature. In the " Vision of Mac

* For this date, see the above-named book of Miss Stokes, p. 11 bot., and 12 top.

† See description of this figure in Miss Stokes's High Crosses of Castledermot and Durrow, p. 10 : but she is certainly mistaken—led astray I suppose by Wilde—in calling this crown a lunula : to which it bears not the least resemblance.

Conglinne " (p. 89, 10) a person is described as wearing a crown of seven *corns*, ' horns,' or fillets ; and in another part of the same tale (123, 31 ; 152, 28), a crown of twenty-seven fillets is mentioned.

The crescents, then, are not *minns*. There is in fact no such thing as a *minn* or diadem in the National Museum ; and I suppose there never will be, for the good reason that such a complex and delicate object would not hold together if buried in the ground. The metallic parts would indeed remain ; and there is good reason to believe that two relics now in the National Museum are of this class. One of them—a beautiful enamelled article—is figured by Miss Stokes in Plate xix., fig. 2, of vol. xxx., Trans. Royal Irish Academy, and described by her at p. 290, same vol., where she records the opinion that it is a portion of an Irish radiated crown. It is figured in outline here : but a proper idea of its exquisite workmanship and beauty of colouring can only be obtained by viewing either the object itself or Miss Stokes's coloured

FIG. 280.

Enamelled metallic object in the National Museum : believed to be a ray or fillet of a crown : drawn half size. (From Miss Stokes, in Trans. Royal Ir. Academy, XXX., Plate XIX., fig. 2.)

representation mentioned above. Mr. Kemble (quoted by Miss Stokes, Early Christian Art, p. 53) says of this and the other corresponding object :—" For beauty of design " and execution [they] may challenge comparison with " any specimen of cast bronze work that it has ever been " my fortune to see."

It is said that an " Irish crown " was found in 1692 at the Devil's Bit Mountain in Tipperary. This " crown " was first figured by Dermot O'Connor in the Preface (p. v.) to his translation of Keating's History of Ireland.

from which it was reproduced in the Dublin Penny Journal (I., p. 72, A.D. 1832).   But we know that O'Connor wilfully perverted Keating; so that no reliance can be placed either on the story told by him or on the picture.   The illustration here shows O'Connor's delineation, which is not like any Irish crown.   Indeed, Wilde plainly hints his opinion that it is a perverted picture of a drinking-cup (Catal., Gold, p. 8, note).

The word *Asionn* appears for the first time as meaning a diadem in O'Flaherty's Ogygia, from which it was copied into various other standard works, including O'Brien's and O'Reilly's Irish Dictionaries.   But in a communication to the Athenæum of 24th August, 1901, I have shown that there is no such word as *asionn*.   It was merely a printer's error. O'Flaherty, in his manuscript, wrote *Mionn*: but as the Irish capital *M* is often written and printed in such a form as to re-

FIG. 281.

Conjectural drawing of an object erroneously supposed to be an Irish crown. Stated to have been found at the Devil's Bit Mountain in 1692.

semble the Irish *As*, the printer changed O'Flaherty's *Mionn* to *Asionn*: and so this spectre of a word has haunted Irish literature ever since.   Of course O'Flaherty did not see a proof; for such a glaring error could not have escaped him.

Earrings.—Men of the high classes wore gold earrings. This custom has been recorded by Nennius, as we have seen (p. 228, *supra*); and it is noticed in Cormac's Glossary (p. 8) under the word *aunasc*, an earring, a word which he correctly derives from *nasc*, a clasp or ring, and *aue*, a form of *o*, an ear.   After this he remarks that the *aunasc* was " a gold ring which is round the fingers or in the ears of the sons of nobles."   As *au-nasc* properly means " ear-ring," O'Curry thinks the insertion here of " the fingers " a corruption of Cormac's text.* But it is not necessary to suppose this, as such extensions of meaning are common in all languages. The passage as it stands merely shows that similar rings were often worn on ears and fingers, so that the name of one got extended to the other. In the ancient tales these ornaments are often mentioned. In the Bruden Da Derga, King Conari's juggler wears " ear-rings (*u-nasca*) of gold round his ears."† And a little farther on the king's nine harpers wore ear-clasps of gold round their ears : but here the word for ear-ring or ear-clasp is *au-chuimriuch.*

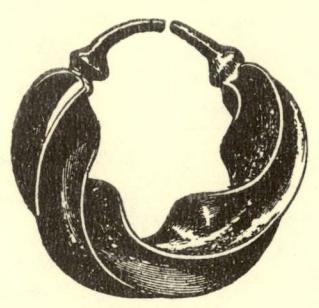

FIG. 282.

Ancient Irish gold Earring, one of a pair found in County Roscommon.

From the names given to earrings, as well as from the manner in which they are mentioned, it is plain that the ears were not pierced ; but a thin elastic ring was clasped round the ear ; and from the lower extremity of this another little ring was suspended (like that represented in fig. 282).

For *cuimriuch,* as already remarked (p. 228), means literally ' binder ' : *au-cuimriuch* ' ear-binder ' : and *au-nasc* means much the same thing : *nasc,* Lat. *nexus,* a bind or tie (see page 224, *supra*). Accordingly, as the Da Derga story tells us, each of King Conari's nine harpers wore an *au-chuimriuch* round (*im*) each ear "‡ : and the chief juggler wore ear-clasps (*u-nasca*) round (*im*) his ears.§ In Cormac's Glossary the *au-nasc* is defined *nasc-aue,* ' binder of the ear ' : and it is said to be worn " in the ear " : but this latter expression is quite consistent with all that is said here.

The mention of Irish earrings by Nennius, and by Cormac under their proper name *aunasc,* may be classed

---

* Man. & Cust., II. 186.   ‡ Man. & Cust., II. 147, note 214.
† *Ibid.,* II. 145, note 206.   § *Ibid.,* II. 145, note 206.

among these remarkable confirmations of the accuracy of the Irish historical romances, so far as incidental details are concerned, mentioned in vol. I., p. 9, *supra*, and in other parts of this book.

Golden Balls for the Hair.—Both men and women sometimes plaited the long hair ; and at the end of the plait they fastened a thin, light, hollow ball of gold, which was furnished for the purpose with little apertures at opposite sides. Sometimes these balls were worn singly—probably behind—and sometimes in pairs, one on each side. In the Book of the Dun Cow the fairy king Labraid (who was sitting in state) is described as having yellow hair, with " an apple (*ubull*) of gold enclosing it."* And in another part of the same book we are told that Cuculainn had " spheres (*cuache*) of gold at his two ears into which his hair was gathered."† The lady Bec Fola, going through a wood, saw a young warrior magnificently attired, and among other ornaments he had " two balls of gold [*da* " *ubuill óir*] on [the ends of] the two divisions of his hair, " each the size of a man's fist."‡ Ladies followed the same fashion : but they had several very small spheres, instead of one or two large ones. Eochaid Feidleach once saw a lady richly attired : on her head were two golden yellow tresses, each plaited into four locks, on the end of each of which was a *mell*, i.e. a little ball or bead : so that this lady wore eight little balls altogether.§

As corroborating all these accounts, there are in the National Museum a number of these golden balls, found from time to time in various parts of Ireland. They are all hollow and light, being formed of extremely thin gold : and each has two small circular holes at opposite sides by means of which the hair was fastened so as to hold the ball suspended. Each is formed of two hemispheres,

---

* Sick Bed, Atlantis, II. 103 : also Man. & Cust., II. 192.
† Kilk. Arch. Journ., 1870–1, p. 377, last line : and Fled Bricr., 65.
‡ Bec Fola, 177.   § Da Derga in Rev. Celt., XXII. p. 14.

which are joined with the greatest accuracy by being made to overlap about the sixteenth of an inch, and very delicately soldered—so that it requires the use of a lens to detect the joining. The largest of these balls is $3\frac{7}{8}$ inches in diameter, and weighs $2\frac{1}{3}$ oz. (figured separately in vol. I., p. 21): so that we see the old story-teller was right enough in describing the two balls worn by the young hero as "the size of a man's fist." Those in the Museum vary in size from $3\frac{7}{8}$ inches down to about two.

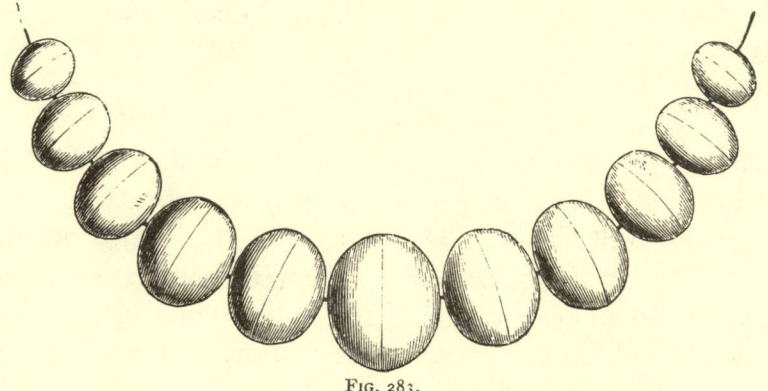

FIG. 283.

Hollow gold Balls, as described in text: erroneously represented as a necklace in Wilde's Catalogue, Gold, 35, from which this illustration has been taken.

Wilde* conjectures that these balls were worn as necklaces, which they certainly were not: for no such form of necklace is referred to in any of the records; and in order to support the conjecture he gives an engraving of eleven of them (found in various localities) arranged, according to size, and connected by a string, as a necklace, as seen here.

The corroboration of the truthfulness of the old records by existing remains has been frequently noticed throughout this book; and this is a very striking example, inasmuch as the custom of wearing gold balls on the hair seems so strange that it might not unnaturally be set down as the invention of story-tellers, if their statements were not supported (see "Corroboration" in Index).

* Catalogue, Gold, p. 34.

4. Short rough classified List of the Gold Objects in the National Museum, Dublin.

More than 30 crescents of the first type (figs. 262, 263) ; five of the second (figs. 264, 265) ; five of the third (fig. 268).

Seven hollow balls for the hair (fig. 283).

Great numbers of bracelets and rings of various shapes and sizes (figs. 252, 253, 254).

A number of long thin bright plates and ribbons.

About 150 open rings called Bunne-do-at (figs. 269 to 275).

About 50 very small open rings without the *ats* or buttons (mentioned at p. 385, below.)

About a dozen thin circular plates with patterns, all with two holes for fastening (fig. 276).

About two dozen torques of different sizes (fig. 260).

A number of small ornamental beads for necklaces, of various shapes (figs. 258, 259).

Four amulets (vol. I., p. 385).

An open spiral, $2\frac{1}{2}$ inches long and 1 inch in diameter, with nine spires, formed of one square wire.

Besides these there are a number of small objects not classified.

(The total weight of all these articles is about 590 oz., which is twelve or thirteen times the weight of the collection of gold antiquities, from all England and Scotland, in the British Museum. See vol. I., p. 556.)

Models.—In 1854 an immense collection of gold articles were found in a stone cist under a small clay mound near Quin in the County Clare, most of them slender delicate rings of the kind called *bunne-do-at*. In one glass-case of the National Museum there are gilt-brass models of a portion of this find, consisting mainly of about 100 *bunne-do-ats*, and five crescents of the third type.*

---

* In 1896 a number of important gold antiquities were found at Broighter in Derry. They were purchased by Mr. Robert Day, F.S.A., M.R.I.A., of Cork, who sold them to the British Museum. They are at this present time the subject of litigation. The question is whether they should not be restored to Ireland, their natural home. See an account of them by Mr. Arthur Evans, F.S.A., in Archæologia, LV., 391, 408 ; and another by Mr. Robert Cochrane, F.S.A., M.R.I.A., in Journ. Roy. Soc. Antiqq , Ireland, ᵗᵒ02, p. 211. (For more on this, see Appendix.)

Ornament: composed from the Book of Kells.

CHAPTER XXIII

AGRICULTURE AND PASTURAGE

SECTION I. *Fences.*

EVER since that remote time when legend and history begin to give us glimpses of the occupations of the inhabitants of this country, we find them engaged in agriculture and pasturage. For both of these purposes open land was necessary; and accordingly, the clearing of plains from wood is recorded in the reigns of many of the early kings as a public service worthy of special notice. But there was always more pasturage than tillage.

Farm Fences.—In very remote times, when the population was small and the land was mostly common property (as pointed out in vol. I., p. 184, *supra*), there was little need for fences, and the country was mostly open, so far as it was free from forest and bog. But in course of time, as tillage gradually increased, and private property in land became more general, it was more and more necessary to fence off the portions belonging to different individuals. Fences are referred to in our oldest literature: and how important they were considered appears from the number of regulations regarding them in the Brehon Law. The general terms for a fence are *ime*, *fál*, *félmae*, and *aile*.

When two or more persons came into possession of adjacent farms, it became their duty to fence off their portions, if not fenced off already. As each fence between

264

two farms would be common property, arrangements for joint action were laid down in the law, so that each man should execute his own part of the work.   In making the fences they had to be up to time.   Three days were allowed for marking out the land : in five the fencing was to be commenced : in ten days the fence should be completed, except the blackthorn crest at top, which was to be finished in a month.

Four kinds of farm-fences are specified in the Law :— *First*, a trench (Irish *clais*, pron. clash) with the earth piled up on one side as a high embankment (called *múr*, or *fert*, or *clad*, pron. cly), a kind of fence still used all through Ireland : *Second*, a six-foot stone wall of dry masonry, which is still very general in stony districts in the west and south : the *Third* was formed of logs laid horizontally and securely fastened : the *Fourth* consisted of pointed stakes standing six feet above the ground, and six or eight inches asunder, bound securely by three bands of interwoven osiers, and having a blackthorn crest on top.   The top of each sharp stake should be blunted by three blows of a mallet.   No man was directly compelled by law to make his fences of any particular height or pattern, or to have them put up by a certain time.   But there was indirect compulsion ; for supposing a lawsuit to arise on a question of trespass or such like, the person owning—or part owning—the fences should be able to show that they were constructed as specified in the law, both as to make and time, otherwise the suit was pretty sure to go against him.   If a fence was carelessly constructed so that some stakes were too sharp-pointed at top, or that sharp spikes projected from the sides, the owner was liable for damages in case cattle got injured.*

* All the preceding regulations will be found in Br. Laws, IV. 71 to 77, 113, 115, and Introd., cxxi. cxxxiii: and vol. III. 291.   Some are also noticed in the general literature : for instance, the thorn-crest is mentioned in Mac Conglinne, 86 18.

Territorial Boundaries.—Fences such as these were too slight and temporary to serve as boundary marks between large districts. Various landmarks of a more enduring kind were assigned for them, some natural, some put down artificially. Suppose a dispute arose as to the exact limits of two adjacent territories, whose boundary had been marked out in times past, the Law (IV. 143) enumerate and recognises twelve different marks, by one or more of which the boundary might be recovered and defined. Among these are :—a " stone-mark," *i.e.* a large pillar-stone ; an " ancient tree " of any kind, or the stump and roots of an old oak, after the tree had fallen and disappeared ; a " deer-mark," namely, the hair-marks left by deer or cattle on the trees of a wood, or the hair-marked footpath made by them along a plain ; a " stock mark," *i.e.* stakes in the earth, or the ruin of a mill, or an old bridge under water ; a " water-mark," *i.e.* a river, lake, or well ; an " eye-mark," *i.e.* a straight line fixed by the eye between any two of the preceding which had been ascertained for a certainty, but which lay some distance asunder ; a " defect-mark," *i.e.* a place or line along which there was no cultivable land, such as a declivity, a sedge, a stony vale, or the track of a disused road ; a " way-mark," *i.e.* a king's road, or a carriage-road, or a cow-road (see pp. 393 to 395, below) ; a " mound-mark," *i.e.* a [great] mound or ditch or foss " or any mound whatever," such as that round the trunk of a tree.

Pillar Stones and Ramparts.—That Pillar-stones were regarded as an important means of marking boundaries is shown by their frequent mention in the records. We are told in one law-tract that when certain tribe chiefs had taken possession of a district, they " erected boundaries or placed pillar-stones there " ; and in another place that after land has been enclosed a hole is made in the ground on the boundary, into which is put the "chief's standing-stone,*

* Br. Laws, IV 7, 17; 9, 9; 19, 1, 2.

in order that his share there may be known." It is stated
in Cormac's Glossary (p. 84, " Gall ") that adjacent settlers
are not considered as neighbours till their properties are
provided with pillar-stone boundaries. The custom was
so general that a legendary origin is assigned to it in the
Cóir Anmann, which says that a certain chief named *Failbe*
[Falvy] " was the first person by whom of old in Erin a
pillar-stone was erected to be set as a boundary ": whence
he was called *Failbe Fál-Choirthech*, i.e. 'of the pillar-stone
boundaries.'* We have seen that a stone set up to mark

FIG. 284.

Pillar-stone, about 10 feet high, now called *Cloch-fada-na-gcarn*, the 'long stone of the carns,' in
the centre of a rath beside Carnfree, the inauguration place of the O'Conor kings, near Tulsk, in
Roscommon. (From Kilk. Archæol. Journ. for 1870, p. 250.)

a boundary was sometimes called a "stone of worship ":
corresponding with the pillar-stone god Terminus wor-
shipped by the Romans (see vol. I., p. 277).

Boundary pillar-stones are found standing all over the
country. But pillar-stones were erected for other purposes,
of which the most usual was as a monument over a grave
(for which, see chap. xxxi., sect. 5, *infra*), a practice that
prevailed in Christian as well as in pagan times. Battles
were often commemorated by pillar-stones as well as by
carns and mounds. Sometimes pillar-stones were set up

* Ir. Texte, III. 293. For other notices of pillar-stones as boundaries
se Kilk. Archæol. Journ., 1867, pp. 5, 6 : and 1899, 221, 12.

on raths, of which a fine example may be seen beside Kilkee in Clare : another is illustrated in fig. 284. It has been already mentioned that pillar-stones were sometimes erected as idols. Many of the standing-stones still remaining have a hole through them from which they are commonly called "holed-stones," but the use of these is a mystery.

FIG. 285.

"Holed-stone," near Doagh, County Antrim. (From Kilk. Archæol. Journ. for 1887-8, p. 78.)

Pillar-stones are called by several Irish names:— *coirthe* [curha] ; *coirthe-cloch* (which is a duplication, for *cloch* is a 'stone'); *gall*; *gallan*; and *legann.* As to the term *gall*, of which *gallan* is a diminutive, Cormac's Glossary tells us that pillar-stones were called "gall" because they were first erected in Ireland by the *Gauls* ; and as a matter of fact we have in Irish legendary literature accounts of a colony of Gauls coming in very early times to Ireland. As to many or most of the pillar-stones now remaining in the country, it is often hard or impossible to tell, in individual cases, for which of the above-mentioned purposes they were erected.*

* It is scarcely necessary to remind the reader that the custom of erecting unhewn pillar-stones for various purposes prevailed among most ancient nations: and such stones are found still standing all through Europe and Asia. Holed-stones are also very general, but, as in Ireland, their original purpose is unknown. "The standing-stones or menhirs" [of the world generally]—says Sir John Lubbock (p. 107)—"were no doubt generally erected in memory of some particular event, the majority being in fact tomb-stones of prehistoric times." See also Wood-Martin, Pagan Ireland, p. 307 : and Joyce's Irish Names of Places, vol. I., pp. 95, 342. Cromlechs,

Many of the great mounds or ramparts also still exist : and there is generally a popular legend that they were rooted by an enormous enchanted black pig. One of the largest of all is that in the valley of the Newry river, which separated the sub-kingdoms of Oriell and Ulidia, and which will be found fully described in the Ulster Journal of Archæology—new series—for 1897. Great artificial dividing dykes are found in every part of the world, some historic like the Roman wall in Britain, and some pre-historic. Offa's Dyke dividing England from Wales is a grand example : but the most stupendous artificial dyke in the world is the great wall of China.

2. Land, Crops, and Tillage.

Classification of Land.—The Brehon Law (IV. 277) specifies three main divisions of " superior arable land," recording in this respect an Irish custom in general use in former times :—*First* : "arable land which takes precedence of all lands," *i.e.* land of the very best kind, which pro-duces " everything good "—corn, and milk, and flax, and *glaisin*, and *roid* (see, for these dyeing plants, pp. 358, 359, *infra*), and sweet herbs, and requiring no manure. There are no " sticking plants," *i.e.* no briars nor burdocks (which stick to one's clothes), so that if a horse should graze on it none of these sticking plants will be found on its mane or tail. Rich land of this kind is often called " land of three roots " (*tir* [or *talamh*] *tri meccon*) : " the richest soil, which, " according to the Irish notion of the present day, is always " known by the presence of three weeds, remarkable for " their large roots, namely the thistle, the ragwort, and the " wild carrot."* *Second* : hilly arable land which is well watered ; groves and copses of ash-trees grow here and

dykes, pillar-stones, &c., are treated of in Lubbock's Prehist. Times, chap. v. For full information on holed-stones, with many illustrations, see Wakeman's Handbook of Ir. Antiqq., 3rd ed., by Mr. Cooke, p. 14.

* Petrie, Round Towers, 218, note †.

there ; and the parts of it that are tilled produce good crops. *Third* : labour-requiring arable land ; what is called axe-land, which requires much labour, but which, when well worked, produces good crops freely.

Besides these three divisions of *good* land, the text gives three divisions of " *weak* land," or arable land of an inferior kind, viz. :—Land in which fern grows : upland with much heath and furze : and lastly, black land with bog on the surface, not absolutely beyond tillage. After this enumeration the values are set forth in milch cows.

Manure (Irish *ottrach*) is very often mentioned in the Laws, showing the importance attached to it. A dung-heap is called in Cormac's Glossary *crum-duma*, which O'Donovan translates ' maggot-mound,' from *cruim*, a maggot, and *duma*, a mound. The manure mentioned in the Brehon Law was chiefly stable-manure : and the law-tract (IV. 277) mentions also the application of shells (*slig*, a shell : pl. *slige*) to land to improve it.* This last law-tract (p. 279), following old custom, enumerates eleven different things that add to the value of land, and estimates in *séds* or cows the amount added by each, or at least the amount to be taken as a basis of calculation. Of these the most important are :—a wood properly fenced in : a mine of copper or iron : the site of an old mill [with millrace and other accessories, rendering easy the erection of a new mill] : a road [opening up communication] : situation by the sea, by a river, or by a cooling pond for cattle.

Digging for Water.—Various passages both in the Brehon Laws and in general Irish literature show that the ancient Irish understood the art of obtaining water by digging deeply into the ground. It must have been a pretty common practice moreover, for the annalists assign a legendary origin for it, a thing they never did except

* The use of shells as a land-improver, is well-known : it will be found noticed in the Ulster Journ. Archæol., IV. 271 : and Boate, Nat. Hist., p. 161, mentions it as common in his time.

where the custom was general.   The Four Masters say, under A.M. 3991 : " It was by this king (Fiacha Finailches) " that the earth was first dug in Ireland in order that water " might be in wells."   The Cóir Anmann (p. 395) assigns the discovery to a different person :—" Findoll Caisirni, " which epithet means *cisternae* or ' earth-rending ' : for he " was the first person by whom of old the earth was dug " to make a pit in which water was found at every time." The Greeks similarly assigned the origin of their custom of digging for water to their old hero Danaus, king of the Argives.

The Cóir Anmann (p. 381) states that the Fir Domnann (a tribe of the Fir Bolgs), during their slavery in Greece, were condemned by the Greeks to dig deeply into the earth to obtain water.   There were in Ireland experts who pretended to discover by a sort of divination the proper places to dig for water.   In the story of the siege of Knocklong we **re**ad that when the Munster army were perishing with thirst, their king called in the aid of the famous druid Mogh Ruith (for whom see vol. I., p. 231, *supra*), who hurled his spear high into the air, and directed his disciple Canvore to dig at the spot where it fell.   He did so : and the water burst forth in a copious stream, which relieved the army.   That same fine well exists to this day, and is universally known by the name of Tober Canvore, Canvore's well.*   This practice is alluded to in a more unquestionable authority, the Brehon Laws (IV. 209, 9), where the gloss on the law of the rights of water has an expression implying that a stream of water was sometimes obtained by digging for it.

Crops.—Most of the native crops now in use were then known and cultivated : chief among them being corn of various kinds.†   Corn in general was denoted by the words

* See Irish Names of Places, I. 103. I found the name familiarly used : but the people—at least those I spoke to—knew nothing of the legend.

† Kitchen-garden vegetables have been already noticed (p. 148, *supra*).

arbar [arrar or arroor], and *ith* [ih] ; besides which there was a special name for each kind. In the " Vision of Mac Conglinne " (p. 98) eight different kinds of grain are enumerated and named ; but some of these were mere varieties. These eight occur also in a 14th century Welsh poem. We know for a certainty that wheat has been cultivated in this country from the most remote ages : for we find it constantly mentioned in our ancient literature : of which an interesting illustration will be found in the record of the death of the two princes in Mailoran's mill, p. 333, below. The most common native Irish word for wheat is *cruithnecht* [crunneght], which in Cormac's Glossary is derived from *cruith* [cruh], blood-coloured or red, and *necht*, clean : the first part of this derivation is probably correct, but *necht* is a mere termination. The etymology, however, sufficiently proves the interesting fact, that the wheat cultivated in the time of the venerable King-bishop Cormac—1000 years ago—was the very same as the Irish wheat of the present day ; for every farmer knows that the old Irish wheat—now fast dying out— is distinguished by its red colour.

It is worthy of remark that in several other languages, wheat—as Pictet shows (Les Origenis, 1. 261)—has been named from its colour, not indeed from its redness as in Ireland, but from its whiteness as compared with other kinds of corn. As one instance, may be mentioned the English word *wheat*, which Pictet shows is only another form of *white*. Three other native Irish words for wheat are *dagh*, *mann*, and *tuirenn*.

The observations made about the early cultivation of wheat apply equally to oats (Irish *coirce*, pron. curk-ya) ; numerous references to its cultivation and use are found in our most ancient literature. In modern times, before the potato became very general, oats formed one of the principal articles of food of the people, as it did of old (p. 141, *supra*). Barley (Irish *eórna* [ōrna]) and rye (Irish *scgal* [pron. shaggal : Lat. *secale*]) were cultivated, and formed an important part of the food supplies.

Corn was cut with a sickle or reaping-hook, anciently called *serr* or *searr* [shărr], which in Cormac's Glossary (p. 149) is derived from Latin *serra*. Mac Firbis explains *serr* by *carrán*, which is the present Irish word for a reaping-hook.   Many specimens of reaping-hooks have been found in Ireland, some of bronze and some of iron, which may be seen in the National Museum in Dublin.   They are all small, and cutting with them must have been slow work. Those of bronze are very ancient—probably beyond the

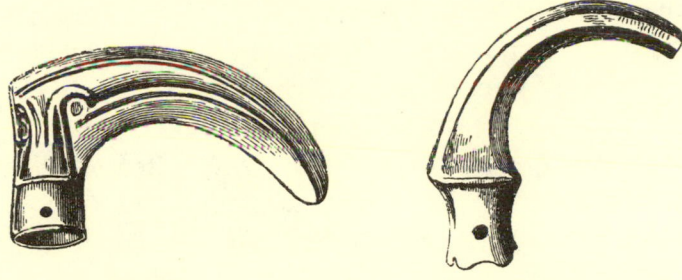

FIG. 286.   FIG. 287.

Ancient Irish bronze reaping-hooks.   Fig. 286 is of beautiful workmanship, 6¼ inches long.   It was fitted with a handle, which was fastened in the socket with a rivet.   Fig. 287 is of much the same construction ; a little imperfect at the top : 7 inches long.   Both now in the National Museum, Dublin.   (From Wilde's Catalogue, p. 527.)

reach of history.   The iron ones are hardly so old ; but still they have the look of great antiquity.   Meadow-grass was cut with a scythe anciently and still called *speal* [spăl] : but an ancient manuscript explains *serr* (sickle) by *speal*, a scythe* ; which may perhaps be taken to indicate that anciently there was little or no difference between a scythe and a sickle.

Corn was reaped as it is at present by cutting the stalks off at the bottom.   But the fact that a *clïab buana*, 'reaping-basket,' is mentioned in some of the tales,† would lead us to think that in very remote ages—in the bronze period—the reaping was sometimes done—as it was, and

* Corm. Gloss., 149.   † Da Derga, pp. 198–9.

is, elsewhere—by cutting off only the tops with the grain, which were brought away in the basket : leaving the straw to be dealt with separately.   If this supposition is correct, it explains the smallness of the reaping-hooks represented above.

The corn, while in sheaves, was stacked in a haggard, which was called *ithlann*, corn-floor or corn-yard.   The word always applied to a corn-rick is *cruach*, which in Cormac's Glossary (p. 44) is derived from a verb meaning ' to sew,' because " it is sewed all round."   From this we learn that the people stacked their corn carefully after reaping, and covered the rick with thatch which they fastened by twining or interweaving with ropes of some kind, probably hay-ropes, or what we now call *sugans*. People do the same still in many parts of Ireland.

Corn was threshed with a flail (*súist*), often on the floor of the kiln-house,* but more commonly on a regularly prepared threshing-floor near the kiln.   In one corner was a little pit or hollow in the floor into which the grain was swept as it was threshed out, and which Adamnan (131) mentions by the Latin name *fossula*, ' little pit.'   A pair of threshers sometimes stood face to face, sometimes side by side : as we see at the present day.   The Book of Aicill has a series of rules for estimating the compensation for injuries to bystanders by an accidental stroke or by the head of the flail flying off,† as I have often seen the *buailteán* or ' striking-stick ' fly off with the latter-day threshers when the *gad* or tying-withe broke.   To get rid of chaff (*cáith* :   pron. caw), the women winnowed the corn by hand, using a winnowing-sheet called *caetig* or *cáiteach*.‡

---

* Br. Laws, III. 221.   Adamnan (p. 131) calls the threshing-floor by the usual Latin name *excussorium*.

† Br. Laws, III. 221 : see also V. 159.

‡ See Todd, Book of Hymns, 17, note 54 : *cáiteach*, in O'Reilly : derived from the same root as *cáith*

Farm Implements.—Most of the common implements employed in farm-work at the present day were used by the ancient Irish, though no doubt they were somewhat different in make. The sickle, scythe, and flail have been already noticed. The use of the plough was universal. The old word for it was *arathar* [arraher], which in Cormac's Glossary (p. 7) is derived from Lat. *aratro*, to plough, as he derives the Irish *ár*, tillage, from Lat. *aro*: but all these Irish and Latin words are cognate, and are not derived one from another, but from an older original. The word *arathar* is now quite obsolete; and the present name for a plough is *céchta* [kaighta], which is also an ancient word. Several of the parts of the plough are

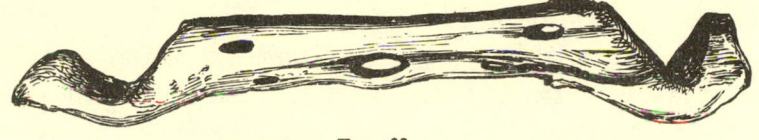

FIG. 288.

A two-horse or two-ox yoke, of timber, 3 feet 9 inches long. Found in a bog in County Monaghan.
(From Wilde's Catalogue, p. 243.)

mentioned in the old records. The coulter or ploughshare was called *socc*, which is the word still used. That it was made of iron we know from many passages—so many that it is unnecessary to refer to instances.

The plough was generally drawn by oxen: but sometimes by horses :—" St. Ciaran had fifty tame horses for tilling and ploughing the ground."[*] Nevertheless when we find ploughing mentioned in old Irish writings, it is nearly always oxen that are in question. The ploughman (*airemh*, pron. arrev) had to see that the several oxen were taken day after day in turn ; and if, under certain circumstances, anyone worked an ox out of his turn without the knowledge of the owner, he was liable to be fined.[†]

[*] Feilire, 61, bottom.   [†] Br. Laws, III. 271, 17.

Cormac's Glossary (p. 43) mentions the *cuing* or yoke, and says it was so called " from the hold (*congbail*) it takes of the oxen " ; and he notices also the *essem*, a rope or strap " uniting one yoke to the other, or to the ox, or to the oxen " (p. 64). The ploughman held each ox by a halter (Irish *cennos*, pron. kennos), and he also carried a sharp goad (Irish *brot*), " so that "—as the law tract expresses it—" the ox may be mastered."* I find no mention in old documents of " ploughing by the tail," which, in comparatively recent times, was so prevalent when horses were employed.†

For breaking clods of clay in a ploughed field farmers used a clod-mallet called *forcca* or *farcha*, which means a mallet of any kind : it had a wooden handle, the head no doubt being also made of wood.‡ They used a spade (*rama*) and a shovel (*sluasat*), both fixed on wooden handles—as noticed in the Brehon Laws (III. 205)—and both probably made of iron. Elsewhere in the laws (IV. 335) a shovel is called by another name *samtach*. In Cormac's Glossary (p. 78) the word for a spade is *fec*, which is still in use even among the English-speaking people of many parts of Ireland, who call a spade *fack* or *feck*. *Ráma* and *sluasad* are also retained as living words for spade and shovel : but the former gets the diminutive form *rámhan*, often shortened to *rán*, both pronounced *rawn*. A rake was used, which, as far as we can judge from the description of it given in Cormac's Glossary (p. 147), must have been much the same as that used at present. There it is stated that " it touches the ground " [when in use], and that " its handle is through a hole." It was, of course, made of wood. It is called in the Glossary *rastal*, which is the word still in use.

---

* Br. Laws, III. 269 ; IV. 304, 305, 306, 307.
† See Irish Names of Places, I. 237.
‡ Br. Laws, IV., 335.

3. *Some Farm-Animals.*

Cows.—From the most remote ages, cows formed one of the principal articles of wealth of the inhabitants of this country ; they were in fact the standard of value, as money is at the present day ; and prices, wages, and marriage portions were estimated in cows by our ancestors (see chap. xxvii., p. 385, *infra*).   As might be expected, therefore, they are constantly mentioned in ancient Irish literature of all kinds ; and they are made the subject of special and important consideration in the Brehon Laws. The most general Irish word for a cow is *bo*, not only at the present day, but in the oldest manuscripts : in one of the eighth-century MSS. of Zeuss it glosses *bos*, with which it is also cognate.   In Cormac's Glossary a passage is quoted from the Senchus Mór to illustrate the word *ferb* as another name for a cow.*   The term *buar* was applied to kine in general, derived from *bo*.   A bull is called in Irish *tarbh* [tarruv], a word which exists in cognate forms in many languages : in the three Celtic dialects—Old Irish, Welsh, and Cornish—it is found in the respective forms of *tarb*, *taru*, and *tarow* while the old Gaulish is *tarvos* ; and all these are little different from the Greek *tauros*, and Latin *taurus*.   *Damh* [dauv], an ox, is evidently cognate with Latin *dama*, a deer.   How it came to pass that the same word signifies in Irish an ox, and in Latin a deer, it is not easy to explain.†   The chief use of the ox was as a draft and plough animal, for which see " Oxen " in Index.

---

* Corm. Gloss., p. 71 ; the original passage of the Senchus Mór, quoted in the ninth or tenth century in the Glossary, may be seen in the present edition of the Senchus Mór (Br. Laws, I. 64, 65), where " teora *ferba* fira," ' three white cows,' are mentioned : one of the evidences of the antiquity of the published edition.

† The transfer of a name from one species of animals or plants to another is a curious phenomenon, and not unfrequently met with.   The Greek *phegos* signifies an oak, while the corresponding Latin, Gothic, and English terms—*fagus*, *boka*, and *beech*—are applied to the beech-tree ; and I might cite several other instances.   See this question discussed in Max Müller's Lectures on the Science of Language, Second Series.

The words *dairt* and *colpa*, meaning a heifer, will be found mentioned in connexion with grazing (pp. 282-3 farther on) and with standards of value (chap. xxvii., p. 386) : and *mart*, an ox, at p. 127, *supra*. The usual Irish word for a calf is *gamuin*, modern Irish *gamhan* [gowan]. Cormac's Glossary (61) gives the old word *dedel* as also meaning a calf : and *lóig* or *laogh* [lay] was still another name. The word *gamhan* must not be confounded with its derivative, *gamhnach* [gownagh], which, according to Cormac's Glossary, means ' a milking cow with a calf a year old ' ; but which in modern Irish is used to signify simply a *stripper*, i.e. a milk-giving cow in the second year after calving. White cows with red ears carried a fictitious and fancy value ; and we often find them mentioned both in the Tales and in the Lives of the Saints. They are also noticed in Cormac's Glossary (p. 72, under " Fir ").

Pigs.—In point of value to the community, pigs came next to cows, and were of more importance to the general run of people than horses. They were kept by almost all, so that they were quite as plentiful and formed as valuable an industry in those days as at present. It has been already stated that pork was valued as food by all persons, from the highest to the lowest ; and the supply was fully equal to the demand. The usual Irish word for a pig was and is still, *muc* or *mucc* : a boar was called *torc*. A very young pig was a *banb* or *banbh* [bonniv], a word which is still known in the anglicised forms of *bonniv* or *bonny*, or with the diminutive, *bonneen* or *bonniveen*—words used in every part of Ireland for sucking-pigs. But an older word for a little sucking-pig was *cumlachtach*, as given in Cormac's Glossary (p. 39). There were many other names for pigs : O'Davoren enumerates eight : but they need not be given here.*

It was cheap and easy enough to feed pigs in those days. Forests abounded everywhere, and the animals

* See Stokes, Three Irish Glossaries, Preface, l. and lxv.

were simply turned out into the woods and fed on mast and whatever else they could pick up. Wealthy people—chiefs and even kings, as well as rich farmers—kept great herds, which cost little or nothing beyond the pay of a swine-herd (*muccaid*, pron. muckee) : and they gave no trouble, for, except in winter, they remained out day and night, needing no sties or pens of any kind, being sufficiently sheltered by the trees and underwood. But in winter they were kept in sties, called in Irish *muc-fhóil* [muckole], as already stated (p. 41, *supra*). The special time for fattening was autumn, when mast abounded ; a practice mentioned by Adamnan (p. 135), whose words imply that the fat pigs were slaughtered at the end of autumn : so that few had to be kept in sties during winter. The Brehon Law mentions pigs feeding on mast (Irish *mes* or *meas* : pron. mas), in wood-covered land : and an expression in another part of the Law implies that wood-land for hog-feeding was sometimes private property, and was of value.* But woodland was generally a part of the " commons " (I. 187, *supra*), where every member of the sept was free to send his pigs to feed.†

When woodland was not convenient, or when for any other reason pigs had to be kept and fattened at home, they were fed on corn or sour milk, and on offal of various kinds : these were managed chiefly by women. A pig kept at home was called a " sty-pig " (Irish *muc-crai* : *cra*, a sty).‡ In Cormac's Glossary (p. 27, " Bacur ") mention is made of " *braiches* round which pigs go " : and in another part of the same Glossary (105) is noticed a " *lotar* or trough in which are *brachles*." *Braiches* and *brachles* both signify the grains or refuse from *brac* or *braich*, malt (p. 117, *supra*) : and from these expressions we learn that the custom of feeding pigs on malt-grains, now so familiar near breweries, was also practised by the

---

* Br. Laws, II. 367, bottom ; III. 39, bottom ; and IV. 103, ₅.
† Br. Laws, IV. 257, last par.   ‡ *Ibid.*, II. 367, bottom ; 369, top.

ancient Irish: for we have seen that brewing was then very common.

The old Irish race of pigs were long-snouted, thin-spare, muscular, and active: and except when fat they could scour the country like hounds. There are many indications in old writings that they were often wicked and dangerous, ready to charge and attack when pro-voked; and sometimes they inflicted fatal wounds. In the Book of Ailill are a number of regulations providing for damages for injuries inflicted by pigs, taking into careful account whether there was provocation or not. For instance it is stated that when an idler provokes a pig, in consequence of which it " charges out on him," and wounds him, the owner is exempt.*   In the remote forests there were plenty of wild pigs: and we have many references to them in our literature.   In the twelfth century Giraldus gives us this testimony :—" In no part " of the world are such vast herds of boars and wild pigs " to be found."   (Top. Hib., I. xix.)

Sheep were kept everywhere, as they were of the utmost importance, partly as food, and partly for their wool: and they are constantly mentioned in the Brehon Laws as well as in general Irish literature.   There was in Ireland a many-horned variety, which however has been long extinct.†   The common Irish word for a sheep was, and is, *cáera*, gen. *cáerech*.

Trespass by Animals.—When two or more tenants held farms next each other, the Law lays down minute regula-tions for the trespass of all kinds of domestic animals, and enumerates many circumstances to be taken into account in fixing fines.   Among these is the presence or absence of " the caretaking which the Law requires."‡   If the animals had not been properly cared, full fines were exacted for trespass ; but if it could be proved that due

* Br. Laws, III. 243, 245.   † Wilde, Catalogue, 249.
‡ Br. Laws, IV. 87, top line.

care had been exercised, the fine was mitigated. The following were some of the precautions that should be taken. Hens should have a hood (*cocholl*), i.e. a heavy rag tied partly on the back and partly up the neck and head. In other cases their wings were clipped, and their feet were tied with *spancels*, i.e. simply bits of twine, or their claws were covered with rag boots. A goat should be hampered by having some kind of leather cover—called a *brogue* or shoe in the Law—tied on each leg : the legs of yearling calves should have a spancel (*urcholl*) : there should be a herdsman with cows, and a shepherd with sheep. At night all animals should be in their proper enclosures, pigs in a sty, horses in a stable (or properly fettered if left outside), and cows in a *bawn* or enclosure. Pigs should have a yoke (Irish *srathar*, pron. srahar) or tie on the back and legs. Pet pigs were, as we might expect, notorious for their mischievous propensities ; and they were very ingenious moreover, for they commonly found an opening through the fence into the neighbour's field, and in this manner showed the way to the whole herd, which were quick enough to follow their pioneer. Accordingly the Law lays down as much fine for a pet pig as for two other animals, for the first offence ; as much as for three for the second ; and as much as for four on the third occasion.*

4. *Herding, Grazing, Milking.*

Herding and Grazing.—The old word for a cowherd was *bóchaill* or *buachaill*, which glosses *bubulcus* (' herdsman ') in one of Zeuss's eighth-century glosses (p. 183, 5). In Cormac's Glossary (p. 20) it is derived from *bó*, a cow, and *cail*, keeping : a ' keeper of cows ' : but in modern times the word *buachail* has come to signify ' boy ' simply without any reference to occupation. Another old name for a cowherd was *bóare* or *boaire* [bo-ar-ĕ : 3-syll.], literally

* For all these see Br. Laws, IV. 87, 109, 111, 117, 119.

' cow-carer.'   The *boare* of Ross, king of Ulster A.D. 248, was *Bairche* or *Boirche*; and from him were named *Beanna Boirche* [Banna Borka], ' Boirche's Peaks,' now the Mourne Mountains in Down, because he herded the king's flocks there.*   The account in the Dinnsenchus adds that when herding, his favourite look-out point was the summit of Slieve Slanga, now Slieve Donard, the highest of the range ; from which he could see southwards as far as the Dublin and Wicklow Mountains, and northwards as far as *Cloch-a-stookan,* or the Giant's Causeway.

There were special keepers of cows, of sheep, of swine : swineherds have been treated of elsewhere.   At the present day a shepherd is called *aedhaire* and *treudaighe* [aira, traidee].   As an aid to herding, bells were sometimes hung round the necks of cows and sheep.   Animals thus furnished are said—in the gloss to the Senchus Mór—to be " privileged " (Irish *uaisli* : singular *uasal* : literally ' noble '), which meant nothing more than that they were distinguished above the rest of the herd.†   There was a fine for removing the bell.   Such bells have continued in use till this day : and in the National Museum may be seen many specimens, some no doubt modern, but some very old.

The nature and use of " commons " have been already explained (vol. I., p. 187, *supra*).   The commons pasture was generally mountain-land, usually at some distance from the lowland homesteads ; and it was grazed in common and not fenced in.   Each head of a family belonging to the tribe or *fine* had the right to send his cattle on it, the number he was entitled to turn out being generally in proportion to the size of his farm.   In regulating the right of grazing, animals were classified, a cow being taken as the unit.   The legal classification was this :—two geese are equivalent to a sheep ; two sheep to one *dairt,* or one-year-old heifer ; two *dairts* to one

* Trip. Life 423.   † Br. Laws, I. 127, 4; 143, middle.

colpthach. or two-year-old heifer ; two *colpthachs* to one cow ; a cow and a *colpthach* equal to one ox. Suppose a man had a right to graze a certain number of cow on the common : he might turn out the exact number of cows, or the equivalent of other animals, any way he pleased, so long as the total did not exceed the amount of his privilege.*

When several persons had grazing farms lying adjacent to each other, or when they grazed their cattle on a common, they often employed one herdsman to attend to all, who was paid by contributions from the several owners, each giving in proportion to the number of his cattle. This is what was called *comingaire* [4-syll.], *i.e.* ' common herding,' from *ingaire* or *gaire*, herding ; and under this name it is mentioned in the Brehon Law. The gloss on the Senchus Mór says that all those owning the cattle should be " in brotherhood with each other,"† and that each one is to be faithful [to the others] : by which is meant that a man, while looking specially after his own cattle, should, so far as he reasonably could, have an eye to those of his neighbours. In the sixteenth and seventeenth centuries it was usual for all the people of a village or townland, after putting down the crops in spring, to migrate to the uplands with their families and cattle, living there in temporary settlements during the summer, and returning to their homes in the beginning of autumn in time to gather in the crops. An upland settlement of this kind was called a *buaile* [booley] : and the custom was known as *booleying* by Anglo-Irish writers, several of whom have described it. Probably this custom descended from early times, for it is noticed in the gloss to the Senchus Mór, in the first volume of the Brehon Laws, p. 133.‡

---

* Br. Laws, IV. 101, bottom.   † Br. Laws, I. 143.
‡ For more information about " booleying," see Irish Names of Places, vol. I., p. 239.

Remnants of the old regulations regarding the use of commons land survive in many parts of Ireland to the present day. There are still " commons "—generally mountain-land—attached to village communities, on which several families have a right to graze their cattle according to certain well-defined regulations; and there are bogs where they have a right to cut peat or turf—a right of turbary, as they call it : and if an individual sells or otherwise disposes of his land, these rights go with it. Grazing in common was lately found, by the Congested Districts Board, in full operation in Clare Island, and in re-arranging the land there they wisely left the old custom undisturbed. A curious instance existing near Swords, seven miles from Dublin, has been described by Judge Kane in a letter which has been published in the Journal of the Roy. Soc. of Antiqq., Irel., for 1890–91, pp. 81, 82. The arrangement for the classification of animals in regard to the right of grazing continues also in force in many parts of the country : the present unit being commonly the *colpthach*, i.e. a cow : now called by the people a " collop." I know one place in Limerick where the people still speak familiarly of a man owning so many collops of grass on the adjacent mountain-common. During the winter, when grass was scarce, cows were often fed on straw—and probably on hay—as at present.*

Farm Life and Milking.—The people of Ireland, not the farming classes merely, but the general community, were early risers, and went early to bed: of which many examples might be cited. One of the *geasa* or prohibitions of the king of Ireland enjoined that while at Tara he should be always out of his bed at sunrise. The two daughters of King Laegaire while living in Cruachan, came out at sunrise to wash their hands, *according to their custom*. The bondmaid of Dubthach, St. Brigit's father, milked the cows at sunrise. From a statement in the

* Br. Laws, III. 151, 13.

Book of Ailill it would seem that the active working-day in the houses of farmers began at sunrise and ended when the cows came to their stalls : and in the houses of chiefs it began when the horse-boy let out the horses in the morning, and ended at bed-time.* A picture of the usual custom of the farmer's homestead in the evening is seen in an incidental entry in the story of the Voyage of the O'Corras, where the three robbers proposed to postpone their evil work *go d-tíosdis ba ocus innile an bhaile dá n-árasaibh ocus dá n-ionnadaibh bunaidh*—" till the kine " and the cattle of the homestead should come to their " byres and their proper places."† Women always did the milking, except of course in monasteries, where no women were employed, and the monks had to do all the work of the community.

From the custom of milking early the word *ambuarach* has come to signify early in the morning : from *buarach*, a cow-spancel, and that again from *bo*, a cow : *am-buarach*, ' in spancel-time.'‡ The *buarach* or spancel was made then as now of a stout rope of twisted hair, about two feet long, with a bit of wood—a sort of long-shaped knob— fixed at one end, and a loop at the other end into which the knob was thrust so as to fasten the spancel round the two hind legs of the cow. That they used a spancel—and a strong one too, with a big knob—in the old times is shown by a story in the Dinnsenchus. An able-bodied idle fellow, roaming about, met a girl herding her cows in the evening in a lonely place, and attempted violence. But he reckoned without his host : for she turned on him and knocked him down with a blow of the wooden end of her spancel, and then twisting the strong hair-rope tightly round his neck, choked him.§

* Br. Laws, III. 419.
† Rev. Celt., XVI. 36 : Old Celtic Romances, 403, 404.
‡ Rev. Celt., XIV. 428, ₂₂; 437. See the word *buarach* in this sense in LU, 61, *b*, top line.
§ Rev. Celt., XIV. 31 : LL, " Contents," 43, *b* ; and Text, 167, *b*, ₁₆.

CHAPTER XXIV

WORKERS IN WOOD, METAL, AND STONE

SECTION I. *Chief Materials.*

imber.—All the chief materials for the work of the various crafts were produced at home. Of wood there was no stint : and there were mines of copper, iron, lead, and possibly of tin, which were worked with intelligence and success. We know that in early ages Ireland abounded in forests ; so that wood as a working material was plentiful everywhere. Even in the time of Giraldus Cambrensis—the end of the twelfth century—when clearances and cultivation had gone on for a thousand years, the greater part of the country was clothed with trees. He says :—" Ireland is well wooded and marshy. The [open] plains are of limited extent compared with the woods."* The common Irish word for a tree was, and is still, *crann* : a wood is *coill* or *fid*. The Brehon Code (IV. 147), in setting forth the law for illegally felling trees, divides them into four classes, with a special fine for each class :—

1. " Chieftain " trees (*airigh feada*) : oak (*dair*) ; hazel (*coll*) ; holly (*cuileann*) ; yew (*ibur*) ; ash (*uindius*, more

* Top. Hib., I. iv

commonly called *fuinnse, fuinnsecnn,* or *fuinnseóg*) ; pine (*ochtach* or *giumhas*) ; apple (*aball*).

2. " Common " trees : alder (*fernn*) ; willow (*sail*) ; hawthorn (*sceith*) ; mountain-ash, or rowan-tree, or quicken tree (*caerthann*) ; birch (*beithe*) ; elm (*leam*) ; and another which is not known from its Irish name, *idha*.

3. " Shrub " trees : blackthorn or sloebush (*draidean* or *droigen*) ; elder or boor tree (*trom*) ; white hazel (*finncoll*) ; aspen (*crithach*, lit. ' shaking ') ; arbutus (*caithne*) ; and two others not known from their names, *feorus* and *crann-fir*.

4. Bramble trees : fern (*raith*) ; bog-myrtle (*rait*) ; furze (*aiteand*) ; briar (*dris*) ; heath (*fraech*) ; ivy (*eideand*) ; broom (*gilcach*) ; gooseberry (*spin*).

The commentator on the Law proceeds to state the qualities or circumstances that give each of the " chieftain " trees its " nobility." The oak : its nobleness in size and appearance, and its *meas* or acorns (for feeding swine : Irish *dearcan*, an acorn). Curious, no mention is made of its bark, which was very valuable for tanning (see p. 367, below). The hazel : its nuts (see p. 155, *supra*), and its wattles, for building wicker-houses. The apple : its fruit and its bark—which was probably used for tanning. The yew : its noble structures : *i.e.* the value of its timber for ornamental furniture, household vessels, and building. This tree was produced in great abundance : so much so that Giraldu; Cambrensis records an opinion that the poisonous juices and exhalations of the yew-trees seriously checked the increase of bees. The holly : because it was made into chariot-shafts ; and for another reason, but here the Irish statement is unintelligible to me. The ash : " supporting a king's thigh " : *i.e.* probably it was used in making the king's throne ; also " half the furniture of arms " ; that is, the handles of spears were made of it. The pine : because its wood was used in making puncheons.

Among the various materials mentioned in the Senchus Mór is whalebone, which is called the *fabra* or ' fringe-bones ' of a *míl-mór* or whale. The gloss says that it was used for making saddle-trees and the bottoms of sieves : and also occasionally for hoops of [small] vessels when suitable wood-hoops were not to be had.*

Metals.—The metallic weapons and tools preserved in our museums are generally either of bronze (sometimes brass, occasionally copper) or iron. The bronze objects far outnumber those of iron, which is partly explained by the fact that iron rusts and wastes away much more quickly than bronze. It is generally recognised that the three materials—stone, bronze, iron—represent three successive stages of human progress : that is to say, stone in its use as a material for tools and weapons, is more ancient than bronze, and bronze than iron. But there was no sudden or well-marked change from one to another : they all overlap. Stone was used in a primitive stage when bronze was not known ; but it continued to be used long after the introduction of bronze. So bronze was used for some long period before iron was known ; but continued in use long after the discovery of iron. And more than that : all three were used together down into Christian times.

That the ancient Irish were familiar with mines, and with the modes of smelting and of extracting metals of various kinds from the ore, is shown by the frequent notices of mines and mining both in the Laws and in the general literature. The Law (IV. 279) enumerates eleven things that add to the value of land, among which is a mine of copper or of iron. The Senchus Mór mentions a penalty for digging a silver mine without the permission of the owner† ; from which we may infer that a mine was, or might be, the private property of the owner of the land : a fact which is still more clearly stated in the Book of

* Br. Laws, I. 125, 10: 135, last paragraph.   † *Ibid.*, I. 167, 171.

Aicill.* An ancient Irish MS. tract of the Brehon Laws, quoted by Petrie (R. Towers, 219), gives the pay of the delver who digs copper ore. When Connall Cernach was fighting the men of Connaught, while retreating in his chariot, he came to a river. "There were miners washing ore" (*batar mianaighe ac nige mianaigh*) in the river above him : and he difficulty he experienced in finding the exact fording place and crossing the turbid and troubled water enabled his pursuers to overtake and kill him.† Here the washing of ore is mentioned as quite an ordinary occurrence ; and in many others of the oldest Irish tracts the smelting of ore is frequently referred to as a matter very familiar. The hard breathing of champions fighting is compared to the bellows-blowing of smiths smelting ore (*tuaircnech nan goband ic méinlegad miannaig* : LL. 218, *b*, 6 bot.). The plain now called the barony of Fermoy in Cork must have been famous for its mines, for it was anciently known as *Magh méine*, the 'plain of minerals.'‡

The truth of all this documentary testimony—and much more might be adduced—is fully confirmed by evidence under our own eyes. Sir Richard Griffith—in his Report to the Royal Dublin Society, 1828—remarks that the numbers of ancient mine excavations still visible in every part of Ireland, prove that "an ardent spirit of mining adventure" must have pervaded the country at some remote period. He instances old copper mines at Mucruss near Killarney, and at Ballydehob in Cork, old coal mines at Ballycastle, Co. Antrim, and the lead mines of Milltown in Clare, the oldest mines perhaps in Ireland. In these last many rude tools were found, such as oaken shovels and iron picks of extraordinary size and weight. O'Halloran also, in the Introduction to his "History of

---

* Br. Laws, III. 203.
† Death of Conall Cernach in Zeitschr. für Celt. Phil., I. 108.
‡ O'Curry, Man. & Cust., I. 215.

Ireland," mentions the antique mining shafts on the Wes-tropp estate in Limerick, near the Shannon : and very ancient copper mines have been found at Knockmahon in Waterford.*

The usual Irish words for smelting metals were *bruth* and *berbad* [bruh, berva], both of which signify ' boiling.' A smelter was called *bruithneóir* [bruhnore], meaning, as O'Clery's Glossary expresses it, " a man [employed in] " boiling or melting [*ag bearbhadh no ag leaghadh*] gold or silver or metal." *Bruth* and *caer* were both applied to a mass of any kind of metal. Of the detailed smelting processes of the Irish we have very little knowledge. But we know that, whether these arts grew from within or were brought hither by the first immigrants, the Irish miners successfully extracted from their ores all the native metals then known.†

In Ireland as elsewhere copper was known before iron. It was almost always used as bronze, which will be treated of at page 297, farther on. We have unques-tionable documentary evidence—such as the " Confession of St. Patrick "—that iron was in familiar use in Ireland in the fifth century of the Christian era : and as we learn from Tacitus that the Caledonians used iron swords in his time, it is certain that this metal was known in Ireland at least as early as the first century : probably much earlier. According to tradition the iron mines of Slieve-an-ierin, east of Lough Allen in the County of Leitrim (*Sliabh-an-iairn*, the mountain of iron), were worked by *Goibniu*, the great Dedannan smith ; and it is now as celebrated for its iron ore as it was when it got the name, long ages ago. In the Book of Rights we find it repeatedly stated that masses of iron were sometimes given as tribute to kings. In the old tale of the Death of Goll and Garbh, from the book of Leinster, steel is mentioned under the

* See Brash's Article on Ancient Mining in Ireland, Kilk. Archæol-Journ., 1870–1, p. 509.   † See Wilde's remarks : Catalogue, 350–7.

name of *crúaid* [croo-ee], which means ' hard ' ; and hence came the name of Cuculainn's sword, *crúadin*, a diminutive form of *crúaid*. Among the pagan remains found in a carn at Loughcrew were many specimens of iron implements, all, as might be expected, very much corroded by rust. One was " an iron punch five inches long with a " chisel-shaped point bearing evidence of the use of the " mallet at the other end."[*]   This was probably used for punching the patterns on gold ornaments (vol. I., p. 566, *supra*).

The Irish word for iron is not very different from the English :—*iarann*, Old Irish form *iarn* [both pronounced eeran], and the word exists in various forms in Welsh and in several of the northern languages ; such as Gothic, *eisarn* ;   Old High German, *isarn* ;   Anglo-Saxon, *íren* ; Welsh, *heyrn*.

Sir Robert Kane[†] says that tinstone has been found only in the auriferous soil of Wicklow. But Smith, in his " History of Kerry " (p. 125), states that he found near the lake of Killarney an ore which contained tin : and, according to Sir Richard Griffith, tin occurs in combination with lead and zinc in Dalkey, near Dublin. There is a very ancient tradition recorded by Nennius as well as by native Irish writers, that one of the " Wonders of Ireland " was the four metallic circles surrounding Loch Lein or the Lake of Killarney, viz. a circle of tin, a circle of lead, a circle of iron, and a circle of copper[‡] : which, so far as tin is concerned, is corroborated by Smith's experience. But whether tin was mined at home or imported from Cornwall—or both, as is more likely—it was constantly used in making bronze : and often without any mixture. " The ores of " lead seem to occur in more places than those of any

---

[*] Fergusson, Rude Stone Monuments, 218.
[†] Industrial Resources, p. 210.
[‡] Irish Nennius, 220. See Kinahan's Geol. Irel., p. 357.

" other metal."* The mines were worked too, so that the metal was sufficiently abundant : the very old lead mines of Milltown have been noticed at p. 289. Zinc, which was chiefly used in making brass, was also found, commonly in connexion with lead. Gold and silver have been already treated of.

2. *Builders.*

From the most remote times there were in Ireland professional architects or builders, as there were smiths, poets, historians, physicians, and druids ; and we find them often mentioned in our earliest literature. Even the very names of the mythical builders of Tara, Emain, Ailech, and other royal residences have been preserved.

There were two main branches of the builder's profession :—stone-building and wood-building. An ollave builder (I. 442, *supra*) was supposed to be master of both, and, in addition to this, to be so far acquainted with many subordinate crafts as to be able to " superintend " them, as the Law (v. 95, 4) expresses it : in other words, to be a thorough judge as to whether the work was properly turned out by the several tradesmen, so as to be able to pass or reject as the works deserved : all which resembles what is expected from architects and builders of the present day.

The most distinguished ollave builder of a district was taken into the direct service of the king, and received from him a yearly stipend of twenty-one cows, answering to a fixed salary of £250 or £300 of the present day : for which he was to oversee and have properly executed all the king's building and other structural works. In addition to this he was permitted to exercise his art for the general public for pay : and as he had a great name, and had plenty of time on hands, he usually made a large

* Kinahan, p. 348.

income. In one of the Brehon Law tracts,* there is a curious classification of the works an ollave builder might undertake, with the payment fixed for each, as taken separately: nineteen classes in all, which are as follows :— The two most important—(1) Building in stone and (2) Building in wood—are named first, as he was to be thorough master of these : six cows each. (3) *Ibroracht*, i.e. ' yew-work ' : six cows. (4) Cook-house or kitchen-building : six cows. (5) Mill-building : six cows. Constructing the three following—(6) [large] ships : (7) *barcas* or ordinary small ships ; and (8) currachs or wicker boats : four cows each. (9) Making wooden vessels, namely vats, tubs, keeves of oak, and small vessels : four cows. (10) *Uamairecht*, conjectured to be ' cellar-making ' (*uam*, a cave) ; perhaps making the subterranean stone-house under a rath (see p. 56, *supra*) : two cows. Constructing the three following—(11) causeways ; (12) stone walls ; (13) *clochans* or stepping-stones across a river : two cows each. For the three following—(14) carvings in wood (*rinnaighecht*, pron. rinneeght) ; (15) crosses ; (16) chariots : two cows each. For these three—(17) wickerwork houses ; (18) shields ; (19) bridges : two cows each. Builders of the inferior grades (below the ollave) had correspondingly lower fees.

It will be observed that in most of the above there is an absence of distinct specification as to quantity or time, as to who supplied materials, or paid the workmen, &c. ; but, as in many others of the Brehon Law provisions, all this was regulated by custom, which was at the time so universally understood and recognised that it was not considered necessary to put it in writing. As illustrating the systematic way in which the Law attempted to provide for all such matters, it is worthy of remark that the permanent stipend of twenty-one cows received by a builder

---

* Br. Laws, v. 93, 95 : Petrie, Round Towers, 346 : O'Curry, Man. & Cust., II. 52, *et seq.*

from the king was calculated on the above charges, in this way :—Full fees allowed for the first two works (stone-building and wood-building) : six cows each ; and one-sixth fees for all the others combined, *i.e.* one-sixth of 54 : 9 cows ; which with the first twelve make 21 cows. Some of the handicrafts mentioned in the above list will be noticed in the present chapter : others have been or will be dealt with in other parts of this book.

By far the most celebrated of all the ancient architects of Ireland was the Gobban Saer, who flourished in the seventh century of our era, and who therefore comes well within historic times. The best accounts represent him as a native of Turvey near Malahide, north of Dublin : and he is mentioned in the Lives of many of the Irish Saints as having been employed by them to build churches, oratories, and houses, some of which still retain his name. This great builder fills a prominent place in all sorts of Irish literature from his own time downwards ; he is men-tioned in the eighth-century poem referred to in vol. i., p. 230, *supra*—almost contemporary with himself ; and to this day the peasantry all over Ireland tell numerous stories about him.*

3. *Braziers and Founders.*

Dán [dawn] is a general word for any art, science, or trade : and *aes-dána* [' men of art '] is applied to those skilled in such arts. In the commentary on the Senchus Mór (Br. Laws, ii. 119), smiths, carpenters, shield-makers, physicians, and poets, are called collectively *aes-dána* : but most commonly the term *aes-dána* meant poets. Some-times an artisan was termed simply *dán* : but there were of course different epithets to distinguish the various callings. It was however usual to restrict the applica-

* Almost everything that is known of his authentic history has been brought together by Dr. Petrie in his Round Towers, 385–7. Several popular stories about him will be found in the Dublin Penny Journal.

tion of *dán* to a poem or poetry : whence a poet was often called *fer-dána*, ' man of poetry.'

The word *goba*, gen. *gobann* [gow, gowan], is applied to a worker in iron—a smith : *cerd* or *cerrd* [caird], to a worker in brass, gold, and silver—a brazier, goldsmith, or silversmith : *saer* to a carpenter, builder, or mason—a worker in timber or stone. Sometimes a bronze or brass-worker was called *umhaidhe* [oovee], from *uma* (p. 297, *infra*). These are the usual applications : but as the arts and trades sometimes overlap, so the words are often applied in somewhat more extended senses : for example, Culann, the mighty smith of the Red Branch Knights, is called a *cerd* in the Book of Leinster.* Still they are generally distinguished, especially in Christian times : and we find *goba* and *cerd* sharply defined in a passage of the Tripartite Life (266, 267), specifying the duties of St. Patrick's household, where we are told that his three smiths (*gobainn* : pl.) made bells for him (which at that time was smithwork, as they were made of hammered iron), while his three braziers (*cerdae* : pl.) made chalices and other brazen and bronze vessels for the altar. The three classes of artists are also well distinguished in a passage in the " Battle of Moyrath " (p. 103), in which the skill of *cerdae*, *gobainn*, and *saeir* (all three words plural) is praised. The three mythical artisans of the Dedannans, the brothers of Diancecht the physician (I. 261, *supra*), were *Goibniu* (gen. Goibnenn) the *goba* or smith, who made their spearheads and swords : *Creidne* the *cerd*, who supplied rivets for the spears, hilts for the swords, and bosses and rims for the shields : and Luchtine the *saer* or carpenter, who made their wooden and wicker shields and spear-handles.† A *goba* and a *cerd* are distinguished also in the Brehon Law rule (III. 193), that goods found in a kiln, a

---

* LL, 63, *a*, 22; *b*, 17.

† Corm. Gloss., 123, under " Nescoit." See also Man. & Cust., I. 246, 248, 249.

kitchen, a forge, or a mill, left in charge of the owner, if they were unconnected with the proper business of the place, were forfeited : and the particular instance of this rule given is :—If gold, silver, or bronze was found in the forge of a *goba* (blacksmith), it was forfeited : because these materials had no connexion with the business of a smith, but belonged to that of a *cérd*.

The word *cérdd* glosses *aerarius* in Zeuss (page 60, 43): and in the form of *caird*—which exactly

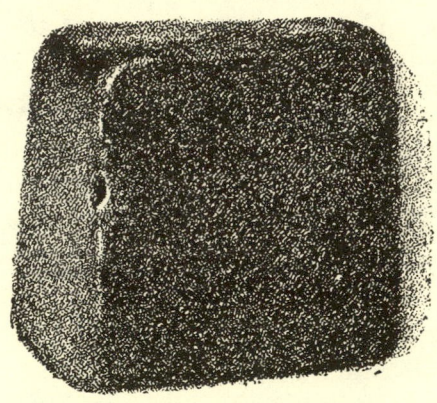

Fig. 289.   Fig. 290.

Braziers' or Goldsmiths' Anvils. Fig. 289 is the natural size, and is much worn : the little shallow holes were for riveting. (From Wilde's Catalogue, p. 523.) Fig. 290 is 3 inches high, and 1¾ inch thick. Two of its corners form right angles: one is rounded : one bevelled : so as to suit the different shapes required. (From Kilk. Archæol. Journ., 1885-86, p. 538.)

represents the sound—it has held its place as a living word in Scotland, even among speakers of English, but it is applied to a tinker :—

> " Her charms had struck a sturdy caird,
>   As weel as poor gut-scraper."
>   BURNS.

Aerarius, which, according to the glossator of twelve hundred years ago, is equivalent to *cérdd*, signifies literally a 'worker in brass'; and, curiously enough, this corresponds exactly with the description the *caird* gives of himself in Burns's poem :—

> " My bonnie lass, I work in brass,
>   A tinkler is my station."

The work of a *cerd* proper has been dealt with in the chapter on art.

We have already seen that the ancient Irish were very skilful in metallic art. Metallic compounds were carefully and successfully studied, copper commonly forming one of the ingredients. The most general alloy was bronze, formed of copper and tin : but brass, a compound of copper and zinc, was also used. The Irish name for copper was *uma*, gen. *umai*, whence the Irish word *umaide* or *umhaidhe* [oo-vee], one of the names of a brazier—a bronze- or brass-worker ; for this word *uma* is used also to denote both bronze and brass. Thus, according to the Tripartite Life, the chieftain Dáre gave St. Patrick a caldron of *uma*, which it is pretty certain was made, not of pure copper, but of bronze ; for all the caldrons still preserved are of that alloy. There were several special terms for different alloys, each no doubt designating a compound of certain metals in definite proportions ; but the exact compounds referred to by some of these terms are unknown to us.

There were two chief kinds of bronze, red and white, or rather reddish and whitish. The red bronze was called *derg-uma* (*derg*, red) or *cred-uma* (for I take it that these two words mean the same thing) and sometimes *créd*, simply ; and the white was called *finn-uma* (*finn*, white) or *findruine* [fin-drĭnă], two terms that also seem to me to be identical. *Findruine* was much more expensive than *creduma*, and was kept for the finer kinds of work. Assuming that the ancient Irish pinginn or penny represented in those times a value equivalent to that now represented by 6s. 8d. of our money—which may be taken as approximately true—a statement in an ancient authority quoted by Petrie ("Round Towers," 219) enables us to assign value on a similar basis to **one ounce** of each of the following metallic materials :—

1 oz. of finn-uma, findruine, or white bronze ⎫	is	⎧ 6s. 8d.
1 oz. of derg-uma, creduma, or red bronze ⎪	represented ⎬	3s. 4d.
1 oz. of zinc . . . . . . ⎬	in present	3s. 4d.
1 oz. of lead . . . . . . ⎭	value by	⎩ 1s. 8d.

The difference in value between the two kinds of bronze is recognised in the tales : as when Queen Maive estimates the comparative merits of the three heroes :— "The difference between *creduma* and *findruine* is between "Loegaire Buadach and Conall Cernach ; and the difference "between *findruine* and red-gold is between Conall Cernach "and Cuculainn." Accordingly she proceeds to give effect to her judgment by presenting the three heroes with three goblets of values according to merit.* The red bronze may be seen in the spear-heads and caldrons in the National Museum, and the *findruine* or white bronze in the ornamental shrines, and other ancient works of art. Many of the spear-heads and other bronze articles belong to a period some centuries before the Christian era.

Metal-casting is very often referred to in general terms in our literature, showing how familiar it was : and through these incidental references we get now and then a glimpse at the artists' tools and appliances. The workmen used charcoal for their fires, that made from birch-wood, as we have seen (vol. I., p. 565, *supra*), giving the greatest heat then attainable, sufficient—with the help of a flux—to melt all ordinary metals. They used a ladle (Irish *liach*) to pour out the melted metal ; and it had to be used carefully, for the Book of Aicill (Br. Laws, III. 213) has a series of provisions for accidents, mentioning damages for injuries to persons or animals during casting, and also

* Fled Bricr., p. 75–79, and 93–95.

during the process of mining. All this indicates how generally metal-founding was practised.

A moulding-compass used by founders was called *luaithrinn* [loo-rin], compounded of *luath* [looa], ashes, and *rinn*, a point. In Cormac's Glossary this word is used characteristically in describing

Fig. 291.

Ornamental inlaid hook, natural size. Possibly for suspending a sword. The scroll-work indicates that it belongs to Christian times (vol. I., p. 551). Now preserved in the National Museum. (From Wilde's Catalogue, p. 572.)

See next page.

the whirlpool of *Coire Brecain*, where he says the waters whirl round " in the likeness of moulding-compasses" (*fo cosmailius luaithrinde*),* showing how familiar the implement was in the ninth and tenth centuries. The exact use of the moulding-compass and the origin of its name, are instructively illustrated in a legendary story quoted from an ancient manuscript by O'Curry.† Mac Engĕ, a shield-maker, was employed to make shields for the Ultonians, and had exhausted all his patterns (for each chief had a special design for himself: see vol. I. p. 125, *supra*) when Cuculainn came to him for a shield, and demanded a design different from all the others. While

Fig. 292.

Spear-head, now in National Museum, where many equally or more beautiful are preserved. Others of very graceful form, and of admirable workmanship, are figured in vol. I., pp. 107, 110, 111, *supra*. (From Wilde's Catalogue, p. 499.)

See next page.

the artist was puzzling his brain trying to invent a new device, a man having in his hand a small fork with two sharp prongs came up to him and said : " Spread ashes (*liath*) on the floor of your workshop" : which he did. Then the man planted one prong of the fork in the ashes

* Corm. Gloss., 41 : Three Irish Glossaries, 13.
† Man. & Cust., I. 329.

and with the other described circular devices for the hero's shield. Accordingly *luaithrindi* or *luaithrind*, 'ashes-engraver,' was thenceforward the name of this sort of fork or compass.

The exquisite skill of the ancient Irish braziers is best proved by the articles they made, of which hundreds are preserved in our Museum. Two illustrations are given on last page (figs. 291 and 292); a beautiful specimen of enamelled metal-work is described at page 258, *supra*, and shown in fig. 280 ; and others will be found in various parts of this book. As to the hook represented in fig. 291, Wilde describes it as " one of the most " beautiful specimens of "inlaying bronze with " silver and some dark " metal (after the fashion " of the ancient *niello*) " which has yet been " discovered in Ireland."

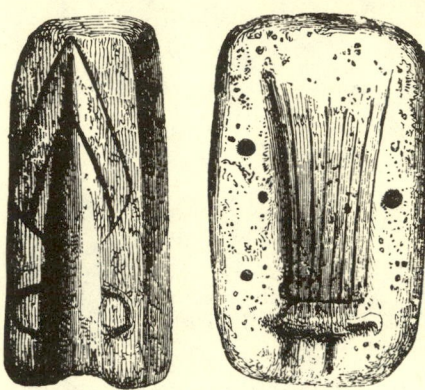

Fig. 293.   Fig. 294.

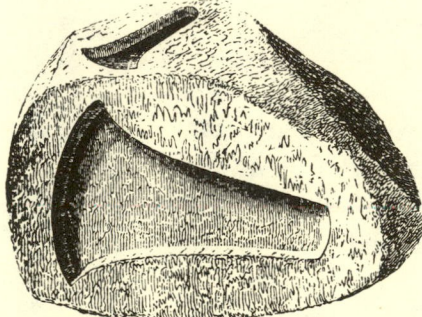

Fig. 295.

Stone Moulds. Figs. 293 and 294 in National Museum, Dublin : fig. 295 in the Belfast Museum. (From Wilde's Catalogue, pp. 91 and 392.)

The gracefully - shaped spear-heads, which, in point of artistic excellence, are fully equal to any of those found in Greece, Rome, or Egypt, were cast in moulds : and we have not only the spear-heads themselves but many of the moulds, usually of stone, proving—if proof was needed—that all these articles were of native manufacture. In one glass case in the National Museum there are more than forty moulds for celts, spear-heads, arrow-heads, &c. : some looking as fresh as if they had been in use yesterday. Probably clay- and sand-moulds were used ; but these would not be preserved.* The old cairds were equally accomplished in making articles of hammered bronze, of which the most characteristic and important are the beautifully-formed caldrons—many of exquisite workmanship—made of a series of bronze plates, hammered into shape and riveted together. Of these numerous specimens may be seen in the National Museum. One will be found figured at page 125, *supra* (fig. 215), and another in vol. I., p. 21, fig. 13. In both of them the heads of the rivets project outwards so as to form ornamental conical studs, a kind of ornament used in other metal-work, as in the bronze trumpets and gold gorgets. But all caldrons had not these cone-headed rivets. A handsome dish, hammered into shape with great skill from a single flat piece of bronze, is shown on fig. 196, p. 71, *supra*.

4. *The Blacksmith and his Forge.*

In a state of society when war was regarded as the most noble of all professions, and before the invention of gunpowder, those who manufactured swords and spears were naturally looked upon as very important personages. In Ireland they were held in great estimation ; and in the historical and legendary tales, we find smiths entertaining kings, princes, and chiefs, and entertained by them in turn. We know that Vulcan was a Grecian god ; and the ancient Irish had their smith-god, the Dedannan Goibniu, who figures in many of the old romances. It sometimes was considered an additional distinction in a chief or warrior to be a good metal-worker. Fergus mac Roy, to show his fitness for the duty of rearing the infant Cuculainn, enumerates his accomplishments, and among other things says, " I am a good craftsman."† Smiths, like the men

* See Wilde, in Catalogue, 392.   † Miss Hull, Cuch. Saga, 19.

of other arts and professions, were of different grades :
an *ollave-goba* or *prim-goba* (' prime-smith ') or *flaith-goba* (' chief-smith ') being of the highest rank.   We find
these distinctions often mentioned in both secular and
ecclesiastical writings,* showing that they were real, and
universally understood and acknowledged.

Cérdcha or *cérddchae* originally meant a workshop in
general, derived, according to Cormac's Glossary (p. 46,
" Ca ") from *cérd*, an artisan, and *ca*, a house : " artisan-
house.'   In " Three Fragments of Irish Annals " (p. 223),
it is applied to the workshop of a fuller of cloth : and in
Zeuss (60, 44) it glosses the Latin *officina*, a workshop of
any kind.   But its most usual application was to a forge :
and it is still so applied, and pronounced *cartha* (the first
syll. long, as in *car*).   A forge was in old times regarded as
one of the important centres of a district.   If, for instance,
horses whose owners were not known were impounded
for trespass, notice had to be sent to the dun or fortress of
the nearest lord, to the principal church, to the fort of the
brehon of the place, and to the forge of the smith (Br.
Laws, IV. 107) ; and in like manner notice of a waif should
be sent to seven leading persons, among them the chief
smith of the district (*ibid.*, III. 273).   For forges were
places well frequented, as they are at the present day,
partly by those who came to get work done, and partly
by idlers.   And sometimes individuals took a nap with
comfort and laziness, as we know from this provision of
the Book of Aicill :—that if any one who had business
at the forge fell asleep while waiting for his turn, it was
the duty of the smith or the bellows-blower to awaken
him when dangerous showers of sparks were flying
about, otherwise they were liable (with some limitations)
for any injury that befell him (Br. Laws, III. 191, and
note 2).

* For instance, Br. Laws, III., p. 273, 22; Oss. Soc., IV. 299, 16; and
Stokes, Lives of SS., 235.

The anvil (*inneoin* : pron. innone) was placed on a block or stock (*cepp* : pron. kepp) : *in cepp i mbái ind inneoin* : " the block on which the anvil is set " (LL. 35, *a*, 5). The anvil must have been shaped something like those in use now ; with a long projecting snout on the side : for in a passage in Cormac's Glossary (p. 135) describing an ugly-looking giant, it is said : " His nose is larger than the *úrbuinde* [oorbinnĕ] or ' anvil-snout ' of a smith." The anvil was large and heavy, as we may infer from the following story. On one occasion King Ochy Moyvane, passing by a large forge, saw his five sons standing inside : and wishing to test their courage, he quietly set fire to the building and shouted to them to save the smith's property. Four of them took out small and portable things ; but Niall seized the heavy and valuable articles and removed them one by one, among them the bellows and the anvil-and-block, while the house was blazing round him.* This young prince subsequently succeeded his father, and is well known as Niall of the Nine Hostages. Yet the anvil of those times could not have been as massive and firm as the present ponderous anvil : for in the Book of Aicill provision is made to meet the case of the sledge (Irish *ord*) breaking or injuring the anvil, or the sledge itself breaking on the anvil, either through the carelessness of the sledger, or because the smith held the red-hot iron in an awkward position† : all which would indicate that neither anvil nor sledge had the solidity or weight of those now in use.

If the anvil was not well secured on the *cepp* or block, it was liable to slip off during working : or the sledge might slip off the anvil if struck awkwardly ; or the head of the sledge might fly off the handle if fastened insecurely ; or the whole sledge might slip from the hand of an awkward sledger ; or two sledges might come into

* O'Curry, Man. & Cust., I. 147 : LL, 35, *a*. See for another version Rev. Celt , XXIV. 195.   † Br. Laws, III. 191.

collision : in any one of these cases injury to persons might result, for which the Law (III. 189) made provision for compensation by the person in fault. So far as I am aware no ancient blacksmith's anvil is to be seen in any of our museums ; but small braziers' anvils made of bronze have been found, two of which are figured at p. 296, *supra*. Another small anvil like these was found in a crannoge in Ulster. Ancient anvils, especially large ones, are rare in all parts of the British Islands.

The smith held the red-hot iron in a *tennchair* [tinne-her], pincers or tongs. In the " Voyage of Maildune," as the boat approached an island inhabited by gigantic blacksmiths, the adventurers heard the thundering sound of smiths' hammers striking a red-hot mass of iron on the anvil : and as soon as the smiths saw the boat one burly fellow rushed out with a great piece of glowing iron in the tongs (*tenchoir*) and flung it after the curragh* : which, however, it missed. A similar incident befell St. Brendan as related in his Voyage† : and both remind us of Ulysses' escape from the Cyclops. While the smith held the glowing iron on the anvil, another person struck it with the *ord* or sledge ; and sometimes two persons were sledging at the same time (Br. Law, III. 189). It is to be presumed that the smith used a hand-hammer like those of the present day.

Making and fixing of rivets (*seman* or *semman*, a rivet) was part of the work of either smith or brazier, but the brazier usually put them in spear-heads and swords. In some of the swords and spear-heads in the museum, the rivets still remain.

A water-trough was kept in the forge, commonly called *umar*, and sometimes *telchuma* ; but this last word is also used to denote a barrel or puncheon. The smith kept a supply of wood-charcoal in bags, called *cual craing*, or

---

* Rev. Celt. **x.** 53 : Old Celtic Romances, **145.**
† Brendaniana, **161.**

cual craind, i.e. " coal of wood."* I do not know if coal from the mine was used : but the distinctive term *cual craing* would seem to imply that it was : and besides, as already remarked (p. 289, *supra*), very ancient coal mines have been found near Ballycastle. The smith wore an apron commonly of buckskin, like those smiths wear now.

The last of the smith's appliances to be noticed is the bellows. The Irish name for a smith's bellows is *builcc* or *builgg* [bullig], which is merely the plural form of *bolg*, a bag, like the English *bellows*; in the Book of Leinster the plural article is in one place brought in, *na builgg*, ' the bags '; all indicating that, in Ireland as in other countries, the primitive bellows consisted of at least two bags, which of course were made of leather. Why two bags were used is obvious—in order to keep up a continuous blast ; each being kept blowing in turn while the other was filling. This word *builcc* the Irish continued to employ for their bellows, even in its most improved form, just as we now call the instruments we have in use " bellows," though this word originally meant ' bags,' like the Irish *builcc*. The following passages relating to the use of the forge-bellows will give us some idea of its construction. In the story of the " Courtship of Emer " we are told that when Cuculainn and the other heroes went to be trained by Domnall, the great Scotch instructor in military and athletic exercises, he set them to practise, in the first instance, on a bellows, and on a spear, as a sort of preliminary exercise to attune their muscles properly for learning—what they came to learn—the special and more difficult battle-feats :—" they were taught by him "—says the old text—" *one thing* on " the flagstone of the small hole, namely, to blow bellows " (*foseted cethar bolcc*) : they had to work on it till the soles " of their feet were all but black or livid : and [they were

* *Telchuma* and *cual* (or *cuail*) *craing*. LL, 35, *a*, 4. see also vol. I., p. 565, *supra*.

" taught] *another thing* on a spear, on which they were set
" to climb up."*

An independent and probably older authority is part
of an elegy on a smith by his wife quoted in Cormac's
Glossary (which itself belongs to the ninth or tenth century),
in which occurs the following passage :—" The red flame
" of his furnace mounted up to the roof : sweet were the
" murmurs that his bellows (*a dí bolg*) used to chant to the
" hole of his furnace."†

In the Book of Aicill‡ the rule is laid down that if
sparks from a smith's fire injured a bystander under certain
circumstances, the bellows-blower was liable for damages
if he had blown with unnecessary violence, so as to scatter
showers of dangerous sparks : but if he had done so by the
direction of the smith, then both were liable in equal
shares.

These passages will enable us in a measure to recon-
struct the old Irish smith's bellows, and exhibit the mode
of working it.   From the Brehon Law extract last quoted
we see that in every forge there was a special bellows-
blower, who blew strongly or gently as occasion required,
sometimes directed by the smith.   From the passage in
the " Courtship of Emer," where the heroes are set to blow,
we may infer that the bellows were worked with the naked
feet, that it took some time to learn how to do so, and that
the bellows was large and laborious to work, since it taxed
the strength of mighty heroes.   That it was large and
heavy we know also from the story of Niall at p. 303.

---

* The original Irish of that part of this passage relating to the bellows,
as printed by Kuno Meyer, is this :—*Forceta leiss aill for licc dercain* [*edon*]
foseted cetharbolcc : noclistis fuiri iarom napdar duba na glassa a fond
(Rev. Celt., XI., pp. 444, 445)   Another version of the same passage,
slightly but not materially, different, will be found in the Stowe MS.,
D, 4, 2, fol. 82, *b*, col. 2, line 8, in the Roy. Ir. Academy, Dublin.

† The original Irish of the above passage, as printed by Stokes, is
this :—*For bir ifraig dercc anis ; babinde nochantais dord friderc aneis
adi bolg* (Three Ir. Glossaries, 32 : Corm. Gloss. 124).

‡ Br. Laws, III. 191.

The passage in Cormac's Glossary speaks of the sweet murmurs of the bellows blowing through the " hole of the furnace " ; while that from the " Courtship of Emer " gives us a somewhat closer view by the expression " the flagstone of the small hole " (*licc,* a flagstone : *derc,* a hole : diminutive *dercan,* with its genitive *dercain,* a small hole). All this means that the smith's hearth or furnace was constructed of flags, in one of which was a small hole through which the pipe directed the air-current from the bellows into the fire. It is doubtful whether this small hole was in the under flag on which the fire was placed, or in the bottom of one of the side-flags : but it is an interesting fact that at the present day, in some parts of Ireland, the fire in ordinary dwelling - houses is often blown — as I have seen done—with a small fan-bellows up through an aperture in the hearthstone by means of a pipe running from the blowing instrument under the floor to the aperture.

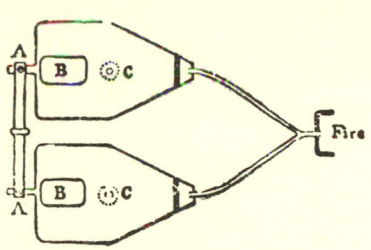

FIG. 296.

Conjectural plan of double or two-chambered forge-bellows. The bellows-blower stood with his feet on BB, and his face towards the fire. AA, the cross-beam or lever, turning on its centre-fulcrum. CC, clapper-valves in bottom boards. The rest of the diagram explains itself.

The name given to the bellows in Cormac's Glossary —*di bolg,* " two bags "—indicates that the bellows in view here had two separate chambers lying side by side. Each of these must have consisted of an upper and an under board with sides of leather : and in the under board of each was a simple clapper-valve as in our present kitchen-bellows. From each chamber extended a pipe, the two pipes uniting into one which was inserted into the hole in the flagstone. The two chambers were placed close to each other, and there must have been a short crossbeam or lever (AA in fig. 296) turning on a centre pivot, with its two ends loosely fastened to the two backward projections of the upper boards. The bellows-blower stood on top, one foot on each board (at BB), and pressed the two down alternately. As each was pressed down, and its chamber emptied through the pipe, the other was drawn up by its own end of the cross-beam, and the chamber was filled through the clapper-valve at bottom : and thus the chambers were compressed and expanded in turn so as to keep up a continuous blast. There was a cross-bar fixed firmly above the bellows for the blower to grasp with his hands, so as to steady him and enable him to thrust downwards with his feet when a strong blast was required, like a modern bicyclist when mounting a hill.

But there was another and a better sort of bellows, having four chambers, as we see by the name employed in the " Courtship of Emer " —*cethar-builcc*, ' four bags ' (of which the *cethar-bolcc* of the above extract is the genitive plural). This was probably constructed and worked

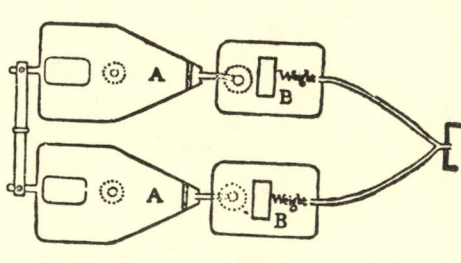

FIG. 297.

Conjectural plan of quadruple or four-chambered forge-bellows. The two pipes through which the chambers AA kept the chambers BB filled are shown: also the four clapper-valves (by little dotted circles) in the four under boards.

in something like the following manner as partly shown in the plan : it is indeed impossible to conceive how four chambers could otherwise be brought into play. The fire was blown from the two chambers BB by pressure of heavy weights like the present smith's bellows. The two chambers AA were worked by the bellows-blower, who stood on them with his face towards the fire. When one of the chambers AA was pressed down, it filled the chamber B in front of it through a pipe communicating with an opening in the bottom board of B (with clapper-valve) : and the other chamber B was similarly filled in its turn. The function of the chambers AA was to keep the two BB filled : the function of BB was to blow the fire. This *cethar-builcc*, or four-chambered bellows, gave a more uniform blast than the two-chambered one. But it was much harder to work : and this doubtless was the reason why old Domnall selected it for the heroes, in order to make sure that, as they needed hard exercise, they should have enough of it.

A bellows — no doubt a very large one, or more probably several worked together — was also used in smelting, as we know from the following comparison in Cormac's Glossary, a part of his description of the Spirit of Poetry disguised as a monstrous giant :—" Like the " blowing of a bellows smelting ore (*oc berbad mianaig*), " was the drawing in and the puffing forth of his breath : " sledge-hammers would not strike from a glowing mass " [of iron] such a shower of fire as his lips struck forth." The comparison of the hard breathing of champions or animals fighting, to the blowing of a smith's bellows, is very common :—*Rabulgsetar a n-óli ocus a srona mar bulgu goband i certchai* : " their cheeks and their noses puffed out like the bellows of a smith in a forge."*

It may be as well to finish this subject here with what there is to say about the domestic bellows. This was totally different in make and mode of using from the forge-bellows, as well as from our present common kitchen-bellows. The Senchus Mór† mentions a bellows among the domestic utensils of a chief's house ; but the name used is not *builcc* but *trefet*, i.e. ' blower.' The gloss upon this (Br. LL., I. 145) explains it thus—bringing in two other names :—" *Trefet* of a chief's house means the *teite*, namely, " that which keeps turning round, and through it the fire is " blown through the leather : or [as another derivation] " it [*trefet*] refers to the strong *fet* or pipe through which " the fire is blown in each chief's house ; *i.e.* the *séitiri*

* LL, 104, *a*, ₂.   † Br. Laws, I. 126, ₅; 127, ₇.

" or blower." So far the gloss. *Séitiri*, as we know, is derived from *séit*, to blow : and the idea put forward in this alternative derivation in the gloss is that *trefet* is shortened from *tre-feit*, which means ' through the pipe,' from *tre*, through, and *fet* or *fead*, a pipe. From this description we must conclude that the bellows used in private houses was one of those made to blow by revolving fans inside. This is further indicated by the fact that in the law-tract it is not called *builg* (' bags '), though three other names are applied to it—*trefet*, *teite*, and *séitiri*. This form of bellows is still occasionally met with, but the body is now made of lacquered tin instead of wood and leather. Moreover, among the English-speaking Irish people it is not called a " bellows " but a " blower," which is the exact equivalent of the old Irish term *séitire*, or in its modern form *séidire* [shaidera], and which is indeed the very term used by O'Donovan in his translation of the Senchus Mór (Br. Laws, i. 127, 7).

5. *Carpenters, Masons, and other Craftsmen.*

Carpenters.—We have seen how carefully handicrafts were classified by the ancient Irish, as set forth at page 293, *supra*. Some of these were sufficiently important and engrossing to give exclusive employment to separate tradesmen : but it is probable that in case of others the same craftsman worked at two or more of them as occasion arose. Woodworkers of whatever kind do not figure near so prominently in the ancient literature as smiths and braziers : yet they must have been more numerous, for there was more work to be done in wood than in metals. One important source of employment for carpenters was the building of houses, which in old times were nearly always of wood. A carpenter who devoted himself to house-building was called *ailtire*, from an old word *alt*, meaning a house : and this branch of the business was called *ailtirecht*.* Accordingly O'Davoren† defines an *ailtire* as *saor denma tighi*, ' a house-building carpenter.'

It has been already stated that the yew-tree was formerly very abundant. Its wood was highly valued and used in making a great variety of articles : so that working in yew was regarded as one of the most important of trades. It required great skill and much training and practice : for yew is about the hardest and most difficult to work of all our native timber : and the cutting tools must have been particularly fine in quality. Yew-work was called *ibraracht*, modern form *iubhraracht* [yooraraght], from *ibar* or *iubhar*, the yew-tree. Various domestic vessels were made from it (p. 69, *supra*), and it was used for doorposts and lintels and other prominent parts of houses, as well as for the posts, bars, and legs of beds and couches, always carved. In the most ancient of the tales we often find mention of houses ornamented with " carvings (*aurscartad*) of red yew " ‡ : and even so late as the first half of the thirteenth century this custom is recorded in the following words written by the Ulster poet Mac Conmidhe in his poetical description of the cathedral of Armagh :—" Upon the arches of this white-walled church are clusters of rosy grapes carved from ancient yew."§ So high was the estimation in which these ornamental carvings in yew were held that the Brehon Law has a special provision for their protection, prescribing fines for scratching or otherwise disfiguring the posts or lintels of doors, the heads or posts of beds, or the ornamental parts of any other furniture.|| It is probable that bows for archers were made of yew as well as of other wood; but I have not met with any passage mentioning this.

Among other tradesmen, there were the *dúalaidhe* [doolee] or painter (from *dúal*, a brush) ; the *rinnaidhe*

---

* Br. Laws, v. 106, ₇ and note ; and 107, ₉, ₁₄.
† Three Ir. Gloss., 54 : Br. Laws, vi., Glossary, " Ailtire."
‡ O'Curry, Man. & Cust., ii. 57.   § *Ibid.*, 58. || *Ibid*, 57.

[rinnee] or metal engraver (from *rinn*, a sharp point, a sharp-pointed instrument) ; and the *erscoraidhe* [erscoree] or wood-carver.*   Carvers were in much request and exercised their art in the highest perfection—as we have seen—on yew-wood.

Various Tools.—Besides other tools mentioned else-where in connexion with certain special arts and crafts, the following, chiefly used by wood-workers, may be dealt with here.   They are often noticed in Irish literature, but more frequently in the Brehon Laws

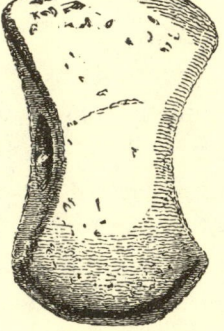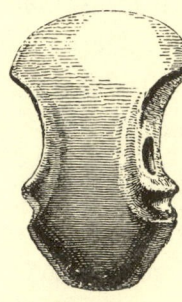

than elsewhere. The old Irish wood- and metal - workers seem indeed to have used quite as many tools as those of the pre-sent day.

There were two names for a saw, *turesc* and *rodhb* [rove], of which *turesc* is still used. Some-

Fig. 298.   Fig. 299.

Stone hatchets, of very hard close-grained stone. Fig. 298 is very large and heavy, being 8¼ inches long. Fig. 299 is 5¼ inches long, beautifully made, and highly polished. (From Wilde's Catalogue, p. 80.)

times it was called *serr*; but this term was more commonly applied to a scythe or a sickle : the point of resemblance between saw and sickle being the teeth on the edge. Sawing (with a *rodhb*) is mentioned in the *Agallamh* (p. 111) as a specially noisy work : and the derivation of *turesc* in Cormac's Glossary (p. 161) makes plain the mode of working : from *tairis*, across, because—says the Glossary—" it cuts everything across."   In the crannoge of Cloonfinlough in Roscommon were found deer-horns neatly sawn in preparation for further manufacture.

There were—as at the present day—several kinds of axes and hatchets variously shaped, and used in different sorts of work, as may be seen by the number of names

* O'Curry, Man. & Cust., II. 209, 210.

for them, and the manner in which they are often distinguished. The common hatchet used in the workshop was called *tuagh* [tooa], which seems to be a general name for a hatchet or axe of any kind : it was applied not only to the hatchet used by tradesmen, but also to a battle-axe. In all forms of axe, the metallic head was fixed on the handle, the same as now, by wedging the wood through the *cro* or opening in the iron or bronze. The head, too, of the carpenter's axe, if not securely fixed, was liable to fly off ; and if this occurred through carelessness, the Law (III. 175) laid down a rule regarding compensation when a bystander was injured. Great numbers of bronze axes are preserved in the National Museum, Dublin. The carpenter's hatchet was probably like some of those figured in vol. I., p. 119, *supra*. Two primitive stone hatchets belonging to prehistoric times, are shown on last page : the originals are in the National Museum, Dublin.

The Crith Gabhlach, in enumerating the various articles that a brewy or keeper of a house of public hospitality should have always ready, mentions three kinds of axes :— a *fidchrann* [feecran], a *fidba* [feeva], and a *biail* [beeal].[*] The *biail* was used in felling and clearing wood. Bishop Olcan, we read, went looking for a place in which to settle, with his " *biail* on his shoulder "[†] ; of course to clear a space from trees and bushes. *Fid*, the first syllable in both *fidchrann* and *fidba*, means wood, and *chrann* or *crann* in the former means a tree or a wooden handle. A *fidba*, or, as it is sometimes called, *fodb* [fove], was something like our bill-hook : we find it mentioned in the Crith Gabhlach as used in making wooden fences.[‡] Again in the Book of Aicill, a decayed king is quaintly said to retain only " the kingship of the three handles, the " handle of his flail, the handle of his *biail*, and the handle

---

[*] Br. Laws, IV.; 310, 12, 13.　　　　　　　[†] Trip. Life, 136, 20.

[‡] Br. Laws, IV. 315, 19, 20. See also Senchus Mór, in vol. I. 124, 14, 15; and Gloss, 141, top lines.

" of his *fidba*."   In the Dinnsenchus* it is said that a man
named Raigne cut down a wood with his *bacc* and his
spade, showing that the *bacc* was a felling axe.   It was
something like the present hedge-cutter's bill-hook.   The
word *bac* or *bacc* means a 'bend' (in this case a *hooked*
blade fixed on a handle); and the gloss on the Brehon
Law mentions a *bac* as used for cutting ivy.†

A *tál* [tawl] or adze—*i.e.* an axe having the edge
across or at right angles to the line of the handle—was
used for special sorts of work; as, for instance, in making

wooden shields; and of course,
in cooperage.   It was an exceed-
ingly common tool, as it is constantly mentioned in all sorts of
records.   More than one historical personage had the epithet
Mac Táil ('son of an adze')
affixed to his name, to denote
that his father was one of
those wood-workers who used
the adze.

Fig. 300.

Bronze adze: in National Museum:
4⅞ inches wide along the edge. (From
Wilde's Catalogue, p. 523.)

An awl, by whatsoever tradesman used, was called
menad or *meanadh* [manna], which is still the Irish word
all through Ireland: but in Munster it takes the form
meanatha [mannaha].   The fanciful derivation of *menad*,
given in Cormac's Glossary (p. 108), is very suggestive :—
from *mín* [meen], small, and *áith* [ā], sharp, as if the
word was contracted from *mín-áith*, ' small-sharp.'   The
old Irish carpenters used an auger and called it *taráthar*
[tarawher], a name which is still in use.   In Cormac's
Glossary the word is fancifully analysed as if contracted
from *dair-uath-air* [dar-oo-ar], meaning ' the oak hates it
(*dair*, oak : *uath*, hatred): " because," as the Glossary
adds—" of its cuttingness, for it cuts through the oak.'

The Crith Gabhlach, enumerating the tools that ought to be in the house of every brewy, includes a *tarathar*.

Irish carpenters and others used compasses which they named *gabulrind* [gowlrin], a word given in Cormac's Glossary* as the equivalent of the Latin *circinus* (a ' pair of compasses '). The Irish term is quite descriptive, being compounded of the two words, *gabal*, a fork, and *rind* or *rinn*, a point : that is to say a fork with two points. Among the pagan relics found under a carn at Loughcrew are many combs engraved with circles by a compass, and also a bit of iron having all the appearance of being the leg of a compass.† The large circles on some of the flat golden gorgets (p. 234, *supra*) were obviously made with a compass: all going to confirm the truthfulness of the records.

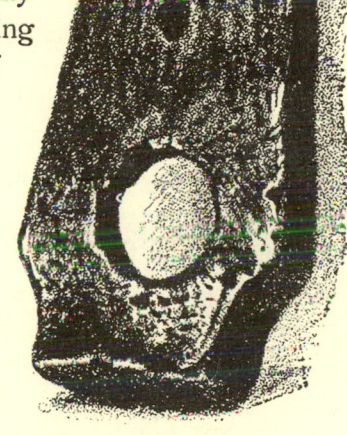

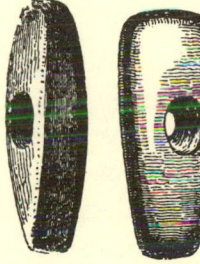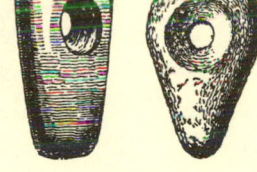

Fig. 301. Fig. 302. Fig. 303. Fig. 304.

Figs. 301, 302, and 303 are small primitive stone hammers. (From Wilde's Catalogue, p. 79.) Fig. 304 is a bronze hammer, found in Sligo: 6 inches long: well worn from work. (From Kilk. Archæol. Journ. for 1885-6, p. 538.)

The mallet used by carpenters, fence-makers, and other workmen, was generally called *farcha* or *forcha*. In the year 512 (FM, A.D. 503), Lewy, king of Ireland, was killed by lightning at a place thence called *Achad-farcha*, a name

* Corm. Gloss., p. 30 : Irish text in Three Ir. Gloss., p. 9.
† Fergusson, Rude Stone Monuments. p. 218.

which is commonly translated the ' Field of lightning,' but which primarily means the ' Field of the mallet.' Indeed the very words used by the Four Masters and other annalists are (in English) " having been struck by a mallet of lightning " (*forcha-teinntighe*) : the idea being the same as that of the Scandinavians, who armed their god Thor with a lightning hammer. A sledge was called *ord* : an ordinary hammer was *lámh-ord* (' hand-sledge ') : but sometimes *cas-ord*, now generally made *casúr* [cossoor]. The *cas* in this, which means ' twisted ' or ' bended,' probably refers to the " claw," so that a *casord* or *casúr* would be a ' claw-hammer.' This is in some measure borne out by the fact that the word *mailin* was used to designate another kind of hammer, no doubt one without a claw : for *mailin* means bald or bare : a " bare or clawless little hammer."

Carpenters used a *rungenn* or *runcan*, a plane : a slightly different form of the name is found in the Brehon Law, where it is stated that the posts of the doors and beds of certain classes of houses were finished off with a *rungcin* [rungkeen], which O'Curry understood as a moulding-plane.* In the Story of Táin bo Fraich (138), 139, bot.) in the Book of Leinster, one of the houses of the palace of Cruachan is described as having decorations of red yew " with variegated planing " (*fo m-brecht-runcain*).

Workers in wood used a sort of press called *cantair*, either for straightening wood or forcing it into certain shapes—after being softened probably by water or steam.† In Stokes's Irish Glosses on Latin Declension *cantair* is the word used to explain the Latin *troclia* : and O'Reilly gives *cantaoir* as a name for any sort of press. The ancient Irish builders used a crane of some kind for lifting heavy articles, as is proved by the following sentence in Cormac's Glossary describing a very repulsive-looking giant :—

* Man. & Cust., II. 29, bottom.
† O'Curry, in Stokes's Irish Glosses on Lat. Decl., p. 60, No. 239.

" *cuirre ina córr auróchala a dhá gruad*, " rounder than a
lifting-crane his two cheeks."*   Here the Irish word corresponding to " crane " is *corr*, which is still the name of any
bird of the crane kind : and it is applied in this passage
to the machine, exactly like the English word *crane,* on
account of the long beak.   The comparison of the giant's
cheeks to the lifting-crane refers to the rounded or bulging
shape of the body of the machine.

The lathe and other turning-wheels were well known
and employed for a variety of purposes.   The Brehon
Law (v. 107) when setting forth the privileges of various
classes of craftsmen has *tornoire* or turners among them,
explaining that these are the men " who do *tornairecht* or
turning."   A much older authority, an eighth-century
Irish glossator, in his remarks on Ps. II. 9, explains a
potter's wheel as " a round wheel (*roth cruind*) on which
the *cérda* or potters make the vessels."†   Mr. Johnson, in
his observations on ancient Irish gold-work, states that he
found the cups of one gold fibula marked with three concentric circles so true as to " have all the appearance of
being done on a lathe."‡   Once the lathe was known it
would of course be used on wood : and in the crannoge
of Cloonfinlough in Roscommon were found, among many
workshop remains, a quantity of shavings exactly such as
would be left by a turner.§   The Irish word for a lathe
is *deil* [dell], which is used by Keating‖ ; and at the present day, speakers, whether using the Irish or English
language, call a lathe a *dell*.   But I have not found the
word in any very old documents.

Chisels of a variety of shapes and sizes were used by
wood-workers : of which the following illustrations will
give a very good idea : the originals—which are all of

---

* Corm. Gloss., 135, bottom : Irish text in Three Ir. Gloss., p. 36, 29.
† Stokes and Strachan, Thesaur., I. 23 : see also p. 79, *supra*.
‡ Proc. Roy. Acad., 1893–6, p. 782.   § *Ibid*., vol. v. p. 211.
‖ See " Deil " in Glossary of Atkinson's Three Shafts.

bronze—are preserved in the National Museum. It has been suggested by Sir John Lubbock that many of the smaller and thinner bronze celts were used as chisels. The Four Masters use the word *fonsura* for a chisel.[*] A large number of bronze gouges are preserved in the National Museum; but I have not found any special Irish name for a gouge. Among the collection of bronze tools found at Dooros-Heath in King's County (p. 320, *infra*) are three gouges with the regularly curved edges, well adapted for excavating and paring wooden bowls and

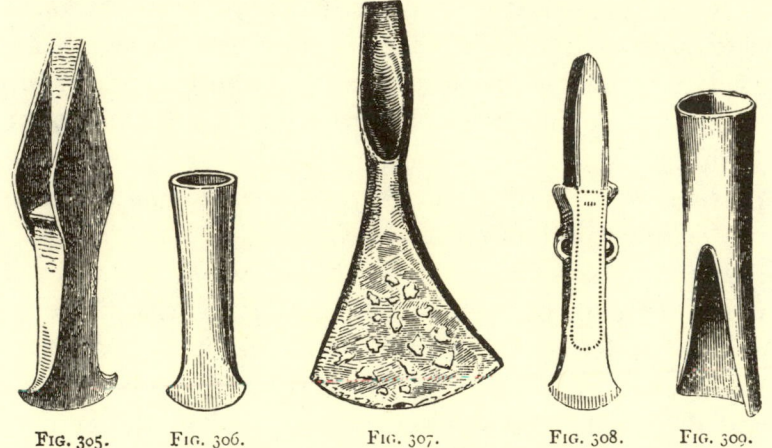

FIG. 305.   FIG. 306.   FIG. 307.   FIG. 308.   FIG. 309.

Figures 305, 306, 307, and 308, bronze chisels: figure 309, a bronze gouge. All in National Museum. (From Wilde's Catalogue, p. 521.)

goblets[†]: and about the same time another was found in Wexford.[‡] The bronze of these and of all the other cutting instruments in the King's County collection is excessively hard. It may be observed that bronze can be made almost or altogether as hard as steel by hammering.

Sharpening.—For sharpening edged tools and weapons, the people used a whetstone, which is called in Cormac's Glossary (p. 42) *cotud*, literally meaning 'hard,' and defined "a *lic* or stone on which iron tools or weapons are ground": but it is often called *lec*, which is the general name for a

<hr />

[*] O'Donovan, Suppl., 647.   [†] Proc. Roy. Ir. Acad., IV. 240.
[‡] Proc. Roy. Ir. Acad., IV. 369.

flat stone, just as we now sometimes call a whetstone "a stone" for shortness. The whetstone is very often mentioned in the Brehon Laws (as in V. 485, line 7 from bottom). But they had also a circular grindstone which was turned on an axis like those now in use. The grindstone was called *liom-brón* [leev-vrone], 'sharpening millstone,' and also *lic-llmad* [lic-leeva], 'stone of grinding'—corresponding exactly with the English name "grinding-stone": and it was turned round by means of a cranked handle. The crank was called *ruiti*, which

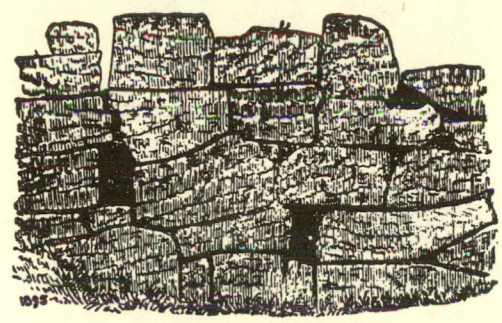

FIG. 310

Specimen of dry or mortarless masonry : portion of the wall of Caher- more, near Kilnaboy, in Clare. The stones are in their natural state— unhammered. (From Mr. Westropp's Article on Prehistoric Stone Forts of Northern Clare, Kilk. Archæol. Journ. for 1896, p. 367. To illustrate observations at p. 323, *infra*.

is defined in connexion with the grinding-stone in a gloss on a sentence of the Book of Aicill (Br. Laws, III. 295) in a manner that leaves no room for doubt as to what it was :—" *Ruitech*, i.e. the thing which runs well from " him and to him [*i.e.* from and to the person turning it], " namely the crooked stick." A grindstone was one of the numerous articles which a brewy was bound to have in his house (Br. Laws, IV. 311). Mr. Wakeman records that in 1872 some whetstones and two circular grindstones were found in a crannoge in Fermanagh, the larger one eight inches across.[*]

[*] Kilk. Archæol. Journ., 1872-3, p. 320.

Remains of Ancient Workshops.—It is worthy of remark that the remains of ancient workshops or factories belonging to several trades have been discovered from time to time in different parts of Ireland. About the year 1820 a brazier's workshop was turned up in a place called Dooros-Heath, in the parish of Eglish near Birr in King's County, where great quantities of gold-coloured bronze articles

FIG. 311.

Clochan-na-Carraige, the 'Stone house of the Rock,' on the Great Island of Aran, Galway Bay. Pagan circular stone house: round outside: inside it is quadrangular, and 19 feet long by 7½ feet broad, and 8 feet high. Walls of dry masonry, converging by overlapping till closed at top by a single stone. Two apertures in roof served for windows and chimney. (From Petrie's Round Towers, p. 130. To illustrate what is said at p. 323, *infra*.). For a Christian house of similar construction, see p. 323, *infra*.

were found—bells, spearheads, celts, trumpets, gouges, and soforth : also whetstones, flat, convex, and concave. That this was a workshop is shown by the fact that many of the articles were unfinished or only half made, while some were mended : and there was one lump of unworked bronze—mere material.* The remains of a glass factory

* See Mr. Thomas Cooke's intelligent article on this find : Proc. Roy Ir. Acad., IV. 423 : see also same vol., p. 239.

will be found mentioned at p. 33, *supra* ; and an old work-shop of a family of goldsmiths near Cullen in Tipperary is described in vol. I., p. 556, *supra*. In parts of Ulster where flints are common, flint workshops are sometimes turned up, with vast numbers of finished and half-finished flint articles.* Ancient Gaulish workshops of various crafts have in like manner been lately found in France.†

Masons and their Work.—A knowledge of the use of lime-mortar and of the arch was introduced by St. Patrick and his foreign missionaries. Before his time the Irish built their stone structures of dry masonry : and not knowing how to construct an arch they brought their walls to converge in a curve—like the ancient Greeks and other nations of antiquity—by the gradual overlapping of the flat-lying stones. Numerous specimens of their handiwork in this department of ancient art still remain, especially in the south and west, in the beehive-shaped houses and stone cahers, which show much skill in fitting the stones to one another so as to form very close joints. Even after the introduction of Christianity the old pagan fashion of building was retained in the erection of many of the ecclesiastical structures : and stone oratories belonging to those primitive ages are still to be seen in various parts of the country, built without mortar and converging upwards by the overlapping of the stones. The outer wall of the cashel enclosing the little hermit-monastic establishment on Inishmurray is of dry masonry and in all respects like the pagan cashels. (See fig. 313 farther on.)

Although the Irish did not employ lime (Irish *ael*) in making mortar till the fifth century, it was used as a whitener in pagan times (p. 63, *supra*). They made lime by burning limestone or sea-shells in a lime-kiln much as is done at the present day : but I find no notice of a kiln for this purpose till far into Christian times—

* Kilk. Archæol. Journ., 1883–4, p. 120.
† De Jubainville, La Civil. des Celtes, p. 130.

yet still before the Anglo-Norman invasion— viz. in 1145, when "a lime-kiln, which was sixty feet every way, "was erected opposite Emain Macha by Gillamacliag, suc- "cessor of Patrick, and Patrick's clergy in general."* The

FIG. 312.

Round Tower of Devenish Island, in Lough Erne: 85 feet high. To illustrate what is said next page as to beauty of outline and general shape. (From Petrie's Round Towers, p. 360.) Round towers are figured also in chap. x., vol. I., *supra*.

Annals record the erection in 1163 of another lime-kiln— which they call *tene-aoil* (literally "fire of lime"—pron. tenneel), seventy feet square, by the abbot of the Columban monastery of Derry—Flaherty O'Brolchain—and his clergy· But the erection of these great structures indicates long-

* Reeves, Churches of Armagh, p. 38.

existing previous knowledge of lime-kilns and of the art of constructing them. There can be no doubt that sea-shells were used for making lime in the old times : this was Petrie's opinion* : and we know that they were turned to this use in the time of Elizabeth : Docwra, in his "Narration," says :—"Cockleshells to make a lyme wee "discovered infinite plenty of, in a little island in the "mouth of the harbour [at Derry] as wee came in."

Fig. 313.

Stone house on Church Island, Valentia, Kerry. Example of a Christian oratory, built of uncemented stones, with walls converging, after the old pagan fashion (see figure 311, *supra*). Interior dimensions, about 19 feet by 11 feet. Near it, on the same little island, is a circular pagan *clochan*, or stone house. (From Journ. Antiqq. Irel. for 1900, pp. 152, 155.) To illustrate observations at p. 321, *supra*.

Numerous structures erected in Christian times, but before the invasion, with lime-mortar, still remain all over the country, chiefly primitive churches and round towers. It is only necessary to point to the round towers to show the admirable skill and the delicate perception of grace-fulness of outline possessed by the ancient Irish builders. A similar remark might be made regarding many of the ancient churches, especially those called Romanesque, for which that part of Petrie's Round Towers relating to churches may be consulted.

* Stokes's Life of Petrie, p. 161.

Blessing the Work.—In old times it was a custom for workmen, on completing any work and delivering it over finished, to give it their blessing. This blessing was called *abarta*, " and if it was omitted, the workman was subject " to a fine, to be deducted from his hire, equal to a seventh " part of [the cost of] his feeding." These are O'Donovan's words, which are merely an expansion of the explanation of *abarta*, given in Cormac's Glossary (p. 9). The same rule is laid down in the Senchus Mór, from which the explanation in the Glossary was borrowed (see Br. Laws, I. 133). This custom is mentioned in the " Small Primer," where *bendacht* (' benediction ') is used instead of *abarta*.* It would appear also that the first person who saw the work after it was finished was bound to give it a blessing on pain of fine : and it was specially incumbent on women to bless the work of other women. The custom has descended to this very day : for the peasantry on coming up to people engaged in work of any kind always say " God bless your work," or its equivalent in Irish, *go m-beannuighe Dia air bhur n-obair.*

6. *Protection of Crafts and Social Position of Craftsmen.*

Artificers of all kinds held a good position in society and were taken care of by the Brehon Law. Among the higher classes of craftsmen a builder of an oratory or of ships was on the same level—in respect to honour-price and *dire*-fine—with an *aire-desa*, the lowest rank of noble : that is to say he was entitled to the same compensation for any injury inflicted on him in person, honour, or reputation. In like manner a chariot-maker and a wooden-house-builder, and some others, ranked with the *tanist*, or intended successor to a *bo-aire* chief. And similar provisions are set forth in the law for craftsmen of a

* Br. Laws, v. 98, 11; 99, 15.

lower grade.* Elsewhere it is stated that the artist who made the articles of adornment of precious metals for the person or household of a king was entitled to compensation for injury to person or property equal to half the amount payable to the king himself for a like injury.† But the most striking illustration of the estimation in which handicraft workers—especially artists of all kinds—were held, occurs in the Brehon Law (v. 383), where, prescribing the fine for the retention or loss of an embroideress's needle,

FIG. 314.

Beautiful window of Castledermot Abbey. (From Miss Stokes's High Crosses of Castledermot and Durrow, p. 7.) To illustrate the statements about the skill of Irish masons, at p. 323, *supra*.

the text winds up with this statement :—" For every " woman who is an embroideress deserves more profit " than even queens." These are a few examples of the provisions found in many parts of the Brehon Law for the protection of craftsmen and the recognition of their proper position.

As illustrating this phase of society we sometimes find people of very high rank engaging in handicrafts. One of St. Patrick's three smiths was Fortchern, son of Laegaire,

* Br. Laws, v. 103–109 : see also Petrie's Tara, 208, note 8.
† O'Curry, Man. & Cust., II. 205.

king of Ireland. Beoan, the father of St. Mochoemoc, and another Beoan, father of St. Ciaran of Clonmacnoise, though both of royal descent, were famous carpenters.* But, on the other hand, a king was never allowed to

FIG. 315.

Doorway of Rahan Church, King's County: dating from about the middle of the eighth century. Specimen of skilled mason-work to illustrate what is said at p. 323, *supra*. (From Petrie's Round Towers, p. 246.)

engage in manual labour of any kind (vol. I., p. 60, *supra*). Many of the ancient Irish Saints were skilled artists. In the time of St. Brigit there was a noted school of metal-workers near her convent, over which presided St. Conleth, first bishop of Kildare, who was himself a most skilful

* Cambr. Eversus, II. 173.

artist.* St. Daig or Dega of Iniskeen in Louth was a famous artificer. He was chief artist to St. Ciaran of Saigir, sixth century, and he was a man of many parts, being a *caird* or brazier, a *goba* or smith, and besides, a choice scribe. In the Martyrology of Donegal it is stated that " he made 150 bells, 150 crosiers : and also [leather] cases or covers for sixty Gospel Books," *i.e.* books containing the Four Gospels. Elsewhere we find it stated that he made " covers or cases for books, some plain, but others covered with gold, silver, and precious gems."†

In the *muinnter*, or *familia*, or household of St. Patrick, there were several artists, all of them ecclesiastics, who made church furniture for him. " His three smiths (*gabaind*) expert at shaping," were Macecht, who made Patrick's famous bell called *Finn-faidhech* or ' sweet-sounding ' ; Laebhan ; and Fortchern, who was son of King Laegaire. His three brasiers (*cérda* ; or, as Evinus calls them in Latin, *tres fabri ærarii*, ' three copper-smiths ') were Aesbuite, Tairill, and Tasach. In the Tripartite Life it is stated that " the holy bishop Assicus (*i.e.* Aesbuite) was Patrick's " coppersmith (*faber ereus*), and he made altars and quad- " rangular tables, and quadrangular book-covers (*leber- " chometa* : lit. ' book-preservers ') in honour of Patrick."‡ We have already seen how highly scribes and book-illuminators were held in esteem. It is to be observed that nearly all the *artists* selected by St. Patrick for his household were natives, though there were many foreigners in his train, some of whom he appointed to other functions : a confirmation of what has been already observed, that he found, on his arrival, arts and crafts in an advanced stage of cultivation.

In common with most civilised people of old time the Irish attempted to fix by law the wages of workmen and

* Todd, St. Patrick, 26.
† Stokes, Féilire, 131 : O'Cl. Cal., 223 : Adamnan, 115, note *c* : Petrie, Round Towers, 202.   ‡ Trip. Life, 97 : FM, A.D. 448.

artists : the rates are laid down in the law, but, as might be expected, they vary a little as given in different authorities. The Senchus Mór states that for making a *lann óir*, i.e. a gold head-band or necklet of gold, the

FIG. 316.

West front of stone-roofed church at Killaloe, the burial-place of Murkertagh O'Brien, king of Munster, and afterwards king of Ireland (died A.D. 1119). An example of skilled mason-work. See observations at p. 323, *supra*. (From Petrie's Round Towers, p. 278.)

caird or artist should be paid in silver one-ninth of the value of the finished article* : and for making a gold ring one-twelfth of its value in silver. A legal commentator, quoted by O'Curry,† says :—" The law tells us that the

---

* Br. Laws, II. 415.   † Man. & Cust., II. 205.

" weight of the *lann-óir* in silver was paid to the *cérd* for " making it " : one of the many proofs—if proofs were needed—that these articles were made by native artists. In another part of the Senchus Mór (Br. Laws, I. 133) it is stated that the price for making any article is one-tenth of its value with food and drink. The Glossator of the Heptads has this remark :—" The payment of all handi- " craft, namely, the tenth of everything made, is the price " of making " (Br. Laws, V. 215) : and in this part of the Laws there are many statements to the same effect. The rule of the tenth was very general, and it was observed in many crafts down to recent times. A little more than a century ago the bakers of Dingle in Kerry charged one-tenth of the value of bread for baking.

No individual tradesman was permitted to practise till his work had been in the first place examined at a meeting of chiefs and specially-qualified ollaves, held either at Croghan or at Emain, where a number of craftsmen candidates always presented themselves. But besides this there was another precautionary regulation. In each district there was a head-craftsman of each trade, designated *sai-re-cérd* [see-re-caird], *i.e.* ' sage in handcraft.' He presided over all those of his own craft in the district : and a workman who had passed the test of the examiners at Croghan or Emain had further to obtain the approval and sanction of his own head-craftsman before he was permitted to follow his trade in the district.* It will be seen from all this that precautions were adopted to secure competency in handicrafts similar to those now adopted in the professions.

Young persons learned trades by apprenticeship, and commonly resided during the term in the houses of their masters. They generally gave a fee : but sometimes they were taught free—or as the law-tract expresses it—" for

---

* Keating, 419, from old authorities.

God's sake." When an apprentice paid a fee, the master was responsible for his misdeeds: otherwise not. The apprentice was bound to do all sorts of menial work—digging, reaping, feeding pigs, &c.—for his master, during apprenticeship.*

CHAPTER XXV

CORN MILLS

Section 1. *History.*

VERY early Irish tradition, transmitted through ancient manuscripts, assigns the erection of the first watermill in Ireland to the illustrious King Cormac mac Art (reigned A.D. 254 to 277). The story is that he had a beautiful *cumal* or bondmaid whose business it was to grind corn with a quern. In order to relieve her from this heavy drudgery, the king sent across "the sea" for a *saer-muilinn*—a 'mill-wright'—who constructed a mill on the stream of Nith, flowing from a well named *Nemnach* ('sparkling') beside Tara. This account is given by Cuan O'Lochain, chief poet of Ireland, who died A.D. 1024, in a poem on Tara preserved in several of our ancient manuscripts. It is given in Petrie's Tara, p. 143: the passage relating to the mill will be found at p. 147. O'Lochain's poem was copied into the present existing manuscripts from much older books. The well *Nemnach* still exists, though not now known by its old name: it was identified more than sixty years ago by Petrie and O'Donovan (see Plan of

* Br. Laws, IV. 237, and note 1.

Tara, p. 81, *supra*). It is remarkable that this ancient written record is corroborated by a vivid oral local tradition of the present day, which gives some details not in the written account, one of which is that King Cormac obtained the mill-wright from the king of Scotland. But here the modern tradition is probably wrong, as it appears that watermills had not been introduced into Britain by the Romans so early as the third century. According to the same oral tradition the name of the imported mill-wright was Mac Lama. It is an interes ing fact that there has been a mill on the spot time out of mind in possession of one family named Mac Lama, having descended from father to son; but in modern times they have translated their name to Hand (Irish *lám*, a hand). It has been always called the mill of Lismullin (the 'fort of the mill'): and the place, which is a mile north-east from Tara, retains the name Lismullin to this day.*

Whatever amount of truth or fiction may be in the tradition of King Cormac's mill, we have ample evidence that f om a period soon after the advent of St. Patrick, watermills were in very general use all through Ireland, and were an important factor in daily life, both in the monasteries and among the people in general. Each *muilenn* or mill was managed by a skilled *muilleóir* [millore] or miller. Mills and millers are mentioned in the oldest Irish literature; and monastic mills are mixed up with the Lives of many of the early Irish saints. In the Tripartite Life (p. 211, 6) there is a passage in which St. Patrick is made to prophesy of certain streams in the present County Waterford that there never would be mills on them. In the Lives of very many of the early saints, we find it recorded, among their other acts, that they built mills at their monasteries. Cogitosus's Life of St. Brigit, written in the tenth century, mentions a millstone (*molaris*

* This account has been taken from Petrie's Tara, p. 162 *et seq.*

lapis), showing that there was a mill in connexion with her nunnery in Kildare. St. Brigit died A.D. 523. The mill built at Fore, in the present County Westmeath, by St. Fechin, in the seventh century, which is recorded in his Life, is noticed by Giraldus Cambrensis; a mill has been kept up there from the saint's time to the present day; and it is still called St. Fechin's mill. There was a mill at the monastery of Mailruan at Tallaght which is frequently mentioned in old Irish writings.* The annals record the burning of St. Ciaran's mill at Clonmacnoise, A.D. 954. In the Story of the Boroma in the Book of Leinster, we are told that certain persons who went in pursuit of St. Molling (seventh century) found him at a place called Fornocht laying out the site of a mill.† Cormac's Glossary (p. 109)—written in the ninth or tenth century—speaks of the mill-shaft and of the millstones, which, it says, were larger than the stones of a quern: and the passage goes on to say that the mill was driven and the corn ground by water-power. Elsewhere (p. 41) in the same Glossary the motion of the great whirlpool of Coire-Brecain is compared to the whirling of mill-paddles: all showing how common mills were in his time. Mills and millers are also often mentioned in the oldest of the tales: as for instance in the " *Féis Emna* " (or " Feast of Emain "), in the " Voyage of Maildune," in the " Fled Bricrenn," in " Da Derga's Hostel," and in the " Courtship of Emer "—in so many indeed that references are needless: and in one passage a warrior's spear is compared to a *mol muilind*, the 'wheel-shaft of a mill." Many of the tales, in which mills are spoken of as objects very familiar, are quite pagan in character, and originated according to the best authorities, in the seventh or eighth century.

A most interesting notice of an ancient Irish mill occurs in connexion with an undoubted historical event,

* Féilire, p. 8, bottom.   † O'Grady, Silva Gad., 423.

the death, A.D. 651, of Donogh and Conall, the two sons of Blathmac (one of the joint kings of Ireland—656 to 664), who were slain by the Leinstermen at " the mill of Mailoran the son of Dima Crón."   This event, which created a great sensation at the time, is recorded in the Annals of Tigernach, as well as in those of Ulster, of the Four Masters, and of Clonmacnoise, and it is commemorated in the form of a short story in an Irish MS. in the Bodleian Library, which has been published and translated by Kuno Meyer in " Hibernia Minora ":   but the storyteller's version differs from the annalists' record in some important details, though non-essential for our purposes.   On a certain occasion the princes were pursued by Mailoran and his party, who determined to kill them. They succeeded in wounding them, near the mill, on which the brothers took refuge among the works, beside the *mol* or shaft :   but the pursuers forced the woman who had charge of the sluice to let the water run, so that the mill was set going, and the young men were crushed to death in the works.   A contemporary poet composed a poem on this event, in which he apostrophises the mill in the following strikingly vivid stanza :—

> " O mill, what hast thou ground ?   Precious thy wheat !
> It is not oats thou hast ground, but the offspring of Kervall [*i.e.* the princes].
> The grain which the mill has ground is not oats but blood-red wheat ;
> With the scions of the great tree (Kervall, their ancestor), Mailoran's mill was fed."

Mageogheghan, in his translation of the Annals of Clonmacnoise, says that " Donogh and Connell were killed " by the Lynstermen near Mollingare, in the mill of Oran " [or Mailoran] called Mollenoran."   This mill was situated on the little river that runs from Lough Owel to Lough Iron, near the point where the river is now crossed by a bridge ; and the place still retains the name of Mullenoran. It is curious that a mill existed there from the time of the death of the princes—and no one can tell how long before —down to the end of the eighteenth century ; and there are some old people still living there whose grandfathers saw it in full work.*

Tigernach and other annalists record that a celebrated pillar-stone called *Lia Ailbe*, which stood at *Magh Ailbe*, now Moynalvy in Meath, fell down in the year 999 (998, FM) : and that from this *lia*, Malachi the Great, king of Ireland (A.D. 980–1002), made four [pairs of] millstones. When St. Columkille dwelt at Clonard under St. Finnen (d. 549), they ground their corn with a quern, which the students worked in turn. But it seems plain that after Columkille settled in Iona, he had a watermill erected. Adamnan speaks of the grain, of the kiln, and of grinding the corn : and though he does not tell us expressly what sort the mill was, he uses an indirect expression that points to a watermill. Speaking of an incident in the life of Columkille, he says it occurred at a spot " where a cross " was afterwards erected and fixed in a millstone, which " may be seen to this day "† (*i.e.* about A.D. 697 : a century after its erection). Innes suggests that this millstone was a quern. But it must have been a large and heavy mill-stone belonging to a watermill to give sufficient support to a stone cross—a conspicuous long-standing memorial. Add to all these early notices that a *mulenn* or mill is mentioned in the St. Gall glosses of Zeuss (p. 778, 20)— seventh or eighth century—at which time the name *mulenn*, which is used in the Irish passage copied by Zeuss, and which was borrowed from Latin, had become well naturalised in the Irish language. We may then take it for certain that watermills—howsoever derived—were in

* See O'Donovan in FM, at A.D. 647. The above poem is in the FM, I., p. 263 : and it is also quoted by the annotator of the Féilire, p. 88.
† " Crux molari infixa lapidi," Adamnan, III. xxiii. (p. 231).

use in Ireland from the earliest ages of Christianity : but there is as yet no sufficient evidence to prove that they were known in pagan times.

2. *The " Eight Parts " of a Mill.*

The Brehon Laws took careful cognisance of mills, descending to minute particulars, in order to determine how far the law of distress applied to them, as well as to fix the amounts of fines and compensations in case of accidental damage or injury to persons. In the Senchus Mór* there is a very interesting enumeration of the " Eight Parts " of a mill, viz.—1. The water : 2. The upper mill-stone : 3. The shaft : 4. The supporting-stone : 5. The shaftstone : 6. The wheel : 7. The axis : 8. The *cup* or hopper. It will be useful to make a few observations on all these, in accordance with the explanations given in the commentaries and glosses,† and with various passages in other Irish writings.

FIRST : The *en* or water consisted of three parts :— The spring (*topur* or *tobar*) : the mill-race (*tuinidhe* : pron. tunnee), from the spring to the mill-pond : and lastly the mill-pond itself. We see from this that in those times the water for a mill was brought from the head source along a channel or mill-race, much the same as at present, till it flowed into a pond, natural or artificial, where it was stored till wanted, when the sluice was raised and the wheel set going. The mill-pond was as familiar an object as the mill, and we find it very often noticed, sometimes by the name *linn* (which means a pool of any kind), and sometimes by the special name *toiden* or *taidhin*. St. Molling is mentioned as being on a certain occasion in his *toiden*,‡ where he often stayed, standing in the water merely to mortify himself.

* Br. Laws, I. 125.　　　　　† *Ibid.*, 141.
‡ Silva Gad. : Irish text, p. 377, 2.

According to the Brehon Law, anyone constructing a mill could bring the necessary supply of water through the intervening farms belonging to his neighbours, acquiring the ground needed for the mill-race by compulsory purchase, and paying the compensation fixed by law : a provision which anticipated by centuries the modern statutes by which persons are compelled to sell any portion of their lands required for certain public works, such as railways. " Every co-tenant "—says the law-tract on the ' Right of Water '—" is bound to permit the " other co-tenants to conduct the water [required for a " mill] across his land "*: " and this "—says the gloss on the text—" is the second instance in the Bérla Féine " speech where the Law commands a person to sell his " land though he should not like to do so."† But certain lands—as the tract goes on to say—were exempted from compulsory purchase, such as a fair-green, the land belonging to a church, the land round a king's residence : water could not be brought through these under any circumstances. In some exceptional cases, where the passage of the water would benefit instead of injuring the owner, the land had to be given without compensation. The owner of the land, when compelled to sell, might take direct payment, or he might choose, as compensation, to have a share in the mill—*i.e.* the use of it for one or more of the rotation days (p. 345 below).

SECOND : the upper millstone, which is called *liae* and *cloch* in the law text : but the general name for a millstone was, and is still, *bro*, gen. *brón* [brone], or *cloch-mhuilinn*.

THIRD : the *mol* [mull] or shaft ; that is, the shaft or axis of the mill-wheel. *Mol* is still the living word for a mill-shaft.

FOURTH : the supporting stone, or lower millstone ; called *indeoin* or *inneoin* [innone].

* Br. Laws, IV. 213. † *Ibid.*, 215.

FIFTH : the *herinthiu* or shaftstone, which is described in the gloss as the little stone which is under the head of the *mol* or shaft, and on which the *mol* turns.

SIXTH : the paddle-wheel or mill-wheel, which is called *oircel* [urkel]. The gloss, in explaining this word, says :— " over its *cel* or paddle the water flows." Here the whole wheel is called *oircel*, and the single paddle *cel* : but in a passage in the " Fled Bricrenn " (p. 67) the paddle is called *oircel*. In this last passage Queen Maive, speaking of Cuculainn's impending attack on her army, says " he will " grind us to mould and gravel . . . like as a mill of ten " paddles grinds very hard malt." This is instructive as giving us an idea of the number of paddles, and as intimating that a mill-wheel with ten paddles was considered a moderately powerful one. The present name for a mill-wheel is *roth* [ruh], which properly signifies any wheel.*

The SEVENTH part was the axis [of the revolving millstone] which is called *milaire* [millerĕ]. This is explained in the gloss, " the burden of the *mol* or shaft, *i.e.* the *gamul*." *Milaire* is now the usual word for the pivot on which the millstone turns.

The EIGHTH " part " was the *cup* or hopper, so called from the Irish verb *cup*, to drop ; " because it *cups* or drops " the corn out of itself into the upper millstone, *i.e.* the " *tual*, i.e. the perforated iron."

From the above description (especially the expression " over its *cel* or paddle the water flows ") we see that the water-wheel here under consideration was an overshot one, and revolved round a horizontal *mol*, shaft, or axis ; that the millstones lay flat ; that the upper or revolving one moved on a perpendicular *milaire* or axis : and that the motion of the shaft was communicated to this axis by cog-wheels.

The writer of the Battle of Moyrath (p. 257), describing two mighty heroes grasping each other and whirling

* Corm. Gloss., p. 143

rapidly round in mortal struggle, says :—" They might be compared to the huge wheel of a mill at rapid grinding." From this and many other such passages in the tales, as well as from the manner in which mills are often mentioned in the Senchus Mór and Cormac's Glossary, and especially from the story of the destruction of the two princes in the works of Mailoran's mill, it may be inferred that some at least of the old Irish mills were fairly large and powerful. The law-tract (on the " Right of Water ": Brehon Laws, IV., p. 219) affords an idea of the cost of what may be considered as an average-sized mill, which is set down as a *cumal*, i.e. three cows, equal to £40 or £45 of our money. This is the expense of the mill alone, and does not include the cost of the building.

3. *Small Mills.*

But a small light mill of much simpler construction was also in use, portions of which are represented in fig. 317. In this little mill the shaft stood vertically, and the wheel horizontally at the lower end of it.* The pivot or gudgeón at the bottom of the shaft worked in a hole in stone or iron, fixed firmly beneath. The two little millstones—which were not larger than querns—were placed horizontally on the top of the shaft, of which the lower one was fixed moveless, by means of the surrounding frame, and the axle (or a round iron bar, a continuation of the axle upwards) passed through a hole in its centre in which it turned freely without disturbing the stone. The top of the axle or bar was fixed firmly in the upper stone, which turned with it. A simple contrivance for slightly altering the distance between the two stones enabled the

---

* Much of the description that follows is abridged from the accounts given by many eye-witnesses, as they saw little mills of this kind working in Ireland and Scotland within the last 250 years : as quoted by Mr. Robert Mac Adam in an interesting article by him on " Ancient Water-mills " in Ulster Journ. Archæol., vol. IV., p. 6.

operator to grind coarse or fine. There was an opening near the centre of the upper stone with a hopper or open box fixed over it (often called the *bél* or mouth), through which the grain was supplied : and the flour or meal, as it escaped at the edges of the stones, was received in a cloth of some kind.

The water was directed through a spout in a powerful stream against the little spoons or paddles, and turned the wheel round very quickly, 100 revolutions or more in a minute ; the wheel whirling with it the axis and the upper millstone. All this corresponds with a passage in the " Montgomery MSS.," written in the seventeenth century, quoted by Mr. Mac Adam in his article. This passage also indicates that these mills were very common in Ulster :—

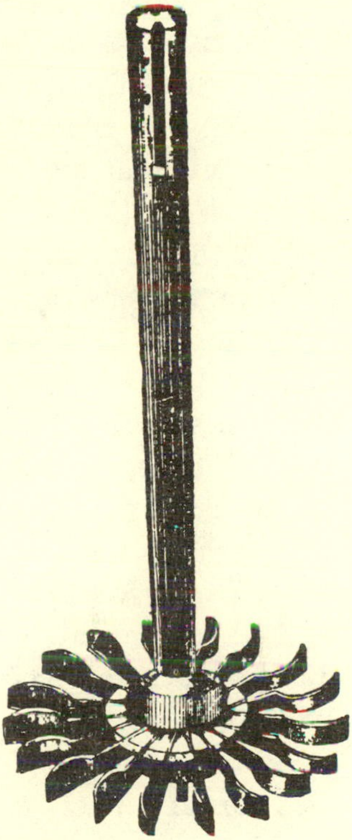

FIG. 317.

Mill shaft and wheel, found near Bally-money, in Antrim. Length of shaft, 6 feet 6 inches : diameter of paddle-wheel, 3 feet 3 inches. (From Ulster Journal of Archæology, IV., p. 6.)

[From a bog near Newtownards in Down] "issue many rills and streams . . .; and on them each townland almost had a little miln for grinding oats, dried in potts or singed and leazed in yᵉ straw, which was yᵉ old Irish custom, the mealle whereof called *greddane* was very cours. The milns are called Danish or ladle milnes ; the axeltree stood upright, and yᵉ small stones or querns (such as are turned with hands) on yᵉ top thereof : the water wheel was fixed at yᵉ lower end of yᵉ axeltree, and did run horizontally among yᵉ water ; a small force driving it."

These little mills were common in other parts of Ireland also, and fifty or sixty years ago they were in full work all over Connaught, and probably also in Munster.

The Irish-speaking people, to distinguish them from mills of a larger and better kind with vertical wheels, gave them the expressive name of *muileann tón re talamh,* " molendinum podex ad terram " ('mill with backside to the ground '). The Connaught people when speaking English called them " gig-mills."* These descriptive details regarding small mills are given here from late authorities ; first, because there is hardly any early literature that enters into particulars regarding their construction and mode of working ; and secondly, because it is pretty certain they descend from ancient times, like many other Irish institutions.

Little mills of this kind, which did not call for much skill, and were very inexpensive, no doubt existed from the earliest period, as well as the larger and more expensive ones. They are not Danish, as they are called in the above extract : for the Danes, who did not begin to arrive till the ninth century, had nothing to do with the introduction of mills, which, as we have seen were known and worked in Ireland long before their time. The popular tradition attributing them to the Danes, referred to by Mr. Mac Adam (p. 14 of his Essay), counts for nothing ; for we know that similar popular traditions attribute all the raths and lisses, as well indeed as most other important works, to that people ; so that the erroneous name " Danish raths "—like " Danish milnes "—was quite prevalent until very lately (see p. 65, *supra*).†

The truth is, as Professor O'Reilly has shown in his instructive article on " Ancient Horizontal Water-mills, Native [Irish] and Foreign " (Proc. R. I. Acad., 14 April, 1902), the little mills of the pattern here described have been found in use, not only in Norway, Sweden, and the

* Ulster Journ. of Archæol., v. 91.

† This tradition or opinion of the Danish origin of the little Irish mills is adopted without further inquiry by Messrs. Bennett and Elton in their History of Corn-Milling.

British Isles, including Ireland, but also in France, Spain, Italy, Roumania, Greece, the Holy Land, Asia Minor, and even Western China. Where the knowledge of them originally came from it seems now impossible to tell. We are only concerned here to assert that howsoever or whensoever they got introduced into Ireland, they were not brought hither by the Norse invaders.

Ancient mill-sites and the remains of old mills have been found in various parts of Ireland buried deep in bog or clay, always beside a stream, many presenting appearances of very remote antiquity. Some are small horizontal-wheel mills like those just described ; some are the remains of larger mills with vertical wheels. In most of those sites millstones have been found, of various sizes up to three feet in diameter : and there is often a long narrow oaken trough or shoot—generally hollowed out from a single tree-trunk—for conveying the water to the wheel. Parts of the framework surrounding the mill, with the flooring, also remain in some of these old sites, mortised together, but never fastened by nails : the woodwork of all generally of oak. Sometimes a large cistern is found : one, for instance, 15 feet by 7, and 20 inches deep ; from which the immediate water-supply was led by the shoot to the little wheel : another is described in Stokes's " Life of Petrie," p. 126.*

4. *Drying and Grinding.*

Preparatory to grinding, the corn had to be dried in a kiln, which was, and is, called in Irish *áith*, gen. *átha* [aw, aw-ha]. The oven containing the fire was called *sorn* or *sorn-na-hátha*, ' oven of the kiln.' It was heated by fire-

---

* For these old mills see the article on ' Ancient Irish Water-mills " by Mr. Prim, in Kilk. Archæol. Journ., 1849–51, p. 154 : see also the vols. for 1860–61, p. 347 ; and 1899, pp. 221 and 223, 8: and Professor O'Reilly's Notes on Horizontal Water-Mills, Proc. Roy. Ir. Acad., 1902. All in addition to Mac Adam's Article in Ulster Journ. Arch., vol. IV.

wood ; and it required some skill and experience to manage, for, if overheated, the kiln might take fire or the corn be scorched. On one occasion when St. Ciaran, during his residence in St. Enda's monastery in Aran, was drying corn, the kiln caught fire. There was a specially experienced man in charge of the kiln. St. Aengus the Culdee, when resident in Tallaght disguised as a working man, had charge of the kiln for some time. A usual plan was to put the grain in a sort of twig-basket or sieve which was held over the fire, while a man kept stirring it up, till the whole basketful was sufficiently dried. The basket was called in Irish *laem* ; and Latin writers of the Lives of Irish Saints refer to it as *rota de virgis contexta*, ' a *rota* or round sieve woven of twigs.' Adamnan (p. 88, 2) calls the drying kiln by the Latin name *canaba*.*

A more primitive way of drying, which was practised down to recent times, was by burning or roasting the corn in the ear. A woman—sitting down at her work—took a handful of unthreshed corn in the left hand and a short stick in the right : she then set fire to the ears, which blazed up ; and watching the right moment, when the outer husk or chaff was burned off, but before the fire had time to reach the grain, she struck off the burning top with the stick. Most country-women could do this work with more or less skill ; but it would seem that certain women followed it as a sort of trade ; and constant practice made them dexterous, so that they separated the grain very quickly. Corn burned off in this manner was called *loisgreán* [lusgraun], *i.e.* ' something burned,' from *loisg*, to burn : and the practice must be an old one, for many places in Ireland are still called by names derived from this word—such as Loskeran near Ardmore in Waterford, probably commemorating the fact that at some former time a professional corn-drier lived there.† In Ulster

* See Adamnan, p. 88, note *c*, and p. 362.
† See Irish Names of Places, I. 238.

and Scotland scorched corn is called *graddan*, as stated in the Montgomery MS. above (p. 339), from the Gaelic *gread*, to burn (with which the English *gridiron* and *griddle* are connected) ; and the Scotch and Ulster peasantry greatly preferred *graddan* bread (which has a slightly burnt taste) to that made from kiln-dried corn. Martin (p. 204) says that in his time, 1703, corn could be dressed, winnowed, ground, and baked, in one hour after reaping (see also Carmichael's " Carmina Gadelica," I. 254).

The ground corn came from the mill in the form of *whole-meal*. If different qualities of bread or of porridge were required, this meal was sifted in a *criathar* [criher] or sieve, which, as well as the baking, was always done by women, as already remarked.

The Brehon Law provided for personal injuries in mills, caused by culpable negligence. In case any one was injured in a kiln during the process of drying, four persons are mentioned in the Book of Aicill, one or more of whom might be liable for damages :—The man who splits the firewood, the man who kindles the fire, the man who puts on the firewood (*i.e.* tends the fire), and the man who dries the corn.*

When the upper millstone was badly set, it was liable, in its rapid revolution, to break from its fastening and slip off the lower one : and so to injure persons looking on or engaged in the work. The Book of Aicill lays down rules for compensation in such cases, and mentions three persons, of whom one, two, or all three might be liable according to the apportionment of the blame :—the owner of the mill, the mill-wright who constructed it, and the person engaged in grinding.† Sometimes accidents happened from the too great force of the water : and here again the proper assignment of liability is provided for.

* Br. Laws, III. 265. † *Ibid.*, III. 281 283

5. *Common Property in Mills.*

A mill was a usual appanage to a ballybetagh or ancient Irish townland, and went with it on sale or other transfer, as is proved by records of many ancient grants and purchases of land. Written into the spare blank pages of the Book of Kells are several such grants, some in Irish, some in Latin : and in the Registry of Clonmacnoise are similar documents. One of those in the Book of Kells records that in the middle of the eleventh century, the *munter* or family of Kells made a grant of Ballyheerin with its mill and with all its land, and Ballycoogan with all its land and with its mill, to God and St. Columkille, meaning that they were granted to St. Columkille's monastery at Kells.* In the Charter of Newry in which King Murkertach O'Loghlin granted several townlands to the monastery there, about the year 1101, this expression (in Latin) occurs :—" These lands, with their mills " [*molendinis*], I have confirmed of my own proper gift " to the said monks."† Several other such grants of townlands of about the same period,‡ in which mills are included, might be mentioned. All the mills in question here were large ones with vertical wheels.

The mill belonging to a ballybetagh or townland was often owned by several families in common, all of whom had a right to the use of it, according to the amount of their several shares. " Whenever a mill was to be erected for the use of neighbours "—writes Dr. O'Donovan in an instructive note on the Brehon Law tract on the Right of Water§—" It was left to the option of the persons " concerned (who were generally the inhabitants of the " three nearest lands) whether they would all join in con- " structing the works and conducting the water thereunto,

* Irish Arch. Misc., 1846, p. 129. † Dub. Pen. Journ., I. p. 102.
‡ For which see Irish Arch. Misc., 1846, pp. 127–160.
§ Br. Laws, IV. 220, 221

" or let all be done by one man, who was to pay his
" neighbours for conducting the water through their lands.
" If the neighbours had assisted in forming the mill-pond,
" mill-race, and other works, they were entitled to certain
" days' grinding at the mill." In order to assign the
number of days belonging to each partner, there was a
regular rotation extending over three weeks, *i.e.* eighteen
working days* ; and the usual arrangement was that the
several owners or claimants had the use of the mill on
certain days of those eighteen, according to their several
claims ; at the end of which the rotation began again and
went on in the same order. An outsider could get his corn
ground by purchasing for a sufficient time the right of one
or more of the owners. When one rich man constructed
the mill with the consent of the neighbours, he paid all
expenses, both of purchase and work, and then the mill
belonged to him. In this case he ground his neighbours'
corn for payment, which usually consisted of a certain
proportion of the corn or flour : commonly a tenth (see
p. 329, *supra*).

Sometimes a man who had a share in a mill had a kiln
of his own, and dried his corn at home ; and occasionally
a kiln, as distinct from a mill, was owned by several people
in common. A brugaid or brewy always had a mill and
kiln on his premises—a thing we might expect, from the
quantity of provisions he needed. In connexion with most
monasteries was a mill for the use of the community.†

6. *Querns and Grain-Rubbers.*

A grinding machine much more primitive and ancient
than the water-mill was the quern or hand-mill. It was
called in Irish *bro*, gen. *brón* [brone] : and often *cloch-bhrón*
[*cloch-vrone*] : *cloch*, a stone : but both these terms were
also applied to a millstone. An older term was *meile*

---

* Br. Laws, IV. 215–219 : see also Introd., clxi ; p. 305, 25 : and vol. I
217, 227   † See Br. Laws, IV. 309, 26 ; and 305, 25 ; 315, 16.

[melle̽ : O'Clery's Gloss.], evidently cognate with English *mill* and the corresponding terms in other languages. Querns were of various forms : sometimes the grinding surfaces were flat : sometimes the under surface was convex and the upper concave : sometimes the reverse—pot-shaped. In all cases the upper stone worked on an axis or strong peg fixed in the lower one, and was turned round by one or by two handles. The corn was supplied at the axis-opening in the centre of the upper stone, and according as it was ground between the two stones flowed out at the edge. Sometimes it was worked by one person, sometimes by two, who pushed the handles from one to the other. In ancient times it was—in Ireland—considered the special work of women, and especially of the *cumal* or bondmaid, to grind at the quern :

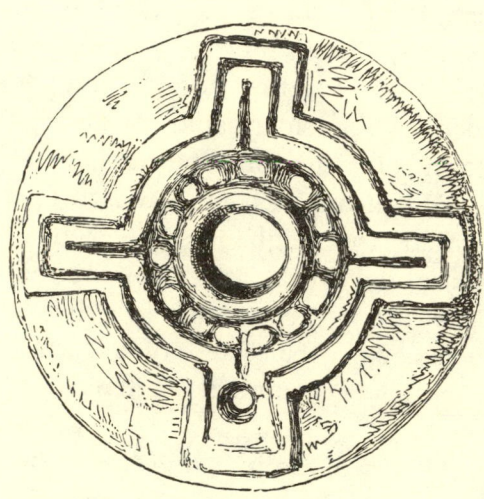

FIG. 318.

Upper stone of a quern : 18 inches in diameter : ornamented with sculptured cross. In National Museum. (From Wilde's Catalogue, p. 107.)

and so generally was this understood that in Cormac's Glossary (p. 42) a *cumal* is explained : "a woman that is "grinding at a quern ; for this was the business of bonds-"women before [water-] mills were made." Querns were used down to our own day in Ireland and Scotland ; and they may still be found at work in some remote localities, especially to grind malt secretly for making *pottheen* or illicit whiskey.

The almost universal use of querns is proved by their frequent mention in the Brehon Laws and other ancient

Irish literature, as well as by the number of them now found in bogs, in or near ancient residences, and especially crannoges. Some of these are very primitive and rude, showing their great antiquity.

In comparatively modern times mill-owners who ground the corn of the people of the neighbourhood for pay looked on the use of querns with great dislike, as taking away custom. Quern-grinding by the poorer people to avoid the expense of the mill was regarded as a sort of poaching; and where the mill belonged to the landlord he usually gave orders to his miller to break all the querns he could find; so that the people had to hide them much as they hide an illicit still nowadays.* In Scotland laws were made in the thirteenth century to compel the poor people to abandon querns for water-mills, all in the interests of landlords and other rich persons. It was the same in England: in 1556 the local lord in one of the western counties issued an order that no

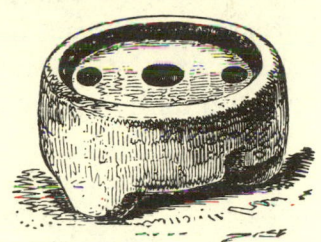

Fig. 319.

Complete pot-shaped quern: 9 inches in diameter. In the National Museum. (From Wilde's Catalogue, p. 108.)

tenants should keep querns " because they ought to grind at their lord's mill."† But these laws were quite ineffective, for the people still kept their querns. Pennant and McCulloch found them in general use in the Scottish Highlands and islands at a recent period.

When two women worked the quern, they sat facing each other, and passed the handle, or both handles, quickly from hand to hand. They ground oats always in the husk and afterwards sifted it. Before grinding—in the absence of a mill-kiln—the corn was very often dried in an iron pot over a fire, and was kept constantly stirred round to pre-

* Dub. Pen. Journ., IV. 295, where there is an interesting and instructive article on this subject: see another good article in Kilk. Archæol. Journ., 1858-9, p. 352.　　　　　　　† Roberts, Social Hist., p. 323.

vent scorching. Quern-grinding was tedious work : for it took about an hour for two women to grind 10 lb. of meal. In Scotland, oatmeal or a preparation from it, is called *broes* or *brose*, which is probably a plural form from *bro*, the Gaelic name of the quern. It is hardly necessary to say that the quern or handmill was in use among all the ancient peoples of Europe, Asia, and Africa : and that it is still extensively employed where water-mills have not found their way.

The most ancient grinding-machine of all, and most difficult and laborious to work, was the grain-rubber, about which sufficient information will be derived from the illustration. Several of these primitive grinding-machines may be seen in the National Museum : they are still used among primitive peoples all over the world.

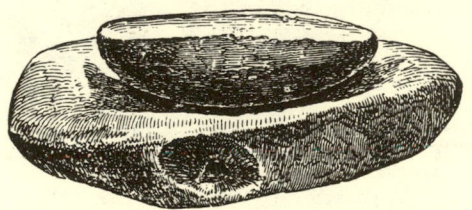

FIG. 320:

Grain-rubber : oval-shaped : 16 inches long. (From Wilde's Catalogue, p. 104.)

Sculpture on a Capital : Priest's House, Glendalough : Beranger, 1779. (From Petrie's Round Towers.)

Ornament on leather case of Book of Armagh. (From Petric's Round Towers.

CHAPTER XXVI

TRADES AND INDUSTRIES CONNECTED WITH CLOTHING

SECTION I. *Wool and Woollen Fabrics.*

Shearing.—Clothing, as may be anticipated, gave rise to many industries, in Ireland as in all other civilised countries. Of these, the most important was that connected with wool. The Irish name of wool was *olann* or *oland*, which is still in use. The wool was taken from the sheep with a shears, which, from the manner in which it is mentioned, must have been much like those used at present. The usual old Irish name is *demess*, which is explained in Cormac's Glossary (p. 55) in a manner that clearly indicates the make of the article itself. He says that it was so called from *mess*, an edge; and that *demess* signifies 'two edges'; for—he goes on to say—it has two knives, and the knives have two handles. This shows that the old Irish wool-shears was like the present hedge-shears. The *demess* is mentioned in the story of the Feast of Bricriu (33 and 162), which throws back the knowledge of the instrument to a still earlier date. In the Brehon Law (IV. 310, 12) it is called *dias*, which means 'a pair,' that is to say, a pair of blades. A small hand-scissors was also in use, and known by the same name. We read in the Tripartite Life (p. 103) that St. Patrick tonsured the druid Caplait : " and Patrick put the *deimess* round his hair." This old name is still used for a shears, in the modern form *deimheas*, which is pronounced *djeeass*. About the year 1849 an ancient iron shears was found in a tumulus at a place called Seskin in the County Kilkenny.* The process of shearing was called *lomrad*, from *lom*, bare.

Preparation for Spinning.—The shearing appears to have been done by men : but after this the whole work up to the finished cloth was regarded as specially pertaining to women : except fulling, which was often or mostly men's work. After being sorted, the wool was greased (*belad*, greasing), adding to the natural oiliness, which rendered it more easy to remove the grease altogether in the next process—scouring. After scouring it was teased or mixed (*cumusc* or *bocad*, i.e. ' mixing '). It was next combed or carded twice, first roughly, and a second time more carefully and finely. The carding (*círad*, pron. keera : from *cír*, a comb) was done by hand : the woman sitting down while at work, and using a pair of cards, much the same probably as those in use for hand-carding now. A quantity of wool lay at her feet in a sort of bag called a *pes-bolg* (which the gloss dervies from *pes*, a foot : ' foot-bag '), from which she drew handfuls as needed. The second carding turned out the wool in the form of soft little *loes*, locks or rolls (*a l-loaib*, ' in locks ' : *lo*, a lock of wool) fit for spinning, just as wool-carders do at the present day.†

Spinning.—In those times spinning was done, in Ireland as elsewhere, by the distaff and spindle ; for the spinning-wheel was not invented till the fifteenth or sixteenth century. The wool or flax in preparation for spinning was wound and fastened loosely on a *rock* or distaff called in Irish *cuigéal* [quiggail]. From the distaff the material was drawn off gradually, with the help of the

* Kilk. Archæol. Journ., I. 9.
† Br. Laws, II. 369, 371, 417, 419 : O'Curry, Man. & Cust., II. 115.

left hand, by the spindle or spinning-stick, which was held in the right hand and manipulated dexterously so as to twist the material into thread, and wind it on the spindle according as spun. When one spindle was full, the operator began with another. The spindle used for flax was called in Irish *fertas* : that for spinning wool was called *snimaire* [sneemara or sneevara], lit. ' spinner,' from *snim*, modern Irish *sniomh*, spin.* But there seems to be some confusion in the gloss in the use of these words—*fertas* and *snimaire* ; and at any rate, the distinction is now forgotten. That a part at least of the process of spinning was often performed by bondmaids appears from the derivation given in Cormac's Glossary (p. 14) for *abras*, a word which was applied to yarn of any kind, or to the material for making thread, rolled on the rock or distaff. He derives it from *abra*, a bondmaid, and *feis*, hand-produce : *abra-feis* (contracted to *abras*), because it is—as the Glossary goes on to say—" the hand-produce of a bondmaid."

The *abras* or thread ready for weaving was rolled up in balls (Irish *certle*, equivalent to Latin *glomus*, a clew or thread-ball : Z, 68, 8), on which it was wound from the spindles according as these got filled. The following quotation from the Law gloss makes matters clear :—
" Abras, *i.e.* the material finished [as thread or yarn] and
" wanting only to be woven, *i.e.* the white balls [*na certle*
" *gela*], i.e. white thread."† The fact that the thread,
" wanting only to be woven," *i.e.* ready for weaving, was white, points to the wool in its natural colour, and is a confirmation of the statement made farther on, that woollen material was dyed in the piece.

Weaving.—The thread was woven into cloth in a handloom, nearly always by women : and like all the rest of the cloth-making process, it was a cottage industry. The complete weaving machinery or loom had two beams :

* Br. Baws, I. 152, 10, 11; 153, 14.
† *Ibid.*, I. 152, 10; 153, 25.

the larger one called *garmain* (and sometimes *gae-mathri*), and the other *lu-garmain* or 'smaller beam' (*lu*, small); which O'Curry believes to have been the front beam on which the warp was rolled up to be woven, and from which it was unrolled as the weaving went on.   Accordingly he

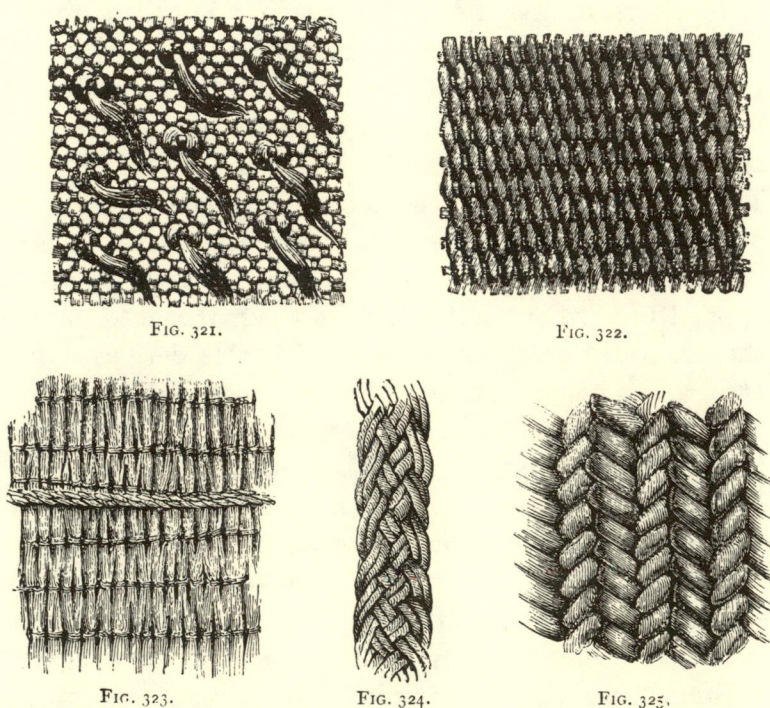

Fig. 321.   Fig. 322.

Fig. 323.   Fig. 324.   Fig. 325.

Specimens of ancient Irish weaving. In 1780 the body of a woman, covered with antique articles of clothing, all wool, was found, buried in hard gravel, under 4½ feet of bog. Figs. 321 and 322 represent portions of two of these. Fig. 323 is part of a long web, made of goat's hair, not exactly woven, but tied or knotted together, as shown in the illustration. The hairs are across, or at right-angles to the length. Found in Cavan, under 14 feet of bog. With this was found a fine plaited or woven woollen band, portion of which is shown in fig. 324. Fig. 325 is portion of a coarse woollen cloth, of which there is a whole suit in the National Museum. It appears from these and other specimens that certain loom-adjustments of the warp, commonly supposed to be of modern inven-tion, were known to the ancient Irish weavers. (From Proc. Roy. Ir. Acad., IX. 103, 104; and Wilde's Catalogue, 295 and 325.)

calls it the "rolling beam." The principal beam must have been large: for we find it recorded that a certain widow cooked a calf in her house for St. Brigit with a fire made from her *garmain*, as she had no other fuel; and the massive spear of a hero, like that of Goliath, is sometimes compared—in Irish tales—to a weaver's beam. In the

Annotations of the Feilire of Aengus* mention is made of the " *nin* of a garmain, *i.e.* the ' fork ' or ' mouth ' on the head of a weaver's beam," which refers to some peculiarity of construction.

What were called the " swords " (*claidim*), or weaving-rods (*slata figi*), were long laths used during the process of weaving, which were nearly or altogether as long as the beam : for in the Bruden Da Derga it is stated that the three great swords of three champions were each longer than a *claidem n-garmnae*, ' the sword of a weaver's beam.'† These swords or laths are what O'Curry calls " heddles," a word used in this application in his own early days in Clare.‡   The warp was called *dluth* [dĺuh] : and the weft or woof *innech*.§   While the woman was weaving she used a *feith-géir* [feh-gair], " which put a smooth face upon her weaving " : and which is represented by the sleeking-stick or " rubbing-bone " still used by hand-weavers.‖

The piece of woven cloth had usually a border or fringe (*corrthar*, pron. curher), which was sometimes woven with the whole piece and formed part of it : and sometimes separately and afterwards sewed on.   In this last case it was woven with a short light *claidem* or lath, altogether apart from the loom, something like the crochet, or netting or meshing work of modern times : and weaving ornamental borders or long scarfs in this manner was practised by ladies of the higher ranks as they practised embroidery.   We read in the Táin that once when Queen Maive was in her chariot, a strange lady suddenly appeared sitting beside her : and " what the woman was doing was, " weaving a border (*corrthar*) with a *claidem* or lath of " *findruine* [findrinně] or white bronze."¶

* Feilire, p. 66, and note *a* ; and " Ninach " in Glossary.
† LU, 95, *a*, 33 : and Man. & Cust., II. 148, note 221.
‡ Man. & Cust., II. 116.
§ Corm. Gloss., 95 : the weft is also called *eanglaim* in O'Cl. Gloss.
‖ Man. & Cust., II. 116.
¶ Man. & Cust., II. 110, note 71   LL, 55, *b*, 32.   See also *corrthair* in

Fulling.—A fuller of cloth was called *ciormhaire* [keervără], literally a comber (from *cior*, a comb) ; or *fúcaire* [fookĕra], or *úcaire*, from *fúcad* or *úcad* [fooka, ooka], to full, and there were persons who practised this as a distinct trade. In the Irish Annals it is recorded that Cerbhall [Kerval] king of Leinster was on one occasion riding a spirited steed through Kildare ; when, passing the shop of a fuller, it happened that a man was sent out to blow the fuller's *congna* or horn : and the horse shied and started at the sudden sound, so that the king was wounded by his own javelin, of which he died (A.D. 909).* This incident tells a plain story. The fuller began his operations on each occasion whenever his materials were prepared, fulling a large quantity at a time, and he fulled his neighbour's cloth as well as his own—for pay of course. When he was ready to begin, he sent out his man to blow the horn at the door, as a signal for the people to bring in their cloth. The custom of tradesmen blowing a horn for such purposes continued to a period almost within our own memory, of which an example, in case of a different *trade*, may be seen in the beginning of the story of " The Whiteboy " in the Dublin and London Magazine, vol. for 1826, pages 73, 74.

2. *Flax and its Preparation.*

The preparation of flax is described in old Irish authorities, especially in the Brehon Law, though not in such detail as that of wool. One of the names of this plant is still preserved in a great number of the Euro-

Corm. Gloss., 44. Besides the special references given here, see for the whole of these details of weaving, Br. Laws, I., pp. 150–153 : and O'Curry, Man. & Cust., II. 116, 117. In the Highlands of Scotland they still preserve most of the ancient methods of manufacturing cloth, from the wool up, including dyeing, as may be seen by the brief, but very interesting, description of the processes as carried on by the Highland women within the last forty years given in Carmichael's Carmina Gadelica, I. 298, 306, 308, 310.

* Three Fragments, 223, notes *c* and *d*. We now know that *congna* means an antler or horn.

pean languages, the forms slightly varying, but all derived from the root *lin*. The Greek word is *linon*; Latin, *linum*; English, *linen* and *linseed*; A.-Sax., *lín*; Russ., *lenû*; &c. This shows that it was cultivated by the western Aryan people since before the time of their separation into the various nationalities of Europe.

The Celtic tribes who first set foot on our shores, brought a knowledge of the plant and its cultivation with them; and corresponding to all the names given above, is the Irish *lín* [leen], which is still the word in universal use for flax. Besides the evidence of philology, our own records show that linen was manufactured in Ireland from the earliest historic times. It was a very common article of dress, and was worked up and dyed in a great variety of forms and colours, and exported besides in large quantities to foreign nations. So that the manufacture for which Ulster is famous at the present day, is merely an energetic development of an industry whose history is lost in the twilight of antiquity.

The flax, after pulling, was tied up in sheaves and dried. It was then steeped, as at present, to rot the woody fibre; and after remaining a sufficient time in the water it was taken up and spread out to dry. After a still further and final drying, over a fire it was beaten with a *smachtín* or flax mallet, to break up the brittle woody covering of the flax fibre. In order to remove this, the operation of scutching (*flescad*) came next, which was done with a scutching-stick called *flesc* or *flesc-lin*.* In the commentary on the Senchus Mór† this process gets another name—*ailgubad*. More than half a century ago, scutching was called *cloving* by the English-speaking people of the south of Ireland, where flax-growing and linen-weaving still lingered on from the days of old: and the forked scutching-stick or *flesc-lin*—which was always

---

* Br. Laws, I. 152, 15; 153, 21: Man. & Cust., II. 116.
† Br. Laws, II. 368, line 3 from bottom.

worked by women—was called a "cloving-tongs": the word "*clove*" being merely the Irish *clómh* or *clóbha* [clove, clova], one of the names for a tongs. But the whole industry—which I saw in full work—is now dead and gone. After the *flescad* or scutching came what was called in English in modern times, "hackling," to divide the fibres into finer filaments, which brought away tangled masses of tow. This was done by drawing it with the hand over the points of a number of strong steel needles fixed closely in a little frame: a work done by certain persons as a special trade. This hackling process is not mentioned in the old account in the law from which the description and names of all the other processes given here are taken: but the flax must have been subjected to it. Next came spinning into thread with a distaff and a spindle, or in later times with a spinning-wheel, which is still found at work in the homes of the peasantry in some parts of Ireland. The thread was made up in hanks or skeins, boiled in home-made potash, and spread in the sun to bleach on a grassy spot called a *tuar* or bleach-green. Lastly, it was wound up into balls or clews (*certle*) and woven into calico or linen.*

3. *Dyeing.*

Dyestuffs and dyeing in general.—The beautiful illumination of the Book of Kells, the Book of Mac Durnan, and numerous other old manuscripts, proves that the ancient Irish were very skilful in colours: and it will be shown here that the art of dyeing was well understood. The dyestuffs were not imported: they were all produced at home: and so important were they considered that among the blessings believed to fall on the country during the reign of a just sovereign, the Book of Leinster and other ancient authorities enumerate "abundance of dyestuffs."†

* For all this about flax, see Br. Laws, I. 150–153: and O'Curry, Man. & Cust., II. 121, where a good abstract of the processes is given.

† Rennes Dind. in Rev. Celt., XVI. 281: O'Curry, MS. Mat., 528, top.

In this Book of Leinster passage the word used for dyestuffs (in general) is *ruaman* (gen. *ruamna*) : and hence the Four Masters (vol. I., 42, 5, 6) use the verbal form *ruamnad* [roomna] for dyeing of any colour—though, as we shall see, *ruam* primarily means red : " whence comes *ruamnaig*, reddening, or blushing, and *ruanaid*, red." The word *ruam*, as it is written in one copy of Cormac's Glossary, or *ruain* as it appears in another, is stated in the Glossary* to be " an herb (*luss*) that gives colour to the face until it is red " (derg) : and in the Cóir Anmann we are told that a person named Diarmait *Ruanaid*, i.e. ' Dermot the Red,' was so called from " ruan," which " is a plant (*lus*) that produces colour on the face."† In an old tract in the Book of Ballymote the tree or bush called *rois*—which is understood to be the elder-bush— is designated " the reddening of faces." *Ruam* is the alder-tree, more commonly called *fearn* or *fearnóg* : and as this plant is used in dyeing a reddish brown, it may be concluded that the words *ruam, ruaim, ruan, ruain*, which we find in the authorities, are all different forms of the name for the alder-tree.

It has been already stated that the Irish people were fond of bright colours : and they wore in fact clothes of all the chief colours then known. But only in a few cases have descriptions of the processes of producing the dyestuffs and of imparting the colours come down to us, and even those we have are often not very precise or clear. The people understood how to produce various shades by the mixture of different colours, and were acquainted with the use of mordants for fixing them. One of these mordants, alum, is a native product, and was probably known in very early times.‡ Dyeing was what we now call a cottage industry, *i.e.* the work was always carried on in the house : as I saw it carried on

---

* Corm., p. 144 : Three Ir. Gloss., 39.   † Ir. Texte, III. 345, 347.
‡ Sullivan, Introduction, 402.

in the homes of Munster more than half a century ago. In the cultivation of the dye-plants, men might take a part : but the rest of the process was considered the special work of women, so that men seldom assisted. In the actual dyeing of the cloth, even the very presence of man or boy was considered unlucky, and liable to mar the process, as is shown by the legend of St. Ciaran given at p. 360 below. It appears from the same story, as well as from what is said about white balls of yarn at p. 351, *supra*, that cloth was dyed in the piece, the wool being left of the natural colour till after weaving and fulling. But woollen cloth was often worn without being dyed at all—just with the shade it brought from the back of the sheep.

Ground Colour.—There were two main stages in the process of dyeing. The first was imparting a ground or foundation colour of reddish-brown, which was done by steeping and boiling the cloth with the twigs of the *ruam* or alder. " *Ruadh* " (red : pron. roo)—says O'Clery's Glossary—" i.e. *ruamann*, the first dye or tinge, or the " stuff that gives it and prepares for the second or last . . . " no colour [can be given] without *ruamann*." In later times this preliminary colouring was called in English *riming*, from *ruaim*. After this the cloth was ready for the second stage—imparting the final colour : which was done by boiling it with the special dyestuff.

Black.—The dyestuff for black was a sediment or deposit of an intense black found at the bottom of pools in bogs, called *dubh-poill*, i.e. ' black-stuff of the *poll*, hole or pool.' It always contained more or less iron, which helped in the dyeing. Boiled with this, the cloth acquired a dull black colour : but if some twigs or chips of oak were added, the colour produced was a glossy jet black, very fixed and permanent.

Crimson.—A crimson or bright-red colour was imparted by a plant anciently called *rud* or *roid*, which required

good land, and was cultivated in beds like table vegetables, requiring great care.*   It was probably a species of
the plant called bedstraw.   In the Senchus Mór provision
is made for dividing the home-stock of this dye-plant, or
rather of the prepared dyestuff, in proper proportions
between husband and wife in case of separation,† which
shows that it was of much value (see p. 11, *supra*).   The
several stages of preparation are indicated by distinct
terms.   First, the plant as gathered from the beds : second
stage, *trilsens* :   third stage, *scriplins*‡ :   fourth and last
stage, the dyestuff, which was a sort of meal or coarse
flour of a reddish colour.§   Some sort of crimson was also
produced from lichen as mentioned below.

Blue.—To dye the cloth blue, after it had been *rimed*,
it was boiled with a dyestuff obtained from woad, called
in Irish *glaisin* [glasheen] :   the Irish word evidently a
descendant of the Gaulish name of this plant—*glastum*.
Pliny records that the ancient Britons used the *glastum* to
dye their bodies blue.   The name *glaisin*, which has long
fallen out of use, was also applied to the prepared dyestuff.   The *glaisin* was cultivated in beds, and was a very
valuable crop, requiring great care and watching during
growth.‖   In vol. I., p. 216, *supra*, has been mentioned a
celebrated lawsuit brought about by sheep eating a crop
of *glaisin*.

That the dye of *glaisin* was blue is indicated by the
name, which is a diminutive of *glas*.   This word *glas* was
however applied to several shades of colour, as for instance
to the green of fields and to bluish-grey coloured eyes.
But it was also applied to pure blue, as is shown by many
ancient passages, as for instance the Voyage of Bran,

* Br. Laws, IV. 277, 10.   † Br. Laws, II. 421.
‡ See *Scriplin* and *Trillsen* in Atkinson's Glossary to Br. Laws.   From
the authorities he quotes one may conjecture that the *trillsen* was a
little wisp of the dried plants : and the *scriplin* a larger bundle in a
further stage of preparation.
§ Br. Laws, II. 421 : see also MS. Mat., 528, 29.   ‖ Br. Laws, II. 371, bot.

where in one place (I. 9. 18) the word *glas* is applied to "the hue of heaven." But as to *glaisin*, the colour it imparted is placed beyond dispute by a legend in the Life of St. Ciaran in the Book of Lismore. On a certain day, when he was a boy, his mother was about to dye some cloth with *glaisin* :—" Then his mother said to him—' Out with thee now, Ciaran ' : for "—continues the old Irish narrative—" they did not deem it right or lucky to have " men [or boys] in the same house in which the cloth was " dyed." Ciaran walked out, saying in a childish pout as he went :—" I wish that there may be a dark grey stripe in it." Accordingly when the cloth was taken out finished, every piece had a dark grey stripe [which spoiled it]. Again the *glaisin* was prepared and the cloth was boiled : and this time—on account of some other words spoken by Ciaran—it came out whitish. A third time the *glaisin* was prepared : and the boy's mother said to him :—" Now " Ciaran do not spoil the *glaisin* any more, but give it a " blessing." He did so : and this time the cloth came out dyed a beautiful intense blue (*gorm*).* Here the word applied to the colour produced by *glaisin* is *gorm*, which means pure blue. The legend attributes to a miracle what must have been a usual occurrence : failure by some mismanagement, followed by success after more careful manipulation.

In the preparation of dyestuffs from *glaisin* there were four distinct stages as in case of the *roid* plant. First, the plant as gathered from the bed : second, a stage called *cro* or *cru* : third, a second stage of *cro* : fourth, the fully-prepared dyestuff, which was in lumps or cakes. But what the first and second *cro* states were we do not know. Here also, as in the case of *roid*, the law provides for the proper division of the *glaisin* between husband and wife if they should separate.†

* Stokes, Lives of SS., 266.
† For all this see Br. Laws, II. 419

Purple was called in Irish *corcur*, which answers to the Latin *purpura* by the usual change from *p* tc *c*. Purple cloaks, purple flowers, and purple colour in general, are very often mentioned in Irish writings, such as the Tripartite Life, the Book of Rights, the Tales, &c.; showing how familiar this colour was. Purple dyestuff was obtained from a species of lichen, and also from a cockle-fish. In one of the pages of an ancient manuscript now in Turin, is a passage written by an Irish hand in the beginning of the ninth century, and published by Chevalier Nigra in his Irish Glosses, which proves that at that early time the Irish were acquainted with the art of dyeing purple by means of a lichen. The gloss which the Irishman wrote in explanation of the Latin text is this :— *Donaib caircib, edon, ar is di lus bis forsnaib caircib dognither in chorcur buide* : which is in English " from the rocks, that " is to say, because it is from a plant which is found on " rocks the yellow purple is made." (In Sullivan's Introd., p. 643, the word *buide* of this gloss is misprinted *buicle*). There is even a more direct notice of rock-purple in a poem of the Agallamh (in LL) in praise of Aran Island in Galway bay, in which it is mentioned that purple-lichens (*corcra*) grow on the rocks there (Silva Gad. 109, 19: Irish text, 102, 7).

The knowledge of dyeing from rock lichen was never lost, but was continued from generation to generation down to recent times. When Martin visited the Scottish Western Islands in 1703, the people there dyed " a pretty " crimson colour with a scurf scraped off rocks and sub- " jected to proper preparation." Joseph Cooper Walker tells us that in his time—the beginning of the last century :—" The purple was obtained from the coarser " kind of arcell [or orchil] growing on rocks, which, being " steeped in urine, and made up into balls with lime, pro- " duced a beautiful purple. Considerable quantities thus " made up are frequently sold in the market at Dingle."[*]

* Memoirs of the Irish Bards, ii. 264

Walker also mentions, in the same passage, that " a fine " bright crimson dye was obtained from a finer kind of " lichen resembling a thin white scurf, which they scraped " from the rocks, dried, and reduced to powder, then infused " in urine for three weeks or a month."

I cannot find any ancient Irish authority in which mention is made of purple being obtained from shellfish. But we may infer from several circumstances that this branch of the dyeing art was known to the ancient Irish. Mr. Franci Joseph Bigger, in the " Proc. Roy. Ir. Academy," vol. for 1893–96, p. 727, gives an interesting account of the remains of a prehistoric settlement in Connaught in which were whole heaps of a species of whelks called *purpura lapillus*—which we know are used to this day for dyeing purple in Ireland and elsewhere. He found all the shells broken uniformly at one particular point—just the point inside which was situated the elongated little sac containing the purple colouring matter : evidently with the object of extracting the precious little globule. In the time of Joseph C. Walker (about 1800) this method of dyeing purple—from " periwinkles and limpets " —was practised in the eastern Irish counties, as also on the opposite coast of Wales. He states (Ir. Bards, II. 265) that the shell was broken at a particular point at the back, very delicately, so as not to bruise the fish, and with a bodkin they picked out what he calls a " white vein," which yielded a few drops of the colouring liquor. This they did several times in succession at proper intervals, the fish renewing the liquor after each occasion. All this corresponds exactly with what Mr. Bigger found : so that the knowledge of this process has descended from prehistoric times to our own day. In like manner this process has been perpetuated from old times in Wales ; for we know that Bede (Eccl. Hist., I. i.) records that in his day the Britons (or Welsh) produced a most beautiful purple colour from shellfish. The reader will scarcely need to be reminded that the celebrated Tyrian purple was produced in a similar way.

The purple dyestuff, however obtained, was produced in very small quantities, so that it was extremely scarce ; and the colour was excessively expensive in Ireland as elsewhere : on the Continent in old times it was worth thirty or forty times it weight in gold. Partly for this reason, and partly for its beauty, purple was a favourite with kings and great chiefs, so that writers often designate it a royal or imperial colour.

Saffron.—Until recent times linen was dyed saffron, probably with the *cróch* or saffron plant (Lat. *crocus*), which was the simplest of all the dyeing operations. But I do not find this mentioned in any ancient authority.

Popular Knowledge of Dyeing.—The Irish peasantry of the present day, as well as the Highland Scotch, possess considerable knowledge of the stuffs—chiefly obtained from herbs—used in imparting various colours, and are skilled in simple dyeing : knowledge and skill that have descended to them from old times. In Donegal they dye woollen cloth yellow with the tops of heather ; and light brown with peat soot : and in various parts of Ireland— as well as in Scotland—they use a sort of lichen called *crotal*, that grows on rocks, to impart a reddish brown. In the County Mayo a species of moss is used for dyeing stockings a reddish brown : and they also dye stockings black with the roots of the blackberry bush.

4. *Sewing and Embroidery.*

Needle and Thread.—The thread used for sewing was generally of wool : all the sewing on the various articles of dress found on the body of the woman mentioned at p. 352, *supra*, was done with woollen thread. In primitive ages fine filaments of gut were often used. The sewing-thread was kept in the form of a *certle*, clew, or ball, like that for weaving ; and women sewed with a needle furnished with a *cro* or eye as at present. From an early age needles were made of steel, but in primitive ages of bronze. In those days a steel or bronze needle was difficult to make ; and its value may be estimated by the fine imposed in the Brehon Law on a person with whom a needle was pledged, for withholding it when the owner demanded it back and tendered the loan. For a common needle it was a *dairt* or yearling calf ; for a needle used in the ornamental work on mantles, it was a *colpthach* or two-year-old heifer ; and for an embroidering needle, an *unga* or ounce of silver.* The word for a needle was *snáthat* [snaw-hat], which is still in use : it is derived in Cormac's Glossary (p. 150) from *snáth* [snaw], a thread, and *sét*, a road or way, i.e. *snáth-shét* [snaw-hait], ' thread-

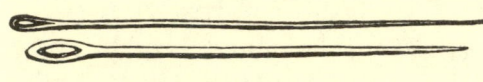

FIG. 326.

Two bronze needles, natural size. These, with a large number of others, are now in the National Museum, Dublin. (From Wilde's Catalogue, p. 547.)

road,' because the thread passes through the *cro* or eye. The first part of this derivation (from *snáth*) is correct, but the second is fanciful. Bronze needles are now often found, which, judging from both material and shape, must be of great antiquity.†

Dressmaking.—Needlework was most commonly practised in ordinary dressmaking. A dress in general, whether for man or woman, was denoted by *étach* or *édach*, and sometimes by *dillat* : and there were, as at present, professional dressmakers—always women—called *étidach*, in modern Irish *éadaigheach* [aideeach], a word derived from *étach*. The old Irish dressmakers were accomplished workers. The sewing on ancient articles of dress found from time to time is generally very neat and uniform, like that on the fur cape mentioned at p. 189, *supra*, which Mr. Mac Adam describes as " wonderfully beautiful and regular."

* Br. Laws, v. 381, 383 : see also O'Curry, Man & Cust., II. 112, 117.
† Kilk. Archæol. Journ., vol. I., p. 260 : Wilde, Catalogue, 546.

When women were at needlework, or any such employment, they kept their materials in a light wooden workbox called a *cusal* : *cusals*, says the law-tract, were " little *crannoges* or wooden boxes in which women kept their *abras* or working materials in old times."*

Embroidery was also practised as a separate art or trade by women. The common word for an embroiderer was *druinech* : but another term sometimes used was *greusaidhe* [graissee], which however more usually meant a shoemaker. An embroiderer kept for her work, among other materials, thread of various colours, as well as silver thread,† and a special needle. The design or pattern to be embroidered was drawn and stamped beforehand by a designer on a piece of leather, which the embroiderer placed lying before her and imitated with her needle : or as it is expressed with perfect clearness by the glossator, who, commenting on the name of the article (" the pattern of her needlework ") given in the Senchus Mór,

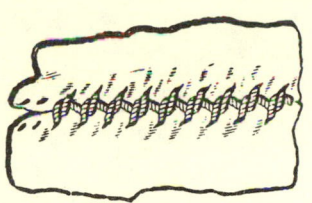

FIG. 327.

Specimen of antique (prehistoric) Irish needlework. A deerskin dress, covering a human body, found, 10 feet deep, in a bog in Galway, in 1821, was sewed together in this manner with fine gut. Stitches very regular all throngh. See Petrie's description in Dublin Philos. Journ. for 1825, p. 433. (From Wilde's Catalogue, p. 277.)

says :—" She [the embroiderer] can the more easily perform " her handiwork by having the leather pattern before her " with the picture of the needlework upon it."‡ This curious and interesting record indicates the refinement, carefulness, and artistic skill of the old Irish embroiderers. This art of stamping designs on leather, for other purposes as well as for embroidery, was carried to great perfection as we know from the beautiful specimens of book covers preserved in our museums (see vol. I., pp. 32, 488).

* Br. Laws, in O'Curry, Man' & Cust., II. 117.

† Br. Laws, I. 151, 14; 153, 7 from bottom ; and v. 315, top : see also Man. & Cust., II. 119, top.

‡ Br. Laws, I. 151, 11; 153, 30: see also Man. & Cust., II. 117.

It was usual for the most eminent of the Irish saints to have one or more embroiderers in their households, whose chief employment was the making and ornamentation of church robes and vestments. St. Patrick kept three constantly at work, namely, Lupait (his sister) ; Cruimtheris, a lady of royal birth ; and Erca, the daughter of Dáre, the chief who granted Armagh to St. Patrick. St. Columkille in like manner had a special embroiderer, namely, St. Ercnait or Coca, from whom is named Kilcock (Coca's Church) in the County Kildare. She is described in a note in the " Feilire of Aengus " as " the embroideress, " cutter, and sewer of clothes to St. Columkille and his " disciples."*

Embroidery was practised in Ireland in pre-Christian times, and was a well-recognised art from the earliest period of legend : for we are told in the Dinnsenchus that Aengus the Firbolg, who gave name to Dun Aenguis on the great island of Aran, had a daughter Maistiu, who was embroideress to the famous Dedannan chief Aengus of the Bruga : " she was the first person that formed the " figure of a cross in Erin, [namely] on the breast border " of Aengus's tunic."† From her also was named the historic fort of *Mullach-Maistenn* or Mullamast near Athy in Kildare—the ' summit of Maistiu.' We know from many ancient authorities that Irish ladies of the highest rank practised needlework and embroidery as an accomplishment and recreation. For this purpose they spun ornamental thread ; and in the Brehon Laws the distaff is constantly spoken of as among the articles in the possession of ladies. In the " Feast of Bricriu " (p. 83), it is casually mentioned, and as a matter of course, that the wives of the great heroes had their needles at the feast, and brought them about with them, no doubt with

---

* O'Curry, Man. & Cust., II. 123. St. Ercnait is commemorated in the Féilire on the 8th Jan. ; but the above note, quoted by O'Curry, is not in Stokes's Féilire under that date.   † O'Curry, Man. & Cust., II. 122.

other articles, in the little bag mentioned below. When Cuculainn came to the house of Fergall Monach at Lusk to woo his daughter Emer, he found the young lady on the lawn before the house with her foster-sisters, whom she was instructing in needlework and embroidery.*

Ladies' ornamental handbag.—Ladies carried a little ornamental handbag, or workbag, called *iadach* or *tiag*, or more usually *ciorbholg* [keerwolg], ' comb-bag,' like the modern reticule, which contained certain choice articles of daily use, and which was closed at the mouth by a string. The handbag of a queen or of a chieftain's wife contained, among other things, a *minn* or diadem of gold, a *lann* or thin band of gold (for the forehead or neck), a veil, a silk handkerchief, needles, and thread both woollen and silver for embroidery.†

5. *Tanning.*

The art of tanning leather was well understood in ancient Ireland. The name for a tanner was *súdaire* [soodĕră], which is still a living word. Oak bark was employed in tanning, and in connexion with this use was called *coirtech* [curtagh : Lat. *cortex*], as we find the word used in the Laws : whence comes the verb *coirtighim*, I tan. It is laid down in the Law (IV. 149) that the penalty for stripping as much bark from another person's oak-tree as would tan a cow-hide was a pair of women's shoes worth half a screpall, and for as much as would tan an ox-hide a pair of men's shoes worth a screpall. A distinction is also made as to the amount of the circumference of the tree that is stripped : and whether the bark had been taken off in the " killing months " or in the " non-killing months." In the Irish Life of St. Columkille it is stated that at Kells there was an oak-tree which was greatly revered, because the saint had at one time lived under it :

---

* Courtship of Emer, 71 : Man. & Cust., II. 122.
† Man. & Cust., II. 113, 114, quoting Br. Laws.

but it was blown down by a storm. "And a certain man "—says the narrative—" took some of its bark to tan " [leather for] his shoes : but when he put on the shoes, he " was smitten with leprosy from sole to crown "—in punishment for the desecration.*

By the process of tanning, the hide was thickened and hardened, as will be seen from the passages quoted below. The tanned leather was of a reddish or reddish-brown colour, as we find by several old passages. In the " Voyage of Maildune," the thieving cook calls his boat *curuch nua co n-derg codail,* " a new curragh [covered] with red hide," i.e. " *tanned* hide " (*codal*, a hide ; *derg*, red). Teigue the son of Cian made a " large curragh which took to cover it forty ox-hides of hard bark-soaked red leather " (*do dhoinn-lethar chruaid choirtigthe* : *donn*, a reddish-brown).† Hence also in the Latin Life of St. Brendan, his vessel is described as covered with cow-hide *rubricatis in cortice roborina,* ' tanned in oak-bark,' where *rubricatis*, though signifying ' tanned,' literally means ' reddened.'‡

6. *Workers in Leather, and the articles they made.*

Tanned leather was used for various purposes, one of the principal being as material for shoes ; but we know that shoes were also made of untanned hide (see p. 216, *supra*). Curraghs or wicker-boats were often covered with leather (see below pages 423 and 424). A jacket of hard, tough, tanned leather was sometimes worn in battle as a protecting corselet : and in connexion with this use, one of the oldest references to leather—in the lay literature— occurs in the Book of the Dun Cow, in the story of the Demon Chariot of Cuculainn. The hero is described as placing around him " his champion battle-girdle outside " of [a jacket of] hard, tanned, smooth leather of the " shoulder of seven ox-hides of yearling heifers, so that it

* Stokes, Lives of SS., 176. † Silva Gad., 386, ₂₇; Irish Text, 343, ₂₆.
‡ Navig. St. Brend. Card. Moran, 90 : O'Donohue, 119.

" extended from the waist of his side to his armpit. It
" [the jacket] was put about him to repel lances and
" sword-points, and spikes, and spears, and darts : because
" they used to fly off him the same as if they had been
" shot against a rock."*   The word *lethar* in the Irish of
this extract, which is still the word for leather, is of
course cognate with the English word.

Bags made of leather, and often of undressed skins,
were pretty generally used to hold liquids : a practice
which is alluded to in Cormac's Glossary (p. 104) in the
explanation of *lesan* as " a [leathern] *bolg* or bag in
which ale is kept."   Adamnan (p. 155) relates that one
of Columba's disciples, preparing for a voyage from Iona
to Ireland, took among other things, a leather milk-bag
(*utrem lactarium*) to bring a supply of milk in his boat :
but before using it he put it to steep for a night in the
salt water at the strand to soften it, placing some large
stones on it to prevent the tide current from carrying
it away.   In the Latin narrative of the " Voyage of
St. Brendan " such bags are often mentioned. On one
occasion he directs his crew to bring on board a number
of skin-vessels (*utres* : sing. *uter*) filled with water. A
leathern bottle was commonly called in Irish *pait* [pot].
Maildune and his companions, when leaving a certain
island, put a quantity of ale into *paits* and brought them
to their curragh† : and in an old Irish translation or paraphrase of 1 Kings xxv. 18, we read, " The women gave him
five sheep, two hundred loaves, and two *paits* of wine."‡
But *pait* is also used to denote a pot of any kind. There
was a sort of leather wallet or bag called a *crioll*, used
like a modern travelling-bag to hold clothes and other
soft articles.§ In Brocan's Hymn occurs the expression
dobert dillat i crioll, " he put a garment in a crioll."

* Kilk. Archæol. Journ., 1870–1, p. 426 : LU, 79, *a*, ₃₆.
† LU, 23, *b*, ₁ and ₂.   ‡ Sullivan, Introduction, 358
§ Silva Gad., 75, ₅   Irish text, 71, ₂₉.

The parts of every article made of leather were joined together by stitching with thongs. A maker of leather bags was called *criollaidhe* [creelee] (sometimes written *cliaraidhe*) from *crioll*, "a leather bag stitched with thongs" ("Man. & Cust.," II. 117). A leather-bottle maker was most commonly called a *pattaire* [pottera], *i.e.* a maker of *paits* or bottles : sometimes also called *sútaire* or *súdaire*.* We have seen that a maker of *cuarans* or un-tanned-leather shoes was called *cuaránaighe* [coorawnee]. The usual name for a shoemaker was, and is still, *greu-saidhe* [graissee] : but an older name was *cairem*, gen. *caireman*, pl. *cairemain*.† O'Clery explains *cairemhain* by *greusaighthe*, shoemakers. But *cairemain* was applied to a maker of leather bottles, as in the Brehon Law, v. 106, ₁₇ ; where also in lines 20, 21, the word is explained as people "who properly sew the round bottles." The word *sútaire* or *súdaire* [3-syll.], cognate with Lat. *sutor*, was sometimes applied to a shoemaker : but it more usually signified a tanner. From the preceding it will be seen that the several terms applied to leather-workers of different kinds were a good deal interchanged one with another. Those tradesmen in leather-work who stitched with thongs, namely, the leather-bottle maker, the shoe-maker, and the leather-wallet maker, worked with a pair of thongs, forming a stitch with each alternately, the workman, while using the free end of one, holding the end of the other between his teeth : exactly like the Egyptian shoemakers as they are depicted in stone and brick records. All this we know from some details given incidentally in a passage of the Brehon Laws (v. 81, top, and line 18).

The artistic uses of leather in making covers for books and embroidery patterns have been already mentioned.

<hr>

* Br. Laws, v. 80, top line.   † Rev. Celt., III. 97.

CHAPTER XXVII

MEASURES, WEIGHTS, AND MEDIUMS OF EXCHANGE

———

SECTION I. *Length and Area.*

IKE other ancient peoples, the Irish fixed their standards of length-measures, for want of better, mostly, but not exclusively, with reference to parts of the human body. The *troigid* [tro-id] or foot was the length of a man's foot, which was counted equal to twelve *ordlachs*—thumb-measures or inches: *ord* or *ordu*, a thumb, now *ordóg*: so that this *troigid* was practically the same as the present English foot. It was so constantly mentioned that it may be considered as the unit for all moderate measurements. Sometimes the space was measured out by the actual length of the person's foot: Conall, the son of Niall of the Nine Hostages, measures the site of a church for St. Patrick, " sixty of his [own] feet " in length.*

The following table of long measures, which is given in the Book of Aicill,† may be taken as the one in most general use. The grain, *i.e.* the length of a grain of

* Trip. Life, 71.   † Br. Laws, III. 335.

371

wheat of average size, was the smallest measure used by the Irish :—

3 grains,	.	.	.	.	1 *ordlach* or inch.
4 inches,	.	.	.	.	1 *bas*, palm, or hand.
3 palms,	.	.	.	.	1 *troighid* or foot.
12 feet,	.	.	.	.	1 *fertach* or rod.
12 rods or *fertachs*,		.	.		1 *forrach*.
12 *forrachs* in length by ⎫			.		1 *tircumaile* (i.e.
6 *forrachs* in width ⎭			.		' *cumal*-land ').

According to this table a *tir-cumaile* [teer-cummala] was equal to a space 576 English yards long by 288 broad : that is, about 34¼ English acres. A *cumal* represented three cows (p. 385, *infra*) ; and a *tir-cumaile* (land for a *cumal*) was as much land as was considered sufficient to graze three cows. This almost exactly agrees with the statement in vol. 1. p. 40—from a different source—that a ballybetagh (which contained 3600 *English* acres) was allowed for 300 cows : one of the many illustrations of the general consistency and accuracy of the old Irish records. When English ideas and practices began to obtain a footing in Ireland, after the Anglo-Norman Invasion, various other measures of land were adopted, the most general of which was the acre. Land was commonly estimated in acres and ploughlands according to the following table* :—

120 acres,	.	.	.	1 *seisrech* or ploughland.
12 ploughlands,	.	.		1 *baile*, bally, or townland.
30 *bailes*,	.	.	.	1 *tuath* or *triucha*.

As all Ireland contained 184 tuaths (vol. 1., p. 40), this gives the (old) Irish acreage of the whole country as 184 × 30 × 12 × 120 = 7,948,800. There are, we know, 20,815,460 *English* acres in all Ireland, which gives the old Irish acre a little more than 2½ of the present English

---

* Comyn's Keating, 113.

acre : exactly bearing out Keating's words :—" The acre " of the measure of the Gaels is twice or thrice greater than " the acre of the division of the Galls or English now."* All this is on the supposition that in the old estimate the whole surface was included, waste as well as arable land. There is some vagueness in all these calculations, which may account for the fact that within recent times the Irish acre is more than once and a half the size of an English acre.

Various other length-measures were in use in ancient Ireland. A *céim* [kaim] or step was $2\frac{1}{2}$ feet : " the lawful step is two feet and a half," says the Gloss on the Law (IV. 215), which gives the full pace (*deis-céim* : pron. desh-kaim), 5 feet. But in another law-tract on the " Division of Land," the full pace is given as 6 feet, making the single step 3 feet.

For small measures the *bas* [boss] and the *dorn* [durn] were in constant use. The *bas* or " palm " was the width of the hand at the roots of the fingers, which was fixed at 4 inches. The *dorn* or ' fist,' with the thumb closed in (called *mail-dorn*, ' bare-fist '), was 5 inches : with the thumb extended (called *airtem*-fist), 6 inches.† We constantly meet with such measures as " a cow 20 fists in girth," " a spear-handle 12 fists in length."

In a part of the Law (IV. 77) relating to fences and their measurement, a foot differing from the tabular one given above is mentioned : not the length of the whole foot, but as far as the separation of the big toe. This foot was considered as 10 inches : but it was rarely used.

---

* Joyce's Keating, p. 37.   For the political subdivisions of Ireland, see vol. I., pp. 39, 40, *supra* : and for various other modern land measures, see Ware, Antiqq., 224 ; Sullivan's Introduction to O'Curry, 96 ; Reeves' paper " On the Townland Distribution of Ireland," Proc. Roy. Ir. Acad., VII. 473 : " On the Territorial Divisions of the Country," by Sir Thomas Larcom, prefixed to the " Relief Correspondence of the Commissioners of Public Works " : and Joyce, Irish Names of Places, I. 241.

† Br. Laws, II. 241.

Lengths and distances were often roughly indicated by sight and sound : a custom that prevailed among nearly all ancient peoples. A chief named Coirbre promised Cuangus all the territory he could see to the north of Sliab Cise, near Assaroe at Ballyshannon, as a reward for expelling St. Patrick* : and many other examples of this sight-measurement might be given. But distances were much oftener estimated by sound. In connexion with the law of distress certain distances, called in the Senchus Mór " magh-spaces," were made use of : and the old commentator defines a magh-space to be " as far as " the sound of the bell (*i.e.* the small handbell of those " times] or the crow of a barn-door cock could be heard."† In the " Second Vision of Adamnan " it is stated with regard to a certain church that " neither the saints nor the " angels come nearer to it than where one hears the voice " of a bell that is struck at the church."‡

A man felling a tree was " bound by law to give warning as far as his voice could reach," so as to avoid danger to cattle or people.§ In some places these old measures are remembered in tradition to the present day. In the parish of Termonmaguirk in Tyrone there is an old burial-ground called *Relig-na-man* (Irish *Reilig-na-mban*), the ' cemetery of the women,' where none but women are buried. It is about half a mile from the church-ruin of Termonmaguirk, and the people of the place give this traditional account of its foundation. The body of a certain woman of bad character was brought to be buried in the church of Termonmaguirk ; but St. Columkille forbade it, and directed that the body should be buried at a spot where the sound of a bell struck at the church began to go out of hearing : and he left an injunction that this new cemetery (now *Relig-*

---

* Trip. Life, 149.
† Br. Laws, II. 107, 109.

‡ Rev. Celt., XII. 425.
§ Br. Laws, III. 227.

na-man) should never be entered by a living woman or by a dead man.*

The crow of a cock and the sound of a bell, as distance measures, are very often met with. The " glockenklang " or bell-clang was also used by the ancient Germans to measure distances.†

Other vague modes of estimating lengths were used. A certain legal distance is laid down in the Law (IV. 139) as being as far as a youth could cast a rod. The legal size of the *faithche* [faha] or green round a house depended on the rank of the owner, and the unit of measure was the distance a man could cast a spear standing at the house (p. 61, *supra*). Very often the human face is taken as the standard of size of a ring or crescent of gold—or silver—to be given as a tribute, or fine, or present. In the Battle of Rossnaree (25) it is stated that the Clanna Dedad of Munster proposed to give to Concobar, king of Emain, among other valuable things, " the breadth of his face of red gold," as an inducement to refrain from invading them. Many other like instances of this standard might be cited. We may form some vague idea of the value of such a ring or crescent from an expression in an ancient poem quoted in Cormac's Glossary (p. 110) :—" Seven ounces of refined gold for my great friend's noble face."‡ So in the Welsh tale of Branwen the daughter of Llyr, Bendigeid Vran offers the offended hero Matholwch a plate of gold of the breadth of his face to appease his anger.§

2. *Capacity.*

The standard unit of capacity adopted by the Irish was the full of a hen-eggshell of moderate size, which perhaps was as good a standard as could be found at the time.

---

* Reeves, Adamnan, 283.

† Stokes (in Rev. Celt., XII. 440) refers for the use of the glockenklang to J. Grimm, Deutsche Rechtsalterthümer, 2te Ausg. 76.

‡ See other instances in Mesca Ulad, 55 ; and Book of Rights, 243.

§ Mabinogion, 30.

Beginning with this there is given in the Book of Aicill*
the following table of measures of capacity :—

12 hen-eggshell-fulls,		=	1 *meisrin.*
12 *meisrins,*	. . =		1 *ollderbh.*
12 *ollderbhs,*	. . =		1 *olpatrick* or *oilmedach.*

Another measure, the *olfeine,* is half an olpatrick : but one
of the law-tracts† gives an olfeine as two olpatricks. I
find by actual trial that twelve times the full of an average-
size hen-eggshell will fill a modern imperial pint ; so that
a *meisrin* was equivalent to a pint, an ollderbh to 12,
and an olpatrick or oilmedach to 144 pints. But there
seems reason to think that the olpatrick was sometimes
reckoned as one-fourth of this size, namely, as containing
36 pints.

A *sellann,* equal to four eggshells, was often used in
measuring honey : it occurs frequently in the Rule of the
Culdees : in which also a *bochtan,* equal to 12 eggshells, is
mentioned as a measure for ale, milk, or whey.‡

A *miach* or sack was much used in measuring corn
and malt : and fines for trespass were estimated, and
payments of various kinds were made, in sacks, so that
the *miach* must have been always much of the same
size. As a standard of value it will be mentioned at
page 386.

As there were vague measures in length, so also in
capacity. In measuring honey in large quantities four
sizes of vessels are often mentioned. A " milch-cow
vessel," or barrel, was one which, when full, a person of
ordinary strength could lift as high as his knee : a " heifer-
vessel," which he could raise to his navel ; a smaller
" heifer-vessel " to his loins ; and a " dairt (or still smaller)
heifer-vessel," which he could raise over his head.§

---

* Br. Laws, III. 335, bottom.   † Br. Laws, III. 337, note 1.
‡ Reeves, Culd., 84, 85 : and Corm. Gloss., 134, under " Pinginn."
§ Br. Laws, IV. 165, note 2.

3. *Weight.*

The smallest weight used was a grain of wheat. We read indeed, in an ancient Irish passage in the Book of Ballymote quoted by Petrie (R. Towers, 218), that there was a smaller weight called an atom : 24 atoms in a grain : but this is evidently fanciful, like some of the minute time divisions (p. 387, *infra*). An attempt was made to render the grain-standard definite and uniform by these two regulations :—First, the grains should be taken from wheat that grew in " land of three roots," *i.e.* land of the best kind (p. 269, *supra*). Secondly, the grains should be in a medium condition as to dryness. The following is the table of weight founded on the average grain of wheat* :—

8 grains,	.	.	1 *pinginn* or penny of silver.
3 pinginns,	.	.	1 *screpall.*
24 screpalls,	.	.	1 *unga* or ounce.

The pinginn and screpall will be again under notice in section 4 (p. 381).

The *unga* or ounce (576 grains of wheat or about 432 grains Troy) was the standard used in weighing metals. The word seems to have been borrowed from the Latin *uncia*. That the Irish did not borrow the standard itself, but had it from the most ancient times, appears from the fact that there was an older native word *mann* for the ounce. In the ninth century the word *unga* had come into general use, and *mann* had become obsolete, so that Cormac thought it necessary to explain it in his Glossary :—" Mann, that is *unga* or ounce." A verse is then quoted from Sencha, a celebrated law-giver and poet of far remote time, to show its application : and the Glossary adds :—" Mann then is ' bright,' that is, a refined ounce."†

---

*Petrie, Round Towers, 218, top : Corm. Gloss., 134, under " Píssíre." Prof. Ridgeway reckons that four of those wheat-grains were equal to three grains Troy. † Corm. Gloss., 110 ; Irish Text in three Irish Gloss., 29.

There was a weight called *dirna*, of which the exact value is not known. It was very much greater than the ounce, as we know from the poem of Colman Mac Lenine, in which an ounce is contrasted with the much heavier *dirna*.* From an old passage quoted in Cormac's Glossary (72, " Fir "), it would seem that a *dirna* of silver was the value of a white cow. In Petrie's R. Towers (p. 219) is a quotation from the Brehon Laws in which a weight called a *dinnra* is mentioned, and it is stated that a *dinnra* of red bronze contains six ounces. Probably *dirna* and *dinnra* are the same : one being changed to the other by metathesis.

The pound weight was used, and was designated by the word *pún*, which is probably a loan-word from Lat. *pondus*. From a passage in the Story of Mongan in the Book of the Dun Cow, it would appear that a pound of silver had twelve ounces and a pound of gold nine. Said Mongan to the poor scholar :—" Go now till you reach the " *sith* [shee] of Lethed Oidni, and bring me a precious " stone which I have there : and take for thyself a pound " of white silver [*pún findairgit*] in which are twelve " ounces . . . thou wilt [also] find a pound of gold, in " which are nine ounces."† But perhaps *pún* here means merely a mass or lump.

From numerous references in the old writings, we learn that the ancient Irish had balances of different kinds and sizes, and with different names. The most usual Irish term for a balance, and also for the beam of a balance, was *med* or *meadh* [ma], which is the word in general use at the present day. Cormac's Glossary (p. 134) explains the word *puincern* [punkern] as meaning two things :—*First*, a *cern* or dish for measuring a commodity called *sella* (probably some kind of corn) : Keating has a " a *cern* of *arbhar* or corn " (p. 78, *supra*) : *second*, " a beam for weighing cattle,

* Corm. Gloss., 10, 11 : O'Curry, Man. & Cust., II. 245.
† Voyage of Bran., I 55, 95

namely, the notched beam." Here the author plainly implies a distinction between a plain beam and one that was notched (*indmeach*) ; and he takes care to explain that the beam called *puincern* used for weighing cattle was a notched one. But it appears from other passages in the glossary that there were smaller notched beams for weighing lighter commodities. Thus *puingcne* (p. 134) is explained " a *screpall* or scruple of the notched beam " : and again under " *cimb* " (p. 39) this quotation is given from the Bretha Nemed :—" A *cimb* or tribute of bronze since I placed the bronze in the notched balance." I take it that the balance with a " notched beam " (*med indmeach*) was a steelyard—a balance having a single weight movable

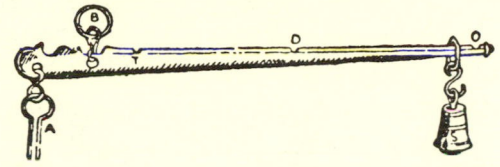

FIG. 328

The small steelyard found in use by Thomas Dineley in the seventeenth century.
(From Kilk. Archæol. Journ., 1858-9, p. 56.)

along a graduated beam *from notch to notch*, which by its distance from the fulcrum or suspension point indicated the weight of the commodity—identical with our modern steelyard. As bearing upon this point it is well to observe that an old steelyard of bronze was found in 1864 in a rath near Ballyshannon in Donegal, ornamented and carefully graduated : the material — bronze — indicating great antiquity.* Thomas Dineley, an Englishman, travelling in Ireland in the seventeenth century, found a " stilyard " in use for weighing foreign coins, of which he gives an illustration (reproduced here, figure 328) : probably a descendant of the ancient *puincern*.

Another balance, which must have been small, is noticed in Cormac's Glossary (p. 134) in these words :—

* Proc. Roy. Ir. Academy, VIII. p. 476.

" *Pissire* [peeshĕrĕ], that is, a broad-headed beam for
" weighing one pinginn of weight.   One pinginn then is the
" burden of that beam."   From the epithet ' broad-headed '
we may conclude that it was a steelyard.   *Pissire* is derived
from *piss* [peesh], an old name for the pinginn or penny.
Still another kind of balance was called *laithe* [lay-he],
always used in this plural form (sing. *laith*).   It is
explained in Cormac's Glossary, but more fully by
O'Clery in his Glossary :—" *Laithe*, a balance for weighing gold or silver."   From an expression in Cormac's
explanation (*etir laithe Lugba*, ' between the scales of
Lugba '), as well as from the fact that the plural *laithe*
is always used (like our " scales "), we may infer that the
balance so designated was the ordinary scales of two
dishes.   We know that the Irish had balances of this
kind ; for on one of the Monasterboice crosses there is
a representation of the general judgment in which the
Archangel Michael is seen weighing souls in a two-dish
balance : the dishes being deep like bowls.   A small
bronze balance of this kind — now in the National
Museum—beautifully finished, was found in 1860 in an
excavation at Kilmainham near Dublin : and another
about the same time in a crannoge in Ulster.*   The
Kilmainham one however is probably Danish.

4. *Standards of Value and Mediums of Exchange.*

In early stages of society in Ireland, as in all other
countries, buying and selling and other commercial
transactions were carried on by means of payment in
kind : and there is hardly any description of valuable
articles that was not used for this purpose.   It will be
seen in many parts of this book that payments were made
for purchases, tribute, fines, &c., in cows, sacks of corn,
salted pigs, butter, mantles, and so-forth : the parties

* Proc. Roy. Ir. Academy, VII., p. 156, II. and p. 368.

determining the values according to the customs of the place. But mixed up with this barter in kind, gold and silver told out by weight, and—after the middle of the eighth century—silver coins, were used as mediums of exchange.

That the Irish were acquainted with the use of coined money, at least as early as the eighth century, is proved by the records; and indeed might be anticipated without the help of records, inasmuch as there was in those times much intercourse, both by traffic and missionary enterprise, between Ireland and the Continent, where coined money was then in constant circulation. A celebrated Irish poet named Rumann, who died A.D. 747, once paid a *cuairt* or professional visitation (see vol. I., p. 449, *supra*) to the Galls or foreigners of Dublin, and composed a poem for them. They at first refused to give him anything, but ultimately agreed that he should name his own reward whereupon he demanded two pinginns from every good Gall and one from every bad Gall. The result was that to a man they gave him two pinginns each.* Half a century later we have another record indicating a familiar acquaintance in Ireland with the use of coined money. There is extant a letter written about the year 790 by the illustrious churchman and scholar, Alcuin, to Colcu the Wise, head of the great school of Clonmacnoise, stating that he had sent, with the letter, a number of *sicli* (small coins), some from himself and some from his great master Charlemagne, and a quantity of pure olive oil (then scarce in Ireland) for use in religious rites.

The coins in circulation among the Irish were the *pinginn* and the *screpall* (or, as it was often called, the *sical*), both of silver: according to the authorities quoted by Petrie (R. Towers, 218, 219), the *pinginn* weighed 8 grains of wheat, and the *screpall* was equal to 3 pinginns and weighed accordingly 24 grains (=18 grs. Troy). It is

---

* Petrie, Round Towers, 353.

curious that in another and older authority, **Cormac's Glossary** (134, under " Pisire "), the weight of the *pinginn* is given as 7 grains : which Petrie (R. T., 220) conjectures may mean that while 8 grains was the normal weight, the *pinginn* then in circulation usually weighed only 7, on account of wear. According to M. d'Arbois de Jubainville, the *screpall* is mentioned in one of the St. Gall eighth-century glosses : which is the oldest Irish notice of it yet discovered.*

The two words *screpall* and *sical,* both meaning the same coin, are borrowed from the Latin *scrupulus* and *siclus* (this last being itself borrowed from the Hebrew *shekel*). In Professor Ridgeway's opinion they were

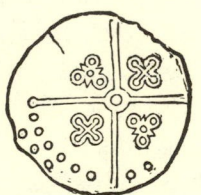 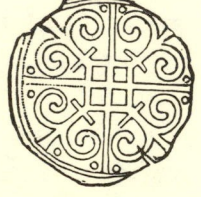

FIG. 329.   FIG. 330.
Irish bracteate coins : now in the National Museum, Dublin.
(From Petrie, Round Towers, p. 278.)

borrowed from the Latin before the time of Constantine, *i.e.*, before the beginning of the fourth century A.D. But the Irish had more than one native name for the *screpall,* which we find in various forms in the different authorities : *puingcne, opuingc, oiffing, faing, fang.* Cormac's Glossary (p. 134) gives the native word *piss* [peesh] as another name for a pinginn-weight.

Many specimens of the pinginn and of the screpall are preserved in the National Museum. The pinginns are what are called " bracteate " coins, *i.e.* struck only on one side ; but the screpalls are impressed on both sides.

We have seen that the Irish were familiar with the use of coins in the eighth and ninth centuries ; and the question

* Rev. Celt., XVIII., p. 114.

has often been debated whether they coined money for themselves before the tenth century. It would be certainly strange if they did not, seeing that they had such constant intercourse with Britain and the Continent in the early centuries of Christianity; and they were—as we have seen—in advance of most nations of Europe in the Middle Ages in artistic metal-working. There is one circumstance that strongly favours the opinion that they had a native mint, namely, that they had a coin with a native name, *crosóc* or *crosóg*, which—both coin and name—fell out of use when the pinginns and screpalls had become well established as the Irish currency. The name—which signifies " little cross "—indicates that it was stamped on the side with the figure of a cross. That this was a very ancient native coin, quite independent of pinginns and screpalls, is rendered pretty certain by three circumstances :—First, the native name *crosóc* ; secondly, that it fell out of use when the coins with the borrowed names " pinginn " and " screpall " came into use ; and, thirdly, and most strongly of all, that in point of value it did not fit in with the tabular arrangement of these two last-named coins, for, according to the native records, it was equal to " two pinginns and a quarter of a pinginn," that is to say, it weighed eighteen grains.* But at any rate this matter of coinage is comparatively unimportant as affecting civilisation, for it has been pointed out that some of the greatest nations of antiquity did not coin money, or coined it only at a late period of their career.

From the very beginning of our records gold and silver were used as a medium of exchange, sometimes as ingots, but more commonly in the form of rings, bracelets, and other ornaments. They were weighed by the ounce,† which, as we have seen, was equal in weight to 576 grains of wheat, or to 432 grains Troy ; and there is the best

---

* See " Crosóc " in O'Donovan's Supplement to O'Reilly ; and Br. Laws v. 437.   † For instances see Irish Miscell., 1846, pp. 133, 143, 147.

reason to believe that, in order to facilitate interchange of this kind, gold and silver rings of various forms, as well as other gold and silver ornaments, were generally or always made of definite weights. Notices of this custom are found everywhere in the literature. In Cormac's Glossary (p. 22), a *briar* is defined as "a pin of one ounce of gold." At A.D. 1150 the Four Masters record that Murkertagh O'Loghlin, king of Ireland, gave the abbot of Derry, among other presents, "a gold ring (*fáil óir*) in which were five *ungas*": in the next year (1151) Cu-Uladh O'Flynn gave the same abbot "a ring of gold in which were two ounces": and Turlogh O'Conor king of Ireland gave the archbishop of Armagh "a gold ring of twenty ounces." In an ancient document in the Book of Armagh certain payments are made for a purchase, among them a *muince* or necklet of three ounces of gold.* St. Finnen once found a gold ring, and gave it to a chief as the price of a certain slave's freedom, for which an ounce of gold had been demanded: the ring was weighed, and it was found to contain exactly an ounce.† Such examples might be multiplied indefinitely. That this custom existed in Ireland is rendered all the more certain by Cæsar's record that in his time the people of Britain "used brass or iron rings *fixed at a certain weight* as their money."‡ But in Ireland, gold, as being comparatively abundant, was used instead of the inferior metals. What is even more to the point, the practice seems to have been universal in other countries:—"I have already shown"—says Professor Ridgeway (p. 399)—"the universality all over the world of making gold ornaments after a fixed weight."§

It may be considered certain that in Ireland the open gold rings called *bunne-do-at* (now often called *fibulæ*:

* Trip. Life, 341.   † Stokes, Lives of SS., 225, bottom.
‡ Commentaries, v. xv.
§ See also on all this M. de Jubainville in Revue Archæologique, 1888, on "Des Bijoux et de l'argenterie employés comme prix d'achat."

see p. 241, *supra*), as well as other gold ornamental articles, were used as money. But besides those called *bunne-do-at*, there are in the National Museum, a great number—fifty or more—of very small open gold rings, from ¼ to ¾ inch in diameter, without the terminal knobs or *ats* : they are *bunnĕs* simply, not *bunne-do-ats*. One is figured here, its natural size, and another is shown in the upper part of fig. 21, vol. I., p. 33, *supra*. These, from their great numbers, and from their simple, unornamental construction, have all the appearance of having been used mainly as currency. Professor Ridgeway has carefully investigated this question in his work " The Origin of Metallic Currency and Weight Standards," and he has fixed on the weight of the smallest specimen in the museum—15 grains Troy—as the standard. He shows moreover that all the larger rings in the Museum are very nearly multiples of this. These little rings then were used in ordinary business transactions, as we use coins now. As the *crosoc* weighed 18 grains of wheat, *i.e.* 13.5 grains Troy, it is likely that it was intended to be in accordance with this standard : in other words, that the smallest of these little rings represented the value of a *crosoc*. Gold rings offered in payment were tested, as we see in case of the ounce ring cited above, paid for the slave's freedom : just as they now weigh gold coins in banks.

FIG. 331.

Gold *bunnĕ* or ring, full size: open, but without the *do-ats*. Used as money. Now in the National Museum.   (From Wilde's Catalogue, Gold, p. 63.)

A full-grown cow, or ox, was in ancient times a very general standard of value, not only in Ireland, but all over the civilised world : and was considered equal in value to one ounce of gold. In this case—as an article of payment—a cow was in Ireland generally called a *séd* [shade]. Cows or *séds* were very often used both in actual payments and in estimating amounts. Next above the *séd* was the *cumal*, which was originally applied to a bondmaid : but the word came to be used very generally to signify the value of a bondmaid, which was counted as three *séds*. The words *séd* and *cumal* are however sometimes used very loosely to denote variable values. Thus in one of the Law Glosses it is stated that the best *séd* is a milch cow, and the worst *séd* a *dartaid* or yearling heifer* : and in Cormac's Glossary (p. 29), under the word *clithar-sét*, there is a sort of classification of *séds*. So also the *cumal* : in a certain Law Gloss a *cumal* of *six* cows is mentioned.†† But the text generally draws attention to exceptional cases of this kind : and in all ordinary statements of value in these standards, a *séd* may be taken as a cow, and a *cumal* as three *séds*.‡

For general convenience it was laid down that where the payment for anything was half a *cumal* or less, it might be legally made in one kind of goods—cows, or horses, or silver : from half a *cumal* to a *cumal*, it should be in two kinds : above a *cumal*, in three. Whenever horned cattle were given in payment, one-third of them should be oxen ; when horses, one-third should be mares ; and silver payment should include one-third of manufactured articles. But under mutual agreement payments might be made in any way.§

A *miach* or sack of corn—generally of oats or barley— which for convenience sake must have been always made of uniform size—was very often used as a standard of value : it is indeed adopted in the Brehon Law as the almost universal standard in estimating fines for trespass, and payments for grazing.‖ Thus for trespass over a full fence there was a fine of four *miachs* of oats or barley : the price that purchased the grazing of certain lands is twelve *miachs* : and the expense of feeding cattle under certain circumstances is a *miach* for every animal per month.¶

* Br. Laws, IV. 29.   See also II. 277, bottom ; and III. 43, bottom.
† *Ibid.*, IV. 25, ₁₇.
‡ See " Séd " in the Index to vol. v. Brehon Laws.
§ See for all these arrangements, Br. Laws, III. 151, 153.
‖ Br. Laws, IV., all through the tract on Judgments of Co-Tenancy, p. 69.   ¶ Br. Laws, IV., pp. 83, 105, 107.

We have no means of ascertaining the exact contents of a *miach* : but we know its value ; for it is stated several times in the Brehon Law that a *miach* was worth a *screpall* of silver.* A *miach* or sack is often mentioned as a standard of value, without any intimation as to what it contains : but in all such cases it is to be understood as a sack of oats or barley.

5. *Time.*

In the works of some ancient writers who touch on technical chronology, such as Bede, Rhabanus, Isidore, &c., are to be found subdivisions of time, based on the day in the higher parts, but in the lower descending to such minuteness as to lead to the conclusion that the smallest measures were purely ideal, and never intended for practical application. The ancient Irish also had their time divisions, with minute denominations, a specimen of which is given in the Tale of the Battle of Moyrath (p. 109). This may be tabulated as follows† :—

Names.	Values.	Equivalents in our present time measures.
1 atom, ...	. . .	$\frac{12}{47}$ of a second.
1 ostent, . . .	376 atoms,	1 min. 36 sec.
1 bratha, ...	564 ,,	2 ,, 24 ,,
1 pars (part), . . .	940 ,,	4 ,, 0 ,,
1 minuit (minute), . .	1,410 ,,	6 ,, 0 ,,
1 pongc (point), . .	3,525 ,,	15 ,, 0 ,,
1 uair (hour), . . .	14,100 ,,	60 ,, 0 ,,
1 cadar (quarter of a day), .	. . .	6 hours.

After this follow a day (called variously in Irish *lá, láa, láe, láthe, dia, die*) ; a week (*sechtman*) ; a month (*mí*) ; a season

* For instance, Br. Laws, I. 61, note 1 ; and II. 251, 8.

† See also Moyrath, p. 331. For another statement of Irish time measures, see Stokes, Trip. Life, Introd., cliv. In the above Table the Irish atom is sufficiently minute : but the Venerable Bede's smallest measure is seven or eight times smaller still, being only the thirtieth part of a second.

(*tréimse*) ; a year (*bliadain*) ; a *saegal* or seculum ; an *aeis* or aeon. As all but one of the Irish words used in the first eight items of the above enumeration are borrowed from the Latin, we may take for granted that the table itself was borrowed from the Latin writers, but probably modified. The exception is *bratha* [braha], a native Irish word, meaning a ' twinkling of an eye.'

The Irish divided their year, in the first instance, into two equal parts, each of which was afterwards subdivided into two parts or quarters. The four quarters were called—*Errach*, now *Earrach* [arragh], Spring ; *Samrad*, now *Samhradh* [sowra], Summer ; *Fogmar*, now *Foghmhar* [fowar], Autumn ; *Gemred*, now *Geimhridh* [gevrĕ], Winter : and they began on the first days of February, May, August, and November, respectively. We have historical testimony that games—which will be described in chapter xxix.— were celebrated at the beginning of Summer, Autumn, and Winter ; but we have no account of any such celebrations at the beginning of Spring. These divisions of the year and the festivities by which they were ushered in originated with the Pagan Irish, and were continued into Christian times.

Errach or Spring began on the first of February. This day was called *oimelc*, *imolg*, or *imbulc* : the first form *oimelc* is given in Cormac's Glossary (p. 127, " *ói* "), where it is derived from *ói*, a sheep, and *melc* or *melg*, milk : " *ói-melg*, ' ewe-milk,' for that is the time the sheep's milk comes." That *oimelc* is the first of February we know from Peter O'Connell's Dictionary, where *oimelc* is identified with *Féil Brighde* (St. Brigit's feast day), which has been, and is still, the Irish name for the first of February all through Ireland, the old Pagan name *oimelc*, being obsolete for centuries.

In Cormac's Glossary (p. 151) *Samrad*, Summer, is fancifully derived from the Hebrew *sam*, the sun, and the Irish *rad*, a course : " the course which the sun runs : then most its brightness and its height delight." Whatever may be the true derivation, the word is obviously cognate with the English *Summer*. The first day of May was the beginning of Summer. It was called *Belltaine* or *Beltene* [beltina], which is the name for the 1st May still always used by speakers of Irish; and it is well known in Scotland, where *Beltane* has quite taken its place as an English word :—

> " Ours is no sapling, chance sown by the fountain.
> Blooming at Beltane, in winter to fade."
>
> —*Lady of the Lake.*

Another name for May Day, according to Cormac's Glossary (p. 36), is *Cedsoman*.

Autumn was called Fogmar, Fogamar, or Foghmhar, which is still its name : according to Cormac's Glossary (p. 74), *Fogamar* was also the name of the last month of Autumn, *i.e.* October. Autumn began on the 1st August, Lammas day. This day has two ancient Irish names :— *Bron-trogain* and *Lugnasad* [Loo'nasa]. The first is derived in an old Irish glossary* from *trogan*, a name for the earth or ground, and *brón*, bringing forth :—Bron-trogain, the bringing forth of fruits by the earth or ground. *Brón* properly signifies ' sorrow ' or distress : the idea here being—in the words of the old Tale of the " Wooing of Emer "†—" It is then the earth sorrows under [the weight of] its fruit " (*is and do-broni trogan ꝼua torthib*). In the Story of the *Agallamh* or " Colloquy of the Ancients "—as well as in the old glossary referred to above—the first day of August, or the " trogan-month," is identified with *Lugnasad,*‡ which is still the Irish name of the first of August everywhere in Ireland. (See page 439, below for the origin of this name.)

* Quoted by O'Donovan in Book of Rights, liii.
† Rev. Celt., XI. 443.
‡ Silva Gad., 216, ₃₀; and Stokes, Acallamh, line 4760

Samain, Samuin, or *Samhuin* [sowin], the first of November, was the first day of *Gemred* or Winter. The name is compounded of the two words, *sam,* which was an old word for *Samrad* or Summer, and *fuin,* an ancient word for end : that is to say, the end of Summer : " for," the old authority adds, " the whole year was [originally] " divided into two parts—Summer from 1st May to 1st " November, and Winter from 1st November to 1st May."* The name *samain* is still used even among the English-speaking people in Scotland and the north of Ireland, in the form of *sowin* or *sowins,* which is the name of a sort of flummery usually made about the 1st November. The term *gemred* for winter is a derivative from the older and simpler word *geim,* meaning the same thing.

For certain legal purposes connected with grazing and trespass, the ancient Irish had another division of the year into two unequal parts :—the Summer division from the 1st March to the 31st July, five months ; and the Winter division from 1st August to the 28th of February, seven months.†

O'Donovan stated in 1847 (Book of Rights, lii) that the season with which the Pagan Irish began their year could not (then) be determined. Some years later O'Curry asserted that according to the authority of an ancient Irish poem, of which he had a copy, the year began on the 1st February.‡ We must presume that this is correct ; but he has not given the stanza in which the statement is made, and I have never seen the poem.

Occasionally time was measured by the fortnight (*coicthiges* : pron. co-keess'). Fothad Airgthech on one occasion rested on a certain hill " till the end of three fortnights." King Concobar—says the " Battle of Rosnaree " (p. 3)—was ill in Emain " for the time of three fortnights " : and in another part of the same Tale (p. 19) Sencha says

---

* Sick Bed, Atlantis, I. 370, note 2 : and Book of Rights, liii.
† Br. Laws, IV. 79, 89, 91.   ‡ Sick Bed, Atlantis, I. 370, note 2.

to Concobar, " I will ask a truce of battle till the distant end of a fortnight in addition to a month."

The ancient Irish counted time rather by nights than by days. Thus in the Life of St. Fechin we are told :— " Moses was forty nights on Mount Sinai without drink, without food."* In coupling together day and night they always put the night first : in other words, the night belonging to any particular day was the night preceding. In the " Vision of Mac Conglinne " a certain thing is spoken of as happening on *Oidche Domnaig*, the " night of Sunday," where it is obvious from the context that the night in question was the night preceding, or what we of the present day would call " Sunday eve " or " Saturday night."† All this is a survival of what appears to have been the universal practice among the Celtic nations of old : for Caesar‡ describes the Gauls as measuring the lapse of time, not by days but by nights : and calculating months, years, and birthdays in such a way as to make the night precede the day. Tacitus§ states that the Germans also gave precedence to the night, and the same custom prevailed among the Jews. Traces of all this still remain in the English language in the words *fortnight* and *sennight* (i.e. fourteen nights and seven nights), and in such words as Christmas-eve and Hallow-eve. In expressing a length of time by nights, the Irish commonly included the two nights at the beginning and end, and hence the word *coicthigis* for a fortnight, which literally means " fifteen-night " ; like the Welsh *wythnos* (" eight-night ") for a week.

The Irish used the word *nomaid* or *nomad* to denote a time, the length of which has not been precisely determined. It evidently means nine time-spaces of some kind,

---

* Rev. Celt., XII. 435. On this custom of measuring time by nights, see Rhys, Hibbert Lectures, 360.

† Mac Conglinne, 18, 20, and 134 : see also Adamnan, 230, last line but one.

‡ Bell. Gall., VI. xviii.   § Germania, cap. XI.

from *nói*, nine. Some take it to mean ' nine nights,' like the Latin *nundinum* : and it has been interpreted ' nine days,' ' five days and four nights ' ; ' the ninth day.' The probability is that its meaning varied, so that two or more of these may be correct.

6. *Enumeration.*

The decimal system was in general use. The mode of enumeration was usually the same as we have now in English, the largest numbers coming first and the smallest last. The Four Masters give all their dates in this order : and Keating reads 2628 as " two thousand and six hundred and twenty-eight." But very often this order was reversed, both in the old and in the more recent writings. In an ancient poem quoted by Keating, 197 years is given as " seven years, ninety and a hundred " : and in another passage 1130 is read " thirty on a hundred on a thousand." Frequently the two systems are mixed, and other denominations besides decimal are brought in, of which the following are examples :—(432 years), " twelve years and twenty and four hundred " : (1978), " eight and seventy, a thousand and nine hundred " : (1130) ships, " ten ships, twenty, on a hundred, on a thousand." Seán Buidhe O'Clery calls 1453 years " a thousand years and four hundred years, and thirteen years, and twice twenty."

It is remarkable that seven is sometimes called " great six." Thus *móir-sheis-ear* is found in old authorities to denote seven persons, literally " great-six persons." This custom as well as the word *móir-sheis-ear* [more-hesher] still continues in use.

Sculpture on Window: Cathedral Church, Glendalough: Beranger, 1779.
(From Petrie's Round Towers.)

CHAPTER XXVIII

LOCOMOTION AND COMMERCE

SECTION I. *Roads, Bridges, and Causeways.*

oads.—That the country was well provided with roads we know, partly from our ancient literature, and partly from the general use of chariots. They were not indeed anything like our present hard, smooth roads, but constructed according to the knowledge and needs of the period, sometimes laid with wood and stone, sometimes not, but always open and level enough for car and horse traffic. There were five main roads leading from Tara through the country in different directions: and numerous roads—all with distinct names—are mentioned in the annals. Many of the old roads are still traceable: and some are in use at the present day, but so improved to meet modern requirements as to efface all marks of antiquity.

The ancient Irish classified their roads in regard to size and use into seven kinds, which are named and partly described in an interesting passage in Cormac's Glossary (p. 141). Cormac gives, as two general terms for a road of any kind, *conair* and *cai*, which are living words at the present day. The following are the names of the seven kinds of *conairs* or ways: they are given here, not in the

Glossary order, but generally according to size :—*Slige, Ramut, Bóthar, Rót, Sét, Tuagrotá* and *Lámrota*.

The *slige* [slee] was the largest of all : it was a main high-road. Cormac says " it was made for the passing of " chariots by each other, for the meeting of two chariots " [of the largest size], *i.e.* a king's chariot and a bishop's " chariot, so that each of them may go [freely] by the other."

" *Ramut* (or *ramat*) "—says the Glossary—" is greater " [*i.e.* wider] than a *rót* : it is an open space or way which " is in front of [*i.e.* leads to] the forts of kings : and every " neighbour whose land comes up to it is bound to cleanse " [his own part of] it." A *ramat* is mentioned in the Senchus Mór, as subject to certain laws ; and the gloss gives the following description of it :—" A *ramat*, i.e. a " great road to which there is no fence [meaning that it is " open on both sides] and to which run all small by-roads : " and the fine for not cleansing the roads has a stay of three " days."* There is here no mention of a king's fort—as there is in Cormac's Glossary—from which we may infer that the *ramuts* were not used exclusively in connexion with the residences of kings.

" A *Bóthar* " [boher]—says the passage in the Glossary —" two cows fit upon it, one lengthwise, the other athwart : " their calves or their yearlings fit on it along with them " [*i.e.* each calf walking beside its mother] : for if the calves " were behind them, the cow that followed would gore " [the calf in front of her]. *Bóthar* is still the common word for a road, and the diminutive *bohereen* or *boreen* (Irish *bóithrín*) is a familiar Anglo-Irish word for a little road or country lane.

Rót (pron. rote : sometimes written *rát*), according to the Glossary, is compounded of *ro*, great, and *sét*, a way : i.e. *ro-shét* [ro-hait], a great *sét* or way—*i.e.* a road which is greater than a *sét*. " A *rót* was made for the horses of a mansion, and there is room on it for a one-horse chariot."

* Br. Laws, I. 233.

The gloss on the Senchus Mór* defines *rót* :—" a small (*i.e.* narrow road), to which there is a fence " (*clád*), namely, a raised bank or " ditch" on each side. *Rót*, written in modern Irish *ród* [road], is still in use, and is evidently cognate with the English word *road* : for Cormac's derivation, above, is fanciful.

Sét [shate], the Glossary says, is less (*i.e.* narrower) than a *rót*, and is " a path of one animal," *i.e.* wide enough for a single cow or horse.

A *tuagrota* is a small road, a farmer's road, such as he makes when he is permitted or purchases a right of way from his farm to an adjacent main road, or to a mountain for the convenience of sending cattle to graze on it, or of bringing home turf.

A *lámrota* (*i.e.* a hand-road : *lám*, a hand) is a small by-road, made for convenience of communication to connect two *sliges* or main roads. " *Lámhród*, as much as to say, *ród láimh le ród eile*, ' a road beside another road ' " (O'Cl. Gloss.).

The five main roads leading from Tara are mentioned in our oldest authorities, as, for instance, in the Story of Bruden Da Derga in the Book of the Dun Cow. They were all called *slige*. 1. *Slige Asail* [slee-assil] ran from Tara due west towards Lough Owel in Westmeath, and thence probably in a north-west direction : it divided the ancient kingdom of Meath into two equal parts, North and South.† 2. *Slige Midluachra* extended northwards towards Slane, through the Moyry Pass north of Dundalk,‡ round the base of Slieve Fuaid near Newtown Hamilton, to Emain, and on to Dunseverick on the north coast of Antrim (Faraday's Táin, p. 59), portions of the present northern highway run along its site. 3. *Slige Cualann* ran southeast through Dublin, across the Liffey by the hurdle-bridge

* Br. Laws, I. 233.
† Book of Rights, Introd., lviii : Three Fragm., 77, 8, 9.
‡ Through the Moyry Pass : see Miss Stokes's Inscr., II. 28 bot.

that gave the city the ancient name of *Baile-atha-cliath* (the town of the hurdle-ford : now pron. *Blaa-clee*) : crossed the Dodder near Donnybrook : then south, still through the old district of Cualann, which it first entered a little north of Dublin, and from which it took its name (the *slige* or road of Cualann), and on by Bray, keeping near the coast. Fifty years ago a part of this road was traceable between Dublin and Bray. 4. *Slige Dála*, the south-western road, running from Tara towards, and through, Ossory in the present Co. Kilkenny. This old name is still applied to the road from Kells to Carrick-on-Suir by Windgap. 5. *Slige Mór* (" great highway ") led south-west from Tara till it joined the Esker-Riada* near Clonard, along which it mostly continued till it reached Galway. Portions of this road along the old Esker are still in use, being traversed by the present highway.

Besides these five great highways, which are constantly referred to, the Annals and other old documents notice numerous individual roads. In the Four Masters we find thirty-seven ancient roads mentioned with the general name *bealach* [ballagh], nearly all with descriptive epithets, such as *Bealach Mughna, Mughain's* or Mooan's Pass, now Ballaghmoon, near Carlow. Many of these are still com-memorated in the names of townlands. This word *bealach*, which is not included in Cormac's List of road-names, though in existence long before his time, is still in use. It means a pass with a road or path constructed through it. Another generic word for a road or way is *raen* or *raon*.

---

* Esker-Riada, a long, natural, wavy ridge formed of gravel, running almost across the whole country from Dublin to Galway. It was much celebrated in olden times, and divided Ireland into two equal parts, Leth-Conn (' Conn's half ') on the north, and Leth-Mow (' Mow's half ') on the south. It may be seen marked on the map in the first volume of this book (squares 33, 34, 35, 36). The Irish *eiscir* means a sand-hill, and *riad*, travelling by chariot, horse, or boat : *Eiscir-Riada*, the ' sand-hill of chariot-driving." For the origin of the names *Leth-Conn* and *Leth-Mow*, see Joyce, Short History of Ireland, p. 131.

In old times the roads seem to have been very well looked after : and the regulations for making them and keeping them in repair are set forth with much detail in the Brehon Laws.   The Book of Aicill lays down that that part of a main road (*prim-rót*) passing through a *tuath* or territory belongs more to the king of the *tuath* than to an inferior chief of the same *tuath* whose land adjoins the road : but that a by-road (*for-rót*), if bounding or passing through the minor chief's land, belongs more to him than to the king of the tuath.   If any person injured a road, he had to pay compensation to the king or chief, or both, of the territory or district : and for the reason stated, if it was a main road, the king got a larger part of the fine than the chief ; but if a by-road, the chief got more than the king.* Care was taken that the roads were kept clean.   According to Cormac's Glossary (p. 142), a road of whatever class had to be cleaned on at least three occasions :—the time of horse-racing, time of winter, and time of war ; which included clearing of brushwood, of water, and of weeds : a statement also found in the gloss of the Senchus Mór.† The Glossary goes on to say that the road was thus cleaned in order that neither chariots going on a journey nor horses going to a fair should be soiled : and it was kept clear of brambles and weeds lest any one going [on horseback] to battle or elsewhere might be upset.

As illustrating the liberal and kindly spirit of the Brehon Laws, it is worthy of mention :—if a man's farm was so situated as that there was no way out of it except through his neighbour's land, he was entitled to purchase from him a *tuagrotae* or small roadway ; or if he did not do so, he could claim a passage in cases of necessity, but under certain restrictions.   If he had occasion to drive his cattle out through his neighbour's farm, six persons were to be sent with them to prevent them spreading over the

---

* Br. Laws, III. 305, 307, 309.
† *Ibid.*, I. 129, II.   See also vol. IV. 145, 27.

land, three from the owner of the cattle and three from the owner of the land. This no doubt was mainly intended to prevent the acquisition of an unlimited right of passage by long usage.*

We find similar equitable ideas running through the rules laid down for the public right of way. Under ordinary circumstances there was a fine for breaking through fences. But it was justifiable to make gaps in a man's hedges or fences where it was necessary for the passage of an army on the march, or of persons bringing a corpse to be buried, or for the passage of carts bringing provisions to an army, or for bringing building materials for a mill, a church, or the fort of a king. No compensation was allowed for these, provided no other convenient way could be found : but in all cases the breaches should be closed up after the passage, so as to leave the fence as perfect as at first, otherwise it was a case for damages. This rule is laid down also, which is very characteristic of the Irish Celt, that in every case permission was to be asked, which of course was always granted :—" Leave is " asked about them all, for it is an old maxim with the " Feini ' every supplication is pleasant.' " If the gap was not closed, the damages therefor were increased if leave had not been asked.†

It seems that certain persons were bound to make a high-road (*slige*) through a wood if required, in time of war ; and to make and keep clean a *rót* at certain other times : but the statement on this point made by the glossator gives no information as to ways and means, or compensation. As an illustration of the favour with which road-work was regarded by all sections of the community, it may be mentioned that according to a statement in the ancient Irish " Life of St. Fechin," when a general three days' fast was enjoined with a certain object, a fast of two

---

* Br. Laws, IV. 157, and Introd., cxxxii.
† *Ibid.*, 155, 157.

days and one night was accepted from anyone who was engaged in making or repairing a bridge, or a causeway through a marsh.*

From the evidence adduced in this short section, we may conclude that Giraldus Cambrensis was mistaken when he asserted—as he did in his " Topography " (I., IV.) —that Ireland " is truly a desert land, *without roads*, but well watered." It may be supposed that he referred to the uninhabited districts, covered with forest, bog, or marsh, which were extensive in his time and for long after : in which case he made no mistake.

Bridges.—There is no evidence to show that the Irish built stone bridges before the Anglo-Norman invasion. The Senchus Mór lays down a law for the erection of a bridge, the gloss on which notices a distinction between stone and wooden bridges.† But the gloss is of much later date than the original text ; and no conclusion can be drawn from this passage as to the erection of stone bridges before the twelfth century. The Annals relate how Aed Allen, king of Ireland (A.D. 734–743), on one occasion stated that he had an intention to build a bridge at Clonard [across the Boyne], and to build it " marvellously " (*i.e.* on an unusually grand scale), " so that my name might live on it for ever " : ‡ but even this grand bridge was no doubt intended to be a timber one. Lynch, in his Cambrensis Eversus (II. 193, top), says :—" I have not " treated of [ancient Irish] bridges because I have not " been able to ascertain whether they were of stone or " of planks."

Droichet, the Irish term for a bridge, is a native word. Cormac's Glossary (p. 54) gives three alternative derivations of it, one of which is *doroichet*, ' he passes,' " for everyone " passes over it from one side to the other of the water or " of the trench." The place chosen for the erection of a bridge was very usually where the river had already been crossed by a ford ; for besides the convenience of retaining the previously existing roads, the point most easily fordable was in general most suitable for a bridge. Bridges were very often built of planks laid across the stream from bank to bank, if it was narrow enough, or supported on rests of natural rock or on artificial piers, if the river was wide : a kind of bridge occasionally used at the present day. There was a plank-bridge across the Shannon in the time of Brian Boru, near his palace of Kincora, that is, either at the very place where the bridge of Killaloe now stands, or near it. For we read in the " War of the Irish with the Danes " (p. 145), that, shortly before the Battle of Clontarf, when Mailmora, king of Leinster, retired in anger from Kincora, a messenger from Brian followed him, and " over- " took him at the end of the plank-bridge of Killaloe on " the east side."   Sometimes bridges were constructed of strong hurdles supported on piles. A bridge of this kind across the Liffey gave Dublin its old name, *Baile-atha-cliath* (see p. 396, *supra*). These timber bridges of the several kinds were extremely common, and they are frequently mentioned in old authorities. The fourteenth abbot of Iona, from A.D. 726 to 752, was Cilline, who was surnamed *Droichtech*, i.e. the bridge-maker, from the number of bridges he got built ; and Fiachna, the son of Aed Roin, king of Ulidia in the eighth century, was called Fiachna Dubh Droichtech, Black Fiachna of the bridges, because " it was he that made *Droichet-na-Feirsi* and *Droichet-Mona-daimh* and others."   These must have been plank-bridges.

Causeways.—In early ages, before the extension of cultivation and drainage, the roads through the country were often interrupted by bogs and morasses, which were made passable by causeways. They were variously constructed ; but the materials were generally branches of trees, bushes, earth, and stones, placed in layers, and trampled down until they were sufficiently firm ; and they were called by the Irish name of *tóchar*, now usually anglicised *togher*. These *toghers* were very common all over the country ; our annals record the construction of many in early ages, and some of these are still traceable. Sometimes a *togher* was covered over with planks laid across, forming what they call in America a corduroy road.

2. *Chariots and Cars.*

Our literature affords unquestionable evidence that chariots were used in Ireland from the most remote ages both in private life and in war. They are mentioned constantly, as quite common and familiar, in the ancient records, both legendary and historical, as well as in the Brehon Laws, where many rules are set forth regarding them. In the ancient historical tales in the Book of the Dun Cow and the Book of Leinster, the great chiefs, such as Cuculainn, Conall Cernach, Laegaire Buadach, &c., are constantly described as going to battle in chariots, each driven by a charioteer. At the Battle of Crinna, near Slane in Meath, about A.D. 254 (Four Masters, 226), Teige, the leader of the Munster forces, used a chariot, and was borne away in it from the field by his charioteer when severely wounded.* When St. Patrick was on his journey to Tara in 433, King Laegaire, as we are told in the Tripartite Life, went from Tara to Slane with nine chariots to arrest him for lighting the forbidden fire. We know from the best authority, such as the Book of Armagh and Adamnan's " Life of St. Columba," that SS. Patrick, Brigit, Columkille, Declan, &c., journeyed in chariots in their missionary progress through the country. And as Cuculainn's charioteer, *Loeg*, is celebrated in the ancient tales, so St. Patrick

* Lynch, Cambr Ev., II. 177 : Keat., 326.

had a charioteer, *Odran*, who is equally well known in ecclesiastical history.

The use of chariots continued without interruption both in military and civil life to a comparatively late period: and they always formed a prominent feature of fairs and other public meetings. In the time of St. Sechnall, fifth century, there was an *aenach* or fair at Dunshaughlin, which in spite of the saint's expostulations was held on the *maigen* or sacred precinct of the church (p. 44, *supra*); but—as the legend tells us—the earth swallowed up thirteen of the chariots with their horses and drivers, and the rest fled off the field glad to escape with their lives.* In the next chapter (p. 447) we shall see the regulations about chariots at the great fairs. Dermot, king of Ireland, when preparing for the Battle of Culdremne, A.D. 561, " gathered an immense army of horse, foot, and chariots."† Adamnan, in his " Life of St. Columba " (p. 33), notices the Battle of Ondemone or Móin-Mór, fought A.D. 563, where the northern Hy Neill defeated the Dalaradians—a battle also recorded in the Annals: and the Dalaradian king, *Eochaid Laib*, " escaped," writes Adamnan, " sitting in his chariot " (*currui insidens*). Chariots played a prominent part in the great Battle of Moyrath, A.D. 637 :—" The snorting and neighing of their " steeds bounding under chariots, supporting and com- " manding the battle around them in every direction " (Moyrath, 193). Chariots are depicted on several of the high crosses (dating from the tenth to the thirteenth century) ; two of which are represented at p. 408, below.

As is usual in case of important articles of every-day life in constant use, the bardic annalists have assigned an origin for the chariot : for we find it stated in the Book of Leinster that the first who invented chariots in Erin was Righairled, a prince of Munster, fourteenth in descent

---

* Book of Hymns, 29, 30.
† Cambr. Evers, II. 177. See also FM., vol. I., 193, note.

from Eber Finn, the son of Milesius—long before the Christian era.*

The usual Irish word for a chariot is *carpat* (now *carbad*), obviously cognate with the Latin *carpentum*, which is itself a Gaulish word. Adamnan always uses the Latin equivalent *currus* : but classical writers call the Gaulish and British chariots *essedum*, which however is another Gaulish word. For all three branches of the Celtic people, the Gauls, the Britons, and the Irish, used chariots. *Carpat*, as we see, is a native word, coming directly from Gaulish : but there are at least three other native terms, for a chariot, all given in Cormac's Glossary (p. 11) :—*A*, ' a wain, or a car, or a chariot ' : *corb*, whence the personal name " Cormac," properly *Corb-mac*, ' chariot-son,' *i.e.* born in a chariot (Corm., 29) : and lastly *cul*, whence comes *culgaire* [3-syll.], *i.e.* the *gáire*, ' voice,' or creaking of a chariot ; and whence also a chariot-maker was called *culmaire*, which in the Glossary is defined *saor denma carpait*, ' an artificer who makes a chariot ' (Corm., pp. 39, 46).

In the old romances there are several descriptions of Cuculainn's chariot, as well as of those belonging to other chiefs ; and in these and many other authorities details are given, from all which we can obtain a good general idea of the construction of the vehicle. They show, moreover, what might be expected, that there were varieties in shape, make, and materials.† The body (Irish *crét*) was made of wickerwork, supported by an outer frame of strong wooden bars ; and it was frequently ornamented with tin, a practice which also prevailed among the Gauls. The ordinary one- or two-horse chariot had two shafts : *fertas*, a shaft, plural, *fertse*, *feirse*, or *feirtse*. The shafts were made of hard wood, often of holly. The charioteer of Orlam, son of

---

* For more about the use of chariots, see vol. i., pp. 87, 89, 90, *supra*.

† See Crowe's Essay on the Irish Chariot, Kilk. Arch. Journ., 1870–71, p. 413.

Ailill and Maive, on one occasion was employed cutting chariot-poles from a holly-tree in a wood* ; and in the Brehon Law we are told that the holly was counted among the noble trees because the *feirse* of chariots were made from it.† O'Donovan translates *feirse* in this Law passage by " axle-trees ' : and as holly is extremely hard and tough it would naturally be used for axle-trees as well as shafts. But that *fertas* was the usual word for the chariot-shaft there is no doubt. St. Brendan says to Iarlaithe (or Jarlath) of Tuam : " Let a new chariot be built by thee ; " . . . and wheresoever the *two* shafts (*dá fhertais*) of the " chariot shall break, there thy resurrection shall be."‡ Again in the Fled Bricrenn, Findabair, looking out from her high-up greenan, sees a hero coming in a *two-wheeled* chariot, which she describes to her mother—and among other things its *feirtse* or *fertas-es*—as hard and straight like a sword.§ Here the *feirtsi* (pl.) were obviously the two front shafts : for there was only one axle, and even that out of sight. Many other passages might be cited in which the two shafts are described in similar terms. But this word *feirtsi* was also applied to the two hind-shafts, on which the chariot rested when it was put by and thrown back, as we see in our present carts. On one occasion Cuculainn, driving his chariot, had a wild ox tied between the two *feirtse* behind.‖

In a two-horse chariot there was a pole (*sithbe* : pron. sheeva) between the two horses. King Laegaire describes Cuculainn's chariot as having hard, sword-straight *fertas-es*, and a *sithbe* [with ornaments] of white silver.¶ This pole is what Caesar calls *temo* when he describes the Britons as running along on it standing on the yoke (*jugum*) while fighting, and running back again to their seat in the

---

* Miss Hull, Cuch. Saga, p. 155 : Lady Gregory's Cuchulain, p. 196 : LL, 68, *a*, 29.

† Br. Laws, IV 151, 3: see also p. 287, *supra*.

‡ Stokes, Lives of SS., line 3495

§ Kilk. Archæol. Journ., 1870–1, p. 376, 16.

‖ *Ibid.*, p. 420, 14.

¶ *Ibid.*, 376, 16, 17; 414, 14.

chariot.*   A one-horse chariot had two shafts but no pole. A two-wheeled chariot, whether with one or two horses, was in very general use.   There was a *cuing* or yoke between the two horses—also called *mám* [maum]—on which the shafts depended : Cuculainn once broke the *cuing* of Conall Cernach's chariot by striking it with a stone, on which the chariot fell down and Conall tumbled out so as to dislocate his shoulder.

There were two words for a wheel, *roth* and *droch*, both of which are given in Cormac's Glossary (p. 61), and the latter corresponding with Gr. *trochos*.   The wheels were spoked—sometimes six spokes, sometimes eight—and were from three to four and a half feet high, as we see by several delineations of chariots on the high crosses (p. 408, below). They were shod all round, generally with iron : Cuculainn's chariot, as we are told in the Táin, had *rotha iarnaidi*, " iron wheels," *i.e.* was iron-shod : and many other such references might be cited.†   This corresponds with what we know of the ancient British chariots, of which some specimens have lately been found in burial-mounds, with iron rims on the wheels.   Sometimes the Irish chariot is described as bronze-wheeled : by which is meant that the wheels were tired with bronze.   Some chariots had four wheels : in the Battle of Rossnaree (p. 19), King Concobar tells Cuculainn to bring horses and to yoke to them " four-wheeled chariots " (*carpait chethir riad*) : and we know that four-wheeled chariots were also in use among the Gauls. The axle pin was fixed immovable in the vehicle, and the wheels revolved on it, and were kept in their place by linch-pins.   In some of the Latin Lives of the Saints the linch-pin is called either *obex* or *roseta* : now called in Irish *dealg-roithleáin* [dallag-rolaun], " the pin of the wheel ' : *roithleán*, modern Irish for a wheel.‡

---

* Gallic War, IV. xxxiii.

† Miss Hull, Cuch. Saga, p. 176 :

LL, 78, *a*, 32. See also Rev. Celt.,

XIV. 417 ; and Kilk. Arch. Journ., 1870–1, 414, 14.

‡ Adamn., 172, *d* ; 174, *g*.

There was commonly an awning or hood overhead, often called *pupall*, which is one of the words for a tent, and is borrowed from the Latin *papilio*. Cuculainn's chariot is described as having a *pupall corcorda*, a " purple hood," from which we may infer that it was of some kind of cloth.* But there was a native word for the hood—*anblúth*—to which more than once is appended an epithet that points to another material as in use. Findabair, describing the chariots of Laegaire the Victorious and of Conall Cernach, says in each case that there was *anblúth n-én n-etegnáith uása creit charpait*,† " an awning of the wings of birds over the body of the chariot," showing that these great warriors used birds' plumage to roof their chariots, as ladies did for the roofs of their greenans (p. 30, *supra*).

Kings, queens, and chieftains of high rank rode in chariots, luxuriously fitted up and ornamented with gold, silver, and feathers. Cuculainn, travelling in his chariot, orders his charioteer, on the approach of night, to spread for him the cushions and skins (*foirtce ocus forgaimin*) of the chariot, preparing to sleep on them.‡ But with all this, the Irish chariot, like those of the Romans and other nations, was a rough springless machine, and made a great deal of noise. They evidently took pride in the noise : and the more distinguished the person riding in a chariot, the greater was supposed to be the creaking and rattle, as is often boastfully remarked by the old Irish writers, " a chariot under a king " being the noisiest of all.§

We occasionally come across expressions that enable us to arrive at some distant estimate of the value of a chariot. One of the annalists|| mentions a chariot—

---

* Kilk. Arch. Journ., 1870–1, 377, 21.

† Windisch, Ir. Texte, 1. 365, " Anbluth " : LU, 106, *a*, 3 and 38.

‡ Sick Bed : Atlantis, 11. 374, bot. of note.

§ Kilk. Arch. Journ., 1870–1, p. 414 (noise twice) : Sick Bed, Atlantis, I. 111, 2nd v. || Three Fragm., 45 : and Rev. Celt., xxiv., 59.

evidently rather a good one—two-wheeled, no doubt, though this is not specified—as worth four cumals or twelve cows, representing £150 or £160 of our money. And one portion of the reward promised by Queen Maive to Ferdiad to fight Cuculainn was a [royal] chariot worth eighty-four cows—something like a thousand pounds.*

The principal person in the chariot, the warrior or master, or chariot-chief, was commonly called *err* or *eirr*,† and sometimes *cairpthech* (' chariot-warrior '). The charioteer or driver was called *ara*. Loeg, Cuculainn's charioteer, is described in the Book of the Dun Cow as wearing a frock (*inar*) of deerskin, close fitting, so as not to impede the free action of his arms : over this was thrown a loose mantle—*for-brat*, i.e. an ' over-mantle ' (p. 200, *supra*). He wore a many-coloured helmet, from which fell a curtain behind down over his shoulders. Across his forehead was a gold-coloured band or fillet (*gipni*), which was worn as a special mark of a charioteer, or, as the old account says, " as a token of his charioteership to distinguish him from his lord."‡ Whether the chariot belonged to an ecclesiastic or a warrior, there was a special seat for the master, and an inferior one for the charioteer, as in case of St. Patrick and his charioteer Odran.§ In the " Phantom chariot of Cuculainn," the charioteer sits in front of the hero (*ar a bélaib*). But generally the charioteer sat on the right of the champion, as we know from Cormac's Glossary (p. 80), where we are told that *fochla* is the name for the champion's seat [in a chariot], which word also signifies both the north and the left-hand side. (See *deas* and *tuaith*, page 521, *infra*.) From this term, *fochla fennida* (' seat of the champion ') came to signify, in an extended sense, any distinguished seat at a banquet or

* Sick Bed, Atlantis, II. 375, last par. of note.

† *Eirr* glosses " curruum princeps " in Z., 255, *n.*

‡ For all this, see O'Curry, Man. & Cust., I. 299 : and Kilk. Arch. Journ., 1870–1, p. 423.

§ Trip. Life, 219 : Three Ir. Gloss, Pref., xxxix.

elsewhere.   For a like reason the word *faitsi*, which signifies *south*, or right hand, means also the charioteer's seat (Corm. 80).

On several of the high crosses chariots are carved, as, for instance, on those of Clonmacnoise, Tuam, and Monasterboice.   The chariots represented here, from one of the Clonmacnoise crosses, have each only one horse and one pair of wheels : but two-horse chariots were more usual, and seem to have been a common vehicle for travelling.*   The chariot ordinarily used in battle had two wheels and two horses.   That four horses were some-times used is plain from the record in the Annals, of the

FIG. 332.

Ancient Irish chariots on base of cross at Clonmacnoise : ninth century. (From Wood-Martin's Pagan Ireland, p. 247.) They are also figured in Miss Stokes's Christian Inscriptions, I., Pl. xxxiii.

death of a prehistoric King Roitheachtaigh [Rohaghty : whose name signifies " possessor of wheels "], FM, A.M. 4176, with the remark, " he was the first that drove a chariot with four horses in Erin."

With rare exceptions, only two persons rode in a chariot, whether in battle or in everyday life : viz. the master (or mistress) and the driver : a custom which pre-vailed also among the Gauls.†   Chariots were generally drawn by horses, especially those of chiefs and military men.   But ordinary persons, and non-military people in

* Two horses : see Fled Bricr., 55, 61, 63 : and Bec Fola, 175.   See also De Jubainville, La Civil. des Celtes, p. 338.

† De Jubainville, La Civil. des Celtes p. 331.

general, often employed oxen : St. Patrick's chariot was drawn by two oxen.*

Besides the chariots hitherto mentioned, both for travelling and for fighting, there was a special war-chariot furnished with scythes and spikes, like those of the Gauls and ancient Britons, which is repeatedly mentioned in the Tales of the Táin : most often in connexion with Cuculainn. It was called *carpat serda*, i.e. " scythed chariot," from *serr*, a saw, scythe, or sickle.   It is thus described in the Book of Leinster :—" The hero of valour [Cuculainn] " leaped into the scythed battle-chariot, with its iron " points, with its sharp edges and hooks, with its hard " spikes, with its sharp nails, projected from its shafts and " straps and tackle."†   There is a similar description in the Book of the Dun Cow.‡   In O'Clery's Glossary is this entry :—" *Searrdha*, an edge : *carbad searrdha*, a chariot in which were sharp edges or sickles " ; and in another more ancient authority we read :—" It is why it was " designated *serrda* from the iron *saws* or scythes which " would be in array out of it."§   These accounts in the lay literature of the use of the scythed chariot are curiously corroborated in one of the ecclesiastical pieces, the commentary in the Amra of St. Columkille.   In the Amra itself Columba is designated " chariot through battle " : on which the ancient commentator utters this remark, or rather prayer :—" That is, as a scythed chariot (*carpat* " *serda*), namely, a chariot armed with swords, goes " through a battle (or a battalion), so may my soul go to " heaven through the battle (or battalion) of demons."‖

<hr>

* Trip. Life, 253, 292.

† LL, 78, *a*, 19 : Miss Hull, Cuch. Saga, 176 : Kilk. Arch. Journ. 1870–1, p. 415.

‡ LU, 80, *a*, 22 : Man. & Cust., I. 300.   See also LL, 76, *b*, 46; and 79, *b*, 3.   § Kilk. Arch. Journ., 1870–71, p. 416.

‖ Stokes, Amra, Rev. Celt., xx. 149.   See the original in LU, 6, *b*, 30.   For scythed- and war-chariots, see De Jubainville, La Civil. des Celtes, 339–341 : also 382 *et seq.*

Farmers and people in general used rough carts, commonly called *carr*, for work of various kinds, but they are hardly noticed in the ancient literature. The name *carr*, which is used in Cormac's Glossary (p. 44), is cognate with Latin *carrus* and English car. In the Senchus Mór, a chariot, as denoted by *carpat*, is distinguished from a *carr*, which is explained in the gloss as a cart for corn or dung :* Another old name for a common cart or wagon or wain was *fén* [fain], which glosses *plaustrum* in one of the eighth-century MSS. of Zeuss (Z., 19, 1 : 776, 19). These carts, whether called *fén* or *carr*, were drawn by oxen trained specially for the purpose, as we know by many references.† They had probably solid wheels—such as the people used in later times—spoked wheels being expensive.

3. *Horse-riding.*

Horses were put to the same uses as at present :—riding, drawing chariots, racing ; and more rarely ploughing, drawing carts, and as pack-animals : all which uses are mentioned in our old literature. The horse is known by various names. *Ech* signifies any horse of a superior kind—a war-horse, a steed ridden by a chief, a chariot-horse, &c. : cognate with Latin *equus*, and Greek *hippos*. *Marc*, another word for horse, is explained in O'Davoren's Glossary, *ech no láir*, " a steed or a mare " : hence the common word *marcach*, a horseman : *marcach*, equestor, Z. 60, 10. *Capall*, meaning a horse of any kind—a term existing in varied forms in several European languages—is the word now in universal use by Irish-speakers. *Gearrán*, a hack-horse, means *equus castratus*, a gelding, from *gearr*, to cut. In ancient Irish documents this word denoted the common beast of burden : in the Anglicised form *garron*, it was constantly used by the Anglo-Irish writers of the time of Elizabeth : and *garron* or *garraun* is in general use

* Br. Laws, I. 166, 22; 171, 2.   † For instance, Todd, St. Patk., 167.

at the present day in Ireland among speakers of English to denote a heavily-worked, half-broken-down old horse. Other terms for a horse, such as *fell* and *gobur*, both of which are given in Cormac's Glossary (80, 83), need not be dwelt upon. The common word for a foal was, and is, *serrach* or *searrach* [shárragh].

The Senchus Mór provides against " over-tying " or " over-fettering " of horses when taken in distress ; *i.e.* it was forbidden to fetter so tightly as to cause suffering or injury : for example, the head was not to be held down by a rope tied to the leg and carried tightly round the neck.* In every chief's house there was an *echaire* [eh'ara] or horse-boy or stable-boy — sometimes called *gilla-scuir*, ' horse-stud boy '—who stabled the horses at night, and let them out in the morning.†

Horses were often let run half wild in droves about the mountains and plains ; and whenever any were wanted, a sufficient number were driven home and trained in. A part of the stipend the king of Hy Blathmaic (the district round Newtownards in Down) received from the king of Ulidia consisted of " eight steeds not driven from the mountains‡ " : that is to say, not wild, but fully trained in. Before the Battle of Rossnaree (p. 19), when King Concobar wanted some horses, he says to Cuculainn :— " Well, O Cuculainn, let the horses (*gabra*) of the plain " of Murthemni be caught by thee ; and let four-wheeled " chariots be harnessed to them," which was accordingly done : for Cuculainn, demigod as he was, subdued and tamed them on the spot.

Besides grazing in the fields, horses were fed on corn of various kinds. When the Red Branch heroes in the palace of Ailill and Maive got their choice of food for their horses, Cuculainn chose barley grain for his, and Conall and Laegaire took *airthend* two years old for

* Br. Laws, I. 169, 5; 175, 8. † Br. Laws, III. 419, bottom.
‡ Book of Rights, 163.

theirs : where *airthend* probably means oats.* An *ógaire*, an inferior chief, was supposed to keep a horse which was used both for working and riding.† The higher classes of chiefs kept horses for riding exclusively, and others specially for work—that is, if they used horses for work at all.

From many passages in the Brehon Laws and other old writings it appears that horses were often imported, and that those from Wales were specially prized. Pichan, the Munster chief, promises Mac Conglinne (p. 44) a gold ring and a Welsh steed (*ech Bretnach*) : and again (p. 110) the same Mac Conglinne is promised a Welsh steed out of every [principal] house from *Carn* [*Ui Neid*] to Cork. The glossator of the " Heptads " in the Brehon Laws (v. 221) includes British (*i.e.* Welsh) mares among the " foreign curiosities " mentioned in the text. According to the Book of Rights (p. 82) the king of Munster was bound to give the king of Ui Liathain, as stipend, among other things, " a steed and trappings brought from over sea." In like manner (p. 247) the king of Tara was to give to the king of Ui Briuin " a noble French steed." Even as late as the fourteenth century the " Tribes and Customs of Hy Many " records that a part of the *tuarastal* of the king of Connaught to his subject king O'Kelly of Hy Many was " ten steeds from across the boisterous brine."‡ In the fourteenth, fifteenth, and sixteenth centuries, those Irish horses called *hobbies* were known all over Europe " and held in great esteem for their easy ample, . . . from " this kind of horse the Irish light-armed bodies of horse " were called hobellers."§

Giraldus Cambrensis‖ tells us that in his time the Irish used no saddles in riding. Two hundred years later, Mac Murrogh Kavanagh had a splendid horse that cost

---

* Fled Bricr., 81. † Br. Laws, IV. 305, 19.
‡ Hy Many, 93. See also Stokes, Lives of SS., line 3128, and p. 348.
§ Sir James Ware, Antiqq., p. 166. ‖ Top. Hib., III. x.

him 400 cows, which he rode with wonderful swiftness without saddle down a hill to meet the earl of Gloucester* ; and the custom must have been very general at a still later time, for laws were made to compel the Irish and Anglo-Irish to ride like the English—with saddles. Yet this custom prevailed among the English themselves in early times, as well as among the ancient Britains, Gauls, and Romans.†

But from the earliest times the higher classes of the Irish used a thick cloth called *dillat*, between them and the horse. Maildune, on one of the islands, saw a lady riding, having a " good adorned *dillat* under her."‡ In another part of the same tale, a lady is seen riding on a horse " with an *ech - dillat* [' horse- *dillat* '] under her." These two last quotations prove too that ladies practised horse-riding as well as men. The *dillat* often

FIG. 333.

Grotesque representation of a horseman, given in the Book of Kells. Man's cap yellow ; cloak green, with bright red and yellow border ; breeches green ; leg clothed ; foot naked. Dillat yellow. (From Wilde's Catalogue.)

covered the whole animal, as is seen in the above illustration taken from the Book of Kells (7th or 8th century)—and also in fig. 334, p. 417, *infra*, from the same old book. This word *dillat* originally meant an outer cloth, garment, or loose vest : in the Cymric Glosses of Zeuss it is given as the equivalent of *vestimentum* or *vestis* : and it is applied in this sense in the following Irish quotation from the Book of the Dun Cow :—*Gabaid-seom dan a dillat n-oenig n-imbi in laa sin* : " He puts his assembly-*dillat* or raiment about him that day."§ As *dillat* was originally applied to the cloth

* Joyce, Short Hist. of Ireland, p. 330.   † Ware, Antiqq., 159.
‡ Rev. Celt., x. 63.
§ LU, 81, *a*, 24 : see " Dillat " in Windisch's Wörterb., Ir. Texte, I. 481.

thrown over the horse's back, the name was retained even when the cloth developed into a regular saddle : and *dillat*, or in its modern form *diallaid*, is now the common Irish name for saddle.   Saddles of some kind were often used by the Irish before the time of Cambrensis, for they are frequently mentioned in the Book of Rights.   The word used in this book is *sadail*, which however appears to be a loan-word from the Norse.   Part of the stipend of the Hy Cennsealaigh from the king of Leinster was ten saddles (pl. *saidle*) : and the king of Ireland was bound to give the king of *Luighne*, among other things, twenty steeds with saddles.*   The Senchus Mór gloss† mentions whalebone as being sometimes used for making saddle-trees—*clár-sadall* : but this is a late authority.

When the Irish employed the horse as a beast of burden, to carry things on his back, they used a pack-saddle.   This is mentioned in Cormac's Glossary (p. 153), under the name *srathar* [srahar], which is still used for it, and which is there derived from *sreth*, a range, because, as Cormac says, " it is set on the range of the [horse's] ribs." The use of the pack-saddle is also mentioned in the " Story of the Eruption of Lough Neagh " in the Book of the Dun Cow, where certain persons pack a *srathar* which is on the back of a great horse with an immense load of household goods.‡

Two kinds of bridle having two different names were in use.   The single-rein bridle, called *srían* (Lat. *frenum*), was used in horse-riding.   This rein (Irish *sreth*, pron. srah] was attached to a nose-band, not at the side but at the top, and came to the hand of the rider over the animal's fore-head, passing right between the eyes and ears, and being held in its place by a loop or ring in the face-band (called *drech-ongdas*, from *drech*, face) which ran across the horse's

---

* Book of Rights, 209, 267.   † Br. Laws, I. 135, last par.
‡ Kilk. Arch. Journ., 1870–1, p. 97.

forehead and formed part of the bridle-gear.* This single
rein was used to restrain merely : it could not be used to
guide, which, as we shall presently see, was done by a
horse-rod. Accordingly a horse for riding is often called
ech-sréine, a " *srian*-steed."†

The two-rein bridle, called *all* or *fall*, was used with
chariot-horses. The charioteer, who sat too far from the
horse's head to use a horse-rod in guiding, had to use
double reins, both to guide and to restrain, like those of
the present day. The two reins were called *sretha* (pl. of
sreth), and also *aradna* (now *earadhain* or *earadhain-sréine*).
The distinction between those two kinds of bridle and their
uses is clearly set forth in a gloss on the Senchus Mór‡ :—
" *Srian*, i.e. [having] one *sreath* or rein : *all* [so called from
" *oll* or *all*, great] because it is greater than the *srian* on
" account of having two reins on it : it is for the horses of
" the chariot it is used." And this distinction is always
observed in the Tales. Where horse-riders are mentioned
they have *srians* or single-rein bridles : but in the descriptions of chariots the two horses have *da n-all*, " two *alls*,"
i.e. each steed has one *all* of two reins. *Essi* or *ési* seems to
be another name for the *all*. Cuculainn says to Loeg :—
Fosta latt éssi fostada th' echraidi, which Stokes translates,
" Fasten the securing reins of thy horses."§ Foill Mac
Nechtain tells Cuculainn's charioteer not to unharness the
horses from the chariot ; to which he answers that he is not
going to do so, inasmuch as he still holds the *ési* and the
aradna in his hands.‖ The bridle-bit was *béilce* or *béilge*
[bailka, bailga], modern Irish *beulmhach* : from *bél* or *beul*,
the mouth.

* Kuno Meyer in Mac Congl., 89, ₂₂: and Glossary.

† Br. Laws, IV. 326, ₁₁.

‡ Br. Laws, I. 139, bot. Other references to the *all* and *srian*, as dis-
tinguished are, :—O'Curry, Man. & Cust., II. 157, bot. and note, p. 158 :
Kilk. Arch. Journ., 1870–1, pp. 376, ₁₇; 413, ₃₀, ₃₉; 414, ₇, ₁₆; Stokes,
Lives of SS., line 317 : Courtship of Emer, 72, top line (LU, 122, *b*, 10) :
Bec Fola, 175 : Fled Bricr., 55 to 63 *passim*.

§ Stokes in Rev. Celt., XIV. 419, top.   ‖ Miss Hull, 149 : LL, 66, *b*, 7.

The bridle was often elaborately and expensively ornamented. Among the royal tributes of the Book of Rights (p. 57) we find " fifty steeds with costly bridles." In the Bruden Da Derga (p. 51) the king's retinue have " thrice fifty steeds with their thrice fifty bridles of red enamel (*srian cruanmaith*) on them." In the Crith Gabhlach the quality of the bridle is set down as indicating the rank of the man :—a certain class of chief (*brugaid*) is stated to have a riding-steed with a bridle of *cruan* or red enamel : another of higher rank (*aire-desa*), a steed with a bridle of silver ; and another still higher (*aire-tuisi*) with one of gold : meaning in all the cases that the bridles were adorned with the several materials.* Accordingly, special provisions were laid down in the Brehon Law (v. 415, 417) for compensation to the owner of a bridle in case a borrower did not restore it ; from five or six cows up to eighteen or twenty, according to the rank of the several owners. In later times the Irish continued or became so extravagant in ornamenting their steeds that the Anglo-Irish parliament passed laws to restrain the use of over-expensive trappings.†

In corroboration of all these accounts, portions of antique bridles and headstalls have been found from time to time, with enamelled ornamentation of beautiful workmanship, some of them now preserved in the National Museum. Petrie, in one of his letters, has an account of a headstall found near Boyle in Roscommon, all covered with a beautiful jet enamel‡ ; and Miss Stokes pictures and describes another, still more elaborate, of exquisite workmanship in coloured enamel.§

Giraldus Cambrensis says that the Irish in his time (1185) used a sort of reins that served for both bridle and

---

* Br. Laws, IV. 311, bot. ; 323, 12; 327, 18. † Ware, Antiqq., 160.
‡ Dr. William Stokes's Life of Petrie, p. 240, bot.
§ Trans. Roy. Ir. Acad., xxx. 291, 293, bot., with plate. For another of a similar kind, pictured and described, see Kilk. Arch. Journ., 1856–7, p. 423. For more about enamelled bridles, see vol. I., p. 559, *supra.*

bit, and did not prevent the horse from grazing.*   The common people generally used a halter, which was, and is still, called *adastar* or *adhastar* [sounded nearly as *oyster*]. Giraldus states that the Irish did not use spurs, but urged on and guided their horses with a rod having a hooked goad at the end.   In this he is correct ; for we find frequent notices of the horse-rod—called *echlasc* and *slatt*—in Irish literature.   In the Story of Aed Baclamh, we read that during a race at Tara, the riders, being dissatisfied with the pace, lashed their horses with their *echlascs*.†   No mention is made of spurs, and none were used.   This *echlasc* was commonly of yew or ash, and must have been—at least in some cases —pretty strong and heavy, not a mere switch : Mailmora, king of Leinster, when leaving Kincora in a rage, struck King Brian's mes- senger with the *eachlasc* of yew, " and broke all the bones of his head."‡   The rider guided with the *echlasc* by touching one side or the other of the horse's head.   In the

Grotesque representation of horse- man, using horse-rod, given in the Book of Kells (seventh century.) (From Wilde's Catalogue, p. 300.)

Táin bo Fraich (p. 137) we read of certain noble riders having *echlascs* [with ornaments] of bronze and with hooked goads (*boccan*) of gold at the end.   In later times the word *echlasc* came, by a natural extension of meaning, to be applied to a whip, or a strong rod with a lash or scourge at the end, which was used both for striking and guiding.   Maildune, coming to a certain island, saw a horse- race a good way off, " and the strokes of their *echlascs* were heard by him "§—notwithstanding the distance.   Here the *echlasc* was no doubt the *slatt* with a scourge.

In some of the above passages the word for goad is *boccan*, which is still in use to denote any hook or crook.

But the more usual word for a goad in the Tales is *brot*, and its diminutive *bruitne* [brit-ně] : " into the horses Loeg " drove the *brot* ; he plied the horse-switch (*slat*) towards road and wayfaring."* In the " Phantom Chariot of Cuculainn " we read :—[Cuculainn] " had a goadlet (*bruitne*) in his hand with which he urged on the horses."†

Horse-riders also used a whip (*sraigell* or *srogell* : borrowed from Lat. *flagellum*). In the Bruden Da Derga, Conaire's three outriders (*ritiri*) had each a *sraigell* in hand‡: and another rider is mentioned in the " Vision of Mac Conglinne " who grasped a *srogell*. *Srogell* glosses *flagellum* and *flagrum* in Zeuss (80, 25 ; 769, 14) ; and O'Clery explains the verb *sroiglim* by *do sgiúrsudh*, ' to scourge.' Whether the same rider carried both a rod and a whip is doubtful ; probably not. The custom of suspending little bells from the necks of horses is noticed in vol. i., p. 376.

It would appear that horses, as well as other domestic and pet animals, were sometimes wholly or partly dyed, for ornament. In the story of " The Courtship of Ferb," we are told that in the train of Prince Mani were fifty white horses with red ears, yoked in pairs to chariots, and having their long manes and tails dyed purple§ : and the circumstance is mentioned as if the practice was usual. From an expression in the story of young Ciaran (told at p. 360, *supra*), we may infer that other animals also were dyed. When the piece of cloth was taken out of the pot for the third time, not only was it dyed an intense blue, but what remained of the colouring liquor in the pot, afterwards " made blue all the dogs and the cats and the trees that it touched " (Stokes's Lives of SS., 267). The seven dogs that accompanied Prince Mani appear to have been

* Death of Goll and Garb, Rev. Celt., XIV. 401.

† Kilk. Arch. Journ., 1870–1, p. 378, top line. See also LU, 122, *b*, 29.

‡ O'Curry, Man. & Cust., II. 146, note 212.

§ LL, 253, *a*, 11, 12 ; Ir. Texte, 462, 463 : Leahy, p. 5.

dyed : for the narrative says that they were of every colour that could be imagined. See also Sullivan's observations in his Introd., p. 405, in which he states that dyeing pet animals is practised in India, where a blue dog is a favourite.

Horsemen rode without stirrups : and every man was trained to spring from the ground by an *ech-léim* or ' steed-leap ' on to the back of his horse.* The chief, Dicho, St. Patrick's first convert, was on one occasion a captive in Tara with some others. But they made their way out of the prison by the help of a cleric, and finding horses ready bridled on the lawn, " they leap on their horses " (*leangait for a n-eochu*) and make their escape. This ready method of mounting continued to the beginning of the seventeenth century in both Ireland and Scotland :—

> " No foot Fitz-James in stirrup staid,
>   No grasp upon the saddle laid,
>   But wreathed his left hand in the mane,
>   And lightly bounded from the plain."
> —*Lady of the Lake.*

It was considered necessary that every young man belonging to the upper classes should be taught horse-riding : and so important was this that even the Brehon Law interfered, just as the law of our day requires children to learn reading. The Senchus Mór prescribes, among other accomplishments, horse-riding " for the sons of chiefs in fosterage."† They began very young ; for the same authority (Br. Laws, II. 159) tells us that *up to the age of seven years* the horse should be supplied by the father : after that by the foster-father. If the foster-father neglected this part of the child's instruction, he forfeited two-thirds of the fosterage fee. A horse was not given to the sons of the *Féini* or farmer grades while in fosterage,

* See Silva Gad., 296, ₁₈; and O Conor, Dissert. 70, note.
† Br. Laws, II. 157, bot.

" for horsemanship is not taught to them " (Br. LL. II.,
p. 161). But the law took care that young farmers should
be taught such things as were considered fit for them (see
I. 441, *supra*). No doubt the horse supplied for learning
was a commonplace animal : but the Law required that the
son of a king should during fosterage be supplied with a
high-class animal in time of races.*

A simile found everywhere in the Irish and also in
Welsh tales is :—" Like flocks of birds over the heroes'
" heads were the sods thrown up by the hooves [or shoes]
" of the steeds." Another not quite so common :—" Like
" a flock of swans pouring over a vast plain was the foam
" which the steeds flung from them over their bridles."
" Like the smoke from a royal hostel was the dust and
" the breath and the dense vapour, because of the vehe-
" mence of the driving which Laeg gave Cuculainn's two
" horses."†

The period of the introduction of the practice of shoeing
horses among the natives of Europe is not very clearly
determined. The Romans had for this purpose a sort of
sock faced with iron, which could be readily taken off and
put on as occasion required, and which was used only
in rough places. That the ancient Irish protected the
horse's hoofs by a shoe of some kind is plainly shown
by the records. This shoe is called *cru* in the oldest Irish
documents : it is given with this meaning in all modern
dictionaries, and *cru* is still the living word for a horseshoe,
not only in Irish, but in Scotch Gaelic and Manx. But
as *cru* was also used for *ungula* or hoof,‡ the inquiry needs
to be conducted with some caution. That the word was
intended to designate a horsehoe in at least some of the
records (which serves our purpose as well as if it was so

---

* Br. Laws, II., Pref., xliv.
† Rev. Celt., XIV. 417 : also LL, 110, *a*, top.
‡ *Cru eich* glosses *ungulus* ; Stokes, Ir. Glosses, 442 : *crua* glosses
ungula in Sg. 46, *b*, 13 ; Stokes in Rev. Celt., XIII., 469.

used in all) is clear from several passages. In the " Demon Chariot " we read that showers of sods were thrown up from the " shoes " of Cuculainn's horses (*a chruib nan ech*). Here the word used is *cru*, which must mean ' shoe,' not hoof, for a few lines farther on, where the hoof is specially mentioned, it is called *bos**: and accordingly Crowe here properly translates *cru* by ' shoe,' and *bos* by ' hoof.'   An entry in the Four Masters, under A.D. 1384, goes to confirm all this :—" Tomaltach Mac Dorcy, chief of Kinel- " Duachain, was killed by his own knife while he was " shoeing a horse " (*ag cur cru* : ' putting on a horseshoe '). It seems plain from the preceding that the ancient Irish shod their horses : but nothing is known that would indicate the particular form of shoe used. Many specimens of iron horseshoes may be seen in the National Museum, generally lighter than the present shoes ; but there are no data on which to found an opinion as to their age.

Giraldus Cambrensis† says that in his time the Irish women rode astride like the men, " their legs sticking out on both sides of the horse " : but I have not found any confirmation of this. Indeed the dress universally worn then by women would render it impossible for them to ride in this manner. It is likely that Giraldus may have witnessed an accidental and exceptional instance, as we may sometimes witness now. Four centuries after the period of his record, Spenser (View, 102) tells us that the Irish women rode, not astride, but on the wrong side of the horse, *i.e.*—as he says—" I meane with their faces towards the right side " [of the horse]. In this he is correct ; and the fashion moreover came down from old times ; for in a delineation of the flight to Egypt sculptured on the high cross of Moone Abbey, the Blessed Virgin sits on the ass with her face to the right—*i.e.* her left hand towards the ass's head, while St. Joseph leads the animal by a halter.* The concurrence of these two unquestionable authorities, one before the time of Giraldus, the other after, renders it all the more likely that he is mistaken.

In old times in Ireland, horse-riding as a mode of locomotion in ordinary life was not very general. But nobles commonly rode and were very proud of their steeds and trappings. Horses were also kept and carefully trained for sporting purposes, chiefly racing, which, as we shall see in next chapter, was a favourite amusement. A poet, praising Sechnasach, king of Ireland (A.D. 664–671), says that his house was " full of bridles " and " full of horse-rods " (*srianach* and *echloscach*).†

The ass hardly figures at all in ancient Irish literature, so that it cannot have been much used.

4. *Communication by Water.*

The boats used by the ancient Irish way be roughly classified as of three kinds‡ :—canoes hollowed out from the trunks of trees ; curraghs, or wicker-boats ; and ordinary vessels—ships or boats—propelled by sails, or oars, or both combined, as occasion required. In the Brehon Law Tract called the " Small Primer " (v. 105), vessels are classified as (1) *ler-longa*, " sea-ships " (*ler*, the sea), viz. large vessels fit for long voyages ; (2) *barca* or barks, small coasting vessels not suitable for long voyages, which are also called *serrcinn* (sing. *serrcenn*, ' saw-head ') ; (3) curraghs. This classification—which is a good one—has reference, not so much to the vessels themselves as to their several builders, in order to set forth their privileges ; which explains why single-piece canoes are not included, inasmuch as they required small technical skill to make them.

---

* O'Neill's Crosses, p. 7, and pl. xvii.   † Rev. Celt., XIII. 97.

‡ This general classification will be quite sufficient here : but that vessels were much varied in shape according to the purposes they were intended to serve is obvious from the fact that Adamnan mentions ten different kinds by their Latin names, which may be seen in Adamn., 176, note *b*.

The single-piece canoes were very common, especially in connexion with crannoges, where they were used to communicate with shore. Many of these have in late times been found in bogs at the bottom of dried-up lakes and near old crannoges, varying in length from 50 or 60 feet down to six or eight : and numbers of them may been seen in the National Museum in Dublin. Adamnan (p. 176) mentions boats of pine and oak, which the monks of Iona dragged overland, and then used them for conveying across the water great timbers both for houses and for ships. These were single-piece boats, and must have been of considerable size.

The curragh (Irish form *curach*, connected with Latin *corium*, a hide) was the best known of áll the Irish boats.

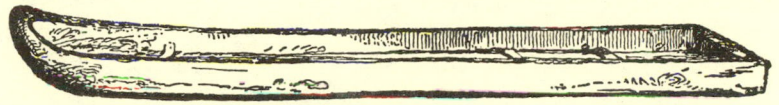

FIG. 335.

Single-piece canoe: in the National Museum, Dublin: 22 feet long; 2½ feet broad. (From Wilde's Catalogue, p. 203.)

It was made of a wicker-work frame, called in Irish *cliabcuraich* [cleev-curry], i.e. *curach*-basket, covered with hides which were stitched together with thongs.* Some curraghs had a double hide-covering, some a triple. These boats are constantly mentioned in lay as well as in ecclesiastical literature, and also by Continental writers, the earliest of whom is Solinus in the third century. They are used still round the coasts, but tarred canvas is employed instead of skins. They were propelled by oars or sails according to circumstances. When there were two or more hide-coverings, they were probably placed in contact. A curragh of one hide was, of course, the least safe : and in the Life of St. Patrick we are told how an Ulsterman named Mac Cuill, a converted sinner, committed himself to the sea in a one-hide boat without oar or rudder, in accordance with a

* See p. 427, line 13, *infra* ; and p. 370, *supra.*

penance imposed on him by St. Patrick, as already mentioned (vol. I., p. 214). In Muirchu's Latin narrative of this incident, the boat is called *navis unius pellis*, while in the Irish Tripartite Life it is *curach oen seiched*, ' a curragh of one hide,' the exact equivalent of the Latin.* Maildune, intending to make a voyage in the Atlantic, had a boat of three hides constructed—*nói tre-chodlidi* (codal, a hide) : here the boat is called *nói* : but a little farther on it is called a *curach*.† Many curraghs were so small and light as to be easily carried on a man's back from creek to creek overland, as Giraldus says the Welsh were accustomed to carry their wicker boats‡ : and as people sometimes do to this day in Ireland.

The mode of constructing curraghs has been described by foreign as well as by Irish writers. Julius Caesar§ tells how he had some curraghs made for his use after the model of those used by the Britons ("ships of the kind that his knowledge of Britain had taught him ") ; and twelve centuries later Giraldus describes in similar terms the Irish curraghs as he saw them.‖ But the most detailed and accurate account we have of the building of a curragh is in the Latin narrative of the Voyage of St. Brendan. The Saint and his companions " using iron tools [saws, " hammers, chisels, &c.] prepared a very light vessel, with " wickerwork sides and ribs, after the manner of that " country, and covered it with cow-hide, tanned in oak- " bark (*rubricatis in cortice roborina* : ' reddened in oak- " bark,' p. 368, *supra*), tarring its joints : and they put on " board provisions for forty days, with butter enough to " dress hides for covering the boat [whenever the covering " needed repair], and all utensils necessary for the use of " the crew."¶ From all these accounts, which might be

---

* Trip. Life, 222, ₁₁; 288, ₁₈.
† Rev. Celt., IX. 459, 460.
‡ Descr. of Wales, I. xvii.
§ Bell. Civ., I. liv

‖ Top. Hib., III. xxvii.
¶ Brendan., Cardinal Moran, 90 ; O'Donohue, 119.

corroborated by many others, we see that curraghs, when intended for long voyages, were made large and strong, furnished with masts and solid decks and seats, and having the hides tanned.*

By far the greatest part of the water-communication round the coasts and across the narrow seas, as well as in the lakes and rivers, of Great Britain and Ireland, was carried on in those early days by curraghs, which indeed were used also in other parts of Europe. The Anglo-Saxon Annals and Florence of Worcester relate that three learned Irishmen, desirous of leading a religious life, went on board a boat which was made of two or three ox-hides, and with provisions for a week, and sailing wherever Providence led them, landed in Cornwall, whence they were brought to the great King Alfred.† We know that in the fourth, fifth, and sixth centuries the Irish sent numerous plundering expeditions to Britain, as mentioned in vol. I., p. 73, *et seq*. These voyages they made in curraghs : and Gildas pictures hordes of them as landing from such vessels (*de curicis*).‡

The native records corroborate these, so far as the general use of the curragh is concerned. In Cormac's Glossary (p. 41) we are informed that Breccán, grandson of Niall of the Nine Hostages, had a fleet of fifty curraghs trading between Ireland and Scotland, till they were all swallowed up in the terrible whirlpool near Rathlin Island. which thenceforward took the name of *Coire-Bhreccain* [corrie-vreckan], Breccan's caldron or whirlpool.§ When the Irish chief Mac Con gathered an army in Britain and Scotland for the invasion of Ireland, leading ultimately to

* See also Silva Gad., 386.   † Ogygia : III. xxiv.
‡ Adamn., 169, note *k*.
§ This whirlpool, which is still well known, but now called Slugnamara (' swallow of the sea '), lies between Rathlin and the coast of Antrim. It was the original Corrievreckan ; but its name was borrowed for the dangerous whirlpool between the islands of Scarba and Jura, in Scotland, mentioned in The Lord of the Isles. See Ir. Names of Places, II. 432.

the great battle of Mucruime, and the accession of Mac Con as king, he conveyed them in vessels of various sizes, so that between Scotland and Ireland " there was "—says the old account—" a continuous bridge of curraghs "* : and when—as we read in the story of " The Siege of Etar "—the Ulster Forces were besieged in Ben Edair (Howth) by Leinstermen, they sent north requesting their friends to come from Ulster either by land or " in curraghs " (*i curchaib*) to relieve them.†

Many of the ordinary vessels used by the Irish in foreign commerce must have been large ; otherwise they could not have traded with Continental ports, as we know they did (p. 429, farther on). In the Book of Rights (p. 39), it is mentioned that part of the yearly tribute from the king of Cashel to the king of Ireland consisted of " ten ships with beds," as much as to say they were large enough to contain sleeping-berths.

The most general Irish name for a ship is *long* ; which in Cormac's Glossary (p. 105) is derived from the Saxon *lang* (Eng. *long*) ; but it is more likely that both the Irish and Saxon words are cognate with Latin *longa*. Sometimes the word *lestar* (' vessel ') was used. A ship filled with men for a warlike excursion was often called *laech-lestar*, ' hero-vessel ' (*laech*, hero), which was the Irish term for a " man-of-war."‡ *Barc*, another Irish word for ship, is not, as might be supposed, a loan-word from English, for it is used in our oldest manuscript tales. In the Senchus Mór§ the word *noe* is used as an equivalent for *curach*, where a " *noe* of one hide " is mentioned ; and in Cormac's Glossary (p. 125) the same word is given in the form of *nai*, as meaning a ship, and derived from Lat. *navis* : here

* O'Grady, Silva Gad., 352 bot. ; Ir. Text, 314, top.

† LL, 115, *b*, 22. For more about curraghs and boats in general, see Ware, Antiqq., xxiv. : Lynch, Cambr. Ev., chap. xii. : O'Flaherty, Ogyg. III. xxxiv. : and Kilk. Arch. Journ., 1852–3, p. 71.

‡ Mac. Congl., 34, bot.

§ Br. Laws, I. 170, top line : see also p. 424, *supra*

no doubt, as in many similar cases, the two words are cognate and derived from a source older than either. This word *noe* or *nai* has been long obsolete : but the diminutive form *noemhóg* or *naomhóg*, which is pronounced *naevogue*, is still in use for a curragh in the south of Ireland. In Kilkee and elsewhere on the western coast you will see plenty of canvas-covered curraghs : but they do not call them *curraghs* or *naevogues* : " canoe " is now the word in Kilkee. It is curious to see the middle *v* sound, which is lost in *noe*, restored in *naomhóg*. Other names for vessels will be brought in as we go along.

In some old texts the word *laidheng* [lee-ang] is used for a boat : and from the expression, " stitched *laidheng*," in one of them, we may infer that it was another name for a curragh.* In O'Clery's Glossary *libhearn* [livern] is given as the equivalent of *long*, a ship. The Irish for an oar is *rámh* or *ramha*, which seems a loan-word from Lat. *remus*. An oar or paddle was sometimes called *sluasat*, which is the common word for a shovel. A sail is called *seól* [shole] or *brat*: and a mast, *crann*, literally a " tree.' The usual word for a pilot is *luamaire* [loomĕrĕ]. For the names of various other parts of ships and boats, see " Mac Conglinne," p. 84.

There were two words to denote a fleet of ships or boats :—*loinges* [ling-as], which is merely a derivative from *long* ; and *cobhlach* [cowlagh], from *cabhal* or *cobhal*, a ship, which seems connected with, or perhaps borrowed from, Lat. *caupulus*, a small ship. What great numbers of boats were in the fleets that navigated the rivers and lakes may be gathered from a record of the Four Masters under A.D. 751, of the shipwreck of the people of Dealbhna Nuadhat in the present county Roscommon, on Lough Ree, when twenty-nine out of thirty vessels were lost in a storm, and their crews were drowned with their chief. Tigernach

* Wars of GG., 40, 5: Moylena, 45, 22.

records that " the large fleet of Cormac mac Airt (third century) was over the sea for the space of three years."

Ferry-boats were in common use in rivers ; and they are often mentioned in the Brehon Laws as subject to strict regulations. Cormac's Glossary explains the word *ethur* or *ethar* : modern form *eithear* : both pron. eher) as a boat that " goes from brink to brink of the river " ; O'Clery's Glossary gives the same word as equivalent to *arthrach iomchuir*, a ' boat for carrying ' or (ferrying) : and the Senchus Mór gives a similar explanation :— " *Ethur* [a boat which] ferries from bank to bank."* These ferryboats were sometimes owned by individuals, and were sometimes the common property of the people living round the ferry. If a church or monastery happened to be near a river where there was no bridge or ford, the inmates usually kept a little ferry-boat for their own convenience and for the free use of travellers.†

A ferry-boat, when not in use, was commonly kept high and dry on the bank for its better preservation. Where a boat was common property, it was usually given in charge to one individual, who was then the regular ferryman. When it was not so in charge, each person used it as he needed : but he was responsible for leaving it on the bank safe and uninjured when he was done with it. Those using it had to bring it down to the water—or help to do so—and where possible bring it back again : and the law is very precise in regulating the fine for any injury in moving it either way.‡ We have seen (p. 66) that the ferry-boat of a crannoge was often kept floating in the middle of the channel, with connecting ropes extending to land on both sides. Pleasure boating parties were usual in those days as well as now ; and young folk were just as inclined to indulge in boisterous merriment ; of which

---

* Br. Laws, I. 126, top line.
† Br. Laws, III. 211, 18: Dr. Healy, Irel. Anc. Sch., 427, 16.
‡ For all these rules about ferry-boats, Br. Laws, III. 209, 211.

it would seem the Brehon Law was in a way conscious ;
for it prescribes compensation in case the boat was injured
during a pleasure excursion.

5. *Foreign Commerce.*

Many passages referring to the communication of
Ireland with the outer world in ancient times will be
found scattered through this book : but it will be convenient to collect here under one heading a few special
notices bearing on the point.   In the native Irish literature,
as well as in the writings of English, Anglo-Irish, and
foreign authors, there are many statements showing the
intercourse and trade of Ireland, both outwards and
inwards, with Britain and Continental countries.   To begin
with early foreign testimony :—The island was known to
the Phœnicians, who probably visited it ; and Greek
writers mention it under the names Iernis and Ierne,
and as the Sacred Island inhabited by the Hiberni.
Ptolemy, writing in the second century, who is known to
have derived his information from Phœnician authorities,
has given a description of Ireland much more accurate
than that which he has left us of Great Britain.   And
that the people of Ireland carried on considerable trade
with foreign countries in those early ages we know from
the statement of Tacitus, that in his time—the end of the
first century—the harbours of Ireland were better known
to commercial nations than those of Britain.*   The natural
inference from these scattered but pregnant notices is that
the country had settled institutions and a certain degree
of civilisation—with more or less foreign commerce—as
early at least as the beginning of the Christian era.

These accounts, and others from foreign sources that
might be cited, are fully confirmed by the native records.
There are numerous passages in Irish literature—in the

---

* For all the above, see Moore, Hist. of Irel., vol. I., chap. i., and the
authorities he refers to.

Book of Rights, for instance—in which are mentioned articles of luxury, dress, gold and silver ornaments, swords, shields, slaves, &c., imported from foreign lands. One of the Law Tracts mentions a foreign axe (probably from Gaul) as in use in Ireland, and in terms too implying that it was highly valued.* In another authority, O'Davoren's Glossary, a foreign axe is noticed in the following curious terms :—" A foreign axe (*Gall-biail*) perfect . . . with its two black ears : "† and here it is set down as worth sixteen *scripuls*, or about the value of a good milch cow. The following incident in the Life of St. Columbanus is illustrative of the intercourse between Ireland and the coast of Gaul in the beginning of the seventh century :—When the authorities of Nantes wished to get rid of him by sending him back to Ireland, in the year 610, there was no difficulty about the conveyance, for they found ready in the harbour a ship which was " engaged in the commerce of the Scots."‡

A section of the Book of Aicill (Br. Laws, III. 423) is given up to *muir-bretha* or ' sea-laws,' namely, those relating to trading vessels arriving on the Irish coast, some from Britain, some from Continental countries: a circumstance that of itself indicates constant traffic by sea. This section mentions, as one of the mediums of exchange between the Irish and their foreign visitors, an " escup-vessel " of wine or of honey: and Cormac's Glossary§ explains a " wine-escop " (*epscop* or *escop-fina*) as being " a vessel for measuring wine among the merchants of the Norsemen and Franks." In the account of the great triennial fair of Carman in Kildare (see page 444, *infra*) we are told that there were three markets, one of which was " a market of foreigners selling articles

* O'Curry, Man. & Cust., II. 29, bot.
† Corm. Gloss., XII. : Three Ir. Gloss. 70, under " Cailech."
‡ Reeves, Adamn., 57, note *d* ; Lanigan, II. 282.
§ Corm., p. 67 : see also " Esbicul," p. 69, same Glossary.

of gold and silver," who sold "gold [ornaments] and noble clothes " : so that the fame of this fair found its way to the Continent and attracted foreign merchants with their goods. In the beginning of the fifth century, when St. Patrick, escaping from slavery—as we are told in his " Confession " —arrived on some part of the coast of Ireland, he found a ship about to set sail : engaged of course in commerce.*

This commerce was not confined to the coasts. In the " Life of St. Ciaran " it is related that on a certain occasion a cask of wine was brought by merchants to Clonmacnoise from the land of the Franks.† Wine was imported too at a much earlier time than this, as we know from the Memoir of St. Patrick written by Muirchu in the seventh century, which mentions that when the saint arrived at Tara on Easter Sunday, A.D. 433, he found King Laegaire [Laery] and his nobles feasting and drinking wine in the palace (manducandibus illis et bibentibus vinum in palatio Temoriae).‡

In the native legends and semi-legendary history, as in the strictly historical Irish writings, there are constant allusions to foreign intercourse and intermarriages : all reflecting historical reality. In the Battle of Rossnaree (Book of Leinster) it is stated that an embassy was sent to some foreign countries from Concobar mac Nessa, and that the pilot who went with them was Cano the foreigner (*Cano Gall*), " to teach them the way over the surface of the sea."§ The wife of Eochaidh, king of the Firbolgs, was Taillte, daughter of the king of Spain, from whom Tailltenn in Meath took its name.|| The various royal families of Ireland, from the fifth to the eighth century, intermarried among those of Scotland and Britain quite as much as among those of their own country : so that in

---

* Trip. Life, 362, top.

† Stokes, Lives of SS., 276 : Adamnan, 57, note *d*.

‡ Trip. Life, 282.

§ Rossnaree, 13.   See also Kuno Meyer, in the Courtship of Emer, p. 303, note 5, illustrative of the intercourse of the Irish with the Scandinavians.

|| O'Curry, Man. & Cust., I. 148

most of the great wars and battles in Ireland we read of the kings and chiefs of both sides being joined by contingents from their relatives in those countries.*

Giraldus Cambrensis has been quoted (I. 164, *supra*) for the statement that slaves were imported in great numbers from England, the chief mart for this trade being Bristol : and our own records show that foreign slaves—" slaves without Gaelic," to quote the old writer's expression, *i.e.* not speaking Irish—were imported (vol I., p. 165, *supra*). The Senchus Mór, in setting forth the law of distress for certain articles, names among them a lock for securing things brought from beyond the sea : and the Gloss explains this as meaning young foreigners ; which possibly may point to slaves imported from the Continent.†

The various articles mentioned here as brought from foreign lands were imported to supplement the home produce ; in which there was nothing more remarkable than our present importation of thousands of articles from foreign countries, all or most of which are also produced at home. The articles anciently imported were paid for in home commodities—skins and furs of various animals, wool and woollens, oatmeal, fish, salted hogs, &c.

At a comparatively late time—the twelfth century— Giraldus Cambrensis tells us that the Irish exchanged their home produce—chiefly hides—with France, especially Poitou, for wine : which agrees with the incident related above about Clonmacnoise. Giraldus also relates that when the Anglo-Normans under Robert Fitzstephen came to attack Wexford in 1169, many ships lay in the harbour, among which was one lately arrived from the coast of Britain laden with corn and wine.

Long after the Anglo-Norman Invasion the export and import trade continued. We know that in the thirteenth century Irish woollen cloth was exported to

* As illustrative of this, see Dr. Healy, Anc. Ir. Sch., 25, bot. : Moyrath, 45, 47, 65 ; and vol. I., p. 79, *supra*.　　　† Br. Laws, I. 127, 3: 143, 16.

England : and in the next century we find Irish frieze—
or " fryseware," as it is called—mentioned as being freed
from " aulnage " or duty when exported to England.   In
1300, the army of Edward I., while in Scotland, was supplied with wheat, oats, oatmeal, pease, beans, wine, beer,
salt, and hogs, purchased in Ireland.*   The " Libel of
English Policie " (about 1430), p. 199, has the following
passage enumerating the exports of Ireland :—

> " I caste to speake of Ireland but a litle :
> Commodities of it I will entitle,
> Hides, and fish, Salmon, Hake, Herrynge
> Irish wooll, and linen cloth, faldinge [a coarse kind of cloth]
> And marterns [martens] goode ben her marchandie,
> Hertes [harts'] Hides, and other of Venerie [hunting].
> Skinnes of Otter, Squirell and Irish hare,
> Of sheepe, Lambe, and Foxe, is her chaffare [merchandise],
> Felles [skins] of Kiddes, and Conies great plentie.
>   *   *   *   *   *   *
> Of siluer and golde there is the oore."

This trade continued and increased as time went on.
There appeared life and activity everywhere, and the
country was becoming great and prosperous.   But all
this came to a sudden end ; for the manufactures and
commercial prosperity of Ireland were swept off the face
of the earth in the seventeenth century by the laws†
made to destroy Irish trade ; a blow which at once reduced
the country to poverty, and from which it has never
recovered.

* " Introduction towards a History of Irish Commerce," by William
Pinkerton : Ulst. Journ. Archæol., III. 177.
† For these laws, see Joyce, A Child's History of Ireland, p. 394.

Ornament: composed from the Book of Kells.

CHAPTER XXIX

PUBLIC ASSEMBLIES, SPORTS, AND PASTIMES

Section i. *The Great Conventions and Fairs.*

ook their rise in Funeral Games.—Public assemblies of different kinds, held periodically, for various purposes and with several designations, formed a marked and important feature of social life in ancient Ireland. Most of the great meetings, by whatever name known, had their origin in Funeral Games. Tara, Tailltenn, Tlachtga, Ushnagh, Cruachan, Emain Macha, and other less prominent meeting-places, are well known as ancient pagan cemeteries, in all of which many illustrious semi-historical personages were interred: and many sepulchral monuments remain in them to this day. In the account given in the Book of Ballymote of the triennial fair of Carman or Garman, in Kildare, we are told that when old Garman, a chief who was contemporary with the heroes of the Red Branch, was dying, " they made his grave there ; and he begged of them to " institute a fair of mourning (*aenach n-guba*) for him, and " that the fair and the place should bear his name for " ever " : and accordingly the place took his name (Carman) and the Fair was held there for ages afterwards.* The double purpose is shown very clearly in the account of the origin of *Carn-Amhalgaidh* [Awly], near Killala :— " *Carn-Amhalgaigh*, i.e. of Amhalgaidh, son of Fiachra- " Ealgach, son of Dathi, son of Fiachra. It was by him " that this carn was formed, for the purpose of holding a " meeting (*aenach*) of the Hy Amhalgaidh around it every " year, and to view his ships and fleets going and coming, " and as a place of interment for himself."† In the Dinn- senchus, as well as in other authorities, we are told that Oenach Macha, *i.e.* the annual fair-meeting at Emain, was established to lament the death of Queen Macha of the Golden Hair, who had founded the palace there.‡

Important affairs of various kinds, national or local, were transacted at these meetings. The laws were publicly promulgated or rehearsed to make the people familiar with them. There were councils or courts to consider divers local matters—questions affecting the rights, privileges, and customary usages of the people of the district or province—acts of tyranny or infringement of rights by powerful persons on their weaker neighbours—disputes about property—the levying of fines—the imposition of taxes for the construction or repair of roads—the means of defence to meet a threatened invasion, and so forth. These several functions were discharged by persons specially qualified. In all the fairs there were markets for the sale and purchase of commodities, whether produced at home or imported.

Some meetings were established and convened chiefly for the transaction of serious business : but even at these there were sports in abundance : in others the main object was the celebration of games : but advantage was taken of

---

* O'Curry, Man. & Cust., 529, 5. For another account see same vol., p. 535, verse 19 : and LL, 215, *a*.

† Book of Lecan, cited in Petrie, Round Towers, 108

‡ Stokes, Rennes Dinds., in Rev. Celt., XVI. 45.

the occasions to discuss and settle important affairs, as will be described further on. The word *Fés* or *Féis* [faish], which literally means a feast or celebration, cognate with Latin *festum* and English *feast*, was generally applied to the three great meetings of Tara, Croghan, and Emain (*Féis Temrach*, *Féis Cruachan*, and *Féis Emna*, respectively). These were not meetings for the general mass of the people, but conventions of delegates who represented the kingdoms and sub-kingdoms, *i.e.* the states in general of all Ireland, who sat and deliberated under the presidency of the supreme monarch.*

The **Féis-Temrach** or convention of Tara, according to the old tradition, was founded by Ollam Fodla [Ollav-Fóla], who was king of Ireland seven or eight centuries before the Christian era. It was originally held, or intended to be held, every third year, but within the period covered by our authentic records, it was generally convened only once by each king, namely at the beginning of his reign, or if at any other time it was on some special emergency. The provincial kings, the minor kings and chiefs, and the most distinguished representatives of the learned professions—the ollaves of history, law, poetry, medicine, &c.—attended. It lasted—as we read in some authorities—for seven days, namely from the third day before Samain (1st November) to the third day after it : but according to other accounts it continued for a whole month, *i.e.* " a fortnight before Samain and the day of Samain, and a fortnight after " ; and still another makes it six weeks.† Possibly the sports lasted for a week, like those of Carman (p. 441, below) : but the meetings of delegates and ollaves for the discussion of important public affairs were held on—like our present parliaments —for some weeks longer. Each provincial king had a

* Keating, 414, 418.
† Stokes, Lives of SS., Pref., xxxiii : Stokes, Acallamh, line 5367, and p. 47, two last lines : see also Silva Gad. 142, bottom.

separate house for himself and his retinue during the time ; and there was one house for their queens, with private apartments for each, with her attendant ladies.   There was still another house called *Rélta na bh-filedh* [Railtha-na-villa], the ' star of the poets,' for the accommodation of the poets and ollaves of all the professions, where also these learned men held their sittings.*   Every day the king of Ireland feasted the company in the great banqueting-hall—or, as it was called, the Tech Midchuarta or ' mead-circling-hall "—which was large enough for a goodly company : for even in its present ruined state it is 759 feet long by 46 feet wide.

In the same hall were held the formal meetings for the transaction of important business, such as proclaiming the Laws, making new regulations for the whole country where necessary, examining and checking the historical records of the kingdom, and correcting them if found defective or wrong.   All these functions were discharged by experts : and at the end of the *féis* the whole proceedings were written by properly qualified ollaves in the national record called the Saltair of Tara.   These are the accounts left us in our oldest traditions.   That the meetings were held here is not however a matter of tradition, but of unquestionable history.   The last *Féis Temrach* was convened by Dermot king of Ireland, in A.D. 560, after which Tara was abandoned as a royal residence, on account of a curse pronounced against it in very solemn fashion by St. Ruadan of Lorrha in Tipperary.

According to the account given by Keating, who took the statement from old authorities now no longer existing, the conventions of Emain and Croghan were largely concerned with industrial affairs.   The ollaves and nobles— as already stated at page 329—selected from many candidates a number, the best of each craft, who were, as we should express it, " certificated " as persons duly qualified

* Keating, 414, from old authorities.

to practise their several trades, each in his own district : which gave them at once legal standing and legal rights in all cases of dispute.*

The **dál** [dawl] was a meeting convened for some special purpose commonly connected with the tribe or district : a folkmote.† A **mórdál** or **árddál** (*mór*, great : *árd*, high) was a great, or chief, or very important assembly. These two last terms are often applied to such assemblies as those of Tara, Tailltenn, and Ushnagh.

The **aenach** or fair was an assembly of the people of every grade without distinction : it was the most common kind of large public meeting, and its main object was the celebration of games, athletic exercises, sports, and pastimes of all kinds. In Cormac's Glossary‡ an *aenach* is well characterised as a place where there were " food " and precious raiment, downs and quilts, ale and flesh- " meat, chessmen and chessboards, horses and chariots, " greyhounds and playthings besides." In a still older authority, the story of the Sick Bed of Cuculainn§ in the Book of the Dun Cow, copied from the Yellow Book of Slane, we read :—" That was the period of time which the " Ultonians devoted to the holding of the fair of Samain " in the plain of Murthemne [the level part of the County " Louth] every year : and nothing whatever was done by " them during that time but games and races, pleasure and " amusement, eating and feasting : and it is from this " circumstance that the *Trenae Samna* (' three days of " Samain ') are still observed throughout Erin."

The Fairs of Tailltenn, Tlachtga, Ushnagh, The Curragh, Nenagh, Aenach-Beag.—The most important of the Aenachs were those of Tailltenn, Tlachtga, and Ushnagh. The Fair of Tailltenn,‖ now Teltown on the Blackwater, midway

---

* See O'Conor, Dissert., 42 : and O'Flaherty, Ogyg., Part III., chap. lvi.: Keating, 419.   † *Dal*, forum, Zeuss, 71, 23.

‡ Corm., page 129, " Orc tréith."   § Atlantis, I. 371.

‖ I have had the advantage of perusing Mr. Edward Gwynn's Todd Lecture on the *Aenach Tailtenn*, of which he lent me the manuscript.

between Navan and Kells, was attended by people from the whole of Ireland, as well as from Scotland, and was the most celebrated of all for its athletic games and sports : corresponding closely with the Olympic, Isthmian, and other games of Greece. It was held yearly on the 1st August, and on the days preceding and following. What vast numbers were congregated during these games will be seen from the Four Masters' record of the last official aenach held there, A.D. 1169, by Roderick O'Conor, king of Ireland, when the horses and chariots alone, exclusive of the people on foot, extended in a continuous line from Tailltenn to Mullach-Aiti, now the Hill of Lloyd near Kells, a distance of more than six English miles. This aenach was originally instituted, according to the old legend, by the De Dannan king Lugad, or Lug of the Long Arms, to mourn and commemorate his foster-mother, Tailltiu, who was buried there under a mound, and from whom the place took its name. From Lug the first of August was named *Lugnasad*, meaning the *nasad* or games of Lug : a name still in use.

Marriages formed a special feature of this fair. " From " all the surrounding districts the young people came with " their parents, bachelors and maidens being kept apart in " separate places, while the fathers and mothers made " matches, arranged the details, and settled the dowries. " After this the couples were married, the ceremonies being " always performed at a particular spot."* Hence, according to Cormac's Glossary (p. 48), a hillock there had the name of *Tulach-na-Coibche*, " the hill of the buying," where the bride-price was paid. All this is remembered in tradition to the present day : and the people of the place point out the spot where the marriages were performed, which they call " Marriage Hollow." The remains of several immense forts are still to be seen at Teltown,

* From Joyce, Short History of Ireland, 90.

even larger than those at Tara, though not in such good preservation.*

O'Donovan carefully examined this historic site in 1836 for the Ordnance Survey, and found among the people vivid traditions of the old customs. Though the younger generation, when speaking English, called it Teltown, the older Irish-speaking people never used any name but *Tailltenn*. They told him too that games were carried on there " down to 30 years ago "—*i.e.* to 1806—but that, on account of the increasing manufacture of *pottheen* whiskey—instead of the old native drinks, ale and mead— there were quarrels and scenes of violence, so that the magistrates at last put a stop to the meetings.†

The meetings at **Tlachtga** and **Ushnagh,** which have already been mentioned, seem to have been mainly pagan religious celebrations : but games, buying and selling, and conferences on local affairs, were carried on there as at the other assemblies. One of the most noted of all the fairs was **Aenach Colmain** on the Curragh of Kildare, which is noticed in sect. 5 below (p. 464) in connexion with races. The memory of one important fair is preserved in the name of **Nenagh** in Tipperary, in which the initial *N* is the Irish article *an*, ' the ': N-enagh, ' the fair.' The yearly fair held here was called *Aenach-Urmhumhan* [Enagh-Uroon], meaning the Fair of *Urmhumha*, i.e. of Ormond or East Munster : and the old people still call Nenagh " Aenach- Uroon " ; but they have quite forgotten the meaning of *uroon*. So also Monasteranenagh in Limerick, the ' Monastery of the Fair,' which in old times, before the monastery was thought of, was called **Aenach-beag,** ' Little Fair,' to distinguish it from the Great Fair of Nenagh.‡

* See Wilde, Boyne, 149, 150 : Stokes, Life of Petrie, 366.

† O'Donovan's Ord. Surv. Letters, Roy. Ir. Acad. (Meath) · Letter on the parish of Teltown.

‡ For more on these see Irish Names of Places, 1. 204–206.

2. *The Fair of Carman.*

The people of Leinster held a provincial *aenach* at Carman, a place situated probably in South Kildare, once every three years, which began on *Lughnasad* [Loonasa], *i.e.* the first of August, and ended on the sixth. It was considered so important to hold this fair that in case the Leinstermen should ever neglect it—a very unlikely thing—the poem in the Book of Leinster (p. 215, *a*) giving an account of the celebration, threatens them with many evils—early greyness ; baldness (see p. 182, *supra*) ; feebleness ; kings without wisdom or dignified manners, without hospitality, without truthfulness. But if the fair was duly held, they were promised various blessings—plenty and prosperity, corn, milk, fruit, and fish, in abundance ; and freedom from subjection to any other province.*

Fortunately we have, in the Book of Leinster, the Book of Ballymote, and some other ancient manuscripts pretty full descriptions—chiefly poems—of this particular *aenach*. The poem in the Book of Leinster was written by a poet named Fulartach, about A.D. 1000. The several accounts, which are printed in the second vol. of O'Curry's " Man. & Cust." (Appendix) differ somewhat in detail : but the following abridged description, drawn from all, will give a good idea of the arrangements and proceedings, not only of this fair, but of all others wheresoever held.† The representative character of the Fair of Carman, as intended for the whole of Leinster, will be seen from the statement in one of the old accounts that forty-seven sub-kings or chiefs of the province [with their people] attended it :— viz. sixteen from Carman itself and the surrounding districts ; eight from the territory of Hy Donoghue around

---

* O'Curry, Man. & Cust., II., pp. 547 and 531.

† Cuan O'Lochain's Poem in the Book of Leinster (LL, 200, *b* ; Man. & Cust., I. 148) describes the Fair of Tailltenn somewhat similarly, but not nearly in such detail.

the River Dodder near Dublin ; twelve from the Plain of Maistiu, *i.e.* the district round Mullamast in Kildare ; five from *Fidh-Gabhla*, now Figile in King's County ; and six from Ossory.*

There was much formality in the arrangements. While the chief men were sitting in council under the king of Leinster, who presided over all, those belonging to the several sub-kingdoms had special places allotted to them in the council-house or enclosure, which were jealously insisted on. The *forud* or sitting-place of the king of Ossory—a sub-kingdom of Leinster—was on the right hand of the king of Leinster, and that of the king of Offaly on his left : and each of the other sub-kings had his own special place assigned to him. Each day but the last appears to have been given up to the games of some particular tribe or class. For instance, we are told the people of Ossory had a special day for themselves for what was called the " steed contest of the Ossorians," *i.e.* for their chariot and horse races.† Another day was set apart for royalty, when *roydamnas* or crown princes contended, and none others were permitted to enter (Man. & Cust., II., p. 539, last verse).

Women played a conspicuous part in this fair, and of course in all others. There were special *cluichi* or games for them in the afternoon which are called *cluichi ban Laigen iar lo*, ' the games of the women of Leinster in the evening,' but what kind they were we are not told. To the *Laisig* (*i.e.* the people of *Laighis* or Leix) was entrusted the important and delicate duty of superintending these games ; and they were responsible not only for the good order of the proceedings, but also for the safety of the jewellery, which the Leinsterwomen wore in abundance, and which they had to lay aside during the games.‡

* O'Curry, Man. & Cust., II., p. 539.   † *Ibid.*, 529, par. 4
‡ *Ibid.*, 539, verses 44, 45.

The women had *airechts* or councils of their own to discuss those subjects specially pertaining to women : and at these assemblies no man was permitted to be present : while, on the other hand, no woman was allowed to enter the special council meetings of the men (Man. & Cust., II., p. 543, ver. 55).   In those formal sittings that were open to both sexes, the women were seated with their own people, in the special places set apart for the representatives of their respective tribes (*ibid.*, p. 529, par. 4).

Conspicuous among the entertainments and art-performances was the recitation of poems and romantic tales of all the various kinds mentioned in I. 533, *supra*, like the recitations of the Rhapsodists among the Greeks :—
" The Tales of the Fena of Erin "—says the old account—
" a never-wearying entertainment : stories of destructions,
" cattle-preys, courtships, rhapsodies, battle-odes, royal
" precepts, and the truthful instruction of Fithil the Sage :
" poets and learned men with their tablets and books of
" trees (I. 480, *supra*) : deep poetry, and Dinnsenchus or
" History of Places : the wise precepts of Carbery and
" Cormac Mac Art " (Man. & Cust., II. 543).   For all of these there were sure to be special audiences who listened with delight to the fascinating lore of old times.

Music always formed a prominent part of the amusements : and among the musical instruments are mentioned *cruits* or harps ; *timpans* ; trumpets ; wide-mouthed horns; *cuisig* or pipes ; and there were plenty of harpers ; pipers ; fiddlers ; bone-men (*cnamh-fhir*), i.e. castanet-players ; " tube-players " ; and *fir-congail* or ' chain-men,' probably men who shook music from chains furnished with little bells like those already described in vol. I., page 586, *supra*.   In another part of the fair the people gave themselves up to uproarious fun, crowded round showmen, jugglers, and clowns with grotesque masks or painted faces, making hideous distortions, all bellowing and roaring out their rough jests to the laughing crowds : for there were " professors of every art, both the noble arts and the base arts."* There were also performers of horsemanship, who delighted their audiences with feats of activity and skill on horseback, such as we see in modern circuses. The Brehon Law (v. 109) mentions " equestrians, namely, those who stand on the backs of horses at fairs."

Prizes were awarded to the best performers of " every " *dán* or art that was just or lawful to be sold, or rewarded, " or exhibited, or listened to " : which excluded from any prize, showmen and all other exhibitors of the baser sort† : and at the close of the proceedings the coveted trophy— always a thing of value, generally a gold ring, or some other jewel—was publicly presented by some important person, such as a king, a queen, or a chief.

Special portions of the fair-green were set apart for another very important function—buying and selling. We are told that there were " three [principal] markets : viz. a " market of food and clothes : a market of live stock and " of horses ; while a third was railed off for the use of " foreign merchants with gold and silver articles and " fine raiment to sell."‡ There was the " slope of the embroidering women," who did their work in presence of spectators (Man. & Cust., II., p. 547, verse 76). A special space was assigned for cooking (verse 76), which must have been on an extensive scale to feed such multitudes.

On each day of the fair there was a conference of the brehons, chiefs, and leading men in general, to regulate the fiscal and other local affairs of the province for that and the two following years : or, as the old account has it, " for " considering the judgments and rights of the province for " three years."§

Possibly some readers may think it strange that in all this detailed list of amusements we do not find a word

---

* O'Curry, Man. & Cust., II. 545, verse 63 : and 531, note, line 16. For showmen's face-distortions, see p. 486, below. † *Ibid.*, 531, note, line 20
‡ *Ibid.*, 531 ; 547, verse 75. § *Ibid.*, 543, verses 53, 54 ; 530 note.

about dancing. There is, in fact, no evidence that the ancient Irish ever danced to music, or danced at all, *i.e.* in our sense of the word " dancing " ; but very strong negative evidence that they did not. Though we have in the old literature many other passages in which the several amusements at popular gatherings are enumerated,* on no-one of them is dancing mentioned. This curious fact has been already noticed by O'Curry, who, after all his vast reading of native literature, says :—" As far as I have ever " read there is no reference that can be identified as con-" taining a clear allusion to dancing in any of our really " ancient MS. books."† So also Stokes :—" Dancing is not " mentioned in the documents now published [in his Trip. " Life], nor, indeed, in any Irish MSS. that I have read." (Trip. Life, clviii). We have now two Irish words for dancing :—*damhsa*, which may be passed over, as it is obviously a modern adaptation of the English " dance " : and *rinncedh*, which is a native word, derived, according to O'Curry,‡ from *rinn*, an old word for foot (see Corm. 145, " Rind "), and the termination *cedh* : so that *rinncedh* literally means ' footing.' But it does not seem to be an old word.

What appears to be a sort of confirmation of all this occurs in a passage in a Homily on the Passion of John the Baptist, published by Dr. Atkinson from the Liber Brecc, where the Irish homilist is giving a free rendering of the Bible narrative about Herodias' daughter dancing before King Herod. He had before him the Vulgate word *saltavit* (' she danced ') : but it would almost appear as if he did not know how to render it into Irish, possibly not knowing what " dancing " was.§ His words are that the girl was skilled in *clesaighecht ocus lemenda ocus opairecht*,

* As, for instance, in the Courtship of Emer, 69.

† O'Curry, Man. & Cust., II. 406.   ‡ *Ibid.*, II. 407.

§ Something like what happened when the Irish annotator, having never seen a *fiber* or beaver, but knowing well what an otter was, explained *fiber* by *dobran*, or ' otter.' (See p. 462 farther on.)

' juggling and *leaping* and activity ' ; where *lemenda* simply means ' leaping,' but not ' dancing ' as such.* So far as I am aware, the Irish words *léim, léimenn, lémenda* mean exactly the same as the English words " leap," " leaping," and nothing more. When we now wish to express in Irish the special sense of " dancing," the word *leimenn*, ' leaping,' will not answer : we have to employ a different word (*rincedh* or *damhsa*) : just as we have to do in English. But the Irish translator had no word but one : and accordingly used the Irish word *lemenda* in its primary sense of leaping merely, to represent " saltavit." In the " Circuit of Muirchertach mac Neill " (p. 45), which celebrates an event that took place A.D. 941, the English translation has— " Music we had on the plain and in our tents, listening to its strains *we danced awhile* " : but the three last words are inserted by O'Donovan (in *italics*), and have no corresponding words in the original. Yet the men kept time with the music—as the poem expresses it—" by the shaking of our hard cloaks " : but not by dancing.

When the evening of the last day had come, and all was ended, the men of the entire assembly stood up and made a great clash with their spears, each man striking the handle of the next man's spear with the handle of his own : which was the signal for the crowds to disperse.† It always took two years to make the preparations for the holding of this fair.‡ After the introduction of Christianity in the fifth century, the pagan customs were discontinued, and Christian ceremonies were introduced. Each day was ushered in with a religious exercise, and on the next day after the fair there was a grand ceremonial : Masses and adorations and singing of hymns.§ But beyond this there was little or no change.

We have seen that a fair-green was usually called *faithche* [faha] : and a small portion of the *faithche* of

---

* Homilies, 66, 307 : Matthew, XIV. 6.   ‡ Man. & Cust., II. 531, note, line 4.
† Man. & Cust., II. 545, verse 70.   § *Ibid.*, II. 545, verse 67.

some forgotten fair-sports still retains the name in " The Faythe," a level spot near the present town of Wexford.

The correspondence between these fairs and the Greek celebrations for similar purposes will be obvious to every-one : and it is worth observing that the Carman festival bore a closer resemblance to the Isthmian games, where there were contests in poetry and music, than to those of Olympia, where there were none.

3. *General Regulations for Meetings.*

The accounts that have come down to us show that the ancient Irish were very careful that there should be no quarrelling or fighting, or unseemly disturbance of any kind that might " spoil sport," at the formal *dáls* or *aenachs*, or meetings, for whatever purpose convened. The Senchus Mór, and the glosses and commentaries on it, mention fines for creating disturbance or being guilty of any misconduct while the people were assembled* : and any serious breach of rule was punished with death. The Poem on Carman says :—

> " Whoever [seriously] transgresses the law of the assembly,
> Which Benen with accuracy indelibly wrote,
> Cannot be spared upon family composition,
> But he must die for his transgression."†

Whatever causes of quarrel may have existed between clans or individuals, whatever grudges may have been nurtured, all had to be repressed during these meetings. Even proceedings likely to lead to disputes were forbidden, such as elopements, repudiation of wives by husbands, or the reverse. There were to be no distraints or other pro-cesses for the recovery of debts, so that a debtor, however deeply involved, might enjoy himself here with perfect safety and freedom from arrest.‡ Hence we find the old

---

* Br. Laws, I. 231, bottom ; 175, bottom ; 177, 12; 233, last line.
† Man. & Cust., II. 543, verse 56. ‡ *Ibid.*, II. 543, verses 53, 54, 55

writer boasting, with natural pride, " the Gentiles of the Gael," *i.e.* the Irish pagans of pre-Christian times, celebrated the fair of Carman " without breach of law, without crime, without violence, without dishonour."* Similarly, Cuan O'Lochain is at great pains to detail the precautions for peace at Tailltenn (LL, 200, *b*, 40–47).

A very few cases of serious violation of the law are recorded, as when " Fogartach O'Carney disturbed the fair [of Tailltenn], for he killed Maelruba the son of Dubhsleibhe " (FM, 715). But the annalists record them as exceptional: as in the present case, where they obviously look upon the breach of the peace as the important and unusual circumstance. The reader will perceive that all this runs parallel with the sacred armistice proclaimed by the Greeks at their Olympic and Isthmian games. Indeed an expression in Cuan O'Lochain's poem is almost identical with some phrases in the Greek accounts, where he tells us (LL, 200, *b*, 46) that among the multitudes attending the fair of Tailltenn, whether from Ireland or Scotland, there was " one universal fair-truce " (*oen chairde oenig*). Where such vast numbers of chariots were congregated there was always liability to accidents. The law took cognisance of these ; and provision was made that in case a chariot should be broken, or anyone was injured by furious driving, or should any other accident occur, the persons responsible should be made liable, but should at the same time be protected from vexatious prosecutions.†

The Law made provision for having the fair-green, and particularly that part of it devoted to special purposes, kept in proper order. This duty was assigned to certain persons of the neighbourhood, whose business it was to clear away the brambles and rubbish immediately before the fair, and to keep the spaces clear during the sports : and for the

---

* Man. & Cust., II. 537, verse 31.   † Br. Laws, III. 265, bottom.

neglect of this duty there was a penalty.* They were of course paid in some way, but on this point we have no information. When to anyone was assigned the task of making a fair-green, he had to furnish it with fences and mounds (*claide* and *ferta*), wherever they were required for such purposes as jumping, racing, special assemblies, &c. : and here also was provided a penalty if the structures were not properly made.†

Besides the large fairs or other assemblies, there were smaller meetings for special purposes, such as councils of representative men to deliberate on local matters. These were generally held in the open air on little hills,‡ and were called *airecht, oirecht,* or *oirechtas,*§ from *oire* or *aire,* a chief or leading man ; for the local king or chief always presided at them. The custom of holding *oirechts* was continued down to the end of the sixteenth century. Spenser (View, 126) notices them as carried on in his time : and the word was familiarly used in an anglicised form by English writers of the time of Elizabeth. In the agreement between the Anglo-Irish council of Dublin and O'Reilly, in 1583, it is laid down :—" He [O'Reilly] shall not " assemble the queen's people [*i.e.* his own people, over " whom in common with all the rest of the Irish the " queen claimed to be sovereign lady] upon hills, or use " any *Irachtes* or parles upon hills."‖

A hill of this kind, set apart for meetings, was sometimes called *tulach,* which is a name for any small hill, or *tulach airechtais,* or *ard-airechtais,* 'hill of meeting' ; and also *ri-bheann,* i.e. royal *benn* or hill : *i.e.* devoted to the king's business.¶ But it was also designated by the special

---

* Br. Laws, I. 123, 24; 129, 13.   † Br. Laws, I. 157, 34; 159, last line.
‡ Moyrath, 67, bottom : Br. Laws, III. 297, 16.
§ See " Aireachta " in O'Donovan, Supplement. The above words will be found in Irish dictionaries.
‖ Hardiman, Irish Minstrelsy, II. 159.
¶ Br. Laws, I. 175, bottom : 177, 12: Sick Bed, Atlantis, I. 384, 18: Moyrath, 92, 5: O'Donovan, Supplement, " Ribheann."

name *aibinn* or *aiminn* [eevin], which the gloss on the Senchus Mór explains by *suide-dála* [see-dawla] *i.e.* the ' seat of the *dál* or meeting ' : ' convention-seat.'* Hills devoted to this particular purpose were held in much veneration, and were not to be put to any other use. Ferflatha O'Gnive, the ollave poet of the O'Neills of Clannaboy in the time of Elizabeth, lamenting the decay of the old Gaelic customs, says that now, alas, the sacred meeting hills are no longer frequented : they are tilled and cropped and used as common market-places.†

Great care was taken that they should be kept in proper order : and anyone who stripped sods from the surface or dug into them for any purpose was fined.   Cows were not permitted to graze on a convention-hill : and if the smooth surface happened to get broken up from any cause it should be strewn with fine clay which was to be trampled down and made smooth before the meeting.   If the meeting had to be held while the hill happened to be bare of grass, or rough, or dirty, the person having the management of the *dál* should have cloths of some kind spread under the feet of kings, and rushes for the other chief people.‡   The very name of these assembly-hills seems to indicate that they were deliberately selected for their pretty appearance : for *aibinn* (or *aiminn* as other authorities have it) denotes anything beautiful, cognate with Latin *amoen-us* : and indeed the Law tells us expressly that, as the name of a meeting-hill, this is the sense it bears.§

At small meetings held in a building or any other confined space, the president, when he wanted silence, shook what was called the " chain of attention " (*slabra éstechta*), which was hung with little bells or loose links that gave forth a musical sound.   In the story of the Sons of Turenn

* Br. Laws, I. 167, ₃₅; 170, ₁₅; 171, ₁₉.
† Hardiman, Irish Minstrelsy, II. 106, second verse.
‡ Br. Laws, I. 171, ₂₀; III. 297.   § *Ibid.*, III. 297 ; IV. 215, ₃₃.

(p. 185) we read that Luga of the Long Arms, sitting beside the king of Ireland in the hall of Tara, and wishing to address the assembly, ordered the chain of attention of the court to be shaken, which procured him silence. More often it was a branch hung with little bells : this was called *craeb* [crave], or *craeb sida*. ' branch of peace.' At the feast in the house of Bricriu, when a dangerous dispute arose and there was a great and noisy contention, Sencha the brehon arose and shook the *Craebh Sencha* (i.e. ' Sencha's branch '), which produced instant silence and attention.* This musical branch with silver bells figures in many of the romantic tales.† There were other ways of procuring attention at feasts and meetings. When there arose some noisy confusion at a feast, King Concobar gave one of his usual signals by striking the bronze pillar that supported the canopy of his couch with his silver *clo* or wand. Sometimes the president hushed all talk and noise by merely standing up, like the Speaker in the House of Commons. At the feast at *Dun-da-bend* (now Mountsandal over the Bann near Coleraine), while the talk and enjoyment went on without restraint, Concobar, sitting on his " hero-seat " at the head, and wishing to speak to the assembly, rose up ; and " mute and silent became the Ultonians when " they saw the king standing, so that if a needle fell from " roof to floor, it would be heard."‡

4. *Some Animals connected with Hunting and Sport.*

The Dog.—Dogs of all kinds were used by the people of Ireland quite as much in ancient times as they are now : but hunting-dogs have, as might be expected, impressed themselves most of all on the literature. By far the most celebrated of the native dogs was the Irish wolf-dog, noted

---

* Fled Bricr., 35 : Ir. Texte, I. 267, 2. See also Hyde, Ir. Lit., 296, top.
† As in Voyage of Bran, I., p. 2 : and the Story of Cormac Mac Art and the Musical Branch, Oss. Soc., III. 213. See vol. I., p. 586, *supra*.
‡ Mesca Ulad., 13, bottom.

for its size and fierceness. There is no doubt that this gigantic animal existed in Ireland from the earliest times, as is proved by unquestionable authorities, one of which is quoted below : but it is curious that it is chiefly from English and foreign writers we get such precise information as enables us to form an idea of its actual size. It was so familiar at home that the native writers did not think it necessary to describe it.

In the ancient Irish tales the hunting-dogs are constantly mentioned in terms of great admiration, as large and strong : but these references are vague, and many persons might regard them as high-sounding poetical exaggerations. There is nothing poetically vague however in the statement of Campion, the English Jesuit, who visited Ireland, and wrote a short history of it in 1571. He says (p. 13) :—" They [the Irish] are not without " wolves, and greyhounds to hunt them, bigger of bone " and limme than a colt." Twelve centuries before his time, a Roman citizen named Flavianus, who had visited Britain, presented seven Irish dogs (*Scotici canes*) to his brother Symmachus, a Roman consul, for the games at Rome (A.D. 391)—though we are left in the dark as to how he procured the animals—a gift which Symmachus acknowledges in a letter still extant :—" All Rome," he says, " viewed them with wonder and thought they must have been brought hither in iron cages."* Among the numerous passages in native Irish writings mentioning this great Irish greyhound I can find only one that gives an idea of its actual size, quoted by the Rev. Dr. Hogan (Wolf-dog, p. 164) fi om the Book of Lismore, a manuscript copied in the fifteenth century from much older sources, which states :—" Each of these hounds is as big as an ass."

* This letter is referred to and partly quoted in Harris's Ware (Antiqq., 166) : the original Latin passage may be seen in the Rev. Dr. Hogan's " Irish Wolfdog," page 153, and a translation of it at page 11 of the same book.

From the fifteenth to the eighteenth century Irish wolf-dogs were, it might be said, celebrated all over the world, so that they were sent as valuable presents to kings and emperors, princes, grand Turks, noblemen, queens, and highborn ladies, in all the chief cities of Europe, and even in India and Persia.* It is strange that Giraldus Cambrensis does not notice these dogs : they must have been in the country in his time ; and if he had seen them he would certainly have mentioned them. After the final extinction of wolves in Ireland in the early part of the eighteenth century, the need for these great dogs ceased. and the race was let die out.†

The word *cu*, genitive *con*, was generally applied to any fierce dog, this term being qualified by certain epithets to denote dogs of various kinds. A greyhound or hunting-dog, whether a wolf-dog or any other, was commonly called *milchu*. In Cormac's Glossary (p. 115) the syllable *mil* is explained *mál*, a king, so that according to this authority *milchu* is *cu-mál*, the hound of a king—which is I fear all fanciful. O'Davoren in his Glossary explains *milchu* by *gadhar* [gy-er g hard] which is still the common word for a beagle or small hound. At the present time the most general name for a dog is *madra* or *mada*, which is also an old word.

A watch-dog for a house was called *archu*, from *ar* or *air*, to watch. These watch-dogs were kept in every house of any consequence ; and they were tied up by day and let loose by night. In accordance with custom and law the watch-dogs of the farming classes were loosed earlier in the evening and tied up earlier in the morning than those of the chieftain grades : in the chiefs' houses so many people were coming and going that the dogs were kept tied up till bedtime to avoid danger to guests : whereas those of farmers were set free at cow-stalling.‡

* Preface to the Rev. Dr. Hogan's " Irish Wolfdog."
† See note on the Irish Wolfdog in Stokes's Life of Petrie, p. 437.
‡ Br. Laws, I. 127, 10; 145. .; III. 419.

A shepherd's dog was called a *cu-buachaill* [coo-boohil], *i.e.* a 'dog-cowherd.' The gloss on the Senchus Mór alludes to a penalty for stealing one of these dogs, and mentions that they were of three kinds, but does not specify them. A story connected with Ireland, in a Norse work of the twelfth century—Snorro Sturleson's Chronicles of the Kings of Norway—written in Icelandic, shows that the ancient Irish trained these dogs as carefully as the shepherd's collie is trained at the present day.

"While Olaf [or Amlaff] was in Ireland [in the ninth or tenth century] he was once upon an expedition which went by sea. As they required to make a foray for provisions on the coast, some of his men landed and drove a large herd of cattle down to the strand. Now a peasant came up and entreated Olaf to give him back the cows which belonged to him. Olaf told him to take his cows if he could distinguish them, 'but don't delay our march.' The peasant had with him a large house-dog, which he put in among the herd of cattle, in which many hundred head of beasts were driven together. The dog ran into the herd, and drove out exactly the number the peasant said he wanted ; and all were marked with the same mark, which showed that the animal knew the right beasts and was very sagacious. Olaf then asked the peasant if he would sell him the dog. ' I would rather give him to you,' said the peasant. Olaf immediately presented him with a gold ring in return, and promised him his friendship in future."*

It appears from some passages in the Laws, as well as from general Irish literature, that lapdogs were as much in favour in Ireland in old times as they are now : women of all classes, from queens down, kept them. We find them even in convents. The virgin saint Cruimtheris, who lived near Armagh in the time of St. Patrick, kept a lapdog which she fed on the milk of a doe.† Their importance in the eyes of the law is attested by the story of the first lapdog brought to Ireland (vol. I., p. 74, *supra*) : and a heavy fine was prescribed for stealing them : which was

* Laing's Translation, quoted in Kilk. Archæol. Journ., vol. I., p. 326.
† Trip. Life, 233.

recoverable by either husband or wife, though the lapdog was always the woman's personal property.

The commonest name for a lapdog was *oircne* [urkina]. a diminutive of *oirc* [urk], which means, among other things, a little dog. Two other terms for these little pets are derivatives from the rootword *mes* or *mess* :—*meschu*, which is very often used by the old Irish writers, and which O'Clery makes equivalent to *oirc* ; and *mesan* or *messan*, which O'Clery's Glossary defines as *cu-beag*, ' little hound.' The Brehon Law (I. 153, bot.) is still more explicit in identifying this word with *oircne*, for the gloss on the Senchus Mór, explaining *oircne rigna* (the ' lapdog of a queen '), says it is identical with *mesan*. In Cormac's Glossary (p. 115) the word *mesan* is derived from *messa*, ' the worst,' because a lapdog is " one that is the worst of hounds," *i.e.* I suppose as being merely a plaything, with no further use. This word is still current in Scotland even among the English-speaking people, and is often met with in Scott's novels. In the Heart of Midlothian (chap. xxix.), Madge speaks to Jeanie Deans about her " little messan dog "—her " puir bit doggie Snap." It has been already remarked that little bells were often hung from lapdogs' necks.

A dog that had the vicious habit of attacking lambs, or fowls, or domestic pets, had a muzzle (*srublingi*) of leather tied on his snout. From the words of the Book of Aicill it appears that dogs were often muzzled as a general precaution. The muzzle should be tested, so that in case a dog did mischief the owner might be enabled to mitigate damages by the plea that proper precaution was taken. An eye-cap, called in Irish *Eirrgi*, i.e. a covering of leather fastened over the eyes, was used for " a dog which does not know its own people from the neighbours," which probably means that he was as ready to bite one of the family as to bite a stranger.*

* Br. Laws, III. 417.

Dogs were liable to run mad then as well as now. When a dog was found to be mad, it was hunted down and killed, its body was burned, and the ashes were thrown into a stream. Here is the quaint language of the Book of Aicill on this point :—" There is no benefit in proclaiming " it [*i.e.* sending round warning of a *cu-confaid* or mad dog] " unless it be killed ; nor though it be killed unless it be " burned ; nor though it be burned unless its ashes have " been cast into a stream."*

Some dogs were " lawful " (*dlighedh*), *i.e.* they were in some way recognised by law, which turned to the advantage of the owner in case of proceedings of any kind in a brehon's court regarding the dog. Others were said to be " unlawful " (*indlighedh*), which did not mean that they were forbidden by law, but simply that they were not legally recognised, and the owner had therefore to take his chance in law proceedings, without any benefit from legal recognition. Some dogs again were fully lawful, some three quarters, and some half lawful ; but these terms are not defined in our copies of the laws. Certain dogs, stated to be lawful, are named ; but the statement is to me not clear. One example of a lawful dog is plain enough— a dog with a duly tested muzzle following a woman as a companion.† The Book of Aicill lays down detailed rules about dog-fights, in view of the injury that might be inflicted on bystanders or on other animals.‡

The Greeks, though they looked upon the dog as the friend of man, did not hold it in high esteem, and they did not use it in war. Among the Celts of Gaul it held a much higher place, and was trained to fight in battles. The high regard in which the Gauls held it remained among their descendants the ancient Irish ; for though I cannot find that dogs were employed in battle in Ireland, they were much valued and esteemed ; and they figure conspicuously

* Br. Laws, III. 273.   † See on all this, Br. Laws, III. 413.
‡ *Ibid.*, 193, to 199.

in Irish literature. The best illustration of this is the very general custom of using *cu* as a name for men, so that large numbers of Irish personal and family names have *cu* or *con* as one of their components; like Cuculainn, O'Conor, Macnamara (*Mac Con-mara*), O'Connolly, Conway, Quin, Quinlan, &c.*

Wolves.—A common name for a wolf was *cu-allaidh* [coo-allee], *i.e.* ' wild-hound.' Another was *mac-tire* [macteera], which literally means ' son of the country,' in allusion to the wild places that were the haunts of these animals. Two other names *fael* and *breach* have long since fallen out of use, though they are commemorated in local names. *Faelchu*, which is formed from *fael*, and *cu*, a dog, is now a general name for a wolf. Cormac's Glossary (p. 87) gives *glademain* (pl.) as a collective name for wolves: which is derived from *glaid* or *glaodh*, a cry (pron. glay).

In old times wolves were so numerous in the woods and fastnesses of Ireland as to constitute a formidable danger to the community: so that in Irish writings we meet with frequent notices of their ravages, and of the measures taken to guard against them. Sometimes when pressed with hunger they killed and ate human beings. But it may be said to have been the only really dangerous wild animal of the country; and one of the old native writers, comparing Ireland to Paradise, and noticing its exemption from baneful reptiles, states that the wolf was its only noxious animal.† In later times, and probably in early ages as well, we know that these animals were hunted down by the great Irish wolf-dog: and they were also caught in traps.‡

* See, on all this, De Jubainville, La Civil. des Celtes, pp. 55-60 : Joyce, Irish Names of Places, II. 156 : and a Series of Papers written in the Irish language by Mr. Thomas Flannery in the first volume of the Gaelic Journal (1882) on the word *cu* as used in Irish names.

† Trip. Life, Introduction, xxx. note.

‡ For wolf-traps in 1659, see Ulster Journ. Archæol., II. 281

The war of extermination against wolves was not left to chance or to individual enterprise. We learn from the Senchus Mór and from the gloss upon it, that in various parts of the country there were organised efforts by the community to keep them down. Once a week a body of men made a regular raid on them under the direction of the chief : and it was a duty owed by every man to his chief to join these parties of attack in turn on the days appointed.* As the population and the extent of open cultivated land increased, wolves became less numerous and were held well in check ; but during the wars of the reign of Elizabeth, when the country was almost depopulated, they increased enormously and became bolder and fiercer, so that we often find notices of their ravages in the literature of those times.†

Bears continued to exist in Scotland—according to Carmichael (II. 306)—so late as the sixteenth century : but they became extinct in Ireland at a much earlier period. The oldest list we have of the chief native wild animals is given incidentally in the treatise already mentioned (vol. I. p. 345, *supra*), written in the year 655, by Augustin, an Irish monk, then living in Carthage ; but bears are not among them. Next in point of antiquity comes the evidence of Bede, who states that the only noxious animals in his time in Ireland were the wolf and the fox.‡ In a Latin poem written early in the ninth century in praise of Ireland by Donatus, bishop of Fiesole, an Irishman, there is a more precise statement ; for one of the points of commendation is that it possessed no bears. Yet there were bears in Ireland at some very early time, while the country was inhabited by men ; for their bones are often found among the remains of human dwellings. Between 1840 and 1846 the skulls of two bears were dug up in a cutaway bog§ : and quite recently the bones of numbers of

* Br. Laws, I. 161, top. ‡ Proc. Roy. Ir. Acad., IV. 417.
† Iar C., 180. § *Ibid.*, IV. 417.

brown bears have been found in the caves of Kesh-Corran in Sligo. The Irish language retains a faint memory of these animals, inasmuch as it has a native name for a bear :—*math*, or more commonly in the compound form *math-gamuin** : but beyond this the bear is totally lost to Irish history, so that it must have become extinct before our earliest legends began.

Deer were plentiful in ancient Ireland, and they are noticed everywhere in the literature, both lay and ecclesi-astical. By far the most remarkable of the ancient deer of this country was the gigantic Irish elk, the bones of which are now often found buried deep in clay, sometimes with a thick layer of bog over it. It is well established that this stately creature lived in the country for some considerable time contem-poraneously with man : but it seems probable that it had disappeared before the time reached by our oldest writings : so that it is lost

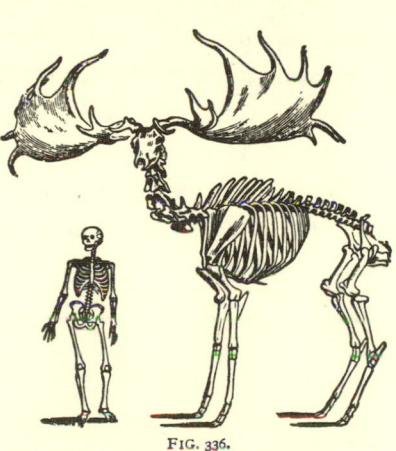

FIG. 336.

Skeleton of Irish Elk in the National Museum, Dublin. (From plate of the Royal Dublin Society.) Human skeleton put in for comparison.

to history ; and those deer so often spoken of in Irish literature are not the great Irish elk, but animals like those of the present day.† The skeleton of the elk in the National Museum has antlers extending twelve feet from tip to tip : and as may be seen from the figure stands nearly twice the height of a man.

The most common word for a deer is *fiad* or *fiadh* [feea], which originally meant wild ; but its meaning has

* See " Math " in Windisch. Wörterb. Ir. Texte, I. : and " Math-gamuin " in O'Donovan's Supplement to O'Reilly.

† See Kilk. Archæol. Journ., 1849–51, p. 166 : and 1856–57, p. 155.

been gradually narrowed, and in Irish writings, as well as in the spoken language, it is almost universally applied to a deer. *Ség* is given in several glossaries, including Cormac's (p. 152), as a name for a wild deer ; and both Cormac's (p. 68) and O'Clery's give *erb* as meaning a kind of deer ; but both these words have been long obsolete. *Os* signifies a fawn. The celebrated Irish poet and warrior who lived in the third century of the Christian era, and whose name has been changed to Ossian by Macpherson, is called in Irish manuscripts *Oisín* [Osheen], which signifies a little fawn ; and the name is explained by a legend.

The Hare.—It has been remarked above that the word *fiadh* [feea] was originally used in the sense of ' wild ' in general. The hare would appear to be the smallest animal to which the term was applied, if we may judge by the composition of its name *gerr-fhiadh* [gerree'] ; *i.e.* short or small *fiadh*, from *gerr*, short or deficient. In Cormac's Glossary (p. 133) is given *patu* [or *pata*], another word for a hare, which still survives in the spoken language in the south of Ireland ; where the diminutive *patachán* is used even by speakers of English to denote a leveret. The same glossary (p. 49) has *cermna* as still another name for a hare. Sometimes a hare was called *mil-maighe* [meel-mee], ' beast of the plain.'

The Cat.—A cat is called by the same name with slight variations, in nearly all the languages of Europe : in Irish the common name is *catt* or *cat* ; but O'Davoren in his glossary gives eight Irish names for this animal. Cormac's Glossary derives *catt* from Latin *cattus* : but it is certain that the two words are merely cognate, *i.e.* both derived from an older source. Wild cats were in old times very plentiful : large wicked rough-looking creatures, very strong and active and very dangerous ; and the race is not yet quite extinct, for wild cats, nearly twice the size of our domestic animals, are still found in some solitary places.

It was these animals that gave origin to the legend, very common in ancient Irish story, of a monstrous enchanted wild cat, dwelling in a cave, and a match for the bravest champion. One of these monsters, named Irusan, that had his dwelling in the cave of Knowth on the Boyne, once seized the poet Senchan in his mouth and ran off with him, till he was rescued by St. Ciaran.* Another tremendous cat named *Luchthigern* (' mouse-lord ' : *luch*, a mouse), lived in *Derc-Ferna*, now the cave of Dunmore near Kilkenny, till he was killed by a *ban-gaisgidheach* or female champion of Leinster.†   Three monstrous cats dwelt in the cave of Croghan, from which Conall Cernach and Laegaire the Victorious had to fly for their lives ; but Cuculainn withstood them though he was not able to kill them.‡   Stories of demon cats have found their way down to modern Irish legend : see " Puss in Brogues," Irish Penny Journal, p. 346.

Otters.—The otter has several names in Irish, the most usual in old writings being *dobor-chu*, ' water-hound ' (from *dabor* or *dobur*, an old word for water, common to Gaelic and Welsh).§ It was also called *madad-* or *madra-uisce*, ' water-dog.'   O'Clery's Glossary explains *dobor-chu* by *madra-uisce*, which is now the general word for an otter ; though *dobar-chu* is still in use in some parts of the country. Cormac's Glossary (p. 40) gives the old word *coinfodorne* (pl. : the singular is *confodorne*) as meaning *dobarchoin*, *i.e.* otters ; and explains *fodorne*, the latter part of the word, as meaning *fo-dobarnai*, i.e. ' under *dobur* or water.' *Confodorne* is given in O'Reilly's Dictionary in the more modern form *confoirne*. Another name for an otter, derived also from *dobur*, is *dobran*, a diminutive, which in

* Tromdamh, pp. 81–85.

† The Poem of Broccan the Pious, in praise of Leinster, in which this cat figures, will be found in LL, 43, *b*, ₇: it has been published, with translation, by Mr. T. O. Russell in his *Fíor Chláirseach na h-Ereann*, p. 118.

‡ Fled Bricrenn, 73.

§ Cormac's Glossary, 40, " Coinfodorne " ; and 53, " Dobur."

Cormac's Glossary is given as the equivalent of *dobarchu*.* In the " Story of the Eruption of Lough Neagh," Liban spends three hundred years as a salmon under the sea, accompanied by her lap-dog in the shape of a *dobran* or otter.† In the tract on Hy Many (p. 90, 16) the compound *condobran* is used for an otter. It is curious that in the Irish Glosses on Latin Declension edited by Stokes (No. 375), the old Irish writer explains the Latin *fiber*, a beaver, by *dobran*, an otter, which possibly may be owing to the circumstance that though he knew well what a *dobran* was, he had never seen a beaver, as there were none in Ireland, and thought that a *fiber* was the same animal as his own native otter (like what happened in case of Dancing, p. 445, and note, *supra*).

Otters abounded in rivers and lakes, and were hunted, partly for sport and partly for their skins. In later times —and probably in the early ages—otter skins formed an important article of commerce, so that they were sometimes given as payment in kind for rent or tribute. We get an indication of the importance of these animals in the fact recorded in the Book of Lecan, that in the end of the fourteenth century the people of the district of Fidh Monach were entrusted with the special charge of the otters and of the fishing of O'Kelly, king of Hy Many (HyM, 93, top).

Of the badger it will be enough to say here that it was called in Irish *broc*, and that the chase of the " heavy-sided low-bellied badger " was a favourite sport.

5. *Races.*

The Irish were passionately fond of racing, even more so than those of the present day. Everywhere, in all sorts of Irish literature, we read of races—kings, nobles, and common people attending them at every opportunity.

---

* Cormac's Glossary, 53, " Dobur "; the Irish in Three Ir. Gloss., p. 15, " Dobur "   † Kilk. Archæol. Journ., 1870–1, p. 100, 6.

The prominence of this sport at the aenachs or fairs is indicated in Cormac's Glossary (p. 127) by one of his derivations of the word *oenach*, a fair, which he says signifies ' contention of horses '—as if racing was the main object of holding a fair. The popularity of the sport affected even the Law : for we find in the Senchus Mór a provision that young sons of kings and chiefs when in fosterage are to be supplied by the foster-fathers with horses in time of races.*

A passage in the " Story of the Second Battle of Moytura " affords another indication of the universality of racing, where it is related that certain visitors arriving at a meeting were asked had they hounds (*coin*) and steeds (*eich*) for races : " for "—the story goes on—" at that time " when a body of men went to another assembly [in a " strange country or district] it was the custom to challenge " them to a friendly contest." Then " the hounds had a " coursing match (*coin cocluiche*, ' hound contest ') and the " horses ran a race " : after which the men themselves engaged in friendly sword-play.† But perhaps the best illustration of the passionate admiration of people high and low for this sport is that it is represented as one of the delights of the pagan heaven, as described to Bran by the fairy lady :—" The hosts run races—a delightful game— " along the plain of sports, the plain on which they hold " games ; a delight to the eye it is to look upon—it is a " glorious sweep of country."‡ This shows, too, that one of the choice plains of heaven was specially set apart for sports. In the races held here there was moreover a variety, namely, races of curraghs on the water against chariots on the low-lying shore adjacent—" curragh con- tends against chariot "§—from which we may conclude that

---

* Br. Laws, II. 155.   † Rev. Celt., XII. 73.

‡ Kuno Meyer, in the Voyage of Bran, vol. I., p. 12, verse 23 ; and p. 4, verse 5. The " Plain of Sports " is *Mag Mon* in the original

§ Kuno Meyer, in the Voyage of Bran, vol. I., p. 4, verse 5.

this odd sort of race was also usual and popular in the mortal world above.   The common name for a race of any kind was *grafand* or *grafann* : plural *graifne* : *cur grafainn*, ' to run a race.'   But this word was most generally confined in its application to a horse-race.   Foot-racing does not appear to have been much practised.

The Curragh of Kildare, or as it was anciently called, the " Curragh of the Liffey " (*Cuirrech Lifè*) was, as it is still, the most celebrated racecourse in all Ireland : and there are numerous notices of its sports in annals and tales. In the Bruden Da Derga it is stated that Conari, king of Ireland in the first century of the Christian era, went once with four chariots to the *Cluichi* or games of the *Cuirrech Lifè*.   The races were held here in connexion with the yearly fair, which was called *Aenach Colmain* or *Aenach Lifè*, as being on the plain of the Liffey.   It was the great fair-meeting of the southern half of Ireland, and especially of the kings of Leinster, when they resided at the palace of Dun-Ailinn (now Knockaulin), which was on the edge, and which, being on a flat detached hill, overlooked the Curragh and its multitudes.   Though sports and pastimes of all kinds were carried on there, races constituted the special and most important feature : so that some of the annalists mention the Curragh under the name of " Curragh of the Races."*   The games here were formally opened by the king, or one of the princes, of Leinster, and lasted for several days : and the great importance attached to them is indicated in the " Will of Cahirmore " in which that king bequeaths to his son Criffan the " leadership of " [*i.e.* the privileges of opening and patronising] the games " of the province of Leinster."†

In Cormac's Glossary *cuirrech* is used as a general word for a racecourse, and derived from the Latin *cursus* : and the scholiast who annotated St. Broccan's hymn on

---

* See Three Fragm., 189, top line : see also FM, A.D. 825, note *n* ; and A.D. 940 and 954.   † Proc. Roy. Ir. Acad., IX. 348.

St. Brigit, referring directly to the Curragh of Kildare gives the same derivation.* showing at what an early time the Curragh was recognised as a racecourse. But it seems more likely that the Irish word *cuirrech* is merely cognate with Lat. *cursus*, and not derived from it. In the hymn itself St. Brigit is designated as " the nun who used to run over the Curragh " ; for her convent was on the edge of it, and no doubt she often drove over the beautiful smooth sward in her chariot.†

Numerous references to chariot-racing are met with in Irish literature. Cormac's Glossary in one place (p. 45) explains the word *cuirrich* by *fich-carpait*, the ' contest of a chariot ' [in a race]. During the first three centuries of the Christian era, chariot-racing was universal in Ireland ; and it was specially popular among the Red Branch Knights. Horse-racing was also very general, almost as much so indeed as racing with chariots. Maildune and his companions come to an island where they find gigantic people eagerly engaged in a horse-race.‡ The sport is alluded to in the ancient Notes on the Feilire of Aengus (p. 105, bot.), where a person striving to earn heaven by doing the will of God is compared to " a chariot that is driven under a king that bears off prizes." The Fena of Erin, as we have seen (vol. I., p. 89, *supra*), did not use chariots, either in battle or in racing ; but they were devoted to horse-racing ; and in many passages referring to them, their chiefs are represented as indulging in this sport.§

A racecourse (*céte* or *cét*) was sometimes in a king's *faithche* or exercise green : and the law in this case laid down rules as to how far the king was liable for accidents,

---

* Todd Book of Hymns, 67, note *j*.

† For much more on the Curragh, and on races, see Hennessy's Paper on " The Curragh of Kildare," Proc. Roy. Ir. Acad., vol. IX., p. 343.

‡ Old Celtic Romances, p. 122.

§ In the Story of Finn and the Phantoms, horse-races alone are carried on : no chariot-races : Rev. Celt. VII. 291.

and when he was exempt : which rules applied to the owners of other racecourses. Thus if accidental collisions occurred from which injury resulted, he was exempt : but he was responsible if injury was caused by a chasm or a deep rut carelessly left unprotected, or not filled up. And the Law follows up this by a series of detailed regulations about the liabilities of the several parties in case of accidents on a course.*

Coursing with greyhounds was another favourite amusement. We have already seen (p. 463) how Irish visitors at a meeting in a distant land were challenged to a coursing match ; which came off with victory for the Irish hounds. The greyhounds (*milchoin* : singular *milchu*) mentioned in Cormac's Glossary as being always found at *oenachs* or fair-meetings, were for coursing contests, as part of the games carried on at the fair. A passage in the Crith Gabhlach, setting forth the distribution of a king's duties among the days of the week, assigns Wednesday for enjoying himself " witnessing greyhounds coursing."†

6. *Chase and Capture of Wild Animals.*

Some wild animals were chased for sport, some for food, and some merely to extirpate them as being noxious : but it will be convenient to include all here in connexion with sports and pastimes.

Our legendary annals relate that the first colonists to Ireland lived by hunting, fowling, and fishing : and though this record is legend, it presents a true picture of the mode of subsistence in primitive times, when the country was nearly all covered with forest and bog, and there was little open land for either tillage or pasture. But even after much land had been cleared and the people had begun to keep herds and to grow food-crops, they continued to hunt, fowl, and fish with the three objects stated above. Every-

* Br. Laws, III. pp. 255–263.   † *Ibid.*, IV. 335, bottom.

where in our literature we meet with notices of hunting, and of various other methods by which wild animals were taken. The hunters led the chase chiefly on foot, with different breeds of hunting dogs, according to the animals to be chased. Maelfothartaig [Mailfoharty], the son of Ronan king of Leinster, visits the king of Scotland, who " had hounds for boars, hounds for deer, and hounds for hares."* The principal kinds of game were deer, wild pigs, badgers, otters, and wolves ; and hares and foxes were hunted with beagles for pure amusement. Pig-hunting was a favourite sport.

For the larger and more dangerous game, such as wild boars, wolves, and deer, the hunters employed wolfhounds and other breeds of large dogs ; and in the romantic literature we have many a passage describing the dangers of the chase, and the courage, skill, and swiftness of hunters and hounds. The tales also reflect the immense delight those observant and nature-loving people took in the chase and all its joyous accompaniments. While Finn rested on the hill of Knockainy in the County Limerick, his companions hunted on the plain beneath ; " and it was sweet music to " Finn's ear the cry of the long-snouted dogs as they routed " the deer from their covers and the badgers from their " dens ; the pleasant emulating shouts of the youths ; the " whistling and signalling of the huntsmen ; and the " encouraging cheers of the heroes, as they spread them-" selves through the glens and woods, and over the broad " green plain of Cliach."† Cailte and his companions once " heard the musical concert (coicedul) of three packs of " hounds hunting round the head of Sliabh Lugda."‡ In another passage a man asks Cailte what pack is it that they hear : " That "—replies Cailte—" is the melodious chase by beagles after the swift and gentle hares."§ Else-where Cailte describes the chase of " the heavy-sided, low-

* Rev. Celt., XIII. 376.
† Old Celtic Romances, 226.
‡ Stokes, Acallamh, p. 206.
§ Ibid., p. 260.

" bellied badgers : and behind the hunt they heard the
" shout of the gillies, and the swiftest of the boys, and
" the readiest of the warriors, and the men who were the
" straightest spear-shots, and the strong attendants who
" bore the heavy burdens." The same keen appreciation
of the chase and its concomitants has descended to
modern Irish sportsmen. The sweetest music in the
world to Daniel O'Connell's ear was the cry of the Kerry
beagles echoing among the woods and hills round Derry-
nane ; and in the modern Anglo-Irish ballad of " Reynard
the Fox " we are told how :—

> " Early next morning the woods they did resound
> With the echo of horns and the sweet cry of hounds."*

Most of the details of the manner of trapping deer we
learn from the Book of Aicill, in the third volume of the
Brehon Laws, chiefly from p. 449, to p. 459. They were
caught in a deep pit or pitfall (Irish *cuithe* or *cuithech*)
with a trap, and a *bir* or spear fixed firmly in a wooden
stock (Irish *cep*, pron. kep) in the bottom, point upwards ;
the whole gin concealed by a *brathlang* or light covering
of sods and brambles.† The spear either had a metallic
head or was merely a stake of hard wood with a sharp
point. Along with the spear there was in the pit a trap
of some kind, the construction of which we do not know,
called *airndil* or *airnil,* from which the spear was called
bir airnil (or *airndil*), literally ' spear of a trap,' or a ' spear
set for a trap.'‡ That this is the correct sense appears
further from Cormac's Glossary (p. 12), which derives
airndel from *air,* noble, and *indel* (now *innil*) a setting :—
" *air-indel,* a noble setting [of a trap] it is."

---

* This ballad and the air will be found in Joyce's Ancient Irish Music,
p. 50.

† *Cuithe*, Br. Laws, III. 452, $_{12}$: *Cuithech*, 272, $_6$ and Trip. Life, 186, $_{25}$,
where *brathlang*, ' a pit-cover,' is also used.

‡ See " Bir " in O'Dovovan's Supplement to O'Reilly : and Br. Laws,
III. 272, $_9$; and 452, $_3$.

The trap—which was also often called *cuichi**—appears to have been set independently of the spear with its stock—though they were beside each other in the pit—so that either spear or trap might be removed without stirring the other : which appears from the expression in the Book of Aicill :—" If the deer [has escaped after falling in and] has carried off the *spear-stock or the trap* out of its place." Spear and trap were both set in the same pit, so that the deer that fell in was pretty sure to be secured by either or both.

A passage in the Rennes Dinnsenchus giving the supposed origin of the name of the ancient district of Magh Cobha, in the present county Down, affords us some idea of how these traps acted :—" Coba [cova], the " *cuchaire* or trapper of Heremon [first Milesian king of " Ireland] son of Milesius : it is he that first prepared a " trap [*airrchis*] and a pit-fall [*cuithech*] in Erin : and he " himself put his foot in it to try if it was in trim, where- " upon his shinbone and his two forearms were fractured in " it : and his drinking-cup, after being emptied, fell down, " so that he died thereof [*i.e.* of the wound and thirst] : " whence is derived *Mag Coba*, Cova's plain."† This passage introduces a new name for a trap—*airrchis* : a word which is in a still older authority, Cormac's Glossary (p. 2, " Airches "), where it is explained " a trap or enclosure," and derived " *ab arceo*, because of its holding whatsoever is put in it." An ancient MS. quoted by O'Donovan, under this passage in the Glossary, states that an *airches* is a trap for catching wild hogs : but the passages just quoted from Cormac's Glossary and the Dinnsenchus show that the word was applied to a trap in general. The quotation by O'Donovan is interesting, however, as it shows that wild hogs were caught in traps as well as deer and other animals. We have already seen that wolves were caught in specially-constructed traps.

* Br. Laws, III. 456, 14 and 17.   † Stokes, in Rev. Celt., XVI. 44.

There were persons skilled in setting traps, following the occupation as a sort of trade, who either worked on their own account, or were employed by others : such a person was called a *cuchaire* or *cuthchaire* [cuh'ara], *i.e.* a trap-maker or ' trapper ' (from *cuichi*). A trapper was, sometimes at least, one of the officials in the employment of a king ; as in the case of Coba. Some trappers or hunters and their pitfalls are designated " lawful " and others " unlawful."* Both are taken into consideration in the Book of Aicill, which, in setting forth fines for damages, distinguishes carefully between them, but gives no explanation of the distinction : because, as in hundreds of other cases, all understood the terms at the time, so that no definition was needed. Probably some sort of license or authoritative legal sanction was prescribed, the possession of which constituted " lawfulness," and its absence " unlawfulness."

A deer-trap was obviously very dangerous to both people and cattle : and the Book of Aicill dwells minutely on the precautions that should be adopted and on the question of responsibility and damages in case of injuries from trap accidents. A deer-trap was generally set in a wild place—mountain, bog, or wood : but sometimes also in the *faithche* or green of the owner's residence, or between the green and the adjacent wild place. The law laid down that in all cases verbal notice should be sent over the nine holdings (*nae n-orba*) nearest to the place.† Sometimes when deer were observed hovering near, they were driven, so far as could be done, towards the trap ; and if they did any damage while being driven, either to the people or to domestic animals, the law provided compensation.‡ Adamnan (p. 154) gives an account of the setting of a sharpened stake in a place frequented by wild animals, on which a poor man caught many

---

* Br. Laws, III. 457. 273, II; 272, ∗   † On these points :—Br. Laws, III. 453 ; ‡ *Ibid.*, 457, bottom.

deer to feed his family. As confirming the preceding records, remains of deer-traps with their sharpened stakes are now often found buried deep in bogs in various parts of Ireland.*

Wooden traps of another kind, quite different from deer-traps, smaller and having no spear, all of much the same pattern, with doors or valves, springs, and triggers, are often found in bogs, of which the illustration (fig. 337) will give a good idea. There has been considerable

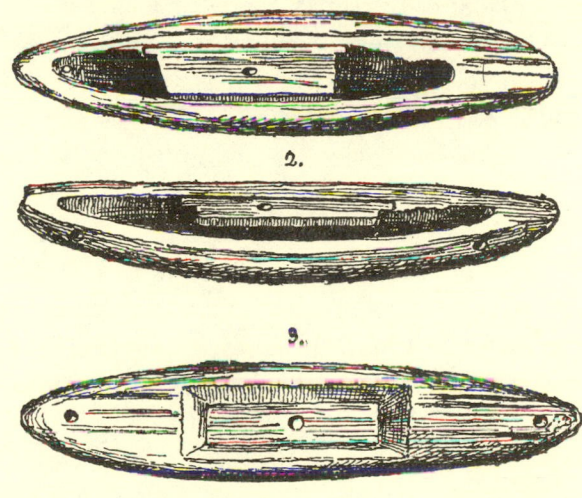

FIG. 337.

Three different views (top, side, bottom) of an otter-trap: found in a bog.
(From Wood-Martin's Pagan Ireland, p. 407.)

divergence of opinion regarding their exact use; but it is now generally considered that they were otter-traps: the animal, while attempting to force its way through, being caught and held by the edge of the door or valve.

There were traps and nets of several kinds to catch birds. The word *sás* [sauce], which means an engine or gin of any kind, is also applied to a bird-trap. A basket-shaped bird-crib, such as is used by boys at the

* Kilk. Archæol. Journ., 1879-82, p. 500, bottom. Mr. G. H. Kinahan has mentioned to me half a dozen places where he has seen the remains of old deertraps. See also his Geology of Ireland, p. 277.

present day, was called *cliabhán* [cleevaun], which is also
the word for a child's cradle: a diminutive of *cliabh*
[cleeve], a basket. A person very much frightened, or
cowardly, or unreliable in time of sudden danger, was
often compared to a bird on which a *sás* or a *cleevaun*
has closed, and also to a salmon caught in a weir-trap.
Cormac's Glossary (p. 152) explains the word *sén* [shain]
as ' a net in which birds are caught,' and illustrates it by
the derivative *sén-bretha*, ' bird-net laws ' : showing that
the practice of catching birds by nets was general ; and
that it was considered of such importance that special laws
were laid down to regulate it. Birds were also caught, as
they are still in the Orkneys and Hebrides, by men let down
in baskets with ropes over the cliffs round the coasts ;
as appears by several entries in the Brehon law-tract
called " Heptads."* O'Flaherty, in his " Iar Connaught "
(p. 67), states that, in his time, birds were caught in this
manner at night by persons who brought down candles,
the light of which fascinated the birds so that they were
easily taken. I have seen birds caught by night in bushes
by boys who carried lanterns : but of this practice I have
found no mention in old Irish literature.

Fish as an important article of food has been already
spoken of (p. 133, *supra*). The general Irish word for a
fish is *iasc* [eesk], cognate with Latin *piscis* and English
fish : and a fisherman was an *iascaire* [eeskerĕ : 3-syll.].
The people fished with the net and with hook and line,
both in the sea and in lakes and rivers : as the records
everywhere show. The *slatt* or fishing-rod was 10 or 12
feet long : the line was called *ruaim* [roo-im] or ruaimnech :
and the hook *duban* [dooan]. Net-fishing came under the
cognisance of the law ; it is mentioned in the Senchus Mór ;
and it appears from the gloss that a fishing-net was called
cochull and *lín* [leen], both words in use still. The net was
sometimes the common property of the *finĕ* or family

* Br. Laws, v. 237, 20; 239, 19; 301, 20·

group of relations, each individual family having a right to use it in turn, or a claim to a share of the fish caught. Both salmon and eels were often caught with trident spears, or with spears of more than three prongs : and sometimes people followed the primitive plan of trans-fixing large fish with a single-point spear. Eels are still caught with forked-spears : and until lately salmon were taken in a similar way, the trident spears having handles about 5 feet long and a cord attached at the end. The spear was flung from the bank with aim that seldom missed : and spear and salmon were drawn back by the cord (see vol. I., p. 112, for a fishing-spear).

Salmon-fishing was the most important of the fishing industries, and it is oftenest mentioned in the old writings : it is constantly noticed by Adamnan. A salmon is desig-nated by several Irish names :—*bratan, ae, eó, tonnem, orcc, éicne* [aiknĕ], and *linnĕ*, besides some others : but the first under the modern form *bradán*, is now the general name. It would seem that in old times *bratan* meant a young salmon, and *eó* a full-grown one : for we find this line in an ancient poem in the Book of Leinster :—" It is from the *bratan* that the *eó* comes : it is from the youth that the king comes."*

Fishing-weirs on rivers were very common. The weir (called in Irish *corad* and *sod*) sometimes belonged to an individual, and sometimes—like the net—it was the common property of the *finĕ*. A man who had land adjoining the stream had the right to construct a weir for his own use : but according to law, he could not dam the stream more than one-third across, so that the fish might have freedom to pass up or down to the weirs belonging to others. If it was found that his dam went more than this, he had to give up two-thirds of the fish he caught to the wronged man, whether living above or below.†

* LL, 148, *a*, 16; " Contents," 34, *a*, 26.
† On all this see Br. Laws, I. 131, 6, 7; 205, 207 IV 211, bottom; 213, 13.

7. *Camán or Hurling, and other athletic games.*

Hurling or goaling has been a favourite game among the Irish from the earliest ages ; and those who remember the eagerness with which it was practised in many parts of Ireland sixty years ago, can well attest that it had not declined in popularity. Down to a recent period it was carried on with great spirit and vigour in the Phœnix Park, Dublin, where the men of Meath contended every year against the men of Kildare. It still continues, though less generally than formerly, to be a favourite pastime, and there is lately a movement to revive it.

Our literature gives us many glimpses of the manner of carrying on this game in old times. It was played with a ball (*liathróid* : pronounced leeroad) about four inches in diameter, made of some light elastic material, such as woollen yarn wound round and round, and covered with leather. Each player had a wooden hurley to strike the ball, generally of ash, about three feet long, carefully shaped and smoothed, with the lower end flat and curved. This was called *camán* [commaun], a diminutive from *cam*, curved : but in old writings we find another name, *lorg* (*i.e.* ' staff '), also used. The game was called *immán*, or in modern spelling *iomán* [immaun], meaning ' driving ' or ' urging ' : but now commonly *camán*, from the *camán* or hurley. In a regular match the players on each side were equal in number. It was played on a level grassy field, at each end of which was a narrow gap (*berna*) or goal, formed by two poles or bushes, or it might be a gap in the fence. The general name for the winning goal was *báire* [bawrĕ]. The play was commenced by throwing up the ball in the middle of the field : the players struck at it with their hurleys, the two parties in opposite directions towards the gaps ; and the game, or part of it, was ended when one party succeeded in driving it through their opponents' gap. It was usual for each party to station

one of their most skilful men beside their own gap to
intercept the ball in case it should be sent flying direct
towards it : this man was said to stand *cúl* [cool], or *cúl-
báire*, 'rear-guard' : *cúl* meaning back.   The preceding
description shows generally how the game was played
down to a period within my own memory ; and so far as
can be judged from the old literature, it was much the
same a thousand years ago.   In old times the field on
which the game was played was commonly the *faithche*
[faha] or green of the dwelling (p. 61, *supra*) : but sometimes a large level space was railed off for games of all
kinds, which was called *cluichi mag*, 'game-plain,' or
mag-mon, 'plain of sports.'

The law required that the sons of kings and chiefs
in fosterage should have their camans mounted or ornamented—or perhaps ringed—with bronze or brass.*   These
bronze-mounted hurleys were valuable, as we may infer
from a record in the annals, that on one occasion Feradach,
king of Ossory towards the end of the sixth century,
collected into one place all his valuable and precious
things—his ingots of silver, ornamented cups, &c.—among
which are enumerated his *camáin creduma*, 'hurleys of
bronze '—that is to say, mounte ' with bronze.†

Provision was made in the Brehon Law for compensation in case of accident by either ball or hurley ; and
in the statements of these rules in the Book of Aicill we
come across other features of the game.   A player is
mentioned as " striking the ball (*liathróid*) with his hurley
" (*lorg*), from the hurling hole (*poll na h-imána*) to the
" place of the *grifid*—or from the place of the *grifid* to the
" place of the division (*comrann*)—or from the hole (*poll*)
" where it [the ball, then] is until it reaches the place where
" it usually lies."‡   Some of these terms and details are
unintelligible to me.

* Br. Laws, II. 147.   † Three Fragments, p. 9.
‡ Br Laws, III. 555.

Hurling is often mentioned in the tales. Cuculainn, when a boy, going to Emain to visit his uncle King Concobar, took with him his playthings to shorten the road, among them *a cammán creduma ocus a liathróit n-argdide*, " his hurley of bronze and his ball of silver."[*] In the tale of the Destruction of Dinnree (see p. 95, *supra*), it is related that Moen Ollam, afterwards Labrad Loingsech (king of Ireland before the Christian era), when a boy, was dumb. But one day as he was playing *immán* in the playgreen, he got a blow of a hurley on the shin, which gave him such a paroxysm of agony that he shouted out and spoke for the first time ; and ever after that he retained his speech.[†] It may be inferred from the careful provisions laid down in the law that the game sometimes resulted in injuries, generally by accident, but occasionally by design, in rare cases ending even in death : and in this respect, too, it resembled the game of our own day. But the mischief was seldom serious.

Various other athletic exercises were practised, some of them like those we see at the present day. We find foot-racing and leaping mentioned, but much prominence is not given to them in the tales. There were contentions in wrestling and swimming. The boys of the Red Branch had a rough sort of game, in which each set strove to tear off the outer garments from their opponents ; and they had another, something analogous to goaling, where they endeavoured to put a ball through a small hole, which those opposed to them tried to prevent.[‡] There was also the " loop and ball game " (*cluiche lúibe ocus liathróidi,*) which was played on the green ; but nothing is said in the tales as to the manner of playing it.[§] What was called the *Roth-chless*, or ' wheel-feat,' consisted in throwing a heavy circular disc or quoit upwards beside the wall of a

---

[*] LL, 62, *a*, ₄₅: Miss Hull, Saga, p. 136.
[†] Stokes's edition, Zeitschr. Celt. Phil., III. p. 10
[‡] Miss Hull, Saga, 138, 139 ; LL, 63, *a*, bottom.
[§] See Kuno Meyer, Ventry, 29, line 530 ; and p. 82, note 529.

large house.   At this the three great Red Branch heroes once contended inside the lofty hall.   Laegaire the Victorious took the first trial and sent the disc half way up the side wall.   Conall Cernach next : and he threw it to the ridge-pole.   Lastly, Cuculainn caught it in mid-air as it came down after Conall's throw, and with a mighty effort hurled it right through the roof, amid the frantic shouts of the spectators.*   Throwing a ball or quoit to a distance, and " putting " a heavy stone forward from hand and shoulder—both of which are noticed in the tales—were in no wise different from the corresponding strength trials of the present day.

8. *Chess.*

In ancient Ireland chess-playing was a favourite pastime among the higher classes.   Everywhere in the Romantic Tales we read of kings and chiefs amusing themselves with chess, and to be a good player was considered a necessary accomplishment of every man of high position.   At banquets and all other festive gatherings this was sure to be one of the leading features of the entertainment.   In every chief's house there was accordingly at least one set of chess appliances for the use of the family and guests : and chess-boards were sometimes given as part of the tribute to kings.†   Chess furniture was indeed considered in a manner a necessity, so much so that in this respect it is classified in the Brehon Law with food.‡

As to the general form and construction of the chess-board there can be no doubt, for Cormac's Glossary (p. 75) describes it with much exactness.   This old authority states first, in regard to the game, that the play demands *ciall* and *fáth* [keeal, faw], *i.e.* attention and judgment : and it goes on to say that the *fidchell* or chess-board was divided into black and white compartments by straight lines : that

* Fled Bricr., 83.   † Book of Rights, 39.   ‡ Br Law, I. 143, 12.

is to say, into black and white squares. The game was called *fidchell* or *fidchellecht* [fihel, fihelleght] : and *fidchell* was used to designate the chess-board. But this was also called *clár-fidchilli*, *clár* being the general name for a board or table. The chessmen were called *fir-fidchilli*, i.e. ' men of chess,' or collectively *foirenn*, which is the Irish word for a party or body of men in general. The whole set of furniture was called *fidchellecht*,* or *fidchell*.

The men, when not in use, were kept in a *fer-bolg* or ' man-bag,' which was sometimes of brass or bronze wire woven. The chiefs took great delight in ornamenting their chessboards and men richly and elaborately with the precious metals and gems. We read in the " Story of the Battle of Mucrime," that when the Irish chief Mac Con was an exile in disguise at the court of the king of Scotland, the king's chessmen were of gold and silver : meaning ornamented with these metals.† The following quotation from a much older authority—the " Courtship of Etain " in the Book of the Dun Cow—is very instructive and very much to the point. Midir the fairy king of Bri-leith, comes on a visit to King Ochy :—" What brought thee hither ? " said Ochy. " To play chess with thee," answered Midir. " Art thou good at chess ? " said Ochy. " Let us try it," said Midir. " The queen is asleep," said Ochy, " and the house in which are the chessboard and men belongs to her." " Here I have as good a set of chess," said Midir. That was true indeed ; for it was a board of silver and pure gold ; and every angle was illuminated with precious stones ; and the man-bag was of woven brass wire."‡ In the Will of Cahirmore, king of Ireland in the second century, we are told that he bequeathed his chessboard and chessmen to his son Olioll Ceadach§—an indication of their great value.

<hr />

* Book of Rights, 201, 17.

† Silva Gad., 351 : see also Keating, 290, top ; and FM, A.D. 9.

‡ See O'Donovan, in Book of Rights, Pref., lxi   § Book of Rights, 201.

The men were distinguished half and half, in some obvious way, to catch the eyes of the two players. Sometimes they were black and white. The *foirenn* or party of chessmen of Crimthan Nia Náir, king of Ireland about the first century of the Christian era, are thus described:—
" One-half of its *foirenn* was yellow gold, and the other half was *findruine* " (white bronze).* Many ancient chessmen have been found in bogs, in Lewis and other parts of Scotland: but so far as I know we have only a single specimen belonging to Ireland, which was found about 1817 in a bog in Meath, and which is now in the National Museum, Dublin. It is figured here, full size. We frequently read in the tales that a hero, while playing chess, becoming infuriated by some sudden attack or insulting speech, flings his chessman at the enemy and kills or disfigures him.

FIG. 338.

Bone Chessman, King, full size; found in a bog in Meath about 1817. (Drawn by Petrie: Book of Rights, page lxii.)

When we remember that chessmen were sometimes made partly of metal and were two and a half inches long, we may well believe this.

The game must, sometimes at least, have been a long one. When St. Adamnan came to confer with King Finachta, he found him engaged in a game of chess: but when his arrival was announced, the king, being aware that he had come on an unpleasant mission, refused to see him till his game was finished: whereupon Adamnan said

* Rev. Celt., xx. 283.

he would wait, and that he would chant fifty psalms during the interval, in which fifty there was one psalm that would deprive the king's family of the kingdom for ever. The king finished his game however; and played a second, during which fifty other psalms were chanted, one of which doomed him to shortness of life. But when he was threatened with deprivation of heaven by one of the third fifty, he yielded, and went to Adamnan.*

That the Irish retained the tradition of the origin of chess as a mimic battle appears from the name given to the chessmen in the story of the Sick Bed of Cuculainn (p. 99) in the Book of the Dun Cow :—namely *fianfidchella*, i.e. as translated by O'Curry, ' *chess-warriors* '; *fian*, a champion or warrior : from which we may infer that the men represented soldiers.

Another game called *brannuighecht*, or ' *brann*-playing,' as O'Donovan renders it, is often mentioned in connexion with chess ; and it was played with a *brannabh*, possibly something in the nature of a backgammon board. A party of Dedannans were on one occasion being entertained ; and a *fidchell* or set of chess furniture was provided for every six of them, and a *brannabh* for every five,† showing that chess-playing and *brann*-playing were different, and were played with different sets of appliances. Among the treasures of the old King Feradach are enumerated his *brandaibh* and his *fithchella*.‡ The Brehon Law prescribes *fithchellacht* and *brannuidhecht* (as two different things) with several other accomplishments, to be taught to the sons of chiefs when in fosterage.§ Notwithstanding that chess-playing and *brann*-playing are so clearly distinguished in the above and many other passages, modern writers very generally confound them : taking *brannuighecht* to be only another name for *fitchellecht* or chess-playing, which it is not.

---

* Silva Gad., 422.

† *Ibid.*, 250 : Ir. text, 220, 50.

‡ Three Fragments, 8, 12.

§ Br Laws, II. 155, 9; 157, bottom.

There is still another game called *buanbaig* or *buanfach*, mentioned in connexion with chess and *brann*-playing, as played by kings and chiefs. When Lugaid mac Con and his companions were fugitives in Scotland, they were admired for their accomplishments, among them being their skilful playing of chess, and *brandabh*, and *buanbaig*.* Nothing has been discovered to show the exact nature of those two last games.

I have headed this short section with the name "Chess," and have all through translated *fitchell* by ' chess,' in accordance with the usage of O'Donovan, O'Curry, and Petrie. Dr. Stokes, on the other hand, uniformly renders it " draughts." But, so far as I am aware, there is no internal evidence in Irish literature sufficient to determine with certainty whether the game of *fitchell* was chess or draughts : for the descriptions would apply equally to both.

9. *Jesters, Jugglers, and Gleemen.*

From the most remote times in Ireland, kings kept fools, jesters, and jugglers in their courts, for the amusement of their household and guests, like kings of England and other countries in much later times. In the tales we constantly read of such persons and their sayings and doings. They were often kept in small companies. Prince Cummasgach, son of Aed mac Ainmirech (king of Ireland, A.D. 572 to 598), had one chief jester named Glasdám, under whom were eight others ; and the whole nine constantly accompanied the prince, forming part of his retinue both at home and on his journeys.†

The most common name for a jester or fool was *drúth* (pron. droo : to be carefully distinguished from *drui*, a druid), which is explained in Cormac's Glossary (p. 59), by *onmit*, a fool, and in another place in the same Glossary

* O'Grady, Silva Gad., 351, top : Ir. text, 312, ₃₀, ₃₁: Revue Celt.
XIII. 443 † Rev. Celt., III. 59 : Silva Gad., 409.

(130) by *midlach*, an imbecile. Another word was *mer*, which generally means a mad person, but which, like *onmit* and *midlach*, appears to have been often used to denote simply an idiot or mental imbecile ; while *drúth* was used as a more general term to include all sorts of fools, buffoons, jugglers, jesters, &c. *Mer* and *drúth* are sometimes used synonymously, as in the Book of Aicill.* The Law (III. 157, 23) fixed seven years as the age when it was to be decided whether a young person was or was not a *drúth*, which here must be understood to have the restricted meaning of an idiot. In Cormac's Glossary (p. 81) *faindelach* is given as still another name for an idiot.

In the *Senchus Mór* the customary functions of a *drúth* are indicated :—He is said to have the power of amusing, and that music was one of the means he employed to do so : for he was a minstrel (*airfidig*) ; and it also states that he had land—at least sometimes—no doubt in reward of his services : while a woman who was a *mer* or mad person was not a minstrel, and had no land.† From a legend given in Duald Mac Firbis's Irish Annals we learn that a *drúth* was trained to give a particular kind of shout, which was easily distinguished from the shout of all other people. At the Battle of Allen in Kildare, fought A.D. 722, the *ríg-drúth* or royal clown O'Maileeny was taken prisoner and beheaded. But just before his execution he was asked to give a "*drúth's* shout," which he did : and it was so loud and melodious that its soft echoes were heard in the air for three days and three nights after his death.‡ And ever afterwards all *drúths* learned to give " a clown's shout," like that of poor O'Maileeny.

These half-witted dependents were always greatly attached to their masters, whose lives, as occasions arose, they sometimes saved by the sacrifice of their own In

* Br. Laws, III. 199, bottom ; 200, 2. † *Ibid.*, i. 137, bottom ; 139, top.
‡ Three Fragments, 43 : and Rev. Celt., XXIV. 55.

the year 598 A.D., Prince Cummascach—as the Story of the Boroma relates—went through Leinster on his " Free circuit of youth." His conduct was on the occasion so intolerably licentious that Branduff, king of Leinster, and his people, at last rose up in a fury and set fire to the house in which the prince and his retinue were feasting, standing all around in close array to prevent escape. Glasdám, the prince's jester, was one of the doomed company : but as he had been hospitably entertained a few days before by Branduff, he now cried out :—" Lo, I " have eaten thy meat : let not this deed of shame be now " wrought on me ! "* And Branduff answered :—" By no " means shall this be done : climb up to the ridge-pole and " leap out over the flames to the ground : we will let thee " pass, and thus shalt thou escape ! " But Glasdám refused to be saved without his master : and tearing off his fool's mantle and cap, while the flames were closing in, he said to Cummascach :—" Take these and escape in guise of me ! " The prince put them on, and, leaping out, was allowed to pass, so that he escaped for the time, while the poor fool remained behind and was burned to death with the rest.†

Fools when acting as professional clowns were dressed fantastically ; and they amused the people something in the same way as the court fools and buffoons of later times—by broad impudent remarks, jests, half witty, half absurd, and odd gestures and grimaces. Concobar's royal fool *Róimid*, who lived in Emania, is thus described in the Story of *Mesca Ulad* as he stood amusing a delighted crowd who surrounded him :—He had a black, pointed, thick head of hair ; his face [painted] a bluish-black, like an Ethiopian ; his eyes were large, wide open, and seemed

---

* For the duty of host towards guest, see p. 168, *supra*.

† O'Grady, Silva Gad., 410 : Stokes's version in Rev. Celt., XIII. 33. Two other equally striking instances may be seen in the story of the jester of Fiachna, king of Ulster (Silva Gad., 427), and that of Mac Con's *druth* at the Battle of Cenn Febrat (Silva Gad., 349, 350).

all white [on account of the blackened face] ; he wore a ribbed *bratt* or mantle all in folds, fastened with a brass clasp at his breast : at his side hung a melodious little bell (*cluicín ceólbind*) which he often struck with a bronze wand to procure attention, making such a sweet tinkle that it gave pleasure and delight to the arch-king and to the whole host. He was a laughable and amusing wight—adds, the old account—and there was no care, fatigue, or sorrow, however great, that a man would not forget for the time, while looking at this droll fellow and listening to his pleasantries.* King Conari's three jesters were such surpassingly funny fellows that, as we are told in the Bruden Da Derga (where they are called *cuitbi*, i.e. jeerers, gibers, mockers), no man could refrain from laughing at them, even though the dead body of his father or mother lay stretched out before him.†

Professional gleemen travelled from place to place earning a livelihood by amusing the people like travelling showmen of the present day. To these the word *drúth* is sometimes applied, though their more usual name was *crossan*, a word which glosses *scurra* in Stokes's " Glosses on Latin Declension," No. 14. When they had given an exhibition it was considered disgraceful to refuse them a contribution : and even St. Patrick, as we are told in the Tripartite Life (205), thought it necessary to comply with this native custom. When he was in Hy Fidgente he was entertained by a chief named Lomman, living beside Mullach-Cae, *i.e.* the mountain now called Knockea, and having his house on a spot lying, as the old record correctly states, to the south of Carn-Feradaig, which is now called Seefin Mountain, rising over the village of Glenosheen in Limerick. One day a number of gleemen came up and asked for some food. Patrick was troubled at this, for he had nothing to give them : but just at the moment a boy

---

* Mesca Ulad, 35.   † O'Curry, Man. & Cust., ii. 150 : Da Derga, p. 311.

passed near with a cooked ram on his back, which the saint asked from him " to save his honour "—*i.e.* that he might not lie under the reproach of refusing the gleemen. The boy gave it gladly, and Patrick handed it over to them ; but before they had time to swallow it they were themselves swallowed up by the earth for their impudence. In the first part of this narrative the gleemen are called *aes ceirdd*, i.e. ' men of art ' : at the end they are designated by *druth* : and in another part of it they are called in Latin *præcones*, i.e. ' public criers,' from their custom of bawling out their jokes. These " men of art " were evidently of the same class as those called *crossans*, who are constantly met with in the tales.

A travelling band of *crossans* had a *fuirseóir* or *obláire* [furshore, oblairĕ], *i.e.* the chief buffoon and juggler of the company. When the sons of O'Corra were about to embark on their voyage of pilgrimage, a band of *crossans* came up and inquired among themselves who they were. " I know them well," said the *fuirseoir* ; " they are the sons " of O'Corra, the robbers and murderers, going on their " pilgrimage : and indeed they do not stand more in need " of it than we do." " I fancy "—said the leader of the band, scoffingly—" it is a long day till you go on a pilgrimage." " Never say so," replied the *fuirseoir*, " for I will certainly go with them " : and so he did. From the same narrative it is clear that they wore dresses of some special sort, which belonged, not to the individuals but to the company : and that if any member left the party he had to leave his dress behind him, as the *fuirseoir* had to do on the present occasion, for they stripped him and sent him off to the pilgrims stark naked.* We may form some idea of one part of the dress from the statement in Mac Conglinne (42), that when he disguised himself as a *fuirseoir*, " he put on a short cloak and short garments :

* Joyce, Old Celtic Romances, p. 409.

" each upper garment being shorter with him, and each
" lower one being longer.   In this wise he began juggling."
See also the description of Roimid's mantle, p. 484, *supra*.

Cormac's Glossary (p. 141, explains the word *réim*
by *fuirseóir*, i.e. buffoon, and does it in such a way as
to give us a peep at one of the buffoon's tricks :—
" *Réim*, the name for a *fuirseoir*, on account of the
" distortions of face he makes towards people " [to make
them laugh].   In the Crith Gabhlach the word is explained similarly :—" *Reimm*, i.e. a *fuirseóir* or a *drúth*,
" a man who brings distortion (*remmad*) upon his body
" and his face, is not entitled to *dire* fine (Br. Laws, vol. I.,
" p. 208), because he goes out of his own shape before
" hosts and crowds."*

There was a *drúth* of a different kind from all those
noticed above, a hand-juggler—a person who performed
sleight-of-hand tricks.   Such a person was called a *cless-
amnach* [classownagh], *i.e.* a ' trick-performer,' from *cless*,
a trick.   In the Bruden Da Derga King Conari's *cless-
amnach* and his trick of throwing up balls and other small
articles, catching them one by one as they came down,
and throwing them up again, are well described :—" The
" blemish of baldness was on him, and the hair on the rest
" of his head was whiter than *canach-slebhe*—canavan or
" cotton grass ; he had clasps (*unasca*) of gold in his ears
" (p. 259,) *supra*) ; and he wore a speckled white cloak.   He
" had nine [short] swords, nine [small] silvern shields, and
" nine balls of gold.   [Taking up a certain number of
" them] he flung them up one by one, and not one of them
" does he let fall to the ground, and there is but one of
" them at any one time in his hand.   Like the buzzing-
" whirl of bees on a beautiful day was their motion in
" passing one another."†   This man seems to have been

---

* Br. Laws, IV. 355, top : see also to the same effect, v. 109, ₇, from
bottom.

† Man. & Cust., II. 144, 145 ; Da Derga, p. 286.

the chief juggler ; for three others are afterwards described, having a number of small balls and of small darts, for performing similar tricks with.*

The Brehon Law lays down fines for injuries to spectators by the careless performance of juggling tricks : and in assessing damages it distinguishes between dangerous articles such as knives, and non-dangerous ones such as balls. The fine for injury was heavier if inflicted by dangerous than if by non-dangerous articles—even though the injury might be the same : which of course was intended to ensure that due care should be taken during the performances.†

It is worthy of remark that the gleemen continued till the time of Elizabeth. Spenser (View, 125) describes them :—" To these may be added another sort of like " loose fellowes, which doe passe up and downe amongst " gentlemen, by the name of Jesters " : and he goes on to say that they were great collectors and carriers of news.

People of all the above classse, *crossans*, *drúths*, jesters, tumblers, distortionists, and soforth, were looked upon as dishonoured and disreputable. This appears from the passage quoted on last page, where we see they were denied certain civil rights enjoyed by ordinary citizens ; and still more pointedly from an ordinance of the Senchus Mór, which, classifying banquets into godly, human, and demon banquets, defines demon banquets as those given to evil people, such as satirists, jesters, buffoons, mountebanks, outlaws, heathens, harlots, and bad people in general.‡ And many other passages in Irish literature might be quoted to the same effect.

* Man. & Cust., ii. 147.   † Br. Laws, iii. 285.
‡ Br. Laws, iii. 25

Ornament on top of Devenish Round Tower. (From Petrie's Round Towers, 400.)

CHAPTER XXX

VARIOUS SOCIAL CUSTOMS AND OBSERVANCES

SECTION I. *Salutation.*

OME of the modes of salutation and of showing respect practised by the ancient Irish indicate much gentleness and refinement of feeling, while others would now be considered degrading. When a distinguished visitor arrived it was usual to stand up as a mark of respect (*uréirge, coiméirge*, rising, or standing up). King Laegaire, sitting with his courtiers, in his council-hall at Tara to receive St. Patrick, ordered that no one should rise when he entered : but Dubthach Maccu Lugair, the king's chief poet, impressed by the saint's commanding presence, disobeyed the order and stood up as he entered. The narrative adds that this Dubthach became a convert, and thenceforward devoted his poetical talents to the service of God.* Mael Fothartaigh, son of Ronan king of Leinster, was so admired and loved, that at meetings of every kind " all would rise up before him."†　St. Molling, on a certain occasion, visited the house of Finaghta the Festive king of Ireland, but was received in a disrespectful manner by the company in general :—" He " found no uprising there [in honour of him] : and he was

<hr>

* Trip .Life, 283.　　† Kuno Meyer's Fingal Ronain, Rev. Celt., XIII. 372.

" ashamed at not getting uprising."* It was not only a mark of respect, but—occasionally at least—something like an acknowledgment of superiority, as we may infer from a passage in the Irish Life of St. Finnchua. The saint having aided the king of Munster to defeat his enemies, stipulated that among other concessions " the king " of Munster should always stand up before Finchua's " successor "† : and still more clearly from the Crith Gabhlach extract given below, about a king and a bishop.

Another mode of saluting to show respect was " raising the knee or thigh " while seated. On the occasion of the above-mentioned visit of St. Molling, while no one actually stood up, Dermot the son of Colcu " raised his knee before him "—as did also his father Colcu—as a mark of reverence. St. Ruadan, when cursing Tara, says to King Dermot :— " The thigh (*sliasait*) that thou liftest not before me to stand up, be it mangled in pieces."‡ Lifting the knee or thigh was not so great a mark of respect as standing up. In the Crith Gabhlach the question is asked, " Which is higher, a king or a bishop ? " Answer : " The bishop is " higher, because the king stands up [to salute him] on " account of religion " : and the sentence concludes—" a bishop however raises his knee to a king."§ This lifting of the knee or thigh admits of an obvious explanation. A person sitting on a low seat—as the Irish generally sat—when about to stand up, naturally drew in one foot, which had the effect of raising the knee. So far this of itself was regarded as a mark of respect, being a preliminary to standing up : but to stand up altogether completed and increased the act of reverence.

Giving a kiss, or more generally three kisses, on the cheek, was a very usual form of respectful and affectionate

---

* Silva Gad., 420, bottom. See also, HyF, 143, 7.
† Stokes, Lives of SS., 241, 17.
‡ See Silva Gad., 74, 1 (thigh) ; 83, 9 (knee).
§ Br. Laws, IV. 339, bottom.

salutation : it was indeed the most general of all. When St. Columba approached the assembly at Drum-ketta, " King Domnall rose immediately before him, and bade " him welcome, and kissed his cheek, and set him down " in his own place."* When Donnchad the son of King Concobar visited Conall Cernach, " Conall put his arms about his neck and gave him three kisses." Similar entries are found everywhere, both in the tales and in the ecclesiastical writings, showing that the practice was as prevalent among Christians as among pagans.

A very pleasing way of showing respect and affection, which we often find noticed, was laying the head gently on the person's bosom. When Erc, King Concobar's grandson, came to him, " he placed his head on the breast of his grandfather."† The old man Cailte, rising up in the morning, came to St. Patrick and laid his head on his bosom : and Patrick blessed him and said : " In whatsoever place God shall lay His hand on thee, heaven is in store for thee."‡ Adamnan (pp. 35, 36) notices this custom, where he relates that King Aedan's son, Ochy Boy, saluted St. Columba respectfully by laying his head on his bosom. Sometimes persons bent the head and went on one knee to salute a superior§ : and in case of eminent saints, laymen often prostrated themselves on the two knees before them : to show both respect and affection.‖

It seems an odd way of manifesting respect for a man, to carry him on one's back for some distance : yet it was in this manner Muiredach, king of Leinster in the sixth century, acted towards St. Finnen of Clonard. Finnen had spent some time in Britain, and returning to Ireland, landed on the Leinster coast ; whereupon the king went down to meet him, and to show reverence carried him on

---

* Adamnan, 38, note, 1st column   ‡ Silva Gad., 137, middle.
† Rossnaree, 55.   § *Ibid.*, 298.
        ‖ Stokes, Lives of SS., lines 381, 2929, 4348, 4693.

his back three several times across three fields near the harbour. Yet this over-condescension on the part of the king was evidently resented by some of his household; for one of them made a sharp remark to the saint: " Thou art oppressive, O cleric, on the king " : on which Finnen replied : " The number of times that I have been " taken on his back will be the number of kings of his race " over the province " ; after which he pronounced a blessing on him.* It somewhat mitigates the humiliation of the king's action here when we know that carrying on the back was not unusual. Some of the early saints had in their household a *fer-imchuir* (' man of carrying ') or *tréin-fher* (' strong-man ') for carrying them over fords or rough places. St. Patrick's " strong-man " has been already mentioned : and St. Ciaran's *fer-imchuir* was Mailoran. When St. Patrick was a boy his foster-father carried him home on his back ; and a man brings his sick mother on his back to St. Brigit to be healed.

In the Life of St. Cormac in the Book of Lecan we are told that a certain chief named Dai " came and put his mouth to the floor out of humility to Cormac."† When St. Patrick visited Moylurg in Connaught, Bishop Maine " drove the [saint's] horses into a meadow, and cleansed their hoofs in honour of Patrick."‡

2. *Pledging, Lending, and Borrowing.*

Although there were no such institutions in ancient Ireland as pawn-offices, pledging articles for a temporary loan was common enough. The practice was such a general feature of society that the Brehon Law took cognisance of it, and stepped in to prevent abuses. The Law did not prohibit charging interest on loans, though laws with this object existed in England, in supposed conformity with the Mosaic dispensation (Exod., xxii. 25).

---

* Stokes, Lives of SS., p. 224.   † Stokes, Lives of SS., p. 343.
‡ Trip. Life, 145.

The Brehon Law, though laying down many precautions, did not contain any provision against usurious or excessive rates of interest : neither did early English law : for the British usury laws are of late introduction.

Portable articles of any kind—including animals—might be pledged for a loan, or as security for the repayment of a debt ; and the law furnishes a long list of pledgable articles. The person holding the pledge might put it to its proper use while in his possession, unless there was express contract against it. But he was to use reasonably—he was not to injure articles of household or of ornament by rough usage, or a horse by overwork. He was moreover obliged to return the pledge on receiving a day's notice, provided the borrower tendered the sum borrowed, or the debt, with its interest : and if he failed to do so he was liable to fine. Suppose it was an ornament of gold or silver, such as a brooch ; and that it was not returned at the time required, so that the owner had to appear at any public function or celebration, such as a fair, without it : in this case the fine for withholding it was increased by a personal or honour fine for the indignity he suffered by being obliged to appear in public without his ornament.* If the pledged article was lost, or not returned, the value—and in some cases double the value—had to be made good.

Sometimes a person borrowed an article on hire for the use of it, engaging to return it by a certain day. If he failed to return it at the proper time, besides what he gave for the use of it, he had to pay interest (*tairgilli*) on it for every day he withheld it. When a man lent an article without any charge—for mere kindness—fixing a day for its return, if it was not returned on the stipulated day, the borrower might be charged interest for it.

There were distinct terms for all these transactions. A loan for kindness was called *óin* : a loan for interest was

---

* Br. Laws, v. 397, bottom.

airlecad : a loan in general was *iasacht*.   Interest or usury
was called *tairgilli*, and also *fogaibthetu*, a very old term,
for it occurs in Zeuss, as noticed below.   Borrowing or
lending, on pledge, was a very common transaction among
neighbours ; and it was not looked upon as in any sense
a thing to be ashamed of, as pawning articles is at the
present day.   The practice moreover continued in use in
Ireland down to comparatively recent times : of which
an instance, occurring in the beginning of the eighteenth
century, may be seen in the Kilk. Archæol. Journal for
1856–7, pp. 168, 169.

It may be observed that the existence in ancient
Ireland of the practice of pledging and lending for
interest, the designation of the several functions by
different terms, and the recognition of all by the Brehon
Law, may be classed, among numerous other customs and
institutions noticed throughout this book, as indicating a
very advanced stage of civilisation.   At what an early
period this stage—of lending for interest—was reached
may be seen from the fact that the MS. from which Zeuss
took *fogbaidetu*, ' usura,' is the Wurzburg copy of St. Paul's
Epistles which was glossed by some Irish monk in the
eighth century.*

3. *Provision for Old Age and Destitution.*

Old age was greatly honoured, and provision was made
for the maintenance of old persons who were not able to
support themselves.   The Brehon Law says :—" Age is
rewarded by the Féine " : and " where there are two chiefs
" of the same family who are of equal dignity and property,
" the senior shall take precedence.   The old man is entitled

---

* *Fogbaidetu*, for *fogaibthetu*, is in the 1st edition of Zeuss, p. 844, last
line : but Ebel has omitted it in his 2nd edition.   Nearly all the regulations regarding borrowing and pledging given in this section, as well as
many others, will be found in Br. Laws, III. 492, and note 3 ; 493, and
495 : and in O'Curry, Man. & Cust., II. 62, III, 112, 113.

" to good maintenance, and the senior is entitled to noble
" election."* The scribe who copied this part of the Law
prefixes a remark of his own which expresses still more
strongly the veneration for age :—[I swear] " by this book
" that so far as I can, I will, in the name of God, bring the
" senior before the junior in every case, as these laws down
" here state."

When the head of a family became too old to manage
his affairs, it was an arrangement sanctioned by the Law
that he might retire, and give up both headship and land
to his son, on condition of being maintained for the rest of
his life. In this case, if he did not choose to live with his
son, a separate house—commonly called a house of *inchis*
—was built for him, the dimensions and furniture of which,
as well as the dimensions of the little kitchen-garden,
are set forth in the law. Three items of maintenance are
distinguished and carefully specified :—food, milk, and
attendance. As to attendance : among other things it is
worth while to mention that he was to have a bath once
at least every twentieth night, and his head was to be
washed every Saturday. His supply of firewood is also
specified.†

If the old man had no children he might make over
his property to a stranger on the same condition of due
maintenance. Or he might purchase from the neighbouring monastery the right to lodge on the premises
and board with the inmates : an arrangement common in
England to a late period, where the purchased privilege of
boarding and lodging in a monastery was called " Corrody."‡
This plan for providing for helpless old age, which was
something like the present practice of purchasing an
annuity, continued to prevail in Ireland down to at least
the sixteenth century. In the seventh volume of the Proc.

---

* Br. Laws, iv. 373 and note.

† O'Curry, Man. & Cust., ii. 30, 31, 479, and note 515 : Br. Laws, iv.
305, note 3.   ‡ Br. Laws, iii., Richey, in Introduction, lxv. lxvi.

Roy. Ir. Academy (p. 18) Dr. Todd has published and translated a deed in the Irish language, dated 1522, by which an old lady gave up her lands to a man who had a mortage on them, on condition that he should support her for the rest of her life.

As to old persons who had no means, the duty of maintaining them fell primarily of course on the children : or failing children, on the foster-child. A son who supported his father in old age had a special distinguishing term applied to him in the Senchus Mór—*mac-gor* or *gormac* : but this last term was also applied to a sister's son.* A son or daughter who was able to support parents but who evaded the duty was punished by having his or her dire-fine lessened (which meant loss of status : 1. 208, *supra*), or in some other way.† The general recognition of the son's duty to support his parents is noticed in a passage in Adamnan's " Life of Columba " (p. 159), where certain brothers who had been supporting their father and mother forced another brother who had been long absent to undertake the duty.

If an old person who had no children became destitute the tribe was bound to take care of him ; for in the words of the Senchus Mór :—" It is one of the duties of the *finé* (circle of relations, tribe) to support every tribesman " : and the Gloss adds :—" They do this by duties which are required of them according to justice."‡ A usual plan was to send the old person to live with some family willing to undertake the duty, who had an allowance from the tribe for the cost of support.

In some cases destitute persons dependent on the tribe who did not choose to live with a strange family, but preferred to have their own little house, received what we now

---

* Br. Laws, I. 207, 19; III. 56, 20; IV. 291, 10; 43, note I ; and v. 71, line 4 from bottom.

† Br. Laws, III. 53, 57, bottom ; IV. 185, 307, 27; see also IV., Richey, Introduction, lxvi. lxvii.   ‡ Br. Laws, III. 55, 2; 57, 9.

call outdoor relief.   According to the Sequel to the Crith
Gabhlach, there was a special officer called *uaithne* [oohina :
lit. a ' pillar '] whose business it was to look after them : **or,**
in the words of the tract, to " oversee the wretched and the
poor," and make sure that they received the proper allowance : something like the relieving officer of our present
poor laws.   He was of course paid for this duty ; and it is
added that he should bear " attacks on his honour " without
his family or himself needing to take any action in the
matter—referring to the abuse and insult he was likely to
receive from the peevish and querulous class he had in
charge.   He was permitted to bear from them insults,
which, if coming from ordinary members of the community, should be resented in the recognised way to wipe
off the disgrace.*

It is plain from some expressions in the Senchus Mór,
as well as from the words of the Glossator, that in those
times, as at the present day, there were poor persons who
preferred the free and easy life of the wandering beggar-
man† : as reflected in one verse of a once popular modern
Anglo-Irish song :—

> " Of all trades a-going begging it is my delight ;
> My rent it is paid, and I lay down my bags every night :
> I'll throw away care, and take a long staff in my hand ;
> And I'll flourish each day courageously looking for chance."

They carried a bag for contributions ; and the Senchus
Mór mentions giving them alms as a commendable deed,
here transmitting a record of a popular feeling that has
continued to prevail to our own day.   Shane O'Neill—
John the Proud — prince of Tyrone in the time of
Elizabeth, always put aside the first dish of food for the
poor :—" to serve Christ first "—as he said.   More than
half a century ago I saw the same custom carried out—

---

* Br. Laws, IV. 351 : Sullivan, Introduction, 251, bottom.
† Br. Laws, III. 19, $_{25}$; 21, top.

though in less regal style—in my grandfather's house, where, just before the family sat down to the noonday dinner, a big dish of laughing potatoes was always laid aside for wandering beggars : and the potatoes rarely survived till night.

From the provisions here described it will be seen that the most important features of our modern poor-laws were anticipated in Ireland a thousand years ago.

4. *Irish Poetry and Prosody : Love of Nature and of Natural Beauty.*

In very early times, not only poetry proper, but histories, biographies, laws, genealogies, and such like, were often written in verse as an aid to the memory. Among all peoples there were—as there are still—certain laws or rules, commonly known as Prosody, which poets had to observe in the construction of their verse : of which the main object was harmony of numbers. The classification and the laws of Irish versification were probably the most complicated that were ever invented : indicating on the part of the ancient Irish people, both learned and unlearned, a delicate appreciation of harmonious combinations of sounds. The following statement will give the reader an idea of this. There are in Irish three principal kinds of verse. Of the first kind, which is called " Direct Metre " (*Dán Direch*), there are five species, all equally complicated. The first of these required the observance of the following rules :—(1) Each stanza to consist of four lines making complete sense ; (2) In each line seven syllables ; (3) Alliteration in at least two principal words of each line ; (4) The lines to rhyme, the rhymes being greatly varied, and occurring very often ; (5) The last word of the second line to have one syllable more than the last word of the first line ; a like relation between the last words of the fourth and third lines.

In Irish poetry of all kinds the rhymes were very frequent, occurring, not only at the ends of the lines, but also within them, once, twice, or even three times. The rhymes were either between vowels—*i.e.* assonances—or between consonants. For this last purpose the consonants were scientifically divided into six classes, " soft," " hard," " rough," " strong," " light, and " the queen," *i.e.* the letter *s* which formed the sixth class : the letters of each of the first five corresponding and rhyming with each other, but not with those of any other class. One-syllable, two-syllable, and three-syllable rhymes were used with equal facility.

That the old writers of verse were able to comply with these numerous difficult prosodial rules we have positive proof in our manuscripts ; and the result is marvellous. No poetry of any European language, ancient or modern, could compare with that of Irish for richness of melody. Well might Dr. Atkinson exclaim (in his Lecture on Irish Metric, p. 4) :—" I believe Irish verse to have been about " the most perfectly harmonious combination of sounds " that the world has ever known. I know of nothing in " the world's literature like it."

Of each principal kind or measure of verse there were many divisions and subdivisions, comprising altogether several hundred different metrical varieties, all instantly distinguishable by the trained ears of poet and audience.* We have seen that there were seven grades of " Poets." Of the lower class, called " Bards," there were also a number of grades. Each of the grades of both had certain metres allotted to them ; and each individual was allowed

---

* See Irish Metric by Dr. Atkinson : the Irish Treatise on Irish Metre from the Book of Ballymote, translated and annotated by the Rev. B. M'Carthy, D.D., in the Todd Lecture Series of the Roy. Ir. Acad., vol. III., pp. 98–141 : Stokes's Féilire, Introduction, 12–15 : Hyde, Lit. Hist., chapters xxxvi. to xxxviii. ; and his little book, Irish Poetry (1903), in which will be found a most useful survey of Irish poets and poetry, with their manifold subdivisions.

to compose only in his own special measure, or in those belonging to the inferior grades ; but he was not permitted to compose in the measure of any grade above him.

Those of the Irish poets—whether clerical or lay—who learned to write Latin, imported many of the Irish prosodial rules into their Latin poetry, using accent instead of quantity, so as to imitate exactly the metres, assonantal rhymes, alliterations, consonantal harmonies, and all the other ornaments common in Irish poetry.*

Some of the greatest Celtic scholars that ever lived— among them Zeuss and Nigra—maintain that rhyme, now so common in all European languages, originated with the old Irish poets, and that from the Irish language it was adopted into Latin, from which it gradually penetrated to other languages, till it finally spread over all Europe.†ature But other eminent men, including the German scholar R. Thurneysen, think that rhyme was mainly borrowed by the Gaels from the Romans. The preponderance of learned opinion is certainly on the side of the Gaels ; but the subject requires to be further investigated before final judgment can be pronounced. One thing is quite certain, that rhyme — as we have already said — was brought to far greater perfection in Irish than in any other language.‡

It has been stated (p. 497) that laws, histories, genealogies, and such like, were often written in verse to make them more easily remembered. Several pieces of this kind have been published, of which the following—all or most mentioned and described elsewhere in this book—are the

---

* See the Irish Liber Hymnorum, by Drs. Atkinson and Bernard, II. xv.

† All that can be said at present in favour of this view will be found in Dr. Sigerson's Introduction to his Bards of the Gael and Gall, and in Dr. Hyde's Irish Poetry, pp. 45–57. See also Hyde's Lit. Hist., chap. xxxvi.

‡ Dr. Douglas Hyde has given, in his Literary History of Ireland, and in his Irish Poetry, English translations of many old Irish poems, in which the rhymes, metres, and alliterations of the originals are exactly imitated. Dr. Sigerson, in his Bards of the Gael and Gall, also often imitates the old rhymes and alliterations.

principal. The *Feilire* of Aengus ; the Book of Rights ; a portion of the Tribes and Customs of Hy Fiachrach ; the *Duan Eirenneach* and the *Duan Albanach,* two long pieces of versified history published by Dr. Todd in his Irish version of Nennius ; and the Topographical Poems of O'Dugan and O'Heeren. This last is an enumeration of the principal tribes of Ireland at the time of the English invasion, with the districts they occupied and the chiefs who ruled over them. The part relating to Leth Conn (North of Ireland) was written by John O'Dugan, who died in 1372 ; and that relating to Leth Mow (South) by Gilla-na-neeve O'Heeren, who died in 1420. The whole poem has been translated and annotated by O'Donovan, and published by the Irish Archæological and Celtic Society. In such compositions as these we could hardly expect to find true poetry, for they are little more than mere catalogues in verse.

The complicated restrictions of their prosody must have greatly hampered the play of the old Irish poets' imagination, so much of their energies were concentrated on overcoming mere mechanical difficulties. Yet in spite of this, they produced a great body of very beautiful poetry. Sufficient materials are not yet available to enable us to pass a general judgment on the character of early Irish poetry : for, as has been remarked, such pieces as the Feilire of Aengus are not, and never were intended to be, poetry, any more than the versified lists of kings and events we often see in modern English school-books. Yet these have been almost the only ancient Irish metrical compositions that have hitherto been brought within reach of the public, and their prominence is due to their historical importance.

The great majority of Irish poetical pieces—poetry in the true sense of the word—are still hidden away in manuscripts scattered through the libraries of all Europe. The few that have been brought to light, through the investigations of scholars of taste, show that many of the ancient Irish poets were inspired with true poetical genius. Most of these pieces are characterised by one prevailing note—a close observation and an intense love of nature in all its aspects. As favourable specimens may be instanced " King and Hermit," lately translated and published (in pamphlet form) by Professor Kuno Meyer (1901), " a singularly beautiful poem," as he designates it, written in the tenth century : Deirdre's farewell to Alban, of which a translation is given below ; the poetical description of the pagan heaven in vol. i., p. 294, *supra*, and another and different one with text and translation by Kuno Meyer in Mr. Nutt's " Voyage of Bran," vol. i., p. 4. Good examples of Irish poetry also are the series of verse-pieces interspersed through the prose of " The Courtship of Ferb," all of which are very simple, and most of them pathetic and picturesque. Many other very beautiful examples will be found in the poetical parts of the Agallamh na Seanorach.*

On this subject I cannot do better than quote a few sentences from Professor Kuno Meyer's Preface to his version of " King and Hermit " :—

" It will then be found that the literature of France and Germany during that period [ninth, tenth, and eleventh centuries] has next to nothing to place by its side [*i.e.* by the side of the poetical literature of Ireland during the above period] ; while even the rich literature of Anglo-Saxon England is quite thrown into the shade when compared, either in wealth or variety, with that of early Ireland. . . . It may be safely predicted that these anonymous and neglected poems, once properly collected, edited and translated, will strongly appeal to all lovers of poetry. There is in them such delicate art, so subtle a charm, so true and deep a note, that, with the exception of the master-pieces of Welsh poetry, I know nothing to place by their side.

* It must be remembered that all these examples—both those referred to and those given here—appear to great disadvantage in translation, inasmuch as the rich melody of the originals is quite lost. All poetry suffers in translation, and perhaps ancient Irish poetry most of any.

The poem here published [" King and Hermit "] affords a good example of that marvellous descriptive art of Irish poets, which they share with the Welsh bards."*

The poet's adage, " A thing of beauty is a joy for ever," found real and concrete application among the ancient Irish. Their poetry, their tales, and even their proper names, bear testimony to their intense love of nature and their appreciation of natural beauty.   Keats, in the opening of " Endymion," enumerates various natural features and artificial creations as " things of beauty," among others, the sun, the moon, " trees old and new," clear rills, " the mid-forest brake," " all lovely tales that we have heard or read." These and many other features of nature and art, not mentioned by Keats—the boom and dash of the waves, the cry of the sea-birds, the murmur of the wind among the trees, the howling of the storm, the sad desolation of the landscape in winter, the ever-varying beauty of the clouds, the cry of the hounds in full career among the glens,† the beauty of the native music, tender, sad, or joyous, and soforth in endless variety—all these are noticed and dwelt upon by those observant old Irish writers—especially in their poetry—in words as minutely descriptive and as intensely appreciative as the poetry of Wordsworth.

It would be easy to multiply instances of this bent of mind, but we must be contented with a few illustrations here.   An excellent example is Midir's address to the lady Befinn, already given (vol. i., p. 294).   In the Life of St. Senan—a plain prose narrative—it is related that a child, playing beside its mother near a cliff in the west of Clare, fell " over the edge of Ireland " into the sea, but was preserved from injury by the intercession of St. Senan.

* Many similar testimonies might be adduced from native Irish writers : but I prefer—for obvious reasons—to quote from this scholarly and discerning foreigner.

† The delight of the Irish, both ancient and modern, in hunting and its accessories has been already noticed (pp. 467, 468, *supra*).

A person who heard the shrieks of the mother went down to look for him, and found him sitting quite safe in the trough of the sea where he had fallen, " playing with the " waves.   For the waves would reach up to him and laugh " round him, and he was laughing at the waves, and putting " the palm of his hand to the foam of the crests, and he " used to lick it like the foam of new milk."*

They loved the music of the wind and the waves.   The sound of the breeze rustling through the foliage so struck the imagination of those spiritual people, that in Cormac's Glossary (p. 132) the word *omna*, one of the Irish names for the oak-tree, is derived from *fuamna*, " sounding " : " because "—in the words of the Glossary—" great is the sound of the wind blowing against it."   In the Life of St. Columkille it is stated that while residing in Iona, he wrote a poem in the Irish language, a tender reminiscence of his beloved native land, in which he expresses himself in this manner :—

St. Columkille's Remembrance of Erin.

" How delightful to be on Ben-Edar† before embarking on the foam-white sea ; how pleasant to row one's little curragh round it, to look upward at its bare steep border, and to hear the waves dashing against its rocky cliffs.

" A grey eye looks back towards Erin ; a grey eye full of tears.

" While I traverse Alban of the ravens, I think on my little oak grove in Derry.   If the tributes and the riches of Alban were mine, from the centre to the uttermost borders, I would prefer to them all one little house in Derry.   The reason I love Derry is for its quietness, for its purity, for its crowds of white angels.

" How sweet it is to think of Durrow : how delightful would it be to hear the music of the breeze rustling through its groves.

" Plentiful is the fruit in the Western Island—beloved Erin of many waterfalls : plentiful her noble groves of oak.   Many are her kings and princes ; sweet-voiced her clerics ; her birds warble joyously in the woods ; gentle are her youths ; wise her seniors ; comely and grace-

---

* Stokes, Lives of SS., p. 212.
† Ben Edar, Howth, a rocky headland near Dublin.

ful her women, of spotless virtue ; illustrious her men, of noble aspect.

" There is a grey eye that fills with tears when it looks back towards Erin.   While I stand on the oaken deck of my bark I stretch my vision westwards over the briny sea towards Erin."*

When the sons of Usna returned from Scotland to Ireland at the treacherous invitation of King Concobar, Deirdrè, the wife of Naisi one of the brothers, seating herself on a sea-cliff of the present county Antrim, looked sadly over the waters at the blue headlands of Scotland, with gloomy forebodings for the future, and uttered this farewell :—

DEIRDRE'S FAREWELL TO ALBAN.

I.

" Dear to me is yon eastern land : Alban with its wonders.   Beloved is Alban with its bright harbours and its pleasant hills of the green slopes.   From that land I would never depart except to be with Naisi.

II.

" Kil-Cuan, O Kil-Cuan,† whither Ainnli was wont to resort :   short seemed the time to me while I sojourned there with Naisi on the margins of its streams and waterfalls.

III.

" Glen-Lee, O Glen-Lee, where I slept happy under soft coverlets : fish and fowl, and the flesh of red deer and badgers ; these were our fare in Glen-Lee.

IV.

" Glen-Masan, O Glen-Masan : tall its cresses of white stalks : often were we rocked to sleep in our curragh in the grassy harbour of Glen-Masan.

V.

" Glen-Orchy, O Glen-Orchy : over thy straight glen rises the smooth ridge that oft echoed to the voices of our hounds.   No man of the

---

* The two Irish poems, with translations, from which the above is extracted, will be found in Reeves's Adamnan, pp. 275 and 285.   They are very ancient ; and they illustrate our theme equally well, whether they were written by St. Columkille or by any other Irishman.

† This and the other places named in Deirdre's Farewell are all in the west of Scotland.

clan was more light-hearted than my Naisi when following the chase in Glen-Orchy.

VI.

" Glen-Ettive, O Glen-Ettive : there it was that my first house was raised for me : lovely its woods in the smile of the early morn : the sun loves to shine on Glen-Ettive.

VII.

" Glen-da-Roy, O Glen-da-Roy : the memory of its people is dear to me : sweet is the cuckoo's note from the bending bough on the peak over Glen-da-Roy.

VIII.

" Dear to me is Dreenagh over the resounding shore : dear to me its crystal waters over the speckled sand. From those sweet places I would never depart, but only to be with my beloved Naisi."*

The singing of birds had a special charm for the old Irish people. Comgan, otherwise called Mac da Cherda (seventh century : vol. I., page 224, *supra*), standing on the great rath of Cnoc-Rafann (now Knockgraffon in Tipperary), which was in his time surrounded with woods, uttered the following verse, as we find it preserved in Cormac's Glossary (p. 7) :—

> " This great rath on which I stand
> Wherein is a little well with a bright silver drinking-cup :
> Sweet was the voice of the wood of blackbirds
> Round this rath of Fiacha son of Moinche."†

Among the numerous examples of Metre given in a treatise on Prosody in the Book of Ballymote is the

---

* From Joyce's " Old Celtic Romances," where the whole tale is given. The original Irish text of this beautiful poem, which was first published, with translation, by Theophilus O'Flanagan, in his version of the Story of the Fate of the Sons of Usna, in Trans. Gael. Soc., 1808, has been lately republished, with the tale itself, by the Society for the Preservation of the Irish language. For a metrical version, see Ferguson, Lays of the Western Gael.

† That is Fiacha Muillethan, king of Munster in the third century, who resided at Cnoc-Rafann : see p. 103, *supra.*

following verse, selected there merely for a grammatical
purpose :—

> " The bird that calls within the sallow-tree,
>   Beautiful his beak and clear his voice ;
>   The tip of the bill of the glossy jet-black bird is a lovely yellow ;
>   The note that the merle warbles is a trilling lay."*

It would be hard to find a more striking or a prettier
conception of the power of music in the shape of a bird-
song, than the account of Blanid's three cows.   When the
Isle of Man was invaded by the Irish Red Branch heroes,
they took the king's castle and brought away all the jewels ;
among them—as the best jewel of all—the lady Blanid,
daughter of the king, together with her great brazen
caldron, her three cows, and also three little birds that
used to sing for them while milking.   These cows were
always milked into the caldron, but submitted reluctantly
and gave little milk till the birds came to their usual perch
—on the cow's ears—and sang for them : then they gave
their milk freely till the caldron was filled.†   See also
vol. i., p. 591, *supra*.

Even the place-names scattered over the country—
names that remain in hundreds to this day—bear testimony to this pleasing feature of the Irish character:
for we have numerous places still called by names with
such significations as " delightful wood," " silvery stream,"
" cluster of nuts " (for a hazel wood), " prattling rivulet,"
" crystal well," " the recess of the bird-warbling," " melodious little hill," " the fragrant bush-cluster," and soforth
in endless variety.‡

---

* Mac Carthy, Cod. Pal.-Vat. 131.   Other examples in Silva Gad. 109 :
Stokes and Strachan's Thes. ii. 290 : and Hyde, Lit. Hist., 275.

† Kilk. Arch. Journ., 1870–1, p. 411.

‡ For the originals of all the above names, and for numerous others of
a like kind, see Irish Names of Places, vol. ii., chap. iv., on " Poetical
and Fancy Names."

Many students of our ancient literature have noticed these characteristics. " Another poem "—writes Mr. Alfred Nutt in his " Studies on Ossian and Ossianic Literature " (p. 9)—" strikes a note which remains dominant throughout " the entire range of Ossianic Literature : the note of keen " and vivid feeling for certain natural conditions. It is a " brief description of winter :—

" ' A tale here for you : oxen lowing : winter snowing : summer passed away : wind from the north, high and cold : low the sun and short his course : wildly tossing the wave of the sea. The fern burns deep red. Men wrap themselves closely : the wild goose raises her wonted cry : cold seizes the wing of the bird : 'tis the season of ice : sad my tale.' "

This is a bald literal translation : what would it be if dressed in the diction of Scott, Goldsmith, or Wordsworth ! Dr. Whitley Stokes, speaking of the " Colloquy of the Ancient Men "—an Ossianic composition consisting of a series of short narratives framed in one connecting story— notices the genuine feeling for natural beauty and the passion for music that pervade the whole of them.*   In this connexion I may again also point to the beautiful poem of " King and Hermit," already mentioned, and Professor Kuno Meyer's Introduction to it.†

So far we have had under consideration the Irish poetry of the early centuries. In later times the Irish poets broke away from their ancient prosodial trammels and produced much excellent poetry. Among the remains of these times—from the fifteenth century down—we have many pieces of great beauty—odes, ballads, elegies, songs, &c.—the products of true poetical inspiration. Spenser, a supreme judge of poetry, but in general a prejudiced

---

* Preface to the Acallamh : Ir. Texte, IV. xii.

† Excellent renderings into English rhymed metre—many of them very beautiful—of about 140 Irish poems, of various ages, from the most ancient to modern times, have been given by Dr. Sigerson in his Bards of the Gael and Gall.

witness for Ireland, and not disposed to praise things Irish, has given the following testimony regarding this poetry of the later Irish bards (View, 124) :—" Yea, truly I have " caused divers of them to be translated unto me, that I " might understand them, and surely they savoured of " sweet wit and good invention, but skilled not of the " goodly ornaments of poetry [*i.e.* they wanted the qualities " that go to form great poetry] ; yet were they sprinkled " with some pretty flowers of their natural device, which " gave good grace and comeliness unto them."*

In modern Irish poetry the old prosodial rules are almost wholly disregarded. The rhymes are assonantal, and very frequent : they occur not only at the ends of the lines but within them—sometimes once, sometimes twice ; and not unfrequently the same rhyme runs through several stanzas. In other respects modern Irish poetry generally follows the metrical construction of English verse.†

* The question of the change from the old order of things in Irish poetry, and its effects on the productions of the bards, is too extensive to be dealt with adequately here. The reader may consult Dr. Hyde's very full treatment of this subject in his Lit. Hist. of Ireland, pp. 479 *et seq.*

† For the metrical laws observed by the Irish poets in the eighteenth century, see the " Introductions " of the Rev. Patrick S. Dinneen, M.A., to his two volumes, the Poems of Egan O'Rahilly, and *Amhrain Eoghain Ruaidh Ui Shuilleabháin* (The Poems of Owen Roe O'Sullivan).

In regard to rhyming, Shelley's poem, " The Cloud," resembles some of these modern Irish pieces : but his rhymes are what are called in English prosody " perfect," not assonantal. This specimen will show what is meant :—

> " I bring fresh showers for the thirsting flowers
>   From the seas and the streams ;
> I bear light shade for the leaves when laid
>   In their noonday dreams.'

The Cork poet, Fitzjames O'Brien, directly imitated the native poetry in his poem on " Lough Hyne " (also with perfect, not assonantal, rhyme) :

> " I know a lake where the cool waves break,
>   And softly fall on the silver sand ;
> And no steps intrude on that solitude
>   And no voice save mine disturbs the strand."

See also, for other instances, Father Prout's " Bells of Shandon," Moore's song, " Wreathe the Bowl," and Curran's " If Sadly Thinking."

The Irish peasant-poets of a century ago, or more, when composing their doggerel songs in English—with which language they were only

5. *Six Stages of Life.*

Shakespeare's seven stages of human life are represented by :—1. the infant ; 2. the schoolboy ; 3. the lover ; 4. the soldier ; 5. the justice ; 6. old age ; 7. decrepitude. The ancient Irish, long before the time of Shakespeare, divided life into six stages—called " Columns of Age " (*colomna áis*)—which are simply enumerated in Cormac's Glossary (p. 41), without any poetical setting :—1. infancy (*náidendacht*) ; 2. boyhood (*macdacht*) ; 3. youth or puberty (*gillacht*) ; 4. adolescence or manhood (*hóclachus*) ; 5. old age (*sendacht*) ; 6. decrepitude (*diblidecht* or *dimligdetu*). Here two of the Irish stages—youth and manhood—are represented by three—lover, soldier, and justice—in Shakespeare.

6. *Human Temperaments.*

Dr. Whitley Stokes, in the Preface to his Three Irish Glossaries (p. xl.), gives a curious myth, from an old Irish manuscript in the British Museum, to account for the different dispositions and temperaments of mankind, which, as he remarks, corresponds with similar legends of Teutonic and Indian origin. The following are the opening words of his translation :—" It is worth knowing " what Adam was made of, namely of eight parts :—the " first part, of earth ; the second part, of sea ; the third " part, of sun ; the fourth part, of clouds ; the fifth part, " of wind : . . . ; the seventh part, of the Holy Ghost ; " the eighth part, of the light of the world."

The old account then goes on to explain the temperaments from these components :—The earth part is man's inperfectly acquainted—imitated, by a sort of hereditary instinct, the assonantal rhymes of their native language. The following is a good specimen the rhyming syllables are *italicised* :—

> " The grand im*prove*ments they would a*muse* you,
> The trees are *droop*ing with fruit all *kind* ;
> The bees per*fum*ing the fields with *mus*ic
> Which yields more *beau*ty to Castle*hyde*."

body, and if this predominates in a man he will be slothful. The part of the sea is the blood, and this in excess makes a man changeful. The part of the sun is his face and countenance, which will be lively and beautiful if that part is prominent. The part of the clouds, . . . The part of the wind is the breath, and if that part prevails he will be of a strong character. The part of the Holy Ghost is the soul, the predominance of which will make him lively, of good countenance, full of grace and of the divine Scripture. The part that was made of the light of the word is piety, and if this prevails he will be a loving, sensible man.*

7. *Blood-Covenant.*

Giraldus Cambrensis, in his " Topography of Ireland " (III., xxii), says that, when the Irish make a very solemn league, they ratify it " by drinking each other's blood, which they shed for this purpose. This custom "—he goes on to say—" has been handed down to them from the rites " of the pagans, who were wont to confirm their treaties " with blood " : after which he proceeds to add some comments, in his usual bitter style. This statement has been considered as one of Giraldus's libels ; and it has been warmly denied by Keating in the Preface to his " History of Ireland " (p. xxvii), by Lynch in his " Cambrensis Eversus " (III., 217, 221), and by Lanigan in his " Ecclesiastical History " (IV., 285). But here Giraldus, though he distorts, and pours forth a volume of rancorous abuse and exaggeration, does not bear absolutely false witness. That the Irish had a *cro-cotaig*, or ' blood-covenant ' (*cro*, blood, cognate with Latin *cruor*), admits of no doubt. In the year 598 A.D., when Branduff, king of Leinster, was preparing to fight the king of Ireland in the Battle of Dunbolg,

* Dr. Stokes has given a poetical paraphrase of this in English (" Man Octipartite "), which may be seen in Stopford Brooke and Rolleston's Treasury of Irish Poetry, p. 348. In the Preface to Three Irish Glossaries, Dr. Stokes refers, for corresponding myths among other ancient nations, to several authorities—German, Sanskrit, Latin, and Old English. See also Rev. Celt., I. 261.

as told in vol. I., p. 141, *supra*, he met, on the side of a mountain at some distance from both camps, a party of Ulidians (from East Ulster), who had formed part of the king of Ireland's army ; and induced them to abandon the monarch and join his own standard. The king of Ulidia then said :—" A blood-covenant (*cro-codaig*) and an agreement shall be made between us ": whereupon—in the words of the old narrative—" they seated themselves on the " mountain and made a *cotach* or bond of fellowship that " should never be broken." The king of Ireland was defeated and slain in that great battle : and the old history adds that the mountain, which had been called before that time *Slieve Nechtain*, was afterwards called *Slieve Codaig*, the ' mountain of the covenant.' This mountain lies on the left of the road as you go from Hollywood to Donard in Wicklow ; and it retains the name to this day in the slightly altered form of Slieve Gadoe.*

Here there is no hint—further than the name—as to the nature of the covenant, or what exactly was done : for the good reason that it was so well understood in the time of the writer, that he needed only to name it. But we get the details from Martin,† as he found the custom practised down to his time, eleven centuries later, among our cousins, the people of the Western Islands of Scotland, who derived it from Ireland. His testimony is moreover independent, as he knew nothing of the early Irish custom. He says of the islanders :—" Their ancient leagues of friendship were " ratified by drinking *a drop of each other's blood*, which was " commonly drawn out of the little finger. This bond was " religiously observed as a religious bond." And he goes on to say that whoever violated it utterly lost character, so that all people avoided him. The ancient Irish custom was something like this : and the blood that each person drank consisted of portion of a single drop, mixed with

* Silva Gad., 413 : Rev. Celt., XIII. 73 : also Irish Names of Places, II. 463.   † Western Isles, 109.

water. So that Giraldus's " drinking each other's blood " must be toned down to this rather mild formality.

Sometimes the Irish ratified covenants by having them written in blood. When St. Cairnech brought about a league between the Hy Neill and the Cianachta, *i.e.* the people of Keenaght in Meath, as we are told in the old tale of the Death of Murkertagh mac Neill, king of Ireland (A.D. 512–533), he mixed the blood of both tribes in one vessel, and wrote with it the treaty : thus rendering it inviolable.* This, as we see, was done under Christian auspices.

The blood-covenant was not peculiar to Ireland and Scotland. It came down from primitive times : it was once prevalent in many countries, and exists among some people to this day. Herodotus, in his account of King Crœsus, records that the Medes and Lydians made oaths in treaties like the Greeks, but added this ceremony :— they scratched their arms till they drew a little blood, and each licked the blood off the other's arm. Professor Max Müller† writes :—

"Another widely-spread custom is the drinking of blood, as the highest sanction of a promise or a treaty. Herodotus (III. 8) alludes to this custom as existing in Arabia ; and how long it prevailed and how firmly it was established we may gather from the fact that Mohammed had to forbid it as one of the heavy sins—idolatry, neglect of duties towards parents, murder, and the blood-oath."

8. *Cremation-ashes thrown into water.*

In some cases the body of an animal or of a human being was burned, and the ashes thrown into water—generally a stream—with the idea of removing some malign influence, or obliterating the memory or the effects of a crime. According to an ancient legend, which is fully given by Keating (pp. 336, 338), a series of calamities fell on Munster in the third century of the Christian era. And

* Petrie's Tara, 121, note   † Anthropological Religion, p. 191

when the nobles inquired into the matter, they were told that all the misfortunes were caused by two sons who were born to their king—the offspring of incest. Whereupon they demanded that the boys should be given up to them, " that they might consume them with fire and cast their ashes into the running stream," with the object of putting an end to the trouble. Whether the design was carried out is not stated.

When Diancecht the Dedannan leech-god (vol. I., p. 261, *supra*) slew Meichi the son of the war-witch Morrigan, he found in the body three hearts in the shape of serpents' heads, which, had they been allowed to grow, would have destroyed all the animals in Ireland. Diancecht burned these three venomous snake-heads, and threw the ashes into the current of the river Barrow, which heated the water and caused it to seethe up so violently that it killed and boiled to rags all the fish along the whole course of the river.* We have already seen (p. 456, *supra*) that the body of a mad dog should be burned and the ashes thrown into a running stream.

Maildune and his companions landed from their currach on an island, where they found a palace inhabited by only one little cat. A great collection of torques and other precious jewels hung round the walls, which Maildune told his men not to interfere with. His foster-brother however, disregarding the injunction, took down one of the torques and brought it away. But the cat followed him and over-took him in the middle of the court, and, springing on him like a blazing fiery arrow, went through his body and reduced it in a moment to a heap of ashes. He then returned to the room, and, leaping up on a low pillar, sat upon it. Maildune turned back, bringing the torque with him, and, approaching the cat, spoke some soothing words ; after which he put the torque back to the place from which it had been taken. Having done this, he

* O'Grady, Silva Gad., 524, top

collected the ashes of his foster-brother, and, bringing them to the shore, cast them into the sea.*   The practice of burning the dead, and throwing the ashes into the sea, prevailed also among the Scandinavian nations.

9. *Something further about Animals.*

There are not, and never have been, any venomous reptiles in Ireland.   There are small lizards, five or six inches long, commonly called in Irish, *art-* or *arc-luachra,* 'lizard of the rushes,' but they are quite harmless. St. Patrick is credited in legend with freeing the island from venomous and demoniac reptiles ; but two centuries before his time, Solinus wrote regarding Ireland, *illic nullus anguis,* " there is no snake." Giraldus Cambrensis, in the twelfth century, testified that there were no snakes or adders, toads, or frogs ; and in an Irish MS., quoted by Stokes,† Ireland is compared to Paradise, which has no venomous reptiles and no frogs.   According to Giraldus, the first frog ever seen in Ireland was found in his own time in a meadow near Waterford : but recently our naturalists have discovered a native frog, or rather a small species of toad, in a remote district in Kerry, which must have cunningly eluded the eye of St. Patrick, for they have been in the place from the beginning.

But though we have no great reptiles in nature, we are amply compensated by legends, both ancient and modern, according to which there lives at the bottom of many of the Irish lakes a monstrous hairy serpent or dragon, usually called *píast* or *béist,* i.e. " beast," from Latin *bestia ;* and sometimes *nathir,* i.e. " serpent " ; chained there by a superior power—commonly credited to St. Patrick—till the day of judgment.   Our most ancient literature, pagan as well as Christian and ecclesiastical, abounds in legends of those frightful reptiles.   Sometimes they guard a *liss*

---

* Old Celtic Romances, 133.   † In Trip. Life, Introduction, xxix.

or fort. The legend is as prevalent to-day as it was a thousand years ago : and very many lakes have now, as the people say, a frightful monster with a great hairy mane, at the bottom.*

But we had a much more gigantic and much more deadly sea-monster than any of these—the Rosualt—a mighty animal that cut a great figure in Irish tales of the olden time. There is a well-known plain at the foot of Croagh Patrick mountain, called Murrisk, where the body of this sea-monster was cast ashore, from which the name is derived. For according to the legendary account in the Book of Leinster, Murrisk is only a shortened form of *Muir-iasc* [Murreesk], meaning ' sea-fish.' When the Rosualt was alive—which was in the time of St. Columkille —he was able to vomit in three different ways three years in succession. One year he turned up his tail, and with his head buried deep down, he spewed the contents of his stomach into the water, in consequence of which all the fish died in that part of the sea, and currachs and ships were wrecked and swamped. Next year he sank his tail into the water, and rearing his head high up in the air, belched out such noisome fumes that all the birds fell dead.   In the third year he turned his head shoreward and vomited towards the land, causing a pestilential vapour to creep over the country, that killed men and four-footed animals.†

St. Brendan, during his celebrated voyage in the Atlantic, once *landed* on the back of a huge fish, thinking it was an island, and his companions made a fire and began to cook their supper ; but the beast, no doubt feeling the heat inconvenient, suddenly sank into the sea, and they barely escaped with their lives into their boat.

* For more about these supernatural aquatic monsters see Adamnan, II. xxvii : IarC., p. 19 : O'Cl. Cal., 145 : Táin Bo Fr., 149, 157 ⁙ Silva Gad., 283 : Joyce, Irish Names of Places, vol. I. 198.

† LL, 167, *b*, ₄₆: Silva Gad., 480, ₂; 527, ₉: Rev. Celt., vol. I. 258.

The name of this great fish was Jasconius,* from which we infer that it was an immense eel, for " Jascon-ius "— pron. Yasconius—is merely the Latin way of writing the Irish *easconn* (pron. ascon or yascon), an eel. This monster was in fact a sea-serpent. An incident similar to that of Brendan is related in the Story of the First Voyage of Sindbad the Sailor. All this will remind the reader of the great Norse sea-animal called the Kraken: the monstrous fish mentioned in the First Book of " Paradise Lost " :—

> " Him, haply, slumbering on the Norway foam,
> The pilot of some small night-foundered skiff,
> Deeming some island, oft, as seamen tell,
> With fixéd anchor in his scaly rind,
> Moors by his side under the lee, while night
> Invests the sea, and wishéd morn delays."

But the Norse Kraken was a dull, listless sort of a beast, with nothing to boast of but mere size; and our Rosualt beats him by long odds in liveliness of temperament and variety of accomplishments.

10. *Animals as Pets.*

Many passages, both in the Brehon Laws and in Irish literature in general, show that tenderness for animals was a characteristic of the Irish people. It appears from a commentary on the Senchus Mór that special care was taken that animals held in distress should be properly fed; and there was generally a person put to care them. When cattle were taken to be impounded, if the journey was long they had to be fed at stations along the way.†

The custom of keeping pet animals was very general; and many kinds were tamed that no one would think of keeping as pets now. We read of lap-dogs, foxes, wolves, deer, badgers, hawks, ravens, crows, cranes, cats, sheep, and

* O'Donoghue, Brendaniana, 127.　　† Br. Laws, II. 77, 104, note I.

even pigs, kept as pets. The favourite pet of the hermit Marban, brother of Guaire Aidne king of Connaught in the seventh century, was a white sow, as we read in the tenth-century poem, " King and Hermit," published by Kuno Meyer : but in the later tale—The Tromdamh—this pet is a white boar. Such animals were so common, and were mixed up so much with the domestic life of the people, that they are often mentioned in the Brehon Laws. Many of the Irish saints were fond of animal pets ; and this amiable trait has supplied numerous legends to our litera- ture, a few of which are given here.* St. Patrick himself, according to Muirchu's seventh-century narrative, showed them a good example of tenderness for animals. When the chief Dáré gave the saint a piece of ground at Armagh, they both went to look at it : and on their arrival they found there a doe with its little fawn. Some of St. Patrick's people made towards it to kill it : but he prevented them ; and taking up the little animal gently on his shoulder, he brought it and laid it down in another field some distance to the north of Armagh, the mother following him the whole way like a pet sheep.†

On one occasion St. Finnen, at Clonard, called to him one of his pupils, named Senach, and told him to go round the monastery and bring a report of how the rest of the pupils were engaged at that moment. We hear only about Colomb, son of Crimthann. He was found on his knees with his mind on the contemplation of God, and birds were resting on his hands and on his head, which he never disturbed. St. Kevin was once at prayers so stead- fastly that birds came and built their nests in the hollows of his outstretched palms. Giraldus Cambrensis has the following version of this legend. The saint retired during Lent—as was his wont—to his little hermitage up the

---

* On the fondness and tenderness of monks for animals, see Kilk. Arch. Journ., 1899, p. 229, bot. : Silva Gad., 2, top Adamnan, 90 ; 91, note *c* : and Reg. of All Hallows, XXI., note *y*.   † Trip. Life, 292.

valley of Glendalough, to spend the time in solitude, contemplation, and prayer; and one morning putting out his hand to raise it towards heaven, " a blackbird perched on the palm and laid her eggs upon it, treating it as a nest." And Kevin, taking pity on the bird, never stirred his hand till the young brood was hatched. Hence, continues Giraldus, all the images of St. Kevin throughout Ireland represent him with a blackbird on his extended hand.*

In the Life of St. Brigit we read that the king of Leinster in her time had a pet fox, which had been taught to amuse him with its tricks and gambols. But one day a shepherd belonging to Brigit's household, going to cut firewood, came upon the fox and killed it, whereupon he was seized by the enraged king to be punished, but was let off by the intervention of the saint.†

Pet cranes were very common and are often noticed: the Brehon Law mentions fines for trespasses committed by them.‡ St. Columkille had one which followed him about everywhere like a dog while he was at home in Iona. St. Brendan of Clonfert had a pet *préchán* or crow (Feil. 73 mid.). St. Colman of Templeshanbo in Wexford kept a flock of ducks on a pond near the church, which were so tame that they came and went at his call. Popular legend subsequently related such marvels of these birds that they became one of the " Wonders of Ireland." It appears that on some occasions one of them was brought home and thrown alive by accident into a pot with other food which was cooking over a fire: but so long as the bird was in the pot the water remained cold, no matter what amount of firewood was lighted up under it; and in the end

---

* See Stokes's Lives of SS., pp. 226 and 344 : and Girald., Top. Hib., II. xxviii. This legend, or rather one corresponding with it, is also current in India.

† Three Irish Homilies, 83. For a similar modern legend of King O'Toole's pet goose, see Dub. Pen. Journ., i., p. 6.

‡ Br. Laws, IV. 115, where several pet animals are mentioned. For pet cranes see also Mac Conglinne, 50, ₃₂; and Stokes's Lives of SS., 270.

the little bird flew back to its companions, hale and hearty.* As to pet pigs, the Brehon Law,† as mentioned elsewhere in this book, anticipating their mischievous propensities, is specially severe on trespass committed by them.

Some small animal called a *tógmall* (for which see p. 128, *supra*) was also tamed and kept as a pet. It is related in the Táin that when on one occasion Ailill and Maive, king and queen of Connaught, were walking out, Maive had a pet *tógmall* on her shoulder, and Ailill a pet bird on his ; and that Cuculainn killed both animals with his sling—merely to show that he could have killed the king and queen themselves if he wished. From this it appears that it was the custom to carry such little pet animals perched on the shoulder—a practice which is curiously illustrated in an authority twelve centuries later, the coloured fresco figures on the walls of Knockmoy abbey in Galway, in which three kings are represented carrying birds, one on the shoulder, one on the arm, and one held by a string.‡   (See vol. I., p. 59, *supra*.)

The English colonists appear to have imitated the Irish in their fondness for animal pets, as they did in many other things. In the Anglo-Irish ecclesiastical annals it is recorded that in 1319 Richard of Exeter, chief justice of Ireland, sued the prior of the monastery of All Hallows (where Trinity College, Dublin, now stands) for sixty shillings damages for the loss of a pet heron he had left in the keeping of the prior, who, however, carelessly suffered it to escape. Sixty shillings was a big sum in those days, equal to £50 or £60 of our present money : indicating how highly these pets were prized. It may be added that the prior had not to pay after all : for the judge pardoned him at the request of the prosecutor.§

---

* Irish Nennius, 217.   These ducks are noticed at length by Giraldus (Top. Hib., II. xxix), who mentions the attempt to boil one of them, and its failure..   † See Br. Laws, IV. 327, 19.

‡ See Stokes's Life of Petrie, 268.   § Reg. of All Hallows, Introd., xxi.

11. *The Cardinal Points.*

A single point of the compass was called *áird*, which is still used in Scotland and Ulster in the form of *airt* : " Of a' the airts the wind can blaw, I dearly like the west " (Burns). The four cardinal points were severally designated by the Irish in the same way as by the ancient Hebrews and by the Indians ; for they got names which expressed their position with regard to a person standing with his face to the east.

East.—The original Irish word for the east is *oir* [ur, er] ; which however is often written *soir* and *thoir* [sur, hur] ; and a derivative form *oirthear* [urher] is used in the oldest Irish writings. Moreover, the first and last are often written *air* and *airther*. Our ancient literature affords ample proof that these words were used from the earliest times to signify both the front and the east, and the same double application continues in use at the present day. As one instance out of many, may be cited the two fold translation of *airther* in the ancient druidical prophecy of the coming of St. Patrick :—*A miasa i n-airther a tighi* (" his dishes [shall be] in the east of his house "). For while Muirchu, in the Book of Armagh, translates *airther* by the Latin word *anterior*, or front, on the other hand, the same word in the same passage has been translated by its more usual equivalent *oriens* or *orientalis* (i.e. east) in the Scholia to Fiacc's Hymn, and in several of the Lives of St. Patrick.*

West.—*Iar* [eer] signifies the hinder part, a meaning which is illustrated in the word *iarball*, applied to the tail of an animal, *i.e.* the hinder *ball* or member. It also signifies the west. There is a derivative form *iarthar*, corresponding with *oirthear*, which is in very general use.

* See Reeves, Adamnan, p. 82.

South.—*Deas* [dass] means literally the right-hand side ; old Irish form *des*, corresponding with Lat. *dextra,* Gr. *dexia,* Sanskr. *daksha* ; and it is also the word for the south, as the right hand lies towards the south when the face is turned to the east. The word is used in both senses at the present day ; and it would be easy to prove by quotations from old Irish authorities, that this was the case in the very earliest ages. It is often written *teas* [tass].

North.—*Tuath, tuaith* [thooa], means properly the left hand ; and as *deas* is applied to the south, so this word is used to signify the north. Corresponding with *deisceart,* we have *tuaiscert,* ' northern part or direction.'

12. *The Wind.*

In the description of the universe in the " Saltair na Rann," already referred to (vol. I., p. 464, *supra*), a prominent place is given to the winds ; and they are described in much the same way in the commentaries on the Senchus Mór. These descriptions deserve to be noticed on account of the curious belief they record of the ancient Irish people that the wind blowing from each quarter has a special colour. God made " four chief winds and four subordinate " winds, and four other subordinate winds, so that there are " twelve winds." The four chief winds blow from north, south, east, and west, and between each two points of these there are two subordinate winds. " God also made " the colours of the winds, so that the colours of all those " winds are different from each other."*

The wind from the north was black (*dub*) ; that from the east, purple (*corcra*) ; the south wind was white (*gel*) ; and the west wind, pale (*odur*). Between the north and east were two winds, speckled (*alod*) and dark (*temin*). Between the east and south two others, yellow (*buide*) ana red (*derg*). Between south and west were the greyish-

* Saltair na Rann, lines 45 to 52 : Br. Laws, I. 27.

green (*glas*), and the green (*uaine*).   Between west and north the dark brown (*ciar*) and the grey (*liath*).   Fig. 339 exhibits the whole fancy very clearly.

The Irish had other beliefs regarding the winds, many of them superstitions connected with the fairy mythology. According to an ancient Irish poem, probably of the tenth century, printed and translated by Prof. Kuno Meyer in

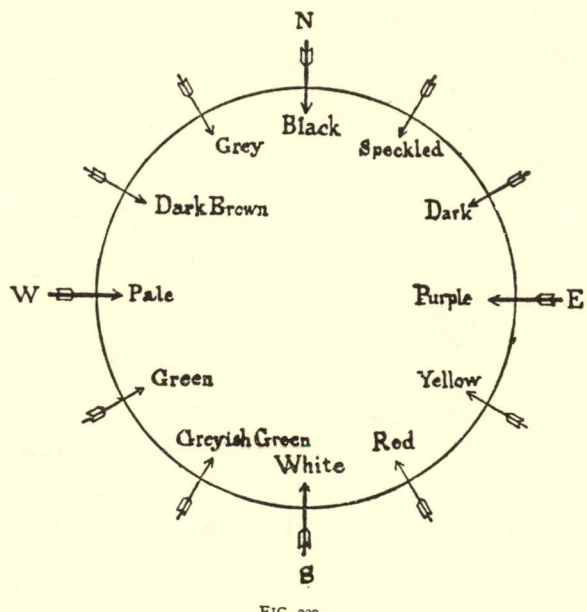

FIG. 339.

The colours of the twelve winds : constructed from the description in Saltair na Rann.

" Hibernia Minora " (p. 39), the fate of the year depends on the wind that happens to blow on the 1st January. The eight principal winds (N., S., E., W., N.E., N.W., S.E., S.W.), and their names, are enumerated, with the particular blessings or calamities that will follow after each, whichever may happen to blow on that fateful day.

There are many modern superstitions in connexion with winds which most probably come down from old pagan times.   The " red wind of the hills " that blasted fruit blossoms and other tender vegetable growths, was caused by the whirling of the fairies in the air, fighting their venomous battles (see vol. I., p. 257, *supra*) : and there were " wise women " who professed to counteract these baneful influences by their charms and spells. The ashes of Irish people buried in foreign lands sometimes returned to their ancestral burial-places on the breezes of summer ; and these winds blighted corn and injured men and animals that happened to lie in their way.*

13. *The Sea.*

The sea was called *muir* (gen. *mara*) ; *fairrge* ; and more rarely *lér* or *léar* (gen. *lir*). Any waif found either floating on the sea or thrown on shore by the waves was called in Irish *frith-fairrgi* [frih-farriga], *i.e.* a ' find of the sea,' or ' sea-waif ' : also called *turcairthe mara*. Of such waifs the Brehon Laws took careful cognisance.† Accord-ing to Cormac's Glossary (p. 67, " Epscop fina "), there was a distinct law-tract to regulate all matters relating to the sea, called *Mur-Bretha*, i.e. " sea-judgments," which is now lost ; but many of its provisions are preserved in the present existing law-tracts. The finder of a sea-waif, or strand-waif, before finally disposing of it, was bound to send notice over the three *trichas* or districts nearest the sea at the place, and to the seafaring people of the fourth district, in view of possible claimants.‡

Anything thrown on the sea-shore belonged to the owner of the shore as far as the value of five *séds* or cows. But if it was worth more than that, the excess was divided according to the " partition of a lawful bark," which was as follows :—One-third belonged to the owner of the shore ; one-third was divided among the heads of families of the *tuath* or district ; one-third went to the king of the same territory, of which he had to give one-fourth to

---

* See Trans. Ossianic Society, II., pp. 94 (note), 113, 114, 115, 144 (note).
† For the seven different kinds of waifs provided for by law, see Br. Laws, v. 321.   See also III. 307, 309.   ‡ Br. Laws, III. 273.

the king of the province, who again had to give one-fourth of his share to the king of Ireland. Accordingly the ultimate distribution was this :—

5 *seds* in the first instance to the owner of the shore.

Of the remainder :—

$\frac{16}{48}$ to the same owner.
$\frac{16}{48}$ to the people of the *tuath* or territory.
$\frac{12}{48}$ to the king of the *tuath* or territory.
$\frac{3}{48}$ to the king of the province.
$\frac{1}{48}$ to the king of Ireland.

Dillesk or dulse cast on the strand belonged wholly to the owner of that part of the shore. When a vessel was cast ashore, if it was merely injured but not broken up, it was the duty of the owner of the port or shore, and of the inhabitants of the place, to preserve it from destruction— we are not told what reward they received : but if it was an utter wreck, then it was regarded as a waif, and the owner of the port might proceed to divide it among the people of the territory in the proportions described above. Any of the crew that were saved were to be lodged and fed by the people of the territory as long as necessary : " for the district on whose shore it [the vessel] is cast is " bound to keep, protect, feed, and make provision for such " parties."

If a man brought in a valuable article floating on the sea, nine waves or more out from land, he had a right to it, no matter to whom it belonged, and whether the owner gave permission or not. But if it was less than nine waves out, the owner's permission was necessary (*i.e.* permission to rescue and keep it) ; and the man who rescued it without this permission could not claim it as his own.* (As to nine waves, see vol. I., p. 308, *supra*.)

* For all these see Br. Laws, I. 129, 167, 203 ; and III. 273, 307, 309, 423 to 433.

The three *Tonns* or Waves of Erin are much celebrated in Irish romantic literature. They were *Tonn Cleena* in Glandore harbour in Cork ; *Tonn Tuaithe* [tooha] outside the mouth of the Bann in Derry ; and *Tonn Rudraidhe* [Ruree] in Dundrum Bay off the County Down. In stormy weather, when the wind blows in certain directions, the sea at these places, as it tumbles over the sandbanks, or among the caves and fissures of the rocks, utters an unusually loud and solemn roar, which excited the imagination of our ancestors. They believed that these sounds had a supernatural origin, that they gave warning of the deadly danger, or foreboded the approaching death, of kings or chieftains, or bewailed a king's or a great chief's death. Sometimes when a king was sore pressed in battle and in deadly peril, the Three Waves roared in response to the moan of his shield (see vol. I., p. 131, *supra*). Instances of all these are so numerous in the tales that it is unnecessary to refer to them. The Welsh people had a similar legend : when the young Welsh hero Dylan was killed, " he was lamented by the Wave of Erin, the Wave of Man, " the Wave of the North, and the Wave of Britain of the " comely hosts."* Though the Three Irish Waves named above were the most celebrated, there were several other noted *Tonns* round the coast.†

Scotland also had its voiceful waves, as our old books record. Adna, the chief ollave poet of Ireland in the time of the Red Branch Knights, had a son Nede [Ney], also a poet, who, when he had learned all that his father could teach him, went to Scotland to complete his education under the renowned Alban ollave, Ochy Horse-mouth (*Eochaidh Ech-bél*). Towards the end of his time in Scotland he went one day to the seashore for inspiration to compose a poem : " for "—as the old book (LL, 186, *a*, 15)

* Rhys, Hibbert Lectures, 386.
† For which see Irish Names of Places, II. 258 ; and Book of Fenagh, 147, note 9.

has it—" poets believed that the place where poetry was always revealed to them was the brink of the water." As he stood on an overhanging rock, he heard a voice in the wave lamenting in sad tones : and he wondered greatly. And believing that some disaster had occurred, he threw a spell on the wave ; and the wave revealed to him the cause of the lament, namely, that his father Adna had just died in his home in Ireland. On this the young poet, bidding farewell to his master, set out to claim the *tugen* or arch-poet's mantle in succession to his father. This is the beginning of the story of the " Disputation of the two Sages " (vol. I., p. 171, *supra* : see also O'Curry, Man. & Cust., II. 315.)

This is a pagan legend. But sometimes the Christian saints could tell what the wild waves were saying as well as any pagan poet. In a legend in the Irish Life of St. Columkille, it is related that he and St. Canice were one day on the shore looking out over the waters, " when a great storm was driving on the main." Said Canice to Columkille :—" I hear the voice of the waves chanting and " calling to us : what are they singing ? " Columkille replied :—" They are telling us that some of the monks of " thy household were in danger at sea a little while ago, " and one of them died : and the voice says that God will " bring the others to us to-morrow safely to this very place " where we are now standing " : which accordingly came to pass (Stokes, " Lives of SS.," 177).

14. *Bishop Ultan and the Orphans.*

St. Ultan, bishop of Ardbraccan in Meath, seventh century, is commemorated in the Calendars under the 4th September, and his death is recorded in most of the Annals. In the Feilire of Aengus he is mentioned as " the great sinless prince in whom the little ones are " flourishing : the children play greatly round Ultan of " Ardbraccan." The annotation explains this in words that give us a glimpse of the havoc wrought by the Yellow Plague, and of the piteous scenes of human suffering witnessed during its continuance. Everywhere through the country numbers of little children, whose mothers and fathers had been carried off, were left helpless and starving. Ultan collected all the orphan babes he could find, and brought them to his monastery. He procured a great number of cows' teats, and filling them with milk, he put them into the children's mouths with his own hands, and thus contrived to feed the little creatures: so that in the words of the annotation, " the infants were playing around him." In one of the accounts, we are told that he often had as many as 150, so that his noble labour of love— even with help—must have kept his hands pretty busy. It would be difficult to find an instance where charity is presented in greater beauty and tenderness than it is in this simple record of the good bishop Ultan.

It is certain that all over Ireland there were many others who exerted themselves to relieve the distress: but Ultan is singled out for special commemoration on account of having hit on the happy idea of using cows' teats as feeding-bottles.

As curiously illustrative of this record, it is worthy of mention that, at the present day in Russia, it is a very general custom for those peasant women who do not suckle their own children, to feed them with a rude feeding-bottle, called by a name equivalent to the English word " hornie," namely, a cow's horn hollowed out, and having a little opening at the smaller end, on which is tied a cow's teat. When the " hornie " is filled with milk, the teat is put into the infant's mouth, who in this manner feeds itself.*

---

* See, for the Irish record, Féilire, pp. 136 and 142 : O'Clery's Cal., at 4th Sept. : and Todd, St. Patrick, p. 213. The account of the use of the " hornie " in Russia I read in an Article in the *Standard* of the 1st April (or thereabout), 1902, from its Moscow correspondent.

15. *Prophecies of Irish Saints.*

The ancient Irish had a universal implicit belief in the prophecies of their native saints.   On the eve of a battle one of the leaders—in order to encourage his men—was pretty sure to bring up and read for the army some prophecy, generally by the patron saint of the tribe, referring to the coming battle, in which victory was predicted for his side.   Just before the Battle of Moyrath (A.D. 637) King Domnall, who was fighting in defence of the kingdom against the rebel Prince Congal and his foreign and native auxiliaries, told his army that their patron, St. Columkille, had foretold this battle nearly half a century before, and predicted that they should gain the victory.   And after a battle lasting for six days, Domnall annihilated Congal's army.   About ten years before this, the same King Domnall was victorious in the Battle of Dun Cethern :   and Adamnan, in his Life of Columba (i. xlix) states that the saint foretold this battle also. When John de Courcy invaded Ulster in 1176, he recalled and spread about, both among his own army and among the Irish, a prophecy of the Welsh wizard and prophet Merlin (who was known and venerated in Ireland as well as in Wales), that Ulster should be conquered by a foreign fugitive knight, white, mounted on a white steed, and bearing birds upon his shield.   And with great astuteness he assumed the very garb described in the prophecy, which materially aided him in conquering Ulster.   Before the Battle of the Yellow Ford, where Hugh O'Neill inflicted a disastrous defeat on the English in 1598, he caused his hereditary *ollave* O'Clery, to read aloud for his army a prophecy of St. Columkille, made a thousand years before, predicting victory for the Irish army.*

* There are extant many prophecies of the Irish saints, some in manuscript, very old, others written in times comparatively recent, and a few forged within my own memory.   O'Curry (in MS. Mat., Lects. xviii., xix.,

16. *Sundry small matters worthy of notice.*

When the four Children of Lir were changed to white swans by their stepmother, the people were so grieved that they forthwith proclaimed a law throughout Erin that no one should ever kill a swan.* On this passage O'Curry ("Children of Lir," p. 132) tells us that in his time the peasantry of Clare had the belief—not derived from books but from immemorial tradition—that the swan, on the approach of death, sings its own dirge as sweet as the plaint of the banshee. This tradition is spread all over Europe ; and it is noticed by Giraldus Cambrensis. The Clare people moreover believe that to this day it is unlucky to kill a swan ; and they give instances where misfortunes befell those that did so. Martin (p. 71) found the same belief in 1703 in the Hebrides. Yet the people there sometimes killed wild swans ; but the man who killed one for food made a " negative vow " before tasting it ; that is, he mentioned some act which was in itself impossible to do, and swore that he would never do it : for instance that he would never jump over his own house. This formality was believed to ward off the evil.

Giraldus (Top. Hib., I., xiv) says that in his time (1185) wild swans were plentiful in the North of Ireland. These birds are migratory, and flocks of them still frequent the west and north-west of Ireland : but they are grey ; not white.

The following incident is often met with in the *Imrama* or Voyages :—The voyagers come to a lonely sea-rock, on which they find a hermit doing penance till the day of judgment ; and he has lived there for so many hundred years that a crop of white hair has grown all over his body

---

xx.) has shown that all or most of these prophecies are spurious : forced to fit certain events, or written after them. For the battles referred to above, see Moyrath, p. 127, and note *b* : and Joyce, Short Hist. of Irel., pp. 153, 271, 273, 492. The belief in prophecies of this kind still prevails in Ireland.   * The whole story of the Children of Lir will be found in Old Celtic Romances.

so long and thick that he needs no other clothing.*　It is curious that this finds a parallel in modern times in England, in what is related of Old Parr, which is best given in the words of Taylor the English " water-poet " :—

> " From head to heel, his body had all over
> A quickset, thickset, natural hairy cover."

Another incident found in Irish tales, as well as in Welsh :—While the champions are feasting or exercising, a strange, gigantic, formidable-looking visitor, with a great sharp axe in his hand, approaches, and utters this challenge to the assembled heroes :—Let any champion come forward and I will cut off his head this night, and he shall cut off my head to-morrow night.　Or if you like better :—let him cut off my head to-night, and I shall cut off his head to-morrow night.　For an example of this challenge and its results, see Fled Bricrenn, pp. 99, and 117 to 129.

On very solemn occasions, when a general fast was enjoined, it sometimes happened that the lower animals were made to fast as well as human beings.　We are told in an ancient Life of St. Fechin, that in order to ward off a plague, a three days' fast was enjoined for every living creature—cattle as well as people.†　When Mahon, king of Munster in the tenth century, was murdered, his blind poet poured forth his sorrow in an elegy, in which he says that among other manifestations of the people's grief, the calves were kept from the cows, as much as to say, that the cattle were made to fast as well as the dead king's human subjects.‡

Maildune, during his voyage, was detained by the queen of one of the islands he visited, as Ulysses was by Calypso :　and he and his men began to long for home. They at last determined to escape :　and one day in the

---

* For instances see Old Celtic Romances, pp. 143 and 165.
† Rev. Celt., XII. 431.　　　　　‡ War of the Gael with the Galls, 101.

absence of the queen they put to sea in their currach. They had not gone very far from land when the queen came riding towards the shore ; and seeing how matters stood, she went into the palace and soon returned with a ball of thread in her hand. Walking down to the water's edge, she flung it after the currach, but held the end of the thread in her hand. Maildune caught the ball as it was passing, and it clung to his hand ; and the queen, gently pulling the thread towards her, drew back the currach to the very spot from which they had started in the little harbour. And when they had landed, she made them promise that if ever this happened again, some one should always stand up in the boat and catch the ball.

The voyagers abode on the island, much against their will, for nine months longer. For every time they attempted to escape, the queen brought them back by means of the clew, as she had done at first, Maildune always catching the ball. At last the men began to suspect that Maildune was doing all this intentionally ; so the next time the thing happened they got another man to catch the ball. It clung as before, and the queen began to draw the currach towards the shore. But Diuran, one of Maildune's companions, drawing his sword, cut off the man's hand, which fell with the ball into the sea ; and the men gladly plied their oars, and the currach resumed her outward voyage. So they escaped, while the island rang with the lamentations of the queen and her maidens.*

There were certain periods of exemption from debt, that is, people could not be forced to pay till the period had expired. On the death of the king of Ireland or of the archbishop of Armagh, debtors were entitled to exemption for a year : on the death of a provincial king the people of the province were exempt for three

* Old Celtic Romances, p. 152.

months ; and the death of the king of a *tuath* or small district brought a month's exemption for debtors within that territory. Every king or chief could, during his lifetime, give exemption for as long a period as would be given at his death.* We have already seen (p. 447) that debtors were exempt while attending a fair.

A noble instance of the self-sacrifice of a king to save his people is related in the story of " The Boroma." Aed mac Ainmirech, king of Ireland (A.D. 572 to 598), once asked St. Columkille how many kings he could remember that certainly won heaven. Columkille named three ; one of whom was Ailill Inbanna, king of Connaught. The two sons of the over-king Murkertagh mac Erca (A.D. 512 to 533) named Domnall and Fergus—who subsequently became joint kings of Ireland—entertained feelings of bitter personal animosity against this king Ailill ; so that they made war on him : and a battle was fought between them at a place called Cúil Conaire in the present barony of Carra, county Mayo : in which Ailill was slain. This battle, and the death of Ailill, are historical facts, which are recorded in the authentic annals† : and there is no good reason to doubt the substantial accuracy of the striking detail given in " The Boroma," as related to King Aed by St. Columkille, of the manner of the king's death. When the battle had gone against Ailill, and he and his army were in full retreat, the king, sitting in his chariot in the midst of the flying multitude, said to his charioteer :—
" Cast thine eyes back, I pray thee, and tell me if there is much killing of my people, and if the slayers are near us." The charioteer did so, and said :—" The slaughter that is made on thy people is intolerable." Then said the king :—
" Not their own guilt, but my pride and unrighteousness it
" is that they are suffering for. Turn now the chariot and

---

* Br Laws, I. 99, note I.
† See Annals of Ulster, A.D. 549 : FM, 544 : HyF, p. 313.

" let me face the pursuers ; for [as their enmity is against
" me only] if I am slain it will be the redemption of many."
The chariot was accordingly turned round, and the king
plunged amidst his foemen and was slain by them ; on
which the pursuit and slaughter ceased. " That man
therefore "—said Columkille to King Aed—" that man
attained to the Lord's peace."*

CHAPTER XXXI

DEATH AND BURIAL

Section i. *Wills.*

ANY passages in our ancient literature, some of
which are quoted below, show that the custom
of making wills at the approach of death
existed among the Irish people from so early
a period that we are not able to trace its beginning.
Private property was disposed of in this way quite without restriction, though not with such strict legal formalities
as are required at the present day.

According to Sir Henry Maine (" Anc. Law," p. 172),
the conception of a will originated with the Romans, from
whom it was borrowed by those western nations that
came in contact with them, namely, the Germans, Gauls,
Scythians, &c., whom they called " Barbarians." Referring
specifically to the Irish or Brehon Law, Maine has the
following passage in his " History of Ancient Institutions "
(p. 55) :—" So far as the published tracts afford materials

* See O'Grady's Silva Gad., p. 416. The original of this narrative of
Ailill's death was put into metrical English, in the form of a short ballad,
by Dr. Whitley Stokes, which may be seen (copied from the *Academy*) in
a recently-published work, a Treasury of Irish Poetry, by Stopford A.
Brooke and T. W. Rolleston, p. 347.

" for an opinion, I am inclined to think that the influence
" of Roman Law [on that of Ireland] has been very slight,
" and to attribute it, not to the study of the writings of the
" Roman lawyers, but to contact with churchmen imbued
" more or less with Roman legal notions. We may be
" sure that the Brehons were indebted to them for one
" conception which is present in their tracts—the con-
" ception of a will." Dr. Richey, the editor of the Third
and Fourth Vols. of the Brehon Law, has a passage much
to the same effect :—" The more educated Irish were not
" wholly ignorant of the Roman law. To any other source
" it is impossible to refer the idea of the right of testa-
" mentary disposition, and the more so as it is found
" chiefly in connexion with the transfer of property to
" the church."* But in this he appears merely to have
followed Maine.

From various considerations that cannot be entered on
here it may be taken for granted that if the practice of
making wills was derived by the Irish from the Romans,
it was derived through the church, as Sir Henry Maine
observes in the above passage. But there is one circumstance that makes it very difficult for us to believe that
this was the origin of the custom in Ireland. We know
that when the Christian missionaries introduced doctrines,
rites, or customs, which had been previously unknown in
Ireland, they also imported Latin words for them : they
were indeed obliged to do so, as no suitable words existed,
or could have existed, in the Irish language. Of this
many examples have been already given (vol. i., p. 316).
If testamentary disposition was unknown in Ireland before
the introduction of Christianity, the Irish language would
have no word for a will, and the missionaries would have
to import one from Latin. But how does the case stand ?
There is in fact in Irish no Latin word for a will, while
there are as many as three very ancient native terms :—

* Br. Law, iii., Preface, xxix.

edoct*, *cendaite*, and *timne*. The first, variously spelled *edoct*, *edocht*, *aidacht*, is found in two passages, both in the Irish language, in the " Additions to Tirechán's Collections of Notes " (belonging to the seventh or eighth century), now preserved in the Book of Armagh : and in both cases the word carries the full meaning of a will. The first passage is this (Stokes's translation) :—" This is Feth Fio's " confession and his bequest (*edocht*) two years before his " death, to the monks of Druim Lias [now Drumlease in " the county Leitrim] and to the worthies of Callrigi, both " laymen and clerics of Druim Lias. That there should " not be a family right of inheritance to Druim Lias, but " that the race of Feth Fio [should inherit it], if there were " any of them [*i.e.*] of the clan, who should be good, should " be devout, should be conscientious "† (after which it goes on to detail the arrangements in case of the failure of Feth Fio's race). The other passage (p. 347), besides mentioning a testament several times by its Irish name, has this :—" Aed [bishop of Sleaty] offered a bequest " (*edoct*) and his kin and his church to Patrick [*i.e.* to the " church of Armagh] for ever." About a century later, Cormac, in his Glossary (p. 5), brings out the sense of the word very clearly, when he derives *audacht* from *uath-fecht*, ' grave journey,' or as he expresses it, " when one sets out on a journey (*fecht*) of the grave (*uath*), that is, of death." In like manner, the Senchus Mór mentions an *udacht* or bequest to the church, which the gloss explains :—" That is, at the point of death."‡ The Book of Leinster§ has a copy of the *audacht* of the great Judge Morann (for whom see vol. I., p. 170, *supra*) to Feradach the Just, king of Ireland (A.D. 95–117), which consists of a series of wise precepts for the king's instruction. This word still continues in use in the form of *udhacht* [oo-aght], which is now the common word for a will.

* On this see Appendix, *infra*.
† Trip. Life, p. 339.   ‡ Br. Laws, III. 33, last line ; 35, 18.
        § LL, 293, *a*, 36; " Contents," 67, *b*.

The oldest document in which I find the second term *cendaite* (or *cennaite*) used is Cormac's Glossary (ninth or tenth century : p. 47) ; and here the signification is brought out very clearly, and in a manner that shows it was then a word of long standing. Cormac derives it from " *cend-laite*, ' fate-day,' the day (*laite*) of a person's fate." After this period it occurs in many documents, always with its technical meaning of a dying testament. For instance, we read in the " War of the Gaels with the Galls " (p. 201) that towards the close of the Battle of Clontarf, the old King Brian Boru, believing he would be killed before the day was over, uttered his last will, while sitting in his tent, to his attendant Laiten, to be conveyed to his son Donnchad :—" My blessing to Donnchad for discharging my last bequests (*ceinnaiti*) after me." : whereupon he made the last disposition of his property. This appears to have been a verbal will : and the circumstances indicate that the obligation to carry it out was regarded as a sacred one.

Timne (or *tiomna*) occurs frequently in the Wurzburg and Milan Glosses quoted by Zeuss—both eighth century —as an explanation of the Latin *mandatum*, a mandate or precept (Z. 884, 30), and in this sense it is used to designate the New Testament—*Tiomna Nuadh*. The best-known example of its use as designating a dying testament is the *Tiomna* or Will of Cahirmore, king of Ireland from A.D. 174 to 177, which is a disposition of property.* Copies of this celebrated will are to be found in the Books of Leinster and Lecan. It is in verse, and has been published with translation by O'Donovan in his edition of the Book of Rights, from the copy in the Book of Lecan.† In its present form it was certainly drawn up centuries after the

* LL, 385, col. 3, line 6 ; " Contents," 78, *b*.

† Book of Rights, Introduction, xxxiii ; and 192. This will, in its tone and spirit, is something like Jacob's death-bed utterance to his sons (Gen. xlix), except that Jacob distributed no property.

reign of Cahirmore : but whether there was an earlier version from which the extant versions were copied, on this point we have no information. In this will the monarch mentions his ten sons one after another, with a detailed statement of the property left to each.

In the Brehon Laws mention is often made of the dying will (generally called *udacht*, but sometimes *timna*) of an ecclesiastic, to be buried in a certain church ; and the

Fig. 340.

Cromlech at Tawnatruffaun, County Sligo: 7 feet high. (From Wood-Martin's Pagan Ireland.)
(See farther on for cromlechs.)

Law specially enjoins that such a will is to be faithfully carried out, and that the body, once buried, is not to be removed.*

From all that precedes it will be seen that the early Christian missionaries found already existing in the Irish language one or more terms for a will—terms that could not possibly have existed unless the conception of a will had grown up previously. So far as we can judge then, from the evidence here adduced, the presumption is that the

* Br. Laws, I. 203, bottom ; 205: III. 67.

conception and practice of testamentary disposition were developed by the Irish. On those who deny this, lies the onus of disproving it. We know that many customs having their germs in the original Aryan community were retained and developed by some of the branches after the separation into different nationalities, while by others they were neglected, so that they disappeared totally. One instance of this is the use of banners in war among the Celts and Romans—a practice quite unknown among the Homeric Greeks (for which see vol. I., p. 136, *supra*); and many others will be found in De Jubainville's "La Civilisation des Celtes." Those who assert that the Irish borrowed the conception of a will from the Romans give no reason beyond the fact that this was found to be the case among all the western Continental "Barbarians." But a question of this kind, beset with difficulties such as are pointed out above, cannot be settled by the mere unsupported assertion of any man, however eminent; and I submit that the whole subject of the origin of testamentary disposition among the Irish demands further inquiry.

There was a merciful provision—called "The rights of a corpse"—to save the family of a dead man from destitution in case he died in debt. Ware (Antiqq., 152) quotes from an ancient Irish canon a section called "The rights of a corpse," to wit :—" Every dead body has in its own " right a cow, and a horse, and a garment, and the furni- " ture of his bed ; nor shall any of these be paid in satis- " faction of his debts ; because they are, as it were, the " special property of his body." Of course this reserved property passed to the family, and could not be claimed by a creditor or any other outsider. Whether the ecclesiastical authorities were the first to introduce this custom, or whether they found it already in existence and confirmed it by this degree, is not known.

2. *Funeral Obsequies.*

There were several words for death :—*és, ég, cro* ; all now obsolete: the word at present in use is *bás* [bauss], which is also an old word.

The pagan Irish, like many other ancient nations, celebrated the obsequies of distinguished persons by funeral games (*cluiche caintech*), as already mentioned (p. 434, *supra*) : and in some cases the games, once instituted, continued to be carried on periodically at the burial-place, far into Christian times. On the death of

Fig. 341.

Sepulchral stone circle, among the seaside sandhills at Streedagh, near the village of Grange, in Sligo. The circle is about 36 feet in diameter. In the centre is a kistvaen or grave, in which were found some calcined bones. (From Col. Wood-Martin's "Rude Stone Monuments" in Kilkenny Archæological Journal for 1887-8, p. 146, in which is a description and illustration of another circle in the same place. See farther on for stone circles.)

ordinary persons there was simply a funeral feast—called *fled cro-lige*, i.e. the *fled* or feast of the death-bed*—chiefly for guests, whether among pagans or Christians. This custom is noticed in Adamnan's " Life of Columba " (p. 79), where it is related that the saint ordered a fat sheep and some corn to be sent to a person named Erc : but meantime Erc died, and the presents " were used at his funeral feast."

* See " Fled " in Glossary to Br. Laws.

On the death of a Christian, a bell was rung :—*clog-estechtae*, ' death-bell,' as it is given in Cormac's Glossary,* from *es*, death.   There was often, or generally, a requiem sung over the grave, called *écnairc* [aiknark] which was an intercession for the soul's repose, and which was often continued by monks at home in their monastery, for a long time after burial.†   The body was watched or waked for one or more nights (Irish *aire* ' watching ').   In case of eminent persons the watch was kept up long : St. Patrick was waked for twelve nights : Brian Boru for the same length of time in Armagh in 1014 ; St. Senan for eight nights ; St. Columba for three at Iona.   Among the pagan Irish, seven nights and days was the usual time for great persons.

In .Christian obsequies lights were kept burning the whole time : during St. Patrick's twelve-night wake, the old Irish writers tell us that night was made like day with the blaze of torches.   This time of watching was called *laithi na canti* (or *caointi* : pron. laiha-na-keenta) : *i.e.* the ' days of lamentation,' or, as Tirechán, in his Latin narrative, renders it, *dies ululationis*.‡   The mourners raised their voices when weeping, like the Egyptians, Jews, and Greeks of old ; a practice mentioned in the most ancient writings, and continued in Ireland to the present day. Spenser (View, 93) notices in his time " their lamentations " at their buryals, with dispairfull out-cries and immoderate " waylings."   This wailing was called *cái*, modern *cáoi* [kee]: verbal form *cáiniud*, or *caoineadh*, or *caoine* [keena], commonly anglicised *keen* or *keening*—weeping aloud.   In the Fled Bricrenn a false report of the death of Cuculainn and Conall Cernach, is brought to Emain ; whereupon the people of Emain began *oc a cáiniud*, ' keening them.' §

* Corm., page 70, under " Es."

† Stokes, Lives of SS., 307, 6: see " Ecnairc " in Atkinson's Glossary to Br. Laws.

‡ Trip. Life, 315.   § Fled Bricr., 91 : Ir. Texte, I. 290, 16.

Sometimes the cry was accompanied by *lám-comairt*, ' clapping of hands ' (*lám* or *lámh*, a hand : pron. *lauv*), a custom which is noticed in an ancient gloss quoted by Stokes,* and which has also descended to our time.

The lamentation was often accompanied by words, expressive of sorrow and of praise of the dead, sometimes in verse, and often extempore. In the old tale of the cattle-spoil of Flidas,† a father " began to lament his [dead] son and to utter his praise " : and in the story of the " Fate of the Sons of Turenn," the father, standing over his sons' bodies, laments and praises them. This custom has also come down to modern times.‡ A regular elegy, composed and recited at the time of death, was usually called *Nuall-guba* (' lamentation of sorrow '). The *Nuall-guba* of Emer on the death of her husband Cuculainn is given in the Book of Leinster.§ An elegy was often called *Amra* or *Amrath*. Dallan Forgall's *Amra* for St. Columkille has long been celebrated, and is one of the most difficult pieces of Irish in existence. It has been translated by J. O'Beirne Crowe : by Dr. Robert Atkinson : and by Dr. Whitley Stokes.|| An elegy is now commonly called *marbhna*, from *marbh* [morrov], dead.¶

Among the Irish pagans it was the custom—which probably continued to Christian times—to wash the body. After the tragic death of King Tuathal's two daughters at the Leinster palace of *Rath Immil*, as we are told in the story of the Boroma, their bodies were washed at Ath - Toncha (' Ford of Washing ': *tonach*, bathing, washing, gen. *toncha*) now Rath-Immil.** The Irish

* Corm. Gloss., 32, " cai."
† Quoted by Kuno Meyer in Ventry, 87.
‡ See Crofton Croker, Researches, 173 : O'Brien's Dict., " Caoine " : and Joyce, Old Celtic Romances, 95.
§ LL, " Contents," 29, *b* : Text, 123, *a*, 20.
|| Crowe's translation forms a separate pamphlet, 1871 : Atkinson in Lib. Hymn., by Bernard and Atkinson : Stokes, in Rev. Celt., xx.
¶ See O'Donovan's article in Kilk. Archæol. Journ., 1856-7, p. 118.
** Rev. Celt., XIII. 39. See also Rev. Celt., XXIII 425.

custom corresponded with that of the Greeks, who washed the bodies of their dead as part of the funeral obsequies*: and the same custom prevailed among the Phœnicians and Romans.

The corpse was wrapped in a *racholl* or *recholl*, i.e. a shroud or winding-sheet : also called *esléne* [3-syll.], which in Cormac's Glossary is derived from *es*, death, and *lénĕ*, a shirt, ' grave-shirt.'†   *Esléine* is the present Irish word for

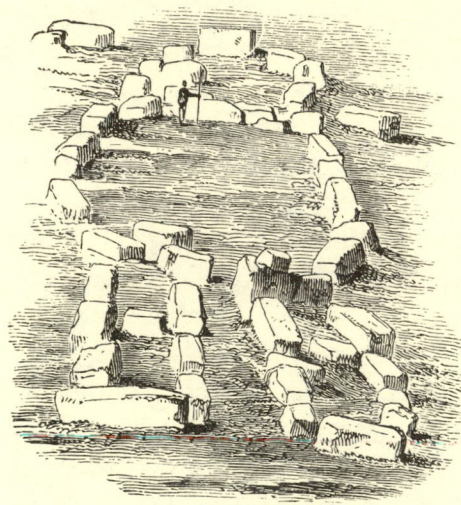

a shroud. When about to be buried the body was placed on a *fuat* or bier, which was borne to the grave, sometimes by men :‡ but if the distance was considerable, on a car, generally drawn by oxen. St. Patrick's body was placed on a little car (*carreine*), which was drawn from Saul to the grave at Dun - leth - glass, now Downpatrick, by oxen:

FIG. 342.

Bird's-eye view of sepulchral stone enclosure in Hazel wood, County Sligo, called *Leacht Con mic Ruis*, ' the grave of Cu, the son of Ros.' Between 90 and 100 feet long, by about 30 feet wide. (From Wilde's Catalogue, p. 130.)

and oxen also drew the bier of King Malachi I. to the grave, A.D. 863.§   The bier that bore the body of St. Cummain Fota to its last resting-place was a boat, in which it was brought up the Shannon to the cemetery of Clonfert.   A poet, who wrote a short elegy on the saint, says : " My eyelids drop tears ; mourning has not ceased since the destruction of his boat"; on which Todd remarks: " It was the custom to destroy the bier after the interment of the corpse."   If this was not done it seems the fairies might use the bier to carry

---

* Iliad., XVIII. 350: Odyss. XXIV. 44.   ‡ Stokes, Lives of SS., lines 2728–9.
† Corm. Gloss., p. 70, " Es."   § Trip. Life, 298: FM, vol I., p. 495.

off the corpse in their nightly excursions and bring it back to the grave before morning.   But when the bier was destroyed they had to let the corpse rest.   This custom has survived to our own time in Scotland.   Carmichael, speaking of a burial-place in one of the Hebrides, tells us :—" When the body is laid in the grave, and the grave " is closed in, the bier on which it was carried is broken " against a certain tree in the burying-ground to render " it unfit for the ' slaugh ' hosts [fairy hosts] to use in " carrying away the dead in their aerial travelling."*

In pagan times the body was sometimes brought to the grave wrapped up in a covering of green bushy branches, commonly of birch.   This covering was called *strophaiss* or *ses strophaiss* or *ses sofais*, which is thus explained in a curious marginal note in the Book of Leinster :—" *Ses* " *strofaiss* means *cained* or lamentation : *strophaiss* is the " broom [or branch-covering] that is round the body when " being taken to the graveyard " (*strophaiss in scuap bís immon corp ica thabairt dochum relggi*).†   This broom-like covering must have been a familiar object, for in an ancient verse, quoted in Cormac's Glossary, the withered beard of certain old men is compared to a grave-broom : but here it is called *ses rapus* or *ses rophuis*, which is explained *scuab adnacail*, a ' broom of a sepulchre.'‡   O'Clery's Glossary explains *ses sobhais* as *sguab adhnacail*, which, the editor, Mr. Miller, assuming that the *scuab* or ' broom ' must have been for sweeping, wrongly translates, " a broom *for sweeping* graves " : whereas *sguab adhnacail* means ' a broom [or branch-bunch] of a sepulchre,' nothing more. That this branchy covering was, sometimes at least, buried with the body appears from a story published by Dr. Todd in the Irish Nennius (p. 207) from an old Irish manu- script :—The monks of Clonmacnoise having heard that

---

* Todd, Book of Hymns, 86, and note 2 : FM, A.D. 661 : and Car- michael, Car. Gad., II. 320.   † Stokes, in Folklore, III. 505 : LL, 161.

‡ Corm. Gloss., 136, verse : Ir. Text in Three Irish Glossaries, 37, 10.

the body of a man—a pagan—had just been interred in their cemetery in some mysterious way without their knowledge, immediately opened up the newly-made grave, and found the body of a great bearded man, covered with blood, and having a covering of green " birch-brooms " [*i.e.* birch-branches] about him, also splashed with blood. No doubt this branchy covering was intended to protect the body from the clay, like our wooden coffins. This of course is legend ; but all the same it indicates that the idea of burying the body wrapped up in branches was familiar.

We read in Cormac's Glossary that the pagan Irish had always a *fé* [fay] or rod, of aspen, with an ogham inscription on it, lying in their cemeteries for measuring the bodies and the graves ; and the following very old verse is quoted there to show the application of the word :—

> " Sorrowful to me to be in life.
> After the king of the Gaels and Galls :
> Sad is my eye, withered my clay,
> Since the *fe* was measured on Flann."

The *fé* is also explained in the marginal note in the Book of Leinster, already referred to (LL, 161) :—" *Fae* is " the tree [or rod] with which a grave is measured, as " Senchan says, ' the tree [or rod] which is called *fae* ' " : and in O'Clery's Glossary the *fé* is defined as a " *slatt* or rod for measuring a grave." The *fé* was regarded with the utmost horror, and no one would, on any consideration, take it in his hand or touch it, except of course the person whose business it was to measure. The worst imprecation a person could utter against another was *fé fris*, ' a *fé* to him,' which was equivalent to saying, " may the *fé* be soon measuring his corpse. ! "*

* For all about the *fe*, see Corm. Gloss., p. 75.

We know from Cæsar* that it was the custom among the Gauls, when celebrating funeral obsequies, to burn, with the body of the chief, his slaves, clients, and favourite animals. But this custom did not reach Ireland. There is indeed in the Book of Leinster one horrible story of a burial which runs as follows :—On a certain occasion the sons of Eochaid Muigmedoin [Ochy Moyvane], king of Ireland (A.D. 358 to 366), went on a predatory hosting into Munster, and gained a battle over the Munstermen, in which however Fiachra, one of the brothers, received a mortal wound. Returning after their dearly-bought victory they brought home their wounded brother and fifty captives taken in the battle. At the end of a month Fiachra died of his wound : and when they buried him, at a place called Foroi, they also buried the whole of the fifty captives alive round his grave.† But this—if it ever occurred—was merely an isolated act of savage vengeance : and there is no reason to think that there was a custom of burying human beings alive or killing them in any manner, as a sacrifice to the dead. It should be noticed that an entirely different version of this story is given in a later authority, the Book of Lecan : obviously taken from older books. Here the captives, as they were marched towards Tara, finding the wounded Fiachra left temporarily without a guard, turned treacherously on him, and buried him alive in the earth.‡ This version of the story is improbable : nevertheless it more or less weakens the testimony of the Book of Leinster narrative.

Cattle were sometimes sacrificed on such occasions : not buried alive however : probably not buried at all, but killed and eaten at the funeral feast. In the story of the Courtship of the lady Etain, the young chief Ailill is on his sick bed dying for love of her, and she is left with

* Gallic War, VI. xix.
† LL, 190, col. 3, line 1 : O'Grady, Silva Gad., 543.
‡ HyF, 309, 345.

him to nurse him and to see that his funeral rites should be duly performed :—"that his grave should be dug, that " his lamentation might be chanted, and *that his quadrupeds* " *might be slain* " : a mode of expression that shows the thing was customary.*

3. *Modes of Burial.*

In ancient Ireland the dead were buried in a variety of ways. One mode was to place the body lying flat in the grave as at present, usually with the feet to the east ;

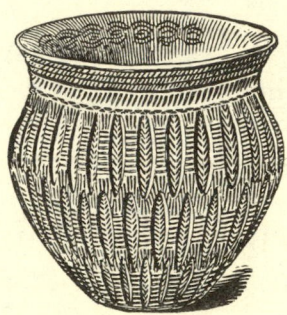

FIG. 343.　　　　　　　　　FIG. 344.

Cinerary urns : now in the National Museum. Fig. 343 is of stone, a very rare and beautiful specimen : 8¾ inches high, 10½ inches broad across the widest part, and 1 inch thick throughout. Fig. 344 is of baked clay : 6½ inches high, and 5 inches across at the widest part. (From Wilde's Catalogue, pp. 134, 177.)

and another was to put it standing up, accoutred and armed, which was often done with the body of a king or warrior. Occasionally it was placed in a sitting posture. Still another mode was to burn the body and deposit the ashes and fragments of bones in an ornamented urn, generally of baked clay, but sometimes of stone. All four prevailed in pagan times : but the first only was sanctioned and continued by Christianity. Of the first two modes of interment—lying flat and standing up—we have ample historical record. That the third—sitting—

* Kilk. Archæol. Journ., 1868-9, p. 334. Trip. Life, Introd., cl., line 13 : Sullivan, Introd., 321 : LU, 130, *a*, 10.

was practised in rare cases we know by the finding of a few bodies in that position, as well as from some delineations on the high crosses. But as to the last—cremation— I can find in the whole range of Irish literature only one direct allusion to it, and even that not in the native writings, but in Latin. Yet we know that cremation was extensively practised in pagan Ireland ; for urns containing ashes and burnt bones are found in graves in every part of the country.

The passage referred to occurs in an ancient Irish ecclesiastical canon, written, or rather copied, in the end of the seventh or the beginning of the eighth century, but then attributed by the writer—no doubt correctly— to the time of St. Patrick—fifth century. It is quoted by Sir James Ware in his " Antiquities " ; and recently attention has again been directed to it by Mr. Warren and Dr. Whitley Stokes, as included in the collection of canons published by Wasserschleben.* The old writer, tracing the origin of the word *basilica* as a term for a church, says that churches were so called " because in " the earliest ages kings [*Gr. basileus*, a king] were so often " buried in them : . . . whereas other people were buried " either by fire or by heaping up [over the body] a carn " of stones " (*nam ceteri homines sive igni, sive acervo lapidum conditi sunt*). It would be much more satisfactory if we could discover a record of some individual instance of the cremation of a body. Yet taking the record as it stands, we may infer from it that in the time of the original writer—fifth century—it was a matter of historical or traditional knowledge that at some previous time the bodies of the dead were burned. This would imply that the practice of cremation was abandoned long before the introduction of Christianity, and not, as some conjecture— for it is only a conjecture—through the influence of the Christian missionaries. But outside of this, it seems

* Ware, Antiqq., 151 : Trip. Life, Introduction, cxxi.

obvious that cremation could not have been practised in
Ireland so late as the fifth century, for if it had been there
would be certainly some mention of it in the Lives of
St. Patrick and of other early Irish saints : and it would
moreover have lingered on, like other pagan customs, down
to a much later time.   Besides all this, in the ancient tales
there are numerous accounts of interments ; but in not one
of them is cremation mentioned : the body is always placed
lying flat or standing erect.

The absence from Irish literature of all direct notice of
cremation is exemplified by a passage in Keating's " Three
Shafts of Death " (159, 162), in which he enumerates the
various modes of interment among different ancient nations,
including the Irish : his notices of the Irish customs being
drawn from old Irish manuscripts.   Although he describes
in detail the various native modes in use among the pagan
Irish, as known to him from his reading, he has no mention
of cremation.   Yet the native writers, including Keating
knew what cremation was, and were aware that other
nations practised it : for we find, in an Irish version of
Marco Polo's Travels, mention of the burning of the dead
by the people of a province on the borders of Thibet, and
enclosing the ashes in an urn (*cronoc cumdoig*, ' preserving
urn '), which they buried among hills and cliffs.   And
Keating himself, in the passage referred to above, notices
that the Romans burned their dead.   If he had any
historical evidence that the ancient Irish practised cremation, he certainly would have mentioned it : and that he
did not do so illustrates how completely the custom had
dropped out of historical and traditional memory.

There is, indeed, a sort of indirect approach to a record
of cremation in the legendary account of the second Battle
of Moytura.   In this great battle, fought many centuries
before the Christian era, the Fomorians were defeated by
the Dedannans, and all their chief men slain.   The whole
narrative is given in a historical tale called " The Second

Battle of Moytura," which has been edited and translated by Dr. Stokes in vol. XII. of the " Revue Celtique." The knowledge of the site has never been lost, but has descended continuously to the present day ; and the place still retains the old name in the slightly altered form of Moytirra, now applied to a townland near the north-east shore of Lough Arrow in Sligo. Moreover, vivid traditions of the battle and of its prominent incidents are still prevalent among the people of the neighbourhood. The whole plain is covered with cromlechs and tombs of many kinds ; it is, indeed, perhaps the most remarkable battle-cemetery in Europe. In all the graves human remains have been found ; and though in none of the old accounts of the battle is there any mention of cremation, by far the greatest proportion of the remains consist of burned bones. Thus, though we have no direct record of cremation, we have a legendary account of a battle in which the bodies of those who fell were cremated.

It is possible that there is a faint echo of the custom in three old Irish words, *adnad, adnacht*, and *adnacul*, all still in use. First, as to *adnad*, or, as it is now written, *adhnadh* [ey-na] : this is the familiar word for kindling, igniting, or burning ; and that it had this meaning in old times is proved by an eighth-century gloss in Zeuss (997, note 12), where the Greek word *asbestes* (*i.e. asbestos*), meaning what is ' un-burnable,' is explained by the Irish equivalent *nephadnachte*, where *neph* is the present Irish *neamh*, a negative particle : and *adnachte*, a derivative of *adna*, is ' burnable.' But this word *adnad* is also used in connexion with burial in the following manner :—In the Book of Ballymote, and also in the Yellow Book of Lecan,* there is a version of the story of the death and burial of Fiachra, and of the burial alive of the fifty captives (p. 545, *supra*), which, after stating that his sepulchre was made and his grave dug, brings in

---

* BB, p. 264, col. 2, lines 25–27 : YBL, 187, *b*, lines 30–33.

the word *adnad* in this passage : *Ro h-adnad a cluiche caentach* (p. 539, *supra*), ' his funeral games were celebrated,' where the word used for ' celebrated ' or ' performed ' is *adnad*.* So also *adnacht* and *adnacul* [ey-nacht, ey-na-cul], both used in the sense of ' burial.' But even supposing that all these three words are derived from *adna* or *adnad*, burning, they may preserve a memory, not of the burning of the body, but of the lighting of fires or torches, as part of the obsequies—a practice that has partially survived to this day in the lighting of candles round the body at wakes : so that no certain conclusion can be drawn from them. Observe that Zeuss, in the passage referred to (997, note 12), queries whether there is not some connexion between *adnad*, ' burning,' and *adnacul*, ' burial,' but ventures no farther : and what perhaps is more significant, in Cormac's Glossary, and in the writings of other ancient Irish glossarists, supposed derivations are given for *adnacul*, but in none of them is any connexion traced with *adnad*, burning.† If there was any such connexion, they could hardly have failed to notice it.

It is curious that, while ancient Irish writings have preserved scarcely any memory of cremation, in Norse literature there are many records of the contemporaneous burning of the bodies of warriors ; and there is, it appears, one such record in the Anglo-Saxon poem of Beowulf.‡

Cremation and ordinary burial were practised in Ireland contemporaneously, as we know from the well-ascertained fact, that in the same cromlech or grave complete skeletons have been found along with urns containing ashes and

---

* Dr. Sullivan, in his Introduction to O'Curry's Lectures (pp. 320 *et seq.*}, has a notice of this, as showing that *adnad* preserves a memory of cremation : but he somewhat weakens his argument by overstatement, and by a strained translation of *ro h-adnad a cluiche caentach*, which he renders " his *cluiche caentach* was ignited."

† Corm. Gloss., 15 : Bernard and Atkinson, Lib. Hymn., 211.

‡ Borlase, Dolmens, 744, 745.

burnt bones.* This is what we should expect ; for cremation was a troublesome and expensive process, and could
not have been practised by poor people, most of whom
must have buried the body without burning.

Occasionally the bodies of kings and chieftains were
buried in a standing posture, arrayed in full battle costume,
with the face turned towards the territories of their enemies.
Of this custom we have several very curious historical
records. In the Book of the Dun Cow it is related that
King Laegaire [Laery] was killed " by the sun and wind "
in a war against the Lagenians : " and his body was after-
" wards brought from the south, and interred, with his
" arms of valour, in the south-east of the external rampart
" of the royal *Rath Laegaire* at *Temur* (Tara), with the
" face turned southwards upon the Lagenians [as it were]
" fighting with them, for he was the enemy of the Lagenians
" in his lifetime."†

The same circumstance is related in a still older
authority, with some additional interesting details—the
" Annotations of Tirechan," in the Book of Armagh. King
Laegaire says :—" For Niall, my father (*i.e.* Niall of the
" Nine Hostages), did not permit me to believe [in the
" teaching of St. Patrick], but [commanded] that I should
" be interred in the ramparts of *Temur*, like men standing
" up in battle. For the pagans are accustomed to be
" buried, armed with their weapons ready, face to face [in
" which manner they remain] to the day of *Erdathe*, among
" the magi, *i.e.* the day of judgment of the Lord." Then
Laegaire goes on to say -—" I, the son of Niall [must be
" buried] after this fashion, namely, as the son of Dunlang
" [was buried] at Maistiu in the plain of Lifè, because of
" the endurance of our hatred." The Dunlang spoken of

* On this point see Wilde's Boyne, 224, 229, 232, 233, 234 : Kilk. Arch
Journ., 1852–3, p. 235 ; 1876–8, p. 178 ; 1879–82, p. 185 : Wood-Martin,
Pagan Ireland, 108 and 353.

† Petrie's Tara, 170 : see also Kilk. Arch. Journ., 1872–3, p. 147.

here was a king of Leinster and a deadly enemy of the family of Hy Neill, to which Laegaire belonged ; and his son was buried at Maistiu, now the hill of Mullamast in Kildare, armed and standing up with his face turned north against the Hy Neill. It appears from Laegaire's words that his own intended burial in Tara after the same manner was, as it were, an answer to the challenge of the son of Dunlang.* A similar account of Laegaire's burial is given in the " Tripartite Life of St. Patrick " (p. 75) and elsewhere.

Keating, in his " Three Shafts of Death " (p. 162), notices this mode of burial and gives one example. Another very distinct statement as to upright burial is found in the Dindsenchus. The Battle of Culliu was fought on a plain, subsequently overflowed by Lough Orbsen or Lough Corrib, where Mannanan mac Lir fell : and the Dindsenchus says : —" And he was killed in that battle and buried standing up in that place " (*ro hadnacht ina shessom*)."†

The truthfulness of all these records is borne out by the actual discovery of skeletons standing up in graves. In 1848 a tumulus called Croghan Erin in the parish of Kiltale, county Meath, near Kilmessan, was opened, and a skeleton was found standing erect in a grave with a large flagstone laid flat near the surface immediately over the skull. Though there were no arms on this skeleton, a bronze sword-blade and an iron spearhead were found near it, with some fragments of an urn.‡ Similar interments have been found in other parts of Ireland.

The pagan Irish believed that, while the body of their king remained in this position, it exercised a malign influence on their enemies, who were thereby always defeated in battle. In the Life of St. Kellach it is stated that his father, Owen Bel, great-grandson of Dathi, and king of Connaught, was killed in the battle of Sligo, fought

---

* Todd, St. Patk., 438. † Rennes Dinds., Rev. Celt., XVI. 277. ‡ Proc. Roy. Ir. Acad., IV. 388.

against the Ulstermen.   And before his death he told his
people to bury him with his red javelin in his hand in the
grave :—" Place my face towards the north, on the side of
" the hill by which the northerns pass when flying before
" the army of Connaught ; let my grave face them, and
" place myself in it after this manner."   And this order
was strictly complied with ; and in every place where the
Clanna Neill and the Connacians met in conflict, the
Clanna Neill and the northerns were routed, being panic-
stricken by the countenances of their foes ; so that the
Clanna Neill and the people of the north of Ireland
resolved to come with a numerous host and raise [the
body of] Owen from the grave, and carry his remains
northwards.   This was done, and the body was buried at
the other side [of the river] with the mouth down, that it
might not be the means of causing them to fly before the
Connacians.*

It is very curious that, in some parts of the country, the
people still retain a dim traditional memory of this mode
of sepulture, and of the superstition connected with it.
There is a place near Garvagh, in Londonderry, called
Slaghtaverty ; but it ought to have been called *Laghtaverty*,
the *laght* or sepulchral monument of a dwarf named
Abhartach [avartagh].   This dwarf was a magician, and
a dreadful tyrant ; and after having perpetrated great
cruelties on the people he was at last vanquished and
slain by a neighbouring chieftain.   He was buried in a
standing posture, but the very next day he appeared in his
old haunts, more cruel and vigorous than ever.   And the
chief slew him a second time and buried him as before ; but
again he escaped from the grave, and spread terror through
the whole country.   The chief then consulted a druid, and
according to his directions, he slew the dwarf a third time,
and buried him in the same place, *with his head downwards* ; which subdued his magical power, so that he never

* Hy. Fiachrach, 472 : Silva Gad., 52.

again appeared on the earth. The *laght* raised over the dwarf is still there, and you may hear the legend with much detail from the natives of the place, one of whom told it to me.

It sometimes happened that the mere exhibition of the body of a dead chief, before burial, paralysed the enemy. When King Dathi (A.D. 405 to 428) was killed by a flash of lightning at the foot of the Alps, Amalgaid [Awly], his son, took command of the army and had the body brought home on a bier. " And," says the old record, " he gained " nine battles by sea and ten battles by land by means of " the corpse : for when his people exhibited the body of " the king, they used to rout the forces that opposed " them."* This superstition about the malign influence of the body of a dead warrior over his living enemies also prevailed among the ancient Britons.† While the head of Bendigeid Vran remained buried in the White Mount in London no invaders could come across the sea to attack Britain (Mabinogion 42).

It is to be noted that the arms of a warrior were often buried with him, whether his body was placed standing up or lying flat.‡

4. *Cemeteries.*

In pagan times the Irish had royal cemeteries in various parts of the country for the interment of kings and chiefs with their families and relatives. Of these there is a short account, called *Senchus na Relec,* " History of the Cemeteries," in the Book of the Dun Cow, with a statement that they were the chief cemeteries of Erin before the introduction of Christianity. This old authority enumerates eight :—Croghan ; Brugh ; Tailltenn ; Luachair Ailbe ; Oenach Ailbe ; Oenach Culi ; Oenach Colmain ; and

---

* HyF, p. 23. See also (for the body of Niall) Otia Mers. II. 91.
† See Sir S. Ferguson, Congal, p. 213 : and Ir. Nennius, 101.
‡ Like Ferbern, LL, " Contents," 49, *b* : O'Curry, Man. & Cust., I. 328.

Temair Erann ; in all of which, as already observed, the illustrious dead were commemorated by annual fairs.

The cemetery of **Brugh**—the burial-place of the De-dannans—lies on the northern bank of the Boyne, a little below Slane, extending along the river for nearly three miles. It is one of the most remarkable pagan cemeteries in Europe, consisting of about twenty barrows or burial-mounds of various sizes, containing chambers or artificial caves with shallow saucer-shaped sarcophagi.

FIG. 345.

New Grange. About 70 feet high, but once much higher: base occupies more than an acre. Formed of loosely-piled stones, with a surface of clay, covered with grass. It was surrounded at base by a circle of great pillar-stones, about a dozen of which remain. Beehive-shaped chamber in centre, about 20 feet in diameter, and 19 feet high, with three recesses, in one of which is a shallow sarcophagus. A passage, 60 feet long, leads to exterior: sides of both chamber and passage formed of enormous stones, covered with carvings like those seen in some of the monuments in sect. 5 farther on. This sepulchre closely resembles some of the ancient Greek tombs. (From Wakeman's Handbook of Irish Antiquities.)

The three principal mounds are those of New Grange, Knowth, and Dowth, which are the largest sepulchral mounds in Ireland. There are numerous pillar-stones : and many of the great stones forming the sides and roofs of the caves are carved with curious ornamental designs of various patterns—circles, spirals, lozenges, and so forth. The term *brugh* (pron. broo), as we have seen (p. 21, *supra*), has several meanings, one of which is a great house or mansion : and it was applied to this cemetery because the principal mound, that now called New Grange, was supposed to have been the fairy palace of the Dedannan chief and magician, Aengus Mac-in-Og (see vol. I., p. 260, *supra*). To this day the name is preserved: for the very field in which the New Grange mound stands is now called Broo or Bro Park, and in it also are Broo or Bro Farm, Bro House, and Bro Mill.*

The cemetery of **Croghan** is called in old documents *Relig na Ríg* [Rellig-na-ree], or the 'burial-place of the kings.' It is half a mile south of Croghan, the seat of the kings of Connaught, near Tulsk in the present Co. Roscommon (see p. 92, *supra*), and is still well recognisable, with numerous sepulchral monuments.† It covers about two acres, and is surrounded by a dry wall, now all in ruins. A little to the north-west of this main cemetery is a natural cave of considerable extent, with artificial alterations and additions, still much celebrated in popular legend. This is the cavern—the "Hell-gate of Ireland" already mentioned (vol. I., p. 265)—from which in old times, on every Samain eve, issued the malignant bird-flocks on their baleful flight, to blight crops and kill animals with their poisonous breath. The great Queen Maive lived at Croghan, and was interred in this cemetery; and to the present day, all over the district, there are vivid traditions about her. More than thirty years ago, Sir Samuel Ferguson found on a stone in the cave an Ogham inscription, which he read as "Medff," a form of Medb or Maive, one of the many striking confirmations of

---

* The Rev. James O'Laverty was the first to call attention to this in Kilk. Arch. Journ. for 1892, p. 430. There are detailed descriptions of the Brugh Cemetery in Wilde's Boyne; in the third edition of Wakeman's Antiquities, by Mr. Cooke; and in Trans. Roy. Ir. Acad., vol. xxx., by Mr. George Coffey. The History of the Cemeteries will be found in LU, p. 50, and, with translation, in Petrie's R. Towers, p. 97. The high ancient mound, now called Millmount, in the town of Drogheda, situated on the south of the Boyne, half a quarter of a mile from the bridge, probably belongs to the Brugh Cemetery.

† A full account of the present state of this cemetery, by Sir Samuel Ferguson, may be seen in Proc. Roy. Ir. Acad., 1870–76, p. 114.

the truth of the old records. Of late years, however, the correctness of his reading has been questioned. On a low mound near the *relig* stands the *coirthe derg* or 'red pillar-stone' marking the grave of King Dathi, mentioned farther on (sect. 5), and figured here.

The kings of Ireland were interred here down to the time of Crimthann Nia Náir, king of Ireland A.D. 74 to 90. Crimthann's wife was a Dedannan lady; and at her solicitation he chose to be buried at Brugh, which after him

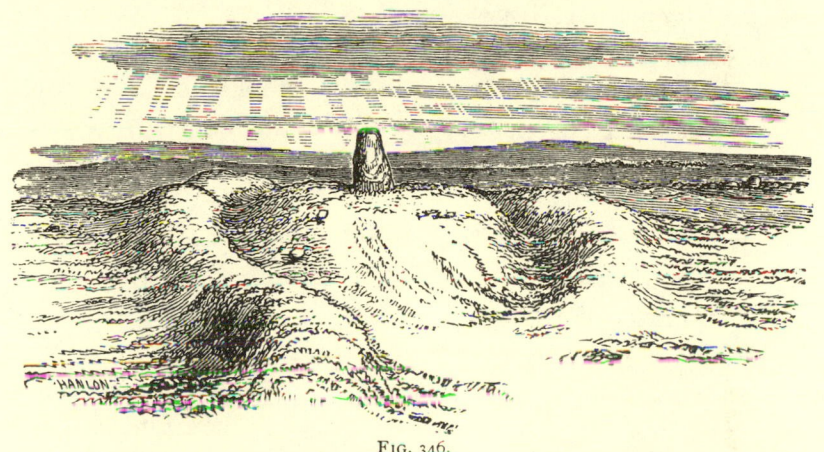

FIG. 346.

King Dathi's grave and pillar-stone at Croghan. (From Proc. Roy. Ir. Acad., 1879, p. 117.)

was adopted as the burial-place of the supreme kings, while the kings of Connaught continued to be interred at Croghan.*

Before noticing the next on the list, Tailltenn, it is necessary to observe that there were other royal cemeteries which are often mentioned in the records, though not included in the list in the " History of the Cemeteries "; such as those at Tara and Ushnagh. And along with these the pagan people had their own local burying-places in every part of the country, of which the remains are still

* From the History of the Cemeteries. See also Keat., 358. In these will be found the names of several illustrious persons interred at Croghan, Brugh, and Tailltenn: for a fuller list see HyF, p. 27.

to be seen in several places, containing the usual mounds and kistvaens. The history of many of these is quite lost. By far the most remarkable and extensive cemetery of this last class in all Ireland is that on the ridge of the Loughcrew hills near Oldcastle in Meath, which was first investigated and described in detail in 1872 by Mr. Eugene A. Conwell of Trim.* It consists of a wonderful collection of great mounds, carns, cromlechs, sepulchral chambers, inscribed stones, and stone saucer-shaped sarcophagi, all of the same general character as those of Brugh. It must have been a noted cemetery; yet it has completely dropped out of history: or rather it should be said there is no passage in any history, tradition, or legend that can be recognised as applying to it.

Tailltenn (now Teltown), as a palace, and as the scene of a great annual fair, has been already noticed. The cemetery, which was the burial-place of the kings of Ulster, and afterwards of the kings of Ireland, was situated near the palace, but has been long obliterated; and no wonder, seeing that the whole site, including raths, sporting-greens, beds of artificial ponds, cemetery, &c., has been for generations under cultivation: so that, with the exception of one large rath—over which however the plough has run—the ramparts and fences have nearly disappeared. Yet traces remain showing that its forts once rivalled or exceeded in size those of Tara.

Mr. Fergusson, the distinguished author of " Rude Stone Monuments," expresses the opinion (at pp. 219, 220)—indeed he all but pronounces dogmatically—that the Loughcrew Cemetery is the real cemetery of Tailltenn,

* In Proc. Roy. Ir. Acad., vol. IX., pp. 42, 355: and vol. for 1870–76, p. 72. It is a pity that Mr. Conwell did not confine himself to simple description; for he indulges in some visionary speculations—especially that about " The Tomb of Ollamh Fodla "—that somewhat detract from the merits of a really valuable paper. Another and more scientific description of this cemetery, by Mr. George Coffey, will be found in Trans. Roy. Ir. Acad., vol. XXXI., p. 23.

rejecting the Teltown site, on the sole ground that it contains no imposing monuments like those at Brugh, which he thinks should be expected in a burying-place of such celebrity.*　But it will be seen that the foundation on which this theory was supposed to rest does not exist, and that the theory itself falls to the ground, in face of the fact first pointed out by Sir Samuel Ferguson,† that Religna-ree at Croghan, which was at least as celebrated as the cemetery at Tailltenn, and also those at Tara, and Ushnagh consist of a number of small mounds over graves, with nothing in the least resembling the immense monuments of Brugh and Loughcrew.

But independently of this, there are other considerations sufficient to show that the cemetery of Tailltenn could not have been that situated on the Loughcrew hills.　The consistent account given in our oldest traditions is that Lug of the Long Arms had his foster-mother, Taillte, buried under a mound *at Tailltenn*, which took its name from her, and that he instituted the yearly games in honour of her, which continued to be celebrated for so many centuries afterwards :　all which were carried on—as in case of the other cemeteries already noticed (p. 434)—*at and around* the original grave.　For instance, Cuan O'Lochain's Poem on Tailltenn in the Book of Leinster (200, *b*, 35) tells us that the fair was held *imman lecht*, ' round the grave.'　This grave was the origin of the cemetery :　and accordingly, in the " History of the Cemeteries," it is stated that the cemetery was *at Tailltenn*.　We are told also in that and other old documents, that Ollam Fodla [Ollave Fóla] and the other illustrious personages who were laid to rest here were buried " in Tailltenn " (*i Tailltenn*).　But the records contain still more conclusive evidence on the point.　The

---

* Mr. Conwell adopted Fergusson's view, evidently without sufficient inquiry.　Mr. Coffey, the latest investigator, a better authority in this matter than either Fergusson or Conwell, does not adopt their theory (see Trans. Roy. Ir. Acad., xxxi., p. 24, note).

† In a Paper in Proc. Roy. Ir. Acad. for 1870–76, p. 114.

places where commemorative fairs and games were held were often called *Oenach* or *Aenach*, followed by the genitive of the proper name of the place : as Croghan was called *Oenach Cruachna* (the ' Fair of Croghan '). The account in the Book of the Dun Cow, speaking of the three cemeteries of Croghan, Brugh, and Tailltenn, says :— There are fifty burial-mounds at each Oenach of these : fifty mounds at the Oenach of Croghan, fifty mounds at the Oenach of Tailltenn, and fifty at the Oenach of Brugh. Here, in all three cases, the cemetery was *at* or *beside* the spot where the fair was held : and thus the writer of this account, who records things as they existed in his time— A.D. 1100—and for immemorial ages previously, tells us that the cemetery of Tailltenn was *at the very spot where the fair was celebrated,* which we know was Tailltenn itself. Tailltenn is a small, circumscribed, well-defined spot, perfectly well known to this day ; so there can be no doubt as to where the " Cemetery of Tailltenn " was situated. To sum up then : after all the evidence that has been here adduced, I suppose no one will now assert that the " cemetery of Tailltenn " was that on the Loughcrew hills, which is *fully fourteen miles off* as the crow flies.

The natural explanation of the difference between the cemeteries of Brugh and Loughcrew on the one hand, and those of Croghan, Tara, Ushnagh, and Tailltenn on the other, is that they belonged to two different races, and probably to different periods. One people had a passion for mighty and enduring monuments, and these have left us the imposing remains at Brugh and Loughcrew : while the other contented themselves with small burial-mounds, covering simple *comrars* or chambers, whose cemeteries were Croghan, Tailltenn, and others like them. It may be added that as the Brugh cemetery is traditionally ascribed to the people called Dedannans, so, that at Loughcrew, which resembles it so closely, belonged doubtless to the same race.

By far the greatest number of interments in pagan times were, not in cemeteries, but in detached spots, where individuals or families were interred. Such detached graves are now found in every part of Ireland. Sometimes they are within the enclosure of raths and cashels. After the introduction of Christianity in the fifth century, the people gradually forsook their pagan burial-places : and the dead were buried with Christian rites in the consecrated cemeteries attached to the little primitive churches. *Reilig*, Old Irish *relec*, means a cemetery or graveyard ; it is the Latin *reliquiæ*, and was borrowed very early, for it occurs in the Zeuss MSS., and Cormac has the word in his Glossary (p. 144). It was applied to a pagan as well as to a Christian cemetery. The most celebrated pagan burial-place in Ireland with this name was Relig-na-rig, mentioned above.

A burial-ground was sometimes called *Ruam* : in the well-known prophecy of the druids regarding the coming of St. Patrick, they say : " *Taillcenns* [see vol. I., p. 357, *supra*] will come who will found churches and lay out *ruams*."* Cormac's Glossary (p. 143) derives the word from " Rome " : the idea being that as Rome was the final resting-place of so many saints, a graveyard in Ireland was a miniature Rome, the resting-place of the faithful. The word continued in use until quite recently, though I think it is not understood now by speakers of Irish.

A sepulchre or grave was sometimes called *otharlige* [ŏharlee], which is literally ' sick-bed '—the bed of a person sick [unto death], from *othar*, sick, and *lige*. a bed (Lat. *lectus*). Olioll Olom's seven sons, who were slain in the Battle of Mucrime (A.D. 250), were buried in an *otharlige* on the north side of the ford† : and we read in the Book of Leinster, that after the death of Cuculainn his head and

---

* Trip. Life, 34, 10.
† Silva Gad., 356, bottom : Ir. Text, 316, 34.

his hand were buried in an *otharlige*.* We have already
seen (vol. I., p. 608) that the cemetery in which the victims
of a plague were interred was called *Tamhlacht*.

5. *Sepulchral Monuments.*

The monuments constructed round and over the dead
in Ireland were of various kinds, very much depending on
the rank of the person buried : and they were known by
several names.   Some were in cemeteries, some—belonging
to pagan times—detached, as already stated.   Many of the
forms of monuments used by the pagan Irish were continued in Christian times.   The most common words for a
grave in general were *uag*, modern form *uaigh* [ooa] : and
fert, modern *feart*.

Carn and Duma.—In our ancient literature, both lay and
ecclesiastical, there are many notices of the erection of
carns over graves.   The Irish word is *carn*, which simply
means a heap : but *card* was another and very old form of
this word.   We have records of carns in documents of the
seventh century.   For example, in Tirechan's " Notes on
the Life of St. Patrick," we read that the saint's charioteer
Totmael died near Croaghpatrick in Mayo, and he [Patrick]
buried him there, *et congregavit lapides erga sepulchrum*,
" and he made a heap of stones beside the grave."†   So
also in Adamnan's " Life of St. Columba " (p. 63) : when
a certain old Pict was buried in the Isle of Skye, his companions raised over him a carn of stones (*congesto lapidum
acervo sepeliunt*).

Endless examples might be cited from the records in
the native language.   Perhaps the oldest is the account in
the " Bruden Da Derga " (p. 169) of the erection of the carn
by the marauders on their way to the Bruden by each man
bringing a stone which they cast all in one heap, as already
related (vol. I., p. 149).   Here it is stated that the carn was

---

* LL, 121, *b*, ₃₉, ₄₀.   † Trip. Life, 322, ₂₆, ₂₇ : see also same, p. 161.

raised for the double purpose of reckoning the slain and commemorating the destruction of the hostel. But the general purpose of a carn was as a memorial of the person or persons buried beneath it. The plan of raising a carn over the grave by each bringing a stone was often resorted to. In this manner—as we are told in the Book of Leinster—Lugaid and his followers, when they had slain Furbaide, son of King Concobar Mac Nessa, piled up a carn over his grave.* The same custom exists to some extent at the present day, for in many parts of Ireland, they pile up a *laght* or *carn* over the spot where any

FIG. 347.

Carn, on Carns Hill, near Sligo. (From Col. Wood-Martin's Pagan Ireland, p. 294.)

person has come to an untimely death; and every passer-by is expected to add a stone to the heap. The tourist who ascends Mangerton mountain, near Killarney, may see a carn of this kind near the Devil's Punch Bowl, where a shepherd was found dead early in the last century.

In or near the centre of almost every carn a beehive-shaped chamber of dry masonry was formed communicating with the exterior by a long narrow passage. The body or urn was placed in the chamber: in some chambers, rude shallow stone coffins shaped like a saucer have been found.

*LL, Contents, 52, *b*, 16: see for another example Contents, 54, *b*, bottom.

In old pagan times people had a fancy to bury on the tops of hills ; and the summits of very many hills in Ireland are crowned with carns, under every one of which—in a stone coffin—reposes some person renowned in the olden time. They are sometimes very large, and form conspicuous objects when viewed from the neighbouring plains, of which one of the finest examples in Ireland is Miscaun Maive near the town of Sligo. It is an immense heap on the summit of the hill of Knocknarea, which hangs over the sea to a height of 1078 feet. The carn is about 600 feet in circumference and 34 feet high ; and for scores of miles round the hill it is a most striking object, whether viewed from land or sea. The popular tradition is that it commemorates the great Queen Maive of Croghan, which may be correct : but, if so, it is a cenotaph, as she was buried in Croghan (HyF, 29, 2). A monumental heap or carn is often called a *lecht* or *leacht*.

FIG. 348

Duma or burial-mound, beside the Boyne, near Clonard : very conspicuous from the Railway, on the left as you go westward. Circumference, 433 feet ; height, 50 feet. (From Wilde's Boyne and Blackwater.)

This word *lecht* is cognate with Lat. *lectus*, and Gr. *lechos* (both meaning a bed) : for in many languages a grave is called a bed (see *leaba* further on). In Cormac's Glossary (p. 101) *lecht* is explained *lige mhairbh*, the grave of a dead [person]. Sometimes entire skeletons have been found under carns and *lechts*, sometimes cinerary urns, and sometimes both together, showing that these monuments were used with both modes of burial (see p. 551, *supra*).

The *duma* or mound—often called *tuaim*—seems to have differed from the *carn* in this :—that whereas the carn was formed of moderately large stones, such as a person could easily carry, the *duma* was made of clay, or of a mixture of clay and small pebbles, having usually, at the present time, a smooth carpet of grass growing on it. While carns were often placed on hills, the *dumas* were always in the lowlands. The *duma*, like the carn, has a cist or chamber in the centre, in which the urn or body was placed : sometimes there is a passage to the outside, sometimes not. Numerous mounds of this class still

FIG. 349.

Sepulchral chamber with shallow sarcophagus: in the interior of one of the Loughcrew carns. Observe the characteristic pagan carvings. (From Col. Wood-Martin's Pagan Ireland, p. 289.)

remain all over the country : they may be generally distinguished from the mounds of *duns* by the absence of circumvallations. They are often mentioned in ancient Irish writings ; and we frequently find it recorded that the bodies of the slain were buried in a *duma*. Very often round a *duma* there was a circle of pillar-stones, some of which remain in position to the present day. But stone circles simply, with a level space within, are often found.

These always mark a place of interment ; being placed round a grave.* (See pp. 539 and 542, *supra*.)

Comrar, Kistvaen, Cromlech.—The stone coffin, chest, or cist in which a body was interred, or in which one or more urns were placed, was called in Irish a *comrar*, a word which means a protecting cover, shrine, or box of any kind. It corresponds with the modern Irish *comhra* [cora], which is now the usual word for a coffin : and also with English *coffer* and *coffin*. In a passage in the Book of the Dun Cow we are given a very clear example both of the *comrar* and of the sepulchral pillar-stone. It is a description of the grave of Eochaid Airgthech, a usurping king of Ireland, who, after reigning a year, was slain, A.D. 280, in a battle fought near the Ollarba or Larne river, in the present Co. Antrim. Cailte, who slew him, tells how he was buried :—" There is a chest of stone (*comrar cloche*)
" about him there in the earth : and there, upon the chest
" are his two bracelets of silver and his two *bunne-do-at*
" (p. 241, *supra*), and his neck-torque of silver : and by his
" *ulad* or tomb there is a stone pillar (*coirthe*) : and on the
" end of the pillar that is in the earth there is an Ogham
" which says :—' This is Eochaid Airgthech : Cailte slew
" me in an encounter against Finn.' "[†]

When a *comrar* is over ground and formed of very large stones, it is now commonly called a *cromlech* or *dolmen* : both words of late introduction and neither of Irish origin : when underground and formed of smaller flagstones, it is generally called a *kistvaen*, meaning ' stone-chest ' : Welsh *maen*, a stone. Many of the kistvaens, and also some of the cromlechs, were made much larger than was needed for the reception of a single body : in these

* See Stokes's Petrie, p. 238, *et seq.* Stone circles are found all through Europe and elsewhere. Of these, Fergusson says they were probably all sepulchral, and that the contention of some persons that the very large ones, both of England and Ireland, were used for religious rites, is not supported by any evidence : which is certainly true so far as Ireland is concerned.

† Petrie, R. Towers, 108 : Voyage of Bran. I, 48, 52 : LU 134, *a*, 3.

were interred several persons, probably all members of the same family. Many of these large *comrars* have been lately discovered and described. The bodies of those who fell in battle were often interred in kistvaens and cromlechs, of which numbers are now found in ancient battlefields.

A cromlech is formed of one great flat stone lying on the tops of several large standing stones, thus enclosing a rude chamber in which one or more bodies or urns were placed. These cromlechs are very numerous in all parts

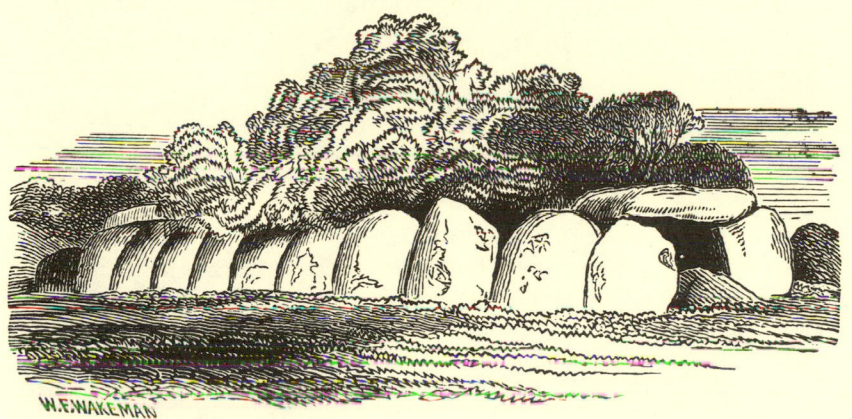

W.F.WAKEMAN

Fig. 350.

Prehistoric "Giant's Grave," near the village of Drumcliffe, County Sligo : about 38 feet in length. A human skeleton was found in it, with a rude necklace round the neck. (From Col. Wood-Martin's "Rude Stone Monuments in Sligo," Kilk. Archæol. Journ. for 1887-8, p. 143.)

of Ireland, and various theories were formerly in fashion to account for their origin ; of which the most common was that they were "Druids' altars," and used for offering sacrifices.* It is now, however, well known that they are tombs, which is proved by the fact that under many of them have been found cinerary urns, calcined bones, and sometimes entire skeletons. The popular name of "Giants' Graves," which is applied to them in many parts of the country, preserves, with sufficient correctness, the memory

* " There is really no sufficient reason "—says Sir John Lubbock in his Pre-historic Times (p. 111)—"for connecting them [*i.e.* cromlechs and other megalithic monuments] with druidical worship."

of their original purpose. Sepulchral monuments of the same class are found all over Europe, and even in India.

There is a village on the east side of the river Moy, a kind of suburb of Ballina, called Ardnaree, a name originally applied to the hill immediately south of the village, which is now called Castle Hill, from a castle that has long since disappeared. The event that gave origin to this name is very fully related by Mac Firbis in his account of the Tribes and Customs of the Hy Fiachrach, and more fully still in the Irish Life of St. Kellach (" Silva Gadelica," p. 50). The same story is told in the Dinn-senchus. The persons concerned are all well-known characters, and the event is far within the horizon of authentic history.

Guairĕ [Guara] son of Colman, was king of Connaught in the sixth century (not Guaire the Hospitable who lived a century later: Miss Eleanor Hull brings this out in " Early Christian Ireland," pp. 55, 56). Though a power-ful monarch, he was not the true heir to the throne ; the rightful heir was a man who in his youth had abandoned the world and entered the priest-hood, and who was now bishop of Kilmore-Moy ; this was Cellach or Kellagh, the son of the last monarch, Owen Bel, and descended directly from the celebrated Dathi. Cellach was murdered at the instigation of Guaire, by four ecclesiastical students—the four Maels, as they were called, because the names of all began with the syllable Mael—who were under the bishop's tuition, and who, it appears, were his own foster-brothers. The bishop's brother however soon after pursued and captured the murderers, and brought them in chains to the hill overlooking the Moy, which was up to that time called *Tulach-na-faircsiona* [Tullanafarkshina], the hill of the prospect, where he hanged them all ; and from this cir-cumstance the place took the name of *Ard-na-riaghadh* [Ardnaree], the hill of the executions.

They were buried at the other side of the river, a little south of the present town of Ballina, and the place was called *Ard-na-Mael*, the 'hill of the [four] Maels.' The monument erected over them remains to this day; it is a cromlech, well known to the people of Ballina, and now commonly called the Table of the Giants.

The account given here, including the statement that the murderers were buried at Ardnaree, is taken from the Life of St. Kellagh (Silva Gad., 66) and from HyF (33): and as the Dinnsenchus states that there was a monument

Fig. 351.

The tomb of the Four Maels at Ardnaree, near Ballina, County Mayo.
(From Col. Wood-Martin's Pagan Ireland, p. 274.)

erected over the murderers, which was called *Lecht-na-Mael*, the 'tomb of the [four] Maels,' the identification of this cromlech may be regarded as complete. The name *Ard-na-Mael* is obsolete, the origin of the cromlech is forgotten, and Bishop Cellach and his murderers have long since ceased to be remembered in the traditions of the people.

Some cromlechs are formed of stones so large that to this day it remains a puzzle how they were heaved up to their places by people devoid of powerful mechanical appliances. The covering stone of the cromlech at Kilternan, on the summit of a hill between Dublin and

Bray, which is figured here, and which is one of the largest of its kind in Ireland, is $23\frac{1}{2}$ feet long, 17 feet broad, and

FIG. 352.

The great cromlech at Kilternan.   (From Wakeman's Handbook of Irish Antiquities.)

$6\frac{1}{2}$ feet thick.   It is lifted so high that a man can stand straight up under its higher end.

Sometimes regularly formed cromlechs—usually small —are found under *dumas* or mounds, like that shown in fig. 353, which still stands in its original place in the

FIG 353.

The Phœnix Park cromlech : example of a cromlech found under a *duma* or burial-mound. Covering stone, 6½ feet long.   (From Proceedings of the Royal Irish Academy.)

Phœnix Park, Dublin.   It was found in the year 1838 under an earthen tumulus of considerable size which was cleared away : several urns were dug out of the mound ;

and under the cromlech lay two human skeletons. But, generally speaking, cromlechs, that is to say, *comrars* formed of a few massive stones, were erected in the open air, and were not covered with a mound.*

Sepulchres are sometimes called *leaba* or *leabaid*, old Irish *lepad* [labba, labby], Manx *lhiabbee* : the word literally signifies a bed, but it is applied in a secondary sense to a grave, both in the present spoken language and in old writings. For example, in the ancient authority cited by Petrie ("R. Towers," p. 355), it is stated that the poet Rumann, who died in the year 747 at Rahan in King's County, "was buried in the same *leabaidh* with Ua "Suanaigh, on account of his (Rumann's) great honour "with God and man." This word *leaba* was applied to stone sepulchres in general, whether the *comrar* was under a mound or in the open air.

Cromlechs are called in many parts of the country *Leaba-Dhiarmada-agus-Gráinne*, the 'bed of Diarmaid and Grainnĕ'; and this name is connected with the well-known legend that Dermot O'Dyna eloped with Gráinnĕ, the daughter of King Cormac mac Art, Finn mac Cumail's betrothed spouse. The pair eluded Finn's pursuit for a year and a day, sleeping in a different place each night, under a *leaba* erected by Diarmaid after his day's journey; and according to the legend there were just 366 of them in Ireland. But this legend is a late invention, and evidently took its rise from the word *leabaidh* which was understood in its literal sense of a bed.

Pillar-stones.—The various purposes for which pillar-stones were erected have been already stated (page 267). Here we have to do only with their sepulchral use. All through the tales we find mention of the head-

---

* For another cromlech, see p. 537, *supra* : and for much more about cromlechs, with many illustrations, see Wakeman's Handbook of Ir. Antiqq., third edition, by Mr. Cooke.

stone or pillar-stone, called by the names *lie* or *lec* and cairthe [curha], placed over a grave. A usual formula to describe the burial of a person is :—His funeral rites were performed, his grave was dug, and his stone erected, with his name inscribed in Ogham. In accordance with these accounts, pillar-stones are found all over Ireland, some with Ogham: the inscription, as already stated, usually telling the name of the person, with the name of his father, and often a few other brief particulars. Some of the sepulchral pillar-stones had no inscriptions. Perhaps the most remarkable and interesting pillar-stone in all Ireland belonging to pagan times is that erected over the body of King Dathi in the cemetery of Croghan, which is figured at page 557, *supra* : it bears no inscription. In later ages the pagan pillar-stone developed into the ordinary headstone with a Christian inscription.

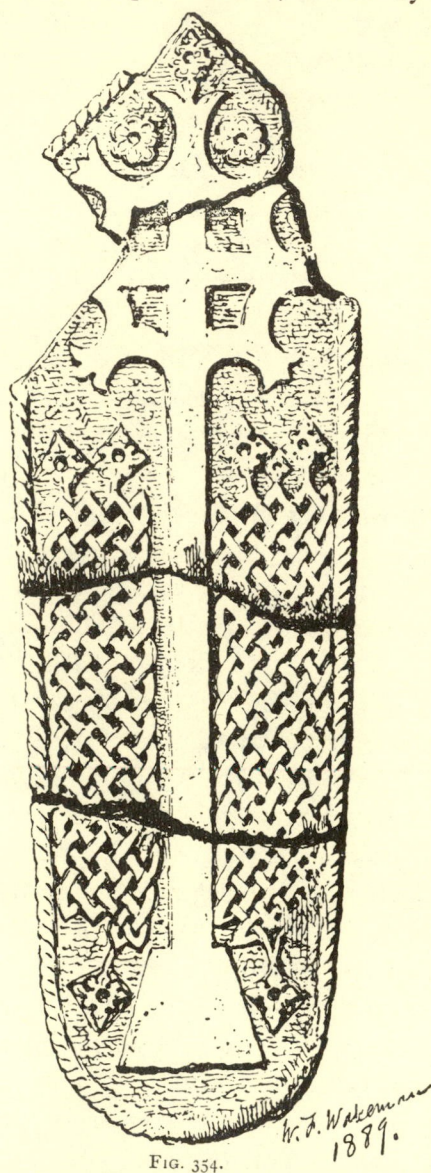

FIG. 354.

Decorated lid of stone coffin found in Devenish Island: belonging to Christian times. (From Journ. Roy. Society of Antiqq. Ireland, for 1896, p. 285.)

Tombs with Christian Inscriptions. — After the establishment of Christianity it became customary to erect a tomb over the grave, having a flat slab on top, especially in the cemeteries of monasteries, with an inscription, generally in Irish, but sometimes in Latin. In many cases the monument was a simple inscribed pillar-stone; so that some of the headstones that are mentioned under the last heading would fall also under this.

A most interesting Christian inscribed pillar-stone, probably the oldest in Ireland, is the headstone of Lugnaed or Lugna, standing about two and a half feet over ground, near the very ancient little church of Templepatrick on the island of Inchagoill in Lough Corrib, of which Dr. Petrie has given a full account in his " Round Towers." It is figured here from his accurate illustration in the same book, page 165. Another accurate drawing of it is in Wilde's " Lough Corrib " (1872, page 136), and a photograph from a paper cast is

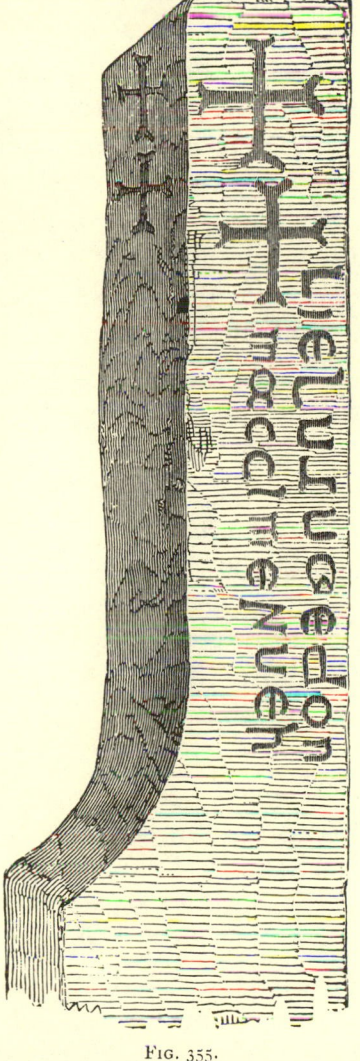

FIG. 355.
Lugnaed's headstone.

given by Sir Samuel Ferguson in his paper (Proceedings Royal Irish Academy for 1870-76, plate ix. at end).

According to the ancient narratives of the Life and Acts of St. Patrick, his sister Liemania had seven sons by Restitutus the Lombard.   These seven accompanied the saint to Ireland, and were settled by him in Connaught in the neighbourhood of Lough Mask.   The youngest was Lugna, Patrick's *Lumaire* or pilot.   Petrie and O'Donovan* concur in reading the inscription LIE LUGNAEDON MACC LMENUEH, " The stone of Lugnaedon [or Lugnaed] son of Limenueh " ;   and they identify this Lugnaed with Lugnaed, the son of St. Patrick's sister, which indeed— according to their reading—they could not avoid doing, inasmuch as—besides the local associations—he is the only saint of the name in all Irish ecclesiastical history.

This monument may be classed among these remarkable corroborations of the accuracy of Irisn historical records, of which so many examples have been given throughout this book : or to quote the words of Petrie :— " The very ancient inscription, which I have copied . . . " will be considered by the learned and unprejudiced as a " very singular and interesting evidence of the truth of " those [aforementioned Irish] authorities."

Dr. Whitley Stokes however reads this inscription differently (Cormac's Glossary, p. 101 : 1868), viz. LIE LUGUAEDON MACCI MENUEH. He is followed by Sir Samuel Ferguson in a paper published in Proc. Roy. Ir. Academy (1872, p. 259), whose words however indicate that he is not very confident in the matter :—" The asso- " ciations originally called up by Petrie may possibly yet " reconstitute themselves around this monument " (p. 260). Miss Stokes (Inscriptions, II., p. 10 : 1878) adopts the same reading, and renders it in English : " The stone of Lugaed, son of Men." Lastly, Mr. R. A. S. Macalister (Journ. Roy. Soc. Antiqq., Irel., 1898, p. 176) gives still the same reading.   All judging from the inscription alone.

Notwithstanding the great authority of these names, I believe that Petrie and O'Donovan were right, and that this venerable little monument marks the resting-place of

* Petrie R. Towers, p. 165 : O'Donovan, Ir. Gram. Introd. LII.,

Lugnaed the son of Liemania. This conclusion has been arrived at, not by an examination of the mere inscription —which is, taken by itself, by no means a safe guide— but by carefully weighing the whole of the evidence, inscriptional, historical, legendary, and topographical The full examination of this question would demand more space than I can afford here ; but it will be dealt with elsewhere (see Journ. R. Soc. Antiqq. Irel. 1906, Opening Paper).

On the monuments now under consideration—whether flat slabs or pillar-stones—the name of the person is sometimes found inscribed, and nothing more : but more usually a prayer is asked for the soul's repose : and occasionally— as in case of Lugnaed's monument—the inscription takes the form of " The stone of such and such a person." The great majority of the persons commemorated on these monuments are men ; but a few women are found.

Some of those whose names are inscribed on ancient tombstones have been identified and are well known in Irish history, which in each such instance fixes the date. But in case of far the greater number, antiquarians have been unable to identify them. The *names* of nearly all however are familiar as occurring frequently in Irish records. As might be expected, many of the inscriptions are mutilated and imperfect ; but a large proportion are as full and perfect as when first they were carved.

In the early part of the last century Dr. Petrie copied, in exact facsimile, all the inscriptions in the Irish language he could find—a great many of them in Clonmacnoise: and the whole collection has been edited and published under the auspices of the Royal Soc. of Antiqq., Ireland, with critical dissertations, descriptions, and translations, by Miss Margaret Stokes in two volumes—" Christian Inscriptions in the Irish Language." In this book—a book essential to every student of Irish antiquities—all Petrie's facsimiles, and many drawn by Miss Stokes herself and by others, are reproduced.

Altar-Tombs.—In the passage quoted above (p. 566), about Eochaid Airgthech, the word *ulad* [ulla], meaning a stone tomb, is applied to the whole structure round the body, including the *comrar* or kist, and probably the *duma* or mound ; but not including the pillar-stone. Here its application is pagan : but in subsequent times it was used to denote the tomb of a Christian : the tomb of Old-Patrick in Armagh is called his *uladh* (Feilire, 133, *a*, 1). As persons often took occasion to pray at the tombs of saints, this word *uladh* or *uluidh* is now, and has been for a long

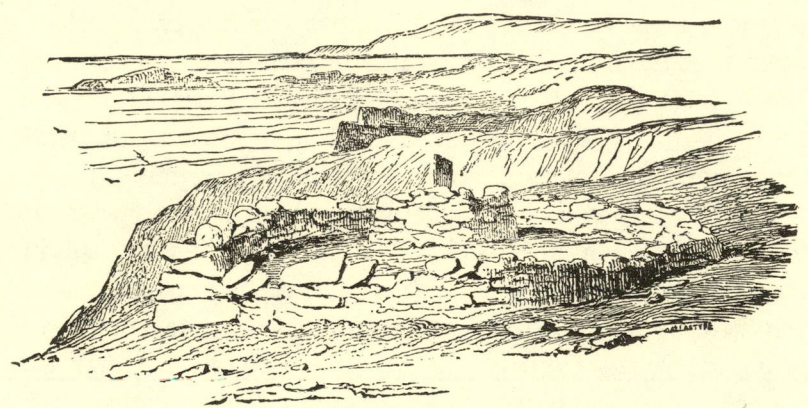

Fig. 356.

Example of an *ulad*: on Inishmurray. It is one of the stations where pilgrims pray in the course of their devotional rounds. It is called *Ulad-Muire* [ulla-murrĕ]. ‘Mary’s Altar,’ because it is dedicated to the Blessed Virgin. (From Kilk. Archæol. Journ. for 1885-6, p. 302. Drawn by Wakeman.)

time, used to denote a penitential station, or a stone altar erected as a place of devotion. It was used in this sense at an early period, for in the “Battle of Moyrath” (p. 298), it is said that “Domnall never went away from a cross “without bowing, nor from an *ulaidh* without turning “round, nor from an altar without praying.” On which O’Donovan remarks :—“*Uluidh*, a word which often occurs “in ancient MSS., is still understood in the west of Ireland “to denote a penitential station at which pilgrims pray, “and perform rounds on their knees.” This is the sense in which it is used in a passage in the Boroma,* in which St. Molling is stated to have been engaged on one occasion in " making *ulads* and altars " : in which the name seems to have no reference to a tomb. Many of these little altar-tombs are still to be seen in the west and south of Ireland.

Ferta.—*Fert*, plural *ferta*, signifies a grave or trench. The old name of Slane on the Boyne was *Ferta-fer-Féic* ; and the account given by Colgan (Trias Thaum., p. 20) of the origin of this name brings out very clearly the meaning of *ferta* :—" There is a place on the north margin " of the River Boyne, now called *Slaine* ; [but anciently] " it was called *Ferta-fer-Féic*, i.e. the trenches or sepulchres " of the men of Fiac, because the servants of a certain " chieftain named Fiac dug deep trenches there to inter " the bodies of the slain."

In the Book of Armagh there is an interesting account, by Tirechan, of the burial, in the *ferta*, of Laegaire's two daughters (see vol. I., p. 255, *supra*), who had been converted by St. Patrick :—" And the days of mourning for " the king's daughters were accomplished, and they buried " them near the well Clebach ; and they made a circular " ditch like to a *ferta* ; because so the Scotic people and " gentiles were used to do, but with us it is called *Reliquiæ* " (Irish *Reilig*), i.e. the remains of the virgins."† *Ferta* was originally a pagan term, as the above passage shows ; but, like many other words, it was adopted by the early Irish Christians.‡

Sepulchral Rath.—In connexion with the *ferta* it is very often mentioned that a *rath* or *raith* was raised round the grave, a custom described by Keating in his " Three Shafts of Death " (p. 161). When Baile (a pagan) was buried, " his *fert* and his *raith* were raised, and his *lia* [pillar-stone]

---

* Rev. Celt., XIII. 99. See also " Uladh " in O'Donovan's supplement.
† Todd, St Patrick, p. 455.
‡ See Reeves's Anc. Churches of Armagh, p. 47.

was set."* When the lady Acall (who gave name to Acaill, now the Hill of Skreen in Meath) was buried, " for " her was raised the rath yonder where she had met her " fate ":† and the Dinnsenchus (Gwynn, 13) mentions the burial of a person named Broccaid in a rath. This rath round a grave, like that surrounding a homestead, was a circular rampart for the mere purpose of protection.

On this point, Keating, in his " Three Shafts " (p. 161), has the following curious observations :— " The second mode [of interment] " was to place the dead under " the earth, with little raths or " entrenchments round them, but " with no stone or *leacht* over them. " And three classes of people " there are who were interred " within these little raths, namely, " men of science or learning, " women, and children. . . . And " there was one door to the grave " of a man of learning, two doors " to the grave of a woman, but " no door to the grave of a child." Keating quotes an old authority for these statements: but I am not able to illustrate them further, either from ancient Irish documents or from existing remains.

FIG. 357.

Monument (lying flat) of Richard de Clare, Earl of Pembroke, better known by the name of Strongbow, and his wife Fva, daughter of Dermot Mac Murrogh, king of Leinster: now to be seen in Christchurch Cathedral, Dublin. Strongbow landed in Ireland in 1170, as the leader of the Anglo-Norman invaders. He died in 1176, and was buried in Christchurch. (From Mrs. Hall's Ireland.)

Effigies.—The custom of carving effigies on tombs was introduced by the Anglo-Normans, and was adopted by the native Irish. But as this subject does not fall within the scope of my inquiry, it will be sufficient to give here

* O'Curry, MS Mat., 473, 20.　　　　　† *Ibid.*, 515.

two illustrations, one representing the monumental effigy of an Anglo-Norman lord, the other that of an Irish provincial king : both as they appear at the present day.

FIG. 358.

Tomb of Felim O'Conor, king of Connaught, in Roscommon Abbey; died, 1265. The two figures at bottom, showing only the heads, are galloglasses, of which there are eight. The rubbish has been recently cleared away, so that all can now be seen. Two of these fine figures are fully depicted in vol. I., p. 146, *supra*. A full-page engraving of the whole tomb, with the eight galloglasses, may be seen in The O'Conors of Connaught, by the Right Hon. The O'Conor Don. (From Kilk. Archæol. Journ.)

The Cross.—From the very earliest period of Christianity in Ireland, it was customary to erect a cross over the grave of a Christian ; of which so many notices occur, both in the Lives of the Saints and elsewhere, that it is unnecessary to give references.

Ornament composed from the Book of Kells.

APPENDIX

NOTES, ADDITIONS, AND CORRECTIONS

Vol. I., p. 118, last two lines of Text.

" Take out the axes quickly " should be " Open the straps quickly." But this does not affect the main argument for the antiquity of the Irish battleaxe. (I am indebted to Dr. Kuno Meyer for this correction, as well as for many other valuable suggestions and criticisms.)

Vol. I., p. 143, line 12.

Dam-dabaich here should be in the nom. form, *dam-dabach*. *Dam-dabaich* is dative, as it correctly appears in the original passage in LL, 79, *a*, 12.

Vol. I., p. 230, lines 8 to 17.

The translation of this poem given in Stokes and Strachan's " Thesaurus," II. 294, differs somewhat from that of O'Curry, and seems to leave it doubtful whether there is here any reference to forecasting by observation of the heavenly bodies. But there is enough of evidence on the point without it.

Vol. I., p. 577, and Note †, same page.

I am indebted to the Rev. Dr. Abbott, s.f.t.c.d., Librarian, for an interesting communication on the age of " Brian Boru's harp." An examination he has recently made has enabled him to bring under observation certain features of this old harp, which, by an accident, were inaccessible to Dr. Petrie, and the discovery of which removes the grounds of some of Petrie's arguments. As a result, Dr. Abbott comes to the conclusion that the harp may be much older than the end of the fourteenth century ; which, so far, agrees with O'Curry's opinion. See Dr. Abbott's detailed account in " The Book of Trinity College," p. 172.

Vol. II., p. 71.

" Keeler." I now doubt that this word is derived from the Irish *cilorn*. It is probably an English word.

Vol. II., pp. 70 to 76.

Dr. Kuno Meyer directs my attention to a passage in YBL, 106, *a*, 40, in which there is a classification, according to size, of seven of the vessels mentioned in the above pages, viz. :— *dabach* (the largest), *ian, drolmach, muide, cilorn, milan, metar*. With this, so far as the last three are concerned, the classification evolved at p. 70, last line (vol. II.), agrees. This YBL passage notes, too, that the whole seven were hooped vessels.

There was another vessel called *mesair* (gen. *mesrach*), glossed *phiala* by O'Mulconry. It was used for drinking ; for we find in YBL, 106, *a*, 21, *mesair senbrogoitti*, " a *mesair* of old bragget," and O'Reilly has " *measair*, a long-handled vessel, a *ʄiggin*."

Vol. II., p. 227.

For Pearls : see also Boate, 187.

Vol. II., pp. 240 to 244.

Do-at, Muince-do-at and *Bunne-do-at*.—It has been established by Windisch that the Old Irish *dóe* means the fore-arm, wrist [or hand ?]. In Middle and Modern Irish, we know that the dative form *doit* or *doid*, besides its use as a dative, is also used as a nominative, in accordance with a well-known linguistic law. Of these applications of *dóit* and *dóid* any number of examples might be cited in Middle and in Modern colloquial Irish. All this would point to a gen. *doat* ; and it has been suggested or asserted that this is the sense of the word in the compounds *muince-do-at* and *bunne-do-at*. But though this will make sense in the case of *bunne-do-at* (' a *bunne* or ring for the hand '), it will not answer for *muince-do-at* (' a *necklet* for the hand '). *Muince* (which is derived from *muin*, ' the neck ') is always applied to something put round the neck, or round anything that might be considered a neck ; but it certainly is not applied to a ring or bracelet for the hand or arm.

I am not aware that the form *doat* has as yet been found as an undoubted genitive of *dóe*, or found at all except in the terms *muince-do-at* and *bunne-do-at*. But I deny that it is here a genitive of *dóe*. It is, in fact, a different word altogether, the identity in form between it and *doat*, gen. of *dóe* (if such a genitive exists) being merely accidental. Even if the gen. of *dóe* should hereafter be found without any doubt to be *doat*, this will not affect the question.

But the main evidence in the case is quite independent of all that precedes—evidence which to most people will be quite conclusive. There, before our eyes, in our Museum, are two classes of objects—*and only two*—with numerous specimens of each, all with the characteristic *do-at*—two *ats*, discs, or buttons —which sharply distinguish them from all other objects in the Museum. To these two types the two terms *Muince-do-at* and *bunne-do-at* exactly answer, and are accurately descriptive of them, while there are no other objects that correspond with the same two terms, and no other terms in the language that correspond with the objects, or (in either case) make any approach to correspondence.

Mere grammatical or linguistic considerations, however valuable within their proper domain, cannot outweigh the evidence of our senses. For all these reasons I adhere to my explanation of *muince-do-at* and *bunne-do-at*.

VOL. II., P. 263.

NOTE ON THE IRISH GOLD ORNAMENTS FOUND IN 1896 AT BROIGHTER.

The litigation mentioned in the footnote of the above page has come to an end. After many witnesses had been examined, and much expert evidence had been given, Judge Farwell, by whom the case was tried, delivered an elaborate and highly instructive judgment, deciding that the articles were treasure-trove, and that consequently they were the property, not of the British Museum, but of the Crown. Soon afterwards they were handed over to the Royal Irish Academy, Dublin, by order of the King : one of the numerous manifestations of His Majesty's gracious and kindly feeling towards Ireland. They are now among the great collection of gold ornaments in the Academy's compartment of the National Museum, Dublin, already mentioned in vol. II., p. 263 : their proper and natural home.

The articles in this Broighter gold-find, which, in point of workmanship, are fully equal to those described in chap. XXII., section 3 (p. 22, *supra*), are as follows :—

1. Model of a boat, 7½ inches long by 3 broad, having originally nine seats for rowers, and a mast; but the mast and one of the seats are missing. The rowlocks are formed of little rings. There are fifteen oars, a miniature grappling-iron (of gold like all the rest), and three forked spears, possibly fishing-spears. The boat was formed from one flat plate of gold by hammering, like the dish shown in vol. II., p. 71, fig. 196.

2. A bowl, 3¼ inches in diameter and 2 inches deep, quite plain, formed, like the boat, by hammering; having four rings on the edge for hanging.

3. A triple chain, 14½ inches in length, to be worn on the neck, with a fastener consisting of a bolt with a pin that slides in and out of a loop. Each of the three separate chains of which this necklace is composed is of exquisite fabric, being formed of spirally-twisted closely-knit links combined in such a way as that the chain itself is four-cornered the whole length.

4. A smaller chain, single, 16½ inches long, worn as a necklace, formed of most complicated plait-work of eight wires, with a fastening like that of the larger one.

5. A collar for the neck, 7½ inches in external diameter, most skilfully and elaborately wrought : formed of a hollow tube, 1⅛ inch in diameter. It had a hinge at one side (which is gone), and an ingenious slot-and-bolt fastener opposite, so that the collar could be opened out for putting on and taking off, and securely fastened when worn. Portion of its ornamentation—a divergent spiral pattern—is depicted in Mr. Cochrane's article, Journ. Roy. Soc. Antiqq. for 1902, p. 217.

6. Two small solid torques, beautifully twisted and ornamented; one complete; the other with only half remaining.

Vol. II., p. 309.

Since writing the article on the smith's forge ending at the first paragraph of the above page, a more careful examination of the Irish Texts has enabled me to arrive at the construction of the old Irish blacksmith's furnace, just as—in the same article—the bellows has been restored from a comparison of similar authorities (pp. 305–309, vol. II.).

In Cormac's Glossary, p. 123, an incident is related of Goibniu, the great Dedannan smith. On one occasion he happened to be in his forge, holding in his hand a *crand* or wooden implement of some kind (*crand*, a tree, a piece of wood, anything made of wood). Cormac goes on to say that *ness* was a special name for this *crand*, and he adds, after his usual happy manner, this short explanatory note showing its use :—" And it is about it the furnace of clay (*urnisi criad*) is made." Here the expression is similar to that used by the old Irish eighth or ninth century commentator already quoted (pp. 79, 317 above), to describe the wooden block on which Irish potters moulded soft clay to make vessels : and observe, that in both passages the block or mould is called *crand* or *crann*. The passage concerning the potter's mould specifying part of the moulding process, is " a round piece of wood (*crann*) about which they [the soft clay vessels] are while being made " (Stokes and Strachan, Thes., I., 23). It appears then that the *ness* or *crand* mentioned by Cormac was a mould round which was formed the soft clay furnace to contain and confine the fire. From all this we infer that whenever the walls of this furnace got burned or worn out—which might be perhaps once a week or so—it was cleared away ; the *ness*, *crand*, or mould was set in the proper place (the exact place for the fire), and a new structure of soft clay was moulded round it in a few minutes with the hands ; after which the mould was lifted up, leaving the furnace (*urnisi criad*) ready for use. At the time the incident related by Cormac occurred, Goibniu happened to be engaged in moulding a fresh furnace, with the *ness* in his hand.

The fuel used in those days was wood-charcoal, which, being lighter than our coal, was liable to be blown about and scattered by the blast of the bellows, if not confined by the furnace. I presume the *ness* or mould was something like what is represented here, either solid or hollow, with a long handle for holding and lifting up. That it had a long handle is also implied by the text of the story, as related by Cormac. Probably a small part of the upright surface of the mould was flat, which was placed up against the upright flag (at the back of the fire) opposite the hole for the bellows-pipe.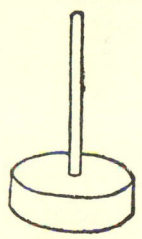

All this is curiously corroborated by a totally independent authority, a passage in the Irish Triads, No. 148, p. 21, edited by Dr. Kuno Meyer :—" Three renovators of the world—the womb of woman, a cow's udder, and a smith's *ness*." In still another MS. this *ness* is explained " a bag of clay," which gives us further insight. The moulding clay of which the furnace was made, was what we now call fire-clay ; and it had to be carefully selected to stand the fire, like all fire-clays. It was of some value ; and was kept in bags like the charcoal to prevent waste. Observe how satisfactorily all this squares in with the main function running through the triad—The function of renovation. From this Triad passage also it appears that the name *ness* was applied both to the shaped furnace and to a bag of moulding clay for making it : as well as to the mould.

I may add that in my young days I have seen, in the county Limerick, furnaces somewhat similar to that described above—but much ruder—used by wandering tinkers, who also practised foundry on a small and simple scale : but they used anthracite coal, not wood charcoal. They made up with their hands a small furnace of moist clay, in a rough and ready way and in a few moments, which they placed securely in a wooden frame, and into which they fixed the pipe of their bellows. By means of this rude contrivance they succeeded in melting small fragments of cast iron, with which they mended—very roughly indeed, but quite effectively—pots and pans, or other cast iron articles that had been gapped or cracked. They formed a strong mould of moist clay round the broken part, into which they poured the white molten metal, which firmly adhered to the broken surface in cooling. The women of the several houses always put their broken vessels aside, waiting for the next visit of the tinker company, who never failed to find plenty to do in every hamlet. (See also the Article on " The Old Irish Smiths' Furnace " in Joyce's book " The Wonders of Ireland.")

VOL. II., 534, LAST LINE ; 535, FIRST LINE.

A Continental scholar, M. Vendryes, derives *edoct* from the Lat. *edictum*. But I cannot believe that at that early time (seventh century, when *edoct* first occurs) the *i* of *edictum* could have been changed to *o* in *edoct*.

VOL. II., 557, NOTE UNDER ILLUSTRATION,

1879 should be 1872.

Sculpture on a Capital or the Church of the Monastery, Glendalough: Beranger, 1779.
(From Petrie's Round Towers, 258.)

LIST OF AUTHORITIES CONSULTED, AND QUOTED OR REFERRED TO THROUGHOUT THIS BOOK.*

1. Abbott, the Rev. Dr., S.F.T.C.D.: Celtic Ornaments of portions of the Book of Kells, consisting of fifty photographic reproductions of the originals: with Preface and short descriptive notes. Hodges & Figgis, Dublin.
2. Acta Sanctorum of the Bollandists ("Acta SS.")
  Adamnan: see No. 237.
  Agallamh or Acallamh: see No. 317.
  Amra or Elegy on St. Columkille: see Nos. 13, 48, 286.
3. Anderson, Joseph, LL.D.: Scotland in Pagan Times (Iron Age): 1883.
4. ———— Scotland in Pagan Times (Bronze and Stone Age): 1886.
5. ———— Scotland in Early Christian Times, First Series: 1879.
6. ———— Scotland in Early Christian Times, Second Series; 1880.
7. Annals (Irish). The chief Books of Annals are described in chapter xiv.: and they are referred to individually as occasion requires.
8. Anonymous: On the Early Relations of Ireland with the Isle of Man (Ir. Eccl. Record: March, 1869).
9. Archdall: Monasticon Hibernicum; and also the later edition of portions of the same work by Cardinal Moran, assisted by various editors.
10. Archiv. für Celtische Lexikographie; edited and partly written by Dr. Whitley Stokes and by Dr. Kuno Meyer.
11. Atkinson, Robert, LL.D.: The Passions and Homilies from Lebar Brecc: Text, Transl., and Glossary.
12. Atkinson, Robert, LL.D.: On Irish Metric: an Inaugural Lecture on Celtic Philology (Pamphlet, 1884).

* When an *Irish* piece is mentioned in this List of Authorities, as having been edited, it is to be understood, unless otherwise stated, that the edition includes Irish text, translation, and notes.

587

13. Atkinson, Robert, LL.D.: The Irish Liber Hymnorum or Book of Hymns: edited by the Rev. Dr. Bernard, F.T.C.D., and Dr. Atkinson. See also No. 327. (See vol. I., p. 510, *supra*.)

———— The Amra on St. Columkille (included in the preceding: see p. 541, *supra*).

14. ———— The Three Shafts of Death by the Rev. Dr. Keating: Text, Glossary, and Appendix, but no translation. (See vol. I., p. 510, *supra*.)

15. ———— Glossary to vols. I.–v. of Brehon Laws.

16. Atlantis (Periodical, Dublin), vols. I., II., III., IV.

Avebury, Lord: see No. 161.

17. Ball, Valentine, LL.D., F.R.S. On Red Glass Enamel, by Dr. Ball and Miss Margaret Stokes: Trans. R. I. Acad., vol. xxx., p. 277.

BB, Book of Ballymote: see No. 22.

Bec Fola: see Nos. 211, viii., and 218.

18. Bede's Ecclesiastical History.

19. Bennett and Elton: History of Corn Milling.

20. Bernard, Rev. J. H., DD. (now Dean of St. Patrick's). On the Domnach Airgid: Trans. R. I. Acad., vol. xxx., p. 303: see also No. 13.

21. Boate's Natural History of Ireland: 1726.

Bollandists: see No. 2.

22. Book of Ballymote ("BB"). (See vol. I., p. 496, *supra*).

———— Deer: see No. 321.

———— Fenagh: see No. 96.

———— Hymns: see Nos. 13, 327.

23. ———— Kells. (See vol. I., p. 546, *supra*.)

———— Kells, Reproductions of: see No. 1.

24. ———— Lecan. (See vol. I., p. 497, *supra*.)

25. ———— Leinster ("LL"). (See vol. I., p. 495, *supra*.)

———— Rights: see No. 194.

26. ———— the Dun Cow, or Lebar na hUidhre ("LU"). (See vol. I., p. 493. *supra*.)

27. Borlase, William Copeland, M.A. The Dolmens of Ireland: 3 vols paged continuously.

Boroma: see Nos. 211, xxviii., and 301.

Boyish Exploits of Finn: see Nos. 42 and 226 iv.

28. Brehon Laws: the ancient Laws of Ireland: 6 vols. (See chap. vi., *supra*.)

Brendaniana: see No. 193.

Bruden Da Chocae: see No. 316.

Bruden Da Derga: see No. 303.

29. Bunting's Ancient Music of Ireland. (See vol. I., p. 593, *supra*.)

30. Bury, J. B., LL.D.: Tirechán's Memoir of St. Patrick: printed in Eng. Hist. Rev. for 1902. (See vol. I., p. 317, note, *supra*.)

31. Butler, the Rev. Richard : Register of the Priory of All Hallows, Dublin : edited by the Rev. Mr. Butler for the Irish Arch. Soc., 1845.

Cambrensis : see No. 80.

Cambrensis Eversus : see No. 162.

32. Campion's Historie of Ireland : ed., 1809.

33. Carmichael, Alexander : Carmina Gadelica ; Hymns and Incantations [in modern Scotch Gaelic] ; orally collected in the Highlands and Islands of Scotland, and translated into English : 2 vols., 1900. (See vol. I., p. 386, note, *supra*.)

Cattle-Spoil of Fraech : see No. 54.

Census : two Reports, 1842, 1851 : see No. 349.

Children of Lir, Story of : see Nos. 125, *a*, and 192.

Circuit of Murkertagh Mac Neill (" Circuit ") : see No. 201.

34. Clanrickard : Memoirs of Marquis of : Dublin edition, 1744 (the original edition was printed in London, 1722).

35. Cochrane, Robert, F.S.A., M.R.I.A. : On Broighter, Limavady, Londonderry, and on the find of gold ornaments there in 1896. See also No. 62. (See pp. 263, note, and 583, *supra*.)

36. Coffey, George, B.A. : On the Tumuli and Inscribed Stones at Newgrange (printed in Trans. Roy. Ir. Acad., vol. XXX.)

37. ———— On the Prehistoric Cemetery of Loughcrew : Trans. Roy. Ir. Acad., vol. XXXI., p. 23. (See p. 558, *supra*.)

38. ———— On the Origins of Prehistoric Ornament in Ireland : Journ. of the Roy. Soc. Antiqq. Irel., vols. for 1892, 1893, 1894.

39. ———— Notes on the Classification of Spear-Heads of the Bronze Age found in Ireland : Proc. Roy. Ir. Acad., vol. for 1893–96, p. 486.

Cóir Anmann : see No. 314.

40. Colgan : Acta Sanctorum.

41. ———— Trias Thaumaturgae. (See, for those two, vol. I., p. 507, *supra*.)

Colton's Visitation : see No. 240.

42. Comyn, David, M.R.I.A. : Boyish Exploits of Finn, Ancient Irish Text with modern Irish Text and translation : forming a small separate vol. (For another edition, see No. 226, iv.)

43. Comyn, David, M.R.I.A. : Keating's History of Ireland, Irish text, translation and notes : published for the Irish Texts Soc., 1902 : only one vol. published so far. See also Nos. 123 and 128. (See vol. I., p. 527, *supra*.)

Cooke's edition of Wakeman's Irish Antiquities : see No. 337.

Corco Laidhe or Corkalee : see No. 206.

44. Cork : Journal of the Cork Historical and Archæological Society.

Cormac's Glossary : see No. 277.

Courtship of Emer : see Nos. 139, and 140.

Courtship of Ferb : see No. 156.

45. Cox, Michael F., M.D. : Notes of the History of the Irish Horse.
Crith Gabhlach, a portion of the Brehon Laws : in vol. IV.

46. Croker, Crofton : Researches in the South of Ireland.

47. ———— Fairy Tales.

48. Crowe, J. O'Beirne : The Amra on St. Columkille : published as a pamphlet : see Nos. 13 and 286. (See p. 541, *supra*.)

49. ———— The Demon Chariot (*Siabar-Charpat*) of Cuchulainn : Kilk. Arch. Journ., 1870–71.

50. ———— *Faeth Fiada*, The ' Guardsman's Cry "—the Hymn of St. Patrick : Kilk. Arch. Journ., 1868–69.

51. ———— Religious Beliefs of the Pagan Irish : Kilk. Arch. Journ., 1868–69.

52. ———— The Destruction of Eochaid mac Maireda (The Overflowing of Lough Neagh) : Kilk. Arch. Jour., 1870–71. (See also Nos. 125, *c*, and 211, XIII.)

53. ———— Scela na Esergi (" Tidings of the Resurrection "). from LU : as a pamphlet : 1869.

54. ———— Táin Bo Fraich—" Spoiling of the Cows of Fraech " : Proc. Roy. Ir. Acad. (Irish MSS. series.)

55. ———— The Vision of Cahirmore : Kilk. Arch. Journ., 1872.

56. ———— Dinnsenchus (part of) : Kilk. Arch. Journ., 1872. (See vol. I., p. 530, *supra*.)
Cuimmin's Poem on the Irish SS. : see No. 312.
Culdees : see No. 239.
Da Chocae : see No. 316.
Da Derga : see No. 303.
Demon Chariot : see No. 49.
Dind Righ or Dinnree, Destruction of : see No. 308.

57. Dottin, G. : La Littérature gaélique de l'Irlande : in " Revue de Synthése historique," Août, 1901.

58. Dublin Penny Journal, 4 vols., 1832–1836.

59. Dunraven, Lord : Notes on Irish Architecture : edited by Miss Margaret Stokes : 2 vols.

60. ———— Description of the Ardagh Chalice in Trans. Roy. Ir. Acad., vol. XXIV., p. 433, Feb. 22, 1869. (See vol. I., pp. 560, 561, *supra*.)

61. Ebel's Celtic Studies : translated from German by Dr. W. K. Sullivan.
Ecclesiastical Antiqq. of Down, Connor, and Dromore (" Eccl. Ant.") : see No. 238.

62. Evans, Arthur J., M.A., F.S.A. : On a Votive Deposit of Gold Objects found on the North-West Coast of Ireland [at Broighter].* See also No. 35.

---

* But they were not *votive* : see pp. 263, note, and 582, *supra*.

63. Evans, John, D.C.L.: The Ancient Bronze Implements of Great Britain and Ireland, 1881.
Facsimiles of Irish National MSS.: see No. 77
Feast of Bricriu: see No. 95.
Feast of Dun-nan-Gedh: see No. 195.
Feilire of Aengus the Culdee: see No. 280.
Fenagh, Book of: see No. 96.

64. Ferguson, Lady: The Irish before the Conquest: 1868.

65. Ferguson, Sir Samuel: On the Legend of Dathi: Proc. Roy. Ir. Acad. Second Series, vol. II. (1879–86).

66. ————— On the Rudiments of the Common Law discoverable in the published portion of the Senchus Mór: Trans. Roy. Ir. Acad., XXIV.

67. ————— On the Patrician Documents: Trans. Roy. Ir. Acad., XXVII.

68. ————— On Sepulchral Cellae: same vol.

69. ————— On the Ceremonial Turn called the Deisiul: Proc. Royal Irish Acad., 1870–76, p. 355. (See vol. I., p. 301, *supra*.)

70. ————— Ogham Inscriptions in Ireland, Wales, and Scotland: 1 vol.

71. ————— Congal, a Poem, with Notes.

72. ————— Poems, with Notes: 1880.

73. Fergusson, James, D.C.L., F.R.S.: Rude Stone Monuments in all countries: their age and uses: 1872.
Fingal Ronain: see No. 142.
Fled Bricrenn, the Feast of Bricriu: see No. 95.

74. Folklore: a Periodical in several volumes.

75. Four Masters, Annals of, edited with Translation and Notes, by John O'Donovan, LL.D. (See vol. I., p. 524, *supra*.)

76. Gaidoz, M. Henri (founder and first editor of Revue Celtique): La Religion Gauloise et le Gui de chene: Paris, 1880.

77. Gilbert, Sir John T., LL.D., F.S.A.: Facsimiles of Irish National MSS.

78. Gildas, the Works of.

79. Gillies, H. Cameron, M.D.: Gaelic Names of Diseases and of diseased states: Pamphlet reprinted from the "Caledonian Medical Journal."

80. Giraldus Cambrensis: Topography of Ireland ("Top. Hib."): Conquest of Ireland ("Hib. Expug."): Itinerary through Wales: Description of Wales. (See vol. I., p. 19, *supra*.)
Goidelica: see No. 285.

81. Graham's Introduction to Surenne's "Songs of Ireland without words."

82. Graves, The Right Rev. Charles, D.D., bishop of Limerick: Several Papers on Ogham in Hermathena, and in Proc. Roy. Ir. Acad. (late vols.).

83. ————— Two Papers on the date of the Book of Armagh in Proc. Roy. Ir. Acad., vol. III., pp. 316, 356.

84. Greaves, C. S., Q.C.: Cannibalism in England [and Ireland]: (proving that there was none). The Archæological Journal, vol. XXXVI. (1879): p. 38.

85. Gregory, Lady: Cuchulain of Muirthemne, the Story of the Men of the Red Branch of Ulster, arranged and put into English: 1902. (See vol. I., p. 543, *supra*.)

86. Guest, Lady Charlotte, The Mabinogion, Ancient Welsh Tales translated into English. (A small and cheap edition of the translation, published by David Nutt, 1902, is the one referred to here.)

87. Güterbock, B., and Thurneysin, R.: Indices Glossarum et Vocabulorum Hibernicorum, quae in Grammaticae Celticae. Editione altera explanantur (Indexes to Zeuss, Gram. Celt.). A supplement to these Indexes will be found in the Rev. Dr. Hogan's Rossnaree, p. 267.

88. Gwynn, Edward, M.A.: Poems from the Dindsenchus (in LL): in Todd Lecture Series, Roy. Ir. Academy.

89. Haddan, A. W., and Stubbs, W., Councils and Ecclesiastical Documents relating to Great Britain and Ireland.
Hakluyt's Voyages: see No. 158.

90. Hanmer's Chronicle of Ireland: Ed. 1809.

91. Hardiman, James: Edition of O'Flaherty's Description of Iar Connaught: Irish Archæol. Soc.

92. ———— Irish Minstrelsy, 2 vols.

93. ———— The Statute of Kilkenny in " Tracts relating to Ireland," printed by the Ir. Archæol. Soc., 1843.

94. Healy, the Most Rev. John, D.D., LL.D., Archbishop of Tuam: Ireland's Ancient Schools and Scholars: 1890. (See vol. I p. 408, note, *supra*.)

95. Henderson, George, M.A., PH.D.: Fled Bricrend, the Feast of Bricriu, Irish text, Translation, and Notes: 1899.

96. Hennessy, William M.: The Book of Fenagh, edited, Text, Translation, and Notes, by Mr. Hennessy, and Mr. D. H. Kelly.
———— The Vision of Mac Conglinne: see No. 154.

97. ———— Mesca Ulad, " The Intoxication of the Ultonians ": Todd Lecture Series, Roy. Ir. Academy.

98. ———— The Irish War Goddess: Rev. Celt., vol I.

99. ———— Cause of the Battle of Cnucha, from LU: Rev. Celt., vol. II.

100. ———— The Curragh of Kildare: Proc. Roy. Ir. Acad., 1866.

101. ———— Irish Ordeals, in Proc. Roy. Ir. Acad., vol. X. (See also No. 315.)
———— Annals of Ulster, vol. I: see No. 168.
Herbert, the Hon. Algernon: see No. 326.
Hibernia Expugnata (" Hib. Expug."): see No. 80.
Hibernia Minora: see No. 144.

102. Hogan, the Rev. Dr. Edmund, s.j.: The Battle of Rossnaree from LL: Todd Lecture Series, Roy, Ir. Acad. (See also No. 87.)

103. ———— Documenta de S. Patricio: The Life of St. Patrick and other Documents from the Book of Armagh. (See vol. I., p. 505, *supra*.)

104. ———— The History of the Irish wolfdog: see p. 451, *supra*.

105. ———— Luibhleabhrán: Irish and Scottish Gaelic names of Plants.

106. Hull, Miss Eleanor: The Cuchullin Saga in Irish Literature: 1898. (See vol. I., p. 542, *supra*.)

107. Hyde, Douglas, LL.D.: A Literary History of Ireland, from the earliest times to the present day: 1899.

108. ———— Two Irish Tales: The Lad of the Ferrule, and the Adventures of the Children of the King of Norway (Irish Texts Society): 1899.

109. ———— Beside the Fire: a collection of Irish Gaelic Folk Stories (1890).

110. ———— Leabhar Sgeulaigheachta, Folk Stories in Irish.

111. ———— Love Songs of Connaught (1893).

112. ———— Irish Poetry: an Essay in Irish, with translation in English: 1903. (See pp. 498, 499. notes, *supra*.)

Hy Fiachrach ("HyF"): see No. 198.

Hy Many ("HyM"): see No. 199.

Iar Connaught ("IarC"): see No. 91.

113. Innes, Thomas: Critical Essays on the Ancient Inhabitants of the northern parts of Britain or Scotland.

114. Irische Texte: A number of ancient Irish texts, some translated, some not: edited by Ernst Windisch (Leipsig): four vols. so far. Vol. I. contains Windsch's valuable Wörterbush or "Glossary." (The several pieces are mentioned elsewhere, and will be referred to as they occur.)

115 Irish Archæological Miscellany, vol. I., 1846 (Irish Archæol. Soc.).

Irish Names of Places: see No. 120.

Irish Nennius: see No. 326.

Irish Ordeals: see Nos. 101 and 315.

116. Irish Penny Journal, The: 1840–41.

117. Irish Penny Magazine, The: 1833–34.

118. Jocelyn: Life of St. Patrick.

Jones, David Brynmor: see No. 249.

119. Jones, the Rev. William Basil, M.A. (afterwards bishop of St David's): Vestiges of the Gael in Gwynedd (North Wales).

Journal of the Roy. Soc. Antiqq., Ireland: see Nos. 132 and 256.

120. Joyce, P. W., LL.D.: The Origin and History of Irish Names of Places: two vols. Seventh or eighth Edition.

121. ———— Ancient Irish Music.

122. ———— A Short History of Ireland to 1608.

123. Joyce, P. W., LL.D.: Keating's History of Ireland (*Forus Feasa air Eirinn*), Book I., Part I. Edited with Text, Translation, Notes, and Vocabulary: see Nos. 43 and 128.

124. —————— A Reading Book in Irish History: 1901 (containing, among many other pieces, translation of "The Fate of the Sons of Usna": see also No. 192).

125. —————— Old Celtic Romances: Third Edition, 1907. The thirteen Stories translated in this book are:—

> (*a*) The Fate of the Children of Lir; or, The Four White Swans.
> (*b*) The Fate of the Children of Turenn; or, The Quest for the Eric-Fine. (For these two, see also No. 192.)
> (*c*) The Overflowing of Lough Neagh, and the Story of Liban the Mermaid, with the Death of Eochaid mac Maireda. (See also Nos. 52 and 211, xiii.)
> (*d*) Connla of the Golden Hair and the Fairy Maiden.
> (*e*) The Voyage of Maildun. (See also No. 295.)
> (*f*) The Fairy Palace of the Quicken Trees.
> (*g*) The Pursuit of the Gilla Dacker and his Horse. (See also No. 211, xvii.)
> (*h*) The Pursuit of Dermot and Gráinne. (See also No. 212.)
> (*i*) The Chase of Slieve Cullinn.
> (*j*) The Chase of Slieve Fuaid.
> (*k*) Oisin in Tirnanoge; or, The Last of the Fena.
> (*l*) The Voyage of the Sons of O'Corra. (See also No. 306.)
> (*m*) The Fate of the Sons of Usna.

126. Jubainville, H. D. Arbois de: Cours de Littérature Celtique: 8 vols., viz. :—

> I. Introduction à l'étude de la littérature celtique.
> II. Le Cycle Mythologique irlandais et la mythologie celtique. 1884.*
> III., IV. Les Mabinogion (contes gallois), traduits en entier en françois.
> V. L'Epopée celtique en Irlande. 1892.
> VI. La Civilisation des Celtes et celle de l'épopee homérique.
> VII., VIII. Etudes sur le droit celtique. (See also No. 247.)

127. Kane, Sir Robert: The Industrial Resources of Ireland: 1844.

128. Keating's History of Ireland, translated by John O'Mahony. This is the edition of Keating always referred to unless otherise specified. See Nos. 43 and 123. (See vol. I., p. 527, *supra*.

129. Keller, Dr. Ferdinand: Essay on "Illuminations and Facsimiles from Ancient Irish MSS. in the Libraries of Switzerland"; translated from German with Introductory Remarks by the Rev. William Reeves, D.D., in Ulster Journ. of Archæol. VIII., 210 and 291.

---

* Within the present year (1903) this has been translated into English by Mr. R. I. Best, and published by O'Donoghue & Co., and by M. H. Gill & Son, Dublin.

Kells, Book of : see No. 23.

Kells, Book of : Reproductions of : see No. 1.

Kelly, the Rev. Matthew : see No. 162.

130. Kennedy, Evory : Opening Address to the Dublin Obstetric Society, Nov. 1838 : in Dub. Journ. of Med. Sci., xv., 168.

131. Kildare : Journal of the Kildare Archæological Society.

132. Kilkenny Archæological Journal : from 1849 to the present (now the " Journal of Roy. Soc. of Antiqq. Ireland ") : see No. 256.

133. Kinahan, G. Henry : Manual of the Geology of Ireland.

134. Kuno Meyer, Dr. : Cath Finntraga, The Battle of Ventry (" Anecdota Oxoniensia ").

135. ————— Gein Branduib, " The Birth of Branduff," king of Leinster ; from LL : in Zeitschr. für Celt. Phil., II. 13?.

136. ————— Goire Conaill Chernaig i Cruachain, ocus Aided Ailella ocus Conaill Chernaig ; " The Christening of Conall Cernach in Croghan, and the Deaths of Ailill and of Conall Cernach " : in Zeitschr, für Celt. Phil., I. 102.

137. ————— The Colloquy of Columkille and the Youth : in Zeitschr. für Celt. Phil., II. 313.

138. ————— Uath Beinne Etair : The Cave or Hiding-Place f Benn Edair : Rev. Celt., XI.

139. ————— Tochmarc Emere : The Courtship of Emer, oldest version : Rev. Celt., XI.

140. ————— The Courtship of Emer, Translation (without Text) : Archæol. Rev. : 1888.

141. ————— The Story of Baile Binnbérlach or Baile Mac Buain : Rev. Celt., XIII. (See also O'Curry, MS. Mat., p. 465.)

142. ————— The Story of Fingal Ronain : Rev. Celt., XIII.

143. ————— Kongs Skuggjo or Speculum Regale, an old Norse book (about A.D. 1250), giving an account of the Wonders of Ireland : Folklore, V. 299.

144. ————— Hibernia Minora : a collection of short Irish pieces from the MS. Rawlinson, B. 512, in the Bodleian Library. It contains the following among others :—

   (a) Fragments of an old Irish Treatise on the Psalter.
   (b) The Story of Mac Dátho's Pig and Hound.
   (c) The Excuse of Guile's Daughter.
   (d) The Death of the three Sons of Dermot Mac Cerbaill, k. of Ireland.
   (e) The Death of Maelodran, son of Dimma Cron.
   (f) Dialogue between King Cormac and Fithel.

145. Kuno Meyer, Dr. : Liadain and Curithir : an Irish Love Story of the Ninth Century. Separate Pamphlet (D. Nutt).

146. ————— Song in praise of the sword of Cerball, king of Leinster : Rev. Celt. xx., pp. 7–12.

147. ————— Two Tales about Finn mac Cumail : Rev. Celt. XIV.

148. Kuno Meyer, Dr.: Cennach ind ruanado, the Bargain of the Strong Man: Rev. Celt. xiv. (Text first printed in Irische Texte, i. 301.)

149. ———— Old Irish Treatise *De Arreis*: Rev. Celt. xv.

150. ———— The Voyage of Bran, son of Febal, to the Land of the Living: translated and edited by Dr. K. Meyer, with an illustrative essay by Alfred Nutt: see No. 182.

151. Kuno Meyer, Dr.: Merugud Uilix Maicc Leirtis, the Irish Odyssey (Pamphlet, D. Nutt).

152. ———— Adventures of Nera: Rev. Celt. x.

153. ———— King and Hermit, a colloquy between King Guaire of Aidne and his brother Marban (Pamphlet, David Nutt).

154. ———— The Vision of Mac Conglinne: translated by Mr. W. M Hennessy: edited by Dr. Meyer: David Nutt (see vol. i., p. 14, *supra*). (See also No. 366.)

155. Lanigan's Ecclesiastical History of Ireland: 4 vols.
Latin Declension, Tract on: see No. 281.
LB (Lebar Brecc): see No. 157.

156. Leahy: The Courtship of Ferb, ancient Irish Tale translated into English (without Irish text), from the German translation of Windisch: David Nutt: see No. 359.

157. Lebar Brecc, the Speckled Book (" LB "). (See vol. i., p. 496, *supra*.)
Lebar Laignech (" LL "), The Book of Leinster: see No. 25.
Lebar Lecain, The Book of Lecan: see No. 24.
Lebar na h-Uidhre, The Book of the Dun Cow (" LU "): see No. 26.

158. Libel of English Policy, in Hakluyt's Voyages, vol. i., p. 187.

159. Lightfoot, Dr. J. B., Bishop of Durham: Leaders in the Northern Church [England], 1890.
LL, Lebar Laignech, the Book of Leinster: see No. 25.
Loca Patriciana: see No. 260.

160. Loth, J.: Bretons Insulairse en Irlande: in Rev. Celt. xviii.
LU, Lebar na hUidhre, the Book of the Dun Cow: see No. 26.

161. Lubbock, Sir John (now Lord Avebury): Prehistoric Times: 2nd edition.

162. Lynch, Dr. John, Bishop of Killala, 17th cent.: Cambrensis Eversus, edited for the Celtic Soc. by Rev. Matthew Kelly.

163. Macalister, R. A. Stewart, M.A.: On an Ancient Settlement in the S. W. of the barony of Corcaguiny, Kerry: in Trans. Roy. Ir. Acad., xxxi.

164. ———— Studies in Irish Epigraphy: 2 vols. have already appeared.

165. MacCarthy, the Rev. B., D.D.: The Codex Palatino-Vaticanus, No. 830 (Texts, Translations, and Indexes). Todd Lecture Series, Roy. Ir. Acad.

166. ———— On the Stowe Missal: in Trans. Roy. Ir. Acad., vol. xxvii.

167. MacCarthy: The Tripartite Life of St. Patrick: New Textual Studies: Trans. Roy. Ir. Acad., vol. XXIX.

168. ————— Annals of Ulster: except vol. I., which was edited by W. M. Hennessy. (See vol. I., p. 522, *supra*.)
Mabinogion: see No. 86.
Mac Conglinne: see No. 154.
Mac Dáthó's Pig and Hound, Story of: see No. 144, *b*.

169. Mac Geoghegan's History of Ireland.

170. Maclean, Magnus, M.A., D.SC.: The Literature of the Celts, its History and Romance, 1902.
M'Sweeny, the Rev. James P., S.J.: see No. 358.

171. Maine, Sir Henry Sumner: Dissertations on Ancient Law, ed. 1883.

172. ————— History of Ancient Institutions, 1875.
Manners and Customs of the Ancient Irish ("Man. & Cust."): see No. 189.
Manuscript Materials ("MS. Mat."): see No. 188.

173. Martin's Description of the Western Islands of Scotland, 1703.
Mesca Ulad: see No. 97.
Meyer: see Kuno Meyer.

174. Miscellany of the Celtic Society: 1849.

174A. ————— Irish Archæological Society: 1846

175. Montalembert: Monks of the West.
Moore, Dr. Norman: see No. 358.

176. Moore, Thomas: The History of Ireland.

177. Moran, Cardinal, Acta Sancti Brendani.
————— New Edition of portion of Archdall's Monasticon Hibernicum: see No. 9.

177A. ————— Civilisation of Ireland before the Anglo-Norman Invasion (republished as a pamphlet from the Irish Ecclesiastical Record, by the Catholic Truth Society).

178. More Madden, Thomas: Ancient Irish Medicine, its Culture and Practice: in The Med. Mag., 1899.
Moylena, Battle of: see No. 190.
Moyrath, Battle of: see No. 195.
Moytura, Story of Second Battle of: see No. 296.
Mucrime, Battle of: see Nos. 211, xxii., and 311.

179. Munro, Robert, M.A., M.D.: The Lake-Dwellings of Europe, 1890.

180. ————— Rambles and Studies in Bosnia-Herzegovina and Dalmatia, 1895.
Nennius: Historia Britonum: see No. 326.

181. Nettlau, Dr. M.: Many articles in the Revue Celtique, embodying a critical examination and comparison of various texts of the ancient Irish Tales.

182. Nutt, Alfred: The Voyage of Bran: Essays on the Irish "Other World," or Pagan Heaven: and on the Celtic doctrine of Re-birth: 2 vols.: D. Nutt: see also No. 150.

183. Nutt, Alfred: Ossian and the Ossianic Literature: one of the series of " Popular Studies in Romance and Folklore ": D. Nutt.

184. ———— Cuchulainn, the Irish Achilles: another of the same series: David Nutt.*

O'Clery's Calendar (" O'C. Cal."): see No. 197.

185. O'Clery's Glossary of Ancient Irish Words, edited by W. K. Miller in Rev. Celt., IV. and V.

186. O'Conor, Charles, of Bellanagar: Dissertations: 1812.

187. O'Connor Don, The Rt. Hon. The: The O'Conors of Connaught: O'Corras, Voyage of: see Nos. 306 and 125, *l.*

188. O'Curry, Eugene: Manuscript Materials of Irish History (" MS. Mat.").

189. ———— Manners and Customs of the Ancient Irish: 2 vols. (See No. 322, " Sullivan," for introductory vol.)

190. ———— The Battle of Moylena (Celtic Soc.).

191. ———— The Sick Bed of Cuchulainn: in Atlantis, vols. I. and II.

192. ———— " The Three Sorrowful Tales of Erin," viz. The Exile of the Sons of Usna, The Fate of the Children of Lir, and The Fate of the Sons of Turenn: in Atlantis, vols. III. and IV. (See also No. 349, for O'Curry.)

O'Davoren's Glossary ; included in Stokes's Three Irish Glossaries : No. 278.

193. O'Donohue, the Rev. Denis, P.P.: Brendaniana, St. Brendan the Voyager in Story and Legend.

O'Donovan, John, LL.D.: Annals of the Four Masters: see No. 75.

194. ———— Leabhar na gCeart, the Book of Rights, Celtic Society. (See vol. I., p. 52, *supra*.)

195. ———— The Battle of Moyrath (" Moyr."), including The Feast of Dun-nan-Gédh: Irish Archæol. Soc.

196. ———— Cormac's Glossary : translated by O'Donovan, edited by Dr. Stokes: see No. 277.   (See vol. I., p. 16, *supra*.)

197. ———— O'Clery's Calendar (" O'Cl. Cal."), also called the Martyrology of Donegal: translated by O'Donovan ; edited by Drs. Todd and Reeves: see vol. I., p. 525, *supra*.

198. ———— The Tribes and Customs of Hy Fiachrach (" HyF "): Irish Archæol. Soc.

199. ———— The Tribes and Customs of Hy Many : Irish Archæological Society. (For these two, see vol. I., p. 17, *supra*.)

200. ———— Three Fragments of Irish Annals : Irish Archæol. and Celtic Soc.

* Mr. Nutt has published a number of Irish pieces which should be in the hands of all students of ancient Irish literature. They are all referred to or quoted in various parts of this book. See also Nos. 86, 145, 150, 151, 153, 154, and 156 of this List.

201. O'Donovan, John, LL.D.: The Circuit of Muircheartach mac Neill ("Circuit") in "Tracts relating to Ireland," vol. I., 1841, by the Irish Archæol. Soc.

202. ————— The Tribes of Ireland : see vol. I., p. 455, *supra.*

203. ————— Topographical Poems of O'Dugan and O'Heeren : Irish Archæol. and Celtic Soc.

204. ————— An Irish Poem attributed to St. Columkille : in the Miscellany of the Irish Archæol. Soc., vol. I., 1846.

205. ————— The Irish Charters in the Book of Kells : in the same vol. as last.

206. O'Donovan, John, LL.D.: The Genealogy of Corco Laidhe : in the Miscellany of the Celtic Soc., 1849. (See vol. I., p. 17, *supra.*)

207. ————— Poem on the Battle of Dun : in the same vol. as last.

208. ————— A Grammar of the Irish Language.

209. O'Donovan, John : Supplement to O'Reilly's English-Irish Dictionary.*

O'Dugan : see No. 203.

210. O'Flaherty's Ogygia.

————— Iar Connacht : A Chorographical Description of West Connaught : see No. 91.

O'Gorman, Martyrology of : see No. 284.

211. O'Grady, Standish H.: Silva Gadelica : vol. I., Irish texts : vol. II., translation and notes. The references are to vol. II. unless where otherwise specified. This book contains the following pieces :—

    I. Life of St. Ciaran of Saigir.
    II. Life of St. Molaise of Devenish.
    III. Life of St. Maignenn.
    IV. Life of St. Cellach.
    V. Story of Aed Baclámh.
    VI. Death of King Dermot, son of Fergus Cerball.
    VII. Birth of Aed Slaine.
    VIII. The Wooing of Becfola : see also No. 218.
    IX. The Disappearance of Caenchomrac.
    X. Panegyric of King Cormac mac Airt.
    XI. Enumeration of Finn mac Cumail's People.
    XII. The Colloquy of the Ancient Men : see No. 317.
    XIII. Death of Eochaid mac Mairidh : see also Nos. 52, and 125, *c.*
    XIV. Death of King Fergus mac Léide.
    XV. Birth of King Cormac mac Art.
    XVI. Fiachna's *Sidh* or Fairy Palace.
    XVII. Pursuit of the Gilla Decair : see also No. 125, *g.*

* This book is carelessly and inaccurately edited, for which O'Donovan has sometimes been censured ; though he deserves no blame. The " Supplement " was a collection of notes for a Glossary or Dictionary, made year by year during his reading, thrown together roughly (such a collection as all students of Irish have to make for themselves), intended to be properly arranged and edited at the right time. But the right time never came : for O'Donovan died : and after his death, the whole collection was edited, apparently with little or no supervision. Even the title-page shows that this supplement was edited after O'Donovan's death.

XVIII. O'Donnell's Kern.
  XIX. The Carle in the Drab Coat : see Ir. Pen. Journ., p. 130
   XX. The Leeching of Cian's Leg.
  XXI. The Enchanted Cave of Keshcorran.
 XXII. Battle of Magh Mucramha : see also No. 311.
XXIII. Battle of Crinna.
XXIV. Story of King Eochaid's Sons.
 XXV. Death of King Crimthann, son of Fidach.
XXVI. The Little Brawl at Almhain or Almu.
XXVII. Teige mac Cein's Adventure.
XXVIII. The Boromean Tribute : see also No. 301.
XXIX. Fragmentary Annals.
 XXX. The Greek Emperor's Daughter.
XXXI. Abacuc the Perjurer. Irish Text of Extracts. Translation
of Extracts.

212. O'Grady, Standish H. : The Pursuit of Dermot and Gráinne : see
Nos. 226, *iii.*, and 125, *h.*

Ogygia : see No. 210.

213. O'Halloran's History of Ireland : 3 vols.

214. O'Hanlon, the Rev. John, Canon : Lives of the Irish Saints :
9 vols., and portion of the 10th, so far. The work will be completed in 12 vols.

215. —————— Life of St. Malachy O'Morgair.

Old Celtic Romances : See No. 125.

216. Olden, the Rev. Thomas : On the Geography of Ros-Ailithir :
Proc. Roy. Ir. Acad. Second Series, II. 219. (See vol. I.,
p. 440, *supra.*)

217. O'Looney, Prof. : Ancient Catalogue of Irish Historical Tales.
(See vol. I., p. 533, *supra.*)

218. —————— Tochmacr Bec-Fola, the Courtship of Bec-Fola · Proc.
Roy. Ir. Acad. (Irish MSS. Series.) ˈ (See also No. 211, viii.)

219. O'Neill, Henry : Illustrations of the most interesting of the
sculptured crosses of ancient Ireland.

220. Memoir of the Ordnance Survey of the Parish of Templemore,
County Londonderry.

221. O'Reilly, Edward : Irish writers : Trans. of the Iberno-Celtic
Soc., 1820.

222. O'Reilly, Patrick : a Series of Articles on Irish Antiqq., photo-
graphically illustrated, in the late vols. of Journ. Roy. Arch.
Soc., Ireland.

223. O'Reilly, Prof. J. P. : Notes on the History of the Irish Wolf-dog :
Proc. Roy. Ir. Acad., 1890.

224. —————— The Milesian Colonisation of Ireland considered in
relation to Gold Mining : Proc. Roy. Ir. Acad., 1900.

225. —————— Notes on Ancient Horizontal Water-mills, Native and
Foreign, in Proc. Roy. Ir. Acad. for 1901 and 1902. (See p. 338,
supra.)

226. Ossianic Society, Transactions of : six vols. : viz.—

> Vol. I. The Battle of Gabra.
> II. The *Feis* of the House of Conan.
> III. The Pursuit of Diarmaid and Gráinne.
> IV. Laoithe Fiannuigheachta (Lays of the Fena) : containing also the boyish exploits of Finn, edited by O'Donovan : see also No. 42.
> V. Proceedings of the Great Tromdamh.
> VI. Laoithe Fiannuigheachta (Lays of the Fena).

226A. Ossory Archæol. Soc., Transactions of : two vols.

227. Pennant's Tour in the Hebrides and Highlands of Scotland.

228. Petrie, George, LL.D. : The Origin and Uses of the Round Towers of Ireland : Second Edition, 1845.

229. ———— On the History and Antiquities of Tara Hill (Ed. 1839).

230. ———— The Ancient Music of Ireland.

231. ———— On the Domnach Airgid, in Trans. Roy. Ir. Acad.
———— Christian Inscriptions in the Irish Language : see No. 270.

232. Pictet, Professor : Les Origines Indo-Européennes ; ou, Les Aryas Primitifs

233. Pinkerton, John : Inquiry in the History of Scotland.

234. Pinkerton, William : Introduction towards a History of Irish Commerce : in Ulst. Journ of Archæol., III. 177.

235. Pollock, Sir Frederick, Bart. : The Forms and History of Swords : " Oxford Lectures," 1890.

236. Proceedings, Roy. Ir. Academy. (The several vols. are referred to as occasion arises.)

237. Reeves, the Rev. William, D.D. (subsequently bishop of Down and Connor) : Adamnan's Life of St. Columba. (See vol. I., pp. 6 and 506, *supra*.)

238. ———— Ecclesiastical Antiquities of Down, Connor, and Dromore (" Eccl. Ant.").

239. ———— The Culdees of the British Islands as they appear in History. (See vol. I., p. 352, *supra*.)

240. ———— Archbishop Colton's Visitation of the Diocese of Derry.
———— The Martyrology of Donegal (" O'Clery's Cal.") : a Calendar of the Saints of Erin. (Edited by Dr. Reeves and Dr. Todd conjointly.) Irish Archæol. and Celtic Soc. : see No. 197.

241. ———— The Ancient Churches of Armagh (Pamphlet).

242. ———— On Augustin, an Irish writer of the seventh century : Proc. Roy. Ir. Acad., 1861. (See vol. I., p. 345, *supra*.)

243. ———— On some Ecclesiastical Bells : Proc. Roy. Ir. Acad., vol. VIII., p. 441.

244. ———— On the Book of Armagh : Proc. Roy. Ir. Acad., 1891–3.
———— Translations, with Notes, of Dr. Wattenbach's Essays : see No. 343.

Reeves, the Rev. William, D.D. : Translation, with Notes, of Dr. Keller's Essay : see Nos. 129 and 344.

245. ———— The Bell of St. Patrick : Trans. Roy. Ir. Acad., vol. XXVII. (1877–1886).

Register of All Hallows : see No. 31.

246. Reinach, Salomon : Les Croissants d'or Irlandais : Rev. Celt., XXI., 75.

Rennes Dindsenchus : see No. 313.

247. Revue Celtique : 22 vols. so far : first edited by M. Henri Gaidoz : now by M. H. D'Arbois de Jubainville. (The several pieces are referred to in the proper places.)

248. Rhys, Principal John, M.A., D.LITT. : Hibbert Lectures, 1888 : On the Origin and Growth of Religion as illustrated by Celtic Heathendom.

249. ———— The Welsh People, by Principal Rhys and David Brynmor Jones, LL.B., 1900.

250. ———— Early Irish Conquests of Wales and Dumnonia : in Proc. Roy. Soc. Antiqq., Irel., for 1890–91, p. 642. (See vol. I., pp. 74–79, *supra*.)

251. ———— The Ogham-Inscribed Stones of the Roy. Ir. Acad., and of Trin. Coll., Dub., in Journ. Roy. Soc. Antiqq., 1902.

252. Richey, Alexander George, LL.D. : a Short History of the Irish People : 1887.

253. ———— Introductions to vols. III. and IV. of the Brehon Laws.

254. Ridgeway, William, M.A. : The Origin of Metallic Currency and Weight Standards : 1892.

255. Roberts, George : The Social History of the People of the Southern Counties of England : 1856.

Rossnaree, Battle of : see No. 102.

256. Royal Soc. Antiqq., Ireland, Journal of : 32 vols., from 1849 to 1903 : referred to as they occur : see No. 132.

257. Russell, T. O. : Beauties and Antiquities of Ireland : 1897.

258. ———— Fior-chláirseach na h-Eireann : a collection of short Irish Poems, text and translation.

Saltair na Rann : see No. 305.

259. Scott's Novels, with Author's Notes.

Second Vision of Adamnan : see No. 300.

260. Shearman, Rev. J. F., Loca Patriciana : a series of articles in one vol., reprinted from the Kilk. Archæol. Journ., 1879 to 1884.

Sick Bed : see No. 191.

261. Sigerson, Dr. George : Bards of the Gael and Gall.

Silva Gadelica : see No. 211.

262. Skene, W. F. : Celtic Scotland, 3 vols.

263. Social England : 6 vols., by various writers : 1895.

Sons of Turenn, Story of : see Nos. 125, *b*, and 192

Sons of Usna, Story of : see Nos. 124, 192.

Speckled Book : see No. 157.

264. Spenser's View of the State of Ireland : ed., 1809.
Statute of Kilkenny : see No. 93.

265. Stern, Ludw.-Chr. : Finn and the Phantoms, prose Irish version with French Translation : Rev. Celt. XIII. See No. 288 for poetical Irish version.

266. Stokes, the Rev. Dr. George T. : Ireland and the Celtic Church (from St. Patrick to the Anglo-Norman Invasion) : and Ireland and the Anglo-Norman Church : two separate vols.

267. ——— The Knowledge of Greek in Ireland between A.D. 500 and 900 : Proc. Roy. Ir. Acad. for 1892, p. 187.

268. Stokes, Miss Margaret : Early Christian Art in Ireland.

269. ——— Early Christian Architecture in Ireland.

270. ——— Christian Inscriptions in the Irish Language, chiefly collected and drawn by George Petrie, LL.D. : edited by Miss Stokes (see p. 575, *supra*).
——— On Irish Ornamentation in Enamel : see No. 17.

271. ——— Three Months in the Forests of France : A Pilgrimage in Search of Vestiges of Irish Saints in France.

272. ——— Six Months in the Apennines : A Pilgrimage in Search of Vestiges of Irish Saints in Italy. (For these two, see vol. I., p. 345, *supra*,)

273. ——— On the Breac Moedog and the Soiscel Molaise (In Archæologia : vol. XLIII., pp. 131–150).

274. ——— The High Crosses of Castledermot and Durrow, with an Introduction on " The High Crosses of Ireland."

275. ——— Christian Iconography in Ireland (in the Archæol Journ., vol. LVII.).
——— Edition of Lord Dunraven's Notes on Irish Architecture : see No. 59.

276. Stokes, Whitley, D.C.L., LL.D. : The Tripartite Life of St. Patrick : 2 vols. paged continuously ; Rolls Series. (See vol. I., p. 506, *supra*.)

277. ——— Cormac's Glossary, translated by O'Dovonan, edited by Dr. Stokes. (See vol. I., p. 16, *supra*.)

278. ——— Three Irish Glossaries, containing Irish Texts of Cormac's and O'Davoren's Glossary, and of a Glossary on the Calendar of Oengus the Culdee : with notes.

279. ——— Lives of the Saints from the Book of Lismore (" Anecdota Oxoniensia ").

280. ——— The Féilire (Calendar) of Oengus the Culdee : Trans. Roy. Ir. Acad., 1880 : Irish MSS. Series. (See vol. I., p. 507, *supra*.)

281. ——— Irish Glosses in a Mediæval Tract on Latin Declension (a separate vol.).

282. ——— Irish Glosses on the Bucolics : in Rev. Celt. XIV.

283. ——— Three Middle-Irish Homilies on the Lives of SS. Patrick, Brigit. and Columba.

284. Stokes, Whitley, D.C.L., LL.D.: The Martyrology of Mael-Muire O'Gorman.

285. ———— Goidelica: Old and Early-Middle Irish Glosses, prose and verse: second edition.

286. ———— The Amra of St. Columkille: in Rev. Celt., vol. xx., at pp. 30, 132, 248, and 400: see Nos. 13 and 48. (See p. 541, *supra*.)

287. ———— Tidings of Doomsday: a Sermon on Doomsday from LU: Rev. Celt., iv.

288. ———— Finn and the Phantoms, a Poetical Tale from LL (page 206, *b*): Rev. Celt., vii.: see No. 265 for prose version.

289. ———— The Siege of Howth (*Talland Etair*): a Historical Tale from LL: Rev. Celt., viii.

290. ———— Middle-Irish Homily on St. Martin of Tours, from LB.

291. ———— Cuchulainn's Death—abridged from LL 76, *a*, 1, to 78, *b*, 2: Rev. Celt., iii.

282. ———— Cath Cairnn Chonaill: the Battle of Carn Conaill: Zeitschr. für Celt. Phil., iii., 203. (See FM, A.D. 645.)

293. ———— The Voyage of Snedgus and Riagla: a Historic Tale from YBL: Rev. Celt., ix.

294. ———— Ancient Irish Treatise on Materia Medica, from manuscript of 14th or 15th cent.: Rev. Celt., ix.

295. ———— The Voyage of Maelduin: from LU and YBL: Rev. Celt., ix. and x.

296. ———— The Second Battle of Moytura: from a 15th cent. MS.: Rev. Celt., xii.

297. ———— The Gaelic Marco Polo from Book of Lismore (15th cent.: abridged with great freedom in Book of Lismore from a Latin version): Zeitschr. für Celt. Phil., i., 245.

298. ———— Irish Life of St. Fechin of Fore: Rev. Celt., xii.

299. ———— Vision of Adamnan from LU: a separate pamphlet.

300. ———— Second Vision of Adamnan from LB (p. 259, *b*): Rev. Celt., xii., 420.

301. ———— The Boroma (Tax on Leinster), from LL: Rev. Celt., xiii.: see also No. 211, xxviii.

302. ———— Paper on the Linguistic Value of the Irish Annals (Philological Society, 1890).

303. ———— Bruden Da Derga; the Destruction of Da Derga's Hostel: Rev. Celt., xxii.

304. ———— The Annals of Tigernach: Rev. Celt., xvii., xviii.

305. ———— Saltair na Rann: Text, Notes, and Glossary, but no transl. (" Anecdota Oxoniensia ").

306. ———— Voyage of the Sons of O'Corra, from the Book of Fermoy: Rev. Celt., xiv. See also No. 125, *l*.

307. ———— Extracts from LL: Rev. Celt., xiv.

308. ———— Orgain Dind Rig, the Destruction of Dinnree, from LL 269, *a*: Zeitschr. für Celt. Phil., iii.

309. Stokes, Whitley, D.C.L., LL.D.: The Gaelic Mandeville, a transl. into Irish of the Travels of Sir John Manderville, made in 1475: Zeitschr. für Celt. Phil., II.,

310. ————— The Violent Deaths of Goll and Garb, from LL: Rev. Celt., XIV.

311. ————— Battle of Magh Mucrime, from LL: Rev. Celt., XIII: see also No. 211, xxii.

312. ————— Poem on the Saints of Ireland by Cuimmin of Conneire: Zeitschr. für Celt. Phil., I. 59.

313. ————— Dindsenchus, from the Rennes MS.: Rev. Celt. XV. and XVI.

314. ————— Cóir Anmann, or Fitness of Names: Derivations and Meanings of the Names of a number of Historical Irish Personages: Irische Texte, III.

315. ————— Ancient Treatise on Irish Ordeals, Cormac's Adventure in the Land of Promise, and the Decision as to Cormac's Sword: all three as one continuous text: Irische Texte, III.

316. ————— Bruden Da Chocae, The Destruction of the Hostel of Da Choca: Rev. Celt., XXI.

317. ————— Acallamh na Seanórach: the Colloquy of the Ancient Men: Irische Texte, IV. (1900). That part of this text in the Book of Lismore has been edited by O'Grady in Silva Gadelica: see No. 211, xii.

318. ————— On the Deaths of some [Irish] Heroes: a poem by Kineth O'Hartigan in LL, pp. 31, 32: Rev. Celt., XXIII., p. 303.*

319. ————— and Strachan, John, LL.D.: Thesaurus Palæohibernicus: a collection of Old-Irish Glosses, Scholia, Prose, and Verse: 2 vols.

320. Stokes, William, M.D.: Life of George Petrie, LL.D. Strachan, John, LL.D.: see No. 319.

321. Stuart, John, LL.D.: The Book of Deer, edited for the Spalding Club, 1869.

322. Sullivan, W. K., PH.D.: Introduction to O'Curry's Manners and Customs of the Ancient Irish: forming a separate vol.: see No. 189.

323. ————— Translation, from German, of Ebel's Celtic Studies. Tables of Deaths: see No. 349.

324. Táin bo Chuailnge (" The Táin "). Táin bo Fraich: see No. 45. Three Fragments: see No. 200. Three Irish Homilies: see No. 283. Three Irish Glossaries: see No. 278. Three Shafts of Death: see No. 14.

---

* In the Introductions to some of his editions—as in the Tripartite Life, and the Lives of the Saints—Dr Stokes has collected all the expressions of the texts that throw light on the social condition of the early Irish: of which notes I have made full use.

Three Sorrowful Stories of Erin : see No. 192.

Thurneysen, R. : Index to Zeuss : see No. 87.

Tigernach, Annals of : see No. 304.

325. Todd, James Henthorn, D.D., S.F.T.C.D. : Memoir of St. Patrick, the Apostle of Ireland.

326. ———— The Irish version of the Historia Britonum of Nennius : Edited by Dr. Todd in conjunction with the Hon. Algernon Herbert : Irish Archæol. Soc.

327. ———— The Book of Hymns : in two vols., paged continuously : Irish Archæological and Celtic Society. (See also No. 13.)

328. Todd, James Henthorn, D.D., S.F.T.C.D. : Obits and Martyrology of Christ Church : Edited by Dr. Todd in conjunction with John Clarke Crosthwaite, A.M. : Irish Arch. Soc.

329. ———— Cogadh Gaedhel re Gallaibh : The War of the Irish with the Galls or Danes : Rolls Series.

———— The Martyrology of Donegal, or O'Clery's Calendar : see No. 197.

330. ———— Descriptive Catalogue of the Book of Fermoy : Proc. Roy. Ir. Acad. : Irish MSS. Series.

Topographia Hiberniae (" Top. Hib.") : see No. 80

Tract on Lat. Decl., Irish Glosses : see No. 281.

331. Transactions of the Gaelic Society, 1808 : 1 vol.

332. Transactions of the Royal Irish Academy.

Trias Thaumaturgæ : see No. 41.

Tribes of Ireland : see No. 202.

Tripartite Life : see No. 276.

333. Tromdamh : constituting vol. v. of the Ossianic Society's Transactions : see No. 226, v.

334. Ulster Journal of Archæology : Old Series : 9 vols.

335. ———— New Series.

Usna, Story of the Sons of : see Nos. 124 125, m, and 192.

336. Ussher's Works by Elrington : 16 vols.

Ventry, Battle of : see No. 134.

Visions of Adamnan : see Nos. 299, 300.

Voyage of Bran : see No. 182.

337. Wakeman's Handbook of Irish Antiquities : third edition, by John Cooke, M.A. : 1903.

338. Walker's Irish Bards : 2 vols.

339. Ware's Works, Harris's Edition : 2 vols.

340. Warren, F. E., B.D. : The MS. Irish Missal in Corpus Christi College, Oxford.

341. ———— The Antiphonary of Bangor.

War of the Gaels with the Galls (" War of GG ") : see No. 329.

342. Waterford, Journal of the Archæol. Soc. of.

343. Wattenbach, " Die Kongregation der Schottenklöster in Deutschland " : translated by Dr. Reeves, with copious notes, in the Ulster Journal of Archæology, vol. VII., pp. 227, 295.

344. Wattenbach: Sur un Evangéliare à miniatures d'origine Irlandaise. Originally written in German; translated into French in Rev. Celt., vol. I. See also this article in English in Miss Stokes's Irish Art, p. 44.

345. Westropp, Thomas, J. M.A.: The Ancient Forts of Ireland: in Trans. Roy. Ir. Acad., vol. XXXI., 1902. Also many papers, chiefly on the Forts of the Co. Clare, in recent vols. of Journ. Roy. Soc. Antiqq. Irel., and Proc. Roy. Ir. Acad.

346. Westwood: Facsimiles of Anglo-Saxon and Irish MSS.

347. Westwood: On the Book of Kells: separate pamphlet.

348. Wilde, Sir William, M.D.: Catalogue of Irish Antiquitise.

349. ———— Census: Two Reports on Tables of Deaths in Census of Ireland, 1842 and 1851 (containing much information translated from Irish Medical manuscripts, all supplied by O'Curry).

350. ———— Lough Corrib and Lough Mask: 2nd edition, 1872.

351. ———— The Boyne and Blackwater: 2nd edition.

352. ———— On the Unmanufactured Animal Remains belonging to the Roy. Ir. Acad., including an ancient Irish Poetical Catalogue of Native Animals: Proc. Roy. Ir. Acad., vol. VII.

353. Williams, T. Hudson: Cairdius Aenius ocus Didanie, the Love of Æneas and Dido, from BB (451, a, 36, to 459, a, 30): Zeitschr. für Celt. Phil., II., 419.

354. Windele, John: On "Irish Medical Superstition" in Kilk. Archæol. Journ., 1864-6, p. 306.

355. Windisch, Ernst: Irische Texte, vol. I., with Glossary: Dr. Windisch, besides compiling the whole of this first vol., has edited and partly written the succeeding vols.

356. ———— L'Ancienne Légende Irlandaise et les Poésies Ossianiques. (Translated from German in Rev. Celt., vol. V.)

357. ———— Text with translation of the following five Ancient Irish Tales in Irische Texte, vol. II.:—Fled Bricrenn, Táin bo Dartada, Táin bo Flidais, Táin bo Regamna, and Táin bo Regamain.

358. ———— A Concise Irish Grammar (chiefly Old Irish). Of this there are two English translations: one by Dr. Norman Moore; the other by the Rev. James P. M'Sweeny, S.J.

359. ———— Tochmarc Ferbe, an ancient Irish Tale, text with German translation, in Irische Texte, vol. III.: see No. 156.

360. ———— De Chophur in dá Muccida: Ancient Irish Tale, text with German translation in Ir. Texte, vol. III.

361. Wood-Martin, Col. W. G.: Pagan Ireland. 1895.

362. ———— Traces of the Elder Faiths of Ireland. 1902.

363. ———— Rude Stone Monuments. (A useful Bibliography of Irish Archæology, very detailed in some departments, will be found in Pagan Ireland and in Traces of the Elder Faiths.)

Wörterbuch, Windisch: see No. 355.

364. Wright's Louthiana.
365. Yellow Book of Lecan (" YBL "). (See vol. I., p. 497, *supra*.)
366. Zeitschrift für Celtische Philologie: Edited by Kuno Meyer and L. Chr. Stern.
367. Zeuss, Grammatica Celtica (" Z "): Ed. Ebel.
368. Zimmer: Glossæ Hibernicæ (one vol.: published in Berlin). Besides many learned articles on ancient Irish Literature, published in the various Continental periodicals devoted to Celtic learning.

ADDITIONAL LIST OF AUTHORITIES

369. Faraday, L. Winifred, M.A.: Tain Bo Cuailnge, translated for the first time, from LU. and YBL (1904).
370. Otia Merseiana, vols. I. and II. (1899–1903). Containing several short Irish pieces, text, translations and notes.
371. Bury, J. B., M.A.: Life of St. Patrick (1905).
372. Moran, Cardinal: Irish Saints in Great Britain.
373. Seebohm, Frederick, LL.D., F.S.A.: The English Village Community (1883). The Tribal System in Wales (1895). Tribal Custom in Anglo-Saxon Land (1902). (Three separate vols.)
374. The Death of Muirchertach Mac Erca: from YBL. 313 *b*.
375. The Death of Crimthan, Son of Fidach, and the Adventures of the Sons of Eochaid Muigmedon; Rev. Celt., XXIV.
376. Wellcome, Henry S.: Ancient Cymric Medicine.

INDEX

Sculpture over a doorway, Cormac's Chapel, Cashel: Centaur shooting at a lion.
(From Petrie's Round Towers.)

INDEX

N.B.—The numbers in parentheses after names of places denote the squares on the map where the names are to be found.

ABBOT, mode of electing, I. 324 ; II. 535.
Abbott, The Rev. Dr., S.F.T.C.D., I. 547 note.
Aberdeen, Breviary of, I. 373.
Abhartagh, a dwarf so called, II. 553.
Acaill, now the Hill of Screen, II. 578.
Acall, her burial, II. 578.
Accallamh or Agallamh na Senórach, story of, I. 539 ; II. 501.
Acéin, King Concobar's Shield, I. 130
Achad-farcha, II. 315.
Achilles, I. 114, 257, 298.
Acta Sanctorum Hiberniæ, I. 507.
Acta Triadis Thaumaturgæ, I. 507.
Adam, I. 529, 571.
Adam and Eve Monastery, Dublin, I. 498.
Adamnan, I. 48, 82, 115, 165, 179, 215, 223, 330, 390, 437, 438, 506, 520 ; II. 13, 84, 334, 402, 422 note, 470, 479, 490, 528, 539 : his cross, II. 81, 85 : his Law, I. 96.
Administration of justice, chap. viii.
Adna the poet, II. 525, 526.
Adonis, legend of, I. 532.
Adoption, I. 166 ; II. 14.
Adventures, a class of tales, I. 533.
Advocates and pleaders, I. 215.
Advocates' Library, Edinburgh, I. 498.
Adze, II. 314.
Aebinn or Aebill, the fairy queen, I. 246, 263.
Aed Allen, king of Ireland, II. 399 : — Baclamh, II. 60 : — bishop of Sleaty, II. 535: — Dubh, k. of Dalaradia, II. 92 : — Finnliath, k. of Ireland, I. 150: — Guaire, k. of Connaught, II. 60 : — mac Ainmirech, k. of Ireland, I. 59, 82, 135, 140, 141, 384, 456 ;

II. 97, 532 : — mac Bric, St., I. 629 to 632: — mac Criffan or mac Criomthainn, I. 490, 495 : — Oirdnidhe, k. of Ireland, I. 96, 460: — Ruad, father of Queen Macha, I. 262 : — Slaine, k. of Ireland, I. 381 ; sons of I. 185, 186 : — Uaridneach, k. of Ireland, I. 614 : — k. of Oriell, I. 266.
Aedan, I. 111.
Aedan k. of the Scotic Dalriada, I. 48, 81.
Aenach or Oenach, a fair, an assembly, I. 30, 179, 211 ; II. 401, 413, 435, 463, 466, 560 : — described, II. 438.
Aenach Ailbe Cemetery, II. 554 : — Beg, now Monasteranenagh, II. 440: — Colmain or A. Life, II. 440, 464: — cemetery of, II. 554 : — Cruachna, II. 560 : — Culi cemetery, II. 554 : — Macha, II. 435 : — n-Guba, a fair of mourning, II. 434 : — Urmhumhan, now Nenagh, II. 440.
Aeneas, I. 246, 280 ; II. 231.
Aeneid, the, I. 104, 246, 280, 492 ; II. 231.
Aengus : see Angus.
Aengus of the Terrible Spear, I. 92 : — Macin-Og, I. 260, 609 ; II. 556 : — mac Natfree, k. of Cashel, I. 280 ; II. 4 : — Ollmucad, k. of Ireland, I. 73 : — the Culdee, I. 413, 423, 426, 507, 508, 509 ; II. 342: see Féilire : — of Dun Aenguis, II. 366.
Aesbuite or Assicus, St. Patrick's coppersmith, I. 489 ; II. 327.
Age of moon, I. 233, 465, 467, 470.
Aghaboe in Queen's Co. (39), I. 468 ; II. 113.
Aghagower in Mayo, I. 370.
Aghowle in Wicklow, II. 33.

Breton or Armoric language, I. 471, 472, 474, 475.

Breviary of Aberdeen, I. 373.

Brewers, II. 118.

Brian, a Dedannan god, I. 261.

Brian Boru, I. 52, 56, 57, 139, 140, 382, 460, 504; II. 19, 100, 107, 400, 536, 540.

"Brian Boru's harp," I. 576, 577.

Briar, briars, II. 287.

Bricin, St., I. 420.

Bricriu, Nemthenga the poet, I. 84, 114 note; II. 34, 230, 451.

Bride, purchased for bride-price, II. 4, 5 note, 6, 439.

Bridges, II. 293: — described, II. 399, 400.

Bridles, I. 559: — described, II. 414 to 417.

Brigh Briugaid, the female lawyer, II. 12.

Brigit, the pagan goddesses of that name, I. 260.

Brigit, St., of Kildare, I. 10, 261, 332, 337, 353, 354, 379, 394, 507, 547; II. 13, 119, 120, 129, 157, 221, 352, 465, 491, 518: — of Cluain-Infide, St., II. 134.

Brigown : see Finnchua.

Bri Leith or Bri Leithe, now Slieve Golry in Longford, I. 253, 294; II. 157.

Bristol, the mart for English slaves, I. 165; II. 432.

Britain, I. 73, 229, 315, 367, 414, 558; II. 24, 31, 425, 429, 430, 431, 432, 490: see England.

British or Britannic languages, I. 471: — marauding parties, I. 133: — Museum, I. 498, 506, 523, 556, 592 note; II. 223, 263 note, 582.

Britons, I. 7, 82, 144, 337, 413, 552; II. 23, 207, 384, 403, 404, 405, 409, 413, 424, 554.

Broccaid, his burial, II. 578.

Broccan, Brocan, or Brogan, St., II. 464.

Broccan the Pious, II. 461 note.

Brocshalach Crion-Ghlúine, II. 210.

Broichan, the druid, I. 223; II. 32.

Broighter in Derry, II. 263, 582, 583; — list of gold ornaments found in, II. 583.

Bróinbherg, the hospital of Emain, I. 616; II. 91 note.

Bronze, II. 68, 71, 126, 288, 297, 298, 318, 364, 405, 475.

Broo or Bro Park, Farm, House, and Mill (anc. Brugh), II. 556.

Brooches, I. 21, 22, 562; II. 196, 200, 202, 207; described, II. 245 to 249.

Brooklime, II. 150.

Brosna, the river, in Westmeath, II. 150.

Brude, the Pictish king, II. 33, 36.

Bruden or brudin, now bruighean, a hostel, a feasting-hall, I. 450; II. 20, 44, 171, 173, 174.

Bruden Blai Briuga, II. 173: — Da Choga, I. 267; II. 173: — Da Derga, I. 106, 132, 149, 232, 310, 492, 495, 539; II. 170, 171, 332,

562: described and identified, II. 171, 172, 173: — Da Ger or of Mac Dareo, II. 173: — of Mac Dáthó II. 173: see Hostels.

Brugaid, a brewy or hosteller, I. 159, 160; II. 39, 54, 134, 167, 174, 185, 313, 319, 344, 416; described, II. 168 to 173: — election court at his house, I. 44: — Cedach, II. 168: — Lethech, II. 169.

Brugh on the Boyne, I. 251, 260; II. 554, 555, 556 and note, 557, 559, 560.

Brunn the son of Smetra, II. 254.

Bruree (44), I. 138; II. 101.

Brussels, I. 506.

Bryan near Athlone, II. 173.

Buanann, a goddess so-called, I. 261.

Buckles, I. 127.

Buffoons and jesters, I. 65; II. 481 to 487.

Bugh, Bodb Derg's daughter, I. 260.

Builders, II. 292, 293, 294, 310, 324: — their works, classification of, II. 352.

Building, I. 544; II. 292, 293, 294: — in stone, I. 354 to 356; II. 23, 65, 292, 293, 294: — in wood, I. 354, 358; II. 21, 23, 292, 293, 294.

Buildings and other material church requisites, I. 354.

Bull Feast, I. 245.

Bunne, buinne, budne, buinni, buinde bouinde, a pipe, a ring, a wave, I. 581, 582, 614; II. 180, 225, 241, 243, 385.

Bunne-do-at, I. 565; II. 240, 384: — described II. 241 to 245.

Bunratty Castle (44), II. 43.

Bunting, Edward, and his music, I. 591, 593.

Burial alive at obsequies, II. 545: — fees, I. 379: — modes of, II. 546: — mounds, II. 564, 565.

Burkes, the, I. 463.

Burning alive as a punishment, I. 212.

Burning the dead : see Cremation.

Burns, Robert, I. 394 note, 448; II. 296, 297.

Burnt Nial, the Norse Saga, I. 519.

Bury, Prof. J. B., I. 317 note.

Bute, Marquess of, I. 317.

Butlers or cupbearers, II. 111.

Butlers (the family), I. 183, 463.

Butter, II. 137.

Buttevant Abbey, I. 362.

Buttons, II. 206, 207, 245.

Byzantium and Byzantine MSS., I. 551.

CABBAGE or Kale, II. 148.

Caeir, I. 453.

Caelchu, the Munster chief, II. 85.

Cael O'Nemhnann, I. 131; II. 30, 177.

Caesar, Julius, I. 26, 207, 221, 239, 296, 384, 391, 404, 424; II. 424, 545.

Caher (51) II. 100, 101.

Caherconree (49), I. 86.

Caher-crofinn at Tara, II. 81, 82.

Cahermore in Clare, II. 319.

Concobar, k. of Connaught, I. 151.

Concubinage, II. 12.

Condiment, II. 132, 134, 150, 152, 156.

Confession of St. Patrick, I. 6, 274, 289 503, 504 ; II. 431.

Cong Abbey, I. 41, 42.

Congal Claen, prince of Ulster, I. 113, 136, 144, 229 ; II. 17, 105, 114, 133, 157, 191, 528.

Congal, king of Ireland, I. 123.

Conleth, St., bishop of Kildare, II. 326.

Conmach, primate, I. 96.

Conn the Hundred Fighter, or Of the Hundred Battles, k. of Ireland, I. 87, 132, 139. 212, 268, 494; II. 71, 88.

Connaught, I. 99, 372, 383, 410, 450, 451, 484 ; II. 114, 170, 553 : — extent of, anciently, I. 37, 39.

Connla's well in Tipperary, I. 446.

Connla the Comely, story of, I. 297, 494, 495.

Conn na mBocht, I. 490.

Consonants, classification of, II. 498.

Constantine, the emperor, II. 382.

Constantius, son of Constantine, I. 77.

Consumption (illness), I. 613.

Contracts, I. 182 ; II. 510.

Conventions and fairs, II. 434 to 451.

Convents and nuns in Ireland, I. 353.

Conversation house, II. 42.

Convulsions (illness), I. 614.

Conwell, E. A., II. 558, 559 note.

Cony or rabbit skins exported, II. 433.

Cooke, Thomas, II. 320 note.

Cooks and cooking, I. 14, 65, ; II. 38, 147, 444 : — described, II. 122.

Coolavin, I. 526.

Coolbanagher in Queen's County, I. 507.

Copenhagen, I. 347, 593.

Copper, II. 288, 289, 290, 291, 297.

Copperas as medicine, I. 623, 624.

Copyright in ancient Ireland, I. 502.

Corc, k. of Munster, I. 173.

Corcalee (Corca-laidhe), genealogy of, I. 17, 530.

Corc-mac-luighdheach, k. of Munster, II. 99.

Corco Luachra in Kerry, I. 98.

Corcomroe abbey in Clare, I. 362, 570.

Corcran the cleric, I. 462.

Cork (56), I. 308, 331, 414, 583, 611 ; II. 140, 217.

Cormacan Ecces, I. 151.

Cormac Cas, I. 617 : — Conlingas, I. 127; II. 173, 247 : — Gaileng, I. 287,; II. 128.

Cormac mac Airt, king, I. 54, 57, 58, 74, 87, 89, 92, 97, 180, 216, 271, 303, 311, 420, 445 ; II. 30, 58, 83, 86, 103, 107, 140, 225, 231, 330, 428, 443.

Cormac Mac Cullenan, I. 147, 150, 400, 475, 476 and note, 526 : Cormac's chapel at Cashel, I. 356, 357 ; II. title-page : — his cup (one of the ordeals), I. 303.

Cormac's Glossary, I. 14, 16, 173, 174, 401, 447, 475, 476 and note ; II. 332, 393, 535, 536, 543.

Cormac, St., II. 491 : — Ua Liathain, I. 349.

Corn (grain), II. 42, 141 : — as crops, 271.

Corn, a horn, a drinking-horn, II. 71, 72, 73 : — a ray or fillet of a diadem, II. 258 : — a trumpet, I. 585.

Cornish language, I. 471, 472, 474, 475.

Corn-ricks, II. 274.

Cornwall, II. 291, 425.

Coroticus, Patrick's epistle to, I. 6, 78 note.

Corpse, rights of a, II. 538 : — branch-covering for, II. 543.

Corroboration of written records by existing remains, I. 8, 9, 11, 13, 20 to 23, 111, 413 ; II. 172, 179, 220, 221, 246, 261, 262, 315, 372, 574.

Corrody, paid maintenance in a monastery, II. 494.

Corrievreckan, II. 332, 425.

Cosmography of Ethicus, I. 403.

Costume illustrated, II. 197, 200, 201, 204, 206, 219.

Cottage industries, I. 34 ; II. 351, 357.

Couches for seats, II. 47: — for sleeping, II. 47.

Council of Cashel, I. 381 : — of Kells, I. 381.

Counting the slain, I. 149.

Coursing with hounds, II. 463, 466.

Courtship of Becuma, I. 246 : — of Emer, I. 495 ; II. 332 : — of Etain, II. 478 : — of Ferb, II. 501 : Courtships or Wooings, a class of tales, I. 533.

Courts of Justice, I. 214.

Covenants or contracts, I. 182 ; II. 510.

Cow-herds, II. 281, 282, 283.

Cows, I. 493 note ; II. 41, 281, 282, 283 : — described, II. 277: — as a standard of value, II. 385, 386.

Cowl, II. 200, 201 : see Cochull.

Coyne and livery, I. 194.

Crafts, protecton of, II. 324.

Craftsmen, social position of, II. 324 : — tested and licensed, II. 329, 437.

Craig-liath, now Craglea, near Killaloe (38), I. 263 ; II. 100.

Crane (the bird) I. 28 ; II. 36, 317, 516, 518 : — for lifting, II. 316, 317.

Crank of grindstone, II. 319.

Crannoge, Ir. crannóg, an insulated dwelling, II. 228, 347, 423 : — described, II. 65 : — a workbox, II. 365 : — various meanings of word, II. 68.

Cream, II. 71, 137.

Crede, the lady, I. 131 ; II. 30, 64, 177.

Credne or Creidne, the Dedannan brazier, I. 261, 555 ; II. 295.

Creduma, red bronze, II. 297, 298, 475.

Creeveroe, Irish Craebh Ruadh, at Emain, II. 20, 90.

Cremation, II. 546 to 551.

Cremation-ashes thrown into water, II. 456, 512.

Crescents, gorgets, and necklets, II. 233 to 240, 250, 328.

Cridenbél, the satirist, I. 627.

Crimson, in dyeing, II. 358, 359, 361.

Crimthan or Criffan Nia Náir, k. of Ireland, I. 73; II. 479, 557: — the great, I. 75: — s. of Cahirmore, II. 464.

Crinna, Battle of, I. 90, 599; II. 401.

Criticism, as a school study, I. 435.

Croagh Patrick, Mt. (26), II. 515, 562.

Crofton Croker, I. 273, 577; II. 103.

Croghan, Ir. Cruachan, palace of (21, 22), I. 64, 237, 265, 536; II. 29, 31, 42, 53, 187, 284, 329, 434, 437, 461, 556: — cemetery of, II. 554, 556, 557, 559, 560, 564, 572, 577: — described, II. 92: — fairy palace at, I. 257.

Croghan Erin tumulus, II. 552.

Cromlechs, II. 537, 566, 569, 570.

Cromm Connaill, the plague so called, I. 608.

Cromm Cruach, the idol, I. 275, 276, 281, 282, 284, 485.

Cromm Dubh, a Connaught idol, so called, I. 276.

Cronan, the poet, I. 445.

Cronn, the river, I. 288.

Croom or Crom in Limerick (44), I. 148.

Crops, II. 271.

Cros-figill, a prayer said kneeling with hands crossed, I. 390, 391.

Crosier, St. Patrick's, I. 276, 364.

Crosiers, I. 485, 610; used in cursing, I. 375.

Crosóc or crosóg, a small coin, II. 383, 385.

Cross of Cong, I. 559; described, I. 563, 564.

Cross placed over graves, II. 579.

Cross, the sign of, II. 43.

Crossan, a gleeman, II. 484, 485, 487.

Crosses, I. 358, 359, 567; II. 293, 402, 547, 579.

Crotal, a lichen for dyeing, II. 363: — a closed bell, I. 377.

Crott or cruit, a harp, I. 576, 587; II. 443.

Crow of a cock as a distance measure, II. 375.

Crowe, J O'Beirne, I. 530; II. 171, 541.

Crown or diadem, I. 59; — described, II. 251 to 259.

Cruachan palace: see Croghan.

Cruadin, the name of Cuculainn's sword, II. 291.

Cruan, red enamel, I. 558, 559; II. 416.

Crucibles, I. 565, 566.

Cruimtheris, St. Patrick's embroideress, II. 366, 454.

Cruise, the harper, I. 574.

Cruithnecan, the priest, II. 15.

Cu, a hound, II. 453, 463: — as a name for men, II. 457.

Cuailnge, now the Carlingford peninsula, I. 38, 536.

Cualann, district of (36), I. 410; II. 172.

Cuanna, I. 113.

Cuangus, II. 374.

Cuan O'Lochain I. 54 note, 462; II. 80, 330, 448, 559.

Cuchorb, I. 110.

Cuculainn, I. 84, 95, 98, 101, 104, 107, 110, 111, 115, 140, 153, 228, 241, 245, 249, 252, 257, 269, 270, 271, 288, 299, 392, 470, 518, 536, 622; II. 6, 17, 26, 50, 110 note, 173, 183, 195, 196, 199, 204, 229, 242, 254, 298, 299, 301, 305, 337, 367, 368, 403, 404, 405, 406, 407, 409, 411, 457, 461, 476, 477, 519, 540, 561.

Cúil Conaire, Battle of, II, 532.

Cuilmen, a great book, I. 436, 490, 493.

Cuirrech, a racecourse; Cuirrech Life, the Curragh of Kildare, II. 464, 465.

Culann, the Red Branch Knights' smith, II. 295.

Culdees, 133, 141, 147, 148, 154: — treated of, I. 352 to 354.

Culdremne Battle of, I. 146, 227, 306; II. 402.

Cullen in Tipperary, I. 556; II. 321.

Culliu, Battle of, II. 552.

Culloden, Battle of, I. 149.

Cumal, Finns father, I. 89, 212.

Cummascach mac Ailello, his bell, I. 374, 375.

Cummascach, prince, II. 61, 481, 483.

Cummian or Cummain Fota, St., I. 224, 411, 458, 510; II. 542.

Cupping and cupping-horn, I. 621.

Cur, a knight or champion, gen. curad, I. 99, 100, 119, 121.

Curad-Mir or Curath-Mír, the champion's bit or share, I. 270; II. 109.

Curds, II. 139.

Curoi mac Daire, I. 86; II. 183, 213, 241.

Curraghs or wicker boats, II. 219, 293, 368, 422, 463: — described, II. 423 to 425.

Curragh of Kildare, II. 440: — fair and races of, II. 464, 465.

Curran, John Philpot, II. 508 note.

Currane Lough in Kerry (54), I. 349.

Custard, II. 138.

Cuthbert, St., I. 337.

Cycles, astronomical and chronological, I. 465, 466, 467, 468: — of Historical Tales, I. 535.

Cyclopean building, II. 57.

DA CHICH DANAINNE, now the Pops in Kerry, I. 261.

Da Choga, the hosteller, II. 173.

Dachonna, St., of Assylin, I. 380.

Da Derga: see Bruden Da Derga.

Dagda, the, I. 251, 260, 627.

Dagobert, k. of France, I. 412.

Dai, the chief so named, II. 490.

Daig or Dagoeus, St., I. 544; II. 327.

Emancipation of sons, II. 13.

Embroiderers and embroidery, I. 441 ; II. 325, 365, 366, 367, 444.

Emer, Cuculainn's wife, I. 228, 249 ; II. 6, 17, 367, 541.

Emeralds, II. 226.

Emetics, I. 622.

Emly College, I. 408 note.

Enamel and enamel work, I. 558, 562 ; II. 73, 258, 299, 300, 416.

Encampments, I. 132 : — a class of tales, I. 533.

Enda, St., of Aran, I. 322, 328 ; II. 342.

Endymion by Keats, II. 502.

Eneclann, honour-price, II. 91 : see Logenech and Honour-price,

England and English, I. 398 ; II. 33, 45, 47, 55, 115, 202, 347.

Enloch, I. 298.

Enna Airgthech, k. of Ireland, I. 557.

Ennis Abbey (38), I. 361, 362.

Envoy or herald, I. 135.

Eochaid or Eochaidh, the leader of a colony to Wales, I. 74 : — king of Leinster, II. 6 : — Airemh, king of Ireland, I. 230 ; II. 478 : — Airgthech, a usurping king of Ireland, I. 108, 397 ; II. 231, 244, 566 : — Beg of Cliach, II. 16 : — Buidhe, s. of King Aedan, II. 490 : — king of the Firbolgs, II. 431 : — Edguthach, king of Ireland II. 192 : — Egeas : see Dallan Forgaill : — Feidlech, king of Ireland, II. 261 : — Horsemouth, the Scotch poet, II. 525 : — Iuil, II. 187 : — Laib, II. 402 : — Muidmedon or Ochy Moyvane, king of Ireland, II. 303, 545.

Eogabail, the fairy chief, I. 262.

Eoghan : see Owen.

Eoghan, Ailill Olum's son, I. 228 ; II. 209, 210 : — Bel, king of Connaught, II. 552, 553, 568 : — Mór, k. of Munster, I. 132, 139, 268 ; II. 195 : — son of Niall 9H., I. 167.

Eorna, barley, II. 272.

Epact, the, I. 467.

Epilepsy, I. 614.

Equestrians, II. 444.

Equinoctial and equinoxes, I. 466, 467.

Epistles, the, II. 230.

Epistle or epistil, a sort of necklace, II. 230.

Erc, a contemporary of St. Columba, II. 539 : — bishop of Slane, II. 87, 133 : — his hermitage, I. 320 : — Concobar's grandson, II. 490.

Erca, St. Patrick's embroideress, II. 366.

Ercnait, St. Columkille's embroideress, II. 366 and note.

Eremitical monasteries, I. 350.

Eremon, k. of Ireland, I. 517, 619.

Erenach, the lay manager of the monastery and monastic farm, Ir. Airchinnech, I. 325, 389.

Eric, a compensation fine, I. 207, 211 : see Compensation.

Eric of Auxerre, I. 341.

Erni, the keeper of Queen Maive's jewels, I. 64.

Erris in Mayo, II. 7.

Erysipelas, I. 624.

Esaia or Isaiah the prophet, I. 548.

Esau, II. 130.

Esker Riada (seem on map as a faint line from Galway Bay by Athenry to Dublin, through squares, 33, 34, 35, 36), II. 396 and note.

Ess mac n-Eirc, II. 29.

Esus, a Gaulish god, I. 249.

Etain, Queen, I. 230 ; II. 478.

Ethicus of Istria, I. 18, 403 to 405.

Ethnea the Fair, K. Laegaire's daughter, I. 233, 255 ; II. 17, 187, 577.

Evangelist, figure of, II. 197.

Eve, I. 571.

Eviction from house and land, I. 196, 204.

Evidence in court of law, I. 55, 215, 216.

Evil eye, I. 309.

Evin, St., of Monasterevin, I. 374, 506.

Exchange, mediums of, II. 380.

Exemption from debt, periods of, II. 531.

Exiles, a class of tales, I. 533.

Exorcist, I. 436.

Exports, two lists of, II. 433.

Extempore composition, I. 443.

Eye-bright in medicine, I. 624.

Eyebrows, dyeing of, I. 343.

Eyes, inflammation of, cure for, I. 624.

FACE, as a measure of a gold ring or crescent, II. 375 : Face, shape of, II. 176.

Failbe of the pillar-stone boundaries, II. 267.

Fail-derg-doid, k. of Ireland, II. 223.

Fairies, I. 494 ; II. 522 : — carrying off corpse, II. 542 : — treated of, I. 250 to 258 : Fairy bath and herbs, I. 626, 627 : Fairy hill, I. 255 : Fairyland, II. 30 : Fairy moat, I. 256.

Fairs, I. 30, 211 : — described, II. 434 to 447, and see Aenach : — green for, kept in order, II. 448 : — modern fairs, I. 106 note.

Fairy Palace of the Quicken Trees, Story of, I. 539.

Fairy palaces, I. 230, 252 : — described, I. 254 to 256 : see Side.

Fairy-struck persons, how cured, I. 624.

Fairy thimble, *digitalis purpurea*, I. 627.

Faithche, a lawn, an exercise green, II. 61, 62, 145, 170, 375, 446, 465, 470, 475.

Faldinge (cloth) exported, II. 433.

Falling sickness, I. 614.

Family, the, chap. xix. and I. 166.

Family names, II. 19.

Fán Comair, I. 311.

Fand or Fann, the fairy lady, I. 228.

Fudir, one of the three unfree classes, I. 162, 163, 164, 209; II. 56: Fudirs on land, I. 194, 195, 196.

Fuel, I. 565; II. 47 : — described, II. 158 to 161.

Fulartach, the poet, II. 441.

Fulling and fullers, II. 354.

Fullon, the druid, I. 225.

Funeral feast, II. 539 ; — games, II. 434, 539, 550 : — obsequies, II. 539.

Fuogh, river in Galway, II. 227.

Furbaide, son of Concobar mac Nessa, I. 622; II. 140, 563.

Furnace for fusing metals, I. 565, 566.

Furniture, II. 37.

Furs, II. 129, 189, 214.

Fursa, St., of Peronne, I. 572.

GABRA, Battle of, I. 89.

Gaela, the territory, I. 124.

Gaelic language, II. 432 : — of Ireland and of Scotland, I. 471 : — three dialects of, I. 471 : Gaelic domestics, I. 67 : — writings, ancient, expounded, I. 425, 426.

Gaels, I. 78, 122, ; II. 499.

Gaidoz, Henri, I. 467.

Galbally, II. 100.

Galen the Physician, I. 605, 606.

Gall, gallán, a pillar-stone, II. 268.

Gall, an Englishman, any foreigner, I. 122, 147, 415 ; II. 381.

Gallagh Castle, I. 461.

Gallen in Mayo, I. 288.

Gallia Braccata, II. 207 : — Comata, II. 178.

Galloglass, Irish gallóglach, a heavy-armed foot-soldier, I. 120, 121, 146, 147 ; II. 215.

Gallows, I. 212.

Gallus or Gall, St., I. 343, 373

Galty Mountains (50, 51), II. 100.

Galway (32), I. 421 ; II. 57.

Gamhanraide of Connaught, I. 86.

Gap of danger, I. 92.

Garland of Howth, I. 505, 547.

Garland Sunday, I. 276.

Garlic, II. 138, 149.

Garman the chief, II. 434 : see Carman.

Garnavilla and its amulet, I. 629.

Garnets, II. 226.

Garters, II. 212, 213.

Gaul, I. 77, 229 ; II. 33, 156, 430.

Gaulish druids, I. 207, 235, 238, 239 : — gods, I. 231, 239 : — inscriptions, I. 400 : — workshops, ancient, II. 321.

Gauls, I. 152, 413, 583 ; II. 95, 109, 207, 232, 268, 321, 391, 403, 405, 408, 409, 413, 456, 533, 538.

Gavelkind, Ir. Gabháil-cine, I. 197.

Geese, I. 28 ; II. 282.

Geis, a prohibition, a thing forbidden, I. 60, 237 ; II. 284 : — described, I. 310.

Geiselberg in Germany, II. 55.

Gelfinne system of holding land, I. 188.

Genealogies, I. 17, 496, 528 : — of the Irish saints, I. 509, 525.

Geography, geographical poem, I. 440.

Geometry studied by Irish, I. 470.

Georgia, churches of, I. 551.

Geraldines, the, I. 463 ; see Fitzgeralds.

Germans, I. 169, 210, 413, 540 ; II. 391, 533.

Germany, I. 626 ; II. 64, 501.

Gertrude, daughter of Pepin, I. 572.

Giant's Causeway, II. 282.

Giants' graves, II. 567.

Giant's Sconce, I. 86.

Gibbet, I. 212.

Gibbon's Decline and Fall referred to, I. 203.

Gibeah, slingers of, I. 101.

Gibson, Bishop, II. 245 note.

Gig-mill, a small mill, II. 340.

Gilbert, Sir John T., I. 547 note.

Gildas, I. 73 ; II. 424, 425.

Gilla, modern giolla, a boy, a gillie or attendant, I. 130, 146, 242, 384.

Gilla Lugan and his son, I. 609 : — Macliag, archbishop of Armagh, II. 322 : — scuir, a horseboy, II. 411.

Gillebert, bishop of Limerick, II. 227.

Gillies, H. Cameron, M.D., I. 616.

Gipne or gipni, a cupping-horn, I. 447, 621 : — a band for the forehead, I. 565 ; II. 181, 250, 407.

Giraldus Cambrensis, I. 19, 48, 116, 119, 120, 164, 277, 299, 383, 547, 549, 555, 556, 573 ; II. 66, 115, 177, 194, 205, 287, 332, 399, 412, 416, 417, 421, 422, 424, 432, 453, 510, 514, 517.

Girdles, I. 487 ; II. 212, 213.

Glám Dichenn (of sorcerers), I. 228, 240, 241, 242, 429 : — (of poets), I. 452 to 454, 456.

Glandore (59), I. 263 ; II. 525.

Glannagalt in Kerry, I. 227.

Glasdam, the jester, II. 481, 483.

Glasnevin near Dublin, I. 408 note, 409, 437.

Glass, I. 562 : — a factory of, II. 33, 320, 321 : ornaments and beads of, II. 32 : — vessels of, II. 32, 33, 68 : — treated of, II. 31 to 34.

Glastonbury, I. 75, 337, 469, 470.

Gleemen, II. 484 to 487.

Glendalough, I. 318, 408 note, 501, 512 ; II. 518.

Glendaroy, Glenettive, Glenlee, Glenmasan, Glenorchy, all in Scotland, II. 504, 505.

Glennasmole, II. 172.

Glenosheen in Limerick, II. 484.

Glossaries, I. 16, 475.

Glosses, I. 16, 17, 433, 439, 467, 473, 495 ; II. 250 : — described, I. 473 : — on the Law, I. 15, 174, 175, 176.

Gloucester, earl of, II. 201, 413.

Gloves, I. 182 ; II. 213, 214.

Glán-iarainn, II. 210.

Goad, II. 217.

Goaling or hurling, II. 474.

Goat-heads, I. 272: Goats, II. 281, 433.

Gobban Saer, the architect, I. 230; II. 294: — St., I. 409.

Gobinet, St., I. 628.

Goblins, I. 248, *et seq.*

God, names for, I. 248.

Gods, pagan, I. 248, *et seq.*, 535.

Goibniu, the Dedannan smith-god, I. 261, 632; II. 84, 290, 295, 301.

Goidels or Gaedels, I. 78, 122; II. 499.

Goidelic or Gaelic language, I. 471.

Gold, I. 554, 565,; II. 49, 68, 222 and following pp., 378, 381, 383, 384, 431 : — balls for hair, I. 21; II. 261, 262: — exported and imported, I. 555; II. 433: — in Ireland and England compared, I. 556: — mines, I. 554, 555: — objects in Nat. Museum, list of, II. 263, 583: — ornaments, I. 33, 34: — and silver as mediums of exchange, II. 381 to 385.

Golden Vale, the, II. 99.

Goldsmiths, II. 321: see Cérd.

Goliath, I. 101; II. 164, 352.

Goll the *Gelt* or Madman, I. 227.

Goll mac Morna, I. 89, 537.

" Good People," (*i.e.* fairies) I. 257.

Gooseberry, II. 287.

Gordon, Bernard, the physician, I. 606.

Gorgets, II. 233 to 240, 301.

Gormac, a son who supports his father; also a sister's son, II. 495.

Gortigern, I. 285.

Gospel worn round the neck, I. 385, 386 : — of Columkille, I. 546: — book, facsimile of page of, I. 553: Gospels, I. 547.

Gossipred, II. 18.

Gougane Barra in Cork (55), I. 350, 351.

Gouge (a carpenter's), II. 318.

Gout in the hands, I. 613.

Grace Dieu, near Swords, I. 333

Graddan, Gaelic greadán, bread made from scorched corn, II. 339, 340, 343.

Grafting, II. 154.

Graham, George Farquhar, I. 594.

Gráinne, d. of Cormac mac Airt, II. 86, 571.

Grain-rubber, II. 348.

Grammar, I. 430, 431, 435: Grammars, Ancient Irish, I. 475, 476.

Grammatica Celtica, I. 472 note, 475.

Granard (22), I. 275, 592, 593.

Gravel (the disease), I. 613, 631, 632.

Graves, the Rev. James, I. 564 note : — the Right Rev. Dr., I. 399, 503 note.

Graves, graveyards, and names of, II. 561, 562.

Gray, Lord Leonard, I. 3:

Grazing, II. 281 to 284.

Grazing animals, classification of, II. 282, 283.

Great Connell in Kildare, I. 333: — cycle, I. 466: — worker, II. 10.

Greaves (for legs), I. 123.

Greece, I. 521, 532, 540; II 3, 64, 439.

Greek and Roman writers on Ireland, 18 note.

Greek language in monastic schools, I. 410, 412, 425.

Greeks, I. 57, 135, 136, 169, 210, 285, 305, 540, 589, 597; II. 29, 109, 110, 112, 127, 173, 177, 271, 429, 443, 447, 448, 456, 512, 538, 540.

Green as a national colour, II. 192.

Greenan-Ely: see Ailech.

Gregor Ghlune Dhu, II. 210.

Gregory, Lady, I. 543.

Gregory, Pope, I. 367.

Grellan or Greallan, St., I. 138.

Grey Abbey in Down, I. 362.

Grian of the Bright Cheeks, the fairy queen, I. 264.

Greyhound, II. 453, 466.

Grianan, *anglicé* greenan, a solar or summer-house, II. 30, 34, 42, 404 : — Lachtna in Clare, II. 100.

Griffith, Sir Richard, II. 289, 291.

Grimm, J., II. 375 note.

Grinding corn, II. 343 to 348.

Grindstone, II. 319.

Groom, the chief's or king's, I. 65.

Ground colour in dyeing, II. 358.

Groups of society, I. 166.

Gryffith ap Conan, k. of Wales, I. 573.

Guaire the Hospitable, I. 205; II. 52, 93, 167, 568.

Guest-house, II. 104.

Guests, I. 330: order of, at table, II. 105.

Gullet of an ox as food, II. 132.

Guy, earl of Warwick, history of, translated, I. 499.

Gwynn, Edward, I. 530; II. 438 note.

Gwyri, the Welsh hero, I. 235.

HAGGARD, II. 62, 274.

Hag's Castle in Lough Mask, II. 67.

Hair, II. 215: — Gold balls for, I. 21; II. 261, 262.

Hair and hair-dressing, II. 177 to 182.

Hake exported, II. 433.

Hallowe'en or All Hallows night, I. 264.

Halter (for animals), II. 417.

Ham, son of Noah, I. 272.

Hammer, I. 566; II. 315, 316.

Hand, the family of the name, II. 331.

Handicrafts taught, I. 441.

Handkerchief, II. 367.

Hands, clapping of, in divination, I. 232: — in mourning, II. 541: — well-shaped, II. 176.

Handstone as a weapon, I. 100.

Hanging as a punishment, I. 212.

Hardiman, James, I. 577: — his Irish Minstrelsy, I. 296 note, 575.

Hare, the, I. 27; II. 433, 460.

THE END.